PAGE
34

ON THE ROAD

YOUR COMPLETE DESTINATION GUIDE
In-depth reviews, detailed listings
and insider tips

Negril &
West Coast
p185

Montego Bay &
Northwest Coast
p143

Ocho Rios &
North Coast
p115

Port Antonio &
Northeast Coast
p93

South Coast &
Central Highlands
p213

Kingston & Around
p36

Blue Mountains &
Southeast Coast
p78

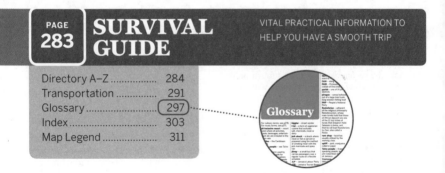

Glossary

THIS EDITION WRITTEN AND RESEARCHED BY

Adam Karlin

Anna Kaminski

welcome to Jamaica

Jah's Garden

Ask any Jamaican in a cold suburb of Toronto or New York or London what they miss about their island, and the answer is inevitably the island itself, the great green garden and natural landscape that constitutes one of the most beautiful islands of the Caribbean. Jamaica's lovely landscape begins with crystalline waters flowing over gardens of coral, lapping onto sand as soft as yellow butter, as dark as ash and white as rice, then rising past red soil and lush banana groves into sheer mountains. This is powerfully beautiful country, captivating to the eyes and soul, and as such, the subject of many Jamaican poems, songs and deep wells of nostalgia. Jamaican culture can be a daunting subject for foreigners to understand, but ultimately it's a matter of appreciating this land and how its cyclical rhythms set the pace of so much island life.

Diving, Spelunking & Cycling

Jamaica cries out to be explored, be it underwater, on hikes, river-bound with a raft, underground with a lamp on your head, or on the road by car or bicycle. You are welcome to spend the entirety of your trip on the beach or in a jerk shack, and we wouldn't blame you for following that instinct. But if you access the Jamaican outdoors you'll be seeing sides of this island many tourists miss. We want to stress: outdoor activities

Jamaica packs in extremes. Flat beaches twinned to green mountains; relaxed resorts and ghettos; sweet reggae and slack dancehall. It's a complicated national soundtrack and it's impossible not to dance to it.

(left) The azure waters and rocky beach at Bluefields (p216).
(below) Rastafarian local.

in Jamaica hardly require you to be as fit as Usain Bolt. There's no physical effort involved when you raft (someone else poles), and even folks in moderate health can accomplish the country's most famous hike: to Blue Mountain peak, to see the sunset and, if you're lucky, Cuba in the distance.

Island Riddims & Recipes

More than any other island in the Caribbean, Jamaica has one foot (and sometimes, it feels, one foot and four toes) planted in West Africa. When you hear the lyricism of the local patois language, or feel the drumbeat behind young men singing along to dancehall, or see the way women sip cups of peanut porridge in the morning, it's hard not to be struck by how strong the bond between the Old and the New World is. Yet this *is* still the New World, and the ways it has evolved from Africa are as interesting as its connections to the mother continent. From the evolution of African folk music into reggae, or the shifting of African spice rubs into delicious jerk, it's rewarding to see how the Jamaican cultural story retains its original voice whilst adapting it to the setting – and of course, rhythms – of the Caribbean.

〉Jamaica

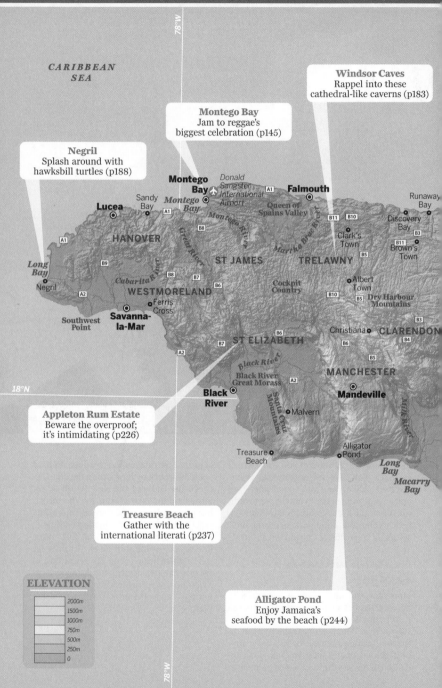

CARIBBEAN SEA

Windsor Caves
Rappel into these cathedral-like caverns (p183)

Montego Bay
Jam to reggae's biggest celebration (p145)

Negril
Splash around with hawksbill turtles (p188)

Montego Bay

Donald Sangster International Airport

Falmouth

Runaway Bay

Sandy Bay

Queen of Spains Valley

Discovery Bay

Lucea

Clark's Town

Brown's Town

HANOVER

Great River

Montego River

Martha Brae River

ST JAMES

TRELAWNY

Dry Harbour Mountains

Long Bay

Negril

Cabarita River

WESTMORELAND

Cockpit Country

Albert Town

Southwest Point

Ferris Cross

Savanna-la-Mar

Christiana

CLARENDON

ST ELIZABETH

MANCHESTER

Milk River

18°N

Black River Great Morass

Black River

Santa Cruz Mountains

Mandeville

Appleton Rum Estate
Beware the overproof; it's intimidating (p226)

Malvern

Treasure Beach

Alligator Pond

Long Bay

Macarry Bay

Treasure Beach
Gather with the international literati (p237)

Alligator Pond
Enjoy Jamaica's seafood by the beach (p244)

ELEVATION

2000m
1500m
1000m
750m
500m
250m
0

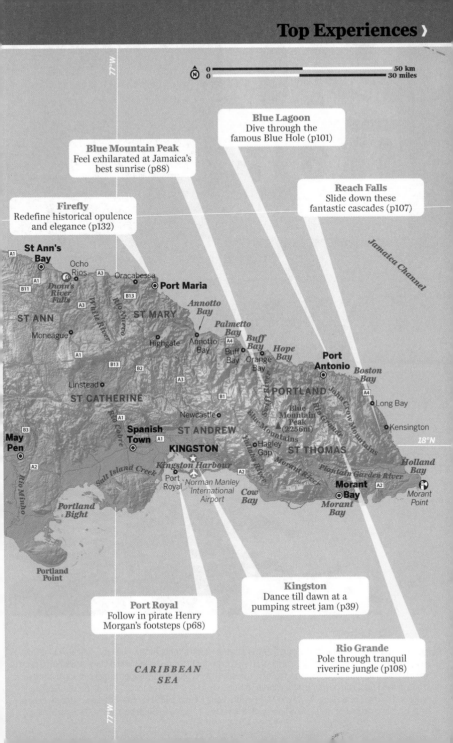

Blue Lagoon
Dive through the
famous Blue Hole (p101)

Blue Mountain Peak
Feel exhilarated at Jamaica's
best sunrise (p88)

Reach Falls
Slide down these
fantastic cascades (p107)

Firefly
Redefine historical opulence
and elegance (p132)

Kingston
Dance till dawn at a
pumping street jam (p39)

Port Royal
Follow in pirate Henry
Morgan's footsteps (p68)

Rio Grande
Pole through tranquil
riverine jungle (p108)

0   50 km
0   30 miles

St Ann's Bay
Ocho Rios
Dunn's River Falls
Oracabessa
Port Maria
ST ANN
Moneague
White River
Rio Nuevo
ST MARY
Highgate
Annotto Bay
Annotto Bay
Palmetto Bay
Buff Bay
Buff Bay
Orange Bay
Hope Bay
Port Antonio
Boston Bay
Linstead
ST CATHERINE
Newcastle
Spanish Town
KINGSTON
Kingston Harbour
Port Royal
Norman Manley International Airport
Cow Bay
Rio Cobre
Salt Island Creek
May Pen
Rio Minho
Portland Bight
Portland Point
Blue Mountains
Blue Mountain Peak (2256m)
Hagley Gap
ST ANDREW
Yallahs River
ST THOMAS
Morant River
Rio Grande
John Crow Mountains
PORTLAND
Long Bay
Kensington
18°N
Holland Bay
Plantain Garden River
Morant Bay
Morant Bay
Morant Point

Jamaica Channel

CARIBBEAN
SEA

77°W

77°W

20 TOP EXPERIENCES

Best Beaches

1 Jamaica's beach experiences are as varied as the island's topography. The tiny, delicate Lime Cay (p71), only reachable by boat from Port Royal, is perfect for snorkeling and picnics. Hellshire Beach (p72) heaves with Kingstonians and reverberates with loud music, its wooden shacks doing a roaring trade in fried fish. The north coast's Winnifred Beach (p104) draws the locals with its azure waters and weekend parties, while Negril's Seven Mile Beach (Long Beach; p189) is criss-crossed by jet-ski riders, and its long crescent of white sand lined with the bodies of sun worshippers. Seven Mile Beach, Negril

IAN CUMMING/PHOTOLIBRARY

Climbing Blue Mountain Peak

2 A night hike to reach Jamaica's highest point (p88) by sunrise, your path lit by the sparks of myriad fireflies, is an experience unlike any other. As you climb, the vegetation becomes less and less tropical, until you're hiking amid stunted trees draped with old man's beard (lichen) and giant ferns. In the pre-dawn cold at the summit, you wait in rapt silence as the first rays of the sun wash over the densely forested mountain peaks all around you, illuminating the distant coffee plantations and Cuba beyond.

Kingston Nightlife

3 Whether you're attending a night-club or a street dance, expect a sweaty, lively, no-holds-barred event (p37). Dress up to the nines and fol-low the locals' lead. At a street dance, two giant speakers are placed facing each other, the street pounding with the bass, while nightclubs provide a similar indoor experience. Expect to be pulled into the melee as the locals will want to see how well you can dance, and bump and grind the best you can; the dancing will be some of the most explicit you'll ever see.

EVERYNIGHT IMAGES/ALAMY

MICHAEL LAWRENCE/LONELY PLANET IMAGES ©

Negril

4 So you've walked on the snowy sands of Negril's Long Beach, wandered past the nude sunbathers, seen the sun sink behind the cliffs, plunged into the ocean to scrub your soul and fended off all the hustlers. How about topping off all of these experiences by donning some scuba gear (p191), getting PADI-certified and watching sea turtles dance their slow ballet in the cerulean waters of Jamaica's westernmost resort? If a full aqualung isn't your thing, just get your snorkel on amid the darting rainbow-colored fish.

Boston Bay

5 The best experiences in Jamaica are extremely sensory affairs, but Boston Bay (p106) may be the only one that is more defined by smell than sight or sound. Well, smell and taste: Boston Bay is the supposed birthplace of jerk, the spice rub that is Jamaica's most famous contribution to the culinary arts. The turnoff to Boston Bay (itself a lovely beach) is lined with jerk stalls that produce smoked meats that redefine what heat and sweet can do as complementary gastronomic qualities. In plain English: it tastes freaking amazing.

NIK WHEELER/ALAMY

SUKI MACDONALD KAPAHI

Reggae Sumfest

6 If there's any cultural trend that defines Jamaica to the rest of the world, it's reggae music – quite literally the soundtrack of the island. And there is no bigger celebration of the island's 'riddims' then Reggae Sumfest (p20), held in Montego Bay in the middle of the broiling Jamaican summer. To be fair, the ocean breezes do cool things down, but you'll still be sweating – from the fires spewing out of homemade aerosol flamethrowers (that means a song is good), the throbbing mass of bodies and the nonstop dancing.

Diving Montego Bay

7 You might find the resorts of Montego Bay to be crowded with people, but wait till you dive in the surrounding waters. They're crowded, yes, although not with human beings – just multicolored fish and swaying sponges. For all the tropical pastels and cool blue hues, this is a subdued seascape, a silent and delicate marine ecosystem that is one of the island's unique natural resources. The best sea walls are to be found at The Point (p153), while more advanced divers should explore the ominous (and gorgeous) Widowmakers Cave (p153).

STUART DEE/GETTYIMAGES

Reach Falls

8 On Jamaica's east coast, past stretches of jungle and beach that are completely off the radar of most tourists, you'll find, up in the hills, one of Jamaica's most beautiful waterfalls (p107) – and this is an island with a lot of beautiful waterfalls. Hire a guide (you'll need one, trust us) and clamber up slippery rocks, over neon-green moss and into cool mountain pools of the freshest spring water. In some areas you can dive under watery tunnels and through blizzards of snowy-white cascading foam.

Bob Marley Museum, Kingston

9 Marley's creaky home (p48) is crammed with memorabilia, but the visitor is drawn to his untouched bedroom, adorned with objects of spiritual significance to the artist, the small kitchen where he cooked I-tal food, the hammock in which he lay to seek inspiration from the distant mountains, and the room riddled with bullet holes, where he and his wife almost died in an assassination attempt. The intimate surrounds and modest personal effects speak eloquently of Marley's turbulent life.

The Perfect Hotel in Treasure Beach

10 The greatest, most interesting variation of accommodations in Jamaica can be found in Treasure Beach (p238), on Jamaica's south coast. Here, instead of huge all-inclusive resorts, you'll find quiet, friendly guest houses; artsy enclaves dreamed up by theater set designers; Rasta retreats favored by budget backpackers and private villas that are some of the classiest, most elegant luxury residences in the country. Did we mention many of these places are involved in admirable community-tourism initiatives, and that there's barely any hustle or hassle here?

Rafting the Rio Grande

11 No less a celebrity then Errol Flynn started the habit of sending discerning tourists on romantic, moonlit rafting trips through the Rio Grande Valley (p109), from Berridale to Rafter's Rest at St Margaret's Bay. These days the experience isn't quite as exclusive as it was when Mr Flynn was running the show – the Rio Grande rafting trips are actually quite affordable as Jamaican tourism activities go – but if the moon is full, you can still pole onto the waters, which turn silver and unspeakably romantic.

Appleton Rum Estate

12 Red Stripe is the alcohol everyone associates with Jamaica, but you may find that rum, the local spirit, provides a more diverse boozing experience. We're not saying Appleton produces the best rum on the island, but it is by far the most commonly available, bottled as several different varieties, and you can sample all these examples of the firewater at the Appleton Rum Estate (p226) in the Central Highlands. A lot of rum is served, so don't expect to accomplish much else on one of these day trips!

PHOTOGRAPHER SEV/IMAGEBROKER

Crocodile-spotting in Black River Great Morass

13 This is one of our favorite ways of exploring wild Jamaica: setting off by boat in the Black River Great Morass (p222), gliding past spidery mangroves and trees bearded with Spanish moss, whilst white egrets and anhinga flap overhead. Your tour guide may tell you about the local women who sell bags of spicy 'swimp' (shrimp) on the riverside, and point to a beautiful, grinning American crocodile, cruising by.

Swimming in the Blue Lagoon

14 From the forested cliffs that surround it, the Blue Lagoon (p101), named after the film starring the teenage Brooke Shields, nestling in its protected cove, is a seemingly bottomless pool of turquoise water – intensely picturesque and perfect for a dip. Fed by several underground streams coming down from the mountains, its waters are a refreshing mixture of warm tidal waves and cool freshwater currents. If you're a diver, you can plumb the lagoon's depths, which reach 55m at its deepest point.

JON DAVISON / LONELY PLANET IMAGES ©

Eating Lobster Fresh from the Ocean

15 So, it shouldn't surprise anyone that Jamaica, being, y'know, a Caribbean island, produces some frankly superlative seafood. But there's seafood and there's seafood, and Little Ochie (p245), in Alligator Pond, decidedly serves up the latter. All of the sea life here, from lobster to fish to crabs, is simply the height of marine food preparation – fresh, sometimes spicy, always complex. The escoveitch, a marinade of vinegar and hot peppers, should be a controlled substance.

ALL CANADA PHOTOS/ALAMY

Spelunking Windsor Caves

16 The Cockpit Country of the island's interior is some of the most rugged terrain throughout the Caribbean, a series of jungle-clad round hills intersected by powerfully deep and sheer valleys. The rains gather in these mountains and the water percolates through the rocks, creating a Swiss cheese of sinkholes and caves. Windsor (p183) is one of the most dramatic and accessible, although the latter is a very relative term when used to describe this cathedral of fantastic rock formations. Oh, and there are bats. Lots of bats.

IAN CUMMING/PHOTOLIBRARY

Sipping Coffee in Mandeville

17 Mandeville (p231) is the fifth-largest city on the island and the unofficial capital of the cool Central Highlands. This is an area that has been settled by many retired Jamaicans who have made their fortunes overseas, as well as many Western volunteers and aid-agency workers. As such, Mandeville has a cosmopolitan feel for a town of its size. Rub shoulders with the local intelligentsia at the Bloomfield Great House, which serves excellent pub fare, and sip some locally grown coffee as the mountain mists are dispelled by the golden sunlight.

MONTY RAKUSEN/ALAMY

Firefly, Noël Coward's Estate

18 From its privileged position on a hill overlooking Port Maria Bay, playwright Noël Coward's former home, Firefly (p132), boasts a magnificent view of the north coast. You can peer through the gun slits at the bar, added by another famous resident who preceded Coward – the notorious pirate-turned-governor, Sir Henry Morgan, or walk through the atmospheric home, untouched since Coward's day. The drawing room once entertained the likes of Sophia Loren and Audrey Hepburn and the table is freshly laid, as if still expecting the Queen Mother for lunch.

Playing Pirates at Port Royal

19 The sleepy fishing village of Port Royal (p68) only hints at past glories that made it pirate capital of the Caribbean and 'the wickedest city on Earth.' Stroll in the footsteps of pirate Sir Henry Morgan along the battlements of Fort Charles, still lined with cannons to repel the invaders; become disorientated inside the Giddy House artillery store, tipped at a jaunty angle; or admire the treasures in the Maritime Museum, rescued from the deep after two thirds of the town sank beneath the waves in the monstrous 1692 earthquake. Fort Charles

Calabash International Literary Festival

20 On the last weekend in May, Treasure Beach explodes with activity as writers, poets and dub lyricists from all over the island, the Caribbean and as far away as the US and the UK descend on the quiet fishing village for three days of outdoor book readings, poetry slams, discussions and after-show music parties (p240). The events are extremely well-attended, the involved audience rewarding their favorites with rapturous applause. Treasure Beach

need to know

CURRENCY
» Jamaican dollar (J$) and US dollar (US$)

LANGUAGE
» English and patois (pah-*twa*)

When to Go

Montego Bay
GO Dec-Mar

Ocho Rios
GO Jan-Apr

Negril
GO Feb-Apr

Port Antonio
GO Feb-May

Kingston
GO Mar-May

Tropical climate, wet & dry seasons
Tropical climate, rain year-round

High Season
(Dec-Mar)
» Expect sunny, warm days, especially on the coast. Little rainfall, except in Port Antonio and the northeast.

» At night it can become chilly, particularly in the mountains.

Shoulder Season
(Apr & May)
» Good time to visit; weather is still pretty dry (again, except in Port Antonio).

» Rates drop for accommodations.

» Far less tourists, especially in the big resorts/cruise ports.

Low Season
(Jun-Nov)
» Sporadic heavy rainfall across the island, except on the south coast.

» Heavy storms, including hurricanes, gear up August to October.

» Many of Jamaica's best festivals happen in midsummer.

Your Daily Budget

Budget less than
US$100
» (J$8500)

» Everything is cheaper outside Kingston, Montego Bay, Negril and Ocho Rios

» Double rooms US$50

Midrange
US$100-200
» (J$8500-17,000)

» Share villas to score luxury rooms for midrange rates

» Fine dine for US$20 to US$30 per head

Top end over
US$300
» (J$17,000)

» Private taxis for transport

» Luxury accommodations from US$200 a night

MONEY

» ATMs, banks and moneychangers widely available in large cities, rarer in rural areas. US dollars (US$) preferred currency at larger hotels, resorts and restaurants.

VISAS

» Not required for American, Canadian, UK, EU, Australian and Japanese citizens for stays of up to 90 days.

CELL PHONES

» US phones must be set to roaming. Local SIM cards work in unlocked phones for most other countries.

DRIVING

» Drive on the left; steering wheel is on right side of car. Automatic drive widely available for rent.

Websites

» **Jamaica National Heritage Trust** (www.jnht.com) Excellent guide to Jamaica's history and heritage buildings.

» **Jamaica Gleaner** (www.jamaica-gleaner.com) The island's most reliable newspaper.

» **Visit Jamaica** (www.visitjamaica.com) The tourist board's version of Jamaica. Listing information may be outdated.

» **Lonely Planet** (www.lonelyplanet.com/jamaica) Succinct summaries on travel in Jamaica, plus the popular Thorn Tree bulletin board.

Exchange Rates

Australia	A$1	J$89
Canada	C$1	J$86
euro zone	€1	J$121
Japan	¥100	J$105
New Zealand	NZ$1	J$68
UK	UK£1	J$136
US	US$1	J$85

For current exchange rates see www.xe.com.

Important Numbers

Jamaica's country code is ✆876, which is dropped if dialing in the country.

Ambulance	✆110
Directory assistance	✆114
International operator	✆113
Police	✆119
Tourism board	✆929-9200

Arriving in Jamaica

» **Donald Sangster International Airport, Montego Bay**

Taxis – US$25 to US$35 to downtown Montego Bay, US$80 to US$100 to Negril, US$100 to US$120 to Treasure Beach

Route taxis – run from near gas station, to the Hip Strip J$80

» **Norman Manley International Airport, Kingston**

Taxis – US$35 to Kingston Pde (Downtown)

Buses – Bus 98, opposite arrivals hall, runs to Kingston Pde J$80

Off the Beaten Path

Jamaica's tourism hot spots are Ocho Rios, Montego Bay and Negril, which stretch (from the last to the first) from the westernmost tip of the island along the north coast to the center of the north coast. This is an undoubtedly beautiful part of Jamaica, and is also the area most heavily populated by all-inclusive resorts and package-tour options. If you want to break away from crowds, we recommend exploring areas like Portland parish, particularly around Port Antonio east towards Long Bay (and even beyond to Manchioneal) and west to Buff Bay; the south coast, especially around Black River and Treasure Beach; and the interior, including large towns like Mandeville, the community tourism sites in the Cockpit Country and the Rio Grande Valley in eastern Jamaica.

if you like...

Diving & Snorkeling

Major dive centers concentrate near resort areas on the northwest coast from Negril through Montego Bay, Ironshore and Ocho Rios; snorkeling opportunities can be found anywhere on the coast. Dive or snorkel and you'll soon discover a plethora of vibrant small fish and good visibility.

Montego Bay Montego Bay gets green points due to protected waters at Montego Bay Marine Park & Bogue Lagoon (p151)

Ironshore Shares operators with Montego Bay. Sights like The Point and the underwater tunnel at Widowmakers Cave are highlights (p166)

Negril The calm waters that generally characterize Negril make it a good place for those newbies seeking scuba certification (p191)

Ocho Rios A reef stretches from Ocho Rios to Galina Point and makes for fine diving and snorkeling expeditions (p121)

Music

It's said Ireland produces a surfeit of authors given its size. That said, we conclude Jamaica (which has a similarly sized population) produces musicians at ridiculous ratios, making it, per capita, one of the most musically influential nations in the world. From the sound-system parties of Kingston to festivals that both bring in international talent and show off local skills, some beats are always in the background here.

Kingston parties Downtown Kingston's sound-system parties are the stuff of legend, but it's best to come with a local (p59)

Reggae Sumfest The world's definitive reggae experience features both the best of old sweet sounds and dancehall's raucous 'riddims' (p155)

Nine Mile Although they've been sadly over-commercialized, the birthplace and tomb of Bob Marley still attract thousands of faithful (p141)

Rebel Salute Held on the beautiful south coast in January, this is the biggest roots reggae festival in Jamaica (p244)

Historic Sites

Jamaica's history begins with the Taino Indians and proceeds through the blood-soaked eras of colonialism, slavery, the long abolition and independence struggle and, since then, fraught efforts to create a stable, prosperous nation. In testament to this legacy, beautiful old architecture has arisen (and occasionally, if not often enough, preserved) while community tourism projects have made a point of leading travelers down the difficult road of Jamaican history.

Falmouth This friendly little town on the north coast boasts the greatest concentration of historic buildings in all Jamaica (p171)

Port Royal Just a skip away from Kingston is this old haven of pirates and streets of Georgian architecture (p68)

Outameni A fantastically comprehensive museum and multimedia and dramatic production that examines the wide sweep of Jamaican history and ethnicities (p174)

Accompong The isolated outpost of the living Maroons, descendants of escaped slaves who have retained deep African cultural roots (p227)

» The indigenous red-billed streamertail hummingbird (also known as the doctorbird)

Wildlife

Jamaicans can be self-deprecating about the wild-life on their island; when we asked a Montego Bay hotelier what he considered the most interesting animal in the country, he shrugged and said, 'Well, there's some wild pigs out there.' Indeed, there are – and American crocodiles, land crabs and a diverse, multihued bird population, to say nothing of the marine fauna, from dolphins to sea turtles, that inhabits the surrounding waters.

Black River Great Morass
Nothing makes a boat trip into a Jurassic-looking swamp cooler than dozens of Jurassic-looking reptiles (p222)

Windsor birding Head into the daunting jungles of the craggy Cockpit Country with trained ornithologists in search of birdlife (p183)

Rocklands Bird Feeding Station In Anchovy, this quirky grassroots tourism project is for birders who want to catch sight of Jamaica's hummingbirds (p178)

Canoe Valley Wetland A series of isolated, lonely roads lead to this lovely window onto Eden, where jungle vines frame a pool sometimes frequented by manatees (p77)

Food & Drink

When home is a garden of an island populated by an ever-shifting cultural mélange of Africans, Chinese, Indians, Spanish and English, you should probably expect food to evolve in some interesting ways. Jamaican cuisine can be as fiery as jerk rub, as comfortably bland as steamed bananas, as heavy as dumplings and as light as fresh seafood. For all that variety, everything goes down well with Red Stripe.

Boston Bay The supposed birthplace of jerk, Jamaica's most famous spice rub, is the best place to sample it (p106)

Appleton Rum Estate Sip the strong stuff in the Central Highlands and realize how much flavor rocket fuel has (p226)

Fine Kingston dining The nation's capital is the place to sample some of the best in haute Caribbean cuisine (p56)

Little Ochie Located at the bottom of Jamaica is this funky beachside restaurant that serves seafood like you've never tasted (p235)

Waterfalls & Rivers

Freshwater rivers have historically been (and in many places still are) the most important arterial routes in Jamaica. It was the rivers that linked the coast to the villages of the interior, in addition to providing all-important drinking water, fish, and bird sanctuaries. Today the rivers and waterfalls of Jamaica are still important for all of these reasons, but they also provide a playground for tourists, domestic and international.

YS Falls Deeply secluded in St Elizabeth parish, you'd be forgiven for thinking YS Falls emerged out of Eden (p226)

Martha Brae River Be gently poled down this emerald-green tunnel, a silent riverine paradise close to MoBay (p173)

Reach Falls These tall falls, which cascade through pools into lush jungle, may be the most beautiful in Jamaica (p107)

Dunn's River Falls They may be slightly overcrowded, but it's still tons of fun to clamber up these slippery falls (p119)

If you like...ghosts, check out Long Bay, where a haunting (some say haunted) road hugs an empty stretch of the island's south coast (p245)

Relaxing at Resorts

For all the adventures and excursions we're mentioning, it's fair to say some of the most fun to be had in Jamaica involves lazing around and getting spoiled like your life depended on it. This is, after all, where the concept of all-inclusive resorts was born. If that isn't your cup of tea, there are plenty of independent hotels where you can still be pampered.

Time 'n Place A cute collection of huts built by a man we'd lovingly call a character, this is beachfront beauty at its quirkiest (p174)

Caves Negril's most exclusive, secluded and beautiful resort promises an unmatched top-end resort experience, likely accompanied by celebrity guests (p198)

Round Hill Classy elegance and innovative design define this preserve of the rich, famous and tasteful, located in the northwest (p177)

Kanopi House One of the most innovative eco-resorts on the island, where green sensibility and uncompromising luxury seamlessly blend (p102)

Spelunking

Jamaica's heavy rains, plus the porous rock that makes up its spine of interior mountains, combine to create a vast system of sinkholes and caves. In fact, this is one of the most extensive cave networks for such a relatively small geographic region. Many of these caves are located within the inhospitable reaches of the rugged Cockpit Country, and as such aren't easily accessed by the average tourist.

Windsor Caves There's something about the entrance and egress of thousands of bats that lets you know you're somewhere special (p183)

Ipswich & Mexico Caves You'll need some initiative to reach these caverns, filled with stunning chambers of rock formations (p227)

Gourie Caves Only the adventurous should apply to enter this complex, where water seeps in and flooding is a possibility (p230)

North Cockpit Country You need a sense of adventure to explore the tunnels that crisscross this rugged corner of Jamaica (p182)

Romantic Getaways

Jamaica is an island where it's pretty easy to fall in love, or fall back into love, or, as the case may be, lust (hey, all those dirty dancehall lyrics start getting to you after a while, what can we say). When you've got a country that zigs between powder beach and misty mountains, and zags from clear waterfalls to molten sunsets, there are lots of perfect-kiss moments.

Treasure Beach A proliferation of small guesthouses, opulent villas and friendly locals – and yes, of course, gorgeous beach (p238)

Long Bay Isolated, friendly, off the tourist trail and fronted by sunrises that emerge fresh out of the ocean (p106)

Negril OK, Negril is over-touristed, but watch that sunset off the west coast and try not to be lovestruck (p188)

Rio Grande River What could make river rafting more romantic? Doing so under the light of the full moon (p109)

month by month

Top Events

19

1 **Reggae Sumfest**, July

2 **Jamaica Carnival**, February

3 **Calabash International Literary Festival**, May

4 **Fi Wi Sinting**, February

5 **Rebel Salute**, January

January

January is prime tourist season, when the rains are few and the weather is pleasantly sunny and warm.

☆ Air Jamaica Jazz & Blues Festival

Locally and internationally acclaimed artists perform a variety of musical genres in a splendid outdoor setting near Rose Hall, Montego Bay. Held in the last week of January; see www.airjamaicajazzandblues.com.

☆ Rebel Salute

The biggest Roots Reggae concert in Jamaica goes down on the second Saturday in January at Port Kaiser Sports Club in Rebel Salute, deep in the south coast.

February

The weather continues to be dry and the sun continues to shine as some of the important cultural festivals on the island occur in the east.

Fi Wi Sinting

This festival (the name means 'It is ours') has grown into the largest celebration of Jamaica's African heritage, with music, crafts and food, Jonkanoo dancing, mentos music and story telling. Held in Hope Bay, Portland parish. See www.fiwisinting.com for more.

☆ Jamaica Carnival

This draws thousands of costumed revelers to the streets of Kingston, MoBay and Ochi. Sometimes spills over into March. Head to www.jamaicacarnaval.com or www.bacchanaljamaica.com for more information.

March

You may find Jamaica less crowded, yet still blessed by good weather, as the high tourism season comes to an end. Until Spring Break kicks in...

☆ J'Ouvert

If you want to see how Jamaican students party (hint: lots of soca dancing, live music and fun), head to the annual carnival celebration of the University of West Indies, Mona, near Kingston. Typically held in late March, but known to occur in April.

April

While this is the beginning of the Jamaican shoulder season, the weather stays largely dry even as the crowds, and accommodations rates, start to plummet.

✕ Trelawny Yam Festival

In ruggedly beautiful Albert Town: yam-balancing races, best-dressed goat and donkey, the crowning of the Yam King and Queen – how can you resist? Perhaps the most idiosyncratic, unique festival on an island full of 'em. See www.stea.net.

May

The rainy season really gears up in May, although things stay dry in the south for the nation's top literary festival.

Calabash International Literary Festival

This highly innovative literary festival draws some of the best creative voices from

Jamaica, plus highly touted international intelligentsia, to Treasure Beach. Head to www.calabashfestival.org for more information.

June

A soupy combination of heat and humidity from the rains begins to take hold, but sea breezes on the coast and mountain chill in the interior keep things fresh.

⭐ Caribbean Fashion Week

You may not be able to access some of the most exclusive tents here, but the vibe of Caribbean Fashion Week can be felt all across Uptown and the posher suburbs of Kingston. Check www.caribbeanfashion week.com.

July

Phew. It's hot. And not just the weather: some of the island's best food and music festivals start heating up the yearly events calendar. The rainy season continues.

🍴 Jamaica Observer Food Awards

Many agree the venerable *Observer*'s affair is the Caribbean's most prestigious culinary event. International talent, tastes and attention turn towards Kingston, where local restaurateurs bring their top game to the kitchen.

⭐ Reggae Sumfest

The big mama of all reggae festivals, held in late July in Montego Bay, this event

brings top acts together for an unforgettable party. Even if you're not attending, you're attending – the festivities tend to take over MoBay. See www.reggae sumfeset.com for more.

August

It's getting as hot as Jamaica gets, and about as humid too. In fact, the rains may be coalescing into ominous storm clouds. Yet the celebrations on the island aren't slowing down.

⭐ Independence Day

August 6 marks Jamaica's independence from the British Empire, and occurs with no small fanfare and delivery of dramatic speeches, especially in the Kingston area. Celebrations mark the event island-wide.

October

Now the rains are coming in hard, and there may be hurricanes gathering off the coast. On the plus side, accommodations prices run dirt cheap.

🍴 Jamaica Coffee Festival

Thousands of coffee lovers converge on the spacious lawns of Devon House in Kingston during the first week of October to slurp up Jamaica's world-famous coffee in an orgy of beverages, liqueurs, ice cream, cigars and classic Jamaican chow.

November

The rains are beginning to slacken off, although the northeast is still getting drenched. This is the end of low-season rates.

🍴 Restaurant Week

Jamaican restaurant week has been building over the years, and organizers clearly hope it will be growing in international cachet. It shows off the dishes of participating restaurants from Kingston, Ocho Rios and Montego Bay. See http://go-jamaica.com/rw/.

December

The weather becomes refreshingly dry again, and resorts start raising their prices accordingly. During Christmas, thousands of Jamaicans fly in from the US, Canada and the UK to spend time with family.

⭐ LTM National Pantomime

The Jamaican take on social satire is pretty raw, irreverent and amusing, and presented at this annual song-and-dance revue in Kingston from December through January. This is some of the best theater you can see in the Caribbean; check www.ltmpantomine.com for more.

🎯 National Exhibition

Kingston's National Gallery shows works by Jamaica's newcomers and old hands at this biennial display; one of the most anticipated cultural events in the Caribbean. The current cycle hits on even-numbered years. See www.natgalja.com.jm.

itineraries

Whether you've got six days or 60, these itineraries provide a starting point for the trip of a lifetime. Want more inspiration? Head online to lonelyplanet. com/thorntree to chat with other travelers.

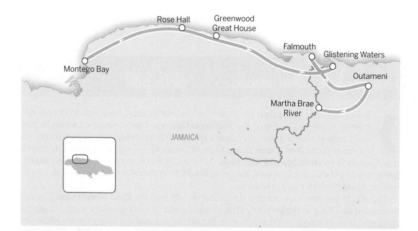

CARIBBEAN SEA

Rose Hall

Greenwood Great House

Falmouth

Glistening Waters

Montego Bay

Outameni

Martha Brae River

JAMAICA

One week
Montego Bay & Around

Start in **Montego Bay**, the gateway to Jamaica for about 80% of international travelers. Hit **Doctor's Cave Beach** for water sports and head downtown to historic **Sam Sharpe Sq**, taking in the historic architecture and the hustle of a real Jamaican city. Are you exhausted by all that energy, or did it invigorate you? Either way, we recommend treating yourself to a fine meal on the Hip Strip afterwards; how about **Native**?

You can spend the next morning relaxing on Montego Bay's beaches and sampling more food, but we don't recommend lingering too long here. Heading east from MoBay you'll find two great houses: the more (in)famous **Rose Hall** and the more authentic **Greenwood Great House**. We recommend the latter. Grab lunch on the north coast and relax on the beach before taking a nighttime boating expedition at **Glistening Waters.**

The next day give yourself a crash course in Jamaican history with a walking tour of **Falmouth** and its crumbling Georgian buildings. Then catch the incredible cultural show at **Outameni**. Finish this itinerary with a rafting trip down the **Martha Brae River**.

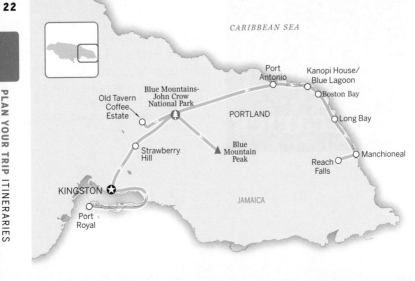

Kingston, Blue Mountains & Portland

Touch down in **Kingston** for three days of sightseeing, excellent food and rip-roaring nightlife. Don't miss the **National Gallery**. Take in historic **Devon House** and lunch at one of Jamaica's famous restaurants; there's plenty to pick from, but we recommend **Red Bones Blues Cafe**. Whether or not you're a reggae fan, there's much to see at the **Bob Marley Museum**. After hours, enjoy some of the liveliest **nightlife** in the Caribbean. For a captivating day trip, visit **Port Royal**, the earthquake-shattered former haunt of pirates and privateers.

Those hills looming over the city are calling, so slip into the **Blue Mountains**. Pamper your mind and body at **Strawberry Hill**, one of Jamaica's most excellent hotels, or spend the night in an economical hut perched on the side of a mountain. Enjoy the breathtaking scenery and crisp mountain air from hiking trails in **Blue Mountains-John Crow National Park**. The main event here is making an early-morning ascent of **Blue Mountain Peak**, Jamaica's highest mountain, from where you can see Cuba if the day is clear enough. If you are truly adventurous, whiz down from the highlands on a **bicycle tour**; if such a trip seems like a bit too much, enjoy a pleasant day seeing how the Caribbean's most prized coffee rises from bean to brewery at the **Old Tavern Coffee Estate**.

Descend from the Blue Mountains to **Portland parish**, on the prettiest stretch of the north coast. Walk the atmospheric streets of **Port Antonio**, taking lodging in one of the many intimate spots to the east of town or within the port's atmospheric historic district. East of Port Antonio, you'll find appealing communities with stellar beaches and attractive places to stay.

You can explore this terrific stretch of coast quickly or slowly, but it lends itself to some lingering. In the course of, say, five days you could go diving in the **Blue Lagoon** and stay at gorgeous **Kanopi House**, take a visit to **Boston Bay**, where you can sample the excellent surfing and jerk, stop in **Manchioneal**, a terrific base for visiting **Reach Falls**, and while away the rest of your trip in quiet **Long Bay**.

CARIBBEAN SEA

Three Weeks
The Sunny South

Start your trip in **Bluefields**, where you'll find comfortable guesthouses, some exceptional stretches of beach and the **mausoleum of reggae star Peter Tosh**. We recommend shacking up in one of the local Rasta-run homestays, where you can begin to slip into the laid-back rhythms of the south coast.

Linger at this quiet fishing beach for a day or three, then continue on to **Black River**, a sleepy port town with lovely historic buildings and vintage hotels. This is the gateway for boat travel into the mangrove swamps of the **Black River Great Morass**, a gorgeous wetlands where crocodile sightings are common. A trip up the river will take up a day of your time; afterwards you can stay at excellent, value-for-money **Idlers Rest Beach Hotel** or the **Ashton Great House**.

In the morning head north to **Middle Quarters** for an unforgettable lunch of pepper shrimp at a crossroads eatery and an afternoon at the lovely **YS Falls**. Wet your whistle at the **Appleton Rum Estate**, then head south to **Treasure Beach**. Check into a hospitable guesthouse, idiosyncratic boutique hotel or luxurious villa and stay awhile in the welcoming embrace of this tight-knit community (folks seem to easily lose a month here). Be sure to take a boat trip to one of the planet's coolest watering holes, the **Pelican Bar**, perched on stilts on a sandbar 1km out to sea.

From Treasure Beach, visit **Lover's Leap** for an astonishing view of the coastlands. You could spend a day here walking around the sweet pastureland of **Back Seaside**. Continue along the coast to the fishing village of **Alligator Pond**. Far from packaged tourism, here you can enjoy traditional village life and unspoiled scenery at its best. You'll also enjoy a delicious seafood feast at a truly extraordinary beachside restaurant, **Little Ochie**.

If you have your own car, preferably a 4WD, and are a confident driver, head east from Alligator Pond on the 'lonely road.' This really is an isolated stretch of road, but you'll find wild, empty beaches here and, after many potholes, **Alligator Hole**, a small preserve where manatees can be spotted.

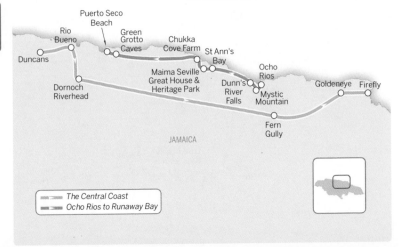

CARIBBEAN SEA

Puerto Seco Beach

Rio Bueno

Green Grotto Caves

Chukka Cove Farm

St Ann's Bay

Ocho Rios

Goldeneye

Firefly

Duncans

Maima Seville Great House & Heritage Park

Dornoch Riverhead

Dunn's River Falls

Mystic Mountain

JAMAICA

Fern Gully

The Central Coast
Ocho Rios to Runaway Bay

One week
Ocho Rios to Runaway Bay

> We'll start this trip from the anchor of tourism on the north central coast: **Ocho Rios**. There's a lot to see around 'Ochi' itself, from history (**St Ann's Bay**, where Christopher Columbus was marooned for a year) to kitschy tourism activities like **Mystic Mountain**, where you can bobsled in Jamaica a la *Cool Runnings*. Give yourself two days to chill out around Ocho Rios, taking full advantage of the tourist menu of activities, and don't forget to head up **Dunn's River Falls.**

Head west to see the **Maima Seville Great House & Heritage Park**, which really ought to be explored on horseback. Nearby in St Ann's Bay you can stop to take a peek at the **Columbus** and **Marcus Garvey monuments**.

Continue your westward expansion to Priory, where you'll want to stop by **Chukka Cove Farm**, where, instead of bobsled rides (done that), you can get pulled around by a dog sled.

Now head to Runaway Bay, where you can eat well, sleep well and base yourself for an exploration of the awesome **Green Grotto Caves** before continuing on to Discovery Bay and the simple charms of **Puerto Seco Beach**.

One week
The Central Coast

> Start in Montego Bay and travel east to **Duncans**, making sure to stop in the atmospheric (and inaccurately named) **Sober Robin** pub. Afterwards you should head to **Rio Bueno** and spend the evening at the highly idiosyncratic hotel-art gallery that is the **Hotel Rio Bueno**. The next day, ask around for a guide to take you into the ghost-town countryside of the **Dornoch Riverhead**. If the thought of treading near ghosts scares you, head to **Braco Stables** instead and canter through the surf.

Now head east toward Ocho Rios and turn south to head through dramatic **Fern Gully**. After this slight detour, return to the coast and continue eastbound towards the towns of Oracabessa and Galina. If this all seems like a long distance, keep in mind it is only a 1½-hour/80km drive back to Duncans, where this tour began! Anyways, head east to see sights associated with a couple of famous British authors: Ian Fleming, who claims the lovely hotel of **Goldeneye**, and Noël Coward, whose former estate **Firefly** is now an excellent museum.

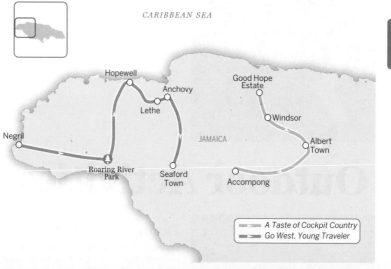

CARIBBEAN SEA

One Week
Go West, Young Traveler

Let your hair down – or get it braided – in **Negril** for a few days, until you've had your fill of peach-colored sunsets and rockin' reggae. Make sure to split your time between the smooth sands of the main beach and the coral cliffs and small guesthouses of the **West End**. You'd also do well to take a trip to **Roaring River Park** near Savanna-la-Mar for a day of incredible scenery and soaking in turquoise mineral pools.

Head east and try to book yourself a grand dinner at the **Round Hill Hotel** in Hopewell (if you've got a lot of cash to spare, stay here for an exquisite luxury experience). Afterwards, head into the western interior, giving yourself time to go rafting in the pretty town of **Lethe** and explore friendly villages like **Anchovy** and **Seaford Town**. There are numerous small farms and adventure-tour groups operating out here, and by all means, you can avail yourself of their services, but much of the joy of traveling here lays in soaking up the scenery. You'd be best served by your own car, though.

One Week
A Taste of Cockpit Country

From Montego Bay, head out to the **Good Hope Estate**, a beautiful great house and working plantation. Enjoy horseback riding, lunch on the terrace and tremendous views.

On narrow roads, travel through cane fields on your way to **Windsor**. Check into a modest lodge and wake to the sound of birds, then head off to explore **Windsor Caves** with a Rastafarian guide, or pay a visit to the **Windsor Great House** to learn about its environmental protection and bird-banding efforts.

Get ready for some challenging but rewarding **hiking**. From Windsor or Albert Town, you can hire a guide and walk the old military trail connecting Windsor (in the north) with Troy (in the south)...but be ready for some gnarly trails.

Exhausted and exhilarated, head east to Clark's Town, then **Albert Town**. This part of the journey is made for soaking up the scenery. Continue south and make sure to stop at **Accompong**, where you can meet Jamaica's remaining Maroons (descendants of escaped slaves).

It's possible to get around on this tour via route taxi, but you'll get the most out of it by renting a 4WD vehicle.

Outdoor Activities

Best Wall Dive
The Point (p153)

Best Wreck Dive
The Kathryn (p121)

Best Long Hike
Blue Mountain Peak Getting to the top just in time for the best sunrise in Jamaica (p88)

Best Short Jaunt
Back Seaside Having a stroll amid the low hills and soft breezes, near Treasure Beach (p240)

Best River-rafting
Rio Grande Heading up into the jungle clad, rain soaked green tunnels of the eastern parishes (p108)

Best Wildlife-viewing
Black River Great Morass A boat trek from Treasure Beach, past jumping dolphins, up the river past sunning, grinning crocodiles (p222)

Diving & Snorkeling

Diving has been a part of the Jamaican tourist landscape since the late 1960s, when the first facilities opened in Montego Bay, even then the tourism capital of the island. Thanks to nearby reefs and the MoBay marine park, the northwest coast, from Negril to Ocho Rios, remains the epicenter of Jamaican diving culture.

Where to Go
Best Dive Sites

Canyons (p138)

Rose Hall Reef (p153)

The Throne (p191)

Best Snorkeling Sites

Seven Mile Beach (Long Beach; p189)

Bear Cay & World Beach (p174)

Belmont (p217)

When to Go
It's best to go from January to April, when the weather is driest and least prone to storms.

Operators
Montego Bay

Resort Divers (☎973-6131; www.resortdivers .com; 2 Gloucester Ave)

Dive Seaworld (☎953-2180; http://diveseaworld .com; Ironshore) Located northeast of Montego Bay.

Jamaica Scuba Divers (☎617-2500 ext 342 (Falmouth), 957-3039 (Negril); www.scuba

---

DIVING COSTS

» **1-tank dive** US$40 to US$50

» **2-tank dive** US$70 to US$90

» **Snorkeling excursion** around US$30

» **PADI or NAUI certification course** around US$400

-jamaica.com) Based out of Falmouth, Negril and Runaway Bay, but does excursions to MoBay.

Scuba Caribe (☑1-888-748-4990; www.scubacaribe.com) Operates out of the Riu Hotel, Montego Bay.

Negril

Jamaica Scuba Divers (☑957-3039; www.scuba-jamaica.com)

Negril Scuba Centre (☑877-7517; www.negrilscuba.com) Has branch offices in numerous Negril hotels.

Sundivers Negril (☑957-4503; www.sundiversnegril.com; Point Village Resort, Long Bay)

Marine Life Drivers (☑957-3245; www.mldiversnegril.com; Samsara Hotel, West End)

Ocho Rios

Garfield Diving Station (☑395-7023; www.garfielddiving.com; Turtle Beach)

Resort Divers (☑881-5760; www.resortdivers.com; Royal DeCameron Club Caribbean, Runaway Bay)

Rafting

Errol Flynn first saw the fun of coasting down the river on a raft of bamboo poles lashed together. Today, you sit on a raised seat with padded cushions, while a 'captain' poles you through the washboard shallows and small cataracts.

Where to Go

The best river-rafting in Jamaica is in the mountainous interior of the northwest, near the Great River and Martha Brae Rivers. Both of these are within easy day-tripping distance of Montego Bay and Ironshore. On the other side of Jamaica, head to the Rio Grande Valley, which sits within day-trip distance between Kingston and Port Antonio in the east.

When to Go

The best time to go rafting is in the dry season (December to April), when the waters aren't too swollen. If you want a white-water experience, head here in summer.

Operators

Mountain Valley Rafting (☑956-4920; Lethe Estate; single/double US$50/80) For trips along the Great River, in the interior, within easy day-trip distance of Montego Bay and Ironshore.

Rio Grande Experience (☑993-5778; Berridale; per raft US$65) For trips along the Rio Grande, in the eastern interior, within day-tripping distance of Port Antonio and, to a lesser extent, Kingston.

Rafters Village (☑952-0889, 940-6398; www.jamaicarafting.com; 66 Claude Clarke Ave, Montego Bay; per raft 1-2 people US$75) For trips along the Martha Brae, near Falmouth on the northwest coast, within easy day-tripping distance of Montego Bay and Ironshore.

Hiking

Hiking is a great way of seeing the Jamaican interior, but keep in mind it's always best to head into the jungles and the mountains with a guide. It's easy to get lost out here, and it's good to have a contact who can vouch for you with locals. Expect to pay at least US$40 a day for local expertise, and possibly a good deal more to head into particularly difficult terrain.

Where to Go

The most developed area for hiking is in Blue Mountains-John Crow National Park, followed by the Rio Grande Valley in Portland parish, where some of the hikes venture into the Blue and John Crow Mountains. The remote Cockpit Country, with its jungle-clad limestone hills, is perhaps the most dramatic landscape on the island; small community-tourism outfits are growing in that region.

DIVE LAWS

By law, all dives in Jamaican waters must be guided, and dives are restricted to a depth of 30m. See p194 for guidelines on protecting the reef.

DON'T WANDER OFF THE TRACK

Wherever your walk carries you, always be sure to stay on the established trails: the mountainous terrain in Jamaica is too treacherous to go wandering off the track, as thick vegetation hides sinkholes and crevasses. You should always seek advice from locals about trail conditions before setting out, and take a good guide even if you think you know the route.

If you're heading into the backcountry, don't forget to take the following:

☐ Hiking boots
☐ Mosquito netting
☐ Bug spray
☐ Drinking water
☐ Sun block

Best Short Trek The one to the summit of Blue Mountain Peak. Reaching it at sunrise is one of the Caribbean's most exhilarating experiences. The view out over the entire island (and as far as Cuba if the day's clear) more than compensates for having got up at an inhuman hour.

Best Long Trek A trek from Quick Step, in South Cockpit Country, to the Windsor Caves in North Cockpit Country. This hike traverses some of the most beautiful, yet simultaneously difficult terrain in the country. Attempting it without a guide would be suicidal. Contact the **Southern Trelawny Environmental Agency** (☎610-0818; www .stea.net; Grant's Office Complex, Albert Town) for more information.

Best Bird-walking Head out in the area around Windsor, in North Cockpit Country, with the biologists of the **Windsor Research Centre** (☎997-3832; www.cockpitcountry.com; Windsor Great House). It's a fun walk (although you need to be fit) and the accompanying scientific expertise is priceless.

When to Go

It's best to go from January to April, when the weather is driest and least prone to storms.

Operators

Grand Valley Tours (☎401-647-4730; www. portantoniojamaica.com/gvt.html; 12 West St, Port Antonio) Specializes in hiking trips in the Rio Grande Valley.

Sun Venture Tours (☎960-6685, 408-6973; www.sunventuretours.com; 30 Balmoral Ave, Kingston) Kingston-based tour operator; specializes in cultural and environmental tours in off-the-beaten-path Jamaica.

Baboo's Garden (☎475-3046; http://baboos garden.wordpress.com; Accompong) The trekking authority when it comes to hiking in the Cockpit Country near Accompong.

Jamaica Conservation & Development Trust (☎960-2848; www.jcdt.org.jm; 29 Dumbarton Ave, Kingston) Manages trails in Blue Mountains-John Crow National Park and can recommend hiking guides.

Southern Trelawny Environmental Agency (☎610-0818; www.stea.net; Grant's Office Complex, Albert Town) Runs Cockpit Country Adventure Tours and can recommend guides in the western interior.

Spelunking

Does caving technically qualify as being 'outdoors'? Well, it certainly attracts outdoor types. Jamaica is honeycombed with limestone caves and caverns, most of which boast fine stalagmites and stalactites, underground streams and even waterfalls. The **Jamaican Caves Organization** (www.jamaican caves.org) provides resources for the exploration of caves, sinkholes and underground rivers. The group regularly sends out expeditions to survey the island's caves. Expect to pay a guide at least US$50 per person for a short, half-day exploration of a cave; if you want to go deeper and longer into spelunking territory, rates for guides start at US$70 to US$85 for full-day treks.

Where to Go
Tourist Caves
You can find guided tours at these caves:

Windsor Cave, Cockpit Country

Green Grotto, Runaway Bay

Roaring River, Savanna-la-Mar

Nonsuch Caves, Rio Grande Valley

Fox Caves, Rio Grande Valley

Advanced Caves
You'll want to contact Jamaica Caves and organize a guide first.

Mexico Cave, near YS Falls

Ipswich Cave, near YS Falls

Gourie Caves, Christiana
Coffee River caves, Troy

Fishing

Deepwater game fish run year-round through the Cayman Trench, which begins just over 3km from shore on the western side of the island. The waters off Jamaica's north coast are also particularly good for game fishing; an abyss known as 'Marlin Alley' teems with game fish. Charters can be arranged for US$500 to US$550 per half-day or US$900 to US$1200 for a full day through hotels or directly through operators in Montego Bay, Negril, Ocho Rios and Port Antonio. A charter includes captain, tackle, bait and crew. Most charter boats require a 50% deposit.

When to Go

Summer is good for game fishing, but major tournaments go off in Montego Bay in late September and October.

Operators

To enquire about charters, see the relevant destination chapters or contact the following:

Errol Flynn Marina (☎715-6044; www .errolflynnmarina.com; Port Antonio) GPS N 18.168889°, W -76.450556°

Montego Bay Yacht Club (☎979-8038; www.mobayyachtclub.com; Sunset Dr, Montego Bay) GPS N 18.462452°, W -77.943267°

Royal Jamaican Yacht Club (☎924-8685; www.rjyc.org.jm; Norman Manley Dr, Kingston) GPS N 17.940939°, W -76.764939°

Surfing

The **Jamnesia Surf Club** (☎750-0103; www. jamnesia.20megsfree.com; PO Box 167, Kingston 2) provides general information about surfing

---

CASUAL ANGLING

In Negril, fishermen congregating by the bridge are often happy to take you down the South Negril River. On the south coast you can find local fishermen at Belmont, Bluefields and Frenchman's Bay in Treasure Beach who are willing to take you along for a fee (US$40 to US$80 depending on how long you want to be on the water).

---

in Jamaica, and operates a surf camp at Bull Bay, 13km east of Kingston.

Boston Beach, 14km east of Port Antonio, has consistent good waves and a small beachside shack from which you can rent boards cheaply. Long Bay, 16km further south, has gentler waves; it's possible to rent boards here as well.

Cycling

You can hire bicycles at most major resorts and many smaller guesthouses. For anything more serious, you should consider bringing your own mountain or multipurpose bike. You will need sturdy wheels to handle the potholed roads. Check requirements with the airline well in advance. Remember to always have, at a minimum, a flashlight for the front of your bike and reflectors for the rear. If you're in the fixed-gear bicycle camp, note that Jamaica's many hills and unpredictable traffic make riding a 'fixie' (a bike with fixed gears) near-suicidal.

Some online resources:

Jamaican Cycling Federation (www .jamaicacycling.com; 14C Benson Ave, Kingston) Good all-around information; organizes many cycling events.

Rusty's X-Cellent Adventures (☎957-0155; http://rusty.nyws.com/bikeshop.htm; PO Box 104, Negril) Offers rentals and tours in the hills near Negril.

St Mary's Off-Road Bike Association (SMORBA; ☎470-8139; www.smorba.com) Holds mountain-biking events and can provide information on cycling on the north central coast.

Operators

The downhill tour from Hardwar Gap (1700m) in the Blue Mountains is very popular (and not for the fainthearted).

Blue Mountain Bicycle Tours (☎974-7075; www.bmtoursja.com; 121 Main St, Ocho Rios; tour adult/child US$98/70) Offers pickup from Kingston or Ocho Rios and transfer to the Hardwar Gap. Potential stops on the tour include a coffee-roasting facility. Up to 43 cyclists can be accommodated.

Mount Edge B&B (☎944-8151, 351-5083; www.mountedge.com; Newcastle) Similar tour with smaller groups.

Bird-watching

All you need in the field are a good pair of binoculars and a guide to the birds of the island. Expect to pay anywhere from US$25 for an hour's jaunt to US$75 for a good half-day of bird-watching in the bush.

Where to Go

Good spots include the Blue Mountains, Cockpit Country, the Black River Great Morass, the Negril Great Morass and the Rio Grande Valley.

When to Go

The best time for bird-watching in Jamaica runs from December to June; at this time of year birds can be expected to show off their best plumage. This is also the dry season, so you're less likely to be drenched in your binoculars.

Operators

Windsor Great House (☑997-3832; www .cockpitcountry.com; Windsor) organizes a bird-banding effort on the last weekend of each month. For more, try the following:

Ann & Robert Sutton (☑904-5454; asutton@cwjamaica.com) Based in Marshall's Pen in Mandeville, they've been leading major bird tours in Jamaica for more than 30 years.

Rocklands Bird Sanctuary (☑952-2009) Near Montego Bay.

Hotel Mocking Bird Hill (☑993-7134, 993-7267; www.hotelmockingbirdhill.com/gvt.html; Port Antonio) Excellent custom birding tours.

Strawberry Hill (☑946 1958; www.islandout post.com/strawberry_hill) Birding trips in the Blue Mountains.

Grand Valley Tours (☑401-647-4730; www .portantoniojamaica.com/gvt.html; 12 West St, Port Antonio) Specializes in trips to the Rio Grande Valley.

Golf

Jamaica has 12 championship golf courses – more than any other Caribbean island. All courses rent out clubs and have carts. Most require that you hire a caddy – an extremely wise investment, as they know the layout of the course intimately. For more information on the island's links, contact the **Jamaica Golf Association** (☑925-2325; www.jamaica golfassociation.com; Constant Spring Golf Club, PO Box 743, Kingston 8).

The two best courses on the island are both near Montego Bay:

Tryall Golf Course (☑956-5660; www.tryall club.com) The championship 6328m, par-71 Tryall Golf Course is one of the world's finest courses and reputedly Jamaica's most difficult.

White Witch Golf Course (☑953-2800, 518-0174; www.whitewitchgolf.com; Ritz-Carlton Rose Hall; green fees Ritz-Carlton guests/visitors US$175/185, 2:30-4:30pm US$109) A par-71 championship course, this is perhaps the most splendid option.

regions at a glance

Kingston & Around

Cuisine ✓✓✓
History ✓✓✓
Nightlife ✓✓✓

Cuisine
As Jamaica's main city, it's only fitting that Kingston should be the culinary capital as well. Feast yourself on jerk chicken, curry goat and other Jamaican delights, as well as exquisite sushi and international gourmet cuisine. Kingston is a great spot for neighbourhood eateries and holes-in-the-wall, but it is also one of the recognized frontier pushers in the field of haute Caribbean cuisine.

History
Visit Port Royal in search of past pirate glory, stroll amid the ruined buildings of Spanish Town, the island's

former capital, or take a walking tour through the streets of Downtown Kingston to trace the capital's development. For decades, Kingston has been a microcosm of the Jamaican experience; understanding the history of this city is reading the history of the nation writ small across the streets of its capital.

Nightlife
The musical heart of Jamaica, Kingston never sleeps and you can join a party on any night of the week. Its nightlife ranges from formal nightclubs to street dances consisting of giant speakers set up at either end of a street, to stage shows featuring the biggest names in dancehall and reggae. Every night of the week, there is some sort of free live music going down somewhere in this city. Make sure you come to downtown parties with a friendly local.

p36

Blue Mountains & Southeast Coast

Hiking ✓✓✓
Birding ✓✓✓
Luxury Retreats ✓✓✓

Hiking
As well as the island's most popular hike – the night-time climb up to Blue Mountain Peak, the island's highest point – the mountains offer numerous other trails to suit all abilities. The mountains in the morning afford some of the best wildlife-spotting in Jamaica.

Birding
The Blue Mountains are home to most of Jamaica's 250 species of bird, including Jamaica's national bird, the streamertail hummingbird (also known as the doctorbird). Also here are the John Crow vulture and the 'patoo' – the Jamaican brown owl.

Luxury Retreats
Those wishing get away from the bustle of the capital by combining the ultimate luxury with superb views and gourmet cuisine will not be disappointed by Strawberry Hill or Lime Tree Farm.

p78

Port Antonio & Northeast Coast

Culture ✓✓
Cuisine ✓✓
Outdoors ✓✓✓

Culture

Portland parish boasts some of Jamaica's deepest, strongest African roots, as evidenced by festivals like Fi Wi Sinting, which explodes in mento music and dancing, and Moore Town, stronghold of the Windward Maroons.

Cuisine

Boston Bay is supposedly the birthplace of jerk rub, Jamaica's great gift to the culinary world. It's not all smoked meat, though; Port Antonio has refreshingly innovative restaurants that serve high-end Jamaican and fusion fare.

Outdoors

Reach Falls is surely one of the most beautiful cascades in the Caribbean. Afterwards, raft up the Rio Grande or relax on lovely, lonely Long Bay. Compared to the crowded northwest coast, tourists are much thinner on the ground when exploring the outdoors in Portland parish.

p93

Ocho Rios & North Coast

Activities ✓✓✓
History ✓✓
Nightlife ✓✓

Activities

The Ocho Rios area arguably has the most activities packed into a relatively small space in Jamaica. Besides Dunn's River Falls, the country's most popular waterfall, the north coast boasts a mountaintop adventure park, good diving spots, horse-riding adventures, ATV safaris and zipline tours that attract active travelers.

History

Explore the ruins of the first Spanish settlement on the island at Maima Seville Great House in St Ann's Bay on horseback, or head over to Firefly, the home of playwright Noël Coward, with its spectacular coastal views.

Nightlife

From karaoke nights, all-you-can-drink swimwear parties and wet-T-shirt competitions, aimed squarely at tourists and cruise-ship passengers, to gritty rooftop dancehall parties and beach sound-system blowouts, 'Ochi' has something to offer everyone.

p115

Montego Bay & Northwest Coast

Activities ✓✓
History ✓✓✓
Hiking ✓✓

Activities

The beaches in Montego Bay are OK, but there's better sand elsewhere; we really recommend swimming in the Glistening Waters and rafting up the Martha Brae. The infrastructure for guided activities is more developed here than elsewhere on the island.

History

Cheerfully chaotic Falmouth is the most historically preserved town in Jamaica, while near Ironshore there are protected great houses and the excellent history/culture show put on at Outameni.

Hiking

Head deep into Cockpit Country, south of Montego Bay, to find fascinating caves and some of the best birding in Jamaica near Windsor and Albert Town. For an easier challenge, you can go on light hill walks in the area near Lethe.

p143

Negril & West Coast

Activities ✓✓
Eating ✓✓
Nightlife ✓✓✓

South Coast & Central Highlands

Outdoors ✓✓✓
Culture ✓✓✓
Relaxing ✓✓✓

Activities

Sure, you can go water-skiing and parasailing and cliff-diving and all that, but a lot of the joy of Negril is in watching that perfect sunset every evening, which is another way of saying: doing nothing at all.

Eating

Negril has a good plethora of eating options, from simple, beach-satisfying fare on Long Bay to the classier confines of the fusion and high-end restaurants of the West End. Sunsets off the island's west coast make for some of the most romantic dining experiences in Jamaica.

Nightlife

If you're looking for a beach party in Jamaica, you can't really do much better than Negril. From folks getting 'sedate' on the beach to rip-roaring, rum-fueled parties, there's a lot to keep you entertained.

p185

Outdoors

From the extensive cave networks of the Central Highlands to the glorious cascades of YS Falls, and even gentler options like the rolling pastureland near Lover's Leap, there's a lot to keep you outdoors.

Culture

Accompong, in dramatic South Cockpit Country, is the best place in Jamaica to interact with the Maroons. For intellectual pursuits, hit Treasure Beach during the Calabash International Literary Festival. Many members of the island intelligentisa are attracted to the laid-back resorts in and around Treasure Beach.

Relaxing

You know what? Crocodiles are relaxing. Look how laid-back they are, chilling on Black River. Even more relaxing? Picking the perfect Treasure Beach accomodations and losing yourself for days, weeks, months...

p213

Look out for these icons:

 TOP CHOICE Our author's recommendation

A green or sustainable option

FREE No payment required

See the Index for a full list of destinations covered in this book.

On the Road

Kingston & Around

Best Places to Eat

» Andy's (p56)

» Red Bones Blues Café (p57)

» Gloria's Top Spot (p70)

» Patrice's Restaurant (p56)

» Prendy's On The Beach (p72)

Best Places to Stay

» Spanish Court Hotel (p54)

» City View Hotel (p54)

» Moon Hill (p54)

» Jamnesia Surf Camp (p66)

» Morgan's Harbour Hotel (p70)

Why Go?

Jamaica's one true city, Kingston is something of an island within the island. It is Jamaica undiluted and unadulterated, its brisk business pace and chaotic traffic contrasting sharply with the timeless languor of resorts and villages elsewhere on the island. Justly proud for having been the launching pad for some of the world's most electrifying music, the city by no means trades on its past reputation; spirited clubs and riotous street-system parties attest to the fact that the beat is still alive and bumping. Kingston's cosmopolitan makeup has given rise to fine international dining but its dynamic galleries and museums remain unapologetically Jamaican.

The capital's proximity to the atmospheric historical ruins and grit of Spanish Town, the original capital, and the faded glory of Port Royal – one-time raucous pirate capital turned laid-back village awaft with the scent of frying fish – makes Kingston an ideal base for exploring eastern Jamaica.

When to Go
Kingston

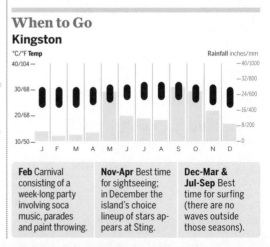

| **Feb** Carnival consisting of a week-long party involving soca music, parades and paint throwing. | **Nov-Apr** Best time for sightseeing; in December the island's choice lineup of stars appears at Sting. | **Dec-Mar & Jul-Sep** Best time for surfing (there are no waves outside those seasons). |

Essential Eating

Visiting the culinary capital of Jamaica demands that you sample at least some of its specialties. Patties with beef, chicken, shrimp and lobster make a great snack, while jerk chicken and pork are a spicy, smoky taste explosion. Curry goat and oxtail and beans are flavorful, filling mains come with rice and peas (beans) and let's not forget the fish – steamed, stewed, fried or escoveitched. Vegetarians will love I-tal vegetable dishes and superb fresh fruit juices. Finish off with sweet potato pudding – a rich, bricklike delight.

STREET PARTY ETIQUETTE

If you attend one of Kingston's famous street parties, you'd do well to follow the locals' lead.

What to wear Batty riders (tight shorts) and figure-hugging tops are de rigueur for ladies, while guys should don jeans, 'puss boots,' clean shirts (pink and baby blue are perfectly manly), bandannas (sometimes worn in the style of Eastern European babushkas) and gold bling. Bring a spare rag for mopping your sweaty brow.

What to do Raise your hand in the air in a mock gun salute and shout 'Bullet, bullet!' or 'Brap, brap, brap!' to signify approval of a particular song. Grind and 'wine' with the best of them and do not show hesitation or fear. Guys may wish to form a dance crew to battle rival dance crews.

What to drink Vendors are always on hand with Red Stripes, rum or fish 'tea.'

Top Five Sound Systems

» Passa Passa (p60), still the biggest Downtown street party that brings Uptown and Downtown together.

» Weddy Weddy Wednesdays (p60) is Uptown's favorite street jam, put on by legendary local DJ, Stone Love.

» Oldies Night (p60), held in the fishing village of Rae Town, attracts a mellow older crowd with a mix of Gregory Isaacs, Horace Andy, John Holt and Bob Marley.

» Bounty Sundays (p62), a weekly favorite held in an outdoor club hosted by Bounty Killer, one of the biggest names in dancehall.

» Street Vybz (p61), a street party with an edgy vibe recreated in an indoor setting and presided over by Vybz Cartel.

AT A GLANCE

Currency Jamaican dollars (J$), US dollars (US$)

Language English, patois

Money ATMs all over; banks open Monday to Friday

Visas Not required for citizens of the EU, Australia or US

Fast Facts

» **Population** 780,000
» **Emergency** ☎110
» **Side of road to drive on** Left

Set Your Budget

» **Budget hotel room** J$3825
» **Two-course evening meal** J$1700
» **Bob Marley Museum admission** J$1000
» **Beer** J$180
» **Bus fare in Kingston** J$80

Resources

» **Jamaica Tourist Board** (www.visitjamaica.com) Introduction to the island's attractions.

» **Jamaicans** (www.jamaicans.com) Jamaican culture, cookery, news, blogs and tourist information.

» **Jamaica Heritage Trust** (www.jnht.com) Detailed info on heritage sites and attractions in Kingston and islandwide.

» **Yard Flex** (www.yardflex.com) News, culture, fashion, dancehall lyrics, message boards and much more.

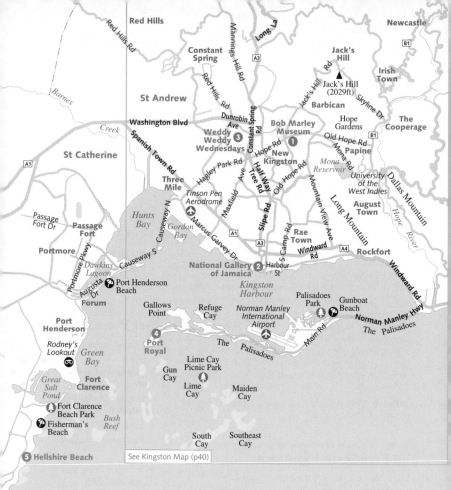

Kingston & Around Highlights

❶ Delving into the life of Jamaica's most revered contemporary hero at his former home and studio, the **Bob Marley Museum** (p48)

❷ Appreciating the vision of Jamaican artists at the internationally acclaimed **National Gallery of Jamaica** (p41)

❸ Getting into the groove at the riotous sound-system party, **Weddy Weddy Wednesdays** (p60), which rattles the windows of Burlington Ave every Wednesday

❹ Retracing the steps of Blackbeard and Henry Morgan at the former pirate capital of the world, **Port Royal** (p68)

❺ Chilling out at **Hellshire Beach** (p72), an atmospheric collection of seaside shacks, where fried fish has been elevated to the status of haute cuisine

KINGSTON

Whether you approach it by air or by land, Kingston – sitting between the world's seventh-largest natural harbor and the wall of Blue Mountains – simultaneously impresses you with its setting and overwhelms you with its sheer size, its noise and its traffic. This is the island's cultural and economic heart, where the political deals are made, where the island's musicians come to follow in the footsteps of the greats, and where you can be exposed to miserable squalor and great luxury within footsteps of each other. A visit to the capital is essential if you wish to understand the complexity of Jamaica's reality and its multifaceted character.

Kingston's been plagued with a negative reputation for decades due to its high crime rate, and while it's not entirely unwarranted – there are certainly areas you'll wish to avoid – with some street smarts, a little luck and an open mind, the visitor is richly rewarded by a firm acquaintance with a city as unbridled and unique to the island as it is to the Caribbean and indeed the world.

Kingston divides neatly into two halves, Uptown and Downtown, and never the twain shall meet. Downtown is the home of many historic buildings, the law courts, banks and factories, Jamaica's greatest art museum and chaotic street markets, centered around Parade (William Grant Park). Its rather shabby streets, busy with higglers, shop assistants and besuited lawyers, reverberate with pounding music – anything from Bounty Killer to Shania Twain – and end by an attractive waterfront park, with the homeless camping out under the palm trees. To the west of Parade lie the notorious 'garrisons' – ghettos such as Trench Town and Tivoli Gardens, with an appalling murder rate but the best street parties – where many houses don't have running water and the streets are particularly 'fragrant' after the rain.

Less than 6km (yet a world) away, Uptown holds the city's hotels, restaurants, and clubs, largely confined to the pocket of New Kingston, with its cluster of tall buildings around Emancipation Park. If you have a light complexion, you are much more likely to blend in here than Downtown. In addition to two of the city's most essential sights, the Bob Marley Museum and Devon House, the capital's diplomatic and commercial status assures Uptown a definite cosmopolitan suaveness – not to mention a certain amount of security, though gated communities with guard dogs abound. Further out, in the foothills, are Kingston's most exclusive neighborhoods and lodgings, with expansive views over the capital.

Uptown and Downtown rarely mix; there are many Kingstonians who never see both halves of their own city, but if you wish to experience Jamaica to its fullest, you should.

You wanted 'real' Jamaica? This is it.

KINGSTON IN...

Two Days

Visit the **Bob Marley Museum** to see where Jamaica's favorite son rested his natty dreads, and the **National Gallery of Jamaica** for a crash course in Jamaican art; tour beautiful colonial manse **Devon House**; eat a meal to remember at the **Red Bones Blues Café** or try **Andy's** for the best jerk in town. At night, hit Knutsford Blvd for some sweaty after-hours excitement at the **Building** or **Quad**.

Four Days

Go to **Port Royal** for a peek into Jamaica's pirate past, and catch a boat to the tiny island of **Lime Cay** for sun worship. Soak in some history by taking a stroll around **Downtown Kingston** and see what influenced the young Bob Marley at the **Trench Town Culture Yard & Village** or what his son Ziggy's up to at **Tuff Gong Recording Studios**. Attend a sound-system party at **Weddy Weddy Wednesdays** or Rae Town's **Oldies Night** (Sundays).

One Week

Head to **Hellshire Beach Recreation Area** for a Kingstonian beach experience; take in **Spanish Town**, Jamaica's capital for over 300 years.

History

Kingston as a city did not even exist when the English captured Jamaica from the Spanish in 1655. For several decades the site of the future city was used for rearing pigs and was known as Hog Crawle. When an earthquake leveled Port Royal in 1692, survivors struggled across the bay and pitched camp with the swine. A town plan was drawn up on a grid pattern, centered on an open square and taking advantage of the harbor.

The port city prospered throughout the 18th century, becoming one of the most im-

Kingston

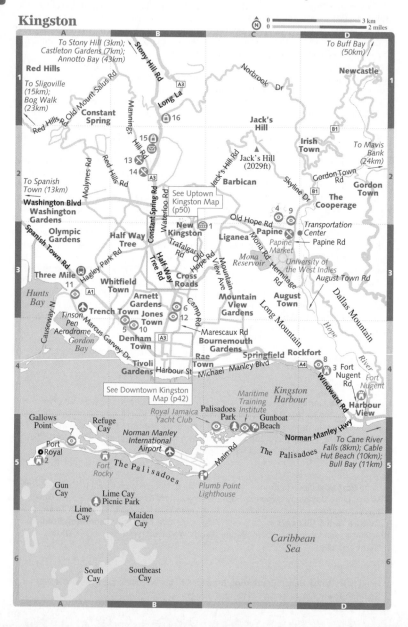

0	3 km
0	2 miles

To Stony Hill (3km); Castleton Gardens (7km); Annotto Bay (43km)

To Buff Bay (50km)

Red Hills

Newcastle

To Sligoville (15km); Bog Walk (23km)

Norbrook Dr

Stony Hill Rd

A3

Long La

Old Mount Salus Rd

Red Hills Rd

Constant Spring

Mannings Hill Rd

16

Jack's Hill

Irish Town

To Mavis Bank (24km)

Red Hills Rd

15

13

14

A3

Jack's Hill (2029ft)

Gordon Town Rd

Skyline Dr

B1

Gordon Town

To Spanish Town (13km)

Molynres Rd

Constant Spring Rd

Waterloo Rd

Jack's Hill Rd

Barbican

B1

The Cooperage

Washington Blvd
Washington Gardens

Olympic Gardens

Half Way Tree

See Uptown Kingston Map (p50)

New Kingston

1

Old Hope Rd

4   9

Papine

Transportation Center

Spanish Town Rd

Hagley Park Rd

Half Way Tree Rd

Trafalgar Rd

Old Hope Rd

Liganea

Mona Reservoir

Papine Market

Papine Rd

Three Mile

11

A1

Whitfield Town

Cross Roads

Mountain View Ave

Mona Rd

Hermitage Rd

University of the West Indies

August Town Rd

Hunts Bay

Arnett Gardens

6

Mountain View Gardens

August Town

Dallas Mountain

Tinson Pen Aerodrome

Marcus Garvey Dr

Trench Town

Jones Town

5   10

12

Camp Rd

Marescaux Rd

Long Mountain

Hope River

Gordon Bay

Denham Town

A3

Bournemouth Gardens

Springfield

Rockfort

8

Tivoli Gardens

Harbour St

Rae Town

Michael Manley Blvd

A4

3 Fort Nugent

Fort Nugent Rd

Fort Nugent

Causeway N

See Downtown Kingston Map (p42)

Maritime Training Institute

Kingston Harbour

Windward Rd

Harbour View

Gallows Point

Refuge Cay

Royal Jamaica Yacht Club

Palisadoes Park

Gunboat Beach

Norman Manley Hwy

To Cane River Falls (8km); Cable Hut Beach (10km); Bull Bay (11km)

Port Royal

7

2

Norman Manley International Airport

Main Rd

The Palisadoes

Gun Cay

Fort Rocky

The Palisadoes

Plumb Point Lighthouse

Lime Cay
Picnic Park

Lime Cay

Maiden Cay

Caribbean Sea

South Cay

Southeast Cay

portant trading centers in the western hemisphere and an important transshipment point for slaves destined for the Spanish colonies, attracting traders and fresh waves of immigrants. As the city expanded and its population swelled, the shanty towns of the poor rural masses mushrooming where today's 'garrisons' are, and the wealthier merchants moved up to the cooler heights of present-day Uptown, where they built more expansive homes.

In 1907 a violent earthquake leveled much of the city, particularly the waterfront, sending Kingston's wealthier elements further uptown and further accentuating the difference between impoverished Downtown and wealthy Uptown. Downtown proved to be fertile breeding ground both for the Rastafarian movement and the pan-African sentiments of the 1930s and served as the stage for major riots during the worldwide economic crisis. The riots were followed by the creation of labor unions and political parties, uniting the workers and clamoring for change.

In the 1960s, Downtown's damaged edifices were given new life, the port expanded and attempts were made to spruce up the waterfront with the introduction of gleaming new offices and bank buildings. The tourist boom, with cruise ships docking in Kingston Harbour and visitors drawn by the city's growing music industry, was short-lived.

The boom years of the 1960s lured the rural poor, swelling the slums and shantytowns that had arisen in the preceding years. Unemployment soared, and with it came crime. The fractious 1970s spawned politically sponsored criminal enterprises whose trigger-happy networks still plague the city. Commerce began to leave Downtown for New Kingston, and the middle class began to edge away as well. That exodus began a period of decline from which Downtown has yet to recover.

Despite ongoing inner-city strife, the Jamaica Tourist Board is pushing to dispel the city's negative image and to resurrect its tourist industry. It has long talked up plans to bring cruise ships back to Kingston and in recent years, Downtown has been showing some signs of rejuvenation, leading you to believe that there is hope.

⊙ Sights

DOWNTOWN

TOP CHOICE **National Gallery of Jamaica** ART GALLERY
(Map p42; www.natgalja.org.jm; 12 Ocean Blvd; admission J$250; ⊙10am-4:30pm Tue-Thu, to 4pm Fri, to 3pm Sat) The superlative collection of Jamaican art housed by the National Gallery is quite simply the finest on the island and should on no account be missed. In addition to offering an intrinsically Jamaican take on international artistic trends, the collection attests to the vitality of the country's artistic heritage as well as its present.

The core of the permanent collection is presented on the 1st floor in 10 galleries representing the Jamaican School, organized chronologically spanning the years 1922 to the present. The first rooms are mainly devoted to the sculptures of Edna Manley and the spectacularly vibrant 'intuitive' paintings (p266), notably the dark landscapes of John Dunkley, the poignant portraiture of Albert Huie and the village life scenes of David Pottinger. Later galleries chart the course of 'Jamaican art for Jamaicans' up to the recent past, including abstract religious works by Carl Abrahams, decidedly surrealist exercises by Colin Garland, ethereal assemblages by David Boxer, Barrington Watson's realist forays and many other works that animate various aspects of Jamaica's national culture. Taíno carvings and colonial-era art are also represented in the permanent collection, the latter contrasting sharply with the vibrant modern works.

Kingston

⊙ Sights

⊗ Eating

⊕ Shopping

TRENCH TOWN

Dumfries St

To National Heroes Park (500m);
New Kingston (4km);

Blount St

Oxford St

Upper Rose La

Slipe Pen Rd

Orange St

Chancery La

Upper King St

North St

Church St

Upper Mark La

Duke St

Upper Johns La

East St

Bond St

Pink La

Rose La

West St

Charles St

7

Survey
Department

3

To Set Me Free (100m);
Passa Passa (150m);
Washington Blvd (6.5km);
Spanish Town (23.5km)

Beeston St

5

6

Spanish Town Rd

29

30

*Liberty
Hall*

Love La

Salt La

Young St

26

28

Heywood St

Produce
Market

N Parade

20

To Downtown
Terminal (200m)

W Queen St

W Parade

17

Parade
(St William
Grant Park)

18

4

Beckford St

S Parade

16

Mark La

Johns La

8

Marcus
Garvey Ave

Pechon St

West St

Matthews La

Princess St

Luke La

Orange St

Peters La

Temple La

15

Georges La

Hanover St

To Tinson Pen Aerodrome
(3.2km); Portmore (10.2km)

Darling St

Water La

13

*Supreme
Court*

14

Church St

Tower St

*Institute
of Jamaica*

11

10

1

New Long-
Distance Bus
Terminal

Water St

Tower
Lane

24

25

27

23

22

21

Harbour St

Port Royal St

2

*National
Gallery of
Jamaica*

Kingston
Mall

Little Port
Royal St

King St

Church St

Ocean Blvd

Nethersole Pl

9

Ocean Blvd

Derelict Wharves

12

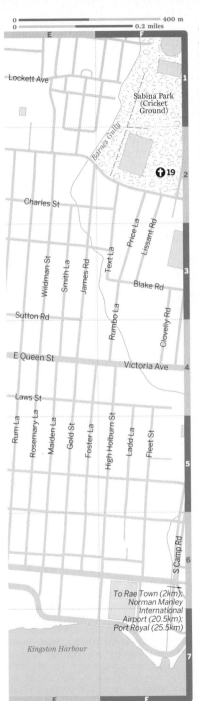

Elsewhere, the various collections and the presentation spaces of the gallery include the AD Scott Collection of Jamaican art, the Cecil Baugh gallery of ceramics, the Edna Manley Memorial Collection, and the eminently enjoyable Larry Wirth Collection, a unique and cohesive assemblage of paintings and African-style sculpture by visionary artist, revivalist bishop and community leader Mallica 'Kapo' Reynolds. Do not miss the realism works, which include Dawn Scott's powerful *A Cultural Object,* a maze-like representation of a Kingston ghetto.

Excellent **guided tours** (☑reservations 922-1561; 45min tour J$1800) are offered, providing illuminating background to the works on show; advance reservations are suggested. The superb **National Biennial temporary exhibition** that takes place on alternate, even-numbered years between mid-December and March showcases the best of contemporary Jamaican art.

Institute of Jamaica   MUSEUM
(Map p42; ☑922-0620; www.instituteofjamaica.org. jm; 10-16 East St; adult/child J$200/100; ☺9:30am-4:30pm Mon-Thu, to 3:30pm Fri) Toward the south end of East St, the Institute of Jamaica is the nation's small-scale equivalent of the British Museum or Smithsonian, housed in three separate buildings. The institute hosts permanent and visiting exhibitions.

You purchase your entrance ticket at the **Natural History Museum**, accessed by a separate entrance around the corner on Tower St. Downstairs there is an array of stuffed birds and a exhibition on the origins of Jamaica's most important crops (currently closed for renovation), while upstairs hosts excellent temporary historical exhibitions, such as 'Jamaican Servicemen during World War II.'

The central building features the **National Library** (www.nlj.org.jm), which incorporates the Caribbean's largest repository of audiovisual aids, books, maps, charts, paintings and documents on West Indian history.

The small but informative **Museum of Music** on the top floor displays traditional musical instruments and traces the history and development of Jamaica's music, from kumina, mento and ska to reggae and dancehall.

Next door, the **Africa Collection** features weapons, carvings and some exquisite craftwork from various African countries. The helmet decorated with cowrie shells is particularly impressive.

The superb **'Guzzum Power: Obeah in Jamaica'** exhibition, accessed through the Africa Collection or the Natural History Museum, offers a fascinating insight into a practice that's currently illegal in Jamaica. Well-labeled exhibits include various ceremonial objects – sinister-looking candles, protection rings and herbs, and there's a replica ceremonial circle on the floor, as well as a typical witch doctor's 'office.' Rocky the curator can not only talk you through the exhibition but also take you on a tour of Downtown on request.

TOP CHOICE **Liberty Hall**   MUSEUM
(Map p42; 948-8639; 76 King St; adult/child J$300/100; 9:30am-4:30pm Mon-Thu, to 3:30pm Fri) At the end of a tranquil tree-lined courtyard, decorated with cheerful mosaics and a mural depicting Marcus Garvey, stands Liberty Hall, part of the Institute of Jamaica and the headquarters of Garvey's UNIA (United Negro Improvement Association) between 1923 and his departure for England in 1935. The restored building now contains an excellent multimedia museum about the man himself and his work, with voiceovers and interactive displays, which allows the visitor to appreciate Garvey's impact on Jamaica as a founder of pan-Africanism.

As in Garvey's day, Liberty Hall has a community outreach program, holding after-school programs for neighborhood children, computer literacy classes and even capoeira lessons on the roof terrace. There is also a reference library with a focus on Garvey. At the time of writing, Liberty Hall was in the process of refurbishing the building next door to accommodate a donation of 10,000 books on the subject of the African diaspora.

Parade   SQUARE
St William Grant Park (Map p42), more commonly known as 'Parade,' is the bustling heart of Downtown, and originally hosted a fortress erected in 1694 with guns pointing down King St toward the harbor. The fort was torn down and a garden, Victoria Park, laid out in 1870, with a life-size statue of Queen Victoria at its center. The park was renamed in 1977 to honor Black Nationalist and labor leader Sir William Grant (1894–1977), who preached his Garveyite message of African redemption here. Her Majesty's statue now stands on the east side of the park, while the north and south entrances

are watched over by cousins and political rivals Norman Manley and Alexander Busta-mante, respectively. At the center of the park is a whimsical four-tiered fountain.

At North Parade, the distinguished **Ward Theatre**, built in 1911, was given to the city by rum baron Colonel Charles Ward, though its location has been the venue for theatrical performances since the mid-18th century. The theater has a 60-year history of staging the annual Boxing Day pantomime – a riotous, irreverent social satire. The building has fallen into disrepair over the years and audiences have dwindled due to the proliferation of Downtown crime, though there were shuttles from New Kingston serving the evening performances. At the time of writing, the theater was undergoing renovation, and tours of its interior were expected once it is restored. For now, you can admire the cracked sky-blue facade with white trim.

The gleaming white edifice facing the park's southeast corner is **Kingston Parish Church**, today serving a much reduced congregation of true Kingstonians – those 'born under the clock' (within earshot of its bell). The original church was destroyed in the 1907 earthquake and was replaced (in concrete) by the existing building. Note the **tomb** dating to 1699, the year the original church was built. Admiral Benbow, the commander of the Royal Navy in the West Indies at the turn of the 18th century, lies beneath a tombstone near the high altar. Marble plaques commemorate soldiers of the West Indian regiments who died of fever or other hardships during colonial wars.

The crenellated **Coke Memorial Hall** facing the eastern side of William Grant Park has an austere red brick facade in the dour Methodist tradition. The structure dates from 1840, but was remodeled in 1907 after sustaining severe damage in the earthquake. It was named after the founder of the Methodist churches in the Caribbean, Thomas Coke.

South Parade, packed with street vendors' stalls, is known as 'Ben Dung Plaza' because passersby have to bend down to buy from hawkers whose goods are displayed on the ground. The place is clamorous, and stores blast reggae music loud enough to

THE YARDS

The ghetto areas of West Kingston are still, as Bob Marley observed during his song of that name, concrete jungles. Acre upon acre of these festering tenements spread out west from the Parade, where much of the city's population growth in recent decades has been concentrated. These areas include Trench Town, Jones Town and sterile housing projects – 'yards' – such as Majesty Pen and Tivoli Gardens, which were conceived as 'model communities' when built in the 1960s.

The region was once a calm residential zone. Alas, during the strife of the 1970s the middle classes debunked and moved to the safety of the suburbs. The poor masses filled the void, and conditions rapidly deteriorated, drawing hoodlums, and other predatory elements called 'yardies.' The situation was exacerbated by the JLP (Jamaica Labour Party) and PNP (People's National Party) currying favor among the ghetto constituencies by patronizing area leaders ('dons'), who in turn encouraged their gangs to recruit voters and intimidate political opponents at election time.

Unlike the 1970s, today the situation is out of the politicians' control, as a large percentage of the gangs' incomes come from drug- and gun-running.

It's easy to tell which party rules behind the stockades. Upfront, no-nonsense wall murals act as territorial markers that tell the tale of a city at war with itself.

Visitors and out-of-towners only venture into the ghettos if they know someone there and, while people from neighboring areas can freely enter the turf of the 'opposition' most of the time, during election times, when tempers are running high and there's much at stake (typical Downtown graffiti reads: 'Vote JLP. We need house.'), crossing into an opposing party's area can be tantamount to a death wish.

The **People's Action for Community Transformation** (PACT; Map p50; ☎920-0334; www.jamaica-kidz.com/pact/; 2-6 Grenada Cres) is a coalition of 26 community-based nongovernmental organizations (NGOs) that works to improve life and community relationships in Kingston's inner city. The organization welcomes donations and will be happy to recommend guides.

drive away even the most determined visitor (locals seem inured).

Tuff Gong Recording Studios
RECORDING STUDIO

(Map p40; ☑923-9380; www.tuffgong.com; 220 Marcus Garvey Dr; tour J$700) Tuff Gong – named for its founder, Bob 'Tuff Gong' Marley – is now one of the Caribbean's largest and most influential studios. Bob Marley's early mixing board traveled with the studio and is still in use today as the studio continues to turn out hit records, not the least of which are those by his son Ziggy, the studio's current chief. Past clients include Damien 'Jr Gong' Marley, Chaka Khan and Capleton. It's a commercial venture and a remastering plant and remixing studio, but visitors are welcome to a 45-minute tour with the entire music production process explained, provided you call in advance. If someone is recording, you may not be allowed to see all sections of the studio. A gift store sells CDs and singles, plus T-shirts, tapes, crafts and a miscellany of Marley mementos.

Trench Town Culture Yard
COMMUNITY PROJECT

(Map p40) Trench Town, which began life as a much-prized housing project erected by the British in the 1930s, is widely credited as the birthplace of ska, rocksteady and reggae music. The neighborhood has been immortalized in the gritty narratives of numerous reggae songs, not the least of which is Bob Marley's 'No Woman No Cry,' the poignant Trench Town anthem penned by Vincent 'Tata' Ford, Marley's mentor, in a tiny bedroom at what is now the Trench Town Museum (Map p40; ☑572-4085; 6-10 Lower First St; yard & museum admission J$1000, with guided neighborhood tour J$1500; ⊗8am-6pm).

The museum, centered around the courtyard, is stocked with Wailers memorabilia, including Marley's first guitar, some poignant photographs from his time here and nyahbinghi drums. There's a rusted-out carcass of a VW bus that belonged to Bob Marley and the Wailers in the 1960s and the small bedroom that was Bob and Rita Marley's home before superstardom. The tour, however, can be rather brisk, with visitors being steered towards the gift shop at the end.

Also on site is the Trench Town Development Association (TTDA; ☑757-6739, 922-8462), singularly responsible for transforming Bob Marley's former home into a community-based heritage site, and dedicated to promoting social justice, self-reliance and human dignity through community-based development.

The Culture Yard, which features a large mural of the man, is one block off Marcus Garvey Dr. It is safe to visit, but don't go wandering elsewhere around Trench Town on your own. To visit, contact the Trench Town Development Association.

Another successful community project is the nearby Trench Town Reading Centre (www.trenchtownreadingcentre.com; First St), established in 1994 in an effort to arm the neighborhood youth with knowledge rather than guns. Book donations are very welcome; see the website for suggestions.

National Heroes Park
PARK

The 30-hectare oval-shaped National Heroes Park (off Map p42) used to be the Kingston Racecourse for over a century before it was shifted to its present location at Caymanas Park. Today its north end is a forlorn wasteland of sun-bleached grass grazed by goats. At the park's southern end, however, National Heroes Circle contains some intriguing statues and memorials. The tomb of Sir Alexander Bustamante is a flat marble slab beneath an arch. More interesting is the Memorial to 1865, commemorating the Morant Bay Rebellion with a rock on a pedestal flanked by bronze busts of Abraham Lincoln and a black slave with a sword.

Marcus Garvey is also buried here, as is ex-Premier Norman Manley, whose body was flown here from England in 1964 and re-interred with state honors. The Manley Monument, honoring his son Michael, was dedicated here in March 2002. Nearby are the final resting places of the beloved 'Crown Prince of Reggae,' Dennis Brown, who died in 1999 and 'Miss Lou,' revered poet Louise Bennett.

Jewish Synagogue
SYNAGOGUE

(Map p42; ☑922-5931; www.ucija.org; cnr Duke & Charles Sts; ⊗service 10am Sat) Jamaica's only remaining synagogue, home to the United Congregation of the Israelites, is an attractive white building dating from 1912 (its predecessor was toppled by the 1907 earthquake) with a fine mahogany staircase and gallery. Sand muffles your footsteps as you roam – the practice of spreading sand on the floor dates back to the days of the Inquisition, when many Jews practiced Judaism in secret, and it's a gesture of solidarity on the part of local Jews, who were never subject to religious restrictions in Jamaica.

The synagogue is usually locked, though on weekdays there is usually someone in the little office around the back who can open up on request, for a small donation. The hall adjacent to the synagogue houses a well-presented **exhibition** on the history of Jamaica's Jewish community and its contribution to Jamaica's commerce, manufacturing, art, music and political system.

FREE **Headquarters House**   NOTABLE BUILDING
(Map p42; 79 Duke St; ☺8:30am-4:30pm Mon-Fri) The brick-and-timber house was originally known as Hibbert House, named after Thomas Hibbert, reportedly one of four members of the Assembly who in 1755 engaged in a bet to build the finest house and thereby win the attention of a much-sought-after beauty. It seems he lost the bet. In 1872, when the capital was moved from Spanish Town to Kingston, the house became the seat of the Jamaican legislature and remained so until 1960, when Gordon House was built next door.

Since 1983, Headquarters House has hosted the **Jamaican National Heritage Trust**, which has its offices in the former bedrooms and in an extension. Visitors are welcome to roam the rest of the building, including the former debating chamber on the ground floor, holding portraits of Jamaica's national heroes and a piano in the corner, which was used to compose Jamaica's national anthem. Upstairs is a lookout tower of the type commonly built by the wealthy merchants of yesteryear to espy incoming vessels.

Gordon House   NOTABLE BUILDING
(Map p42; ☎922-0200; cnr Duke & Beeston Sts; admission to public gallery free) Jamaica's parliament meets at Gordon House, immediately north of Headquarters House. The rather plain brick-and-concrete building was constructed in 1960 and named after national hero the Right Excellent George William Gordon (1820–65); see the boxed text, p253.

You can visit Gordon House by prior arrangement to watch how the Jamaican parliament conducts business. The legislature has a single chamber, where the House of Representatives and the Senate meet at different times – the former at 2pm on Tuesday (and sometimes, during pressing business, on Wednesday at the same hour), and the latter at 11am on Friday. When the legislature is not in session, the marshal sometimes lets visitors in at his discretion.

Rock Tower   ART GALLERY
(Map p42; ☎922-9229, 509-0480; 8 Pechon St; ☺9am-5pm Mon-Fri) This gallery-cum-art-workshop is the brainchild of Australian artist Melinda Brown who moved her studio to Kingston from Manhattan's meat-packing district in 2005 and took over the old Red Stripe Factory. The sprawling warehouse project aims to rejuvenate the surrounding area and to help channel local creativity into sustainable living. Rock Tower (aka 'Rocktowa') artists include potters and sculptors, and one of the ongoing projects is the creation of a medicinal forest as a living art installation, using waste from nearby Coronation Market as compost – a metaphor for the renewal of the neighboring communities.

Wolmer's School & Mico Teachers' College   NOTABLE BUILDINGS
At the northern end of National Heroes Park you'll find **Wolmer's School** (Map p40), a venerable educational establishment founded in 1729 that has produced many notable figures, including prime ministers and governor generals.

The impressive 1909 wooden colonial structures nearby house one of the oldest teacher-training colleges in the world, **Mico Teachers' College** (Map p40), which owes its existence to the 11th-hour refusal by Lady Mico's nephew to marry one of her six nieces in 1670. The unused dowry was invested, and a century and a half later, the considerable accumulated assets were used to establish the Mico College with a mission to educate former slaves after emancipation.

African-Caribbean Heritage Centre & Jamaica Memory Bank   CULTURAL CENTRE
(Map p42; ☎922-4793; www.instituteofjamaica.org.jm; 12 Ocean Boulevard; ☺8:30am-4:30pm Mon-Thu, to 3:30pm Fri) Presided over by the Institute of Jamaica, the Heritage Centre houses an extensive library dedicated to the history of the Middle Passage and a sociocultural exploration of the African diaspora. It is also home to the Memory Bank, an engrossing audiovisual history archive created to preserve Jamaica's rich folkloric traditions. The center is mainly used for research, but its Outreach program stages cultural events, from lectures and symposia to readings and dance performance.

Bank of Jamaica   NOTABLE BUILDING
(Map p42; Nethersole Pl) The national mint and treasury stands at the east end of

Ocean Blvd, fronted by a tall concrete statue of Noel 'Crab' Nethersole (minister of finance from 1955 to 1969). Inside the bank building you'll find the surprisingly absorbing **Museum of Coins & Notes** (admission free; ◷9am-4pm Mon-Fri), displaying Jamaican currency through the centuries, and chronicling the history of money worldwide, from the early bartering systems to the Chinese invention of coins and notes.

Secret Garden Memorial   MONUMENT
(Map p42; cnr Tower & Church Sts) Consisting of a stylized dark head with silver tears running down its cheeks, this memorial was unveiled by Prime Minister Bruce Golding in 2008 as an official acknowledgement of the impact of the existing culture of violence on Kingston's youth. It commemorates children who have died in tragic or violent circumstances, with the names and ages of the victims carved into the plinth. Most are boys between the ages of 11 and 17.

St Andrew's Scots Kirk   CHURCH
(Map p42; 43A Duke St) This octagonal Georgian brick structure (entrance on Mark's Lane) serves the United Church of Jamaica and Grand Cayman. It was built from 1813 to 1819 by a group of prominent Scottish merchants and is surrounded by a gallery supported by Corinthian pillars. Note the white-on-blue St Andrew's cross in the stained-glass window. You'll be amply rewarded if you visit during a service, when its acclaimed choir, the St Andrew Singers, performs.

Trinity Cathedral   CHURCH
(Map p42; 1 George Eddy Dr; ◷5:30pm Mon-Fri, 8:30am Sun) Open only for services, this partially restored church is noted largely for having been the site of Norman Manley's funeral (attended by such dignitaries as Fidel Castro) as well as a small wall of mosaics dating back to Spanish times.

Negro Aroused Statue   MONUMENT
(Map p42; King St) This controversial bronze statue depicting a crouched black man breaking free from bondage is the work of Jamaica's foremost sculptor, the late Edna Manley. This is actually a replica; the original is in the National Gallery of Jamaica.

Ba Beta Kristian Church of Haile Selassie I   CHURCH
(Map p42; Oxford St) A Sunday afternoon service here is a colorful affair. To attend, women must sit on the right-hand side, wear dresses and keep their hair covered.

UPTOWN

TOP CHOICE ⟩ **Bob Marley Museum**   MUSEUM
(Map p40; www.bobmarley-foundation.com/museum.html; 56 Hope Rd; adult/child J$1000/500; ◷9:30am-4pm Mon-Sat) For many, Jamaica means reggae, and reggae means Bob Marley. If this sounds like you, a visit to Kingston definitely means a visit to the reggae superstar's former home and studio. The large, creaky colonial-era wooden house on Hope Rd where Marley lived and recorded from 1975 until his death in 1981 is the city's most-visited site. Today the house functions as a tourist attraction, museum and shrine, but much remains as it was during Marley's day.

The house is shielded by a wall painted in Rasta colors – red, green and gold – and adorned with photos and Rastafarian murals, including those of his seven sons (though not his daughters). Dominating the forecourt is a gaily colored statue of the musical legend; when conducting interviews, Marley used to sit on the front step behind the statue. Some of the guides are overly solemn (focusing with eerie earnestness on the room where Marley survived assassination, the bullet holes left untouched), but the hour-long tour provides fascinating insights into the life he led after moving uptown. His gold and platinum records (*Exodus,* 1977; *Uprising,* 1980; and *Legend,* 1984) are there on the walls, alongside Rastafarian religious cloaks, Marley's favorite denim stage shirt, and the Order of Merit presented by the Jamaican government. One room upstairs is decorated with media clippings from Marley's final tour, with prominence given to concerts played in Africa. Another contains a replica of Marley's original record shop, Wail'n Soul'm, and his little kitchen showcases the blender he used to make fruit juices. Perhaps most powerfully, Marley's simple bedroom has been left as it was, with his favorite star-shaped guitar by the bedside.

The former recording studio out back is now an exhibition hall with some wonderful photos of Bob on tour and playing football, and a theater, where the tour closes with a 20-minute film composed of footage from the 'One Love' concert and snippets of interviews. There is another recording studio inside the house, which his sons occasionally use for solo projects. A recently upgraded shopping court offers 'official' Marley products, including Bob's Honey, produced by a hive of bees that's been buzzing on the site since the musician adopted them in the mid-1970s, and the excellent 'Catch a Fire' line of clothing designed by his daughter Cedella.

(Map p50; ☎929-6602; www.devonhousejamaica. com; 26 Hope Rd; admission J$700; ⊙9am-4:30pm Tue-Sat) This restored colonial home nestles in landscaped grounds on the northwest side of Hope Rd at its junction with Waterloo Rd.

MARLEY'S GHOST

Although Bob Nesta Marley (1945–81) was born and buried in Nine Mile in St Ann parish, it was from Kingston that Jamaica's most famous son made his indelible mark on the global music scene. In many ways, the city still bears his footprint as much as reggae does.

Migrating to the capital in 1955, Bob and his mother (his father, Norval Marley, a white superintendent of the Crown's lands, had little contact with the family and passed away the same year) moved into a 'government yard in Trench Town' similar to the one he would later sing of in 'No Woman, No Cry.' Not yet the gang-war zone it would become in the 1970s, Trench Town was a desirable neighborhood as well as fertile soil for the emerging music scene. Bob met Bunny Livingston and Peter Tosh here, and in 1963 they formed the Wailin' Wailers and received tutelage from fabled Trench Town vocalist Joe Higgs. The band's first single, 'Simmer Down,' reached number one on Jamaica's radio charts.

Success was slow, however, and it wasn't really until the band signed with Island Records in the early ' 70s (and became Bob Marley and the Wailers) that it began to receive international acclaim with the 1973 albums *Burnin'* and *Catch a Fire*. Excellent marketing made Marley an international superstar and brought reggae as a genre to the world stage. Peter Tosh and Bunny Wailer quit in 1974 due to professional differences with Chris Blackwell ('Chris Whiteworst' to Marley supporters who believe that he exploited Bob and the band). Unsurprisingly, fame made living in increasingly volatile Trench Town impossible, and in 1975 Marley moved into the house at 56 Hope Rd that is now his museum. The move uptown alienated many back in Trench Town – and also disturbed his affluent new neighbors, who were unused to the trail of Rastafarian visitors and the football matches in the front yard.

Nothing could have prepared them for the night in 1976 when a gang, likely siding with the conservative Jamaica Labour Party, crashed the gates of the Hope Rd home and shot Bob, his wife Rita, and his manager just before a major concert sponsored by the socialist-leaning People's National Party. Remarkably, everyone survived, and Marley even played at the concert, his wounds wrapped in a sling. After the concert, Bob and Rita went into exile in Britain for two years.

In 1978 Marley made his legendary homecoming at a moment when messages of peace and unity were being all but drowned out by open street warfare. On April 22 a ceasefire was declared between the PNP and the JLP in honor of the 'One Love' peace concert at the National Stadium. With 100,000 people in attendance, including the PNP's Michael Manley and the JLP's Edward Seaga seated in the front row, Marley took to the stage around midnight. During 'One Love' he invited the feuding Manley and Seaga onstage and performed the near-impossible feat of joining their hands together, with his own, in a gesture of unity that probably saved Jamaica from a bloody civil war.

The transformation was not permanent. Before the elections of 1980 almost 800 people were killed when Kingston erupted again in violence, and political gang clashes continue to this day.

During his far-flung world tour in 1980, Marley was diagnosed with cancer and passed away in a Miami hospital eight months later, though not before being awarded Jamaica's Order of Merit. Some may argue that Marley was not the greatest reggae musician who's ever lived, but there's no denying that his music has touched more people worldwide than that of most other artists. Marley's legacy lives on through his own music and that of this children – Ziggy, Cedella, Sharon, Steve and Damien 'Junior Gong' – successful musicians in their own right.

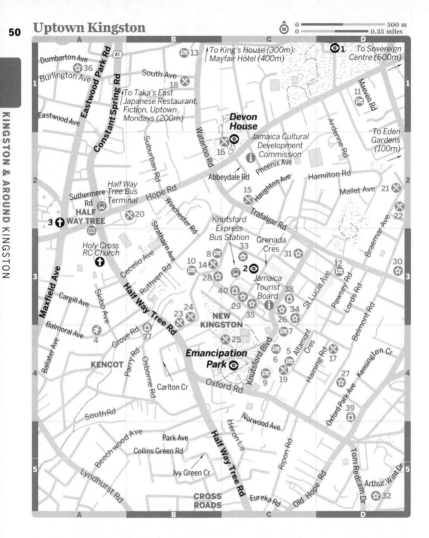

The beautiful ochre-and-white house was built in 1881 by George Stiebel, a Jamaican wheelwright who hit pay dirt in the gold mines of Venezuela after being shipwrecked off the country's coast. He rose to become the first black millionaire in Jamaica, as well as the first black custos (representative of the Crown at parish level) of St Andrew. The Stiebel family occupied the house until 1922, when the last descendant passed away.

Antique lovers will enjoy the visit, whose highlights include some very ornate porcelain chandeliers. Note the trompe l'oeil of palms in the entrance foyer and the round-

about chairs, corners pointed forward, designed to accommodate a man wearing a sword. Stiebel even incorporated a gameroom with whist and cribbage tables, a sewing room, and a gambling room discreetly tucked away in the attic. Admission includes a mandatory guided tour.

The tree-shaded lawns attract Kingstonians who come here to canoodle and read. The immensely popular former carriage house and courtyard are home to two of Jamaica's more famous restaurants, the Grog Shoppe and Norma's On The Terrace, as well as the island's best ice cream and a few quality shops.

For Emancipation Day, August 1, Devon House puts on a rousing celebration complete with roots plays, a maypole ritual and, naturally, a booming sound system.

Emancipation Park
PARK

(Map p50; Knutsford Blvd) Finally unveiled in 2002 after decades of planning, the spacious Emancipation Park has become the pride of New Kingston. This wide open space, carved from the dense urban jungle, has a jogging track, stately fountains and, winningly, reggae music emanating from tiny speakers hidden in the grass. It's a grand place for a stroll, particularly in the early mornings and at sunset, when the walkways fill with cheerful Kingstonians just liberated from their workplaces.

A controversial focal point is the US$4.5 million statue, *Redemption Song*, by Laura Facey Cooper. Depicting a couple of nude, 3m-tall slaves gazing to the heavens, the epic work sometimes elicits prurient comments by passersby due to certain larger-than-life physical attributes of the figures.

FREE **Hope Gardens**
GARDEN

(Map p40; Old Hope Rd; ☉5:30am-6:30pm) These 18-hectare gardens, replete with manicured grounds, exotic plants and beautiful flowers, date back to 1881 when the government established an experimental garden on the site of the former Hope Estate. The Ministry of Agriculture, which administers the gardens, maintains a research station and nursery, and attempts have been made in recent years to spruce up the grounds. The spacious lawns, towering palms and flower-scented walkways provide a lovely respite from the urban jungle.

Among the attractions are cycads ('sago palms') from the antediluvian era. There's a sunken garden, forest garden, orchid house, greenhouses, a small aquarium, ornamental ponds and a privet-hedge maze.

**National Stadium &
National Arena**   LANDMARK
(☎929-4970; Arthur Wint Dr) Around 2km east of New Kingston, the 40,000-capacity stadium, built in 1962 when Jamaica hosted the Commonwealth Games, is the venue for most of Jamaica's sporting events of importance, such as the track and field events. It's also the home of the national football team, the **Reggae Boyz** (www.thereggaeboyz.com). During national games, the stadium tends to be packed to bursting point, and the atmosphere is electric.

There's a so-called **Celebrity Park** on the north side of the stadium, although the only statue at present is one of Bob Marley holding his guitar.

The adjacent **National Arena** is used to stage fashion shows during Fashion Week and for smaller-scale sporting events.

| FREE | **King's House**   NOTABLE BUILDING
(off Map p50; ☎927-6424; W Kings House Rd; ☺by appointment 9am-5pm Mon-Fri) Hidden amid trees behind Jamaica House is the official residence of the governor-general, the representative of the Queen of England. King's House was initially the home of the Lord Bishop of Jamaica. The original house was badly damaged in the 1907 earthquake. Today's visitors explore the remake, built in 1909 to a new design in reinforced concrete. The dining room contains two particularly impressive full-length portraits of King George III and Queen Charlotte by Sir Joshua Reynolds.

Jamaica House   NOTABLE BUILDING
(Map p50; Hope Rd) About 500m from Devon House on the left, Jamaica House is faced by a columned portico and fronted by expansive lawns. Initially built in 1960 as the residence of the prime minister, the building today houses government offices. The **prime minister's office** is located in an unattractive modern building, partially hidden by vegetation, to the left of Jamaica House. Visitors are restricted to peering through the fence.

Half Way Tree   NEIGHBORHOOD
This neighborhood (Map p50), road junction and major bus terminal is named for a venerable silk cotton (kapok) tree that stood here until the 1870s; its shaded base became the site of both a tavern and market. Today, the spot is marked by a **clock tower** sure to tell the correct time every 12 hours. It was erected in 1813 as a memorial to King Edward VII, whose bust sits on the south side of the tower.

Sculpture Park   PARK
(Map p40; 237 Old Hope Rd) This sculpture garden, on the grounds of the University of Technology, just north of the University of the West Indies campus, was unveiled in 2000. It features nine sculptures by acclaimed Caribbean artists, including Laura Facey's sculpture of a woman's torso stretched in a yoga position, and Basil Watson's *The Compass*, depicting humanity shaping the environment with the use of technology.

St Andrew Parish Church   CHURCH
(Map p50; cnr Hagley Park & Eastwood Park Rds) This brick church is more popularly known as the 'Half Way Tree Church.' The foundations of the existing church were laid in 1692. The exterior is austere and unremarkable, but the stained-glass windows and organ are definitely worth a peek. Outside, there's a very atmospheric graveyard.

☞ Tours

Sun Venture Tours   CULTURAL TOURS
(Map p50; ☎960-6685; www.sunventuretours.com; 30 Balmoral Ave) Offers a city tour of Kingston,

---

THE MARLEY STATUE FIASCO

In 1981 the Jamaican government commissioned expressionist sculptor Christopher Gonzáles to create a fitting memorial to Bob Marley for the newly created Celebrity Park. The result was a visually arresting 2.7m half-man, half-tree, the defiant-looking Marley and his microphone apparently growing out of the ground. The roots flowing seamlessly into his locks and upper body symbolised both his growth as an artist and his being a 'Roots' man, but unimpressed Marley fans pelted the statue with rocks and fruit upon its unveiling. It has now been relocated to Ocho Rios' Island Village (p119), replaced by a rather bland representation of Marley by Alvin Marriott.

starting either at the Bob Marley Museum or Tuff Gong Studios, and incorporating a walking tour of Port Royal and a visit to Devon House (US$65 per person for four people or more). Sun Venture also has hiking tours of the Blue Mountains and Maroon country, excursions to coffee plantations and more.

Beat'n'Track Culture Tours   MUSIC TOURS
(395-8959) Innovative, unconventional tours of Kingston's music scene run by Andrea Lewis. Choose your own itinerary – anything from hanging out with local musicians to visiting Tuff Gong and other recording studios to trips to Hellshire Beach, Trench Town Culture Yard or even the city's best music shops. From US$100 per person for transportation and guide.

Our Story Tours   HISTORICAL TOURS
(377-5693) Historical tours of Kingston, Port Royal and Spanish Town. Itineraries tailor-made to suit your needs.

☆☆ Festivals & Events

Befitting a Caribbean capital city, Kingston is the site of engaging festivals and events year-round.

Jamaica School of Dance Concert Season   DANCE
(☉Jan) Creative, Caribbean-themed dancing at the Little Theatre.

Carnival   SOCA
(www.jamaicacarnival.com, www.bacchanal jamaica.com; ☉Feb) A week of costumed revellers taking to the streets, two carnival camps – Jamaica Carnival and Bacchanal Jamaica – paint- and rum-throwing, parades, all-night parties and live reggae, calypso, and particularly soca. Highlights

include **J'Ouvert**, an epic night-long party, and the **Road March**, when the two camps parade through the streets of New Kingston in carnival costume.

EME Awards   MUSIC
(☉early Feb) The Excellence in Music and Entertainment Awards honor the best in Jamaican music with a lavish awards ceremony.

Carib Cement International Marathon   MARATHON
(☉mid-Feb) Attracts top national and international athletes.

Miss Universe Jamaica Beauty Pageant   BEAUTY PAGEANT
(☉mid-Mar) Determines who represents the island in the Miss Universe contest.

Devon House Craft Fair   CRAFTS
(☉Apr) This fair has quality arts and crafts displays, and Jamaican foods.

Jamaica Horticultural Society Show   HORTICULTURE
(☉May) The best of the island's plants and flowers showcased in the National Arena.

Kingston on the Edge   ART
(www.kingstonontheedge.com; ☉Jun) Week-long urban art festival featuring the best of new painting, photography and sculpture, as well as gallery shows, concerts and readings.

International Reggae Day   REGGAE
(☉early Jul) This festival shines a spotlight on Jamaica's finest reggae artists, with shows and workshops all over Jamaica.

National Gospel Song Contest Finals   MUSIC
(www.jcdc.gov.jm; ☉Jul) Held the last week of July, it's a spirited competition to name the most outstanding original gospel song of the year.

World Reggae Dance Championships   DANCE
(www.jcdc.gov.jm; ☉Aug) The finals of the reggae, dancehall and reggaeton dance competition, with troupes of young dancers battling it out among themselves at the Ranny Williams Entertainment Centre.

Caribean Heritagefest   CULTURE
(www.jcdc.gov.jm; ☉mid-Oct) A two-day event at the Jamworld Entertainment Complex at Portmore, southwest of Kingston. It features food and crafts fairs, folk theater, traditional dance and drumming, and musical performances.

Devon House Christmas Fair FAIR
(☺Dec) Promotes a colorful display of arts, crafts and culinary delights in the week before Christmas.

LMT National Pantomime PANTOMIME
(☺Dec) Annual event at the Little Theatre, with traditional Jamaican song and dance, saucy humor and fabulous costumes.

Biennial Art Exhibition ART
(www.natgalja.org.jm; ☺Dec-Mar) Exhibition featuring the very best of contemporary Jamaican art, held on alternate even-numbered years.

🛏 Sleeping

Many lodging options cater more to business travelers than tourists, and rates do not vary year-round. Most hotels are in Uptown, with some of the more luxurious retreats further out, in the hills.

⭐ TOP CHOICE Spanish
Court Hotel BOUTIQUE HOTEL $$$
(Map p50; ☎926-0000; www.spanishcourthotel. com; 1 St Lucia Ave; r US$189-289, ste US$379-1499; P❄@🛜🏊) The newest addition to Kingston's high-end set has rapidly become a favorite with the discerning business elite. Thoroughly modern rooms, decorated in warm tones, exude minimalist chic and come equipped with plasma-screen TVs and iPod docks. Small touches, such as the single fresh flower by the bedside, are appreciated. Relaxation options include the rooftop infinity pool and a luxury spa with a full range of treatments. The elegant Gallery Café serves an excellent selection of gourmet coffees and beautifully presented international and Jamaican dishes, and guests are treated to cocktails and hors d'oeuvres at the manager's reception on Thursdays.

⭐ TOP CHOICE City View Hotel BOUTIQUE HOTEL $
(☎969-4009; www.cityviewjamaica.com; Mannings Hill Rd; r incl breakfast J$2781, ste J$3217-3894; P❄🛜) This family-run pocket of splendor overlooking Kingston offers an intimate, luxurious experience combined with an incredible panoramic view of Kingston. The five rooms, named after Jamaica's different parishes, feature delightful antique furnishings, including four-poster beds in two of the suites. St Andrew Suite, the plushest option, particularly popular with newlyweds, boasts a Jacuzzi. The genial hosts, Mr and Mrs Bent, treat guests like family and the staff

are always on hand to let you in after a 3am clubbing session or to help you plan a local excursion. There's a typical Jamaican breakfast (ackee and saltfish, callaloo, dumplings, with fresh fruit for lighter eaters).

Moon Hill BOUTIQUE HOTEL $$
(☎620-8259; 5 Roedeen Cl; r US$120, entire villa $600; P🛜🏊) A combination of seclusion and close proximity to the capital's attractions, this luxurious four-bedroom villa located in the Blue Mountain foothills is ideal for romantic or small-group getaways. The airy bedrooms feature firm queen- and king-sized beds; there are fans but no air-con, though you won't miss it, thanks to the cool breeze from the mountains. The Jamaican and international menu will be tailored according to your needs, using fresh produce from the on-site organic garden.

Mikuzi Guest House GUEST HOUSE $$
(☎978-4859, 813-0098; www.mikuzijamaica. com; 5 Upper Montrose Rd; r/ste J$7819/11,851; P❄🛜) Friendly yellow colonial-era guest house with comfortable rooms – all bright colors and funky furnishings, most with kitchenettes. All but the 'backpacker rooms' (J$3386) have air-con. There's a cushion-strewn gazebo in the lush garden for relaxing in. There was an armed robbery on the premises in 2009, putting security into question.

Hilton Hotel HOTEL $$$
(Map p50; ☎926-5430; www.hilton.com; 77 Knutsford Blvd; r US$170-265, ste US$273-357; P🛜❄@🏊) Strongly oriented toward the business traveler, the spacious rooms and suites at the Hilton boast contemporary furnishings and a full complement of facilities, including an Olympic-size swimming pool and 24-hour fitness center. The Jonkanoo Lounge bar hosts the popular Latin Night on Thursdays and special events sometimes take place in the hotel's lush grounds.

Terra Nova All-Suite Hotel HOTEL $$$
(Map p50; ☎926-2211; www.terranovajamaica. com; 17 Waterloo Rd; ste incl breakfast US$145-580; P❄@🏊) Though the colonial mansion was built in 1924, the spacious junior suites in three two-story wings have a contemporary feel, with tropically vibrant fabrics. The suites vary from regular to ultra-luxurious, but king-size beds and cable TV are standard – and thumbs up for the marble bathrooms, some of which have Jacuzzis. The

elegant Venetian Room is the venue for one of the city's top Sunday brunches.

Jamaica Pegasus
HOTEL **$$$**

(Map p50; ☎926-3690; www.jamaicapegasus.com; 81 Knutsford Blvd; s/d US$280/300, ste US$400-800; P�’✳@☎) This glitzy 17-story property overlooking Emancipation Park has been a long-term favorite of airline crews and high-end business travelers. On Wednesday there's poolside happy hour (6pm to 7pm), featuring a complimentary buffet of Jamaican finger foods and all the rum punches you can drink. For an unparalleled view, ask for a room facing the mountains.

Alhambra Inn
HOTEL **$$**

(☎978-9072; 1 Tucker Ave; r US$110-120; P✳☎) Across from the National Stadium, this is an attractive, two-story property with appealing rooms in Spanish style, the ones upstairs with lofty ceilings and king-size beds. You can dine in the lush courtyard, overflowing with flowers, to the sound of trickling water from the little waterfall. Particularly popular with the business set, the hotel often attracts conventions and standards of service are accordingly high.

Eden Gardens
HOTEL **$$**

(off Map p50; ☎946-9981; www.edengardensjamaica.com; 39 Lady Musgrave Rd; r US$140; P✳☎) Set amid lush vegetation – a nod to its name – this condo and wellness center complex attracts those who like to mix business with pleasure. Each of the spacious, light rooms comes with fully equipped kitchenette and large desk, while the Therapeutic Spa has a full range of massages and other treatments. Long term–stay discounts available.

Altamont Court
HOTEL **$$**

(Map p50; ☎929-4497; www.altamontcourt.com; 1 Altamont Cres; r incl breakfast US$120, ste incl breakfast US$160-180; P✳@☎) A secure though rather nondescript-looking business hotel, livened up somewhat by all the greenery between buildings. The clean one-bedroom studios and suites have standard furnishings and a Jamaican breakfast is served in the attractive Mango Tree restaurant. The real draw here is the central location, within easy walking distance of New Kingston's attractions.

Shirley Retreat Hotel
HOTEL **$**

(Map p50; ☎946-2679; 7 Maeven Rd; r incl breakfast J$6600-7180; P✳☎) Operated by the United Church of Jamaica, this simple retreat down a quiet road has simply furnished, well-lit

rooms with hardwood floors, brisk management and polite clientele. Meals are cooked on request.

Knutsford Court Hotel
HOTEL **$$**

(Map p50; ☎929-1000; www.knutsfordcourt.com; 16 Chelsea Ave; s US$105-135, d US$115-145, ste US$155-205, townhouse US$350-360; P�’✳@☎) Agreeable hotel with a garden setting, popular with Jamaican and international families alike. The rooms – some with private balconies and work desks – are clean and well appointed. Rates include continental breakfast, served in the Lobby Café, and the Melting Pot Restaurant provides exemplary Jamaican fare and room service.

Mayfair Hotel
HOTEL **$**

(off Map p50; ☎926-1610; 4 W Kings House Close; r US$76-90, ste US$105-160; P✳☎) A popular option with Jamaican travelers, this hotel sports a columned portico entrance that hints at grandeur within, but the rooms in eight individual houses are fairly basic. The cheaper rooms have fans rather than aircon and the suites come with kitchenettes. There's a good Jamaican-Japanese fusion restaurant on the premises, but the hotel's best feature is the view toward the Blue Mountains.

Courtleigh Hotel & Suites
HOTEL **$$**

(Map p50; ☎929-9000; www.courtleigh.com; 85 Knutsford Blvd; r US$167-195, ste US$249-445; P�’✳@☎) Next door to the Hilton, this is a splendid contemporary option with Chinese-style decor in the lobby, deluxe rooms and one-bedroom suites featuring four-poster beds and tasteful mahogany furnishings. The local execs let their hair down at the pool bar on Fridays during the live music session and rates include a buffet breakfast.

Hotel Prestige
HOTEL **$**

(☎927-8244; 70 Sandhurst Cres; s J$4656, d J$5502-6772; P✳☎) In a quiet residential neighborhood in Liguanea, this renovated hotel is a favorite option with budget travelers and families. The spotlessly kept rooms with their black-and-white tile floors, utility furniture and plastic flowers conjure images of Miami in the 1960s. Some have a private veranda. A large dining terrace shaded by mango trees affords views toward the Blue Mountains.

Indies Hotel
HOTEL **$**

(Map p50; ☎926-2952; www.indieshotel.com; 5 Holborn Rd; s/d/tr J$5502/5926/6875; P✳@♿)

SUNDAY BRUNCH SPOTS

Sunday brunch is a local tradition, and many Kingstonians make an occasion of it by heading to a couple of best-loved local institutions to indulge themselves after a morning at church. 'Brunch' typically commences at noon and lasts well into the afternoon. After such a meal, you may never need to eat again:

» Boon Hall Oasis (p57)
» Terra Nova All-Suite Hotel (p58)

This family-friendly 'home away from home' is highly rated for its cheerful ambience and accommodating atmosphere. Take an upstairs room for sunlight. A small restaurant serves economical pizzas and great fish and chips and the attractive patio is a good spot for alfresco dining.

Gardens   HOTEL $$
(☎927-8275; 23 Liguanea Ave; s US$85-100, d US$180; [P][✳][🛜][⊛]) In a quiet, leafy neighborhood north of the Bob Marley Museum, this wonderful hotel is composed of seven stately townhouses offset by well-tended gardens. The townhouses, which feature large, airy living rooms, can be reserved as double ensuite rooms or shared doubles and are ideal for longer-term stays. Wi-fi reaches most of the property.

🍴 Eating

As in other matters, Kingston is Jamaica's capital of food; it is here that the national cuisine was born and it is here that it continues to thrive and evolve. Let your taste buds run free!

Most of the notable eateries, which include international and fusion cuisine, are found in Uptown Kingston, where the culinary adventurer is spoiled for choice.

DOWNTOWN

TOP
CHOICE ▷ Patrice's Restaurant   JAMAICAN $
(Map p42; Temple Lane; meals J$400; ⊙lunch Mon-Fri) An unmarked hole-in-the-wall down an equally unmarked little lane, this dimly lit little eatery run by the indefatigable Patrice is more than worth seeking out for its generous portions of superb home cooking. The three daily specials, chalked up on the little board, often include brown stew fish, stew

chicken and melt-in-your-mouth curry goat, each accompanied by a mountain of pumpkin rice, salad and festival (sweet fried cornmeal dumpling). Those in the know claim that Patrice's stew pork and dumpling is among the very best in Jamaica.

Moby Dick   JAMAICAN $$
(Map p42; 3 Orange St; meals J$1100-2000; ⊙9am-7pm Mon-Sat) Don't let the plastic tablecloths and the jolly whale murals fool you: this is one of Kingston's priciest restaurants. Popular with besuited lawyers and judges, this Muslim-run former sailors' hangout has been a restaurant for nearly a century. The curried goat (J$1000) is outstanding, as is the conch version (J$1700) when available, served with roti, rice and salad and washed down with one of the excellent fresh fruit juices.

Swiss Stores   CAFE $
(Map p42; cnr Church & Harbour Sts; meals J$450; ⊙lunch) Jerk sausage, hearty pepperpot soup, Black Forest ham sandwiches and wine inside a welcome bubble of air-con – what more could you ask of a jewelry store! The stools are not conducive to sitting on for long, but all the items on the small menu are fresh and tasty and the Blue Mountain coffee (J$125) comes in a cup the size of a soup tureen.

Chung's   JAMAICAN $
(Map p42; cnr Mark Lane & Harbour St; meals J$500; ⊙lunch Mon-Fri) In spite of the name, this simple canteen-style place – a favorite of Downtown office workers – serves only Jamaican specialties. Choose your mains, such as stew peas, fried chicken or curry goat, and then either take your overflowing container to the bustling dining area next door or go picnic on the waterfront.

UPTOWN

TOP
CHOICE ▷ Andy's   JERK $
(Map p40; 49 Mannings Hill Rd; meals J$500; ⊙lunch & dinner) If you're after the best, authentically prepared jerk chicken and pork in Kingston, then Andy's is well worth the travel. This nondescript-looking corner stop gets particularly busy in the evenings, when locals line up for their meats, accompanied by fried breadfruit, festival sweet potato or plantain. The meat, smoked for hours over pimento wood, is permeated with that wonderful, distinctively smoky flavour, the pork

is beautifully tender and...enough! We're drooling on the page!

Boon Hall Oasis
TOP CHOICE

JAMAICAN $$

(☑942-3064; 4 River Rd, Stony Hill; buffet lunch J$2000; ⊙noon-5pm Thu-Sat, 10am-3pm Sun) The Sunday brunch at this lovely spot near Stony Hill is worth the drive from Kingston. A footpath leads down through curtains of vines and flowers to a true oasis by a trickling stream. Take a seat among the churchgoers and wedding parties and help yourself to a buffet of mackerel rundown, curry goat, ackee and saltfish, stew fish, jerk chicken and other Jamaican favorites. Desserts include sweet bricks of potato pudding and rum cake. To get here, turn right on Eerie Castle Rd from Stony Hill Sq, then left onto River Rd. A steep dirt road leads down from River Rd to the car park.

Red Bones Blues Café
FUSION $$$

(Map p50; ☑978-8262; 1 Argyle Rd; mains US$20-40; ⊙noon-1am Mon-Fri, from 6pm Sat) The in-crowd is in at this former colonial house, long a beehive of cultural and culinary activity. Inside, the walls are beguilingly bedecked with photographs of jazz and blues legends. Stellar dishes include callaloo strudel, smoked marlin salad, or the pasta with seafood trio of shrimp, mussels and salmon sautéed in a spicy coconut sauce, though leave room for the sweet potato pudding! In the evenings, call ahead to snag a table overlooking the garden stage – they're in high demand. On busy nights, service can be very leisurely.

Guilt Trip
FUSION $$

(☑977-5130; 20 Barbican Rd; meals J$1600-2500; ⊙dinner) The name alludes to the imaginative, decadent desserts, such as white chocolate Guinness madness, the unrestrained consumption of which will leave you feeling very indulgent. That's not all: the chef constantly experiments with Caribbean-French fusion cuisine, so you'll be constantly surprised by such tantalising concoctions as coconut curry sea bass with mango and chestnut salsa and roast chicken with whiskey sauce. The experience is worth dressing up for.

Taka's East Japanese Restaurant
JAPANESE $$$

(off Map p50; ☑960-3962; Market Pl, 67 Constant Spring Rd; meals J$2500-4500; ⊙lunch & dinner Wed-Sun, dinner Tue) Part of the upmarket cluster of restaurants known as the Market Place, this established Japanese restaurant, popular with New Kingston's business set, serves an exquisite selection of authentic, imaginative sushi. The Fiction Roll, with raw tuna and spicy fish roe, is deserving of its own fan club. Though the menu is fish-heavy, noodle dishes abound and the vegetable tempura hits the spot. The heavily air-conditioned interior will make you glad there's a dress code: no sleeveless shirts or shorts.

Starapple
JAMAICAN $$

(94 Hope Rd; meals J$1300-1700; ⊙lunch & dinner) Feast on flavorful Jamaican dishes inside this attractive wooden house with creaky floors, popular with Uptown families and groups of friends. The starters are outstanding – the jerk sausage and the salt fritters are arguably the best in town, though the portions fall short of generous. Brown stew snapper, stew pork and curry goat are standout mains. Be prepared for a leisurely meal, as the staff live on Zen time.

Café Blue/Deli Works
CAFE $

(Sovereign Centre, Hope Rd; meals J$700-900; ⊙8am-8pm Mon-Sat, 9am-3pm Sun) Always full of Uptowners with laptops, this bright, air-conditioned cafe serves an array of delicious though not cheap Blue Mountain coffees (try the Café Blue Special) as well as cakes, filled bagels and sandwiches. The smoked marlin baguette (J$500) is consistently superb. Next door, you can choose from a number of Jamaican specials (J$500 to J$650), consumed in a lively canteen setting. Free wi-fi available to customers.

Norma's on the Terrace
FUSION $$$

(Map p50; ☑968-5488; Devon House; meals J$3000-5000; ⊙10am-10pm Mon-Sat, closed public holidays) Although its popularity has somewhat declined, the seasonal menu at this love child of Jamaica's leading food emissary, Norma Shirley, still explores Caribbean-fusion food with great finesse. Long standing favorites include the smoked pork loin in teriyaki sauce and smoked marlin salad with grapefruit. Creative desserts (try the English trifle) are not to be missed. Even if a meal is beyond your budget, it's worth having a drink on the candlelit terrace.

Scotchies
JERK $

(2 Chelsea Ave; meals J$550; ⊙11am-11pm Mon-Sat, until 9pm Sun) The extremely popular jerk joint, made famous in Montego Bay and Ocho Rios, has come to conquer the capital,

and very successfully, too. The chicken, pork and jerk sausage are all done to perfection, as testified to by the discerning crowds of repeat customers. There is even a lush garden area with gazebos, perfect for group gatherings – an oasis of tranquillity in the midst of Uptown's perpetual traffic snarl.

Sweetwood Jerk JERK $
(Knutsford Blvd; ¼lb lamb J$370; ☺lunch & dinner) This lively jerk center, opposite Pegasus Hotel, is popular with Uptown office staff and gets particularly busy after work. Spicy, flavourful meaty offerings can be enjoyed in the outdoor sitting area facing Emancipation Park. Accompaniments include festival, sweet potato and particularly good fried breadfruit, and this is one of the few jerk joints in Jamaica to feature jerk lamb.

Terra Nova All-Suite Hotel INTERNATIONAL $$$
(Map p50; ☎926-2211; 17 Waterloo Rd; Sunday brunch J$2500; ☺lunch & dinner; ☞) The European menu has hints of the Caribbean as well as Jamaican favorites such as pepperpot soup and grilled snapper. However, the bigger draw for well-heeled, hungry Kingstonians and visitors alike is its famous Sunday brunch, comprising an all-you-can-eat buffet of 80 or so quality international and Jamaican dishes. Gorge yourself on curry goat, jerk chicken, pasta salads, ribs, and more. The only downside is that there's only so much you can eat!

Ashanti Oasis I-TAL $
(cnr Trafalgar Rd & Haughton Ave; meals J$450-600; ☺noon-5pm; ☞) Having made the move from its former tranquil home at Hope Garden to a more central location, Ashanti may have lost some of its character but not its taste or popularity. Feast on excellent vegetarian food from a changing daily menu featuring hearty soups, veggie burgers and combo platters starring mains such as lentil curry. Fresh juices or a glass of the homemade aloe wine are a must.

Chez Maria LEBANESE $$
(7 Hillcrest Ave; meals J$750-1800; ☺lunch & dinner; ☞) Whether you sit in the garden beneath the mango tree or grab a table on the front terrace, you'll be treated to fine Lebanese and Italian cuisine. The mezes, notably the hummus, are excellent and are complemented by homemade pita bread. A host of shawarmas and kebabs awaits if you still have an appetite. Alternatively, go for some

of the best pizza in town or the outstanding penne ala vodka.

White Bones SEAFOOD $$
(Map p40; 1 Mannings Hill Rd; meals J$1500-2200; ☺dinner) The decor of fishing nets and fish tanks gives away the restaurant's specialty the moment you walk through the door. Choose your fish of choice from the extensive menu and have it fried, steamed or stewed, preceded by an appetizer of grilled or raw oysters.

Hot Pot JAMAICAN $
(Map p50; 2 Altamont Tce; meals J$500-650; ☺breakfast, lunch & dinner Mon-Sat, dinner Sun) Unfussy, indisputably delicious Jamaican home-style cooking with dishes such as ackee and saltfish, escoveitch fish and garlic chicken. Wash it down with a fresh tamarind juice, coconut water or a Red Stripe. Take-outs come at a discount.

Jade Garden CHINESE $$
(☎978-3476/9; Sovereign Centre, 106 Hope Rd; dim sum brunch J$2000; ☺lunch & dinner) Highlighting the à la carte menu at this elegant spot are the Dragon & Phoenix (chicken wings stuffed with minced pork and shrimp; J$1660) and a variety of excellent seafood dishes. If you feel like spending, the two-course Peking duck (J$7200), traditionally prepared and carved at the table, is a delight, but the Sunday dim-sum brunch is still the big draw here.

So-So Seafood Bar & Grill SEAFOOD $$
(Map p50; 4 Chelsea Ave; meals J$1200-2000; ☺lunch & dinner) A casual place, known for its mellow after-work scene, its seafood menu belies the modesty of the name. The garlic shrimp and stew fish are particularly good, as is the weekly conch soup (Thursday and Friday), and delicious mannish water (miscellaneous goat-part soup) on Sundays.

Rib Kage Bar & Grill GRILL $$
(12 Braemer Ave; meals J$1000-2000; ☺lunch & dinner) While catching a lot of the spillover from ever-popular Red Bones Blues Café across the street, Rib Kage attracts its own following with its succulent beef or pork ribs and an array of southern US soul food, served in a relaxed, wood-accented setting. Steaks, burgers, pizzas and a selection of fish dishes are also available.

Devon House Bakery BAKERY $
(Map p50; Devon House; patties J$120-300; ☺lunch; ☞) While nearby Norma's and the

Grog Shoppe get all the raves, those in the know swear by the lobster patties served up in this small bakery located next to Devon House I-Scream. An array of tempting cakes and juices is also available at this excellent option for a picnic on the grounds.

Akbar
INDIAN $$$

(Map p50; ✆926-3480; 11 Holborn Rd; mains J$900-2500; ◷lunch & dinner; ✎) Kingston's best Indian restaurant draws crowds for its gracious service, garden graced by a fountain and pricey but well-executed menu that includes tandoori and vegetarian dishes, complemented by excellent Indian breads. Be sure to insist on extra spiciness, if fire's what you crave. Offers a buffet lunch special (J$1500).

Grog Shoppe
JAMAICAN $$

(Map p50; Devon House; meals J$1500-2500; ◷lunch & dinner Mon-Sat) Lodged in an expansive brick building that used to be the servants' quarters for Devon House, this atmospheric choice has the look and feel of a colonial pub. A separate dining room serves good Jamaican specialties, while the pub menu features burgers, crab cakes and other finger food.

Sovereign Centre
FOOD COURT $

(off Map p50; 106 Hope Rd; ✎) Most large malls have food courts, and this is one of the best. **Pastry Passions** does great cakes – try the pumpkin cinnamon strudel (J$300) or the red velvet cupcakes (J$80). **Jamaica Juice** serves a great range of fruit juices and smoothies (J$100 to J$250) and the chickpea roti (J$260) is a meal in itself.

Cannonball Café
CAFE $

(Loshusan Shopping Centre, Barbican Rd; meals J$500-700; ◷7am-7pm Mon-Fri, 9am-5pm Sat & Sun; ✎) Popular and busy cafe with wireless internet, serving excellent Blue Mountain coffee and cakes. Light dishes – quiches, sandwiches and salads – are also on offer here.

Devon House I-Scream
ICE CREAM $

(Map p50; Devon House, 26 Hope Rd; scoops J$120; ◷10am-10pm Mon-Sat, 11am-10pm Sun & holidays) Some of the island's best ice cream in over 20 flavours. Devon Stout and pistachio are superb.

Gaucho's Grill
INTERNATIONAL $$

(Map p50; 20A South Ave; meals J$900-2600; ◷lunch & dinner) Meat-heavy menu of Jamaican and Italian dishes in an attractive open-air setting. The steaks are good but pricey.

Earl's Juice Garden
BAKERY $

(Map p50; 28 Haining Rd; ◷10am-5pm Mon-Fri) Excellent fruit-juice mixes (J$200) and baked goods.

Thai Gardens
THAI $$

(Map p50; 11 Holborn Rd; meals J$1400-2500; ◷lunch & dinner; ✎) This restaurant offers an extensive menu of noodle and curry dishes that's a little hit-and-miss.

Self-caterers can try the following:

Loshusan Supermarket
SUPERMARKET $$

(Barbican Centre, 29 East Kings House Rd) Good selection of imported goods, a sushi counter and bakery.

Empire Supermarket
SUPERMARKET $

(Lane Plaza, Liganea) Inexpensive, mostly local products.

Sovereign Supermarket
SUPERMARKET $$

(Sovereign Shopping Centre, 106 Hope Rd) Good selection of local and imported foodstuffs, though not cheap.

☆ Entertainment

Kingston is the best town in Jamaica for bar-hopping and clubbing. From copacetic watering holes to throbbing nightclubs – with a few all-night sound-system street jams thrown into the mix – you'll never want for after-hours action in this town.

Many bars, nightclubs and sound-systems feature regularly scheduled events and theme nights, making it possible to get a groove going every night of the week. For

Patties – pastries with spicy beef, chicken, lobster, shrimp, cheese or vegetable filling, often consumed as part of a coco-bread 'sandwich' – are a Jamaican institution. They're cheap, filling and delicious, and sold by the **Juici Patties**, **Tastee Patties** and **Mother's** franchises. Juici has an edge over its rivals by not limiting itself to patties alone; the larger branches serve ultra-filling hominy and peanut porridge for breakfast, and lunch mains such as salt fish with callaloo or cabbage. Try **Juici Patties** (Map p42; cnr Harbour & King Sts), which is downtown, or pretty much everywhere else.

listings, check out the Friday *Observer* and keep an eye out for flyers around town advertising one-off music events. Drinking and music invariably go hand-in-hand in Kingston (unless you're drowning your sorrows in a seedy rum bar), though at sound-system parties your choice of beverage will be limited to rum and Red Stripe beer.

Without question, the high point of Kingston's nightlife is its free outdoor sound-system parties. A raucous combination of block party, dance-offs between neighborhood posses, fashion show and all-out stereo war, sound-system parties can be heard blocks away and go well into the night. They kick off around 10pm and, due to a recent government crackdown on street events, are obliged to shut down at 2am rather than dawn. Certainly not for the fainthearted or anyone who dislikes dancehall, sound-system dances are, nevertheless, unforgettable cultural experiences.

It's perfectly safe to attend street parties, as the neighborhood dons are responsible for security and most people don't take kindly to violence spoiling the event, but it's best to come with a local and to leave any obvious valuables behind. The locals want to

---

DON'T MISS

KINGSTON WEEKLY PARTY PLANNER

Monday	**Hot Mondays At Limelight** (p62)
	Uptown Mondays (off Map p50; Savannah Plaza, Half Way Tree) Dancehall sound-system.
Tuesday	**Passa Passa** (off Map p42; cnr Spanish Town Rd & Beeston St) Still the definitive Downtown sound-system, though not as extravagant as when Dudus was in charge.
	Set Me Free (off Map p42; cnr Spanish Town Rd & Chestnut La) Rooftop dancehall event.
	Ladies' Night At the Building, p61.
Wednesday	**Weddy Weddy Wednesdays** (Map p50; Stone Love HQ, Half Way Tree) One of the best Uptown sound-systems.
	Retro Night At Quad, p61.
	Inclusive Wednesdays At Medusa, p61.
Thursday	**Street Vybz** At the Building, p61.
	Latin Night At Jonkanoo Lounge, p61.
	I Love v.O.D.k.a. At Privilege, p62.
Friday	**After Work Jam** At the Deck, p61.
	Stress Free At the Building, p61.
	Friday Night Party At Privilege, p62.
	Club Night At Fiction, p62.
Saturday	**Inclusive Saturday** At the Building, p61.
	Latin Night At Pepper's, p61.
	Privilege Saturday At Privilege, p62.
	Club Night At Fiction, p62.
Sunday	**Oldies Night** Sound-system playing the best of reggae outside the Capricorn bar in Rae Town.
	Bounty Sundays At Limelight, p62

see how well you can move, so be prepared to be thrown in the deep end.

Kingston has frequent live stage shows, which are announced on streetside billboards. Top-name artists often perform at the **National Arena** (☑929-4970; Arthur Wint Dr).

Bars

Red Bones Blues Café   BAR
(1 Argyle St; ⊘11am-1am Mon-Fri, 7pm-1am Sat) This could easily become your favorite spot in town – it's a hip bar with cool ambience, good conversation and great music. The last Wednesday of the month there's poetry with musical accompaniment, and on Fridays and Saturdays there are quality live music events, which include blues and jazz, showcasing well-chosen local and international talent. And this says nothing of the food.

Deck   BAR
(Map p50; 14 Trafalgar Rd; ⊘from 4:30pm) This cavernous open-air bar, festooned with fishing nets, is a long-standing favorite with the older crowd for its easygoing atmosphere and good bar food. On Fridays things get particularly lively during the ever-popular oldies After-Work Jam.

Pepper's   BAR
(31 Upper Waterloo Rd; ⊘5pm-3am) You'll feel like a local after a night at this rousing spot, which gets going early for the after-work crowd and continues hopping with a younger crowd on the outdoor dance floor well past midnight. Rack up the balls on one of the many pool tables or show off your salsa skills during the excellent Latin Night (Saturdays).

Escape   BAR
(Map p50; 24 Knutsford Blvd) A typical night here starts with a dominoes tournament amongst older clientele, fuelled by the inexpensive drinks, followed by a loud music mix of hip hop, dancehall and reggae that attracts a younger crowd.

Cuddy'z   SPORTS BAR
(Map p50; 25 Dominica Dr) Perhaps the best sports bar in Jamaica, this hip establishment is the creation of the 'Big Man Inna Cricket,' Courtney Walsh. TVs in each booth and a lively bleachers section with an oversized screen make this a great place to catch the latest football, cricket and baseball games.

Medusa   BAR
(96 Hope Rd) The airy upstairs deck makes for relaxing evening drinking and the Inclusive

Wednesdays (all-you-can-drink for J$800) are particularly popular with local students. It's behind Treasure Hut Shopping Plaza.

Jonkanoo Lounge   LOUNGE
(Map p50; Hilton Hotel) This pleasant cocktail lounge most nights heats up on Thursdays when well-heeled locals and tourists take to the dance floor to Latin Night's lively beats.

Carlos' Café   BAR
(Map p50; 22 Belmont Rd; ⊘11am-2am) A pleasant, open-air bar with lively tropical decor – an ideal spot to shoot some pool or quaff martinis on Martini Mondays.

Cinema

First-run Hollywood movies can be seen at the following:

Carib 5 Cinema   CINEMA
(☑926-6106; cnr Slipe & Half Way Tree Rds) Five screens.

Palace Cineplex   CINEMA
(☑978-3522; Sovereign Centre, 106 Hope Rd) Two screens.

Nightclubs

TOP
CHOICE **Quad**   NIGHTCLUB
(Map p50; ☑754-7823; 20-22 Trinidad Tce; admission J$1270) You can easily spend all night here, moving between the four different levels of this upmarket superclub as the mood takes you. On the main floor is Christopher's Jazz Club, a tasteful jazz bar where the city's movers and shakers gather on a nightly basis. Every Wednesday, Friday and Saturday, two clubs open up: the top-floor Voodoo Lounge, which tends to draw an older, more urbane crowd with an oldies mix; and, on the level below it, Oxygen, which attracts a 20-something set always ready to get sweaty to rocking dance beats until 4am. In the basement is Taboo, a so-called 'naughty gentleman's club' with 'exotic' dancers (separate J$847 admission charge).

Building   DANCEHALL
(Map p50; ☑906-1828/9, 69 Knutsford Blvd; admission J$300-800) The renamed club, formerly known as Asylum, is still part of the happening scene, packing in a young, lively crowd from Tuesday through Sunday. Tuesday is still Ladies' Night, and the street reverberates with dancehall beats from the Street Vybz Thursday, hosted by Vybz Cartel, and Inclusive Saturday events, fuelled by the venue's lethal Street Vybz rum.

Privilege
DANCEHALL

(Map p50; ☎622-6532; www.clubprivilegejm.com; 14-16 Trinidad Tce; admission J$1000; ☺10pm-4am Thu-Sat) Kingston's most exclusive club with a smart dress code, large dance floor and the most extensive collection of high-end liquors of any Jamaican club, including Black Hennessey. The 'I Love v.O.D.k.a. Thursdays' features two-for-one vodka cocktails, 'Friday Night Party' lets two women in for the price of one and features locally famous and international DJs, while 'Privilege Saturday' is fuelled by free shots as well as DJ skills.

Limelight
DANCEHALL

(☎908-0841; Half Way Tree Entertainment Complex, 5-7 Hagley Park Rd; ☺midnight-5am) Popular bar-club venue that has several parties weekly, hosted by local dancehall stars, such as Bounty Killer's Bounty Sundays, Uptown Mondays and Boasy Tuesdays.

Fiction
NIGHTCLUB

(off Map p50; ☎631-8038; unit 6, Market Place, 67 Constant Spring Rd; admission J$800; ☺6pm-4am Mon-Sat) Pretty young things rub shoulders (and not just shoulders) with each other at one of Kingston's most popular elegant new clubs, which wouldn't look out of place in Miami.

Sports

Sabina Park
SPORTS

(☎967-0322; South Camp Rd) *The* place for cricket in Jamaica. The 30,000-seat arena hosted its first Test match in 1929. The atmosphere during international Tests makes it a must – whether or not you're a fan.

National Stadium
SPORTS

(☎929-4970; Arthur Wint Dr) Track-and-field events and matches featuring the Reggae Boyz, Jamaica's national football (soccer) team.

Theater

Little Theatre
THEATER

(Map p50; ☎926-6129; www.ltpantomime.com; 4 Tom Redcam Dr) Puts on plays, folk concerts and modern dance throughout the year. The National Dance Theatre Company performs July to August. Pantomime from late December through April.

Pantry Playhouse
THEATER

(Map p50; ☎960-9845; 2 Dumfries Rd; ☺Wed-Sun) Presents comedies and plays at an outdoor New Kingston playhouse year-round.

Centre Stage Theatre
THEATER

(Map p50; ☎968-7529; 70 Dominica Dr) Musicals in patois and English, particularly popular with families.

🔒 Shopping

Kingston has it all, from modern shopping malls to street craft stalls. Good crafts are found Downtown, whereas Devon House is your port of call for specialty shops. Art galleries and souvenir shops are scattered around Uptown, though many are to be found in shopping malls off and along Hope Rd.

Wassi Art Pottery
CRAFTS

(Map p50; Devon House, 26 Hope Rd) This pottery store sells marvelous vases, planters, plates, bowls and so on, each hand-painted and signed by the artist.

Patoo
SOUVENIRS

(Map p40; Manor Hill Plaza, 184 Constant Spring Rd) Local treasures – Tortuga puddings laced with rum, Busha Brown sauces, ceramic tableware, decorative ornaments and batik sarongs.

Cooyah
CLOTHING

(96 Hope Rd) This is the place to go for licensed reggae T-shirts and assorted tops and dresses in Rasta colors. *Cooyah* means 'look here' in patois; you should.

Bookland
BOOKSTORE

(Map p50; 53 Knutsford Blvd) Stock includes a strong selection of titles on Jamaica and the Caribbean, including guidebooks. Good black literature section.

Bookophilia
BOOKSTORE

(92 Hope Rd) Very good selection of books and magazines. The Blue Mountain coffee and muffin counter makes you want to linger longer.

Crafts Market
SOUVENIRS

(Map p42; cnr Pechon & Port Royal Sts; ☺Mon-Sat) Stall upon stall of wood carvings, bead jewelry, wickerworks, batiks, handbags and Jamaican clothing.

Jubilee Market
MARKET

(Map p42; Pechon St) Anything from flip-flops in Jamaican colors to string vests favored by Downtown tough guys.

Bolivar Bookshop & Gallery
ART GALLERY

(Map p50; ☎926-8799; 1D Grove Rd) Works by Jamaica's leading artists are on offer here, but there are also rare books, antiques and maps.

Rockers International MUSIC STORE
(Map p42; ☎922-8015; 135 Orange St) The best pick of reggae music in town, both CDs and LPs. Find your Burning Spear, Horace Andy and John Holt here.

Mutual Gallery ART GALLERY
(Map p50; ☎929-4302; 2 Oxford Rd) Excellent little gallery at the base of North Tower, with constantly changing exhibits of Jamaica's most exciting modern art.

Techniques Records MUSIC STORE
(Map p42; ☎967-4367; 99 Orange St) Oldies, dancehall and traditional Jamaican music.

Grosvenor Galleries ART GALLERY
(Map p40; ☎924-6684; 1 Grosvenor Tce) Excellent contemporary art by exciting new artists.

Tuff Gong Recording Studios MUSIC STORE
(Map p40) A great back catalogue of artists who've recorded here.

Contemporary Art Centre ART GALLERY
(☎927-9958; 1 Liguanea Ave) Good selection of contemporary art.

Gallery Pegasus ART GALLERY
(Map p50; Jamaica Pegasus hotel, 81 Knutsford Blvd) Some contemporary art gems occasionally spotted here.

Coronation Market MARKET
(Map p42) Similar to Jubilee Market.

Two of the largest shopping centers are **Sovereign Centre** (106 Hope Rd) and **New Kingston Shopping Centre** (Map p50; Dominica Dr).

ⓘ Information

Dangers & Annoyances

Kingston has a reputation as a dangerous destination with a high murder rate, but most murders take place in the ghettos and are gang- or drug-related. Visitors can enjoy the sights and sounds in reasonable safety as long as a few common sense guidelines are followed.

» Try to stick to the main streets – if in doubt, ask locals to point out the trouble areas.

» New Kingston and upscale residential areas such as Liguanea and Mona are generally safe for walking, as are most main roads and Downtown (though it's certainly *not* an area to be wandering alone at night).

» Avoid Kingston entirely during periods of tension, such as elections, when localized violence can spontaneously erupt. At such times, absolutely avoid Downtown and adhere to any curfews that police may impose.

» Take care in West Kingston (especially Trench Town, Jones Town, Denham Town and Tivoli Gardens), particularly west of Parade, Downtown; those areas are best explored with a local guide.

» Watch out for pickpockets at the markets.

Emergency

Ambucare (☎978-2327) Private ambulance service.
Emergency (☎119)
Police headquarters (☎922-9321; 11 East Queen St); Half Way Tree (142 Maxfield Ave); Cross Roads (Brentford Rd)
St John Ambulance (☎926-7656) Free ambulance services in Kingston.

Internet Access

Most upscale and midrange hotels provide free in-room wi-fi access. Prices in hotel business centers tend to be outrageous. Cafes offering free wi-fi include **Cannonball Café** and **Café Blue**. Digicel, **LIME** and **Claro** shops offer island-wide USB modems for laptops (from J$2700).
Kingston and St Andrew Parish Library (2 Tom Redcam Ave; per 30min J$100; ⊙9am-6pm Mon-Fri, 9am-5pm Sat) The cheapest option, though not the quietest.

Media

Daily Gleaner (www.jamaica-gleaner.com) Jamaica's dominant newspaper since 1834.
Jamaica Observer (www.jamaicaobserver. com) A boisterous alternative.

Medical Services

Andrews Memorial Hospital (☎926-7401; 27 Hope Rd) Well-equipped private hospital with well-stocked pharmacy.
Kingston Public Hospital (☎922-0210; North St) Public hospital with emergency department.
Liganea Drugs & Garden (134 Old Hope Rd) Uptown pharmacy.
Monarch Pharmacy (Sovereign Centre; ⊙9am-10pm Mon-Sat, 9am-8pm Sun)
University Hospital (☎927-1620; University of the West Indies campus, Mona) The best, most up-to-date public hospital with 24-hour emergency department.

Money

Banking hours are 9am to 2pm Monday to Thursday, 9am to noon and 3pm to 5pm Friday. Uptown, there are half a dozen banks along Knutsford Blvd. Most banks have foreign-exchange counters as well as 24-hour ATMs. There are also ATMs along Hope Rd, particularly by the shopping malls.
Scotiabank foreign exchange center (cnr Duke & Port Royal Sts); ATM (cnr King & Tower Sts)
Western Union (7 Hillcrest Ave)

Post

DHL (19 Haining Rd; ⊙8:30am-5pm Mon-Fri, 8:30am-1pm Sat)

FedEx (75 Knutsford Blvd; ⊙8:30am-5pm Mon-Fri)

Post office (⊙8am-5pm Mon-Thu, 9am-4pm Fri, 8am-1pm Sat) main post office (Map p42; 13 King St); Liguanea Post Mall (115 Hope Rd); Half Way Tree (Map p50; 18 Hagley Park Rd) Main PO gets crowded; Liguanea is a speedier option.

Telephone

You can make international calls from most hotels. You'll find plenty of public call centers around town. International call centers are located off the Half Way Tree roundabout.

SIM cards for cell phones are inexpensive and convenient. **Digicel**, **LIME** and **Claro** offer good deals for international customers, such as calling the UK or USA for 30 minutes but paying only for the first five minutes. There are numerous Digicel, LIME and Claro stores, mostly uptown. Top-up cards are sold in most kiosks.

Tourist Information

Jamaica Tourist Board Uptown (Map p50; ☎929-9200; www.visitjamaica.com; 64 Knutsford Blvd); Norman Manley International Airport (Map p40; arrivals hall) The Uptown office offers maps, brochures and limited travel advice. Island maps featuring Jamaica's heritage sites for sale (J$250).

❶ Getting There & Away

Air

Norman Manley International Airport (Map p40; ☎924-8452/6; www.nmia.aero), 27km southeast of Downtown, handles international flights; see p291 for more details on international services. Domestic flights depart and land at **Tinson Pen Aerodrome** (Map p40; Marcus Garvey Dr) in west Kingston; see p293 for details.

Air Jamaica (☎888-359-2475; 4 St Lucia Ave) Daily service to and from Montego Bay and Ocho Rios from Norman Manley International Airport.

Jamaica Air Shuttle (☎906-9026/30; www.jamaicaairshuttle.com) Air-taxi services connecting Kingston with Montego Bay and Ocho Rios from Tinson Pen Aerodrome. Charter flights to Port Antonio available.

Car

FROM THE NORTH COAST The busy A3 artery leads to Kingston via the outlying communities of Stony Hill and Constant Springs. The more scenic but difficult B3 takes you to Papine from Buff Bay via the Blue Mountains but is sometimes closed due to landslides.

FROM THE WEST Spanish Town Rd enters Kingston at the Six Miles junction. For Uptown Kingston, veer left on Washington Blvd. Its name changes to Dunrobin Ave; it eventually joins Constant Springs Rd for a straight shot into Uptown.

FROM THE EAST Windward Rd passes the turnoff for Port Royal and the airport. For New Kingston turn right on Mountain View Ave or South Camp Rd (the latter has helpful 'follow the hummingbird' signs directing the way).

Public Transportation

Buses, minibuses and route taxis run between Kingston and every point on the island. They arrive and depart primarily from the chaotic **Downtown terminal** off Darling St, seven blocks west of Parade. Exercise caution as the terminal adjoins the occasionally volatile district of Tivoli Gardens. At the time of writing, the Downtown terminal was due to be relocated to the brand new **long-distance bus terminal** (Map p42; cnr Port Royal St & Ocean Blvd). Buses (fewer departures on Sundays) depart when full and are often packed beyond capacity.

Comfortable **Knutsford Express** (Map p50; ☎971-1822; www.knutsfordexpress.com) buses run from their own bus terminal in New Kingston to Ocho Rios (J$1250, two hours) and Montego Bay (J$2000, four hours). Departures are at 6am, 9:30am, 2pm and 5pm Monday to Friday, 6am, 9:30am and 4:30pm Saturday and 8:30am and 4:30pm Sunday.

Book the Montego Bay ticket more than 24 hours in advance and get a discount for J$250.

BUSES FROM KINGSTON

DESTINATION	COST (J$)	DURATION (HR)	FREQUENCY
Mandeville	200	1½	5-6 daily
May Pen	120	1	6-8 daily
Montego Bay	280	4½-5	6-8 daily
Ocho Rios	200	2	8-10 daily
Port Antonio	240	2½	6-8 daily
Santa Cruz	180	2	6-8 daily

All bus fares within Kingston are J$80, with the exception of the express bus to the airport, which is J$90.

BUS NO	DESTINATION	FREQUENCY	DEPARTURE POINT
1/1A	Hellshire Beach	hourly	Parade/Half Way Tree
21B/22, 22A	Spanish Town	hourly	Half Way Tree/Parade
42/42A	Constant Spring	hourly	Parade/Half Way Tree
60, 68	Papine	hourly	Parade
61	Gordon Town	several daily	Parade
74/76	Barbican	hourly	Parade/Half Way Tree
97	Bull Bay	hourly	Parade
98	Airport, Port Royal	every 30min	Parade
99	Harbour View	hourly	Parade
500/600/700	Parade	every 30min	Half Way Tree

Be at the bus station 30 minutes before departure to register your ticket.

Buses to Port Antonio arrive and depart from the revamped **Half Way Tree Bus Terminal** (Map p50). There are numerous buses from Half Way Tree to various parts of Kingston. If you're traveling to Kingston, find out where you will be dropped before boarding a bus. (See p293 for information about Jamaica's bus system.)

🛈 Getting Around

To/From the Airport

BUS Bus 98 operates between the international airport and Parade Downtown (J$80, 35 minutes, every 30 minutes). The bus stop is opposite the arrivals hall. For Tinson Pen Aerodrome, take bus 22 or 22A from Parade (J$80, 15 minutes, hourly).

TAXI Between the international airport/Tinson Pen Aerodrome and New Kingston costs about US$35/15.

Car

Driving in Kingston is not for the faint-hearted. Be prepared for erratic and aggressive driving. Do not drive in the Downtown area after dark and do not linger at red lights anywhere late at night. All hotels and shopping centers offer parking. Secure car parks are nonexistent Downtown but you can park on the street.

Most car-rental companies offer free airport shuttles. Some reputable companies with offices at Normal Manley International Airport:
Avis (🖉924-8293; www.avis.com)
Budget (🖉759-1793; www.budget.com)
Hertz (🖉924-8028; www.hertz.com)
Island Car Rentals (🖉924-8075; www.island carrentals.com)

Public Transportation

Buses, minibuses and route taxis arrive and depart from North and South Parade in Downtown, Half Way Tree bus station in Uptown, Cross Roads (between Uptown and Downtown) and Papine, at the eastern edge of town off Old Hope Rd.

Jamaica Urban Transport Co Ltd (JUTC; www.jutc.com; fares J$80-170) operates a fleet of white and yellow Mercedes-Benz and Volvo buses. Most are air-conditioned. JUTC buses stop only at official stops.

Minibuses and route taxis ply all the popular routes (J$50 to J$80), stopping on request. It's easy to confuse white route taxis with red license plates with identical chartered taxis.

Taxi

Taxis are numerous in Kingston except when it rains, when demand skyrockets. Call a taxi from one of the recommended taxi companies, rather than flagging down the first driver to pass. Use licensed cabs only (they have red PP or PPV license plates). Taxis have no meters, so negotiate the fare in advance. Fares from New Kingston to Downtown are about J$500.

Some reputable taxi companies:
El Shaddai (🖉925-1363)
Express (🖉923-2868)
On Time (🖉926-3866)

AROUND KINGSTON

Whether it's Downtown's perpetual slope toward the harbor or the Blue Mountains beckoning from high above Uptown, there's something about Kingston's topography that tempts the visitor to take a break from the intensity of city life.

Most popular among day trips is a visit to Port Royal, a former pirate's den of iniquity, easily combined with a visit to Lime Cay, the best (and closest) swimming spot in the area. Other good seaside options include Hellshire Beach – a quintessential Kingstonian seaside experience – and Bull Bay, a rapidly growing surfing community. If it's greenery you crave, Castleton Gardens, a half-hour drive north of Kingston, are the finest botanic gardens in Jamaica. Finally, Jamaica's second city and former capital, Spanish Town, is noted for its Georgian architecture as well as the red brick splendour of St Jago de la Vega, the oldest Anglican cathedral outside of England.

Castleton Gardens

These **gardens** (admission free; ◉9am-5pm), straddling the A3, 27km north of Half Way Tree, are spread over 12 hectares on the banks of the Wag Water River. Many exotic species introduced to Jamaica, such as the poinciana, were first planted here.

The gardens, which rise up the hillside on the west side of the road, date back to 1862, when 400 specimens from Kew Gardens in London were transplanted on the former sugar plantation owned by Lord Castleton. More than 1000 species of natives and exotics are displayed.

East of Kingston

Watching Long Mountain close in on the sea from Downtown Kingston, it's easy to think there's nothing east of Kingston beyond the turnoff to the Palisadoes, home to Norman Manley International Airport and Port Royal. Yet the A4 does manage to squeeze past and make it to St Thomas parish and up into Portland. Before it does, the road brushes through Bull Bay, a gritty village that draws surfers and pilgrims to a fundamentalist Rasta community.

ROCKFORT MINERAL BATHS

Providing respite from the urban environment, these **baths** (Map p40; Windward Rd; adult/child J$250/100; ◉8am-4pm Mon-Fri; 7am-6pm Sat & Sun), 5km east of Downtown Kingston, are fed by a cold spring that made its first appearance following the earthquake of 1907. There's a large public pool and 11

private pools of varying sizes, all with whirlpools and wheelchair access (being refurbished at the time of writing). The slightly saline and radioactive water is said to have therapeutic properties. One hour is the maximum allowed in a bath. There's a cafeteria and juice bar, plus changing rooms and lockers. **Massage** (J$2963 per hour) is offered.

Adjacent to the baths is **Fort Rock**, an English fort with rusty cannons. It was built in 1694 amid rumors of an imminent invasion by the French.

To get here, take bus 99, 98 or 97 from Parade (J$80).

PALISADOES

This narrow, 16km-long spit (Map p40) forms a natural breakwater protecting Kingston Harbour. It extends due west from Windward Rd. At the western end, reached via Norman Manley Hwy, lies the historic town of Port Royal. The spit earned its name for the defensive palisade that was built across the spit to defend Port Royal from a land-based attack. The Palisadoes is fringed on its harbor side by mangroves that shelter crocodiles and colonies of pelicans and frigate birds.

The 22m-tall, stone-and-cast-iron **Plumb Point Lighthouse**, built in 1853 but still functioning, lies midway along the Palisadoes at its elbow. Despite the lighthouse's presence, in 1997 a freighter ran aground nearby on the windward side of the spit. It is still rusting away.

BULL BAY & ENVIRONS

Bull Bay is a small, spread-out town, 14km east of Downtown Kingston, with little to recommend it, but nearby is an interesting Rastafarian encampment and Jamaica's most notable surf camp.

To get to Bull Bay, take bus 97 or a route taxi from Parade (J$80).

Jamaica is continuing to gain stature as a surfing destination and Billy 'Mystic' Wilmot, once Jamaica's best surfer, has done as much as anyone to raise the profile of Jamaican surfing. Along with his family, he runs **Jamnesia Surf Camp** (☏750-0103; Cable Hut Beach; camping per person J$847, with provided tent J$1270, s/d J$2116/3386) – a destination in itself for those interested in surfing in Jamaica. Jamnesia has a wide array of boards for rent (J$2116 per day), from short minithrusters to a 2.9m-long board. Individual surfing instruction is also available. The famous 'Board Hut' is packed with boards

Around Kingston (Southern Plains)

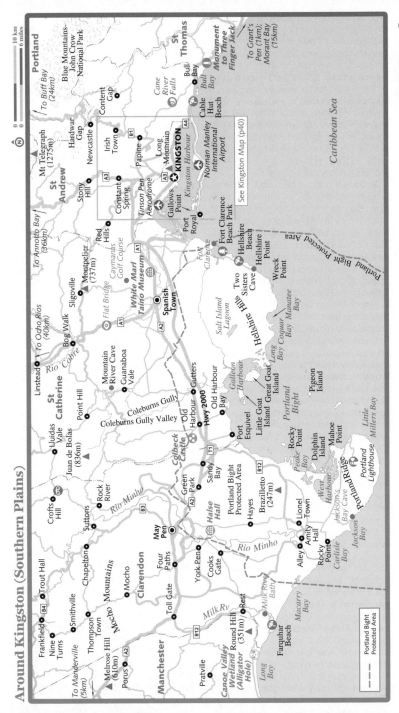

Portland

To Buff Bay (24km)

Blue Mountains–John Crow National Park

Content Gap

St Thomas

Bull Bay

Monument to Three Finger Jack

To Grant's Pen (1km); Morant Bay (15km)

Cane River Falls

Bull Bay

Cable Hut Beach

Mt Telegraph (1275m)

Hardwar Gap

Newcastle

Irish Town

Papine

B1

Long Mountain

A4

KINGSTON

Caribbean Sea

St Andrew

To Annotto Bay (36km)

Stony Hill

A3

Constant Spring

Tinson Pen Aerodrome

A3

Gallows Point

Norman Manley International Airport

See Kingston Map (p40)

Red Hills

Caymanas Golf Course

Port Royal

Fort Clarence Beach Park

Fort Clarence

Hellshire Beach

Hellshire Point

Montpelier (737m)

Sligoville

White Marl Taino Museum

Spanish Town

Wreck Point

To Ocho Rios (40km)

Flat Bridge

A1

Two Sisters Cave

Portland Bight Protected Area

Linstead

Bog Walk

St Catherine

A1

A2

Salt Island Lagoon

Hellshire Hills

Long Bay

Coquar Bay

Manatee Bay

Rio Cobre

Point Hill

Mountain River Cave

Guanaboa Vale

Galleon Harbour

Pigeon Island

Lluidas Vale

Juan de Bolas (836m)

Coleburns Gully

Coleburns Gully Valley

Old Harbour

Gutters

Hwy 2000

Old Harbour Bay

Little Goat Island

Great Goat Island

Portland Bight

Rocky Point

Dolphin Island

Mahoe Point

Portland Lighthouse

Crofts Hill

Rock River

Colbeck Castle

Green Park

A2

Sandy Bay

T1

Port Esquivel

Peake Bay

West Harbour

Jackson's Bay Cave

PortlandRidge

Little Millers Bay

Suttons

Rio Minho

B3

Halse Hall

Hayes

Brazilletto (247m)

B12

Frankfield

B4

Trout Hall

Nine Turns

Smithville

Chapelton

Mocho

Mocho Mountains

Clarendon

Four Paths

May Pen

York Pen

Cooks Gate

Rio Minho

Lionel Town

Amity Town

Alley

Rocky Point

Carlisle Bay

Jackson Bay

Macary Bay

To Mandeville (5km)

Thompson Town

Melrose Hill (610m)

Porus

A2

Manchester

Toll Gate

Pratville

Canoe Valley Wetland (Alligator Hole)

Round Hill (351m)

B12

Rest

Milk Rv

Milk River Bath

Farquhar Beach

Long Bay

Portland Bight Protected Area

10 km

6 miles

Portland

donated by traveling pros and friends of the burgeoning Jamaican surfing scene. The backyard, full of cats, dogs and Billy's sons, has a rustic outdoor bar, and on Saturdays there's often live music, courtesy of musician friends. During the summer months, three of Billy's sons host a learn-to-surf camp for youngsters who want to learn how to shred.

The camp offers simple rooms and camping, with shared kitchen facilities and bathrooms. You can pitch your own tent, or use a provided tent that comes with bedding. Multinight lodging packages are also offered, including meals and surf shuttle.

Bobo Hill (Ethiopia Africa Black International Congress; ☏578-6798), or the Black Sovereign Ethiopian Embassy, painted in the Rasta colors of red, gold and green, is the home of the Bobo Ashanti ('Bobbaheads') and sits on Queensbury Ridge above Bull Bay. About 100 fundamentalist Rastafarians live here and, true to the principles of self-respect and self-reliance, make a living from farming or selling natural-fiber brooms in Kingston. Other than that, they disassociate themselves from 'Babylon' and don't venture outside their commune.

Guests with a sincere interest in learning about Bobo and their beliefs are welcome as long as they respect 'manners and principles.' If you're male, you're greeted by the head priest in a room festooned with portraits of Haile Selassie, who will give you a spiel rich in clever metaphor that offers a fascinating insight into Rastafarian philosophy. If you're female, you'll be met by a female elder (if it's your time of the month, you will not be allowed inside the commune).

You are welcome to stay overnight or as long as you wish in simply furnished rooms, but you must contribute 'something' and 'come to salvation' through performing duties on 'campus.'

It's little more than 1km uphill from the bridge on the A4, 20m east of the Red Lion Pub. You'll need a 4WD and it's best to call ahead as the Bobo prefer advance warning.

Beyond Bull Bay, the main road climbs the scrub-covered hill before making a hairpin descent to Grants Pen and St Thomas parish. Near the summit you'll pass a **monument to Three Finger Jack** (Map p67), one of Jamaica's most legendary folk heroes. The marker was erected by the National Heritage Trust to recall the deeds of Jack Mansong, who in 1780 and 1781 often singlehandedly waged a war of terror against English soldiers and planters and who ended up enslaving his own master. He finally met his demise at the hand of Quashie the Maroon who presented Jack's head, preserved in rum, to the authorities in Spanish Town in exchange for a large reward.

Back on the coast, 1.5km west of Bull Bay, is **Cable Hut Beach** (Map p67). It's strewn with litter but surfers rave about the waves that roll into shore here. Surf seasons are June to September and December to March.

Port Royal

POP 3300

Once the wealthiest (and 'wickedest') city in the New World, the pirate capital of the Caribbean – and for more than 200 years the hub of British naval power in the West Indies – Port Royal today is a sleepy fishing village replete with important historic buildings, with children playing amid ramshackle, brightly painted houses and upturned fishing pirogues.

Port Royal Development Project has long touted the tourism potential of Port Royal, with planned projects ranging from semiplausible to completely bonkers, such as a 32-hectare theme park, cruise-ship pier, entertainment center and arcade, and heritage reenactments, including townsfolk in period costumes. Mercifully, the projects show no signs of getting off the ground.

There are few hints of the town's former glory, though landmarks such as Fort Charles and the Old Naval Hospital have been given a new lease on life by the Jamaica Heritage Trust. The excellent eateries, serving the freshest fish in Kingston, and doubling as party spots after hours, the proximity of Lime Cay with its white-sand beach and a laid-back, friendly vibe make this one of the best-loved spots near Kingston.

History

The English settled the isolated cay in 1655. They called it 'Cagway' or 'The Point' and built Fort Cromwell (renamed Fort Charles after the Restoration in 1660) as well as four other forts to defend Kingston Harbour.

At the time, England sponsored freelance pirates in their raids against Spanish ships and possessions. Almost as soon as the English had captured Jamaica, buccaneers – organized as the Confederacy of the Brethren of the Coast – established their base at Port Royal until the anti-piracy laws, passed in

1687, marked the end of the safe haven for buccaneers.

Admirals Lord Nelson and Benbow and Edward 'Blackbeard' Teach once lived here, but of all Port Royal's seafaring visitors the best-remembered buccaneer is Henry Morgan, whose celebrated exploits included a daring raid on Havana in the 1660s.

The lawless buccaneers were also big spenders. The wealth flowing into Port Royal attracted merchants, rum traders, vintners, prostitutes and others seeking a share of the profits. Townsfolk even invested in the expeditions in exchange for a share of the booty and by 1682 Port Royal was a prosperous town of 8000 people.

At noon on June 7, 1692, a great earthquake shook the island, followed by a huge tidal wave, and two-thirds of the town disappeared underwater. Around 2000 people died instantly, and numerous survivors were claimed by the pestilence that followed, caused by the hundreds of unburied corpses.

The defensive works were repaired in time to repel a French invasion mounted against Jamaica in 1694. Increasingly overshadowed by the growing city of Kingston, the rebuilt Port Royal never regained its former importance as a merchant town.

The near-constant state of war between England and Spain, France and Holland throughout the 18th century marked the beginning of Port Royal's 250-year tenure as headquarters of the Royal Navy in the West Indies; though, after being struck by one natural calamity after another, the old port went into decline. In 1838 Jamaica ceased to be a separate naval command and with the development of steam warships in the early 20th century Port Royal's demise was sealed.

⊙ Sights & Activities

TOP CHOICE **Fort Charles**   FORT
(Map p40; adult/child J$200/100; ⊙9am-4:45pm) Jamaica's latitude and longitude are measured from the flagstaff of Fort Charles, a weathered redoubt originally laid in 1655. Among Port Royal's five original forts, only Fort Charles withstood the 1692 earthquake, though it sank 1m. Originally washed by the sea on three sides, the fort is now firmly landlocked due to the gradual silt build-up.

At its peak, 104 guns protected the fort. Many cannons still point out from their embrasures along the restored battlements.

In the center of the courtyard stands the small, well-presented **Maritime Museum**,

If you've ever wondered why there's no large-scale tourist development in Port Royal, look no further than the little blue house behind Gloria's eatery. The village is governed by the Brotherhood – a council of Port Royal elders whose families have lived in the village for generations, and it is they who decide who can build – or even live – in Port Royal. Their headquarters may be unmarked, but everyone knows who wields the power.

containing a miscellany of objects – from glassware and pottery to weaponry – retrieved from the sunken city, plus a fabulous model of the *Jamaica Producer* cargo ship. Horatio Nelson, who later became one of Britain's greatest naval heroes, lived in the small 'cockpit' while stationed here for 30 months.

Behind the museum is the restored raised platform known as **Nelson's Quarterdeck**. It was here that the young Nelson was said to keep watch for enemy ships when put in charge of the fort amid fears of a French invasion. Once you climb to the top you'll agree that it does offer a splendid vantage point. A plaque on the wall of the King's Battery, to the right of the main entrance of the museum, commemorates his time here.

A small red-brick artillery store, the 1888 **Giddy House** (so known because it produces a sense of disorientation to people who enter), sits alone amid scrub-covered, windblown sand just behind Fort Charles. The 1907 earthquake, however, briefly turned the spit to quicksand and one end of the building sank, leaving the store at a lopsided angle.

Next to the Giddy House is a massive gun emplacement and one of two equally mammoth cannons – part of the easternmost casement of the **Victoria & Albert Battery** that lined the shore, linked by tunnels. The cannon keeled over in the 1907 earthquake and the second one disappeared.

Museum entry includes a guided tour.

St Peter's Church   CHURCH
Built in 1725 of red brick, this church is handsome within, despite its faux-brick facade of cement. Note the floor paved with original black-and-white tiles, and the beautifully

decorated wooden organ loft built in 1743 and shipped to England in 1996 for restoration. The place is replete with memorial plaques. The communion plate kept in the vestry is said to have been donated by Sir Henry Morgan, though experts date it to later times.

Most intriguing is a churchyard tomb of Lewis Galdy, a Frenchman who, according to his tombstone, '...was swallowed up in the Great Earth-quake in the Year 1692 & By the Providence of God was by another Shock thrown into the Sea & Miraculously saved by swimming until a Boat took him up.' He went on to live until 1739.

Come dressed up for a Sunday service or else call **Rhonda 'Molly' Wade** (☏899-1315) to arrange a visit.

Old Naval Hospital   NOTABLE BUILDING
Behind the old garrison wall off New St stands the dilapidated two-story Old Naval Hospital, built by Bowling Ironworks in Bradford, UK, shipped to Port Royal and reconstructed at this site in 1819. Though it suffered considerable damage by Hurricane Gilbert, the Jamaica National Heritage Trust is taking steps to renovate it and there are plans to open it to the general public. The ground floor currently contains a multimedia room where visitors will be able to watch a video dramatization of Port Royal's history once the renovation is complete. Contact the **Jamaica National Heritage Trust** (☏922-1287; www.jnht.com) for more information.

Naval Cemetery   CEMETERY
(Map p40) Less than 1km east of the dockyard, also enclosed by a brick wall, is the intriguing naval cemetery, where sailors lie buried beneath shady palms. The entrance is marked by an anchor in memory of the crew of HMS *Goshawk*, who perished when the ship sank in the harbor. Alas, the cemetery's most ancient quarter, which contained the grave of the famous buccaneer Sir Henry Morgan, sank beneath the sea in 1692.

Old Gaol House   HISTORICAL SITE
The only fully restored historical structure in town is the sturdy Old Gaol House, made of cut stone on Gaol Alley. It predates the 1692 earthquake, when it served as a women's jail, and has since survived a host of disasters, including 14 hurricanes and two major fires.

🎊 Festivals & Events

The **Port Royal Seafood Festival**, held each year on National Heroes Day, the third Monday in October, is a rollicking good time with scores of vendors selling fried fish, bammy and fish or conch soup, and live onstage entertainment.

On the last Friday of every month, there is a **sound-system party** inside Fort Charles.

🛌 Sleeping

TOP
CHOICE **Morgan's Harbour Hotel**   HOTEL **$$**
(☏967-8040; www.morgansharbour.com; s/d US$130/142, ste US$199-206; P✳✳) This hotel is a bit pricey for what it is, but it's atmospheric and the location is lovely; it stands within the grounds of the old naval dockyard. Sporting the largest marina in the Kingston area, a restaurant and a waterside bar, the hotel is a favorite haunt of sea salts. The spacious rooms have terra-cotta tile floors; most have balconies. Room 105 is where James Bond was woken up by a spider in *Dr No*, and the bar was the *Pussfeller's Club*.

Admiral's Inn   GUEST HOUSE **$**
(☏353-4202; d J$3809; ✳) The spotless rooms inside this cheerful yellow guest house, run by a friendly and helpful family, have fridges and microwaves, and you can chill in the back garden while the owners cook your fish supper on the grill. Trips to Lime Cay can be organized with advance notice. Follow the road round past Gloria's Top Spot and past the park on your right-hand side. The guest house is on the left.

🍴 Eating & Entertainment

On the main square are several food stalls serving good fried fish.

TOP
CHOICE **Gloria's**   SEAFOOD **$**
(5 Queen St; stew fish J$900; ☉lunch & dinner) This informal outdoor eatery may not look like much, but the plastic seats fill up daily with locals who drive here from miles around. Get here early, particularly on Friday nights and Sunday lunchtimes, place your order and then take a stroll around Port Royal, as your food will take a while. Avoid the other seafood, which is average, and go straight for the fish. When it finally arrives, Gloria's fish is nothing short of glorious – a large plate of melt-in-your-mouth perfection, accompanied by bammy, festival or rice. The brown stew parrotfish is par-

ticularly good. On Sundays, a mellow vibe prevails during oldies' music night.

Gloria's Top Spot
SEAFOOD $$

(1 High St; meals J$1100-1400; ⊙lunch & dinner) Also run by the children of the dearly departed Gloria, this restaurant perches by the water, with a large, attractive upstairs dining area that's particularly popular with tourists and large groups. The menu is largely the same as at Gloria's, though here you pay slightly more for the attractive setting. Particularly lively on Friday and Saturday nights when gussied-up locals pile in to flirt and dance to the latest sounds.

Red Jack Restaurant
INTERNATIONAL $$

(Morgan's Harbour Hotel; meals J$1000-2500) Offering gratifying panoramic views of Kingston Bay from its outdoor waterfront setting and top-notch seafood, this is Port Royal's more upscale dining experience. Lobster and fish dishes figure prominently on the menu, as do Jamaican specialties, salads and sandwiches.

Y-Knot
SEAFOOD $

(meals J$800-1100; ⊙10am-7pm Sun-Thu, 9am-1am Fri & Sat) On a large deck over the water, this spot serves particularly good conch soup, as well as sumptuous grilled chicken, fish, shrimp and lobster. The bar draws a younger crowd on weekends for drinking and dancing.

Fisherman's Tavern
BAR $

(40 New St) This is a funky watering hole drawing locals who wash in and out, overindulge in white rum, munch on fried fish and pick fights. It has tremendous character on Friday night when a mountain of speakers is built 7m high in the main square and ska music reverberates across the harbor, attracting a friendly crowd of Kingstonians.

❶ Getting There & Away

From Kingston's Parade take bus 98 (J$80, every 30 minutes, less frequently on Sundays) or a taxi (about US$45 one way).

Around Port Royal

The idyllic **Lime Cay** is one of half a dozen or so uninhabited, white sand-rimmed coral cays sprinkled about 3km offshore from Port Royal. In 1948 this was also the site of the fatal standoff between the police and Ivan 'Rhygin' Martin, the real-life cop-killer immortalized in the film *The Harder They Come*. It's the perfect spot for sunbathing and snorkeling and there's a shack selling snacks and refreshments.

Maiden Cay, a smaller, shadeless option nearby, is popular with nudists.

En route to Lime Cay, you'll pass what little remains of **Rackham's Cay**; it was named for the infamous Jack Rackham, one of scores of pirates hanged here in metal casings after execution. Nearby is **Gun Cay**, named for the cannons that can still be seen, legacies of a British fortification.

You can catch a ride to Lime Cay with **Y-Knot** (round trip per person J$1000), which runs daily (minimum four people) or from **Morgan's Harbour Yacht Marina** (Wednesday to Sunday only) for the same price; the latter also offers customers a two-hour tour of the cays (J$1694). You might talk the local fishermen into taking you to Lime Cay for a reduced rate on their motorized boats ('canoes'); agree a round-trip rate first and only pay half until they come to pick you up, or risk getting stranded.

West of Kingston

The Nelson Mandela Hwy (A1) connects Kingston to Spanish Town, Jamaica's second-largest city, before becoming the A2 and soldiering on to May Pen, the capital of Clarendon Parish and home to **Halse Hall**, a former plantation. From here, it's a mere 20-minute drive to Milk River Bath, the island's most celebrated mineral spa. You can bypass Spanish Town and the congested A1 by taking the **T1 Hwy** (toll J$80) towards May Pen instead.

Much closer, the Portmore–Kingston Causeway leads to the drab commuter city of Portmore, from which you can reach Hellshire Beach.

PORTMORE

There is little of interest in this sprawling residential suburb besides **Fort Augusta**, at the eastern end of Port Henderson Beach, dating from 1740. The original fort was destroyed when lightning struck the magazine holding 3000 barrels of gunpowder, killing 300 people. The fort is now a women's prison, housing a number of Western inmates guilty of drug smuggling.

At the west end of the beach is **Port Henderson**, a fishing hamlet backed by some fine examples of Georgian architecture, notably **Rodney Arms** (Old Water Police Station, Port Henderson Rd; meals J$1200-1700; ⊙lunch & dinner), a restaurant and pub serving very good seafood, though now the sea view is spoiled by the malodorous squatter settlement across the road. About 200m uphill from the Rodney Arms are the ruins of a semicircular gun emplacement replete with cannon, and an old fort and the **Apostles Battery**. It is worth the visit for the views across the harbor, especially at sunset, when Kingston glistens like hammered gold.

The horse races at **Caymanas Park** (☑988-2523; www.caymanaspark.com; Caymanas Dr; admission J$150-350; ⊙Wed & Sat), one of the best race tracks in the Caribbean, make for a lively outing; it's best to come with a local to understand the complicated betting system.

A nearby outdoor area is the Jamworld Entertainment Complex, the venue for **Caribbean Heritagefest** in mid-October and the edgy all-night dancehall event, **Sting**, at the end of the year.

❶ **Getting There & Away**

Buses 17, 18, 20, plus frequent route taxis and minibuses run from Kingston's Parade; buses 17A, 18A, 20A (J$80) from Half Way Tree.

HELLSHIRE BEACH RECREATION AREA

White-sand beaches fringe the eastern Hellshire Hills and are reached via a road that leads south from Portmore via Braeton Newtown to Hellshire Point, 13km south of Braeton.

The road meets the coast at **Great Salt Pond**, a circular bay lined with briny mangrove swamps where snook, mullet, stingrays and crocodiles ('alligators') can be seen.

At the southeasternmost point of Great Salt Pond is **Fort Clarence Beach Park** (adult/child J$250/150; ⊙10am-5pm Mon-Fri, 8am-7pm Sat & Sun), popular with Kingstonians on weekends. It hosts beauty contests and live dancehall concerts. It has clean sand, showers and toilets plus secure parking. A restaurant and bar are open weekends only.

A road to the left of the second, more southerly roundabout leads east to Hellshire Beach, also called **Fisherman's Beach**, which is the setting of a funky fishing and Rasta 'village' with dozens of gaily painted huts and stalls selling beer, jerk, and particularly good fried fish and festival. It's a boisterous, party-hearty place on weekends, with sound systems on Sunday nights. In

the morning, fishing pirogues come in with their catch. On any day of the week, though, it's a fascinating visit, a slice of the 'real' Jamaica up close.

The best place to eat is **Prendy's on the Beach**, where you can select your fish or lobster (in season) and instruct them how you want it cooked, though most other places turn out decent fish for cheaper prices if you bargain.

❶ **Getting There & Away**

Bus 1 (J$80, 30 minutes), minibuses and route taxis (J$200) run from Kingston's Parade; bus 1A (J$80, 35 minutes) from Half Way Tree.

PORTLAND BIGHT PROTECTED AREA

Created in 1999, this 1876-sq-km **protected area** (PBPA; www.portlandbight.com.jm) comprises Jamaica's largest natural reserve with 210 sq km of dry limestone forest and 83 sq km of wetlands, as well as precious coral reefs (two-thirds of the protected area lies offshore). Its convoluted boundaries extend westward from Kingston Harbour across St Catherine and Clarendon parishes as far as Canoe Valley Wetland (p77), on the border with Manchester parish.

This vital habitat for birds, iguanas, crocodiles, manatees, marine turtles and fish – and 50,000 human beings – is managed by the **Caribbean Coastal Area Management** (CCAM; ☑986-3344).

The CCAM has plans to move forward with 'community tourism' programs that utilize local fishermen to lead guided boat tours and hikes. An Eco-Heritage Trail, beginning at Hellshire Beach and ending at Canoe Valley Wetland, was in development at the time of writing, as was a visitor center to be part of a Biodiversity Conservation Centre and botanical garden (with trails) in the Hellshire Hills, where native plants will be propagated.

Spanish Town

POP 160,000

Spanish Town, Jamaica's capital for more than 300 years, was once considered to boast exemplary town planning. Today, for visitors traveling from Kingston through the city's blighted outlying ghettos, it's somewhat of a stretch to envisage the former capital's erstwhile grandeur. However, this changes the moment one arrives at the evocative historic center, where you'll find the Caribbean's most extensive assortment of Georgian ar-

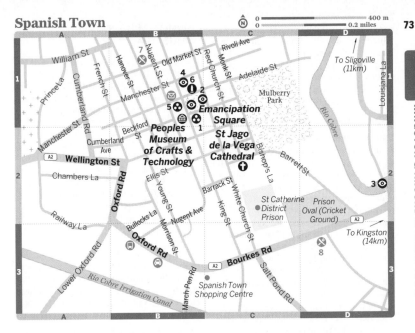

chitecture (albeit in a sad state of repair), its greatest cathedral and Jamaica's national archives.

The island's second-largest urban center and the gritty, busy capital of St Catherine parish, Spanish Town is frequently the locus of Jamaica's most wrenching urban strife. Consider this a day trip only.

History

After the settlement at Sevilla la Nueva failed in 1534, the Spanish established a new capital at Villa de la Vega – 'the Town on the Plain' – atop foundations that had been laid down earlier by Christopher Columbus' son, Diego. The town grew modestly as the administrative capital, helped along by a silk-spinning industry. However, Villa de la Vega (later renamed St Jago de la Vega) languished, and at its peak had a population of only about 500 people.

The town was poorly defended and was ransacked several times by English pirates. Eventually, in 1655, an English invasion fleet landed and captured the city. The English destroyed much of the town, then they renamed it 'Spanish Town' and made it *their* capital.

For the next 217 years, the town prospered as Jamaica's administrative capital but it

was eventually outpaced by Kingston, which took over as the island's capital in 1872.

Today, the town's most notorious building is St Catherine District Prison. Hangings have been carried out inside this fortress-like prison since 1714. Today, eight prisoners are on death row in narrow cells that date back almost three centuries. Conditions in the prison, Jamaica's largest, are very basic: cells contain a mattress and a slop bucket, and an area separate from the main prison yard retains scaffolding where inmates were hanged until 1988. Though capital punishment still exists, no one is likely to be hanged anytime soon: death sentences are automatically commuted to life imprisonment after five years and the legal process takes a very long time.

Sights

Emancipation Square   SQUARE
Spanish Town's finest old buildings enfold this square, established by the Spanish as the center of Jamaica's capital city in 1534. Dominating the square on the north side is the elaborate **Rodney Memorial**, built in honor of Admiral George Rodney, who crowned his four-year service as commander-in-chief of the West Indian Naval Station in 1782 when he saved Jamaica from a combined French and Spanish invasion fleet at the Battle of the Saints. He stands within a cupola temple, with sculpted panel reliefs showing the battle scenes.

The building behind the memorial is the **National Archives** (984-2581; admission free; 9am-4:30pm Mon-Thu), with national documents dating back centuries, including the proclamation of the abolition of slavery.

On the eastern side of the plaza is the red-brick **House of Assembly**, erected in 1762 and today housing the offices of the St Catherine Parish Council. It has a beautiful wooden upper story with a pillar-lined balcony. The Assembly and Supreme Court sat here in colonial days, when it was the setting for violent squabbles among feuding parliamentarians.

Moving to the south side of the square, you pass the fenced-off **Courthouse Ruins**, destroyed in 1986 by fire. The Georgian building dates from 1819, when it was used as a chapel and armory, with the town hall upstairs.

On the west side of the plaza is the porticoed Georgian red-brick facade of the ruins of the **Old King's House**, a once-grandiose building erected in 1762 as the official residence of Jamaica's governors. The building was destroyed by fire in 1925, leaving only the restored facade. Both the Courthouse Ruins and the Old King's House are now propped up by beams so that they won't collapse further, though there are no immediate plans to restore them.

Today the stables, to the rear, house the **People's Museum of Crafts & Technology** (adult/child J$300/100; 9:30am-4:30pm Mon-Thu, to 3pm Fri). A reconstructed smith's shop and an eclectic array of artifacts –

WHITE MARL TAINO MUSEUM

Jamaica owes much to the influence of the Taíno Indians, whose history is on display in a small **museum** (Map p67) atop a large pre-Columbian settlement. Hunting and agricultural implements, jewelry and carvings are featured and a reconstructed Taíno village is up the hill behind the museum. The museum is 200m north of the A1, about 3km east of Spanish Town. At the time of writing, the museum was closed, and potentially due to be moved to a more central location. Contact the Institute of Jamaica (p43) for more information.

from Indian corn grinders to early sugar-processing and coffee-making machinery – provide an entry point to early Jamaican culture. A model shows how Old King's House once looked and the outdoor section features carriages used in colonial times.

St Jago de la Vega Cathedral   CHURCH
Built in 1714, this is the oldest Anglican cathedral in the former British colonies. It's also one of the prettiest churches in Jamaica, boasting wooden fluted pillars, an impressive beamed ceiling, a magnificent stained-glass window behind the altar, and a large organ dating to 1849. The church stands on the site of one of the first Spanish cathedrals in the New World: the Franciscan Chapel of the Red Cross, built in 1525. English soldiers destroyed the Catholic church and used the original materials to build their cathedral. Note the handsome octagonal steeple with faux-Corinthian columns, and gargoyles with African features, considered unique in the world, above the south window.

Many leading local personalities are buried within its precincts. The oldest tomb dates to 1662 and is inset in the black-and-white transept aisle laid by the Spanish.

Iron Bridge   LANDMARK
At the bottom of Barrett St, turn left onto Bourkes Rd and follow it east to the narrow Iron Bridge spanning the Rio Cobre. The span was made of cast iron prefabricated at Colebrookdale, England, and was erected in 1801 on a cut-stone foundation that dates to 1675. The only surviving bridge of its kind in the Americas, it is still used by pedestrians, if barely.

📛 Sleeping & Eating

Spanish Treasure Hotel HOTEL **$**
(📞984-2474; Sligoville Rd; d J$4656, ste J$6772;
🅿️❄️🏊) If you have to stay the night, this motel-style hotel 2.5km northeast of town is the one good choice, with its basic but clean rooms, a restaurant and bar, a pool area and a skating rink.

Cecil's JAMAICAN **$**
(35 Martin St; meals J$450-650; ⏰breakfast, lunch & dinner Mon-Sat) Curry goat, oxtail and beans, brown stew chicken and a host of chow mein dishes served on plastic tablecloths under dim lighting.

La Cocina for Mom's Cooking JAMAICAN **$**
(shop 31, St Jago Shopping Centre, Bourkes Rd; meals J$300-450; ⏰lunch) Popular lunch spot cooking up a slightly Spanish take on Jamaican favorites such as stew pork, red pea soup and curry mutton.

❶ Information

Parts of Spanish Town are heavily affected by gang violence. Beware pickpocketing, especially at the market, and avoid driving near the market and exploring away from main downtown streets.

Police (📞984-2775; cnr Oxford Rd & Wellington St)

Post office (cnr King & Adelaide Sts)

Scotiabank (27 Adelaide St)

Spanish Town Hospital (📞984-3031; Bourkes Rd) Has a 24-hour emergency department.

Spanish Town Pharmacy (Spanish Town Shopping Centre, 17 Bourkes Rd)

❶ Getting There & Away

BUS From Half Way Tree: 21B; Parade: 22, 22A (J$80). In Spanish Town, buses, minibuses and route taxis leave from the **municipal bus terminal** (Bourkes Rd).

CAR Take Washington Blvd from Uptown Kingston or Marcus Garvey Blvd to Spanish Town Rd from Downtown; both join the A1.

TAXI A ride between Kingston and Spanish Town will cost about J$2540. Taxis depart from the taxi stand to the east of the bus terminal on Bourkes Rd.

Around Spanish Town

SLIGOVILLE

This peaceful village – the first free village, post-emancipation – sits on the upper story of Montpelier Mountain (737m), 8km east of Bog Walk at a junction with roads for Kingston (via Red Hills) and Spanish Town.

During the colonial era the area was a popular summer retreat for white society, and the second Marquis of Sligo, the pro-emancipation governor of Jamaica from 1834 to 1836, had a home here. **Highgate House**, a good example of Georgian architecture, has been recently restored by the National Heritage Trust with the help of US Peace Corps volunteers.

BOG WALK GORGE

About 11km north of Spanish Town the A1 cuts through a beautiful limestone canyon – **Bog Walk Gorge** – carved by the slow-moving, emerald-colored Rio Cobre, lined with vine-draped trees. You drop into the gorge and cross the river via the Flat Bridge, an 18th-century stone bridge, formerly a notorious place for bottlenecks. Bog Walk Gorge is closed to northbound traffic (7am to 9am Monday to Friday), and to southbound traffic (4pm to 7pm Monday to Friday).

Every rainy season, landslides block the road, disrupting traffic and adding to the damming effect of the narrow gorge. Flat Bridge is frequently under water after heavy rains; the high-water mark of August 16, 1933, when the river rose 8m above the bridge, is shown on the rock face. Halfway through the gorge, on the western side, you can see the huge **Pum Pum Rock**, named after a part of the female anatomy that it resembles.

COLEBURNS GULLY

This off-the-beaten-track valley extends northwest from Spanish Town into the central highlands. The road via Guanaboa Vale leads 8km north to **Mountain River Cave**, a National Trust site of archaeological importance, 3km above Guanaboa Vale. Guides will lead you down 1.5km and across the river, where the cave entrance is barred by a grill gate; the steep track is sweaty going, but there's a good spot for swimming in a small river with a waterfall. Inside, you'll discover Taíno petroglyphs painted on the walls and ceiling using a mix of ash and bat guano, many dating back up to 1300 years. The cave itself is not particularly spectacular-looking, but it's worth visiting for the scenic walk alone.

Contact the **Jamaica National Heritage Trust** (📞922-1287; www.jnht.com; 79 Duke St, Kingston) to arrange a guided tour for around US$45 (J$3830).

OLD HARBOUR

This otherwise nondescript town with a busy market vibe along its main street is famous for its iron **clock tower** in the town square. The Victorian tower is marvelously preserved, as is the clock, which was installed shortly after the English invasion in 1655. Other points of interest include the **Church of St Dorothy**, one of the oldest on the island.

The ruins of the **Colbeck Castle great house** stand amid scrubby grounds 2.5km northwest of Old Harbour; to reach them, follow the road north from the clock tower.

OLD HARBOUR BAY

This large fishing village, facing Portland Bight, 3km south of Old Harbour, is the site of the south coast's largest fish market. Fishermen land their catch midmorning, and it makes a photogenic sight with the nets laid out and the colorful pirogues drawn up on the otherwise ugly shore. The village is a squalid place of tin and wood shacks and is prone to flooding in the rainy season.

May Pen & Around

MAY PEN
POP 48,500

The capital of Clarendon parish, 58km west of Kingston, is a teeming market and agricultural town. It's bypassed by the A2 (Sir Alexander Bustamante Hwy), which runs about 1.5km south of town, and is due to join the T2 highway which will eventually link Kingston with Montego Bay. Expect pandemonium on Friday and Saturday when the market is held south of the main square, with the terrible congestion adding to the general mayhem.

The annual **Denbigh Agricultural Show** is held on the Denbigh Showground, 3km west of town, on Independence weekend in early August. It's a muddy, smelly, noisy and enjoyable affair, with farmers from each parish showcasing the fruits of their labor, from yams to livestock. Live entertainment and food vendors round out the bill. For information, contact the **Jamaica Agricultural Society** (☎922-0610; 67 Church St, Kingston).

WORTH A TRIP

MILK RIVER BATH

This well-known **spa** (☎449-6502; adult/child per bath J$400/200, hotel guests free, massages J$1000-4500; ☉7am-10pm), 23km southwest of May Pen, is fed from a saline mineral hot spring that bubbles up at the foot of Round Hill, 3km from the sea. The waters are a near-constant 33°C (92°F). Immersion is said to cure an array of ailments ranging from gout and lumbago to rheumatism and nervous conditions.

The spa, which is attached to the Milk River Hotel, is owned by the government. The six timeworn public mineral baths and three private baths are cracked and chipped, though clean.

These are the most radioactive spa waters in the world; 50 times more so than Vichy in France and three times those of Karlsbad in Austria. Bathers are limited to only 15 minutes, though you are allowed three baths a day. Imbibing the waters is also recommended by the spa staff as a stirring tonic. Kingstonians flock on weekends seeking treatments. Indulge yourself with the massages on offer.

About 200m north of the spa is the open-air **Milk River Mineral Spa Swimming Pool**, belonging to the Milk River Hotel. It was under renovation at the time of writing.

Beyond Milk River Bath, a dirt road lined with bush and tall cacti leads 2.5km to the black-sand **Farquhars Beach** (be careful how you pronounce that!), a funky fishing village at the river mouth, where you can watch fishermen tending their nets and pirogues.

Milk River Hotel (☎449-6502; Clarendon; d without/with bathroom J$5164/7449) is a rambling, homey, white-porched hotel with shady verandas, louvered windows, etched wooden motifs above the doors, well-worn pine floors and 20 modestly furnished, pleasant rooms. Meals are served in a cozy dining room, where the menu includes Jamaican favorites such as mutton stew and stewed fish. Full board available.

Farquhars Beach has two good eateries: **Dian's Three Star Seafood Restaurant**, a sky-blue shack serving steamed fish (J$650) and basic Jamaican fare; and **Jaddy's** Rasta shack at the end of the beach, great for fried fish (J$650), fish tea and dumpling.

A bus operates from May Pen (J$140, 45 minutes) twice daily.

Halse Hall (☑986-2215; tours by arrangement) is a handsome great house, on the B12, 5km south of May Pen, situated up on a hillock with commanding views. After the English invasion in 1655, the land was granted to Major Thomas Halse, who built the house on an old Spanish foundation and whose grave is behind the house in a small cemetery. For a time the house was occupied by Sir Hans Sloane, the famous doctor and botanist, whose collection of Jamaican flora and fauna formed the nucleus of what later became the Natural History Museum in London. Today, it is owned by the bauxite concern Alcoa Minerals, which uses it for conferences and social functions. To take a tour, call and ask for Mrs Thomas.

The pleasant, modern **Hotel Versalles** (☑986-2775; 42 Longbridge Ave; r J$7195, ste J$8042; [P][✿][@][≋]), 1km southwest of town, has modestly furnished rooms, suites and studios featuring cable TV. Take the second left at the Mineral Lights Roundabout.

At **Toll Gate**, 10km west of May Pen on the A2, **Fyah Side Jerk** serves tasty jerk chicken and pork, while just beyond is the **Juici Patties** factory, restaurant and drive-through, featuring reliably good patties, peanut porridge and saltfish-and-cabbage combos.

❶ Information

May Pen Hospital (☑986-2528; Muirhead Ave) Three kilometers west of the town center.

Police station (Main St) Around 100m west of the main square.

Scotiabank (36 Main St)

❶ Getting There & Around

The transportation center on Main St, 200m southeast of the main square, has frequent buses, minibuses and route taxis to and from Spanish Town, Kingston, Ocho Rios, Mandeville, Negril and Milk River.

CANOE VALLEY WETLAND

This is a government-owned **wildlife reserve** (☑377-8264; admission free; ☺Mon-Sat), commonly known as 'Alligator Hole.' It's notable for its family of three manatees (all females) that inhabits the diamond-clear water, in which crocodiles (called 'alligators' locally) also hover. They live amid dense, tall reeds in jade-blue pools fed by waters that emerge at the base of limestone cliffs, and are not always easy to see. Herons, grebes, jacanas, gallinules and other waterfowl are abundant.

The best time to see the manatees is on Tuesdays and Fridays between 2pm and 4pm, when they come out to be fed sea grass. There's a small visitor center with displays on local wildlife. You can take an hour-long trip by canoe with a guide for J$847 (tip expected).

The turnoff is signed 1.5km north of Milk River Bath on the B12. Otherwise you can take the beautiful 17km-long coastal road from **Alligator Pond**, which is often deserted. The road conditions tend to be poor after autumn rains.

Blue Mountains & Southeast Coast

Best Places to Eat

» Strawberry Hill (p85)

» Cafe Blue (p82)

» Crystal Edge (p83)

» Gap Café Bed & Breakfast (p84)

Best Places to Stay

» Strawberry Hill (p85)

» Lime Tree Farm (p87)

» Forres Park Guest House & Farm (p87)

Why Go?

Looming over Kingston, the majestic, forest-covered Blue Mountains throw the rest of the island into sharp relief. Their slopes, crags and fern forests seem light years from the capital's gritty streetscape, allowing you to hike old Maroon trails, go in search of the elusive streamertail hummingbird (Jamaica's national bird) or simply perch on a mountaintop, watching the valleys unfold out of the mist below.

A steep walk through a highland working plantation reveals the nuances of the coffee cultivation process, culminating in a cup or two of Blue Mountain coffee – which tastes even more heavenly when you can smell the beans from a nearby field.

The least-explored corner of the island, the southeast coast is a place of bloody rebellions, obeah rituals, and traditional rural life, largely undisturbed by visitors. Dirt trails lead you through cane fields to rustic hot springs or a picturesque lighthouse on a lonely coast.

When to Go

In February, Holywell Recreation Area hosts the Misty Bliss festival, celebrating the island's Maroon heritage. Predawn hikes up Blue Mountain between June and August are enlivened by a proliferation of peeny-wallies (fireflies), and September is a good time to join in the parade and the dancing at Bath's Breadfruit Festival to commemorate the arrival of the first breadfruit.

BLUE MOUNTAINS

Deriving its name from the azure haze that settles lazily around it's peaks, this 45km-long mountain range looms high above the eastern parishes of St Andrew, St Thomas, Portland and St Mary. The Blue Mountains were formed during the Cretaceous Period (somewhere between 144 and 65 million years ago) and are the island's oldest feature. Highest of the highlights, Blue Mountain Peak reaches 2256m above sea level, and no visit to the area should neglect a predawn hike to its summit for a sunrise view.

Unsurprisingly, the Blue Mountains' largely unspoiled character owes much to the difficulty in navigating around the area. Roads are narrow and winding, and some are dirt tracks that are utterly impossible to pass without 4WD, especially after heavy rains. If you are spending time in the area, renting a hardy vehicle, contacting a tour guide or making arrangements with your hotel are highly advisable.

History

With dense primary forests and forbidding topography, the prospect of life in the Blue Mountains has discouraged all but the most determined settlers. During the 17th and 18th centuries, these same formidable qualities made the territory the perfect hideout for the Windward Maroons, who from their remote stronghold at Nanny Town resisted enslavement and British colonialism for more than 100 years. But this region's primary claim to fame has always been coffee cultivation; it has been a mainstay since the very first coffee factories were erected around Clydesdale in the mid-18th century. Meanwhile, back down at sea level, the southeast coast of St Thomas parish is notable for its long history of protest and rebellion, and the independent spirit of the region has kept it at odds with the government even up to this day.

National Parks

The Blue Mountains-John Crow National Park protects 78,210 hectares and is managed by the Natural Resources Conservation Authority (NRCA). The park includes the forest reserves of the Blue and John Crow Mountain Ranges and spans the parishes of St Andrew, St Thomas, Portland and St Mary. Ecotourism is being promoted and lo-

cals are being trained as guides. Camping is only permitted at designated sites. Camping 'wild' is not advised.

Dangers & Annoyances

The roads in the Blue Mountains consist of endless switchbacks; they are narrow, often overgrown with foliage and can be badly rutted. Many corners are blind. Honk your horn frequently and watch out for reckless local drivers.

Ask about trail conditions before hiking in the mountains. If a trail is difficult to follow, turn back. Mountain rescue is slow and you could be lost for days.

ℹ Information

There are **ranger stations** (⊙9am-5pm) at Holywell Recreation Area and Portland Gap, and at Millbank in the Upper Rio Grande Valley. Entry to the park is free, except for Holywell Recreation Area. Other than the station at Holywell, the other stations might keep more erratic hours.

Jamaica Conservation & Development Trust (JCDT; ☑920-8278; www.jcdt.org.jm; 29 Dumbarton Ave, Kingston) Provides management and supervision of the national park.

ℹ Getting There & Away

BUS Minibuses and route taxis arrive from and depart to the mountains from the Park View Supermarket on the square in Papine. The frequency of service depends on demand. There is at least one morning run and one in the afternoon for the two main routes. Destinations include Mavis Bank (J$250, 15km, 1½ hours) and Newcastle (J$270, 23km, 1¼ hours). There is no regular bus service from Buff Bay up the B1.

CAR There are no gas stations; fill up in Papine. From Kingston, Hope Rd leads to Papine, from where Gordon Town Rd (B1) leads into the mountains. At the Cooperage, the B1 (Mammee River Rd) forks left steeply uphill for Strawberry Hill resort (near Irish Town) and Newcastle. Gordon Town Rd continues straight from the Cooperage and winds east up the Hope River Valley to Gordon Town, then steeply to Mavis Bank and Hagley Gap. From the north coast, the B1 heads into the mountains from Buff Bay (closed at time of writing due to a landslide).

ℹ Getting Around

Traveling by your own vehicle is the best way to enjoy the Blue Mountains as public transportation between villages is infrequent and it's difficult to reach many points of interest. You'll need a sturdy 4WD with a low gear option to handle the road conditions.

Blue Mountains & Southeast Coast Highlights

❶ Setting out before dawn to experience the greatest high in Jamaica, **Blue Mountain Peak** (p88)

❷ Rewarding yourself with a meal, spa treatment or night of romance at one of Jamaica's best hotels, **Strawberry Hill** (p85) near Irish Town

❸ Seeing a red berry transformed into the world's best coffee bean at **Old Tavern Coffee Estate** (p85)

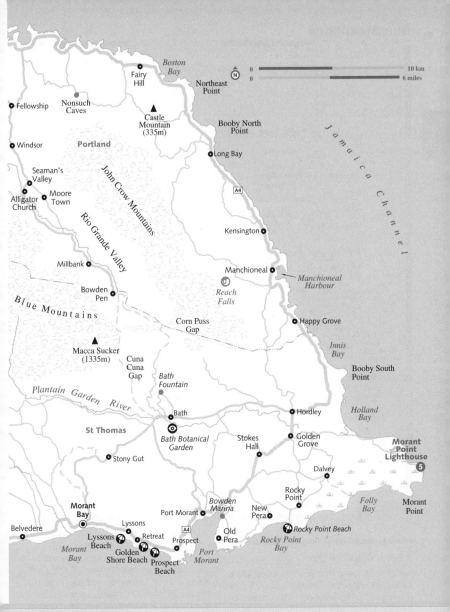

- Fairy Hill
- *Boston Bay*
- Northeast Point
- Fellowship
- Nonsuch Caves
- ▲ Castle Mountain (335m)
- Booby North Point
- Windsor
- **Portland**
- Long Bay
- *J a m a i c a   C h a n n e l*
- Seaman's Valley
- John Crow Mountains
- Alligator Church
- Moore Town
- Kensington
- Millbank
- Rio Grande Valley
- *B l u e   M o u n t a i n s*
- Bowden Pen
- Corn Puss Gap
- Manchioneal
- *Manchioneal Harbour*
- 🎵 *Reach Falls*
- Happy Grove
- ▲ Macca Sucker (1335m)
- Cuna Cuna Gap
- *Innis Bay*
- Booby South Point
- *Plantain Garden River*
- *Bath Fountain*
- Bath
- **St Thomas**
- ◎ *Bath Botanical Garden*
- Stokes Hall
- Hordley
- Golden Grove
- *Holland Bay*
- Stony Gut
- Dalvey
- **Morant Point Lighthouse** ❺
- Rocky Point
- *Folly Bay*
- **Morant Bay** ◉
- Belvedere
- Lyssons
- Port Morant
- *Bowden Marina*
- New Pera
- Morant Point
- Lyssons Beach 🏖
- Retreat
- A4
- Old Pera
- 🏖 *Rocky Point Beach*
- Golden Shore Beach 🏖🏖 Prospect Beach
- Prospect
- *Port Morant*
- *Rocky Point Bay*
- *Morant Bay*

0 — 10 km
0 — 6 miles

Ⓝ N

A4

❹ Cycling from **Hardwar Gap** (p83), quickening your pulse with a rip-roaring descent from the high mountains, through coffee plantations and villages

❺ Finding your way to the remote **Morant Point Lighthouse** (p91) to enjoy a privileged view of coast and mountains

BLUE MOUNTAINS & SOUTHEAST COAST BLUE MOUNTAINS

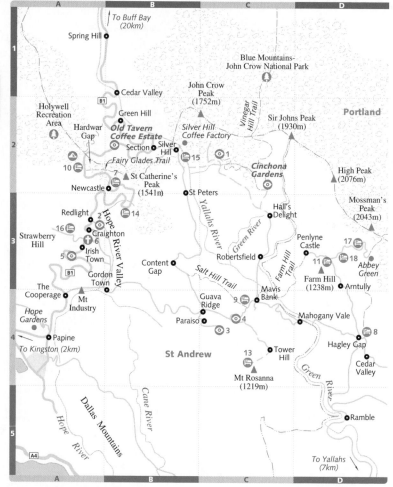

The Cooperage

About 3km above Papine via Gordon Town Rd is the Cooperage, a hamlet named for its community of Irish coopers who made the wooden barrels in which coffee beans were shipped in the 19th century.

Buses to Redlight, Hardwar Gap and Gordon Town all pass the Cooperage.

Irish Town

Mammee River Rd climbs to Irish Town, a small village where the coopers lived dur-

ing the 19th century. Potatoes are still an important crop, reflecting the Irish influence. Largely famous for one of the Caribbean's most luxurious resorts, it also contains **St Mark's Chapel**, an attractive white clapboard church restored after damage from Hurricane Gilbert. The pleasant **Observation Deck Gallery** (☎944-8592; ☺Thu-Sun) features sculpture and painting by local artist Tiffany Recas; it can be found just below the town. A little further up the road, the excellent **Cafe Blue** (meals J$700; ☺lunch), the offshoot of the popular Kingston institution, serves sumptuous gourmet

when they come down to hold a Nyabinghi Sabbath Service consisting of drumming and dancing.

To get to Irish Town, take a minibus (J$80) or route taxi (about J$100) from Papine.

Newcastle

The road climbs to 1220m where you suddenly emerge on a wide parade ground guarded by a small cannon. The military encampment clambers up the slope above the square. Newcastle was founded in 1841 as a training site and convalescent center for British soldiers. Since 1962 the camp has been used by the Jamaica Defense Force.

Note the insignia (which dates back to 1884) on the whitewashed stone wall, commemorating those regiments stationed at Newcastle. Visitors are allowed only around the canteen, shop, roadways and parade ground.

Three kilometers above Newcastle you reach **Hardwar Gap** (1700m), at the crest of the Grand Ridge – the start on an exhilarating cycle track.

Sights & Activities

Craighton Coffee Estate   COFFEE ESTATE
(www.craightonestate.com; adult/child J$1270/593; ⊙8am-4pm) Just north of Newcastle, you can take a one-hour tour of the attractive 200-year-old Craighton Estate Great House and coffee plantation. During the tour, your guide explains to you the basics of coffee cultivation and a mildly steep walk leads you up to a gazebo with wonderful views of the mountains and the villages below.

Cycling   CYCLING
An exhilarating way to see the Blue Mountains is by mountain bike – the sturdier the better as the going can be steep and arduous. Blue Mountain Bicycle Tours (p122) in Ocho Rios offers pickup from Kingston or Ocho Rios, transfer to the Hardwar Gap and an exhilarating downhill **cycling tour** (adult/child J$8296/5923). Potential stops include a coffee-roasting facility. Up to 43 cyclists. Mount Edge B&B (p84) offers a similar tour with smaller groups, also from Hardwar Gap. Check bike condition before setting out!

Hiking   HIKING
A steep dirt road runs from the parade ground up to **St Catherine's peak** (one

sandwiches and Blue Mountain coffee, while the adjoining **Crystal Edge** (meals J$1000; ⊙lunch) specializes in Jamaican favorites, such as curry goat.

Further uphill is **Redlight**, a hamlet so-named because it used to serve as a brothel for soldiers from the Newcastle barracks.

From Irish Town, a dirt road runs up to the fundamentalist Rastafarian commune called **Mount Zion Hill**, consisting of just over 50 adults and children who rely on subsistence farming for a living. Though fierce in their rejection of Babylon, the residents can be seen on Papine Sq every Saturday

hour). You need to get permission first from the military encampment.

🛏 Sleeping & Eating

TOP CHOICE **Mount Edge B&B** GUEST HOUSE $
(☑944-8151, 351-5083; www.mountedge.com; r with shared bathroom J$2540-4233, with private bathroom J$3386-6772; ℗@☑) Run by an eccentric host, this quirky mountainside maze of brightly painted rooms and rustic bathrooms is a great budget option. Some rooms have great views over the valley below and the owner's vegetable patches where he grows organic produce for the little restaurant above the guest house. The spacious, no-frills lounge has a guest library, kitchen and wide windows on all sides. Birding and cycling tours are on offer. Meal packages can be arranged and weekly and monthly rates are negotiable.

Gap Café Bed & Breakfast B&B $
(☑579-9528; r J$5926) Just below the entrance to Holywell Recreation Area, the Gap Café Bed & Breakfast has a cosy Hansel-and-Gretel-style, one-bedroom, self-catering cottage with a veranda. The cafe (☺breakfast & lunch) is a fabulous place to rest and take in the vistas. Dine alfresco on a wooden terrace, sampling the succulent curry goat and smoked pork chops, as

well as lighter fare in the form of fancy sandwiches. Dinner is by reservation only.

Barbecue Heritage Gardens GUEST HOUSE $$
(☑960-8627/0794; www.heritagegardensjamaica.com; cottages J$8465) Set 400m east of New-castle parade ground, this is a simple yet exquisite two-bedroom, fully equipped wooden cottage (with kitchen, lounge and live-in caretakers) set in a coffee estate (circa 1750) with wonderful views towards Kingston. The old coffee-drying barbecues are now laid out as gardens.

Holywell Recreation Area

Spanning Hardwar Gap, this **area** (☑960-2848; www.jcdt.org.jm; adult/child J$846/423; ☺9am-5pm) protects 120 hectares of remnant woodland, lush with dozens of fern species, epiphytes, impatiens, violets, nasturtiums, wild strawberries and raspberries. The mist-shrouded uppermost slopes are densely forested with rare primary montane forest, dominated by pine trees. The **bird-watching** is fabulous. The manned ranger station is a short distance beyond the entrance. The orientation center hosts occasional live entertainment such as traditional music and dance, plus outdoor games, storytelling and a treasure hunt for the kids (contact the Jamaica Conservation & Development Trust for information). On the last Sunday in February, the **Misty Bliss** mountain festival is held here, involving Maroon drumming, food and storytelling.

Well-maintained, easy hiking trails lead off in all directions through the ferny dells, cloud forest and elfin woodland. The 2.4km **Oatley Mountain Trail**, best seen with a guide (US$20) who can point out the different flora, leads to a river good for bathing. The 2km **Waterfall Trail** leads down along a stream to the Cascade Waterfalls – more trickle than cascade, due to recent landslides.

Camping (per person J$423) is allowed. You can also rent rustic **cabins** (1-/2-bedroom cabins J$4233/5926) with basic kitchens. Bring your own bedding and food (there's a gas ring and fridge) and reserve cabins in advance, particularly on weekends and holidays.

Section

Heading northeast from Holywell, the road drops steeply toward the hamlet of Section and then curls its way down to Buff Bay, 29km north (impassible at the time of writing due to landslides). A turnoff to the right at Section leads 1.5km to the ridge crest, where the main road loops south and drops to Content Gap, eventually linking up with the road from Gordon Town to Mavis Bank. A steep and muddy dirt road to the left drops to the simple Silver Hill Coffee Factory.

TOP CHOICE **Old Tavern Coffee Estate** (924-2785; www.exportjamaica.org/oldtavern; admission free) lies about 1.5km southwest of Section. You would surely pass by the small cottage, marked only by the presence of a severely disused Land Rover, if you didn't know that its occupants, Dorothy Twyman and her son David, produce the best of the best of Blue Mountain coffee. The late Alex Twyman emigrated to Jamaica from England in 1958 and started growing coffee a decade later, his son now keeping up the tradition. Dorothy oversees the roasting, meticulously performing quality control by taste. The environmentally conscious Twymans keep their use of chemical pesticides and fertilizers to a minimum and compost all by-products before returning them to the soil.

Although the Twymans' coffee is widely acclaimed as the best on the island, they weren't allowed to sell an ounce (due to Kafkaesque government regulations) until 1997, when they were granted an exclusive license to self-process coffee under an 'estate' label – the only estate on the island permitted to do so at the time.

The Twymans welcome visitors by prior arrangement. You are treated to a lesson on coffee growing and production as well as a tasting session of two of the three arabica bean roasts: dark, medium-dark and medium. Additionally, they produce the rare peaberry variety with a mild, subtle flavor. Though hard hit by recent hurricanes, the Twymans hope to restart the

---

DON'T MISS

STRAWBERRY HILL

One of the finest resorts in Jamaica and record mogul Chris Blackwell's pet, **Strawberry Hill** (946-1958; www.islandoutpost.com/strawberry_hill; r/ste/villa incl breakfast & transfers US$295/395/595;) is a luxury retreat just north of Irish Town. Gaze at Kingston and the harbor 950m below from a deckchair by the infinity-edge pool, roam the bougainvillea-draped grounds or relax at the ayurvedic spa after an 'elemental nature consultation' to determine your customized treatment based on five elements (earth, air, fire, water and infinity).

The Caribbean-style cottages range from well-appointed mahogany-accented studio suites, each with canopied four-poster beds with heated mattresses, to a four-bedroom, two-story house built into the hillside. A sumptuous breakfast is included in the rates, as are transfers. All-inclusive rates are US$300 extra per night. Bird-watching, hiking and other tours are available and Strawberry Hill also hosts a calendar of special events throughout the year.

Many Kingstonians make the tortuous drive to Strawberry Hill for some of the finest nouvelle Jamaican cuisine on the island (dinners US$25 to US$55, Sunday brunch J$3000). Reservations advised.

Since coffee grows best on well-watered, well-drained slopes in cooler yet tropical climates, it is no surprise that it thrives in Jamaica's Blue Mountains. The region's distinctly flavored coffee, with its lack of bitterness, is acclaimed by connoisseurs as among the world's best. To be designated 'Blue Mountain,' it must be grown – and roasted – at a certain altitude in a prescribed area.

In 1728, at Temple Hall Estate, north of Kingston, governor Sir Nicholas Lawes introduced coffee to Jamaica and other planters followed suit, prompted by the growing demand in Europe. During the peak years (1800–40), production rose to 17,000 tons a year and Jamaica became the world's largest exporter.

Emancipation in 1838 brought an end to many of the plantations. Many slaves left the estates and planted their own coffee. As steeper slopes were planted, coffee quality began to decline. The end of Britain's preferential tariffs for Jamaican coffee further damaged the industry at a time when high-quality coffee from Brazil was beginning to sap Jamaica's market share. By the close of WWII, Jamaica's coffee industry was on its last legs, prompting the Jamaican government to establish quality guidelines for coffee cultivation, thus saving the plantations.

There has been a resurgence in the popularity of Blue Mountain coffee in the last decade, largely thanks to interest from Japan, where it is a treasured commodity and sells for US$140 or more per kilogram. More than 80% of Blue Mountain coffee is sold to Japan at a preferential rate, which means that the beans that make it to North America and Europe can be quite expensive.

Sadly, this profitability only encouraged deforestation at home. Tearing down trees brought coffee farmers more valuable land, but also chased away migratory bird populations and has made Blue Mountain coffee especially vulnerable to hurricane damage. Over the past few years the industry's small farmers have been particularly hard hit by natural disasters, highlighting the need both for greater regulations and greater investment.

---

production of homemade mead, honey and coffee liqueur in the near future. You can purchase their coffee at the Cannonball Café in Uptown Kingston or at the estate itself for a reduced price after the free tour.

Starlight Chalet & Health Spa (☑969-3070; www.starlightchalet.com; s/d US$80/90, ste US$95-285; **P**) is set amid a flower-filled hillside garden with dramatic alpine vistas. The three-story plantation-style retreat sits at the turnoff for the Silver Hill Coffee Factory. A great base for birding and hiking, it also offers massages at the no-frills spa, as well as nature walks and yoga; book ahead of arrival. If you come in the off-season, you're likely to have the place all to yourself. Pickup from Kingston available.

Around Section

Clydesdale is a derelict old coffee plantation and a good spot for camping. The much-battered waterwheel and coffee-mill machinery are partially intact. There is a small waterfall where you can skinny-dip and a natural pool in the Clydesdale River below, rumored to have healing properties.

From Section take the horrendously potholed road south towards Guava Ridge; the turnoff for Clydesdale is about 1km above the hamlet of St Peters. Then you will cross over the Chestervale Bridge above the Brook's River and take the left, steeply uphill road at the Y-fork. It's a terribly rocky drive, suited for a 4WD only.

It was the cultivation of Assam tea and cinchona (whose quinine – extracted from the bark – was used to fight malaria) that led to the founding of **Cinchona Gardens** (admission free, tip to caretaker expected) in 1868. The grounds were later turned into a garden to supply Kingston with flowers. In 1903 the Jamaican government leased Cinchona to the New York Botanical Gardens and, later, to the Smithsonian Institute.

A dilapidated old house full of weathered antiques sits atop the 2.5-hectare gardens, fronted by lawns and exquisite floral beds. Today, the gardens are a little run-down, but the views are fabulous: to the north stand the peaks, but you can also peer down into the valleys of the Clyde, Green and Yallahs Rivers. The **Panorama Walk** begins to the east of the gardens, leading through a glade of towering bamboo and taking in the juniper cedar, camphor and eucalyptus trees, as well as a striking display of orchids.

Most of the trails that snake off into the nether reaches of the mountains are overgrown, but the 16km **Vinegar Hill Trail**, an old Maroon trail leading down to Buff Bay, can be negotiated with an experienced guide.

Finding Cinchona can be difficult without a guide. From Clydesdale you can either hike (1½ hours) or drive uphill along the muddy dirt track for about 3km. There are several unmarked junctions; ask for directions at every opportunity. Don't underestimate the awful road conditions; *a 4WD with low-gear option is absolutely essential*. Alternatively, you can drive up the more populated route via Mavis Bank, though the road conditions can be as atrocious.

Gordon Town & Guava Ridge

Gordon Town, at 370m, is a hamlet centered on a wide square with a police station, and tiny courthouse. It began life as a staging post for Newcastle in the days before the Mammee River Rd was cut from the Cooperage. Turn right at the square and cross the narrow bridge to reach Guava Ridge, a ridge-crest junction for Content Gap and sights to the north, while Mavis Bank and Blue Mountain Peak are straight ahead.

Part dirt road, part footpath, the **Bermuda Mt Trail** begins in Gordon Town and follows the Hope River Valley for part of the way before leading northwest to Redlight via Craighton.

A road signed for 'Bellevue House' 50m east of Guava Ridge, leads through pine and eucalyptus forests to the coffee plantation of **Flamstead** (☑960-0204) – visits by prior appointment. This former great house of Governor Edward Eyre (see p257) was a lookout from which Horatio Nelson and other British naval officers surveyed the Port Royal base. You can admire the awe-inspiring views over the Palisadoes and Kingston Harbour.

Buses and minibuses to Gordon Town operate from Parade, Half Way Tree and Papine in Kingston (J$80).

Mavis Bank

Mavis Bank, around a one-hour drive from Kingston, is a tidy little village in the midst of coffee country.

◉ Sights & Activities

Mavis Bank Coffee Factory   COFFEE FACTORY
(☑977-8015; tour J$846; ☺10am-2pm Mon-Fri) Established in 1923 and located 1km southwest of Mavis Bank is the largest coffee factory in Jamaica, producing Blue Mountain coffee sold under the 'Jablum' label. Ask the chief 'cupper' to demonstrate 'cupping' (tasting), the technique to identify quality coffee. You can tour the factory to see the coffee beans drying (in season) and being processed; call in advance. At the end of the 'from the berry to the cup' tour you can purchase roasted beans at bargain prices.

Farm Hill Trail   HIKING
This trail begins beside the Anglican church, crossing Yallahs River and Green River and leading uphill for 8km (1½ to two hours) to Penlyne Castle and on to Blue Mountain Peak.

🛏 Sleeping & Eating

TOP CHOICE **Lime Tree Farm**   BOUTIQUE HOTEL $$$
(☑881-8788; www.limetreefarm.com; cottage with full board US$312; ℗) This combination of a small working coffee farm with exclusive all-inclusive lodging is one of the most appealing retreats near Kingston. Owned by Lord Caradon, the grandson of former governor Hugh Foot, the property offers three large, luxurious cottages with jaw-dropping mountain views as well as fine meals, prepared by his wife and consumed in the attractive open-air lounge. All-inclusive packages comprise wine with dinner, transportation to and from Kingston and a variety of tours, such as bird-watching in the Blue Mountains, hikes to Blue Mountain Peak, excursions to the Cinchona Gardens and local scenic hikes along the Governor Bench trail.

TOP CHOICE **Forres Park Guest House & Farm**   GUEST HOUSE $$
(☑927-8275; www.forrespark.com; cabin US$75, r US$90-220; ℗) This working coffee farm run by the Lyn family has an enviable hillside setting amid lush gardens and tiers of coffee bushes. The farm is home to all three of Jamaica's hummingbird varieties, and 25 other bird species, making this a top choice

for bird-watchers. All rooms have balconies and the plushest sports a whirlpool tub. Excellent meals, cooked on request and available to non-guests, include coffee barbecued shrimp and steamed fish in coconut sauce. You can rent mountain bikes and enjoy the on-site spa treatments after tackling the steep, rewarding hiking trail. Tours and guided hikes offered by appointment.

❶ Getting There & Away

Buses run twice daily from Papine via Gordon Town (J$100); route taxis more frequently (J$250). A taxi from Kingston costs about US$35.

Hagley Gap & Penlyne Castle

The ramshackle village of Hagley Gap sits abreast a hill east of Mavis Bank and is the gateway to Blue Mountain Peak. The road forks in the village, where a horrendously denuded dirt road to Penlyne Castle begins a precipitous ascent.

Penlyne Castle is the base for the 12km hikes to and from Blue Mountain Peak. Most hikers stay overnight at one of several simple lodges near Penlyne Castle before tackling the hike in the wee hours.

Bring warm clothing. One minute you're in sun-kissed mountains; the next, clouds swirl in and the temperature plunges.

🛏 Sleeping & Eating

Jah B's Guest House   GUEST HOUSE **$**
(☏377-5206; bobotamo@yahoo.com; dm/r J$1270/2963; P🅿) This friendly place, run by a family of Bobo Rastas and particularly popular with shoestring travelers, has a basic but cozy wooden guest house with bunks and simple rooms, on the left 400m below Wildflower Lodge. Jah B's son Alex himself cooks I-tal meals (about J$847) amid a cloud of ganja smoke and a nonstop volley of friendly banter; he can help arrange transfers from Kingston and will guide you up Blue Mountain Peak for J$4656.

Whitfield Hall   GUEST HOUSE **$**
(☏878-0514; www.whitfieldhall.com; camping per tent J$254-593, dm adult/child J$1270/1693; s/d J$4233/2540; P🅿) About 400m uphill from Wildflower Lodge, nestled amid pine trees, this former plantation dating from 1776 is an atmospheric but basic option, with bunks for up to 40 people, shared bath-

rooms and kitchen. The dark, cavernous lounge has a huge fireplace and smoke-stained ceiling. Camping is allowed on the lawn beneath eucalyptus trees. Order a large breakfast (J$650) or lunch/dinner (J$750) in advance. Reliable guides to the peak charge J$3386.

Wildflower Lodge   GUEST HOUSE **$**
(☏929-5395; r with shared/private bathroom J$1693/2963, cottage J$5502; P🅿) A hardwood lodge amid attractive gardens, with solar-heated water and an assortment of bunks and ensuite rooms. An atmospheric dining room has hammocks on the veranda and meals can be arranged. The lodge offers horseback rides and guides for the climb.

❶ Getting There & Away

Many hotels in the Blue Mountains offer 4WD transfers to Penlyne Castle from Mavis Bank (from J$4232 per vehicle one way) or Kingston (from J$8465). Booking in advance is essential; no transfers after 6pm.

BUS Regular minibuses and route taxis run from Papine to Mavis Bank. Less frequent transport to Hagley Gap via Gordon Town. Avoid starting out on Sunday.

CAR Continue through Mavis Bank to Mahogany Vale and cross the Yallahs River. Penlyne Castle is reached via a 5km dirt road that ascends precipitously from Hagley Gap. Only 4WD vehicles with low-gear option can handle the dauntingly narrow and rugged road.

Blue Mountain Peak

From Penlyne Castle to the summit of Blue Mountain Peak (2256m) is a 950m ascent and a three- or four-hour hike one way. It's not a serious challenge, but you need to be reasonably fit.

Most hikers set off from Penlyne Castle around 2am to reach the peak for sunrise. Fortified with breakfast of coffee and cereal, you set out single file in the pitch black along the 12km round-trip trail (you'll need a flashlight and a spare set of batteries, just in case). The first part of the trail – a series of steep scree-covered switchbacks named **Jacob's Ladder** – is the toughest. Midway, at Portland Gap, there's a ranger station and cabin.

As you hike, reggae music can be heard far, far below, competing with the chirps of crickets and katydids. A myriad peeny-wallies flit before you, signaling with their phosphorescent semaphore.

You should arrive at the peak around 5:30am, while it is still dark. Your stage is gradually revealed: a flat-topped hump, marked by a scaffolding pyramid and trig point (in the cloud it is easy to mistake a smaller hump to the left of the hut near the summit – **Lazy Man's Peak** – for the real summit). If the weather's clear, Cuba, 144km away, can be seen from the peak, which casts a distinct shadow over the land below. After a brief celebratory drink and snacks, you'll set off back down the mountain, passing through several distinct ecosystems – stunted dwarf or elfin forest, with trees like hirsute soapwood and rodwood no more than 2.5m high, an adaptation to the cold, followed by cloud forest, dripping with filaments of hanging lichens and festooned with epiphytes and moss and dotted with wild strawberries, while further down you encounter bamboo and primordial giant tree ferns. Your guide points out Blue Mountain coffee growing and you arrive at your accommodations in time for brunch.

Don't hike without a guide at night. Numerous spur trails lead off the main trails and it is easy to get lost. Although hiking boots or tough walking shoes are best, sneakers will suffice, though your feet will likely get wet. At the top, temperatures can approach freezing before sunrise, so wear plenty of layers. Rain gear is also essential, as the weather can change rapidly.

Guides can be hired locally at Hagley Gap or Penlyne Castle, or through most local hotels, for J$4656/5926 per half/full day. For organized hikes, see below.

The **Jamaica Conservation & Development Trust** (☎960-2848/9; www.jcdt.org.jm; 29 Dumbarton Ave, Kingston 10; tent J$170, dm J$423) maintains two basic wooden cabins halfway up the trail at Portland Gap (4km above Abbey Green). You can camp outside, where there's a cooking area and water from a pipe. Bring your own tent, sleep on a bunk bed (bring own sleeping bag) or on the floor (foam mats available for rent; J$150). Reserve in advance.

HIKING IN THE BLUE MOUNTAINS

The Blue Mountains are a hiker's dream, and 30 recognized trails lace the hills. Many are overgrown due to lack of funding and ecological protection programs, but others remain the mainstay of communication for locals.

By far the most popular route is the steep, well-maintained trail to 'The Peak,' which in Jamaica always means Blue Mountain Peak.

These trails (called 'tracks' locally) are rarely marked. Get up-to-date information on trail conditions from the main ranger station at Holywell. When asking for directions from locals, remember that 'jus a likkle way' may in fact be a few hours of hiking.

If you're hiking alone, normal precautions apply:

» Wear sturdy hiking shoes

» Bring snacks, plenty of water and a flashlight (torch)

» Let people know where you're headed

» Buy the 1:50,000 or 1:12,500 Ordnance Survey topographic map series, available from the **Survey Department** (Map p42; ☎750-5263; www.nla.gov.jm; 23½ Charles St, Kingston)

Guides for the Blue Mountain Peak hike can be hired at Hagley Gap or Penlyne Castle, or through most local accommodations, for J$4656/5926 per half/full day. Guided hikes in the Blue Mountains are also offered by the following:

» Forres Park Guest House & Farm (p87)

» Jamaica Conservation & Development Trust – manages trails in the National Park and can recommend hiking guides

» Mount Edge B&B (p84)

» Strawberry Hill (p85)

» Sun Venture (p52)

SOUTHEAST COAST

Jamaica's southeast corner, the parish of St Thomas, is one of the least-developed parts of the island, which is part of its charm. Don't be surprised if you come across obeah circles in isolated villages. This parish is strongly associated with the practice (see p263), so if you have a grudge against someone and wish to scare them, you tell them: 'St Thomas me a go.' Life here revolves mostly around toiling in the cane fields and factories, and small fishing villages, where the work is still performed by canoe and net. There are several attractive beaches – including the ones by Morant Point Lighthouse – among the majority of unappealing gray-sand ones, and surfers rave about more than a dozen prime surf spots. Further inland lies the semi-forgotten village of Bath, its hot springs rumored to have healing properties.

Yallahs & Around

Southeast of Bull Bay and the parish boundary between St Andrew and St Thomas, the A4 from Kingston makes a hairpin descent to **Grants Pen**, then winds through scrub-covered country until it reaches the coast at **Yallahs**, its name deriving from that of a Spanish family that ran the Hato de Ayala cattle ranch here. The excellent **jerk stands** of Yallahs' Main St are a cheerful pit stop. Past Yallahs, a series of long, dark-gray beaches, with colorful pirogues drawn up, extends eastward to **Morant Bay**, and a pitted dirt road, only navigable by 4WD, heads north into the mountains to Hagley Gap.

East of Yallahs, the two large **salt ponds** are enclosed by a narrow, bow-shaped spit of sand. The ponds are exceedingly briny due to evaporation and legend has it that they were formed by the tears of an English planter whose beloved married his brother. Algae flourishes and often turns the ponds a deep pink, accompanied by a powerful smell of hydrogen sulfide ('bad egg gas').

Morant Bay

POP 9400

Morant Bay, the town that played a pivotal role in Jamaica's history, squats on a hill behind the coast road. These days, it's a nondescript place with a lively central market, its sugar-producing heyday long behind it.

Most of the town's early colonial-era buildings were burned in the Morant Bay Rebellion of 1865, led by the town's national hero, Paul Bogle (see p257), but a couple of gems remain.

October 11 is **Paul Bogle Day**, when a party is held in the town square and a 10km road race sets out from Stony Gut.

◉ Sights

Just east of Morant Bay lies the attractive, palm-fringed **Lyssons Beach**, rejuvenated by a Kingston-based NGO. It's one of the very few public beaches in Jamaica with free access for locals (though paid parking).

Courthouse & Around   HISTORICAL BUILDING
Edna Manley's **sculpture** depicting Paul Bogle normally stands grimly in front of the courthouse, hands clasped over the hilt of a machete. At the time of writing, the statue has been taken away for restoration. The **courthouse** was rebuilt in limestone and red brick after being destroyed in the 1865 rebellion and burned down again in early 2007, its ruins standing defiant behind Bogle's empty plinth. Bogle is buried beside the courthouse alongside a mass grave holding the remains of many slaves who lost their lives in the rebellion. The spot is marked by a moving memorial dedicated to 'those who love freedom.' Prominent citizens are campaigning for the statue not to be returned to its rightful place until the courthouse is restored to 'a place from which justice is delivered'. To do any less, they say, is to deny the sacrifices of Bogle and the others.

Diagonally across from the courthouse is a handsome, ochre-colored **Anglican church** dating to 1881.

Stony Gut Monument   MONUMENT
The marker, commemorating Bogle's birthplace, stands opposite the Methodist church, 8km inland at the tiny hamlet of Stony Gut. His great grandson Phillip Bogle is buried behind the marker.

ℹ Information

Police station (7 South St) Next to the old courthouse.
Scotiabank (23 Queen St) Opposite the Texaco gas station.

ℹ Getting There & Away

Buses serve Kingston (J$160 to J$250, two hours, three daily) and Port Antonio (J$160 to J$300, 2½ hours, two daily). Minibuses and route taxis arrive and depart from beside the Shell gas station on the A4 at the west end of town.

Retreat

A small beachside residential community about 5km east of Morant Bay, Retreat draws Kingstonians on the weekends. It sits between two of the few pleasant beaches along Jamaica's southern coast. The aptly named **Golden Shore Beach** is hidden from view from the road. Watch for the hand-painted sign. Further east is **Prospect Beach**, a 'public bathing beach.'

Whispering Bamboo Cove (☑982-1788; www.discoverjamaica.com/whisper.html; 105 Crystal Dr; r J$4233-6772, ste J$7619; **P** ❋) is a comfortable, contemporary villa-style hotel facing the beach in Retreat. It offers airy, spacious and tastefully furnished rooms with tropical fabrics and antique reproductions. It's worth paying a little extra for the seafront view and balcony. Full board can be arranged with advance warning.

Port Morant

Five kilometers east of Retreat lies Port Morant, a formerly important banana-, rum- and sugar-shipping point, reduced to a small village reliant on fishing and oyster farming at nearby Bowden Wharf. Two kilometers east of Port Morant, a road forks south towards a fenced-off property by the sea on your right. Place your orders with

the fishermen there and they'll bring you several dozen small, sweet oysters fresh from the oyster beds (J$100 per dozen), shucking them in front of you and seasoning them with a delicious sauce of their own concoction, made of sugar, vinegar, allspice, thyme, Scotch bonnet peppers and spring onions. Bring an icebox to take away.

Bath

This village, 10km north of Port Morant by a very attractive road, lies on the bank of the Plantain Garden River, amid sugarcane and banana plantations. The town owes its existence to the discovery of hot mineral springs in the hills behind the present town in the late 17th century, which attracted socialites for a time.

Minibuses and route taxis run daily from the downtown bus terminal in Kingston (J$250).

◉ Sights & Activities

Bath Fountain   HOT SPRINGS

Local legend says that in 1695 Jacob, a runaway slave, discovered hot springs that cured the leg ulcers he'd had for years. He was so impressed by this miracle that he returned to tell his master. In 1699 the government bought the spring, created the Bath of St Thomas the Apostle, and then formed a corporation that would administer mineral baths for the sick and infirm. The waters have high sulfur and lime

---

WORTH A TRIP

MORANT POINT LIGHTHOUSE

Golden Grove is the gateway to Morant Point, a peninsula that juts into the Caribbean Sea. Cast in London and erected in 1841, the 30m-tall, red-and-white-striped **Morant Point Lighthouse** (admission free; ◷no set hr) marks Morant Point, the easternmost tip of Jamaica. Ask the lighthouse keeper to show you the way to the top (don't forget to tip the lighthouse keeper if he takes you up and gives you a quick tour). The powerful view and the windy silence make for a profound experience as you look out over rippling sugarcane fields toward the cloud-haunted Blue Mountains and the deserted, wave-lashed eastern shore. The beaches here are unsuitable for swimming but you will have their wind-whipped beauty all to yourself.

The lighthouse is best reached by car; take a right in Golden Grove to the one-street village of **Duckenfield**, stopping for lunch at the excellent **Miss Nora's Cookhouse** (dishes J$300; ◷daily), which offers Jamaican favorites. Drive past the Duckenfield sugar factory on your left and take the dirt road that runs straight into the cane fields. Several lesser trails branch off from it, but as long as you stick to the main one it's very difficult to get lost. The dirt road meanders through cane for around 8km before emerging by the lighthouse. A 4WD is strongly recommended during the rainy season.

content, and their slightly radioactive waters have therapeutic value for skin ailments and rheumatic problems.

You can walk to the free hot springs 50m north of the Bath Hotel and Spa, though you will then have to fend off the attentions of persistent 'guides' offering **massages** (J$2000), or you can have a peaceful soak in the spa at the Bath Fountain Hotel & Spa.

Two springs issue from beneath the **bath house** (20min bath for 1/2 people J$350/550; ⊗8am-9:30pm). The water here can be scorching (it varies from 46°C to 53°C). You soak in deep, ceramic-tiled Turkish-style pools or whirlpool tubs. The homey spa also offers a variety of massages. Arrive early on weekends. To get there, turn up the road opposite the church in Bath and follow the road 3km uphill.

FREE **Bath Botanical Garden**   GARDEN

(⊗dawn-dusk) At the east end of town is an old limestone church shaded by royal palms that flank the entrance to a somewhat rundown horticultural garden established by the government in 1779. Many exotics introduced to Jamaica were first planted here: bougainvillea, cinnamon, mango, jackfruit, jacaranda and the famous breadfruit brought from the South Pacific by Captain William Bligh aboard HMS *Providence* in 1793. Every September, Bath holds a **Breadfruit Festival** to commemorate what's now a firm Jamaican staple.

Hiking   HIKING

A former Maroon trading route, for experienced hikers only, leads from Bath Fountain up over **Cuna Cuna Gap** to Bowden Pen. Obtain Sheet 19 (showing St Thomas parish) and Sheet 14 (Portland parish) of the Ordnance Survey 1:12,500 map series from the **Survey Department** (☎922-6630; www.nla.gov.jm; 23½ Charles St, Kingston) for more detailed information or hire a guide from Sun Venture Tours in Kingston or the JCDT (p89).

🛏 Sleeping & Eating

Bath Fountain Hotel & Spa   HOTEL $

(☎703-4154; r with shared/private bathroom J$3600/4450, deluxe r J$6000; P) Your only option is this recently renovated, pink colonial hotel that dates to 1747 and contains the spa baths on the ground floor. The clinically white bedrooms are modestly furnished, lacking air-con and TVs. It has a small restaurant serving Jamaican dishes such as curry goat and stew chicken (J$350 to J$400), as well as breakfast.

Golden Grove

Golden Grove is 10km northeast of Port Morant (and 11km east of Bath). It's a desperately poor hamlet of corrugated-tin and wood huts on stilts, housing workers employed at the Duckenfield sugar plantation and factory to the east of the road, and the banana plantations of Fyffes to the west.

Port Antonio & Northeast Coast

Why Go?

Sleepy Portland parish is by far the least developed resort area in Jamaica, yet also the most rugged and scenic. Forested mountains with deep gorges and rushing rivers spread their fingers towards fringes of white sand and cool-blue surf that rolls into beach-lined coves. The folks are friendly, the hustle comparatively small. The only drawback is the constant rain but, hey, that's what keeps the parish green and gorgeous.

The only town of any size, colonial Port Antonio, hugs a half-moon bay that seems to be in a permanent state of mildewed – but romantic – entropy. Inland are lush expanses of tropical rain forest and the Rio Grande Valley, one of Jamaica's best territories for hiking and bird-watching. Along the coast you'll find a string of fishing villages and beach communities that possess two notable features: they're utterly charming, and oddly untouristed. Break some vacation frontiers, traveler.

Best Places to Eat

» Blueberry Hill Jerk Centre (p112)

» Dickie's Best Kept Secret (p99)

» Mikey's (p106)

Best Places to Stay

» Gee Jam (p102)

» River Lodge (p113)

» Kanopi House (p102)

» Ambassabeth Cabins (p111)

When to Go

Port Antinio

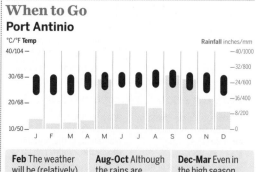

°C/°F Temp   Rainfall inches/mm

Feb The weather will be (relatively) dry and you'll have a chance to see the Fi Wi Sinting festival (p19).

Aug-Oct Although the rains are vicious, you'll also likely get good wind for serious adventure surfing.

Dec-Mar Even in the high season this region doesn't see nearly as many crowds as the rest of Jamaica.

History

The last of Jamaica's lands to be officially settled, Portland parish was the final great stronghold of the Windward Maroons, who survive to this day in the Rio Grande Valley with many African-based traditions intact. In the late 19th century Portland's economy enjoyed a precipitous spike thanks to the United States' newfound appetite for the banana. The fruit cargo ships that sailed to and from Port Antonio served double duty as transportation for some of Jamaica's first tourists, making 'Portie' the island's first destination resort. In recent years, Portland parish has led the nation in establishing 'green' tourism practices.

Climate

Port Antonio enjoys a tropical climate with relatively high rainfall. The temperature hits an average of 33°C in summer and 28°C in winter. The evenings are cooled by wonderful breezes floating in off the mountains.

It rains most May to June and October to November.

❶ Getting There & Away

Minibus and route-taxi traffic is high in and out of Port Antonio, where it's a simple matter to find local transportation to Ocho Rios, Kingston and beyond. Lots of yacht traffic goes in and out of Errol Flynn Marina. Ken Jones Aerodrome, near Port Antonio, was not receiving flights at the time of our visit; there was some talk of resurrecting service, but the operative word is 'talk.'

PORT ANTONIO

POP 14,400

If you took an ice-cream scoop out of the rainy northeast coast and surrounded it with a mess of markets, higglers and Georgian architecture slipping into various states of disrepair, you'd get Port Antonio, the laid-back yet endearingly real capital of laid-back, endearingly real Portland. There's definitely

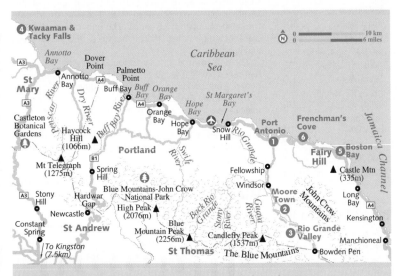

Port Antonio & Northeast Coast Highlights

❶ Wandering the streets of picturesque, crumbling **Port Antonio** (p94)

❷ Listening to the stories of the elders of the Windward Maroons at **Moore Town** (p110)

❸ Drifting merrily, merrily, merrily, merrily on a raft down the Rio Grande past the former banana plantations in the verdant **Rio Grande Valley** (p108)

❹ Contemplating the wonderful primordial **Kwaaman & Tacky Waterfalls** (p113) from the pools below

❺ Stuffing your face with fine Jamaican jerk and shredding some waves with local surfers at **Boston Bay** (p106)

❻ Enjoying **Frenchman's Cove** (p101), the pretty white- sand beach that hugs a blue estuary no Margaritavilles here; just a capillary-like tangle of backstreets, browsing goats and friendly locals. Wandering away from the bustle, past the dilapidated houses lining the potholed streets of Titchfield Peninsula, it's very easy to think you've roamed onto the set of some quaint colonial ghost town.

Ironic, then, that the tentacles of Jamaican tourism first found purchase in Port Antonio. The town came to prominence as the island's major banana port, and its prosperity began luring visitors at the turn of the 20th century. Celebrity visitors, led by cinematic and real-life swashbuckler Errol Flynn, descended on the town in the 1930s. And when the tourist attentions moved on to the west of the island, Port Antonio went back to bananas. That's been bad news for big resorts seeking a presence here, but perfect for travelers seeking a laid-back urban alternative to Jamaica's big cities.

History

The Spanish christened the bay 'Puerto Anton' in the 16th century, but made no serious effort to settle. In 1723 the British laid out a rudimentary town on the peninsula and named it Titchfield; a fort was added in 1729. But rampant fevers in the swampy coastlands and constant raids by marauding Maroons deterred all but a few settlers.

Following peace with the Maroons in 1739, Titchfield expanded. Many settlers grew sustenance crops, including bananas. Enter the Yankee skipper Captain Lorenzo Dow Baker (1840–1908), a fruit-shipping magnate, who arrived here in 1871 and established the banana trade that created a boomtown overnight. Baker and his Boston Fruit Company went on to own 40 banana plantations from Port Antonio to Buff Bay, making Port Antonio the 'banana capital of the world.' Port Antonio grew so wealthy that, it is said, planters would light their cigars with US$5 bills.

In the 1890s Baker began shipping tourists from the cold US northeast in his empty banana boats. Although Portland's banana bonanza was doomed in the 1930s by the onset of Panama disease, the arrival of movie star Errol Flynn and, later, numerous bluebloods and Hollywood stars, gave new cachet to Port Antonio as a tourist resort.

In the 1960s a second brief heyday occurred when a luxurious resort was built overlooking Frenchman's Cove. This was followed by Prince Alfonso de Hohenlohe's equally exclusive Marbella Club at Dragon Bay. The regal resorts attracted the jet-set crowd, and the coves east of town were colonized by the very rich, setting a trend that still continues.

Today, as in the past, all the bananas exported from Jamaica depart from Port Antonio's dock. The loading of the fruit is now mechanized, so you will no longer see the tallyman tallying bananas or stevedores 'working all night on a drink of rum.'

⊙ Sights

Town Square & Around NOTABLE SITES
Port Antonio's heart is the **Town Sq**, at the corner of West St and Harbour St. It's centered on a clock tower (which has a city directory painted on it) and backed by a handsome red-brick Georgian courthouse that dates back to 1895; the building is surrounded by a veranda supported by Scottish iron columns and topped by a handsome cupola. About 50m down West

---

ERROL FLYNN

Errol Flynn (1909–59), the infamous Hollywood idol, arrived in Portland parish in 1946 when his yacht *Zacca* washed ashore in bad weather. Flynn fell in love with the area and made Port Antonio his playground and home (his acting career was by then washed up). In his autobiography, *My Wicked, Wicked Ways*, he described Port Antonio as, 'more beautiful than any woman I've ever seen.'

Flynn bought the Titchfield Hotel and Navy Island, where he threw wild, extravagant parties. Locals tell exaggerated tales of his exploits: 'Remember de day 'im drove de Cadillac into de swimming pool?' Flynn's beguiling ways inevitably attracted the attention of other stars of stage and screen, like Clara Bow, Bette Davis and Ginger Rogers.

With his third wife, Patrice Wymore, Flynn later established a cattle ranch at Boston Estate. He also planned a lavish home at Comfort Castle and had grandiose plans to develop Port Antonio into a tourist resort. But heavy drinking and a profligate lifestyle added to his ill health. He died in 1959 before his plans could be brought to fruition. The wild parties are no more, but his legend lives on.

St is the junction of William St, where the smaller **Port Antonio Sq** has a **cenotaph** honoring Jamaicans who gave their lives in the two world wars.

On the west side is **Musgrave Market**, decked out in yellows and blues, a sort of quintessential chaotic developing-world market supported by thick limestone columns. Following William St south to Harbour St, you can turn left to peek inside **Christ Church**, a red-brick Anglican building constructed in neo-Romanesque style around 1840 (much of the structure dates from 1903). Look for the brass lectern donated by Captain Lorenzo Dow Baker, who made his fortune in the banana trade.

On the north side of the Town Sq is the imposing facade of the **Royal Mall**, a beautiful three-story complex painted a striking red, now more or less a covered shopping parade decorated and designed in a plethora of styles, including Tudor and Renaissance.

Errol Flynn Marina   MARINA
(☎715-6044; www.errolflynnmarina.com) Port Antonio has, undoubtedly, one of the finest natural harbors in Jamaica, which has been converted into a posh yachting dock where white sailboats (but as of yet, no light cruise ships, perhaps to the chagrin of local politicos) moor and the well-to-do wander. At night it's a popular place for young couples to stroll along the paths that snake around a few upmarket restaurants and shopping centers. It's a quiet retreat from the bustle of town, and a good place to meet some oddball sailing types.

Titchfield Peninsula   NOTABLE BUILDINGS
Along this hilly peninsula – known locally as 'the Hill' – are several dozen Victorian-style gingerbread houses, most notably **DeMontevin Lodge** (21 Fort George St), an ornate rust-red mansion, now a hotel. Many of the finest homes line King St, which runs down the center of the peninsula (parallel

Port Antonio

⊙ Sights

1 Cenotaph C3
2 Christ Church C4
3 DeMontevin Lodge C2
4 Errol Flynn Marina B3
5 Fort George..D1
6 Musgrave Market..............................C3
7 Royal Mail...C3
8 Titchfield School D1

⊕ Activities, Courses & Tours

9 Grand Valley Tours B4
  Lady G'Diver ....(see 4)
10 Valley Hikes C4

▣ Sleeping

  DeMontevin Lodge ....(see 3)
11 Holiday Home......................................C2
12 Ivanhoe's...C2
13 Ocean Crest Guest House B&B C2

⊗ Eating

14 Golden Happiness...............................C3
15 Norma's at the Marina B2
16 Rusalka..B3

⊕ Entertainment

17 Club La Best C4
18 Roof Club B4
19 Shadows A4

Shopping

  Musgrave Market.........................(see 6)

to Queen and Fort George Sts); other roads were in a shocking state of disrepair at the time of research. The peninsula is now a National Heritage Trust site and has been slated to receive restoration for a while now. This is a relatively well-off area, and there's a touchingly sad sense of glamour gone by that's quite romantic.

Fort George

Further north at the tip of the peninsula are the ruins of **Fort George**, dating from 1729. The parade ground and former barracks today house **Titchfield School**, not open to the public. Beyond the school, several George III–era cannons can still be seen mounted in their embrasures in 3m-thick walls.

Navy Island   ISLAND
This lushly vegetated 25-hectare island is popular with local day-trippers on weekends – or it was, when the ferries ran.

In colonial days the British Navy used it to career ships for repair, built a small battery, jetties and warehouses and imported breadfruit, now a staple of Jamaican cuisine. In the mid-20th century Errol Flynn bought the island and built a home that became a hotel, which later fell into decay. In early 2002 the Port Authority and the Urban Development Corporation (UDC) jointly took over the island with a view to developing the jaded property as an upscale resort and ecological theme park, but nothing has developed so far. Talk to fishermen on the docks or, more reliably, the folks at **Dickie's Best Kept Secret** (☑809-6276); they may be able to get you out here for a good day of stomping through the ruins.

Folly   RUIN
This rather appropriately named two-story, 60-room mansion on the peninsula east of East Harbour was built entirely of concrete in pseudo-Grecian style by North American millionaire Alfred Mitchell in 1902. Short-sightedly, sea water was used in the concrete mix, causing the iron reinforcing rods to rust and the roof to collapse in 1936. What's left is a fantastically evocative ruin that deserves a place on the cover of *The Great Gatsby*. The shell of the structure remains, held aloft by limestone columns, and makes a perfectly peculiar locale for a picnic.

Folly Point Lightouse

Near the Folly mansion stands the orange candy-striped **Folly Point Lighthouse**, built in 1888, which overlooks **Woods Island**. Said island adds even more Gatsbyesque pathos to the story: Mitchell once housed his colony of pet monkeys there. You can't make this stuff up, people.

🏃 Activities

Fishing   FISHING
You can charter sport-fishing boats on the docks at Errol Flynn Marina. **La Nadine** (tour per person US$25) also does harbor tours (minimum of four people). **Jamaica Deep Sea Adventures** (☑909-9552; half day US$550-750, full day US$800-1200) is a reliable operator.

Lady G'Diver   DIVING
(☑715-5957, 995-0246; www.ladygdiver.com; 2-/4-dive package costs US$84/152; Errol Flynn Marina) Located at the new marina, this is a full-service dive shop; dive boats leave at 11am and 2pm daily. It has a retail store, PADI instruction

and equipment rentals. The folks here are pioneering the largely undiscovered dive sites in the area, including **Courtney's Rest** and **Fisherman's Reef**, a series of drops, canyons and outcrops of coral.

☞ Tours

Port Antonio makes an excellent base from which to take excursions into the forests of the Rio Grande Valley and into the Maroon country towns of Moore Town and Nanny Town.

Grand Valley Tours   HIKING TOURS
(☑993-4116, in the USA 401-647-4730; www .portantoniojamaica.com/gvt.html; 12 West St) Treks to Scatter and Fox Caves as well as hikes to Moore Town, Nanny Falls, Nanny Town and along the White River Trail.

Carla Gullotta   CULTURAL TOURS
(☑993-7118; carla-51@cwjamaica.com) Carla runs Drapers San Guest House, east of Port Antonio. She occasionally leads small contingents by minibus to some of the best reggae shows island-wide. She arranges tickets and will act as your intermediary at the show.

Jamaica Explorations   ADVENTURE TOURS
(☑993-7267; www.jamaicaexplorations.com) Professional outfit based at Hotel Mocking Bird Hill that aims to promote ecocultural tourism in Portland and the Blue Mountains. Tailor-made guided soft-adventure tours include walking, hiking and cultural excursions.

Port Antonio Tours   SIGHTSEEING TOURS
(☑831-8434, 859-3758; www.portantoniotours. netfirms.com) Portland enthusiast and all-round local character Joanna Hart offers excellent custom tours of the area. *Se habla español.*

✯✯ Festivals & Events

Portland Jamboree   CARNIVAL
(☉mid-Aug) Full on one-week carnival with jonkanoo dancing (traditional Caribbean dancing with West African roots).

Port Antonio International Marlin Tournament   FISHING
(☑927-0145; www.errolflynnmarina.com; ☉early Oct) Weeklong fishing extravaganza.

🛏 Sleeping

Guest-house owners are served by the **Port Antonio Guest House Association** (☑993-7118; www.go-jam.com). Port Antonio has no top-end hotels, but to the east in nearby Fairy Hill (p102) are several exceptional choices. The Port Antonio area has many luxurious villas, situated both on the water or in the hills with soaring views, where couples, families and small groups can spend a few days or more in style. Contact the **Jamaican Association of Villas & Apartments** (JAVA; ☑800-845-5276; www.villasinjamaica.com).

TOP CHOICE **Jamaica Heights Resort**   HOTEL $$
(☑993-3305; www.jahresort.com; Spring Bank Rd; d US$75-125, cottage US$175; P ☀) Seriously, who doesn't have a thing for hilltop plantation homes with plucked-from-Eden gardens offering incredible views over Port Antonio Bay? And we haven't even gotten started on columned verandas, whitewashed walls, dark hardwood floors, louvered windows, French doors and a cool white-and-blue color scheme. The six rooms and two cottages are tastefully furnished with white wicker and antiques, plus four-poster beds; a spa offers massage and treatments, and there's a beautiful plunge pool plus a nature trail. A small gatehouse can house backpackers for US$45 a night, or you can rent the whole property for US$500.

Ivanhoe's   HOTEL $
(☑993-3043; 9 Queen St; r US$50-65; ☀🛜) Fantastic views across the whole of Port Antonio from breezy verandas, spotless white rooms and bargain rates are the hallmarks of this spot, the oldest guest house on historic Titchfield Hill. Lovely meals are cooked to order. Be sure to ask for a room with a view out over the harbor.

DeMontevin Lodge   HOTEL $$
(☑993-2604; demontevin@cwjamaica.com; 21 Fort George St; r US$50-160; ☀) This venerable Victorian guest house has a homey ambience that blends modern kitsch and antiques reminiscent of granny's parlor. The place could be the setting of a tropical Sherlock Holmes novel were it not for the Disney-character bedsheets in some rooms (the effect is actually quite cute). The simple bedrooms (six with private bathrooms) are timeworn, but clean as a whistle.

Holiday Home   HOTEL $
(☑816-7258, 993-2425; holidayhomesilverabuck ley@yahoo.com.sg; 5 Everleigh Park Rd; s/d/tr US$38/45/60; ☀) This creaky old house is full of rooms that define diversity across aesthetic and quality categories. Some are little

more than Victorian cupboards; others are wood-paneled antique pockets of charm. It's hardly a place that embraces modernity, but we love it for its relentless nostalgia.

Ocean Crest Guest House B&B
B&B $
(☎993-4024; 7 Queen St; r US$40-55; ✱) A favorite with the backpacker crowd, this B&B has bouncy rooms with tile floors and an ice-creamesque pink-and-white color scheme that's sure to emasculate. We don't mind; the lounge has a large-screen TV and the balconies have a stunning view of Port Antonio and its picturesque bay.

Hotel Timbamboo
HOTEL $$
(☎993-2049; www.hoteltimbamboo.com; 5 Everleigh Park Rd; s US$50-70, 1-/2-/3-bedroom ste US$85/150/200; P✱@≋) Offering rare comfort for a Port Antonio hotel so centrally located, the Timbamboo has spacious, sunny rooms with modern furniture, carpeted floors and cable TV. Suites have sizable kitchens, while some rooms have balconies with views of the Blue Mountains. The hotel's sun deck is a great place to unwind.

Eating

Dickie's Best Kept Secret FUSION $$
(☎809-6276; dinner US$20-40; ☾dinner) Almost too well kept a secret for its own good, Dickie's – an unsigned seaside hut on the A4, less than 1km west of Port Antonio – offers enormous five-course meals in rooms that look as if they were decorated by Bob Marley after reading *Alice in Wonderland* too many times. Dickie and his wife promise to cook anything you want (provided they have the ingredients); believe us, that anything will be delicious. Invariably, the meal begins with a palate-cleansing fruit plate followed by soup and a callaloo omelet. Reservations essential.

Anna Banana's Restaurant & Sports Bar
JAMAICAN $$
(7 Folly Rd; breakfast J$300, seafood dinners J$800-1500; ☾breakfast, lunch & dinner) Need seafood? Jerk? An open-air bar? Great; head to this breezy restaurant-bar, overlooking a small beach on the southern lip of the harbor, which specializes in jerk or barbecued chicken and pork and groaning plates of conch and lobster. Hit up the pool table or toss some darts afterwards.

Rusalka
RUSSIAN $$
(☎298-8773; Ken Wright Cruise Ship Pier; mains J$700-1800; ☾lunch & dinner) Russian? Why not? One of Port Antonio's finer fine-dining spots happens to have an open-air veranda, wickerwork furniture, gracious service and Russian cuisine (plus all the Jamaican favorites). There is even some Russian-Jamaican fusion going on (one of the culinary world's admittedly weirder marriages), including chicken baked in a sort of cheese-mushroom sauce that's seriously addictive.

Golden Happiness
CHINESE $
(cnr Fort George & West Sts; mains J$300-750; ☾lunch & dinner) Thank you, life's pleasant surprises. Latest on the list: good Chinese food in Port Antonio, including a vast menu of chop sueys and sweet-and-sour dishes. The dining room is spartan, but it's a good place to take in the hustle and bustle of West St – or to order takeout.

Survival Beach Restaurant
JAMAICAN $
(24 Allan Ave; mains US$5-10; ☾breakfast, lunch & dinner; ✎) In addition to the usual local fare, natural juices and the best jelly coconut in town, this choice shack serves a tasty dish made with coconut milk, pumpkin, Irish potato, garlic, scallion, thyme, okra, string beans and three kinds of peas, served with sides of cabbage and callaloo. Just ask for the vital I-tal stew.

Norma's at the Marina
FUSION $$
(☎993-9510; Ken Wright Cruise Ship Pier; mains US $11-20; ☾lunch & dinner) Fronting a lovely white-sand beach, this quality restaurant can be a forlorn place – but some might find the solitude blissfully peaceful. It helps if you have a date. Steaks, chops and fish prepared in the continental style are served at outdoor tables overlooking the Errol Flynn Marina.

Entertainment

Roof Club
NIGHTCLUB
(11 West St; ☾8pm-late Thu-Sun) This is Port Antonio's infamous hang-loose, rough-around-the-edges reggae bar. Young men and women move from partner to partner. You're fair game for any stranger who wants to try to extract a drink from you. It's relatively dead midweek when entry is free, but on weekends it hops and on Thursday – 'Ladies Nite' – this place gets nuts.

Club La Best
NIGHTCLUB
(5 West St; ☾9:30pm-late) The newest, liveliest spot in Port Antonio, La Best assumes a different identity depending on the evening.

Dancehall throbs into the wee hours on Fridays; Sundays groove to a mellow blend of reggae and old-school R&B; ladies' nights are Fridays; and periodic live shows occur on Saturdays.

Hub
BAR

(2 West Palm Ave) The name says it all – the Hub is a preferred drinking hole for Portland youth and grizzled old-timers alike. It's friendly, but in a pretty rowdy way; it might be best to show up here in a group.

Shadows
BAR

(40 West Palm Ave) A less rowdy option than most, this place plays vintage music on Tuesday and Sunday. Other nights it can verge on comatose.

Anna Banana's Restaurant & Sports Bar
BEACH BAR

(7 Allan Ave) This beachside bar is the place to go for darts, pool and a rum punch. Friday heats up with the help of local DJs.

Shopping

Musgrave Market
MARKET

(West St) There's a small craft market on the north side. Look for a stand called **Rock Bottom** selling well-made crafts and reggae-inspired duds.

Portland Art Gallery
ART

(☑882-7732; 2 West Palm Ave) A simple gallery and studio staffed by Hopeton Cargill, a Port Antonio realist painter. He's delighted to act as an ambassador for the local art scene.

Information

Dangers & Annoyances

A few locals try to eke out a living by scamming tourists. Guard your valuables when browsing Musgrave Market and stick to the main streets if walking at night.

Emergency

Police station (☑993-2527/46; Harbour St)

Resort Patrol Services (☑993-7482) Based in the police station, it patrols to guard the welfare of tourists.

Internet Access

Don J's Computer Centre (☑715-5559; Village of St George, Fort George St; per hr J$300; ☺10am-4pm Mon-Fri)

Portland Parish Library (☑993-2793; 1 Fort George St; per 30min US$1; ☺9am-6pm Mon-Fri, 9am-1pm Sat)

Internet Resources

Port Antonio (www.portantoniotravel.com) The official online visitor's guide.

Medical Services

City Plaza Pharmacy (☑993-2620; City Centre Plaza, Harbour St)

Port Antonio Hospital (☑993-2646; Nuttall Rd; ☺24hr) Above the town on Naylor's Hill, south of West Harbour.

Square Gift Centre and Pharmacy (☑993-3629; 11 West St)

Money

CIBC Jamaica Banking Centre (☑993-2708; 3 West St)

FX Trader Cambio (☑993 3617; City Centre Plaza, Harbour St)

National Commercial Bank (☑993-9822; 5 West St)

RBTT Bank (☑993-9755; 28 Harbour St)

Scotiabank (☑993-2523; 3 Harbour St)

Post

Post office (☑993-2651; Harbour St) On the east side of Town Sq.

Getting There & Around

The town center lies at the base of the Titchfield Peninsula, where the two main drags meet at a right angle in front of the main plaza and courthouse.

Air

Ken Jones Aerodrome (☑913-3173), 9km west of Port Antonio, was no longer receiving flights on our last visit. Most upscale hotels offer free transfers to and from the aerodrome for guests. There's no shuttle-bus service, although you can flag down any minibus or route taxi passing along the A4. A tourist taxi will cost about US$10.

Boat

Errol Flynn Marina at Port Antonio (☑924-8685; www.rjyc.org.jm; Norman Manley Dr, Kingston) Customs clearance for private vessels(GPS N 17.940939°, W -76.764939°).

Car

There are gas stations on West Palm Ave, Fort George St and Harbour St.

Eastern Rent-a-Car (☑993-4364; 16 Harbour St)

Public Transportation

There's a **transportation center** (Gideon Ave) that extends along the waterfront. Buses, minibuses and route taxis leave regularly for Annotto Bay, Port Maria (where you change for Ocho Rios) and Kingston.

Taxi

For licensed taxis, call **JUTA/Port Antonio Cab Drivers' Co-op** (☎993-2684). Taxis hang out by hotels. They can also be found pretty easily in town, notably along Gideon Ave and the intersection of Bridge St and Summers Town Rd. Licensed taxis to Port Antonio cost about US$100 from Kingston and US$250 from Montego Bay.

EAST OF PORT ANTONIO

Port Antonio to Fairy Hill

Beyond the turnoff for Folly the A4 meanders east of Port Antonio through thick fog and thicker jungle past jagged-tooth bays, pocket coves and the coastal villages of Drapers, Frenchman's Cove and Fairy Hill. This is where most visitors to Port Antonio, and indeed to Portland, will find accommodations and explore the nearby Rio Grande Valley, Nonsuch Caves and Blue Lagoon as well as the luxuriant sands of Frenchman's Cove, San San Beach and Winnifred Beach. Back in the 1950s and '60s, the amount of vacationing A-listers in this part of Portland earned the area the nickname the 'Jamaican Riviera.'

While the hotels and restaurants of Drapers, Frenchman's Cove and Fairy Hill will accommodate most budgets and tastes, be sure to venture into the local communities, small as they are. Portlanders are among the most gracious of all Jamaicans, and their acquaintance enhances any visit to their parish. The following sites are listed in the order you will encounter them heading east from Port Antonio.

⦿ Sights

Trident Castle   NOTABLE BUILDING

Just 3km east of Port Antonio, the road circles around Turtle Cove (which frankly looks like a turtle when the water is green and packed into the bay). Squatting atop the western headland is a magnificent castle, on one of the largest residences in the Caribbean. This is Trident Castle, built in the 1970s by the (in)famously eccentric Baroness Elisabeth Siglindy Stephan von Stephanie Thyssen, also know as Zigi Fami. When the castle was first built it wasn't nearly as ostentatious as the baroness' full name, but new owners have added layer after layer to this rather magnificent wedding cake. The architect, Earl Levy, known locally as the Earl of

Trident, eventually took over the property and now hosts the occasional grand ball event, still attended by Hollywood glitterati and European nobility. Thus at the time of writing the castle was closed to the public, but it still makes one hell of a landmark from the road. See www.tridentcastle.com for an amusing tour of the interior.

Frenchman's Cove   BEACH

(admission US$6; ☉9am-5pm) This little cove, just east of Drapers, 8km from Port Antonio, boasts a small but perfect white-sand beach, where the water is fed by a freshwater river that spits directly into the ocean.. The area is still technically owned by the **Frenchman's Cove Resort** (www.frenchmans cove.com). There's a snack bar serving jerk chicken and fish (US$7 to US$9), bike rental (US$20 a day), alfresco showers, bathrooms, a secure parking lot and the option of taking boat tours to the Blue Lagoon (US$20). Look for the entrance opposite the San San Golf Course.

San San Beach   BEACH

(admission US$6; ☉10am-4pm) San San is another gorgeous private beach used by residents of the villas on Alligator Head, and guests of the Goblin Hill, Fern Hill and Jamaica Palace hotels. The whole thing is fenced off (to the chagrin of locals, we note), but passersby can gain access to the bay, enclosed by a reef that's wonderful for snorkeling (US$10 per day) and kayaking (US$25 per hour). Undeveloped Monkey Island (there are no monkeys. Damn) is a good snorkel spot, and you can swim here if you're in decent shape.

Blue Lagoon   LAGOON

The waters that launched Brooke Shields' movie career are by any measure one of the most beautiful spots in Jamaica. The 55m-deep 'Blue Hole' (as it is known locally) opens to the sea through a narrow funnel, but is fed by freshwater springs that come in at about a depth of 40m. As a result the water changes color through every shade of jade and emerald during the day thanks to cold freshwater that blankets the warm mass of seawater lurking below. You're welcome to take a dip – David Lee (whose folks run the G'diver shop in Port Antonio) did back in 2002, when he set a world record here freediving to a depth of 60.35m.

You may encounter boat operators eager to take you on a short boat ride (US$25) to

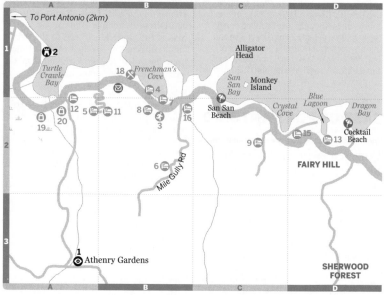

nearby **Cocktail Beach** (where parts of the Tom Cruise vehicle *Cocktail* was filmed) and rustic **Monkey Island**, a short distance away.

The lagoon is accessible from the road and is technically public property, but touts in the parking area will demand an entrance 'donation' – J$200 (about US$3) should assuage them.

🏃 Activities

Scuba Diving   DIVING

Good scuba diving abounds: the shoreline east of Port Antonio boasts 13km of interconnected coral reefs and walls at an average of 100m to 300m offshore. **Alligator Head** is known for big sponge formations and black corals. Hammerhead sharks are common at **Fairy Hill Bank**.

For dive tours, instruction and equipment, contact Lady G'Diver (p97) at the Errol Flynn Marina in Port Antonio.

San San Golf Course &
Bird Sanctuary   GOLF

(☑993-7645; 9/18 holes US$50/70; ⊙8am-5pm) The 18-hole golf course is laid out along valleys surrounded by rain forest. The bird sanctuary comprises primary forest and is not developed for tourism.

🛏 Sleeping

TOP CHOICE **Kanopi House**   HOTEL $$$

(☑632-3213, in the USA 305-677-3525, from UK 0203-318-1191; www.kanopihouse.com; Hwy A4, Drapers; r from US$300; ❋☀🖙) This Blue Lagoon ecoresort really deserves the title, as well as many other well-deserved accolades given in honor of its considerable luxury and comfort. Staying in these dark-wood chalets that seemingly grow from the jungle feels like staying in a laid-back five-star hotel carved into a banyan tree. The property makes great efforts to leave a low ecological footprint (gray-water system, local sustainable hardwoods used in construction, none of which were cut) and is stuffed with elegant Caribbean art. Fresh organic dinners are prepared on site, and the Jamaican owners are a dream to chat with.

TOP CHOICE **Gee Jam**   HOTEL $$$

(☑993-7000/302; www.geejamhotel.com; off Hwy A4, San San Bay; r US$595-795, ste US$995-1895; ᴾ❋☀🖙☀) The home of Gee Jam recording studios is the inheritor of the legacy of Portland's old status as the Jamaican Riviera. If old-school celebrities once stayed in gingerbread Victorian guest houses, today rock stars and hip-hop moguls come to Gee Jam

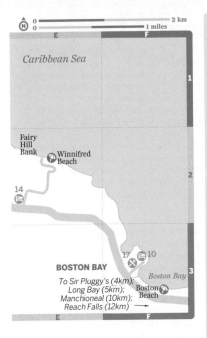

for ultra-modern design, cuisine and a high bar of exclusivity. There's a definite Manhattan penthouse vibe, except these penthouses are connected by jungle walkways with views of essentially the whole of the northeast coast. Rooms are all individualized and could be the setting of MTV music videos, which makes sense as visiting luminaries include No Doubt, Keith Richards and India Arie. The owner, Jon Baker, is a music-industry veteran with a taste for hip-hop and reggae. He can be choosy about accepting guests, preferring 'characters' with a 'good story.'

TOP CHOICE **Hotel Mocking Bird Hill**   HOTEL **$$$**
(☑993-7267/134; www.hotelmockingbirdhill.com; Mocking Bird Hill Rd; r US$190-295, ste US$348-600; ✸☎⛬) The Mocking Bird deserve a lot of credit: not just for being a great hotel (although that it is) but for being one of the most vigorous proponents of ecotourism in Portland parish. The place runs a laundry list of activities aimed at getting you out into the 'real Jamaica,' including tours to the Maroon country and bird-watching walks. The property itself is a lovely *maison* at the end of a trek up a winding dirt road; all rooms are lovingly appointed with well-chosen fabrics and modern art,

and boast ocean views from private balconies. Facilities include a Caribbean-bright lounge and a bar and a variety of health and wellness services, including massage. Meals at the Mille Fleurs restaurant are sublime. Trails lead through the lush hillside gardens, fabulous for the aforementioned bird-watching.

Mikuzi Vacation Cottages   COTTAGES **$**
(☑978-4859, 480-9827; www.mikuzijamaica.com; Hwy A4, Fairy Hill; r US$45-85, cottages US$100) Mizuki is wonderful: kind of funky, kind of romantic, set in pleasingly landscaped grounds and run by some of the warmest, most attentive staff in Jamaica. It's a perfect hideaway, especially for couples. The property is divided between candy-bright cottages (the cheaper one lacks a kitchen), a small house and nicely kitted out studio apartment. Discounts are given for longer stays.

THE FIGHT FOR A FREE WINNIFRED BEACH

Perched like a baby bird on a cliff 13km east of Port Antonio you'll find the little hamlet of Fairy Hill and a rugged dirt track. Follow that road steeply downhill and you'll reach Winnifred Beach, yet another totally gorgeous beach that puts a lot of the sand in more famous places (ahem: MoBay, Negril) to shame. Remember the Robin Williams movie, *Club Paradise* (not quite as famous or eponymous as *Blue Lagoon*)? It was filmed here.

Since around 2007, locals have been fighting to keep this, the last public beach in the area, free. The Jamaican government has been intent on developing Winnifred into a private ecoresort, a move which will result in the displacement of a fair few local businesses and the cause of no small tension, although that tension is between the government and local vendors. Foreign visitors still seem to be treated with a lot of grace; you get the sense that the locals genuinely believe a beach can be shared with tourists without hustle or hassle on either side. The fight is still ongoing as of this writing; in the meantime, locals continue to keep the beach sparkling clean for visitors and some may ask you for a donation if you visit.

Drapers San Guest House
GUEST HOUSE $

(☎993-7118; www.go-jam.com/drapersan-e.html; Hwy A4, Drapers; s incl breakfast US$30, d incl breakfast US$48-52; ☞) Run by Carla Gullotta, an Italian expat and activist who is quite culturally and politically plugged in to the goings on in Portland parish, this rambling yet cozy little house comprises two cottages with five doubles and one single room (two share a bathroom), all with fans, louvered windows and hot water. There's a small beach with snorkeling just a few meters from the house. It's all very family-oriented; there's a comfy lounge and communal kitchen and dinner can be served by arrangement. Thanks to Carla, a lot of Italian bohemian types tend to stay here.

Jamaica Palace
HOTEL $$

(☎993-7720; www.jamaica-palacehotel.com; Hwy A4; r deluxe/superior US$170/190, ste US$230-320; P☀☀) A charmingly eccentric, if aloof neoclassical property overlooking Turtle Cove, Jamaica Palace almost feels like an art gallery before a hotel. We think that's quite appealing; of all the resorts studding this northeast coast, the Palace feels the most like one of the original grande dames of the Jamaican Riviera. The cavernous rooms and suites boast king-sized beds, crystal chandeliers, period antiques and Georgian bay windows. In the landscaped grounds is a 35m-long pool shaped like the island of Jamaica.

Fan
VILLA $$

(☎390-0118; www.go-jam.com/thefan-e.html; Drapers; villa incl breakfast US$120-150; ☀) In the hills behind Drapers, overlooking the harbor, is this beautiful, staffed villa rental with gingerbread trim, a large living room and a lovely set-off separate dining room in the guest apartment. Meals can be provided on request. The experience is a good deal more luxurious and attentive than at resorts priced several times higher.

San San Tropez
HOTEL $$

(☎993-7213; www.sansantropez.com; Hwy A4, San San Bay; s/d US$190/210, 2-bedroom ste US$195; P☀☞@☀) This friendly Italian-run hotel has gracious, well-lit rooms and suites and a palpably European small-resort feel. The furnishings are modern and graced by bright tropical decor, there's a nice sun deck and the adjoining restaurant has splendid views and better food (meal plans are offered). Gives passes to San San Beach.

Moon San Villas
VILLA $$

(☎993-7600; www.moonsanvilla.com; Hwy A4, Fairy Hill; r incl breakfast US$145-195; P☀@☀) Sitting above Blue Lagoon, this is a tastefully decorated three-level house with a big-windowed lounge and bedrooms you could get lost in, all with wide windows, good views, fans and pretty romantic (in a frilly way) decor. Two rooms have king-sized beds. The bargain rates include a gourmet breakfast and passes to San San Beach. French-inspired meals are offered on request. You can rent the whole place out if you like.

Goblin Hill Villas
RESORT $$$

(☎993-7443, 925-8108; www.goblinhillvillas.com; Goblin Hill Rd; 1-bedroom villa US$155-215, 2-bedroom villa US$235-295; P☀☀) Popular with families, this 5-hectare hilltop estate above San San Beach has a cluster of two-bedroom and one-bedroom villas, fully equipped, frankly huge and surrounded by lawns and forest; when the mists accompany the frequent rains, you can see why they call it 'Goblin Hill.' A meandering nature trail encircles the property. The villas come with their own private maid and butler (optional), and the resort has a TV lounge and reading room, two tennis courts and the fabulous Tree Bar, built around a massive fig tree.

Fern Hill HOTEL **$$**
(☑993-7374/5; www.fernhillclubhotel.com; Mile Gully Rd, San San; r/ste US$95/115, 1-/2-bedroom villas US$140/182; P☕) On a breezy hilltop at San San, up Mile Gully Rd, the spacious if slightly coldly functional twin-level units are spread across the hillside, and each has a balcony beyond French doors. Suites have mezzanine bedrooms and their own hot tubs; most have gratifying views of the sea. When there's a full house, a mento band entertains on weekends.

Frenchman's Cove RESORT **$$**
(☑933-7270; www.frenchmanscove.com; Hwy A4, Frenchman's Cove; r/ste US$95/135, 1-/2-/3-bedroom cottages US$140/225/295; P☀☕) This old great house frankly feels its age; back when Errol Flynn was the talk of the town we're sure this hotel was a big deal too, but today the stone cottages and '70s modernist condos feel a bit dated. Lovely staff and ready access to one of Jamaica's prettiest beaches makes some amends.

✖ Eating & Drinking

This stretch of road has many accommodations but few independent restaurants. Most folks eat at their hotels – which generally have restaurants open to nonguests – or are catered to by the staff of their villa.

Mille Fleurs JAMAICAN **$$$**
(☑993-7267; Hotel Mocking Bird Hill, Mocking Bird Hill Rd; 3-course dinner US$90; ☉7am-10pm; ☞) This overwhelmingly romantic candlelit restaurant offers some of the best haute Jamaican cuisine on the island, savored on a gorgeous terrace and served with a sense of elegance, yet also unrushed intimacy, providing a classical fine-dining experience. The changing organic menu is influenced by what ingredients are seasonally available, includes vegetarian options and ends with a cleansing trolley of regional liqueurs. Reservations required.

Bush Bar FUSION **$$$**
(☑993-7000; Gee Jam; set meal US$70; ☉dinner) Set in a veranda that overlooks the jungle and the ocean and ensconced in multiple layers of hip, the restaurant at Gee Jam offers an immaculate Asian-Jamaican fusion experience, replete with cocktails as neon-bright as Vegas, chilled background music and that ineffable sense of being part of life's winning team, the perpetual in-crowd. The menu varies, but you can expect your socks to be pretty well blown off. Call ahead.

San San Tropez ITALIAN **$$**
(☑993-7213; Hwy A4, San San Bay; mains US$12-25; ☉breakfast, lunch & dinner) The enormous menu here has one focus: Italian food, home-cooked and cooked right. It's relatively simple stuff (if you've ever been to an Italian restaurant, you can probably recite the menu from rote memory), well-prepped and filling; the seafood and pizza are standouts. There's a large wine list as well.

Woody's JAMAICAN **$**
(Hwy A4, Drapers; mains J$300-800; ☉lunch & dinner) This pleasant spot – with an outdoor patio and an indoor counter that doubles as a local meeting place – prepares tremendous hotdogs and burgers, grilled cheese and Jamaican dinners to order. Vegetarians are catered for by a veggie burger heaped with stewed callaloo. Just east of Jamaica Palace.

Sir Pluggy's JERK **$**
(Hwy A4, Drapers; mains J$400-800; ☉lunch & dinner) There are two things that can't be beat about Sir Pluggy's: the name and the jerk. Smell that sweet smoke, order by the pound and fill dem belly up.

🛍 Shopping

Gallery Carriacou ART
(☑993-7267; Hotel Mocking Bird Hill; ☉10am-5pm Thu-Tue) Has a fabulous array of paintings, ceramics, sculptures and other quality works of fine art by local artists. It also hosts workshops for rural children and cultural events, so it tends to be a social anchor for this part of the island.

Philip Henry's Art Bus CRAFTS
(☑993-3162; Hwy A4) En route, you might call in at this roadside place at Turtle Cove, to check out Philip Henry's array of woodcarving and assorted crafts.

R Stewart ART
(Hwy A4, Drapers) In Drapers you'll find the roadside gallery of renowned self-taught artist R Stewart, who more than likely will be working on his latest canvas at the edge

of the road. His whimsical, masterful depictions of Jamaican life regularly inspire impulse buys from passersby.

ℹ Information

In the little hamlet of Drapers is a small **post office** (Hwy A4; ⊘8am-4pm Mon-Fri, 8am-noon Sat), and a **police station** (☑993-7315) just east of Frenchman's Cove.

ℹ Getting There & Away

Buses run infrequently between Port Antonio and Boston Bay and to other points beyond. Minibuses and route taxis (J$100) run more frequent services.

Derron's Rent-a-Car (☑993-7111; Hwy A4) has an outlet in Drapers.

Boston Bay

Boston Bay, 2.5km east of Fairy Hill, is a pocket-sized beach shelving into jewel-like turquoise waters. High surf rolls into the bay and locals spend much of their time surfing. Few dispute its reputation as the best surfing spot in Jamaica. Although the bay has been damaged by hurricanes in the past, eroding much of the beach, surfers say this has actually improved the quality of local waves. You can rent boards on the beach for around US$15.

Alongside its surfing hot-spot status, Boston is equally famous for the highly spiced jerk chicken and pork sizzling on many smoky barbecue pits along the roadside. Today, jerk has a worldwide fan base and is pretty much synonymous with Jamaican cuisine, but until the 1950s the stuff was virtually unknown outside this area. The practice of marinating meat with jerk seasoning was first developed centuries ago not far from here by the Maroons, and the modest shacks at Boston Bay were among the first to invite attention.

TOP CHOICE **Great Huts** (☑353-3388; www .greathuts.com; Boston Beach Lane; African-style tent per person US$60-80, huts US$200-250; 🛜) perches on a scenic crag overlooking Boston Bay. There are four luxury tents and eight elegant 'huts' (including three tree houses), all lavishly decorated with distinctive Afrocentric designs. These two-story open-air structures have verandas, bamboo-walled bedrooms, Jacuzzi baths and kitchenettes and are generally romantic as hell. Alfresco showers are enhanced by the squawking of a small aviary of parrots. If you can tear yourself from your room, the Cliff Bar, featuring excellent pizzas and superlative views of the sea, and the hotel's own beach on the rocks below will demand attention.

When it comes to eating, as you approach the entrance to Boston Bay you'll see a clutch of smoky pits. Lots of vendors will vie for your custom; we say go for **Mikey's**, right off the roadside, which produces a complexity of heat and sweet that has us shuddering at the memory. At all of the jerk places (and honestly, they're all quite good) you can expect to be filled up for around J$400 to J$800, depending on your appetite.

A frequent habitué of the beach is the **Maroon Prophet**, a roots bush doctor selling his handmade tonic and blood cleanser made from roots and 'bush' according to tradition. Other roots tonic specialists sell their bitter brews here as well.

ℹ Getting There & Away

Boston Bay is 15km east of Port Antonio; buses (J$100) leave early in the morning (8am) and around 5pm, and minibuses and route taxis ($J200 to J$250) will get you there or back.

Long Bay

Guess what – there is a beach in Jamaica where there are barely any hustlers and free spirits congregate out of sight of big-shot resorts. And it ain't Negril. Come to Long Bay, a rugged 1.5km-wide harbor and hamlet of freaks, geeks, backpackers, bohemians and surfers. A number of expats have put down roots and opened guest houses here, and it's not hard to see why. There's not much to do but chill or surf.

The bay has rose-colored sand, deep turquoise waters and breezes pushing the waves forcefully ashore. Canoes are drawn up on the beach, with fishing nets drying beside them. There's a dangerous undertow, so avoid swimming, but surfers love the waves. Surfboards are often available for rent on the beach (per half-day US$10), as are boogie boards (US$3).

The **public library** (☑913-7957; Hwy A4; per 30min US$1; ⊘Mon-Sat) offers internet access, which is becoming increasingly common in local guest houses as well.

🛏 Sleeping

Rose Hill Cottage   COTTAGE $
(☑913-7452; Rose Garden Rd; cottage US$40-90) This private cottage is offered by Peter-Paul

Zahl, a seasoned German author who has long called Jamaica home. Perched above the main road and affording tremendous views of the beach, the self-contained cottage has a small bedroom, sleeping loft, living area and kitchen. There are plenty of German-language books lying about. Your host, who inhabits a house a stone's throw away, has an insouciant air and the gift of the gab; he's a good character with a lot of insight on island life. The cottage is self-catering, but a delicious Caribbean dinner is offered nightly.

Likkle Paradise GUEST HOUSE $
(913-7702, 528-8007; www.likkleparadise.com; r from US$40;) Up an unnamed lane just south of the library, the home of lovely Herlett Kennedy includes two handsomely furnished rooms. Your host provides the extras: loads of charm, advice and hospitality. Guests enjoy full kitchen privileges, while Herlett lives upstairs.

Glass House GUEST HOUSE $
(913-7475, 891-0516; http://themorgansglass house.wordpress.com; r US$50) This pretty property is run by Mama Lou Morgan, who'll make you feel right at home. The rooms are all well kitted out and tastefully decorated, and you're left to do as you please or interact with the friendly Morgan family as much as you care to.

Villa Seascape VILLA $
(576-0082; saintsteven1@gmail.com; Hwy A4; d/villa with shared bathroom incl breakfast US$60/130;) At this well-maintained guest house the sea licks the walls of the veranda; inside you'll find modest, nicely furnished rooms with fans. There's a congenial vibe and meals are prepared to order.

Blue Heaven Resort RESORT $
(715-4336, 448-9605; www.blueheavenjamaica .com; r US$30-60;) This friendly spot consists of three funky cottages offered at an absolute steal. The digs may be a little basic, but c'mon – you get privacy and an oceanfront.

Hotel Jamaican Colors HOTEL $$
(913-7716, 893-5185; www.hoteljamaican-colors.com; Hwy A4; 1-/2-/3-bedroom cottage US$65/75/100, house US$110-264;) This spiffy hotel, run by a French host, is located on the cliffs 2km south of Long Bay and consists of 12 comfortable cottages, all with attached bathrooms and plush double beds draped with mosquito netting (there's also a private home for rent that can sleep six;

rates go up based on number of guests). It's a nice option if the above guest houses seem a bit too intimate and you want more privacy. An open-air restaurant features the proprietor's astonishing sand collection, displayed on the wall in labeled test tubes, and there's a large Jacuzzi bath. The owners arrange excursions and dispense good information for surfers.

Eating

Numerous rustic beachside shacks sell inexpensive Jamaican fare and double as no-frills 'rum shops' with music at night; find the one with guests, music and laughter, pop in and enjoy yourself. The following restaurants are all located on the beach. For classy French fare, head to Hotel Jamaican Colors.

**Cool Runnings
Beach Bar & Grill** JAMAICAN $
(meals J$350-800; ⊙lunch & dinner) This beach bar and restaurant is a good first stop in Long Bay; the proprietor represents local guest houses and can help you find accommodations. Food is well prepared and tasty – everything is made from scratch, including a wickedly rich mayonnaise. One of the signature dishes is a lovely coconut cream fish. On Saturday night there's a beach party playing old roots reggae and R&B.

Chill-Out JAMAICAN $
(meals J$350-800; ⊙lunch & dinner) Just down the beach from Cool Runnings, this is another popular thatched beachfront eatery and bar. Try the steamed fish and vegetables liberally seasoned with allspice. Sound-system parties are frequently held in the evenings.

Sweet Daddy's JAMAICAN $
(meals J$400-900;) A locals' favorite with an emphasis on seafood and big hearty breakfasts. The cook and proprietor says she takes good care of vegetarians.

Getting There & Away

Minibuses and route taxis run between Port Antonio and Long Bay (J$300).

Reach Falls

Reach Falls is one of the most beautiful places in Jamaica, a spot that screams island paradise and should rightfully be your desktop screensaver. The white rushing cascades are surrounded by a bowl of virgin rain forest; the water tumbles over limestone tiers from one hollowed, jade-colored pool into the next.

Once you enter the **falls** (adult/child US$10/5; ⊙8:30am-4:30pm Wed-Sun) a guide will offer his services. This is actually pretty crucial if you want to climb to the upper pools, which we highly recommend (there's a little underground, underwater tunnel a bit up the falls; plunging through is a treat). Tip generously! The **Mandingo Cave**, the crown jewel of the falls, can be accessed at the top of the cascades, but you need to bring climbing shoes and rope and be prepared for a long, arduous climb. Outside the entrance to the falls, locals congregate and will offer to lead you to the highway through a series of rugged jungle paths, usually for around US$15. It's a beautiful walk, but don't attempt it in anything less than real walking shoes.

❶ Getting There & Away

Catch any of the minibuses and route taxis that run between Kingston and Port Antonio via Morant Bay; get off in Manchioneal, then walk or hitchhike 3km uphill to Reach Falls (the turnoff is signed, 1km south of Manchioneal). A charter taxi from Port Antonio costs about US$60 to US$75 round-trip. Private taxis will take you up the hill to the falls for around US$10.

Manchioneal

POP 2300

Keep heading about 2km south past Reach Falls and the road rises, then humps into a series of silly curves and waves around a deep bay – and we mean 'deep,' both the depression the bay carves out of the surrounding hills and the vivid blue of the water. Surrounding said bay is the sleepy fishing village Manchioneal (Man-kee-oh-neal), where colorful pirogues are drawn up on the wide, shallow beach. It's a center for lobster fishing and the surf is killer – July is said to be the best month.

Just as Boston Bay is famous for its jerk pork and chicken, Manchioneal is a culinary destination for roast fish or conch in foil, which you can purchase from small shacks on the beach; try them later in the day after fishermen have come in with their catches, or the fish might not be ready for your eager consumption. There are plenty of jerk stalls and rum shops, some serving steamed fish, fish tea, roast conch and such.

Three kilometers southeast of Manchioneal, **Ennises Bay Beach** is a great place to spend a lost afternoon shooting the breeze with local Rastafarians. There's a refreshment stand and lovely views of the John Crow Mountains. The beach is half gravel, half sand; on Sunday nights there's usually a sound-system party, and a local club spins tunes on many other nights.

Appropriately under Zion Country cottages is **Under the Rock Beach**, a small cove with a bar that's a good spot to sip beer and basically let the day slip away. Again, live music goes off on Sundays.

The best place to stay around here is **Zion Country** (☑993-0435, 451-1737; www .zioncountry.com; s US$45, d US$55-75), a series of cottages, hammocks and huts built over the green cliffs that overlook Machioneal bay. An excellent backpacker and ecotourist haven, it holds four appealing hillside log-and-bamboo cottages sharing two bathrooms, with hammocks on the veranda and three showers. There is a bar and small restaurant set in a lush garden, and the owner, Dutchman/Rastafarian Free-I, is a chill fellow who is a good resource for exploring the surrounding area; he offers trips to Blue Mountain Peak and transfers to Kingston and Montego Bay. A private beach receives year-round visits from manatees.

Inexpensive food stalls are ubiquitous, especially on the beaches. A good option is **Bryan's Restaurant** (Main St; meals J$200-600), a rooftop eatery that offers simple but delicious Jamaican fare, served on a sunny veranda. Pay for your meal at the B&L Supermarket on the 1st floor before heading up the stairs.

For masks and other fine woodwork, Winsome Shaw operates a **crafts' stall** (☑335-6057) on the road to Reach Falls.

❶ Getting There & Away

Minibuses and route taxis run between Port Antonio and here (J$350).

RIO GRANDE VALLEY

The Rio Grande river, fed by the frequent rains of wet Portland parish, rushes down from 900m in the Blue Mountains and has carved a huge gorge that forms a deep V-shaped wedge between the Blue Mountains to the west and the John Crow Mountains to the east. While not as remotely rugged as the Cockpit Country, the Rio Grande comes pretty close; if you need an escape from anything resembling a city, we recommend heading out here. The Maroons, descendants of escaped slaves who have retained a strong sense of their African cultural heritage, have a strong presence here; to distinguish themselves from their cousins in the Cockpit Country, they are referred to as the Windward Maroons.

Red Hassell Rd runs south from Port Antonio and enters the Rio Grande Valley at Fellowship.

🏃 Activities

Hiking

HIKING

Popular hikes include those to White Valley, known for its large population of giant swallowtail butterflies; to Dry River Falls; and to Scatter Falls and Fox Caves.

Other hikes are demanding, with muddy, overgrown trails and small rivers that require fording. Don't attempt to hike off the beaten path without a guide. The Corn Puss Gap trail is particularly difficult, as is the wild path from Windsor to Nanny Town.

Scatter Falls & Fox Caves

An excellent and easy hike takes you to Scatter Falls and Fox Caves, reached by crossing the Rio Grande on a bamboo raft at Berridale, then hiking for 30 minutes through a series of hamlets and banana groves. The falls tumble through a curtain of ferns into a pool where you can take a refreshing dip. There are changing rooms nearby as well as toilets, a campground, a bamboo-and-thatch bar, and a kitchen that serves a hot lunch – though this must be ordered in advance through Grand Valley Tours, based in Kingston.

A steep, 15-minute hike from the falls leads to the caves, which have some intriguing formations, some of which resemble Rasta dreads. The roof is pitted with hollows in which tiny bats dangle, and you can see where the falls emanate from the caves.

As the path is unsigned and you'll be passing through private property, it's imperative that you visit accompanied by a guide.

Nanny Town

This former village stronghold belonging to the Windward Maroons is perched on the brink of a precipitous spur on the northeastern flank of Blue Mountain Peak, about 16km southwest of Moore Town as the crow flies. It is named for an 18th-century Ashanti warrior priestess and Maroon leader, now a national hero. In 1734 English troops brought swivel guns into the valley and blew up most of Nanny Town, but the local Maroons remained defiant. Essentially, they proved more trouble to subdue than they were worth, and Nanny Town was granted a sort of semi-autonomy that persists to this day.

It's a tough 16km hike from Windsor, 5km north of Moore Town. Grand Valley Tours has a three-day guided hike. There are numerous side trails, and it's easy to get lost if you attempt to hike on your own.

Organized Hikes

The following are all good outfits to contact before setting off on a hike; all of the below can organize homestays in the Rio Grande Valley, which is preferable to rocking up on your own or camping in an area you're unfamiliar with.

Sun Venture, based in Kingston, offers hiking and also cultural tours in the area. In Port Antonio, contact Jamaica Explorations at Hotel Mocking Bird Hill, or Grand Valley Tours, which offers treks to Scatter Falls and Fox Caves as well as hikes to Moore Town, Nanny Falls and Nanny Town. **Valley Hikes** (☑993-3881; Unit 41, Royal Mall, Port Antonio) is another locally run trekking outfit.

Rafting

RAFTING

Errol Flynn supposedly initiated rafting on the Rio Grande during the 1940s, when moonlight raft trips were considered the ultimate activity among the fashionable.

Today paying passengers make the 11km journey of one to three hours (depending on water level) from **Grant's Level** (Rafter's Village), about 2km south of Berridale, to **Rafter's Rest** at St Margaret's Bay. When the moon is full, unforgettable moonlight trips are offered. These are less regimented; your guide will be happy to pull over on a moon-drenched riverbank so that you can canoodle with your sweetie or just open the ice chests to release the beer.

Reserve at **Rio Grande Experience Ltd** (☑993-5778; Berridale; per raft US$65, full-moon rides US$130; ☺8:30am-4pm). You can buy tickets at Rafter's Village at Grant's Level if you don't have reservations. This is a one-way trip, so if you're driving you need to hire a driver to bring your car from Berridale to St Margaret's Bay (Rio Grande Experience will help for US$15; the drivers are insured, but make clear to them that you expect them to drive slowly and safely) or take a taxi from Port Antonio (US$20).

A route taxi from Port Antonio to Grant's Level costs J$200; they depart from the corner of Bridge St and Summers Town Rd. Licensed taxis cost about US$20 round-trip.

Athenry Gardens & Nonsuch Caves

Athenry Gardens, high in the hills southeast of Port Antonio, is a former coconut plantation and agricultural research center, now a lush garden that boasts many exotic and native species. The highlight is bat-filled **Nonsuch Caves** (☎9779-7144; admission US$8.80; ⊙9am-5pm), 14 separate chambers full of stalagmites and stalactites once inhabited by Taínos. Tour groups come out here, about the only sign of package tourism (besides rafting trips) in the Rio Grande. It's all kind of corny, but charmingly so. Also, your entrance ticket scores you a free rum (or fruit) punch, so hey.

❶ Getting There & Away

The caves and garden are about 11km southeast of Port Antonio via Red Hassell Rd. After 3km along Red Hassell Rd there's a Y-fork at Breastworks. The right fork leads to Berridale and the Rio Grande; take the left for Nonsuch.

You can also reach Nonsuch Caves from Drapers via the same road that circles back to Port Antonio.

Moore Town

This one-street village, 16km south of Port Antonio, stretches uphill for several hundred meters along the Wildcane River. Today it looks like any other Jamaican village, but historically it occupies a space of some importance as the former base of the Windward Maroons. The village was founded in 1739 following the signing of a peace treaty granting the Maroons their independence. Moore Town is still run semi-autonomously by a council of 24 elected members headed by a 'colonel.' The locals attempt to keep alive their lore and legends, and still bring out their *abengs* (goat horns) and talking drums on occasion, but many youth are emigrating to the cities.

Visitors expressing interest in the fascinating history of the Windward Maroons will be warmly welcomed. On arrival, it's considered polite to pay respects to the local colonel (Wallace Sterling during research; just ask about and someone will take you

to him). If he's not about, you may be approached by one of his emissaries and asked for a small donation. Trails lead from Moore Town, including one to a series of lovely pools at **Nanny Falls**, about 45 minutes away.

Grand Valley Tours in Port Antonio leads trips, including a 'Moonlight at Moore Town' community tour that aims to connect visitors to the spirit of the Maroons.

Moore Town's main site of interest is **Bump Grave**, at the southern, uppermost end of town. Topped by a flagpole flying the Maroon and Jamaican flags, the oblong stone and plaque mark the grave of Nanny, warrior woman freedom fighter and chieftainess of the Maroons. There's a gate protecting the grave, but it can be opened for a small donation. Also be on the lookout for the church of Mother Roberts (the building is bedecked in flowers); it's the AME Zionist Deliverance Center, and is a major destination for faith healings.

❶ Getting There & Away

Moore Town is unsigned and lies in a hollow to the left of a Y-junction at Seaman's Valley; the road to the right continues via Alligator Church through the Upper Rio Grande Valley. In Moore Town the road dead-ends in the village.

Minibuses and route taxis operate to Moore Town from Port Antonio (about J$150). A minibus from Port Antonio runs in the early morning and again in the early afternoon (J$100).

Upper Rio Grande Valley

The road to the right of the Y-junction at Seaman's Valley leads via Alligator Church to Bowden Pen, 16km or so up the river valley. The paved road ends at Alligator Church. Beyond here, the dirt road is extremely rough and narrow and you'll need a 4WD.

The ranger station for Blue Mountains-John Crow National Park is at **Millbank**, 3km before Bowden Pen, near the summit ridge of the John Crow Mountains, which parallels the valley like a great castle wall. A trail leads to the **White River Falls**, a series of seven cascades, while beyond you may find the ruins of abandoned Maroon villages – just beware. This is a tough trek through some serious rain forest. In Millbank itself, avail yourself of the wisdom of local Maroon elders (there's a preponderance); they're very friendly and seem to genuinely enjoy the chance to relate the stories of their forebears to international visitors.

A short distance above Bowden Pen the track begins rising more precipitously and the vegetation closes in. Don't push too far, for there is nowhere to turn your vehicle back. You can continue on foot across the Corn Puss Gap.

Valley Hikes and Grand Valley Tours in Port Antonio offer tours; the latter operates a campsite just beyond Millbank. You must arrange with the company in advance. Both companies can also arrange lodging in private homes in the area.

You can also try to stay in **Ambassabeth Cabins** (☑395-5351; www.bowdenpenfarmers. com; cabins US$50), a community tourism outfit in Bowden Pen that's a real gem. These (very) rustic wooden cabins have running water but no electricity. You'll be treated to a true Maroon cultural experience, with indigenous folklore, Maroon cooking and local guides all on offer. This is as educational and fun as stays in the Jamaican bush get.

❶ Getting There & Away

A minibus from Port Antonio goes as far as Millbank, as do route taxis (J$200).

WEST OF PORT ANTONIO

Port Antonio to Hope Bay

There's nothing inspirational about Hope Bay, which has a somewhat sad, gray beach fronted by rows of everyday shops. A loop drive, however, can be made from here up the Swift River Valley, where plantations grow cacao.

◉ Sights

Somerset Falls   WATERFALL
(☑383-6970; www.somersetfallsjamaica.com; Hwy A4; admission J$750; ☺9am-5pm) This dark waterfall is hidden in a deep gorge about 3km east of Hope Bay. The Daniels River cascades down through a lush garden of ferns, heliconias, lilies and crotons into glistening teardrop black pools. Visitors have to negotiate some steep, twisty steps to get here.

The recently renovated site has a restaurant, bar, jerk pit, ice-cream shop and massage therapy space, but further in the falls themselves are mercifully unspoiled and

certainly less touristy than those at Dunn's River.

The entrance fee includes a guided tour through a grotto by boat to the Hidden Fall, which tumbles 10m into a jade-colored grotto. Bring a swimsuit to enjoy the large swimming area.

🛏 Sleeping & Eating

Rio Vista Resort & Villas   HOTEL **$$**
(☑993-5444; www.riovistajamaica.com; Rafter's Rest; r US$65-115, villa US$155-185; P❀☀) This chintzy option sits atop a ridge near the turnoff for Rafter's Rest on the Rio Grande, 6km west of Port Antonio. The house itself, built into the remains of an old plantation home, has an enviable setting high above the Rio Grande, with mountains behind – you'll find it hard to concentrate on breakfast from the patio. The actual villas and rooms are a bit old-fashioned but lovely nonetheless. Airport transfers and car rentals are available. The attached Buccaneer restaurant does a good trade in chops, steaks, seafood and such, plus the usual Jamaican favorites.

Ital Village   HOTEL **$**
(☑898-5323; www.italvillage.com; Hope Bay; s/d US$40/50; P❀) Run by Italian expats, Ital Village is good for that Rasta-friendly beach vibe and is popular with backpackers and adventurers who want to get far away from the tourist trail. Rooms are simple, comfortable and clean, all dark wood and bright sheets. The on site restaurant does plenty of both Italian and Jamaican cuisine and can happily accommodate vegetarians. Located a little ways west of Hope Bay, about two minutes inland on a dirt track; call ahead to get directions.

❶ Getting There & Away

Both route taxis (J$150) and minibuses (J$100) pass Somerset Falls and Hope Bay between Annotto Bay and Port Antonio.

Orange Bay

The road between Hope Bay and Orange Bay takes an inland route and is wonderfully scenic with dense jungle foliage, open forests of towering palms and hillsides covered with tropical plants boasting leaves the size of elephant ears. You'll pass by huge stands of bamboo up on the ridge and expansive plantations of banana. Along the way there are simple roadside stands that sell produce and pepper shrimp, as well as **Pon Di Corner** – which you'll smell before you see it: this excellent jerk center is famous in these parts, as much for the colorful murals that adorn the walls as the succulent meat.

At Orange Bay the road rejoins the coast. Keep an eye out for the old **rail station** that served the Kingston–Annotto Bay line until it ceased operation in 1983; it's sadly atmospheric, a relic of bygone days. The building now houses a video store as well as the daughter of the former stationmaster. Across the street is **Marsha's Pub**, which hosts sound-system parties in the evenings, rattling windows for miles around.

Almond Lodge (☑385-4139; www.almondlodge.com; d US$40; ℗), a roadside lodge with plenty of personality, offers several simple but clean fan-cooled rooms and bathrooms with no hot water, each containing one double bed. There's a pebble and black-sand beach, which you are likely to have all to yourself, and a small restaurant and bar with pool table that occasionally hosts parties for the local villages, inevitably a fun way of meeting some friendly locals.

Buff Bay

POP 11,000

This is a small, neatly laid-out town in the midst of a major banana-producing area, with several colonial-era buildings of modest interest, centered on the Anglican church.

One of the largest African heritage events in the Jamaican cultural calendar, **Fi Wi Sinting** (p19) is held on a Sunday in February at **Nature's Way**, 5km east of Buff Bay. An African marketplace offers robes, batiks and jewelry, and performances are staged throughout the day. In a moving ritual, the official celebration comes to a close when libation is poured in remembrance of those who survived the 'middle passage,' a term designating the passage of slaves to Jamaica from Africa. A boat covered in flowers is released into the sea. The festival provides a rare opportunity to witness Kumina drumming, a tradition with direct ties to Africa, believed to be a form of communication with the dead. A Kumina drum circle keeps a sizable crowd dancing deep into the night.

Fishdone Waterfalls is a beautiful spot on a private coffee plantation near Buff Bay. The falls are surrounded by rain forest, and there are trails for hiking.

Two miles inland from Buff Bay you can find the **Asafu Yard** (☑445-2861; admission by donation) in the Maroon settlement of Charles Town. The Yard is a sort of house complex/gardens/museum operated by Maroon Colonel Lumsden, who's happy to clue visitors in to the nuances of his culture while leading you on a small walk past historical artifacts and plants and herbs used in traditional Maroon medicine. He may also take you on a short trek to some Maroon ruins; just remember it's crucial to call beforehand.

For a snack or meal, head to the colonial-era **Kildaire Villa Great House** (☑996-1240; Main St), at the eastern end of town. Besides serving as a sort of community center for all things Buff Bay, this used to be the plantation house for the United Fruit Company, which once basically ran this part of the parish as its own playground. Today the Kildaire House has a well-stocked gift store selling patties and desserts, while upstairs a Jamaican seafood restaurant offers patio dining, ackee, saltfish and brown stew chicken (J$500).

[TOP CHOICE] **Blueberry Hill Jerk Centre** (jerk meat J$300-750), located on the coastal side of the road to Orange Bay, has developed a well-deserved reputation for its pork and chicken, drenched in a punishing sauce that will clear your sinuses (whilst filling them with a lovely smoky odor). A serious case is made by aficionados that this could be the best jerk in Portland parish, which is really saying something.

The post office is 100m east of the church. Buff Bay also has a small **hospital** (☑996-1478), and the **police station** (☑996-1497) is at the east end of town.

Buff Bay River Valley

The B1 heads south from the town center and climbs 32km through the valley of the Buff Bay River to Hardwar Gap, at an elevation of 1700m, before dropping down to Kingston. Note that during the rainy season, the road is sometimes put out of commission by landslides, so check conditions before setting out.

Annotto Bay

This erstwhile banana port is a downtrodden one-street town that springs to life for the Saturday market. Depressing shanties line the waterfront, while the paltry remains of **Fort George**, and some gingerbread colonial-era structures with columned walkways, stand on Main St. The most intriguing is the venerable yellow-and-red brick **Baptist chapel**, built in 'village baroque' style in 1894, with cut-glass windows and curious biblical exhortations engraved at cornice height.

Three kilometers west of town is the junction of the A4 with the A3.

There's no real reason to stay in Annotto Bay, but 13km inland on the banks of the Penscar River at Long Road, you'll find the **River's Edge** (☎944-2673; riveredge99@hotmail.com; camping per person US$10, dm/apt per person US$20/35). This is a relaxing little escape with plenty of rural character; primarily a campsite, it also has basically furnished dorm rooms and one simple studio apartment with kitchenette and private bathroom. You can camp on the lawns (tents are rented) and order meals by request.

The best place to eat in Annotto Bay is the **Human Service Station** (mains J$200-600), at the side of the road to Buff Bay as you're leaving town. It serves fish stews as well as chicken, many of which can be seen roaming around the yard.

The town has a small **hospital** (☎996-2222), a **police station** (☎996-9169; Main St) and a **National Commercial Bank** (☎996-2213; Main St). The **Annotto Bay Branch Library** (☎996-2508; Hwy A4; per 30min US$1.25) offers internet access.

Robin's Bay

Midway to Port Maria from Annotto Bay, on the A3, you'll pass a turnoff to the north that hugs a lonesome shoreline with gray-sand beaches backed by lagoons. After 4km you'll emerge in **Mt Pleasant Heights**, a fishing village nestled atop Don Christopher's Point, named for the Spanish guerrilla leader Don Cristobal Arnaldo de Ysassi, who led the resistance against the 1655 British invasion, culminating in the Battle of Rio Nuevo.

The paved road ends at **Robin's Bay** (known as Strawberry Fields in the 1970s, when it was a free-love haven for American hippies). There are persistent rumors about pirate's treasure still hidden away in the area's sea caves. Sadly, creating an eyesore at the far end of Robin's Bay is the Robin's Bay Village & Beach Resort.

◉ Sights & Activities

Kwaaman & Tacky Waterfalls   WATERFALLS
In refreshing contrast to Jamaica's more famous – and thus more visited – waterfalls, Kwaaman and Tacky are so pristine and isolated that, if you stumbled across them wandering up the coast from Robin's Bay, you might be tempted to claim them as your own. Kwaaman Waterfall is a 32m cascade that tumbles into a clear pool you can swim in.

Gazing up from the water at the contorted rockface behind the falls, you'll be able to make out what appears to be dreadlocks formed in the rock by the continual flow of water over centuries. Tacky Falls lacks the dreads but is equally worth the visit, particularly if the weather's calm and you can take a boat ride from Robin's Bay.

Hiking   HIKING
You can reach Robin's Bay from Port Maria by a hiking trail that leads along one of the few stretches of Jamaican coastline that remains pristine. Locals can lead you to remote **Black Sand Beach**, and the Kwaaman and Tacky Waterfalls.

🛏 Sleeping & Eating

TOP CHOICE **River Lodge**   HOTEL $
(☎995-3003, in Germany 089-74-999-797; www.river-lodge.com; s/d US$50/80, d cottages US$90-100; ℗) This is a truly atmospheric option that has sprouted up from the ruins of a centuries-old Spanish pirate fort, established by longtime Jamaica resident Brigitta Fuchslocher. The rooms – which probably once were barracks for buccaneers – have white bleached-stone walls and blood-red floors, and are lit by skylights. The bathrooms (cold water only) are festooned with climbing ivy; the bathroom in the upstairs 'tower' room is alfresco. Meals are a social affair, served in a small thatched restaurant; rates include breakfast and dinner. There are two cottages with privileged sea views located less than 1km from the lodge. One is an octagonal bamboo hut with private bathroom and fridge, the other a Moorish-style cottage with kitchenette and a delightful hearth on the patio, perfect for roasting fish. The whole complex is complemented by the aptly named Natural Vibes bar.

Strawberry Fields Together   RESORT $$
(☎999-7169; www.strawberryfieldstogether.com; camping per person US$15, junior cottage US$70-90, deluxe cottage US$180-220; ℗❄)

This series of romantic cottages is often hired out by foreign and domestic honeymooners, but is also popular with counterculture types and those on a budget due to the campground and general vibe of Robin's Bay. (You need to bring your own tent, by the way.) The cottages (which can sleep four to six people) all have good views to the hills and the sea, and some come equipped with luxuries such as whirlpool baths. The surrounding land has been left undeveloped and is lovely to trek through; some areas are a naturalist's dream, especially if you love birds. Delicious home-cooked meals available through a meal plan.

❶ Getting There & Away

Any one of the public vehicles that travel between Ocho Rios and Annotto Bay or Port Antonio will let you off at the junction to Robin's Bay on the A3. It's then a 6km walk to Robin's Bay. With good timing, you can connect with bus JR16A, which operates between Kingston and Robin's Bay, or with the few route taxis that run to Robin's Bay from the A3. Or just contact your accommodations choice in advance to arrange a transfer.

Ocho Rios & North Coast

Why Go?

Ocho Rios is the ideal base for the widest range of outdoor activities in Jamaica, such as horseback riding, scuba diving, mountain biking, and swimming with dolphins. The area around the third-largest town in Jamaica features some of the most beautiful (and popular) natural attractions on the island. Along the north coast you will find pleasant white sand beaches, clear waters, spectacular waterfalls and lush mountainous terrain.

The town can sometimes feel rather like an American theme park, with cruise ships disgorging hordes of passengers, all-inclusive hotels, and appropriately tourist-friendly nightlife, but if you grow tired of pre-fab commercialism you can retreat to the luxurious villas and exclusive elegant hotels east of town, take the winding mountain roads inland to pay your respects to Bob Marley, visit a working plantation, or retrace the footsteps of Columbus near St Ann's Bay, the site of Jamaica's earliest Spanish settlement.

Best Places to Eat

» Toscanini (p125)

» Passage to India (p125)

» Scotchies Too (p125)

» Tamarind Great House (p131)

Best Places to Stay

» Cottage at Te Moana (p123)

» Goldeneye (p131)

» Itopia (p138)

» Bolt House (p133)

When to Go
Ocho Rios

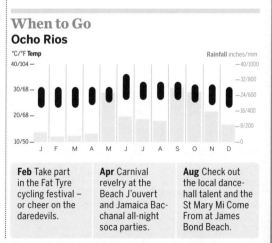

Feb Take part in the Fat Tyre cycling festival – or cheer on the daredevils.

Apr Carnival revelry at the Beach J'ouvert and Jamaica Bacchanal all-night soca parties.

Aug Check out the local dancehall talent and the St Mary Mi Come From at James Bond Beach.

Ocho Rios & North Coast Highlights

1 Climbing one of the world's most famous waterfalls, **Dunn's River Falls** (p119)

2 Savoring the jaw-dropping view from author Noël Coward's well-preserved former home, **Firefly** (p132)

3 Paying your respects to Jamaica's best-known son at Bob Marley's birthplace and final resting place, **Nine Mile** (p141)

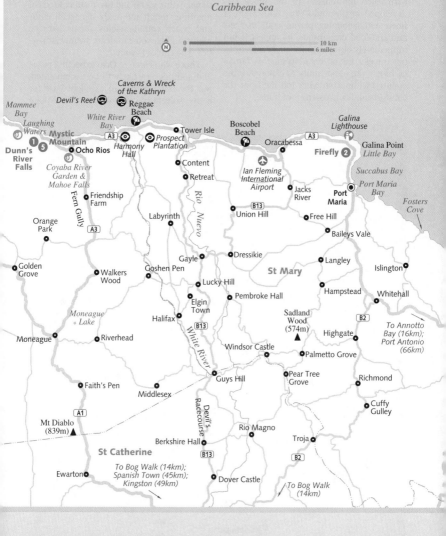

Caribbean Sea

N
0 ———————————————— 10 km
0 ———————————————— 6 miles

Mammee
Bay
Laughing
Waters
**Mystic
Mountain**
**Dunn's
River
Falls**
Ocho Rios
*Coyaba River
Garden &
Mahoe Falls*

Devil's Reef
*Caverns & Wreck
of the Kathryn*
Reggae
Beach
*White River
Bay*
Tower Isle
Prospect
Plantation
Harmony
Hall

Boscobel
Beach
Oracabessa

Galina
Lighthouse
Firefly
Galina Point
Little Bay
Succabus Bay
*Port Maria
Bay*

*Fosters
Cove*

Content
Retreat
Friendship
Farm

Ian Fleming
International
Airport
Jacks
River
**Port
Maria**

Fern Gully
Orange
Park
A3
Labyrinth

Rio Nuevo
B13
Union Hill
Free Hill
Baileys Vale

Golden
Grove
Walkers
Wood
Goshen Pen
Gayle
Dressikie
Lucky Hill
Pembroke Hall

St Mary
Langley
Islington
Hampstead
Whitehall

*Moneague
Lake*
Moneague
Riverhead
Elgin
Town
Halifax
B13

Windsor Castle

Sadland
Wood
(574m)▲
B2
Highgate
Palmetto Grove
*To Annotto
Bay (16km);
Port Antonio
(66km)*

Faith's Pen
Middlesex
White River
Guys Hill
Pear Tree
Grove
Richmond
Cuffy
Gulley

Mt Diablo
(839m)▲
A1
Berkshire Hall
B13
Devil's Racecourse
Rio Magno
B2
Troja

St Catherine
Ewarton
*To Bog Walk (14km);
Spanish Town (45km);
Kingston (49km)*
Dover Castle
*To Bog Walk
(14km)*

④ Exploring Jamaica's
first Spanish settlement,
**Maima Seville Great House
& Heritage Park** (p135), on
horseback, finishing off by
riding into the sea

⑤ Admiring panoramic views
of the coast from the chairlift
and zipping down Jamaica's
longest canopy line at **Mystic
Mountain** (p120)

OCHO RIOS

POP 17,000

Wrapped around a small bay with postcard-worthy snugness, Ocho Rios is a former fishing village that the Jamaica Tourist Board earmarked for tourism in the 1960s and developed in the mid-1980s. With Main St lined with shopping plazas, craft markets and fast-food emporiums, its appeal is not immediately obvious to the more adventurous traveler, but others welcome this 'Jamaica Lite' – the opportunity to experience the country without straying too far from the comforts and conveniences of home.

The frequent docking of cruise ships at the central pier that commands the town's focus gives 'Ochi' a decidedly 'packaged' feel, spiced up by the incessant entreaties of 'guides' and souvenir sellers. However, it has also endowed the town with an international eating scene and two distinct kinds of nightlife: rough-and-ready dancehall clubs and beach sound-systems versus karaoke nights and all-you-can-drink swimwear parties. The choice is yours.

Those who come to Ochi expecting peace and solitude are likely to be disappointed, but the town makes an excellent base for active, solvent travelers who wish to explore

Ocho Rios

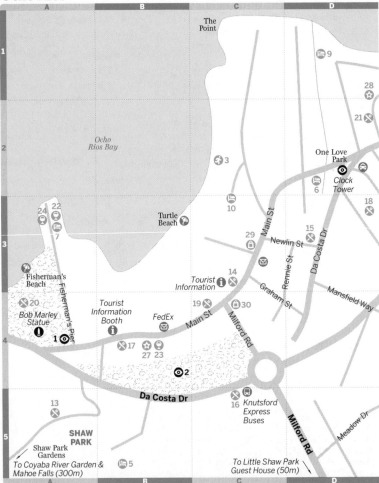

the scenic north coast and to partake in slick, well-managed 'adventures' such as dog sledding, zip-line tours, horseback riding and waterfall climbing.

History

The name Ocho Rios is a corruption of the Spanish term *chorreros,* which means, roughly, 'swift water.' Not only was the area west of Ocho Rios the site of Columbus' first landing in Jamaica and the first Spanish settlement, but it was also one of the last strongholds of Spanish dominion over the island. The site of Spain's last stand in Jamaica can be found at Rio Nuevo, east of modern-day Ocho Rios. It was here that the British instituted huge sugar and pimento (allspice) plantations, crops that defined the region until the mid-20th century, when bauxite mining and tourism took over.

◉ Sights

TOP CHOICE **Dunn's River Falls**   WATERFALL
(www.dunnsriverfallsja.com; adult/child J$1270/1016; ⊘8:30am-4pm Sat-Tue, 7am-4pm Wed-Fri) Widely held to be one of the most beautiful waterfalls in the world, these famous falls, on the A3, 3km west of town, are Jamaica's top-grossing tourist attraction.

A morning at Dunn's River Falls is an enjoyable and invigorating experience – as long as you're not expecting a peaceful communion with nature. Join hands in a daisy chain at the bottom and clamber up the tiers of limestone that step 180m down to the beach in a series of cascades and pools. The water is refreshingly cool and the falls are shaded by a tall rain forest and a number of magnificent tree specimens.

Today, the place seems more like a theme park than a natural wonder, and you are likely to encounter great throngs of people, though this doesn't make the climb any less exhilarating.

You must buy a ticket at the roadside ticket booth, then follow the stairs down to the beach. Guides congregate at the bottom of the falls and can assist you with you climb (a tip is expected) and carry your camera, but their services are not necessary. The powerful current can sweep your feet from the slippery rocks, and you climb at your own risk – yes, occasionally people hurt themselves – but as long as you stick to the left side of the falls (which is easier to climb), the ascent is easily achieved by most able-bodied people. There's a first-aid station. You can always exit to the side at a convenient point if your nerves give out.

It's a 30-minute climb, and swimwear is essential. There are changing rooms, and you can rent lockers (J$500) and rubber booties (J$500). It's best to leave any valuables in your hotel safe, as the lockers are reputedly not secure.

The facility now includes a mento yard for live music, an orchid garden, a children's playground, a crafts market, jerk stalls, a gazebo for weddings, snack bars and a restaurant. As you leave the complex, you are obliged to walk through a mazelike craft market where the hard sell is laid on thick.

Mallards Bay

James St

To Bibibips Bar & Grill (100m); H2O (600m); Five Star Watersports (800m); Cottage at Te Moana (1.2km); Blue Mountain Bicycle Tours (1.6km); Sandals Royal Plantation (1.8km); Jamaica Inn (1.9km)

Transportation Center (Buses, Taxis)

Ocho Rios Bypass

Evelyn Rd

Main St

Ardite Rd

Catterton Rd

Almond Rd

Pitlandia Pl

Perth Rd

Methven Rd

Rennie Rd

Murray Rd

Mansfield Way

To Wassi Art (500m); Fern Gully (1km); Ewarton (43km); Spanish Town (61km)

Ocho Rios

Plan to arrive before 10am, when the tour buses arrive, or around 4pm after they depart. Also try to visit when the cruise ships aren't in town (usually Saturday to Tuesday). Avoid Easter. Route taxis (J$80) head west to Dunn's River Falls and beyond from Main St; it's a simple matter to flag one down.

TOP CHOICE **Mystic Mountain** THEME PARK
(www.rainforestbobsledjamaica.com; ⊙9am-4pm)
Following in the footsteps of other Rain Forest Adventure ecotourism theme parks (in Costa Rica, St Lucia and Dominica) comes one of Ochi's biggest attractions, featuring a series of zip lines crisscrossing the forest in what is possibly the best canopy tour in Jamaica, as well as the signature attraction: a thrilling 'bobsled' ride through the dense foliage.

To get to the park, you take the obligatory Sky Explorer chairlift through the forest canopy to the top of the mountain (J$3555), with superb views of the coastline along the way. The visitor center has an excellent exhibition on Jamaica's sporting heroes, in-

cluding the bobsled team that inspired the film *Cool Runnings* (and this theme park), as well as the **Mystic Dining** restaurant specializing in contemporary Caribbean cuisine, an infinity pool with 25m water slide (included in ticket price) and a gift shop. You can either go in an individual 'bobsled' or link yours to your friends'; you also control the speed of the ride, which can thus range from mild to exhilarating. One thing it isn't is cheap: a Sky Explorer and Bobsled combo is US$68.20; a Sky Explorer and Zipline combo is US$114.40, whereas a combination of all three is US$136.40. You can add on more rides once in the park. Avoid the park on cruise ship days.

Mystic Mountain lies 3km west of Ocho Rios; to get here, catch one of the numerous route taxis heading towards St Ann's Bay (J$80).

Coyaba River Garden & Mahoe Falls GARDEN
(www.coyabagardens.com; Shaw Park Rd; admission incl Mahoe Falls adult/child J$847424; ⊙8am-

6pm) *Coyaba* being the Arawak word for 'paradise', this garden seems aptly named, its walkways and trails leading through the best-kept gardens in Ocho Rios, with streams and pools filled with carp, crayfish and turtles. The thoughtful **Coyaba Museum** traces Jamaica's heritage from early Taíno days to independence and there is a splendid panoramic view of Ocho Rios from the Ysassi's Lookout Point, adjoining the Mahoe Falls, an attractive waterfall suitable for swimming. Coyaba is just shy of 2km west of St John's Church (on the A3), not far from Shaw Park Gardens; follow the signs.

Shaw Park Gardens　　　　GARDEN
(www.shawparkgardens.com; Shaw Park Rd; admission J$847; ⊙8am-5pm) This is a tropical fantasia of ferns and bromeliads, palms and exotic shrubs, spread out over 11 hectares centered on an 18th-century great house. Trails and wooden steps lead past waterfalls that tumble in terraces down the hillside. A viewing platform offers a bird's-eye vantage over Ocho Rios. The gardens are signed from opposite the public library on the A3.

Island Village　　　ENTERTAINMENT CENTER
(admission to village/beach free/J$200; ⊙9am-midnight) Since its 2002 opening, this self-contained entertainment park, at the junction of Main St and DaCosta Dr, has changed the face of Ocho Rios. The 2-hectare development, brainchild of resort and media visionary Chris Blackwell, claims to resemble a 'Jamaican coastal village.' It doesn't. Quibbles aside, you will find a peaceful beach, upscale craft shops, a cinema, **Jimmy Buffett's Margaritaville** bar and restaurant and **Blue Mont** cafe, a video-casino, and a village green and amphitheatre for live performances. There are admission charges for some special events.

Wassi Art　　　　CRAFTS
(☎974-5044; www.wassiart.com; Bougainvillea Dr; ⊙9am-5pm Mon-Sat, 10am-4pm Sun) Family-owned Wassi Art employs over 50 artists to make its colorful, richly decorated terracotta pottery. It is named for the 'wassi' wasp, or potter wasp, which makes a mud pot for each of its eggs and stuffs it with a caterpillar for food for her hatchlings. Free tours are offered, detailing the entire process including clay processing, painting and firing. A store sells work (US$5 to US$5000). The owners get discounts from FedEx and will ship your purchases abroad.

Wassi Art is in the Great Pond District, signed from Milford Rd (the A3), from where it's a convoluted (but signed) drive.

Turtle River Park　　　　PARK
(⊙8am-6pm) Near Island Village on Main St, this welcome new green space in the middle of downtown represents a positive new trend in Jamaica's approach to urban development. The lushly gardened park with manicured lawns also provides a zone free from the hustle of the main drag.

🏖 Beaches

The main beach of Ocho Rios, popular with tourists, is the long crescent known variously as **Turtle Beach** and **Ocho Rios Bay** (admission J$200; ⊙8am-5pm), stretching east from the Turtle Towers condominiums to the Renaissance Jamaica Grande Resort, fenced off and topped with barbed wire. There are changing rooms and palms for shade. **Island Village Beach** (admission J$254; ⊙6am-6pm), located at the west end of Main St, is a peaceful, smaller beach that offers lockers (J$423), towels (J$423) and beach chairs and umbrellas (J$423 apiece). Both beaches offer a complete range of water sports.

Immediately west of Island Village Beach is tiny **Fishermen's Beach** (admission free), with colorful pirogues (fishing boats) and several eateries serving fresh fish and more. The small and charming **Mahogany Beach** (admission free), 1km east of the town center, is particularly popular with locals; it comes to life on weekends with loud music, smells of jerk cooking and impromptu football matches.

🏃 Activities

Virtually the entire shoreline east of Ocho Rios to Galina Point is fringed by a reef, and it's great for **snorkeling** and **scuba diving**. One of the best sections is **Devil's Reef**, a pinnacle that drops more than 60m. Nurse sharks are abundant at **Caverns**, a shallow reef about 1km east of the White River estuary; it has many tunnels plus an ex-minesweeper, the *Kathryn*. Most resorts have their own scuba facilities. As well as operators listed here, upscale hotels also offer water sports.

Dolphin Cove　　　DOLPHIN ENCOUNTER
(☎974-5335; www.dolphincovejamaica.com; admission US$45, dolphin packages US$67-195; ⊙8:30am-5:30pm) This popular cove, adjacent to Dunn's River Falls along the A3, allows you to swim with bottlenose dolphins.

Three dolphin packages are offered, notably 'Swim with Dolphins' (US$195), which grants you 30 minutes in the dolphin lagoon with two dolphins, the thrill seeker grabbing the dorsal fins of two dolphins and being lifted out of the water by means of a foot push. 'Encounter Swim' (US$129) is just that, with a single dolphin, while the tamer 'Touch Encounter' (US$67) allows you to stroke the dolphins while standing in knee-deep water.

Professional trainers direct the dolphins. More adventurous visitors can touch and feed nurse sharks (US$119) – under the Cove's watchful supervision. Basic admission includes an aquarium and pools with tropical fish, sharks, stingrays and eels, as well as a mini zoo with exotic species to be experienced on a 'Jungle Trail', a chance to shop at a tacky 'Little Port Royal', and the opportunity to snorkel with stingrays (tail barbs removed) and take to the waters in a glass-bottomed kayak.

Note that the **Jamaica Environmental Trust** (JET; www.jamentrust.org) opposes the display of captive marine mammals, as mortality rates increase during capture, transport and captivity. The trade and harvesting of wild dolphins (mostly females) also has an adverse impact on local populations (most of the ones on display in Jamaica were captured in Cuban waters). JET has been trying to ensure proper governmental oversight of the facility yet, despite its opposition, another dolphinarium was opened in Lucea.

Reservations advisable in winter. Bring a towel and leave your jewelry behind.

Garfield Diving Station   DIVING
(☑395-7023; www.garfielddiving.com; Turtle Beach) Ocho Rios' longest-running water sports operator with 29 years' experience. Dive packages include one-tank dives (J$5079), wreck dive (J$5926) and PADI certification course (UD$420). Other water sports offered, such as snorkeling excursions (J$5926), glass-bottom boat rides (J$2116) and jet-ski rental (J$5926 for 30 minutes). Boat charter available for deep-sea fishing (half day for up to four people US$500).

Five Star Water Sports   WATER SPORTS
(☑974-2446; www.fivestarwatersports.com; Shop 14, 121 Main St) Specializes in three catamaran cruises: **Wet'n'Wild** (J$5926; ⊘2:30-5pm Thu) is an adults-only, clothing-optional cruise with all the booze you can guzzle; **Taste of**

Jamaica (J$5926; ⊘5-8pm Fri) is a combination of buffet-style Jamaican dinner, open bar and romance; and the **Dunn's River Falls Cruise** (J$7819; ⊘12:30-4pm Mon-Wed, Fri & Sat) includes an hour's snorkeling and entry to the falls.

Resort Divers   DIVING
(☑881-5760; www.resortdivers.com; Royal DeCameron Club Caribbean, Runaway Bay) Dive packages available with pickup from Ocho Rios (see p138 for more details).

Calypso Rafting   WATER SPORTS
(☑974-2527; www.calypsorafting.com) Reliable operator offering bamboo rafting (J$4233) and inner tubing (J$1694) on the White River, as well as half-day deep-sea fishing trips on fully equipped yachts (US$600 to US$750) and jet-ski rental (J$5079 for 30 minutes).

Island Village Beach   WATER SPORTS
(Island Village; ⊘8am-4pm) Rents snorkeling gear (J$1270 per day), kayaks (single/double J$847/1270 per hour), windsurfing gear (J$4656 for 30 minutes) and Hobie Cats (J$3386 for 30 minutes).

☛ Tours

The Ocho Rios area offers more organized outdoor adventure tours than any other Jamaican resort area. All operators offer transportation from hotels.

Chukka Caribbean Adventure Tours
ADVENTURE TOURS
(☑972-2506; www.chukkacaribbean.com/jamaica; tours J$3555-7819) Established multi-adventure specialist offering horseback-riding tours, river tubing, zip-line canopy tours, ATV safaris, adventure jeep drives to Bob Marley's birthplace and even dog-sleigh tours.

Hooves   HORSEBACK RIDING
(☑972-0905; www.hooves-jamaica.com; 61 Windsor Rd, St Ann's Bay; US$65-115) Offers guided horseback tours from the Maima Seville Great House to the beach, with a bareback ride into the sea (beginners welcome) and the 'rain forest honeymoon ride,' for experienced riders. Reservations required.

Blue Mountain Bicycle Tours   CYCLING TOURS
(☑974-7075; www.bmtoursja.com; 121 Main St; Blue Mountain downhill tour adult/child J$8042/6349) Exhilarating downhill cycling tour of the Blue Mountains, week-long eco-adventures in Portland and tours of Kingston.

BLUE HOUSE

This intimate little gem of a B&B, **Blue House** (☑994-1367; www.thebluehousejamaica .com; White River Bay; s/d J$4233/5926; P✷@✿☎) offers a wonderful get-away-from-it-all luxurious experience. True to the name, the four tiled, luxurious bedrooms are decorated in blue hues. All beds have mosquito nets. The separate two-bedroom Cozy Cottage offers even greater seclusion, with its private patio with hammock hidden behind a curtain of flowers. Darryl the Barefoot Chef cooks up some of the best fusion cuisine on the island, drawing on Chinese and Indian influences, and the lavish three-course dinners are worth every penny. The meals are taken in the dining room in a family atmosphere. And if the above were not enough, a share of the B&B's profits goes to support the area's destitute elderly, women and children. To get here, drive around 4km east of Ocho Rios to White River Bay. The guesthouse is signposted.

Captain John's Island Hoppers HELICOPTER TOURS
(☑974-1285; www.jamaicahelicopterservices .com; tours for up to 4 people US$440-1280) Specializes in memorable aerial tours of Jamaica. Choose from 'James Bond's Jamaica,' 'Memories of Jamaica,' or the all-encompassing 'Jamaica Showcase.'

Wilderness Tours QUAD-BIKE TOURS
(☑382-4029; www.wildernessatvtours.com; Reynolds Pier, Main St; tours per person J$4994-6772;⊙9am & 1pm Mon-Sat) Two all-terrain-vehicle tours into the mountains and through the forest, the more expensive one including Dunn's River Falls.

Dolphin Cove PLANTATION TOURS
(☑974-5335; www.dolphincovejamaica.com) Horseback, camelback and open-air jitney tours of Prospect Plantation.

★ Festivals & Events

Fat Tyre Festival MOUNTAIN BIKING
(⊙Feb) This rip-roaring mountain-bike race and festival is the nation's premier mountain-biking festival, and is definitely not for the weak of heart (or calves). See www .smorba.com for more information.

Follow Di Arrow DANCEHALL
(⊙Feb) Annual dancehall music event featuring big local artists, held at James Bond Beach on the last weekend in February.

Beach J'ouvert SOCA
(⊙Apr) Popular soca music night held at James Bond Beach during the carnival season, with all-night revelry and paint throwing.

Bacchanal Jamaica CARNIVAL
(www.bacchanaljamaica.com; ⊙Easter) Part of the nationwide carnival season, celebrated in a big way in Ocho Rios, this riotous all-night party featuring soca music is held at Chukka Cove.

Ocho Rios Jazz Festival JAZZ
(⊙Jun) This eight-day event (which also goes off in Kingston, Port Antonio, Montego Bay, Negril and the south coast) draws some of the biggest names in jazz and stages concerts under the stars. Check www.ochoriosjazz.com for further details.

St Mary Mi Come From DANCEHALL
(⊙first Sat in Aug) Dancehall event headlined by Cappleton and featuring other popular dancehall artists, held at James Bond Beach.

Harmony Hall Anniversary Crafts Fair CRAFTS
(⊙late Nov) Showcases local art.

🛏 Sleeping

Villas of varying ranges of opulence are represented by **Sun Villas** (in the USA ☑888-625-6007; www.sunvillas.com), **Jamaican Association of Villas & Apartments** (JAVA; ☑in the USA 800-845-5276; www.villasinjamaica.com) and **Royal Plantation** (☑in the USA 877-845-5275, in the UK 800-022-3773; www.uniquevillasofjamai ca.com). See p285 for more information on renting villas.

TOP CHOICE **Cottage at Te Moana** COTTAGES **$$**
(☑974-2870; www.harmonyhall.com; cottages US$130-150; P✷) With its small clifftop garden overhanging a reef, this exquisite reclusive property with two delightful cottages offers a wonderful alternative to Ochi's resorts. You imagine that this is the kind of setting where great novels are crafted. At the Seaside Cottage, the bedroom is reached via an external staircase and has

a king-size bed and ceiling fan, and a magnificent artist's aesthetic. The Garden Cottage is decorated in light hues and features comfortable wicker furniture. Both have fully equipped kitchens, separate living areas, plus verandas with hammock. Steps lead down to a coral cove good for snorkeling, and kayaks are available. Three-night stay minimum.

TOP CHOICE Jamaica Inn
GUEST HOUSE $$$

(974-2514; www.jamaicainn.com; ste US$479-746, cottages US$1164-1570; P🐕❄🛜🏊) Winston Churchill's favorite hotel, this exquisite family-run 'inn', tucked in a private cove, exudes patrician refinement. The suites are a soothing combination of whites and Wedgwood blues, with mahogany beds, Edwardian furnishings and colonial-theme prints. The West Wing veranda suites hang over the sea (East Wing rooms nudge up to the pristine, white-sand beach). There's a library and a bar with a warm clubby feel and the 4-Hand Bliss at the on-site KiYara Spa is just that. Dining requires a jacket and tie for men. Water sports include scuba diving, snorkeling and fishing. Breakfast, half- and full-board available on request.

Sandals Royal Plantation
RESORT $$$

(in the USA 800-022-3030; www.royalplantation.com; ste US$750-1390; P🐕❄🛜🏊) From the neoclassical lobby decked in Victorian furnishings to the C Bar (Jamaica's only caviar-and-champagne bar) to the orchids that grace the garden areas to the pillow menu for your room, the Royal Plantation goes the extra mile. All rooms face the sea and feature marble bathrooms, and there are three gourmet restaurants, notably Le Papillon, an intimate French *boîte* with a dress code. An array of water sports is on offer and full-board is available.

Hibiscus Lodge
HOTEL $$

(974-2676; www.hibiscusjamaica.com; 83 Main St; r US$140-152; P🐕❄@🏊) A stairway descends alongside a cliff overhang, past flowering gardens overflowing with bougainvillea, and down to a private sunning deck, perfect for a spontaneous jump in the sea. A small gallery of contemporary Jamaican art complements the main building nicely. All rooms are modestly furnished; the deluxe ones are worth the extra expense for their large private balconies. There's also a breezy bar and the Almond Tree, a fine restaurant.

Sans Souci Resort & Spa
RESORT $$$

(994-1206; www.couples.com; d US$735-745, ste US$756-1341, cottages US$1391; P🐕❄@🏊) On the A3, east of town, this sophisticated resort has a sublime setting in a secluded cove. The top-end suites have Jacuzzis and one of the two beaches is for nude bathing. Rates include gourmet dining, trips to Ochi's attractions, and all the golf you can play. Charlie's Spa is set on mineral springs rumored to have rejuvenating powers. The huge range of water sports on offer includes scuba lessons.

Silver Seas
HOTEL $$

(974-2755; www.silverseashotel.com; 66 James Ave; r US$135; P🐕🏊🛶) Ocho Rios' first-ever luxury resort is somewhat worn and creaky, but wonderfully atmospheric and particularly welcoming to families. Inside the colonial-style building with a cavernous entrance hall with creaky wooden floors, each well-kept room has a large, private patio with a stellar ocean view. Dining takes place on the delightful waterfront patio and there's good snorkeling to be had off the jetty.

Little Shaw Park Guest House
GUEST HOUSE $

(974-2177; www.littleshawparkguesthouse.com; 21 Shaw Park Rd; r J$3809-4656, apt J$5502, ste J$6349; P🐕🛜) This restful retreat, set among beautifully tended lawns and a garden overflowing with bougainvillea, is justifiably popular with the young, fabulous and broke. The furniture may be somewhat worn, the cheaper rooms are spacious but rather dark, but the well-lit studio apartments with kitchens are great value for money. While away the day in the gazebo or one of the hammocks. Meals available on request.

Mahoe Villa & Guesthouse
GUEST HOUSE $

(974-6613; 11 Shaw Park Rd; r with shared bathroom J$2116-2963, with private bathroom J$3809, with spa bathroom J$7195; P) One of the few decent budget digs in town, this large guest house, run by the effusive Michael and replete with original works of art, is great value for money. The spic-and-span, fan-cooled rooms share a communal kitchen and a chilled vibe prevails; you'll usually find a fellow traveler or two lazing in the hammocks strung up in the yard.

Crane Ridge
RESORT $$

(974-8050; www.craneridge.net; 17 DaCosta Dr; ste US$130, deluxe 1-/2-bedroom ste US$190/270; P❄🛜🏊) Offering a convenient hilltop location, this modern resort, popular with Kingstonian families, features spacious, fully equipped suites, some with loft bedrooms. The airy restaurant serves Jamaican dishes with an emphasis on fresh fruit. If you miss the weekly poolside BBQ and mento band performance, you're still treated to pounding beats at the swim-up bar during the day. There's a complimentary shuttle service to the beach.

Rooms RESORT **$**
(☎974-2008; www.roomsresorts.com; Main St; r incl breakfast US$87-105, apt US$123; [P][✳][@][✳][✷]) Right in the center of Turtle Beach, this affordable, family-friendly resort has all the trappings of an all-inclusive without being one. Everything (apart from continental breakfast) – from meals to internet access to a full range of water sports – costs extra, but the location is superb, the beachfront pool and gym are bonuses and the spacious, tiled rooms boast sea or pool views.

Fisherman's Point APARTMENTS **$$$**
(☎974-2837, 888-790-5274; www.fishermanspoint. net; 1-/2-bedroom apt US$243/480; [P][✳][✺][✷]) This attractive low-rise condo, close to the beach and overlooking the cruise-ship pier, is the more appealing of the self-catering options. All apartments are fully equipped with kitchenettes and cable TV, and there's an excellent restaurant on the premises. Not a Christmas option, since the apartments get taken over by their owners.

Ocean Sands Resort GUEST HOUSE **$**
(☎974-2605; 14 James Ave; s/d incl breakfast J$5079/6772; [✳][✷]) This quiet, attractive property offers an oceanfront setting and its own pocket-size beach, with coral, at your doorstep. A tiny restaurant sits at the end of a wooden wharf. The spacious, tiled rooms have French doors that open onto private balconies.

Carleen's Villa GUEST HOUSE **$**
(☎974-5431; 85A Main St; r J$3809; [P]) Serviceable budget option, popular with European backpackers. Rooms are rather worn but fan-cooled and have cable TV. The seafront communal terrace is a good jump-off point for snorkeling.

Executive Inn B&B **$**
(☎795-4070; 60 Main St; r US$110; [P][✳]) The 20 air-conditioned rooms may have little character but the very central location makes this guest house a convenient stopover.

✖ Eating

Ocho Rios has a good range of international cuisine and several economical Jamaican restaurants; many places are open late. After dark, you'll find many smoking oil-drum barbecues along the roadside, particularly in the area surrounding the clock tower.

TOP CHOICE **Toscanini** ITALIAN **$$$**
(☎975-4785; Harmony Hall; meals J$3300-4600; ⊙lunch & dinner Tue-Sun; ✎) One of the finest restaurants on the island, this roadside spot is run by two gracious Italians who use the freshest local ingredients in recipes from the motherland. The proprietress greets all the guests and explains the use of local herbs in the cooking. The daily menu ranges widely, encompassing such appetizers as prosciutto with papaya or marinated marlin and mains like garlic lobster pasta, or shrimp sautéed with garlic and Appleton rum. Leave room for sumptuous desserts such as strawberry tart or the profiteroles. Treat yourself!

TOP CHOICE **Scotchies Too** JERK **$**
(☎794-9457; Jack's Hall Fair Ground; meals J$500-700; ⊙lunch & dinner) This consistently excellent roadside offshoot of the famous jerk center in Montego Bay lies adjacent to an Epping Gas station just west of Dunn's River Falls. Its pork and chicken, traditionally smoked over pimento wood, water the mouths of locals and visitors alike; the jerk sausage is good, but doesn't match the pork and chicken in taste. Accompaniments include roast breadfruit, *festival* (sweet fried cornbread) and yam.

Passage to India INDIAN **$$$**
(☎795-3182; Soni's Plaza, 50 Main St; meals J$1800-3200; ⊙lunch & dinner Tue-Sun, lunch Mon; ✎) On the rooftop of a duty-free shopping center, Passage to India offers respite from the crowds below in addition to very good northern Indian fare. The naan is crisp, the lassis flavorful, the curries sharp, and the menu divided into extensive chicken, mutton, seafood and vegetarian sections. Tandoori options are also on offer. Try the 'vegetable bullets' with the tangy garlic and coriander dip (J$677) and the curried conch (J$1524). The 'recession lunch' thali combos, available Monday to Saturday, are particularly good value and come with rice and naan: choose from tandoori chicken, Goan fish curry or mattar paneer (J$847 to J$1100).

Ocho Rios Jerk Centre
JERK $

(☎974-2549; 16 DaCosta Dr; meals J$500-1000; ☺lunch & dinner) Its existing popularity further boosted by it being the official Knutsford Express stop, the liveliest jerk joint in town serves excellent jerk pork (J$325), chicken (J$295) and conch (J$795), as well as BBQ ribs. There are daily specials, the best being curry goat (J$450) and goat head soup (J$100). Grab a Red Stripe and watch sports on the big-screen TV while you're waiting for your jerk. 'Spicy Fridays' feature weekly DJ sets (free entry) and the last Friday of the month is Retro/Soca Nite.

Lion's Den
JAMAICAN $

(A3; meals J$650-1000; ☺breakfast, lunch & dinner) West of town between Dolphin Cove and Dunn's River Falls, this place looks like a tourist trap but it is worth a stop for the excellent, well-priced Jamaican fare and unique, artistic decor. The dining room resembles a Rastafarian chapel with hand-carved columns and wicker 'tree limbs' reaching to the ceiling. The menu boasts local specialties such as curry goat, stew pork and dumpling and fried chicken.

Evita's
ITALIAN $$

(☎974-2333; Eden Bower Rd; meals J$1400-2500; ☺lunch & dinner; ✍) This slightly overpriced charmer sits high above Ochi in a romantically decorated 1860s house – an airy setting with exquisite views. The Italian-Jamaican menu includes jerk spaghetti, the ackee and callaloo 'Lasagna Rastafari' and the delectable, fish- and seafood-filled 'Lasagna Capitano'. Lighter dishes include a selection of salads; half-portions of the pasta dishes are also available. If you're lucky the gregarious proprietor, Eva, will stop by your table and give your shoulder a squeeze.

Whalers
SEAFOOD $

(Fishermen's Beach; meals J$800-1000; ☺breakfast, lunch & dinner) Rising up above the wooden shacks on tiny Fishermen's Beach, adjacent to Island Village and awaft with ganja smoke, this cheerful eatery with an upstairs terrace is the best place in town for fresh fish dishes. Besides the fish that comes in steamed, brown stew or escoveitch form, there is delicious conch soup (lunchtimes only) and breakfast specials like ackee and saltfish.

Centre Spot
JAMAICAN $

(75E Main St; meals J$400-500; ☺breakfast & lunch) This unassuming hole-in-the-wall place whips up local favorites such as cur-ried goat; specials include the ever-popular cow head, tripe and beans and cow foot. For breakfast, if you're hungry consider the porridge – a cup of the cornmeal or peanut variety really sticks to your ribs – or the ackee and saltfish.

Almond Tree Restaurant
INTERNATIONAL $$

(☎974-2813; Hibiscus Lodge, 83 Main St; meals J$1000-2800; ☺breakfast, lunch & dinner) Providing a splendid perch for a sunset dinner, this clifftop spot features a dining pavilion that steps down the cliffside. Candlelit dinners are served alfresco. The menu ranges from seafood and continental fare, such as steaks and cheeseburgers, to steadfast Jamaican dishes.

Bibibips Bar & Grill
INTERNATIONAL $$

(93 Main St; meals J$1000-3000; ☺lunch & dinner) This popular, touristy oceanfront bar and restaurant with a porch overlooking Mahogany Beach serves up a range of tasty seafood, burgers, jerk and barbecue dishes that don't quite live up to their pricing. Wash it down with a cocktail from the extensive list.

World of Fish
SEAFOOD $

(3 James Ave; meals J$850; ☺lunch & dinner Mon-Sat) Popular with locals, this casual and economical eatery has been serving fried fish, stew fish and steamed fish for years. Get it with bammy (cassava flatbread), rice and peas or *festival*.

Healthy Way
VEGETARIAN $

(Ocean Village Plaza; meals J$650; ☺breakfast & lunch Mon-Sat; ✍) A vegetarian kitchen and health-food store selling herbs, teas, I-tal juices and supplements, plus hearty chow such as a delicious tofu cheeseburger, stew peas and large fruit plates to go.

Mama Marley's
INTERNATIONAL $$

(50 Main St; meals J$1690-2800; ☺lunch & dinner) Popular Bob Marley–themed restaurant, bar and gift shop, formerly run by Marley's mother, Cedella, offering a somewhat overpriced non-I-tal menu of pasta, seafood, burgers and fish dishes.

Blue Mont
CAFE $

(Island Village; meals J$700; ☺breakfast, lunch & dinner) Pleasant coffee shop opposite Margaritaville, serving wraps, sandwiches and a range of Blue Mountain coffees, packs of which are also available for purchase.

Tropical Kitchen
BAKERY $

(Main St; ☺breakfast, lunch & dinner; ✍) Cakes, pastries and the best potato pudding on the north coast.

Juici Patties
JAMAICAN $

(1 Newlin St; ☺breakfast, lunch & dinner) The local branch of the best patty chain on the island, serving coco bread as well as cheese, beef, chicken, shrimp and lobster patties (J$80 to J$120).

Devon House I-Scream
ICE CREAM $

(Island Village; per scoop J$200) Serves some of the best ice cream on the island.

General Foods Supermarket
SUPERMARKET $

(Ocean Village Plaza) There are also smaller grocery stores scattered along Main St.

Produce market
MARKET $

(☺daily) You can buy fresh produce at the market on the south side of DaCosta Dr by the clock tower.

♟ Drinking

There's a healthy bar scene and a decent choice of nightspots, but in general Ochi after hours lacks the verve of Negril or the authenticity of Kingston. Nonetheless, it's not hard to find a good party atmosphere *somewhere* on any night of the week.

Many all-inclusive resorts sell night passes permitting full access to meals, drinks and entertainment.

TOP CHOICE Jimmy Buffett's Margaritaville
BAR

(Island Village; ☺9am-4am Mon, Wed & Sat, to 10pm Tue, Thu, Fri & Sat) This corporate franchise has turned getting drunk into big business. As with its counterparts in Montego Bay and Negril, the music is loud and the signature margaritas don't come cheap, but many tourists and locals find the orchestrated good-time vibe to be irresistible. Those hankering for trappings of Western civilization can order a 'Cheeseburger in Paradise', Caesar salads and pizzas to go with their margaritas. Admission is charged for special events. The Wet'n'Wild Pool Party (J$1692) on Wednesday nights is particularly debauched, with free drinks until 1am and half-price entry for guests in swimwear.

Ocean's 11 Watering Hole
BAR

(Fisherman's Point) With its prime spot on the cruise-ship pier, it's little surprise that it's exceedingly popular with cruise-ship passengers, who fill the barrel-shaped seats, knock back the Red Stripes (J$280) and potent cocktails and cheer each other on during Tuesday night karaoke. The upstairs space doubles as a small art gallery–coffee shop and serves excellent Blue Mountain coffee

(J$339), which you can also purchase by the pound.

H2O
BAR

(Shop 22, Coconut Grove Shopping Centre; ☺noon-4am) Run by reggae singer Tanya Stephens, this inviting resto-bar specializes in vegetarian and seafood dishes during the day, and fills up by night when locals and visitors alike stream in for the music events. Live band karaoke takes place on Friday nights, the H2O Flow event on Saturdays features appearances from local and international artists, while Sunday is the night to live out the glory days of reggae, ska and mento.

Baywatch Grill & Bar
BAR

(Fisherman's Point; ☺from 6pm Fri-Sun) Lively bar right by the cruise ship pier. Saturday nights offer two-for-one cocktail specials and free tequila shots for the ladies, presumably to encourage them to take part in the Wet T-Shirt Competition. Fridays feature live music at the After Work Jam, while Retro Music Sundays are just that.

John Crow's Tavern
SPORTS BAR

(10 Main St) The big TV above the bar screens the latest football games and the outdoor terrace is perfect for a beer, burger and a spot of people-watching.

★ Entertainment

On the A3 east of town, the **White River Reggae Park** infrequently hosts sound systems. **Priory Beach** has a regular Sunday sound system on the beach (7pm onwards). Also look for posters around town advertising live music or sound systems at **Reggae Beach**.

Amnesia
DANCEHALL

(70 Main St; ☺Wed-Sun) A classic Jamaican dancehall, this remains the happening scene. Theme nights include an oldies jam on Sunday, ladies' night on Thursday and an after-work party on Friday. This is all leading up to Saturday's dress-to-impress all-night dance marathon. Expect lots of sweat, a tightly packed dance floor and some of the raunchiest dancing you've ever seen. Admission J$350 to J$550.

Blitz
DANCEHALL

(60 Main St; admission J$500; ☺10pm-6am Tue & Fri) Though this is essentially an after-party for the Ocean 11's karaoke crowd on Tuesday nights, on Fridays be prepared to wine and grind your way through the batty-rider- and

puss-boot-clad local crowd at the weekly 'Thank God It's Friday' (admission free for women) dancehall event. Big names perform occasionally.

Nexus
NIGHTCLUB

(8 Main St; ☺9pm-4am Tue & Fri, 7-11pm Sun) Rooftop lounge that comes to life on cruise-ship days. Tuesday is Ladies' Night, Friday nights feature local DJs and the street reverberates with the pounding beats. Live bands on Sundays play a mix.

Roof Club
DANCEHALL

(7 James Ave; admission J$300) The gritty Roof sends earth-shattering music across the roofs of town; it's the place to get down and dirty with the latest dancehall moves. It can get rough.

Cove Theatre
CINEMA

(☎675-8886; Island Village) Try this cinema for the latest Hollywood releases.

🛍 Shopping

Sellers of CDs hawk mix CDs of the latest sounds on Turtle Beach and along Main St, where crafts vendors also sell their goods, though for the more exceptional souvenirs, you'll have to travel further out.

Olde Craft Market
CRAFTS

(Main St) A better (and less expensive) choice than rows and rows of identical crafts at Ocho Rios Craft Park and Dunn's River Craft Park, this market features quality ceramics and art, as well as the usual T-shirts with chirpy Jamaican slogans and Rasta tams with fake dreadlocks attached.

Harmony Hall
ART

(www.harmonyhall.com; ☺10am-5:30pm Tue-Sun) Art gallery featuring the best of local art, located 7km east of Ocho Rios. Renowned for its Christmas, Easter and mid-November craft fairs, and regular exhibitions.

Ocho Rios Craft Park
SOUVENIRS

(Main St) For all your tacky T-shirt, batik, wooden sculpture and crafts-made-of-coconut-shells needs. Some of the sellers also sell quality music-mix CDs.

Wassi Art
CRAFTS

Excellent pottery and ceramics; and you can watch it being made.

Reggae Yard
SOUVENIRS

(Island Village) Reggae wear in Rasta colors, Usain Bolt T-shirts, and a good selection of reggae music.

Vibes Music Shack
MUSIC STORE

(Ocean Village Plaza) Reggae and dancehall CDs, as well as some mento and calypso.

Scent of Incense & Things
SOUVENIRS

(79 Main St) Incense, scented oils and a variety of herbs.

Herba Kadabra
SOUVENIRS

(Island Village) Potions, spices and healing herbs.

ℹ Information

Dangers & Annoyances

Good humor and a firm 'no' should be enough to deal with the persistent taxi drivers, hustlers and would-be tour guides. Avoid the area immediately behind the produce market, south of the clock tower and the seedy, poorly lit James Ave, a hang-out strip of ill repute. Use caution at night anywhere.

Emergency

Police station (☎974-2533) Off DaCosta Dr, just east of the clock tower.

Internet Access

Computer Whizz (Shop 11, Island Plaza; ☺8:30am-7:30pm Mon-Sat; per 30min/1hr J$150/250) Has 10 computers as well as wi-fi access for those with own laptops.

Jerkin'@Taj (☺9am-5pm Mon-Sat; per 15min/1hr J$170/680) Inside Taj Mahal shopping center.

Medical Services

Kulkarni Medical Clinic (☎974-3357; 16 Rennie Rd) Private practice, between RBTT and Jamaica National Bank, used by upmarket hotels in the area.

Pinegrove Pharmacy (☎974-5586; Shop 5, Pinegrove Plaza; ☺9am-8pm Mon-Sat, 10am-3pm Sun)

St Ann's Bay Hospital (Seville Rd; ☎972-2272) The nearest hospital.

Money

There are numerous banks along Main St, including Scotiabank. All have foreign-exchange facilities and ATMs.

Post

FedEx (17 Main St; ☺9am-5pm Mon-Sat)

Post office (Main St; ☺8am-5pm Mon-Sat) Opposite the Ocho Rios Craft Park.

Telephone

There are payphones aplenty downtown, though it may be more convenient to pick up an inexpensive SIM card for your cell phone.

Call Direct Centre (74 Main St) Economical calls overseas.

Digicell (70 Main St) East of the clock tower. Sells SIM cards, cell phones and phone cards.

Tourist Office

Tourist information (☎974-7705; Shop 3, Ocean Village, Main St; ☺9am-5pm Mon-Thu, to 4pm Fri) Represents the Jamaica Tourist Board. Staff can help you suss out Ochi's transportation, lodging and attractions options. Also operates an information booth on Main St, but it's open only when cruise ships are in port.

❶ Getting There & Away

Air

At the time of writing, the former Boscobel Airport, about 16km east of town, had just reopened as the **Ian Fleming International Airport** (☎975-3101), expanded primarily to accommodate private jets, as well as chartered flights (see p291). **Jamaica Air Shuttle** (☎906-9026/30; www.jamaicaairshuttle.com) offers several weekly flights to Kingston.

Public Transportation

Buses, minibuses and route taxis arrive at and depart Ocho Rios at the **transportation center** (Evelyn Rd). During daylight hours there are frequent departures (fewer on Sundays) for Kingston and destinations along the north coast. There is no set schedule: they depart when full. If heading to Port Antonio by bus, you will have to change buses at Port Maria (J$140) and possibly Annotto Bay. Sample destinations:
Discovery Bay J$150, 35 minutes
Kingston J$320, two hours
Montego Bay J$330, two hours
Port Maria J$140, 50 minutes
Runaway Bay J$140, 30 minutes
St Ann's Bay J$80, 15 minutes

Knutsford Express (www.knutsfordexpress.com) has scheduled departures to Kingston and Montego Bay from its office in the car park of the Ocho Rios Jerk Centre. Arrive half an hour prior to departure to register your ticket. Departures:
Kingston (J$1200, two hours) 6:20am, 10:25am, 2:30pm and 6:30pm Monday to Friday; 7:20am and 5:55pm Saturday; 9:45am and 6pm Sunday.
Montego Bay (J$1200, two hours) 7:45am, 11:20am, 3:45pm and 6:40pm Monday to Friday; 7:45am, 11:20am and 6pm Saturday; 10am and 6pm Sunday.

Taxi

JUTA (☎974-2292) is the main taxi agency catering to tourists. A licensed taxi will cost about US$110 for Montego Bay, and about US$100 for Kingston (US$110 to the international airport at Kingston).

❶ Getting Around

To/from the Airport

There is no shuttle service from the airport to downtown. Local buses (J$100), and minibuses and route taxis (J$150) pass by. A tourist taxi will cost about J$2116.

Car & Motorcycle

Shopping malls along Main St have car parks, though not secure ones. Most hotels offer parking; all upmarket hotels offer secure parking. Main St during rush hour is one long traffic jam.
Some car-rental outlets:
Bargain Rent-a-Car (☎974-8047; Shop 1A Pineapple Place Shopping Centre, Main St).
Budget (☎974-1288; 15 Milford Rd)

Public Transportation

Minibuses and route taxis ply Main St and the coast road (J$80 for short hauls; J$150 to Boscobel or Mammee Bay).

Taxi

Chartered taxis are in great abundance along Main St. Negotiate the fare before setting off, as the drivers will quote any figure that comes to mind. If you want the driver to wait for you, do not hand over the full fare in advance.

EAST OF OCHO RIOS

While the signal of **IRIE FM** (Hwy A3) carries all over the island, the limits of Ocho Rios are immediately apparent once you pass the radio station's studios at the town's eastern edge. The seaside resorts quickly give way to isolated villas and fishing villages like Port Maria as the coastal road winds its way east along cliffs and bluffs. The sense of leaving tourist Jamaica behind is enhanced by the drop-off in road quality.

Drawn by the coastal beauty and unspoiled character, two of Jamaica's most famous visitors, author Noël Coward and James Bond creator Ian Fleming, made their homes in the area. While Coward settled in Firefly, with its spectacular view down on the coastline, Fleming found refuge at Goldeneye, now one of the island's most elegant hotels.

Reggae Beach to Boscobel Beach

East of Ocho Rios, habitations begin thinning out along the A3. Several beaches lie hidden below the cliffs; notable among them is Tower Isle, 9km east of Ocho Rios, with its

OCHO RIOS & NORTH COAST REGGAE BEACH TO BOSCOBEL BEACH

cluster of resorts. The Rio Nuevo meets the ocean about 1km west of Tower Isle.

Sights & Activities

TOP CHOICE Prospect Plantation PLANTATION

(☎994-1058; www.prospectplantationtours.com; tours J$2963-5418; ☺Mon-Sat) If you've been wondering why St Ann is called 'the garden parish,' you'll find your answer at this beautiful old hilltop great house and 405-hectare property, less working plantation and more tourist attraction, 5km east of town. On a pleasant, educational tour you'll travel by tractor-powered jitney (J$2963) through scenic grounds among banana, cassava, cocoa, coconut, coffee, pineapple and pimento. **Dolphin Cove** (p123) offers tour combos including either a horseback (J$5418) or camelback ride (J$5418), an ostrich feeding session and a visit to Dunn's River Falls.

Harmony Hall ART GALLERY

(☎974-2870; www.harmonyhall.com; ☺10am-5:30pm Tue-Sun) A beautiful great house by the A3 about 6km east of town, Harmony Hall dates to 1886 when it was a Methodist manse that adjoined a pimento estate. The restored structure is made of cut stone, with a wooden upper story trimmed with gingerbread fretwork and a green shingled roof with a spire. Reborn as an arts-and-crafts showcase, it holds shows in the Front Gallery throughout the year; an exhibition season runs mid-November to Easter. The Back Gallery features fine arts and crafts by local artists such as Albert Artwell and Cebert Christie. An acclaimed restaurant on the ground floor serves outstanding Mediterranean fare.

Reggae Beach BEACH

(admission J$847; ☺9am-5pm) Located east of Harmony Hall on the A3, this clean yellow-sand beach is hustler-free and popular with tourists only, due to the high admission rate. Kayaks are available for rent, and jerk chicken and fish are readily available. Raucous sound-system parties are held here now and then.

Rio Nuevo Battle Site HISTORICAL SITE

(admission J$424; ☺10am-5pm Mon-Fri, 10am-2pm Sat & Sun) On the bluff west of the Rio Nuevo river mouth is this little-visited site where, in 1658, the English forces fought their decisive battle against the Spanish, sending them fleeing to Cuba. A plaque here records the events and there's a small exhibition on the area's historical heritage.

Boscobel Beach BEACH

This beach, 6km east of Rio Nuevo, is a hamlet dominated by Boscobel Beach Spa Resort & Golf Club, a resort especially geared towards families with young children. The Ian Fleming International Airport is located nearby.

Jamaica Beach BEACH

Between Tower Isle and Rio Nuevo, it is renowned for its dive sites offshore. The offshore reef, known as the Rio Nuevo Wall, supports turtles, barracudas and other marine life.

Getting There & Away

Minibuses and route taxis traveling between Ocho Rios and Oracabessa serve Rio Nuevo and Tower Isle (J$100).

Oracabessa

POP 10,300

Taking its name from the Spanish *oro cabeza* (golden head) Oracabessa, 21km east of Ocho Rios, is a small one-street, one-story village with a vague aura of a Wild West town. The street itself is lined with Caribbean vernacular architecture, its wooden houses trimmed with fretwork. This was a major port for shipping bananas in the 19th century. While the boom era has passed, the town itself is far from derelict.

Below Oracabessa is the marina (formerly a banana-loading port), in the lee of a tombolo on whose western flank pirogues and fishing boats bob at anchor.

Sights

James Bond Beach BEACH

(adult/child J$423/254; ☺9am-6pm Tue-Sun) The attractive strip of white sand hosts large-scale annual music events, such as **Follow Di Arrow**, **Beach J'Ouvert** and **Fully Loaded** (watch out for event posters in Ocho Rios). During the week it's pretty quiet but on weekends, in particular, visitors flock to **Stingray City** (www.stingraycity jamaica.com; adult/child J$4656/2116) to snorkel and swim with the resident stingrays or to take part in jet-ski safaris (J$5502) and glass-bottom boat rides (J$2963) along the coast. A small bar and restaurant provides refreshment.

Adjacent to the Bond beach is **Fisherman's Beach**, a rootsy alternative where one can enjoy simple I-tal and seafood fare and the occasional sound-system party.

Sun Valley Plantation PLANTATION
(☑995-3075, 446-2026; tour incl snack J$1016; ☺9am-2pm) This working plantation and botanical farm is at Crescent on the B13, some 5km south of Oracabessa. Owners Lorna and Nolly Binns offer enjoyable garden tours in a plantation setting, which teach visitors about banana and sugar-cane – two staple crops that have played an important part in the development of the area. You can opt to visit the groves of coconuts – the current main crop – and other tropical fruits and medicinal herbs.

🛏 Sleeping & Eating

TOP CHOICE **Goldeneye** HOTEL **$$$**
(☑946-0958; www.goldeneye.com; ste US$832, 1/2/3-bedroom cottage US$1120/1520/2280, villa US$6800; ⓟ❄☎📶☑) If this looks like the type of place James Bond might have retired to, it's possibly because his creator Ian Fleming used to live here. Jamaica's most exclusive property features eight villas, including Fleming's abode (spectacular decor, highlighted by Balinese fabrics and a remarkable outdoor bath), sprinkled across expansive grounds on a quaint cove. Additional waterfront cottages, built of wood and stone and painted in autumnal colors, have ceiling fans, a kitchen, a TV room and pampering yet discreet stewards. The two restaurants serve gourmet meals and there's a communal entertainment room where 007 movies are shown, but the coup de grâce is the hotel's secluded, private island with its own beach and water sports.

Located on the A3 immediately east of Oracabessa.

Tamarind Great House GUEST HOUSE **$**
(☑995-3252; Crescent Estate; d J$5502-7195; ⓟ☎) Nestled atop a hill 6km south of Oracabessa, this 'plantation guest house' is run by delightful English hosts Gillian and Barry Chambers. The setting is sublime, with lush valleys and mountains all around, and the house boasts gleaming wood floors cut from a single tree and offbeat antiques. The large bedrooms with four-poster beds open to a vast veranda. The excellent restaurant serves stick-to-your-ribs breakfasts (J$1016) and full-course dinners (J$2963). From the minibus and taxi stand at Oracabessa, take Jack's River Rd. The rough 6km drive from the main road is worth it for the gourmet food alone. Keep a keen eye out for the directional signs along the way.

Nix-Nax GUEST HOUSE **$**
(☑975-3364; dm/r J$1270/2540) Northeast of the town center at the school crossing, this inimitable hostelry offers cheerful dorms, rooms, and communal kitchens. On the site is a Montessori-style preschool, and a holistic healing center. Your host, Domenica, a Harlem transplant who has run the guest house for more than 20 years, prides herself on flexible arrangements for travelers, saying that it's a 'good place for the broke and busted.'

Nix Nax CAFE **$**
(Main St, opposite Nix Nax guesthouse; meals J$500; ☺breakfast & lunch; ☑) Cafe serving Blue Mountain coffee and a selection of vegetarian sandwiches.

Tropical Hut BAR **$**
(Racecourse; ☺lunch & dinner) Popular local watering hole serving delicious Jamaican dishes.

FLEMING...IAN FLEMING

Ian Fleming, inventor of legendary superspy James Bond, first came to Jamaica in 1942 while serving with British Naval Intelligence. In 1946 he bought a house on the shore at Oracabessa and named it 'Goldeneye,' and he wintered here every year until his death in 1964. It was here that Fleming conceived his secret agent 007, the creation of whom the author attributes to living in Jamaica.

'Would these books have been born if I had not been living in the gorgeous vacuum of a Jamaican holiday? I doubt it,' he wrote in *Ian Fleming Introduces Jamaica*. All 14 of Fleming's James Bond novels were written here, and five were set in Jamaica.

In the same book, he related, 'I was looking for a name for my hero – nothing like Peregrine Carruthers or Standfast Maltravers – and I found it, on the cover of one of my Jamaican bibles, *Birds of the West Indies* by James Bond, an ornithological classic.'

The house is now part of Goldeneye hotel and can be rented.

❶ Information

Oracabessa Medical Centre (☑975-3304; Vermont Ave; ☉8am-2:30pm Mon & Tue, 7am-noon Wed-Sat) By the Esso gas station at the east end of town.

Scotiabank (Main St) Bank with ATM.

❶ Getting There & Away

Minibuses and route taxis pass through, en route between Ocho Rios and Port Antonio, and between Ocho Rios and Kingston (J$140).

Galina Point & Little Bay

Five kilometers east of Oracabessa, the A3 winds around the promontory of Galina Point. A 12m-high concrete lighthouse marks the headland. South of Galina you'll pass Noël Coward's first house, **Blue Harbour**, squatting atop 'the double bend,' where the road and shoreline take a 90-degree turn and open to a view of Cabarita Island. The road drops steeply from Blue Harbour to Kokomo Beach in Little Bay.

The beach is unappealing, but the bay and around makes a more pleasant stop-over than Port Maria if you wish to visit Firefly.

◉ Sights

TOP CHOICE Firefly   HISTORICAL HOUSE

(admission J$847; ☉9am-5pm Mon-Thu & Sat) Set amid wide lawns high atop a hill 5km east of Oracabessa and 5km west of Port Maria, Firefly was the home of Sir Noël Coward, the English playwright, songwriter, actor and wit (see the boxed text), who was preceded at this site by the notorious pirate Sir Henry Morgan. When he died in 1973, Coward left the estate to his partner Graham Payn, who donated it to the nation.

Your guide will lead you to Coward's art studio, where he was schooled in oil painting by Winston Churchill. The studio displays Coward's original paintings and photographs of himself and a coterie of famous friends. The drawing room, with the table still laid, was used to entertain such guests as the Queen Mother, Sophia Loren and Audrey Hepburn. The upper lounge features a glassless window that offers one of the most stunning coastal vistas in all Jamaica. The view takes in Port Maria Bay

NOËL COWARD'S PEENY-WALLY

The multitalented Sir Noël Coward first visited Jamaica in 1944 on a two-week holiday. He found peace of mind here and dubbed his dream island 'Dr Jamaica.' Four years later he rented Ian Fleming's estate, Goldeneye, at Oracabessa, while he hunted for a site to build his own home. He found an incredible view over Little Bay near Galina, 6km east of Oracabessa.

In 1948 Coward bought the 3-hectare estate and set to work building Coward's Folly, a three-story villa with two guest cottages, and a swimming pool at the sea's edge. He named his home Blue Harbour and invited his many notable friends, a virtual 'Who's Who' of the rich and famous. The swarm of visitors, however, eventually drove Coward to find another retreat.

While painting with his lover Graham Payn at a place called Lookout (so-named because the pirate Henry Morgan had a stone hut built atop the hill to keep an eye out for Spanish galleons), Coward was struck by the impressive solitude and incredible view. The duo lingered until nightfall, when fireflies ('peeny-wallies' in the Jamaican dialect) appeared. Within two weeks Coward had bought the land, and eight years later he had a house built. He named it Firefly.

Coward lived a remarkably modest lifestyle in Jamaica; he set up the now-defunct Designs for Living shop in Port Maria, the profits from which went to train local children in arts and crafts. Coward himself recorded his love of the island and islanders on canvas in bright, splashy colors.

Coward had spent 30 years in Jamaica when he suffered a heart attack at the age of 73, and was buried on the lawns of Firefly beneath a marble slab. Lines from his last poem, inscribed on one of Firefly's walls, are a suitable epitaph: 'When I have fears, as Keats had fears, Of the moment I'll cease to be/I console myself with vanished years, Remembered laughter, remembered tears/And the peace of the changing sea.'

and the coastline further west. Contrary to popular opinion, Coward didn't write his famous song, 'A Room with a View' here (it was written in Hawaii in 1928).

Coward lies buried beneath a plain white marble slab on the wide lawns where he entertained many illustrious stars of stage and screen; a pensive statue of the man graces the lawn.

🛏 Sleeping & Eating

TOP CHOICE **Bolt House**   BOUTIQUE HOTEL $$$
(☏994-0303; www.bolthousejamaica.com; villa US$2200; ⓟ❄🌐⛱) This secluded cliffside villa, built by Blanche Blackwood, mother of Chris Blackwood, owner of Island Records, is the ultimate in luxury. Offering the same spectacular views as nearby Goldeneye, it has an infinity pool, a yoga deck and private hiking trails on its 18 hectares of land. The five rooms (four nights minimum stay) are splendidly decorated with contemporary art, and guests have access to the exclusive beach at Goldeneye, after which they can relax at the separate Spanish Elm cottage and its waterside terrace. Delectable fusion cuisine (US$60/day) is served in the airy dining room and it's possible to dine at Goldeneye with 24 hours' notice.

Blue Harbour   HOTEL $
(☏725-0289, in USA 505-586-1244; www.blueharb.com; r per person US$70, full board US$120; ⓟ⛱) Once owned by Noël Coward and visited by Marlene Dietrich and Errol Flynn, this is a rather offbeat retreat with a laid-back atmosphere, consisting of three villas by a tiny beach and saltwater pool. Spacious rooms feature some original furniture from Coward's day. Blue Harbour comes fully staffed with cook and housekeeper; meals are served on a wide veranda with bay views and full board is worth it for the delicious home-cooked Jamaican specials.

Galina Breeze   HOTEL $$
(☏994-0573; www.galinabreeze.com; r US$85-95, ste US$120; ⓟ❄🌐) This small hotel with superb views of the coast has just 14 light, spacious rooms, all equipped with firm king-size beds and cable TV. The hotel sponsors two local primary schools and guests interested in the community outreach program are welcome to try their hand at teaching. More conventional tours are also organized.

Little Bay Inn   HOTEL $
(☏994-2721, 373-5871; r J$2540-2963; ⓟ) On the main road, just at the turnoff for Firefly, this modest hotel offers 10 simple, fan-cooled rooms with double beds and private bathroom; the pricier rooms have TVs. There's a small restaurant and jerk center and the downstairs disco may keep you awake.

ℹ Getting There & Away

Minibuses and route taxis pass through, en route between Ocho Rios and Port Antonio, and between Ocho Rios and Kingston.

Port Maria

POP 8000

Gazing down from the lawn at Firefly, you might think Port Maria is a quaint fishing village nestled around a deep turquoise and aquamarine bay with mountains rising behind, but up close it's largely unappealing.

St Mary's Parish Church, at the extreme west end of town, was built in 1861 in quintessential English style. Facing it is the **old courthouse**, destroyed in 1988 by fire but since partially restored and today housing a **Civic Centre**. A **monument** in front commemorates Tacky, a runaway slave who led the local slave rebellion in 1760 which was brutally suppressed by the British forces with the aid of Maroons, with 50 of the captured rebels hung in irons or burned alive as a deterrent to others.

For a good meal, head to **Almond Tree Club & Restaurant** (56 Warners St; meals J$400-550; ⏰breakfast, lunch & dinner), offering curry goat, fried chicken, chop suey and, for breakfast, a selection of porridges. **Juici Patties** (Stennet St; patties J$80-110), on the southeast side of the town square, sells reliable patties.

You can catch buses or minibuses to Port Maria from Ocho Rios (J$160, 40 minutes) and Kingston (J$220, 2½ hours).

Brimmer Hall

This 809-hectare working **plantation** (☏994-2309; 1hr tour J$2540; ⏰9am-4pm Mon-Fri), near Bailey's Vale, 10km southwest of Port Maria, grows bananas, coconuts, sugarcane, pineapple and citrus for export. It's centered on a wooden great house dating back to the 1700s, with an impressive interior furnished with oriental rugs and antique furniture, and even an original suit of armor. The one-hour plantation tours are in a canopied jitney. It is signed from the A3.

SOUTH OF OCHO RIOS

The A3 winds through sweeping pastoral country on its way south. At Moneague, the road meets up with the A1 from St Ann's Bay, continues over Mt Diablo and drops dramatically to Kingston.

Fern Gully

Passing through this lush **gorge** is one of the prime attractions of Ocho Rios. Milford Rd (the A3) zigzags uphill through the 5km canyon of an old watercourse that was planted with hundreds of different fern species around 1880. Today the trees form a canopy overhead, filtering subaqueous light, while crafts vendors ply their wares at the side of the road.

Moneague

This small crossroads town, at the junction of the A3 and the A1, 19km south of Ochi, was favored during the 19th century as a hill resort, and before that as a staging post on the journey between Spanish Town and the north coast. The Moneague Training Camp of the Jamaica Defense Force is here, with two **Saracen armoured cars** at the gateway.

Faith's Pen

South of Moneague, the A1 climbs steadily to Faith's Pen, 27km south of Ocho Rios. Pull into the little side road parallel to the main road and choose your meal from the many shacks offering jerk pork and chicken, fried fish and fresh fruit juices. You'll be immediately surrounded by the competitive roadside cooks; insist on sampling the wares first. **Shack 2** is best for soursop juice (J$250 a bottle) while **shack 8** is great for jerk pork and accompaniments.

The road continues up the pine-forested slopes of **Mt Diablo** (839m). At 686m the A1 crests the mountain chain and begins its steep, winding descent to Ewarton and the lush Rosser Valley, beautiful when seen from these heights.

WEST OF OCHO RIOS

Mammee Bay

Formerly a favorite with Jamaican beachgoers, Mammee Bay – 5.5km west of Ocho Rios and 4km east of St Ann's Bay – has several little beaches, some hidden away, but is now firmly dominated by the monolithic Club Hotel Riu Ocho Rios. Much of the beachfront is a private residential estate, but access is offered to the public beaches.

At **Laughing Waters** – also called Roaring River – 1km east of Mammee Bay and 1km west of Dunn's River Falls, a river appears from rocks amid a shallow ravine about 3km from the sea and spills to a charming little **beach** (admission free). This is where Ursula Andress famously appeared as Honey Ryder, dripping with brine, in the James Bond movie *Dr No*. Look for the large fenced-in electrical power structure beside the A3. Follow the river to the beach. Public access to the falls is by foot, though sometimes access to the beach is blocked by guards stationed along the road.

At Old Fort Bay, on the east side of Mammee Bay, the secluded **Cannon Villas** (☎927-1852; www.cannonvillaja.com; 3-/4-bedroom villas US$396/451; P✳@) is a good choice for groups and families. The six spacious villas each come with a living and dining area, satellite TV, fully equipped kitchen and a patio with a barbecue pit. A housekeeper and cook is provided and the location – steps away from an attractive white-sand beach – can't be beat.

WALKERSWOOD FACTORY

As you climb from Fern Gully on the A3, you enter the village of Walkerswood. Its main claim to fame is the tongue-searing jerk sauce made by **Walkerswood Caribbean Foods** (☎917-2318; www.walkerswood.com), as well as marinades, pickles and barbecue sauce, now available all over the world. Walkerswood began as a local farmer's co-op dedicated to providing irrigation and jobs for the community. Today, close to 200 people work full time at the environmentally conscious plant.

At the time of writing, the factory was not running the popular tours that allow visitors to taste its products, though tours may restart in the near future.

COLUMBUS MAROONED

As any experienced island traveler will tell you, in Jamaica the best-laid plans can veer wildly astray. Such was the case with Christopher Columbus. In 1503, on his fourth voyage to the New World – and his second trip to Jamaica – the explorer's two remaining ships were pummeled by a storm. Leaking badly, the ships managed to make land on Jamaica's north-central coast near modern-day St Ann's Bay. With one of his worm-eaten ships nearly submerged and all the rigging gone, Columbus and his downtrodden crew dug in and tried to make friendly with the locals.

Fortunately they were able to come to agreeable terms with the Taínos living nearby in the village of Aguacadiba. And so began the short-lived honeymoon between the European interlopers and Jamaica's indigenous people.

Now that they could depend on all-inclusive service, Columbus turned to other matters. He sent Mendez off in a canoe to Hispaniola to fetch help – that's another story! – and sank dejectedly into a period of idleness. Predictably, his Taíno friends soon tired of their obligation to the moody explorer, who was derelict in paying his bills.

To frighten them back into submission, Columbus performed a disingenuous parlor trick by consulting his trusty almanac and 'predicting' that their vengeful God would express his consternation with a sign of anger in the sky. When night fell, a lunar eclipse caused the moon to have an eerie 'bloody' quality and the Taínos fell into a panic. The next morning room service resumed, and Columbus and his men survived for 12 more months until help arrived from Santo Domingo.

St Ann's Bay

POP 12,400

This small market town and parish capital, 11km west of Ocho Rios, rises up the hillside above the bay.

Christopher Columbus landed here in 1494 during his second voyage to the Americas and christened the bay Santa Gloria. During his fateful fourth and final voyage in 1503, he was forced to abandon his ships in the bay; Columbus and his crew were stranded for more than a year before finally being rescued.

In 1509 the Spaniards built the first Spanish settlement on the island about 700m west of St Ann's Bay, at Sevilla la Nueva. The site was abandoned within four decades and it was later developed as a sugar estate by a British planter. Other planters established sugar estates nearby, and the town grew and prospered as a bustling seaport with forts on opposite sides of the bay.

Marcus Garvey, founder of the Black Nationalist movement, was born here and is honored each August 17 with a parade.

◉ Sights

TOP CHOICE **Maima Seville Great House & Heritage Park**　　　HISTORICAL SITE

This historical park, less than 1km west of present-day St Ann's, marks the site of the first Spanish capital on the island – Sevilla la Nueva – and one of the first Spanish settlements in the New World.

When the English captured Jamaica from the Spanish, the land on which Sevilla la Nueva had been built was granted to Richard Hemming, an officer in Oliver Cromwell's army. Hemming's descendants developed the property as a sugar estate, dominated by the Seville Great House, built in 1745 by Hemming's grandson. Just outside are the Hemming family tombs.

The restored great house contains an engaging **museum** (☑972-2191; www.jnht.com; adult/child J$423/170; ◷9am-5pm) depicting the history of the site from Taíno times through the era of slavery and the colonial period, each room displaying numerous artifacts from a particular historical period.

Traces of the original Spanish buildings, including a church, a sugar mill and the castle-house of the first Spanish governor, are visible, accessed via a grassy track leading to the ocean from the A1. This was also the site of the Taíno village of Maima; the inhabitants were forced to work as serfs under the Spanish *encomienda* system, and quickly died out through a combination of disease, overwork and suicide.

The best way to explore the sprawling property is by joining a **Hooves** (☑972-0905; www.hoovesjamaica.com; half-day horseback tour incl refreshments J$5926) horseback tour that ends with a jaunt into the sea.

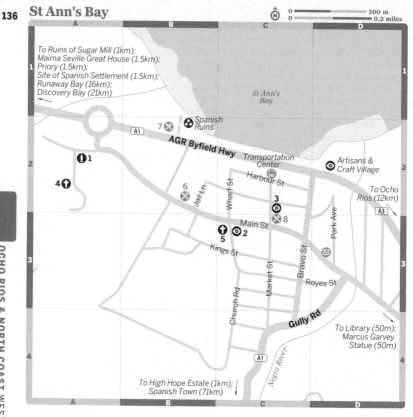

St Ann's Bay

Other Sights LANDMARKS

The grassy forecourt of the parish library on King St is dominated by the **Marcus Garvey Statue**, with the hero portrayed larger than life in gray bronze (see the boxed text, p258).

At the corner of Market St is the **courthouse**, erected in elegant cut limestone and red brick in 1866 with a pedimented porch bearing the scales of justice. Across the way is the **market**, which gets busy on Fridays and Saturdays. Further west lies quaint **St Ann's Bay Baptist Church**.

At the west end of Main St stands the **Columbus Monument**, topped by a bronze figure of the explorer dolled up as a Spanish grandee.

Up the hill from the Columbus Monument is the exquisite Catholic church of **Our Lady of Perpetual Help**, built in contemporary Spanish design by an Irish priest in 1939 with stones recovered from the ruins of Sevilla la Nueva. Inside, great beams support the organ loft.

★ Festivals & Events

Emancipation Jubilee CULTURE

(⊙ Jul 31-Aug 1) Held annually on the grounds of Maima Seville Great House overnight from July 31 to August 1. Celebrations consist of dancing and traditional folk music, such as Kumina and mento.

🛏 Sleeping & Eating

TOP CHOICE High Hope Estate   B&B $$

(📞972-2277; www.highhopeestate.com; r US$110-185; P 🌀 @ 🐾 🐕) Set amid 16 hectares of manicured gardens, lawns and woodland high in the hills above St Ann's Bay, this quirky yet chic Venetian-style villa built in 1961 resembles a location from a Fellini film. Each of its seven rooms, decorated with antiques, has a minibar and mini-library of books; three have wonderful ocean views and verandas. There's a well-stocked library, and you're welcome to peruse and play the original owners' collection of vinyl records. A mixture of Jamaican and Italian dishes, lovingly prepared with ingredients hand-picked from the property's fruit trees and garden, are available and cooking courses are held on request. To get here, take Church St south (uphill) three blocks from downtown St Ann's and continue uphill for about 1.5km.

There are street **food stalls** along Main St dishing up fish tea and jerk. Also recommended:

Seafood Specialist   SEAFOOD $
(cnr Jail Lane & A1; meals J$500-850; ⊙lunch & dinner) Wholesome local fare such as brown stew, plus excellent steamed or fried fish with yams and rice and peas, washed down with natural juices.

Spicy Nice Patties & Pastries   JAMAICAN $
(22 Main St; patties J$90) Sells chicken, saltfish and vegetable patties.

ℹ Information

Library (2 King St; internet per 30 min J$100) Internet access, 100m east of Braco St.

Police station (cnr Main & Braco Sts)

Scotiabank (18 Braco St) Has a 24-hour ATM.

St Ann's Bay Public General Hospital (📞972-2272) At the far west end of Main St, with an emergency clinic.

ℹ Getting There & Away

Frequent minibuses and route taxis traveling between Montego Bay and Ocho Rios call at St Ann's.

Priory & Around

Priory, about 1.5km west of St Ann's Bay, has a small beach with water sports and several hotels. You can turn inland and head into the hills for views down the coast. Here you'll find Lilyfield Great House, about 8km east of Brown's Town.

⊙ Sights & Activities

TOP CHOICE Chukka Cove Farm   ADVENTURE CENTER
This former polo field west of Priory is now the home of **Chukka Caribbean Adventures** (📞972-2506; www.chukkacaribbean.com), which offers an ever-growing list of guided excursions and adventures. The trips are sometimes a mite crowded, but the quality of service and expertise of the guides is high. Chukka works closely with a dog-rescue center, and offers 'dog-sledding' on land (J$7195), the exhilarating 50km/h buggy ride pulled by a trained dog team. Other popular excursions include the three-hour Horseback Ride 'n Swim (J$6264), which culminates with an exciting bareback trot into the sea; Zion Bus Line (J$7111) to Bob Marley's Nine Mile resting place; River Kayak Safari (J$7619); and Zip Line Tour (J$3555). Rates include transfer from Ocho Rios.

In April, Chukka Cove Farm hosts the exuberant all-night **Carnival party**, complete with soca music and paint throwing, though purists are grumbling about the introduction of dancehall to the event.

H'Evans Scent   ECO-ADVENTURE CENTER
(📞564-6467; www.hevansscent.com; ⊙8am-5pm Mon-Fri, 9am-4pm Sat & Sun) In the tiny hill town of Free Hill, 10km south of Priory, this evolving ecotourism experiment is the brainchild of Derek Evans, better known in the UK as fitness celebrity Mr Motivator. The sprawling hilltop property is the site for four adrenalin-charged but family-friendly experiences: paintballing, ATV rides, a zip-line tour and – the tour de force: the Screamer – a 17m giant swing that sends you hurtling across the valley. Activity package combos are available, with discounts for groups of 10 or more; if you want to sample everything on the menu, the 'Zips, ATV and Paintball Extreme' (J$6250) gives you access all areas. Meals are available in the bright-yellow main house.

Cranbrook Flower Forest   GARDEN
(www.cranbrookff.com; adult/child J$847/424; ⊙9am-5pm) This 53-hectare botanical garden is a treat, crafted in the lush valley that carves up into the hills south of Laughlands, about 5km west of Priory. The garden is built around a colonial-era building and includes theme gardens, a hothouse orchid display,

pools, and lush lawns (with croquet) fringed by banks of anthuriums and other tropical flowers.

Guided nature walks (about 90 minutes) lead to the river, reflecting giant tree ferns, spectacular torch ginger, heliconia and other exotic species, and there are perfect spots for picnicking. River tubing, horseback rides and adrenalin-packed canopy zip-line tours are available.

🛏 Sleeping

Circle B Farm Guest House   GUEST HOUSE **$**
(☎913-4511; dm/r J$1693/4656) The working Circle B Plantation owns this simple backpackers' lodge offering several dorm-style rooms, a communal kitchen and lounge. Meals are not offered; you may want to consider bringing food to prepare. The farm runs engaging tours that demonstrate the raising of avocados, bananas, coconuts and vegetables. The farm is reached via a turnoff 1km west of Sevilla la Nueva at Priory, 3km west of St Ann's Bay.

ℹ Getting There & Away

Minibuses that run between St Ann's Bay and Runaway Bay can drop you off at the bus stop right in front of Chukka Cove Farm. To reach H'Evans Scent and Cranbrook Flower Forest, you need you own vehicle.

Runaway Bay

This bay (16km west of St Ann's) is low on cultural attractions, though sun worshippers, snorkelers and divers find much to celebrate. This one-street village, lined with all-inclusive resorts and nondescript local shops, stretches along the A1 for 3km, merging with the small community of Salem to the east.

🏃 Activities

Several small beaches are supposedly public, although most are the backyards for a few all-inclusive resorts. If you're hankering for a dip in the big blue, head to the white-sand **Cardiff Hall Public Beach**, opposite the Shell gas station. There is a livelier (but littered) **fisherman's beach** in Salem, where the occasional sound-system party is staged on the weekend.

Runaway Bay has excellent **diving**. There's a wreck in shallow water in front of Club Ambiance, plus two cars and a plane offshore from Club Caribbean. A reef complex called Ricky's Reef is renowned for its sponges. More experienced divers might try the eponymous **Canyon**. Here, too, is the *Reggae Queen*, a 30m-long sunken tugboat. Potty Reef will have you flush with excitement; divers can't resist having their photo taken sitting on, er, King Neptune's throne.

Resort Divers   DIVING
(☎881-5760; www.resortdivers.com, Royal DeCameron Club Caribbean, Runaway Bay) Besides one/two tank dives (J$3809/7195), there are certification courses (from US$300), night dives (J$5079) and a plethora of other water sports on offer, such as banana-boat rides (J$1693), parasailing (J$4656), snorkeling excursions (J$2540) and jet-ski rental (J$6772 for 30 minutes).

Scuba Jamaica   DIVING
(☎381-1113; www.scuba-jamaica.com; Franklyn D Resort, Runaway Bay) Offers one-/two-tank dives (J$5079/8465), as well as PADI Open Water certification programs (US$420) and night dives (J$5502). Discounts for own equipment. Pickup J$1270.

🛏 Sleeping

The **Jamaica Association of Villas & Apartments** (JAVA; ☎974-2508, in the USA 800-845-5276; www.villasinjamaica.com) offers fully-staffed beachside and hilltop villas.

TOP CHOICE **Itopia**   VILLA **$$$**
(☎948-1958; www.islandoutpost.com/itopia; villa US$595; P❋🛜) The area's best accommodation is found not on the beach but in the quiet isolation of the hills, a 15-minute drive from Runaway Bay. A historical-home-cum-luxury-retreat, this beautiful 1660 colonial house belongs to the Henzel family, of Perry Henzel and *The Harder They Come* fame. The three bedrooms combine antique furnishings with modern conveniences and the price includes the services of a housekeeper and cook who prepares wonderful Jamaican meals made of fresh local produce in accordance with your needs. To get here, head south by the gas station next to the Breezes Runaway Bay Hotel Golf Course, take the second left after the Runaway Heart Hotel, keep left until you pass the Cardiff Hall Great House on your left and then take the second left and first right.

Club Ambiance   RESORT **$$**
(☎973-6167;   www.clubambiance.com;   s/d US$156/222, 3-bedroom villa US$980; P❋🛜🏊)

This lively budget alternative to the grander all-inclusives down the road, is popular with 20- and 30-somethings and features two small private beaches, a pool with a raucous poolside bar and a secluded three-bedroom villa that sleeps up to six people and has its own swimming pool. All bright colors and kitschy art, the spacious rooms feature firm king-sized beds and tiled floors. Guests must be over 18.

Little Savoy Guest House GUEST HOUSE $$
(☑474-5889; www.jamaica-holiday.net; 150 Rickets Dr; r incl breakfast J$7619; P🅿❋@🏊) This grand new guest house with marble floors, faux-Grecian columns and the odd burst of color in the shape of fresh flowers livening up the austere black-and-white exterior, is proving a hit, particularly with wedding parties. Each light, double room has its own color scheme and there's a good buffet breakfast.

Franklyn D Resort RESORT $$$
(☑in the USA 800-654-1337; www.fdrholidays.com; all-incl 1/2/3 bedrooms US$490/595/650, child 6-15/16-19/under 6 US$50/80/free; P🅿❋@ 🛜🏊🛗) At this Spanish hacienda-style, all-inclusive family resort, there are kid-friendly facilities and a personal nanny assigned to each child. The resort has three restaurants and a bar, plus an oceanfront spa and water-slide. Three nights minimum stay.

House Erabo GUEST HOUSE $
(☑973-4813; www.house-erabo.com; r J$3725; P🅿🛜) A small, bright-yellow guest house hiding behind flowering shrubbery, House Erabo offers spic-and-span rooms on the western edge of Runaway Bay with access to a small secluded beach.

✕ Eating & Drinking

TOP CHOICE Food Fa Life I-TAL $
(West Salem; meals J$450; ☉closed Sun; 🍽) Excellent I-tal food served from a nondescript container near Devon House I-Scream. Try the June plum juice (J$150), the ackee or the tasty vegetable stew.

Sharkie's SEAFOOD $
(Salem Beach; meals J$1000) Locals head for this informal seafood restaurant on one of the prettier stretches of public beach for steamed and fried fish, conch (curried, soup or fritters) and non-fishy standards.

Tek It Easy BAR $
(A1; meals J$500-700; ☉lunch & dinner) At this economical rooftop haunt, Jamaican fare

– primarily chicken and fish – competes for attention alongside the freely flowing overproof rum. There's music most nights.

Cardiff Hall Restaurant INTERNATIONAL $$
(☑973-2671; Runaway Bay Heart Hotel; meals J$1270-2400) This cheerful restaurant serves well-made Jamaican and continental fare. The service is great and reservations highly recommended.

Papa Rome's Pizza ITALIAN $
(A1; meals J$1000-1300; ☉lunch & dinner) Good thin-and-crispy pizzas with numerous toppings. Next to Shell gas station.

Jerkie's JERK $
(Salem; meals J$550; ☉lunch & dinner) Main-street jerk joint serving better jerk chicken than pork.

For snacks:

Devon House I-Scream ICE CREAM $
(Salem; ☉breakfast, lunch & dinner)

Bayside Pastries BAKERY $
(A1; ☉breakfast, lunch & dinner)

☆ Entertainment

Most fun-hungry visitors make the short journey to Ocho Rios for their after-hours kicks or settle for what's on at their resort. Subsequently, most resorts offer expensive night-passes for US$50 to US$100, granting unlimited booze, food and entertainment.

Local entertainment consists of a few rum shops and insalubrious go-go clubs.

ℹ Information

Police (cnr Main St & B3)
Post office (Main St)
Scotiabank (Main St, Salem) ATM.

ℹ Getting There & Around

BUS Minibuses and route taxis ply the A1 between Montego Bay (J$150 to J$200, 1½ hours) and Ocho Rios (J$100 to J$140, 40 minutes). They can be flagged down anywhere in Runaway Bay.

CAR In Salem, **Salem Car Rentals** (☑973-4167; www.salemcarrentals.com) and **Caribbean Car Rentals** (☑973-3539) are located on the main road.

Discovery Bay

This wide flask-shaped bay, 8km west of Runaway Bay and 8km east of Rio Bueno, is a popular resort spot for locals drawn to Puerto Seco Beach and many of Jamaica's wealthiest families have holiday villas up in

DISCOVERY BAY MARINE LABORATORY

The largest marine ecology laboratory in the world, the Discovery Bay Marine Laboratory (DBML) is part of the University of the West Indies' Centre of Marine Sciences, dedicated to the study of the geology of coral reefs and the life forms they support. Ongoing projects focus on environmental issues that have led to severe degradation of coral reefs in Jamaica and other parts of the Caribbean over the last two decades and include monitoring programs. The goal of the projects is 'to detect environmental changes in order to inform conservation priorities.' The DBML welcomes researchers and students from around the world; accommodations and meals available on request. For more information, contact the **University of the West Indies** (☑985-8835).

the hills here. The town itself has only marginal appeal.

Resembling a kind of giant nipple, the Kaiser Bauxite Company's Port Rhoades bauxite-loading facility dominates the town (it was used for the headquarters of Dr No – Crab Cay – in the James Bond movie, *Dr No*). Large freighters are fed by conveyor belts from a huge storage dome that looks like a rusty pumpkin. You can follow the road signed 'Port Rhoades' uphill 1km to a lookout point offering fantastic views over the bay. Note the metal likeness of Anancy, the folkloric spider, in the playground of the Kaiser's Sports Club, en route.

Locals believe this to be the location where Christopher Columbus first landed on Jamaican soil in 1494, though others say it was at Rio Bueno.

◉ Sights

Green Grotto Caves   CAVES
(www.greengrottocavesja.com; adult/child J$1692/847; ☺9am-4pm) This impressive system of caves and tunnels, 3km east of Discovery Bay, extends for about 45km. The steps lead down into the impressive chambers, where statuesque dripstone formations are illuminated by floodlights. Pre-Columbian Taíno people left their artwork on the walls. Much later, the caves were used as a hideout by the

Spanish during the English takeover of the island in 1655. Runaway slaves in the 18th century also took refuge here, and between the two world wars the caves were used by smugglers running arms to Cuba. The highlight is Green Grotto, a glistening subterranean lake 36m down. The entrance fee includes a guided one-hour tour, which is particularly family-friendly. The guides conduct their tours with humor and attempt to amaze you by tapping stalactites to produce hollow drum-like sounds, as well as pointing out the different species of bat that live in the cave, and their imported predator, the Jamaican yellow boa.

Puerto Seco Beach   BEACH
(admission J$350; ☺9am-5pm) The eastern side of the bay is rimmed with white-sand beaches. With its soft sand and limpid waters, Puerto Seco Beach, in the center of town, is a real charmer. Open to the public, it sports rustic eateries and bars and a fun park with a waterslide for kids not interested in suntanning. On weekends and holidays the beach is teeming, but during the week the place is often deserted. You can rent fishing boats, sea bikes and jet skis.

FREE **Columbus Park**   MUSEUM
(☺9am-5pm) This eclectic open-air roadside museum sits atop the bluff on the west side of the bay. Highlighted by a mural depicting Columbus' arrival in Jamaica, it features such memorabilia as anchors, cannons, nautical bells, sugar-boiling coppers and an old waterwheel in working condition that creaks and clanks as it turns. There's also a diminutive locomotive formerly used to haul sugar at Innswood Estate. Nearby are the stone and ironware remains of Quadrant Wharf, built in 1777 by the British, with a plaque commemorating Columbus' landing.

🛏 Sleeping & Eating

Some of the most luxurious fully-staffed villas on the island are found in the hills above Discovery Bay and can be booked with the **Jamaica Association of Villas & Apartments** (JAVA; ☑974-2508, in the USA 800-845-5276; www.villasinjamaica.com).

Paradise Place   GUEST HOUSE $
(☑862-2095; www.paradiseplace54.com; 54 Bridgewater Garden; r/apt J$5936/7819; P✳) The pick of the Bay's budget accommodations, this attractive eight-room guest house is set back from the A1. The hot tub in the yard is

a nice touch. Look for the bright murals by the white gates.

Ultimate Jerk Centre JERK **$**
(meals J$500-750; ☺lunch & dinner) This popular rest stop and bar opposite Green Grotto Caves caters to a captive audience. The curry goat is very good, as is the bammy and festival, but the jerk is far from ultimate – in fact, it's downright disappointing.

❶ Getting There & Away

Minibuses and route taxis ply the A1 between Montego Bay and Ocho Rios. They depart from the Texaco gas station, opposite the entrance to Puerto Seco Beach.

DRY HARBOUR MOUNTAINS

Paved roads lead south from Discovery Bay, Runaway Bay and St Ann's Bay and ascend into the Dry Harbour Mountains. In this off-the-beaten-track area, the badly potholed roads twist and turn through scenic countryside as they rise to the island's backbone.

Only two main roads run east–west. The lower, the 'Great Interior Rd' (the B11), parallels the coast about 11km inland. It begins at Rock, 2km east of Falmouth, and weaves east to Claremont.

Brown's Town

Brown's Town is a lively market town 11km south of Runaway Bay. Many noble houses on the hillsides hint at its relative prosperity. The town is at its most bustling during market days (Wednesday, Friday and Saturday), when the cast-iron **Victoria Market** (cnr Main St & Brown's Town Rd) overflows with higglers (street vendors).

Irish estate-owner Hamilton Brown (1776–1843) financed the building of **St Mark's Anglican Church** (cnr Main St & Brown's Town Rd) in Victorian Gothic style. Note the fine cut-stone **courthouse** (Brown's Town Rd) with neoclassical columned portico.

Minibuses and route taxis run to St Ann's Bay, Kingston and Nine Mile from the east end of Top Rd, a block off Main St.

Nine Mile

The small community where the 'King of Reggae' was born on February 6, 1945, is set dramatically in the midst of the Cockpits. Despite its isolated location, 60km south of Ocho Rios, the village of Nine Mile is decidedly on the beaten path for pilgrimages to Bob Marley's birth site and resting place, particularly on his birthday.

> **WORTH A TRIP**
>
> ### NINE MILE MUSEUM
>
> The **Nine Mile Museum** (📞999-7003; www.ninemilejamaica.com; admission J$1600; ☺9am-5pm) is in the house in which Bob Marley spent his early years before moving to Kingston. After showing the room displaying various gold discs awarded for the reggae icon's albums, Rastafarian guides given to impromptu singing of Marley's songs lead pilgrims uphill to the plainly furnished two-room house on Mt Zion – now festooned with devotional graffiti. You'll see the single bed he sang of in 'Is This Love.' Another highlight is the Rasta-colored 'rock pillow' on which lay his head when seeking inspiration. Marley's body lies buried along with his favorite Gibson Les Paul guitar, his football, the Bible and some marijuana in a 2.5m-tall oblong marble mausoleum inside a tiny church of traditional Ethiopian design, its stained-glass windows the red, green and yellow of the Ethiopian flag. A single window depicts three flowers, symbolizing the 'three little birds' from the song of the same name. His brother is interred with him and nearby is the mausoleum of his mother, Cedella.
>
> Bob's widow, Rita, periodically expresses disdain at how her husband's legacy has been turned into a tourism 'product,' and she has spoken of exhuming him for burial in Africa, though there are rumors that his remains have already been secretly spirited away to Ghana.
>
> The museum shop that you're steered through after the tour sells Marley paraphernalia of every description. Note that the expensive entry fee does not include a tip for the guide.

❶ Getting There & Away

BUS Infrequent minibuses and route taxis operate between Brown's Town, Alexandria and Claremont, stopping in Nine Mile. **Chukka Caribbean Adventures** (☑972-2506; www.chukka caribbean.com; tour US$65) runs the 'Zion Bus Line' tour from Ocho Rios.

CAR Getting to Nine Mile is fairly straightforward as it's well-signposted and locals are happy to give you directions. From the A3, take the turn towards Claremont or, if you're coming down the A1, follow the signpost from Claremont. The road to Nine Mile is in good condition, though there are some narrow sections as it winds through the hills.

Montego Bay & Northwest Coast

Why Go?

Montego Bay serves as both a gateway to Jamaica for countless travelers, and a stage for some of the island's most obvious contrasts, from the geographic to the cultural to the socioeconomic. The city is a typical Jamaican resort town, divided between an unapologetically tourist-oriented stretch of gaudiness and a rough-and-real city center. Most major Jamaican towns related to the tourism industry are thus, but within are bubbles of independent cool, with flashes of the 'real' Jamaica, although the glimpse you get may not be beautiful. Some people love it here – there are some beautiful beaches – and some can't leave soon enough. Nearby are more stretches of groomed coastline studded with enormous all-inclusive resorts, the occasional independent one, and crumbling Georgian architecture. To the south are mountains, crossroads, jungle and Cockpit Country – as wild and free of visitors as Montego is domesticated and crowded with them.

Best Places to Stay

» Time 'n Place (p174)
» Windsor Great House (p183)
» Round Hill Hotel & Villas (p177)
» Hotel Rio Bueno (p176)

Nights to Not Miss...

» Reggae Sumfest (p20)
» Fridays at Pier One (p163)
» Dancing at Blue Beat Jazz & Blues Bar (p162)
» Parties on Cornwall Beach (p145)

When to Go
Montego Bay

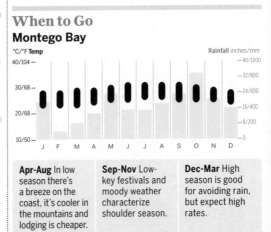

Apr-Aug In low season there's a breeze on the coast, it's cooler in the mountains and lodging is cheaper.

Sep-Nov Low-key festivals and moody weather characterize shoulder season.

Dec-Mar High season is good for avoiding rain, but expect high rates.

Montego Bay & Northwest Coast Highlights

1 Blitzing through the course of Jamaican history at the cultural show at **Outameni** (p174)

2 Soaking up the sun with tourists and returned Jamaican expats at **Doctor's Cave Beach** (p145)

3 Exploring the halls of the **Greenwood Great House** (p169)

4 Hiking into the heart of the wild **Cockpit Country** (p181)

5 Watching the algae glow on your fingers as stars twinkle overhead in the **Glistening Waters** (p173)

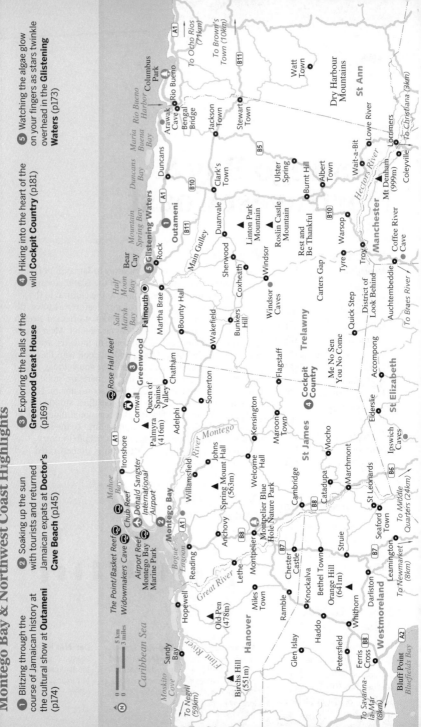

ⓘ Getting There & Around

AIR

Most international visitors fly into Jamaica through **Montego Bay and Sangster International Airport** (MBJ). Dozens of carriers regularly fly here, including the following:

Air Canada (www.aircanada.com)

Air Jamaica (www.airjamaica.com) Also flies at least once daily to Kingston.

American Airways (www.aa.com)

US Airways (www.usairways.com)

Virgin Atlantic (www.virgin-atlantic.com)

BOAT

During the high season, as many as a dozen cruise ships will dock at Montego Bay every week, carrying thousand of passengers. A new port in Falmouth will also be docking mega-liners by the time this book comes out. Thousands of yachties (yacht crews) party in Montego Bay and smaller towns on the Northwest Coast annually.

BUS, CAR & TAXI

The city of Montego Bay is a major land transportation hub serviced by regular minitaxis, regular taxis and an express bus service to Kingston. The well-paved, well-maintained A1 highway runs from Montego Bay east along the coast through Ironshore and Falmouth to Saint Ann's Bay (west of Ocho Rios), and west, again along the coast, through Lucea to Negril. Smaller roads like the B8 (accessible from MoBay) and B9 (accessible from Lucea) run into the interior; expect potholes and twisty mountain driving. Public transportation on the coast road is reliable and relatively quick, but the same cannot be said in the mountains. To access areas like Cockpit Country, we strongly advise hiring a driver or renting your own vehicle.

MONTEGO BAY

POP 110,000

There's a good chance MoBay (as everyone calls it) will be your introduction to Jamaica – some 80% of travelers choose the second-largest city in Jamaica as their port of entry. And we mean 'port' – many folks fly here, but enormous cruise ships dock alongside sweating cargo container boats as well. Nestled in front of a wall of green hills, Montego has made an interesting progression from local port to tourist-packaged commodity to an intriguing, if not terribly attractive, blend of both. As a result, while the Hip Strip (Gloucester Ave), a long stretch of commercialized cheesiness, is initially off-putting, it has also become a place to sample genuinely creative cuisine and a nightlife scene where surprising amounts of locals rubs shoulders with cruise passengers. Past the Hip Strip, MoBay is colorful, chaotic and occasionally dangerous. We recommend not spending too much time here – the beaches are better elsewhere, while the 'real' Jamaica and its attendant music scene is more authentic in Kingston. That said, Montego is a decent first stop, and a good base for day-tripping around Western Jamaica.

◉ Sights

HIP STRIP & THE BEACHES

Doctor's Cave Beach BEACH
(Map p156; ☎952-2566; www.doctorscavebathingclub.com; adult/child J$500/250; ☺8:30am-sunset) It may sound like a rocky hole inhabited by lab-coated troglodytes, but this is actually Montego Bay's most famous beach. A pretty arc of sugary sand fronts a deep blue gem studded with floating dive platforms and speckled with tourists sighing happily. Er, *lots* of tourists – and a fair few Jamaicans as well; if you're coming in winter you may have trouble finding a beach under all the suntanners. The upside is an admission charge keeps out most of the beach hustlers. Founded as a bathing club in 1906, Doctor's Cave earned its name when English chiropractor Sir Herbert Baker claimed the waters here had healing properties. Folks flocked to Montego Bay, kick-starting a tourism evolution that would culminate in the appearance of *Homo Margaritavillus* decades later. There are lots of facilities on hand including a food court, grill bar, internet cafe and water sports, and lots of things to rent (beach chairs, towels, snorkeling gear). Parties tend to pop off here, especially in the high season; dates change, so ask your hotel when the fun goes down.

Cornwall Beach BEACH
(Map p156; ☎979-0102; www.cornwallbeachja.com; admission $J350; ☺8am-6pm) Cornwall Beach has the most coolness cred out of Montego's beaches – if you're looking for a beach that feels like the spot where the cool locals hang out (well, the cool locals willing to shell

ⓘ **CHRISTMAS CROWDS**

Be warned: Montego Bay is filled with nightmarish crowds of returning expats, tourists, and folks in from the country during Christmas.

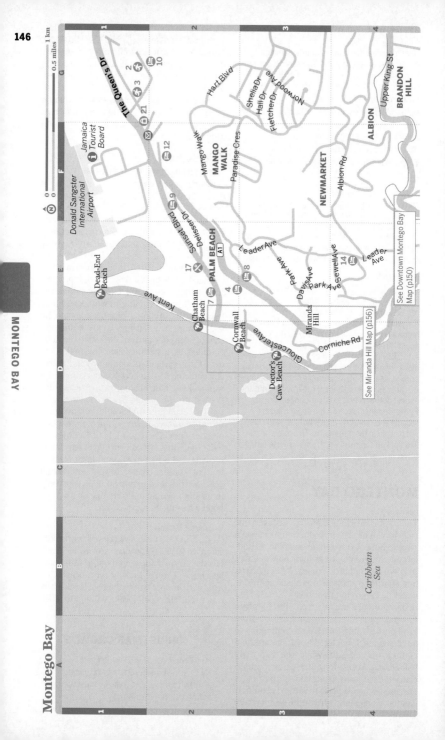

Montego Bay

MONTEGO BAY

Caribbean Sea

Donald Sangster International Airport

Jamaica Tourist Board

The Queen's Dr

Dead-End Beach

Kent Ave

Chatham Beach

Cornwall Beach

Doctor's Cave Beach

Sunset Blvd

Delisser Dr

PALM BEACH A1

Gloucester Ave

Mango Walk

MANGO WALK

Paradise Cres

Hart Blvd

Shella Dr

Hall Dr

Fletcher Dr

Norwood Ave

NEWMARKET

Albion Rd

ALBION

Upper King St

BRANDON HILL

Leader Ave

Park Ave

Davis Ave

Sewell Ave

Leader Ave

Miranda Hill

Corniche Rd

See Miranda Hill Map (p156)

See Downtown Montego Bay Map (p150)

1 km
0.5 miles

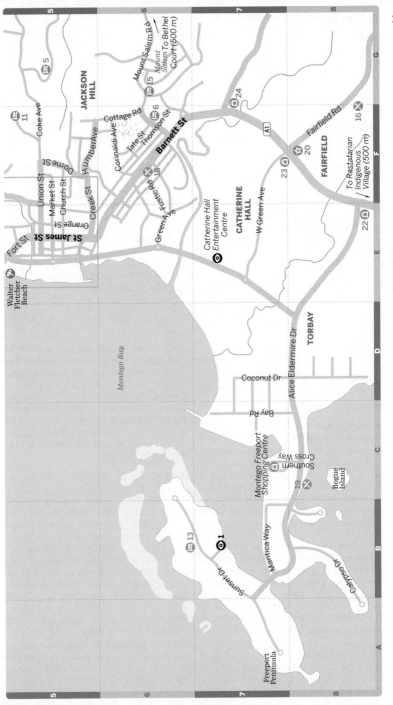

MONTEGO BAY

out $J350), this is your spot. There's a nice shallow shelf for snorkeling, clear water for swimming and white sand for you to look good on. Every Wednesday an (open bar) beach party goes down here from 9pm til *oh-god-is-that-the-sun?*

**Walter Fletcher Beach &
Aquasol Theme Park** BEACH
(Map p146; ☎979-9447; www.aquasoljamaica.com; adult/child US$5/3; ◷10am-10pm) Locals still call it Fletcher Beach, but officially this is now the Aquasol Theme Park: a complex full of go-karts, boat rides, snorkeling excursions and swimming. The whole place is pretty much structured for kids, although the state of the facilities (ie rusty go-kart track) could have used some improvement when we visited. There's a good deck-bar on hand for sundowner drinks and more locals than you'll find at Doctor's Cave but this unfortunately includes hustlers. As the sun sets, this place evolves from kids' park to adult playground, and a definite party atmosphere starts to take over.

FREE **Dead End Beach** BEACH
(Map p146) Beside Kent Rd just north of Gloucester Ave this narrow strip, also known as Buccaneer Beach, is popular with locals.

When we say narrow, we mean narrow; at high tide it's pretty accurate to drop the 'beach' from 'dead end.' There are no facilities here (except those at a few hotels over the road), but the lack of crowds makes the sunsets over the bay all the more gorgeous. Sunset Blvd heads east from here towards the airport past the Summit Police Station, the only police precinct office we've heard of that gets its own pool.

DOWNTOWN
Sam Sharpe Square SQUARE
(Map p150; Fort St) This bustling cobbled square, formerly called the Parade, is named for the Right Excellent Samuel Sharpe (1801–32), national hero and leader of the 1831 Christmas Rebellion. At the square's northwest corner is the **National Heroes Monument**, a bronze statue of Paul Bogle and Sam Sharpe, Bible in hand, speaking to three admirers. The sculpture is the work of Jamaican artist Kay Sullivan and has an appealing rawness to it. Also on the northwest corner is the **Cage**, a tiny cut-stone and brick building built in 1806 as a lockup, now a small souvenir shop. The Cage was originally built of wood, but unruly prisoners damaged it so much it was remodeled in stone.

Civic Centre
NOTABLE BUILDING

(Map p150; ☎971-9417, 952-5500; admission J$200; ☺9am-5pm Tue-Fri, 10am-3pm Sat, noon-5pm Sun) At the southwest corner of Sam Sharpe Sq you'll find the copper-domed Civic Centre, an elegant colonial-style cut-stone building on the site of a ruined colonial courthouse. It contains the small, not terribly well assembled (if informative) **Museum of St James** (Map p150), replete with relics and other exhibits tracing the history of St James parish from Taíno days through the slave rebellions to the more recent past. An art gallery and 200-seat theater are also on site, both of which host various events on the MoBay cultural calendar.

Church Street
STREET

Many of the most interesting buildings in town are clustered along Church St (Map p150), the most picturesque street in MoBay, although you shouldn't expect a quiet historic district – this thoroughfare is as alive and chaotic as anywhere else downtown. Note that if we do not provide admission hours these buildings either cannot be entered or are occupied by modern businesses.

The highlight is **St James Parish Church** (Map p150; ☎952-2775; Church St), regarded as the finest church on the island. It was built between 1775 and 1782 in the shape of a Greek cross, but was so damaged by the earthquake of March 1, 1957, that it had to be rebuilt.

With luck, the tall church doors will be open (if they're not, call the rector at the above number) and you can view the interior, one of the most beautiful rooms in the whole of Jamaica. Note the wonderful stained glass and marble monuments, including some fine works by John Bacon, the foremost English sculptor of the late 18th century. One is a memorial to Anne May Palmer, whose virtuous life was upended in

literature to create the legend of the White Witch of Rose Hall. Look carefully at her neck and you'll detect faint purple marks. Locals consider this proof of the fable that the 'witch' was strangled. Outside are the neglected (yet romantic, in a decaying way) gravestones of old planters.

The pretty **Town House** (Map p150; ☎952-2660; 16 Church St), fronted by a stately red-brick exterior, is buried under a cascade of bougainvillea and laburnum. The house dates from 1765, when it was the home of a wealthy merchant. It has since served as a church manse and later as a townhouse for the mistress of the Earl of Hereford, Governor of Jamaica. In the years that followed it was used as a hotel, warehouse, Masonic lodge, lawyer's office and synagogue (its current incarnation is a clothes store).

At the corner of Water Lane is a plantation-style octagonal structure that today houses a police station. About 50m west, at the corner of King St, is a redbrick Georgian building harboring the **National Housing Trust** (Map p150; ☎952-0063; 1 King St). A more impressive structure is the three-story Georgian building at 25 Church St (Map p150) – headquarters of **Cable & Wireless Jamaica**.

Burchell Memorial Baptist Church
CHURCH

(Map p150; ☎952-6351; Market St) Two blocks east of Sam Sharpe Sq is one of the churches in which Sam Sharpe is said to have been a deacon: Burchell Memorial Baptist Church. The building, which dates to 1835, is an attractive bit of brick, a slice of British countryside architecture smoldering handsomely away in the tropical heat. The original church was founded in 1824 by Rev Thomas Burchell. An angry mob destroyed the church in reprisal for Burchell's support of the emancipation cause, but the missionary escaped to sea. Sam Sharpe's remains are

---

FORT MONTEGO'S QUIET CANNONS

At the southern end of the Hip Strip a set of stairs leads (very) steeply up to a rough square of old rocks dubbed, somewhat ambitiously, **Fort Montego** (Map p150). Well, the ruins of Fort Montego, complete with rusty cannons. A sign describes the nitty-gritty of the production of said armaments, while leaving out the depressing details: the cannons were only fired twice, and both times were a fiasco. The first shot, in celebration of the capture of Havana in 1760, was a misfire that killed an artilleryman. The second time the cannoneers screwed up and shot at one of their own ships, the *Mercury*, which was carrying a dangerous cargo of...dogs. Fortunately the cannon crews (as you may have guessed by now) weren't the best at their jobs and missed the *Mercury*. There's a fairly uninspiring craft market next to the fort.

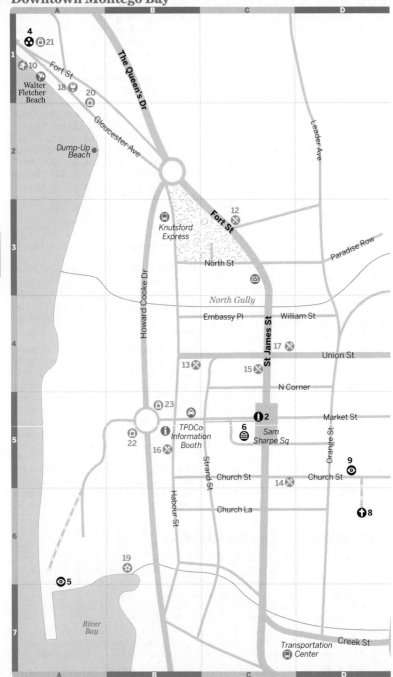

buried in the vault. There are no official admission times here, but if the church doors are open you're welcome to wander around inside.

Creek Dome NOTABLE BUILDING
(Map p150; cnr Dome St & Creek St) Lurking at the end of Creek St is the bizarre-looking Creek Dome, built in 1837 above the underground spring that supplied drinking water for Montego Bay. The structure is actually a hexagon with a crenellated castle turret in which the 'Keeper of the Creek' lived and collected a toll on the dispensation of drinking water.

AROUND MONTEGO BAY

Bellefield Great House NOTABLE BUILDING
(✆952-2382; www.bellefieldgreathouse.com; basic tour US$20, lunch tour adult/child US$40/20; ⏰9am-5pm Mon-Sat) The sea of sugarcane south of Montego Bay is part of the Barnett Estate, a plantation owned and operated since 1755 by the Kerr-Jarretts, one of Jamaica's preeminent families; their holdings once included most of the Montego Bay area. Today the family (now in its 11th generation) holds the land in trust for the government and manages it accordingly.

The Bellefield Great House, built in 1735, has been restored and is now a showcase of 18th-century colonial living and Jamaican culinary history, which makes for an interesting mash-up of historical tourism catering (pun intended) to the traveler-cum-foodie demographic. You'll get to see the local gardens, meander past an on-site jerk pit, get pleasantly drunk on rum punch, wander the house and then gorge yourself at a delicious lunch buffet. Decadent eating, drinking and lolling about while being catered to by servants – a pretty accurate depiction of being an 18th-century plantation owner. Many hotels in MoBay offer property tours (with lunch) of the Great House for US$60/30 per adult/child.

The estate is about 800m to the east of Doctor's Hospital, about 15 minutes from downtown Montego Bay. It's poorly signed: take the right turn at the Y-fork marked for Day-O Plantation, then the signed right turn at Granville Police Station.

**Montego Bay Marine Park &
Bogue Lagoon** NATURE RESERVE
(MBMPT; Map p150; ✆952-5619; www.mbmp.org; Pier One Complex, off Howard Cooke Dr) The waters of Montego Bay are gorgeous to behold both above and below the surface, but they

have long been compromised by the effects of fishing, water sports and pollution. With the creation in 1991 of the Montego Bay Marine Park, Jamaica's first national park, environmental regulations at last began to be strictly enforced to protect the area's coral reefs, rich flora and fauna, and shoreline mangroves. The park extends from the eastern end of the airport westward (almost 10km) to the Great River, encompassing the mangroves of Bogue Lagoon.

You can hire canoes or set out with a guide to spot herons, egrets, pelicans and waterfowl – swimming and crawling below are barracudas, tarpon, snapper, crabs and lobsters. Request a guide two days in advance; there's no charge but donations are gladly accepted. Authority is vested in the Montego Bay Marine Park Trust (MBMPT), which maintains a meager **resource center** (☉9am-5pm Mon-Fri) with a library on the vital ecosystem.

Indigenous Rastafarian Village   RASTAFARIAN VILLAGE
(off Map p146; ☎285-4750; Fairfield Rd; 2hr/1-day tour US$25/100; ☉tours by appointment) If you want to learn about the Rastafari movement past the effort it takes to pop in an old Bob CD, come out to this…hmmm. 'Theme park' is definitely not the right description. How about 'living interpretive exhibit?' There's

not exactly a natural mystic floating in the *ay-er*, but this 'village' is still a good introduction to Jamaica's most famous indigenous religion. You'll be taken through a pretty, jungly settlement, shown medicinal plants (not what you're thinking) and given a coherent breakdown of what the Rasta faith traditionally believed in. As most travelers don't learn much about Rastafari past the ramblings of dreadlocked hustlers, this is a pretty valuable experience, and the all-day tour includes some lovely treks into the surrounding countryside, complete with swimming in paradisial natural pools.

It's located on Fairfield Rd, about 3km inland from MoBay. You'll need either your own wheels (it's a lovely drive) or to prearrange a visit – which can easily be done through your accommodations. Even if you drive yourself, we recommend calling ahead; the village may not be ready to deal with drop-in visitors.

Freeport Peninsula   NEIGHBORHOOD
(Map p146) The artificially made Freeport Peninsula is located southwest of downtown Montego Bay and serves (among other functions) as the docking point for cruise ships. You might even see actual banana boats out this way, although if you sing 'Day-O' while they unload we wouldn't blame the police for arresting you. It's fun to drive

out here, past the mangroves of the Bogue Lagoon and through a series of high-end time-shares, condos and shopping plazas – in some ways this area feels more insulated from the grittier realities of downtown Montego Bay than the Hip Strip.

Montego Bay Yacht Club
(Map p146; 979-8038; www.mobayyachtclub.com; Sunset Dr; ⊙10am-10pm) If you come out to the peninsula, try to stop by the pretty and posh Montego Bay Yacht Club for a meal and a drink; the hours indicated above are for the on-site restaurant, **Robbie Joseph's Seahorse Grill**. Technically the club is only open to members, but if you present yourself at the entrance and ask politely to look around, you'll likely be invited inside. If you're coming by boat and want to dock here, contact the cub on VHF Channel 16; the club will contact customs and immigration to have you cleared for arrival. To get here by car, head down Howard Cooke Blvd and head right at the crossing with Alice Eldemere Dr.

🏃 Activities

Diving
MoBay offers a few good dive sites. For advanced divers, the **Point** north of the airport has a good wall dive due to the fish, sharks, rays and dense coral that are fed by crystal-clear waters scoured by currents. The wall here starts at 20m and drops to at least 90m. **Airport Reef**, off the southwestern edge of the airport, is considered by some to be the best site on the island, with masses of coral canyons, caves and tunnels, and a DC-3 wreck that's become a multicolored mansion for masses of fish.

Besides boasting the sort of name you'd rightly expect in a *Pirates of the Caribbean* movie, **Widowmakers Cave** is an incredible tunnel filled with sponges, barracuda and schools of smaller fish. This is a site for experienced divers, who can navigate through the 21.3m (70ft) passage and out the top of its chimney. **Chub Reef**, a 12.2m (40ft) dive site located far to the east of the city, is named for the preponderance of Bermuda chub, rather than any physical squatness. **Rose Hall Reef**, a few kilometers east of the city, is a shallow reef more suitable for less-experienced divers. The main attraction is the **Fairy Castle**, a pretty coral pillar as fantastic as its name suggests.

With all this said, don't dive here expecting top-rate macrodiving (ie lots of big fish). There are mantas, nurse sharks and the like in these waters, but most divers report seeing nothing larger than barracuda, reef fish and rock lobsters.

Most dive centers also offer snorkeling trips. All of the following provide multiple levels of PADI certification.

PREACHING RESISTANCE

The weeklong Christmas Rebellion, which began on Kensington Estate on December 27, 1831 and engulfed much of the Montego Bay region, was the most serious slave revolt to rock colonial Jamaica. Its impact and the public outcry over the terrible retribution that followed were catalysts for the British parliament passing the Abolition Act in 1834.

The instigator of the revolt was Samuel Sharpe (1801–32), the slave of a Montego Bay solicitor. Sharpe acted as a deacon of Montego Bay's Burchell Baptist Church and became a 'Daddy' (leader) of the church. He used his pulpit as a forum to encourage passive rebellion.

In 1831 Sharpe counseled fellow slaves to refuse to work during the Christmas holidays. Word of the secret, passive rebellion spread throughout St James and neighboring parishes. Inevitably word leaked out, and warships and extra troops were sent to Montego Bay.

The rebellion turned into a violent conflict when the Kensington Estate was set on fire. Soon plantations and great houses throughout northwest Jamaica were ablaze, and Sharpe's noble plan was usurped by wholesale violence. Fourteen colonists were murdered before authorities suppressed the revolt. Swift and cruel retribution followed.

As part of the colonists' punishments, more than a thousand slaves were killed. Day after day for six weeks following the revolt's suppression, magistrates of the Montego Bay Courthouse handed down death sentences to scores of slaves, who were hanged two at a time on the Parade – among them 'Daddy' Sam Sharpe. He was later named a national hero and the Parade was renamed Sam Sharp Sq.

Resort Divers
DIVING

(Map p156; ☎973-6131; www.resortdivers.com; 2 Gloucester Ave) Located on the Hip Strip in the Royal DeCameron Hotel.

Dive Seaworld
DIVING

(☎953-2180; diveseaworld.com; Ironshore) Located northeast of Montego Bay.

Jamaica Scuba
DIVING

(☎617-2500 ext 342 (Falmouth), 957-3039 (Negril); www.scuba-jamaica.com) Based out of Falmouth, Negril and Runaway Bay, but does excursions to MoBay.

Scuba Caribe
DIVING

(☎1-888-748-4990); www.scubacaribe.com) Operates out of the Riu Ironshore, Montego Bay.

Fishing

The waters off Jamaica's north coast offer spectacular game fishing. Deep-water game fish like blue marlin, sailfish, wahoo, kingfish, dolphin and yellowfin tuna use the abyss known as Marlin Alley as a migratory freeway (June and August are peak months for marlin). The **Montego Bay Marlin Tournament** is held in late September; contact the **Montego Bay Yacht Club** (☎979-8038).

Charters can be booked through hotels, or you can contact **Chokey Taylor** (☎381-3229; chokey@reggaefimi.com; half-day charter US$450; Pier One Marina), a local reggae musician who loves to reel in big-game fish. Chokey also offers fishing excursions out to Ocho Rios for US$1250, which covers up to four passengers. At time of writing the going rate at other charters was US$500/1000 per boat for half/full day (up to six passengers).

Boat Trips

The number of party boat tours in Montego Bay is stupefyingly diverse. Most companies charge US$45 to US$80 for three-hour party cruises with open bars, and US$35 to US$45 for sunset and dinner cruises. You can also charter yachts for private group sailing trips from the Montego Bay Yacht Club at Montego Freeport.

Jamaica Cruise Excursions
BOAT TRIPS

(Map p146; ☎979-0102; Shop 204, Chatwick Plaza) We've had a reliably good time with this outfit that offers a catamaran adventure (US$65, 10am to 1pm and 3pm to 6pm Monday through Saturday) on swift boats specially designed for partying, with an open bar and a snorkeling stop in the marine park. Cruises depart from Doctor's Cave Beach Club. A bus will pick you up at your hotel.

☞ Tours

To paraphrase Yakov Smirnov, 'In Jamaica, tour company finds YOU.' Between your hotel or guest house and touts on the Hip Strip, someone's gonna approach you about taking a tour. There are always customization options available; trips to places like Negril, Dunn's River Falls (near Ocho Rios) and Nine Mile (the birthplace of Bob Marley, south of Ocho Rios) are de rigeur. If you find a taxi driver you get along with who offers to give you a personalized tour, consider the option: your money may go directly to someone you like, rather than being split among commission-takers.

Countrystyle Tours
CULTURAL TOURS

(☎962-7758; www.countrystyletourism.com) Technically based in Mandeville in St Elizabeth parish, Countrystyle operates tours all around Jamaica and is our favored option for community-based tourism activities on the island. Tours cater for individual tastes, and you're guaranteed an educational experience that exceeds the standard tour-group speeches. Contact a bit in advance.

Barrett Adventures
ADVENTURE TOURS

(☎382-6384; www.barrettadventures.com) Run by the organized and efficient Carolyn, Barrett specializes in nature and adventure tours around Montego Bay and across the country. White-water rafting, diving, horseback riding and bird-watching, plus some nice city tours, are all on offer.

Island Routes
SIGHTSEEING TOURS

(☎local or in the USA 1-877-768-8370, outside USA 1-305-663-4364) A large professional outfit. Does good tours around the country, and has a nice spread of options in Montego Bay and Falmouth (including a horse-and-buggy ride for those so inclined to *really* feel like plantation owners).

Winston Tours
SIGHTSEEING TOURS

(☎957-2075, 324-1419; www.winstontoursjamaica.com; winstontours@anbell.net) We recommend calling Winston for a personalized, intimate tour via his own JUTA-approved minibus. He'll tailor schedules for individual itineraries, which provides a nice level of flexibility.

Phillip Country Tours
SIGHTSEEING TOURS

(☎843-9840; www.phillipcountrytours.com) Like Winston Tours, Phillip provides personal (and personable) tours of his home island catering for individual travelers. A nice break from being herded around in a big bus.

Michael G CULTURAL TOURS
(www.toursbylocals.com/maroontour) Contact Michael through the Tours by Locals website for individually personalized tours of the Maroon country, Cockpit Country, and other areas not covered by the big package-tour dealers.

Maroon Attraction Tours CULTURAL TOURS
(Map p150; ☑971-3900, 700-8805; 32 Church St) Runs a cultural, educational and historical tour (US$60, 8am to 3:30pm Tuesday, Thursday and Saturday) to Maroon Town, south of MoBay.

Johns Hall Adventure Tours ADVENTURE TOURS
(Map p146; ☑971-7776; www.johnshalladventure tour.com; 26 Hobbs Ave) Includes fairly comprehensive tours of the south coast.

Tropical Tours SIGHTSEEING TOURS
(Map p156; ☑952-1126; www.tropicaltours-ja .com; 49 Gloucester Ave) Has a huge menu of tours, including a recommended US$20 half-day historical tour of Montego Bay.

Caribic Vacations SIGHTSEEING TOURS
(Map p156; ☑953-9895/6; www.caribicvaca tions.com; 1310 Providence Dr, Ironshore Estate) Caribic is a pretty big outfit, with well-trained tour guides. You'll be in the tourist herd, but the service is very reliable.

✪ Festivals & Events

Held in the fall, alternating between October and November, **Africa Jamfest** celebrates the African roots of Afro-Caribbean culture.

🛏 Sleeping

The following places are within Montego Bay proper; the top-end resorts and all-inclusives tend to cluster east of town in Ironshore. Note that all prices are high season (ie December–March) rates, which can be double or more during events like Reggae Sumfest (p20).

GLOUCESTER AVE (HIP STRIP)

Toby Resorts HOTEL **$$**
(Map p156; ☑952-4370, outside Jamaica 1-888-790-5264; www.tobysresorts.com; Cnr Gloucester Ave & Sunset Blvd; r from US$100; ❄☀🕾) Located just off the 'top' of the Hip Strip, Toby's provides admirable local vibe with amenities geared for discerning international travelers. In plain language: in terms of staff mood and attention, Toby's feels like a gracious guest house, except it also has large grounds, comfy (although not luxurious) rooms, a big pool, a good bar and restaurant and easy access to the beaches. A great midrange option.

Altamont West HOTEL **$$**
(Map p156; ☑620-4540, 979-9378; www.altamont westhotel.com; 33 Gloucester Ave; r US$110-180; ❄☀🕾) A brightly colored, vaguely art deco option well placed near Walter Fletcher Beach, the Altamont is popular with travelers who want a low-key but slightly luxurious place to stay amid the strongest beat of Jamaica's tourism heart. An airy common area offset with mustard yellow and rust-red interior accents adds to the warm yet breezy conviviality of the place. Rooms are fine – well decked out, a match for most all-inclusives.

Wexford HOTEL **$$**
(Map p156; ☑952-2854; www.thewexfordhotel.com; 39 Gloucester Ave; r from US$120, ste from US$200; ❄☀@☀) This hotel has undergone quite a few sprucings, and they've all been for the better. Rooms in the older wings are efficient but comfortable, while the newer wing offers elegant digs decked out in minimalist boutique-style elegance – they're a better option but a bit more expensive. The Wexford is convenient for Walter Fletch Beach, to which guests have free access. May have wi-fi by the time you read this.

Beachview Apartments APARTMENTS **$**
(Map p156; ☑971-3859, 952-8784; www.jamaica beachviewapartments.com; 39 Gloucester Ave; apt US$75; ❄☀☀) These self-contained apartments are excellent value for money. You're near all the Hip Strip action, bar-, restaurant- and beach-wise, but have the quiet and comfort of, essentially, your own place. Come with two or more people (each apartment has two double beds) and this is a great budget choice. The interior decor is kind of frilly (almost feels like your Jamaican grandmother's place), but we think this actually adds to the charm, as does the friendliness of the owners and staff.

Knightwick House B&B **$**
(Map p156; ☑952-2988; knightwick@hotmail. com; Corniche Rd; r from US$85; ❄☀) Behind and above the Coral Cliff Hotel, this wonderful B&B is close to the action without being overwhelmed by it. Run by a

charming couple, Jean and Stanley Magnus, the colonial structure – boasting terra-cotta floors, wrought-iron railings and abundant artwork – has three modest yet appealingly furnished bedrooms with one, two and three beds. All are well lit and airy, and each has a balcony.

Casa Blanca · HOTEL $$

(Map p156; ☑952-0720; Gloucester Ave) Casa Blanca is one of the older hotels on the Hip Strip, and was undergoing a major retrofit at the time of research (expect room rates to be in the high midrange category). From the look of the already completed lobby, reception area and a few rooms, the end product will be a boutique property that captures the glamour and style of the Jazz Age. Dark wood furnishings offset by white walls and floors, tasteful brass and copper accents – think of the Algonquin Round Table in the tropics, all set in a beautiful position above wave-battered cliffs.

Ridgeway Guest House · GUEST HOUSE $

(Map p146; ☑952-2709; www.ridgewayguesthouse. com; 34 Queens Dr; r US$45-80; ❈☎) This homey guest house makes you feel just like a guest in a friendly house, where the rooms surround a pretty garden and are as good a deal as any you'll find in MoBay. In fact they're comparable to midrange digs: cozy beds, tiled floors, nice furnishings, all kept quite clean and presentable. The cheapest ones are fan-cooled, which isn't really a problem, especially in winter. Located away from the beaches near the airport, but a free shuttle gets you to the sea and sand.

Hotel Gloriana · HOTEL $

(Map p146; ☑970-0669; www.hotelgloriana.com; 1-2 Sunset Ave; r US$46-65; ℗❈☎) Just east of the end of Gloucester Ave en route to the airport, this large family-run option has well-worn, somewhat dark rooms. There's a big pool, no-nonsense restaurant, and very friendly vibe – this is a popular spot with tourists and middle-class Jamaicans, which is the main draw for us: holidaying as the locals do. They've even made a movie about the Gloriana, entitled *Glory to Gloriana*. So nice they used the word twice.

Royal Decameron Montego Beach Resort · RESORT $$$

(Map p156; ☑952-4340; 2 Gloucester Ave; all-incl r US$185-220; ℗❂❈@☎) The Decameron gets good marks in the all-inclusive game. This welcoming low-rise beachfront resort has 143 rooms with creamy orange-and-white color schemes and its own pretty, private beach overlooked by a competent restaurant. Rooms all have ocean views and balconies. The range of activities is huge, as per normal at all-inclusives, including tennis, golf and water sports.

Doctor's Cave Beach Hotel · HOTEL $$

(Map p156; ☑952-4355; www.doctorscave.com; Gloucester Ave; r US$145-185; ℗❈@❂☎) If convenient beach access is a priority, this large hotel across the street from the main beach is an all-right choice. Labyrinthine corridors lead to well-appointed rooms and suites

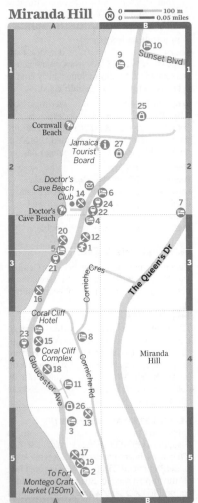

Miranda Hill

decorated in tropical themes. The lush gardens at the back are right up against the cliff face, where there's a whirlpool. There are complimentary yoga classes for guests and a topless sunbathing pool (which is a draw for those who are into that sort of thing who don't want to be gawked at on the beach).

Caribic House
HOTEL $

(Map p156; ☑979-6073; 69 Gloucester Ave; r US$35-70; ✳) This no-frills spot across the street from Doctor's Cave Beach is a favorite for budget-minded party people. The rooms are basic, the hot water doesn't always work and there's no real communal area, but that's not why folks come here. They come for cheap beds and easy access to fun on the Hip Strip. If you're into that (and not peace and quiet) this a good option.

MIRANDA HILL

TOP CHOICE **Richmond Hill Inn**
HOTEL $$

(Map p146; ☑952-3859; www.richmond-hill-inn.com; Union St; s/d/ste US$85/115/189; ⓟ✳🛜❄) It's hard to understand why anyone who can afford a night at the Richmond three times over (and that's *a lot* of tourists in Jamaica) would sleep elsewhere. This charming property is built of limestone, molasses and character. It's chock-full of antiques (some dating back to the early 1800s) and, with its wooden furnishings, plush sitting rooms and elegant verandas, feels like that rarest of things: a modern hotel that successfully captures the elegance and opulence of the colonial era without descending into cheap imitation. Worth checking out for the views over MoBay and excellent on-site restaurant alone.

Big Apple
GUEST HOUSE $

(Map p146; ☑952-7240; www.bigapplejamaica.com; 18 Queen's Dr; d/ste US$55/80; ⓟ✳❄) This pleasant hilltop inn is a good low-key option: simple and sweet. It's basic, and lovely for that. The property has a commanding view over Montego Bay, and tiled and air-con rooms with satellite TV. Rooms are all clean and well-kept, but vary in size (most come with two double beds) and quality of views; ask about both if booking ahead and the pleasant staff will accommodate.

Palm View Guesthouse
GUEST HOUSE $

(Map p146; ☑952-8321; www.montego-bay-jamaica.com/palmview/; 22 DeLisser Dr; d US$55, 2-/3-bedroom ste US$132/198; ⓟ🔆✳❄) Lacking in pretension, this secure, well-kept property five minutes from the airport offers rooms and suites with balconies, phones, small TVs and spacious bathrooms, all for a bargain rate. The old furniture and friendly staff make the place feel more comfortable.

Miranda Hill

Verney's Tropical Resort
GUEST HOUSE $

(Map p146; ☎952-2875; www.verneyhousehotel.com; 3 Leader Ave; r from US$77; P❋≋) Popular with Jamaican families, this option feels secluded (there are nice views over sugarcane fields) but is really only about a 10-minute walk from the heart of Montego Bay. Rooms are homey and clean and have cable TV. The open-air bar is pleasant, perfect for an after-beach drink under the stars.

El Greco
APARTMENTS $$

(Map p156; ☎940-6116; www.elgrecojamaica.com; 34 Queens Dr; 1-/2-bedroom apt US$135/195; P❋⊗≋) More like a condo-rental than a hotel, El Greco is a nice choice for those who value their comfort and their independence. The apartments have cable TV and kitchens, and private balconies that look out over a well-equipped complex that includes a pool, laundry service, tennis courts and kiddie play area (speaking of which, there's a babysitting service on site). This is an efficiently run operation, and booking from overseas tends to be refreshingly headache-free.

Jamaica Grandiosa Resort
GUEST HOUSE $

(Map p146; ☎979-3205; jamaicagrandiosa@hotmail.com; 3 Ramparts Close; r US$70; P❋≋) This unassuming hilltop property has 38 rooms with modest furnishings, cable TV, grandiose views and varying quality – some are kept quite clean, but others have faulty hot water and rusty furnishings. Being 20 minutes away from town, you do feel a little isolated (especially if there aren't many guests), but a free shuttle service to the beach is available. The dining room has a lofty vista. There's a small breeze-swept pool and sundeck, plus a pool table and an undistinguished bar.

AROUND MONTEGO BAY

In the following places you're a taxi ride (shared and public, or private and pricey) away from the Hip Strip.

View Guest House
GUEST HOUSE $

(Map p146; ☎952-3175; 56 Jarrett Tce; r $50; ❋≋) On the southeast edge of town on the downslope of the road that leads to Mt Salem is this family-run, extremely friendly option. Rooms are basic but clean and come with a lot of love – return guests (and there are many) are fanatic in their loyalty to this place, which should tell you something. Home-cooked meals are served, and it has a communal kitchen and bar, plus a view overlooking the city. There's no website as such, but there's a Facebook page (just search 'The View Guest House Montego Bay').

Brandon Hill Guest House
GUEST HOUSE $

(Map p146; ☎952-7054; www.brandonhillguesthouse.com; 28 Peter Pan Ave; s US$45-55, d U$50-60; P❋≋) Yet another smallish, family-run guest house with loyal returning clientele, a homey feel, basic amenities and much love. It has attractive gardens and a nice view, plus modestly furnished, well-lit rooms. The pool is a nice touch. Try to get a room with an airy balcony – with the right breeze you might not even need air-con.

Bethel Court
HOSTEL $

(☎476-7239, 971-0134; bethelcourt.wordpress.com; Federal Ave; dm/r from US$20/40; P❋⊗) Located in the outer neighborhood of Mt Salem, Bethel Court was one of the few dedicated hostels we found – not just in Montego Bay, but in Jamaica as a whole. It's run by Steve, a friendly guy who works hard to help set up tours and arrange transportation if you need it. The dorms are communal and clean but just remember: backpackers in Jamaica tend to love their reggae, so don't expect peace and quiet. But it's friendly and convivial, as hostels tend to be. The private rooms are fine, but you'll get more bang for your buck at similarly priced guest houses, although those aren't as conducive to meeting other travelers.

Sandals Montego Bay
RESORT $$$

(☎952-5510; www.sandals.com; N Kent Ave; all-incl r from US$435; P⊝❋⊗≋) This is the original Sandals, one of the great-granddaddies of all-inclusive resorts. With, at last count, no less than five restaurants, four bars (including a swim-up, natch) and more activities than a summer camp, you're spoiled for choice for things to do. The resort beach is beautiful, the plantation-style furnishing is actually quite tasteful and guests get free access to Sandals' other Jamaican properties. Located north of the city just a few miles past Sangster International Airport.

Sunset Beach Resort & Spa
RESORT $$$

(Map p146; ☎979-8800, 800-888-1199; www.sunsetbeachjamaica.com; Sunset Dr; all-incl r from $US270; P❋⊗≋) At the end of the Montego Freeport Peninsula is this 430-room, twin high-rise, upscale, all-inclusive resort. Rooms have ocean or bay views, mahogany beds, a whole mess of tropical prints and private balcony. Ask for one with a Jacuzzi. There are restaurants, discos and bars on the grounds, plus tennis courts, pools, gym and spa, business center and three beaches (with a nudist section) with water sports.

Relax Resort
RESORT $$
(Map p146; ☑979-0656; www.relax-resort.com; 26 Hobbs Ave; r US$78, studio US$141, 1-/2-/3-bed-room ste US$151/221/297; ❂❄@☀) This breeze-swept resort is an agreeable choice – not as flashy as larger all-inclusives, but not as informal as a normal hotel either. There are a lot of grounds to wander and a good range of large rooms with floral prints, tile floors and ocean views. The larger three-bedroom villas are definitely the best deal, a great option for those traveling with a lot of friends who book well in advance.

Comfort Guest House
GUEST HOUSE $
(Map p146; ☑952-1238; 55 Jarrett Tce; r US$50; ❂❄) Run by a devoutly Christian family, the Comfort is a nice option for people who eschew the party atmosphere and want a quiet vacation. Everything is kept spick-and-span, there's a nice sundeck for relaxing and the owning family is lovely in the extreme.

🍴 Eating

Montego Bay is a good place to sample 'haute' Jamaican food – fancy takes on traditional Caribbean cuisine. The steady influx of free-spending vacationers, many of whom are desperate to escape the tyranny of the all-inclusive meal plan, means there are plenty of upmarket restaurants. Cheap local eats are tough to find on the Hip Strip. As per usual, if you see a jerk stand on the side of the road billowing clouds of blue smoke and attracting lots of locals, eat at it.

DOWNTOWN
Adwa
VEGETARIAN $
(Map p150; City Centre Mall; mains J$180-400; ❂breakfast & lunch; ☑) As is often the case in Jamaica, the diamonds are in the rough – or in this case, the 2nd floor of a shopping mall. By 'diamond' we mean fantastic cheap vegetarian fare, fruit juice so fresh it tastes like liquid sunlight (OK, it was a long, hot and dusty day when we stopped in) and silky smoothies. Curry tofu and soy patties are delicious, even if you're a dedicated carnivore.

MoBay Proper
JAMAICAN $
(Map p150; 44 Fort St; mains J$300-800; ❂lunch & dinner) The name is both revealing and misleading. 'Proper' is located in proper (as opposed to tourist) Montego Bay, but the

behavior inside, attire and attitude is totally casual, and we mean that in the best possible way. This is a Jamaican sports bar that's as friendly to tourists as it is to locals. That may be because it's popular with returning Jamaican expats as well as guys from around the block, so it knows how to cater to local, foreign, and locals-influenced-by-foreign tastes. The usual brown-stewed dishes, rice and peas, and curried loveliness are on offer, although their preparation is anything but run-of-the-mill; this stuff is delicious. Turns into a raucously fun bar at night.

Nyam 'n' Jam
JAMAICAN $
(Map p150; 17 Harbour St; mains J$300-700; ❂breakfast, lunch & dinner) This is where Jamaicans who crave something a little different head. When we say different, it's just an *ickle* (little) bit different, but enough to be interesting. Sure, there's jerked meat, callaloo and saltfish – but we've also seen cow mouth, soups that use hooves as a base and a frankly bewildering array of goat dishes, all of them lovely. The name, by the way, is patois for 'eat and relax.'

Pier One
AMERICAN $$
(Map p150; Howard Cooke Blvd; mains US$8-18; ❂lunch & dinner) Best known as a nightclub, Pier One also has a restaurant with a good, clean, waterfront setting – all of which are more of a draw than the average sandwiches, burgers and seafood.

GLOUCESTER AVE (HIP STRIP)
Native Restaurant & Bar
JAMAICAN $$
(Map p156; 29 Gloucester Ave; ☑979-2769; mains US$8-25; ❂breakfast, lunch & dinner) The Native is one of Montego Bay's best practitioners of the haute Jamaican cuisine trope. Eating here educates you on Jamaican cuisine while opening new vistas of the genre's possibilities – chicken cooked in a citrusy ginger sauce is a delicious example. If you're really hungry, consider the 'Boonoonoonoos' sampler (composed of ackee and saltfish, jerk chicken, curried goat, escoveitched fish, plantains and pineapple) – it's like taking a crash course in Jamaican food.

Dolly's Café
JAMAICAN $$
(Map p146; Hotel Gloriana Plaza, 1 Sunset Blvd; mains US$6-20; ❂breakfast, lunch & dinner) This cozy pub-style dining room is the place for *real* Jamaican cooking. The menu features time-honored favorites like pepperpot soup, roast pumpkin and a unique, delectable snack that you'll want to take along for

SELF-CATERING YOUR MONTEGO BAY STAY

Self-caterers are served by well-stocked modern supermarkets and open-air **farmers markets** (note: not yuppie farmers markets with artisanal cheese, but markets where farmers sell scallions, yams and carrots). Look for higglers selling bags of delicious (and cheap) pepper shrimp – fair warning, these usually have some kick. You can haggle with local fishers over fresh lobster and the morning catch in **Whitehouse Village** at the northern edge of town if you want to prep your own fresh seafood.

For fresh produce downtown, head to the **Gully Market** (Map p146; Orange St) between Union and William Sts, and **Fustic Street Market** (Barnett St).

Downtown supermarkets include those at **MoBay Shopping Centre** (Map p150; cnr Howard Cooke Dr & Market St) and **Westgate Shopping Centre** (Map p146; Barnett St) on the A1 south of town, but the largest and most modern is the **Super Plus** (Map p146; ☏953-6980; Fairview Shopping Centre, Alice Eldemire Dr).

the ride: baked coconut chips. You can't do much better than Dolly's hearty Jamaican breakfasts; standout selections include 'steam fish and bananas' and 'mackerel rundown' (salted fish stewed in coconut milk).

Pelican   JAMAICAN $$
(Map p156; Gloucester Ave; mains J$400-1000; ☺7am-11:30pm; ☻) The Pelican perches just over the Hip Strip both in terms of location and quality of fare. This is one of many places in MoBay that does Jamaican food with a sit-down, refined twist: red snapper in parchment paper, cooked in a wine-and-béchamel sauce, is a rich, delicate evolution of peasant fare. The rest of the menu is a study in this sort of upgraded traditionalism, but don't think of this place as fancy; it feels more like an ambitious diner.

Toby's Good Eats   JAMAICAN $$
(Map p156; Toby Resorts, cnr Gloucester Ave & Sunset Blvd; mains J$500-1200; ☺breakfast, lunch & dinner) As casual eats go, Toby's is a good choice, especially if you're staying on Sunset Dr and don't feel like venturing onto the actual Hip Strip. The menu features red snapper prepared the local way (steamed in foil with Jamaican veggies and spices), vegetable dishes and pasta. Stick around for some stick (ie pool) after dinner.

Twisted Kilt   BRITISH $$
(Map p156; Gloucester Ave; mains J$450-1200; ☺11am-2am) One of the more pleasant surprises on the Hip Strip is that this English pub, with Irish-themed signs and a technically Scottish-themed name, does genuinely lovely pub grub. If you need a shepherd's pie or a juicy burger you could do a lot worse than this spot, which also happens to have a lovely outdoor deck. Opt to eat there, as they

keep the interior air-con set to 'winter's day in the Arctic.'

Ma Lou's   JAMAICAN $$
(Map p156; Coral Cliff Casino, Gloucester Ave; mains US$14-31; ☺dinner) You expect kind of tacky African-themed corniness in the Coral Cliff Casino; the surprise is that the gaudiness hides an exciting nouvelle-Jamaican restaurant. Ma Lou is either humble or marketing-savvy enough to refer to herself as a 'gourmet food shack.' A hole in the wall this ain't, but enough with the setting: how about the food? Roasted Peking chicken, curry with coconut and fried plantain, and specialty jerks grace this menu and, if you're smart, your taste buds.

Pork Pit   JERK $
(Map p156; 27 Gloucester Ave; mains J$300-800; ☺11am-11pm) For many visitors, the Pork Pit is their first jerk-in-Jamaica experience. Makes sense; the place smells great, and while it's an open-air, picnic table sorta joint (shaded by a gargantuan silk-cotton tree that the chef reckons to be 300 years old), it's on the Hip Strip, so it's accessible to all tourists. That said, we want to make something clear: while quite good, this is not the best jerk in Jamaica, or even Montego Bay. It's a solid 7 out of 10, and the *festival* (fried sweet cornbread) is a 9 out of 10, so have at it and enjoy. Just don't limit your jerk quest to the Pork Pit, which many people seem to do.

Brewery   AMERICAN $$
(Map p156; Miranda Ridge Plaza; mains US$8-16; ☺11am-2am) Open-air balcony, loud music, groaning portions of burgers, tacos and Jamaican standards, cold Red Strip – sounds all right. As it'll take you a while to finish

your invariably large meal, maybe you can stick around afterward – when the Brewery becomes more of a bar.

Marguerite's
JAMAICAN $$$
(Map p156; Gloucester Ave; mains US$12-33; ⊙6-10:30pm) Adjoining Margaritaville, this celebrated restaurant provides a lovely setting from which to watch the sunset while drinking cocktails, followed by dinner on the elegant clifftop patio. The pricey menu edges toward nouvelle Jamaican and fresh seafood, but also includes sirloin steak and inventive pasta. The chef displays his culinary chops at a central flambé grill.

Golden Dynasty
CHINESE $
(Map p156; 39 Gloucester Ave; mains J$400-800; ⊙lunch & dinner) Sometimes you just you need basic Chinese food, which is to say rice and fried things and glistening, oily sauces, a meal that is solidly middle of the road: mid-priced, mid-flavor, mid-satisfying. Enter the Golden Dynasty: the Hip Strip's answer to your chow mein dilemma. Middle of the road, but comfortably so.

Groovy Grouper
AMERICAN $
(Map p156; Doctor's Cave Beach; mains US$6-14; ⊙9am-1:30am) Location is the attraction of this spot on Doctor's Cave Beach. The food – burgers, seafood and such – is average, you get to eat it with the sand between your toes and the salt water drying on your back, so who gives a toss?

AROUND MONTEGO BAY

TOP CHOICE Houseboat Grill
JAMAICAN $$$
(Map p146; ☑979-8845; Southern Cross Blvd; mains US$15-32; ⊙dinner Tue-Sun) Moored in Bogue Bay at Montego Bay Freeport, this converted houseboat is one of the best restaurants in the country. The changing menu offers eclectic Caribbean fusion cuisine: tiger shrimp in a fiery red curry, or beef medallions with goat's cheese and plantain mashed potatoes, plus homemade ice cream. You can dine inside, or reclusively out on the moondeck. The bar draws the local middle class and is open from 4:30pm until the last guest goes home. Reservations are strongly recommended, especially on weekends. Dress up, but not too much (ie smart casual).

Day-O Plantation
JAMAICAN $$
(Map p146; ☑952-1825; Fairfield Plantation; mains US$8-22; ⊙9am-9pm Mon-Sat, 10am-6pm Sun; ☑) Ignore the cheesy name of this place if you can and just focus on the fact that

this spot, about 3km west of Montego Bay proper, is romantic as hell, housed in a beautiful mansion that elegantly makes use of colonial furnishings and serves some very fine food. Snapper done up with sweet peppers and olives is a surprisingly fresh take on the Jamaican original, as is a delicate curried shrimp. Maintains one of the best high-end vegetarian menus in the area as well – give the curry caribe, a bend of local fruits and vegetables doused in spicy gravy, a try.

Evelyn's
JAMAICAN $
(☑979-8822; Kent Ave, Whitehouse; mains J$300-700; ⊙9am-9pm Mon-Sat, 10am-6pm Sun) Fantastic choice: a true local's spot, essentially a rustic seafood shack (near Sandals Montego Bay) that's also patronized by some very in-the-know tourists. The food tends to be rich yet refined – layered and pleasantly oily without being overwhelmingly heavy (as is often the case in Jamaica). They know how to utilize spice here: ask for something mild and mild it shall be (but still tasty); ask for it spicy and you will get a heat/flavor combination of the gods. Anything that comes in curry form will be one of your best meals in Montego Bay.

Richmond Hill
INTERNATIONAL $$$
(Map p146; Richmond Hill Inn, Union St; mains US$20-45; ⊙lunch & dinner) Need class? Get off the Hip Strip and head 150m above town to this terrace restaurant, where the elegant

QUICK EATS IN MO BAY

If you're in a rush or on the cheap or both: meat patties are always a good snack that could double as a meal. **Butterflake Pastries** (Map p150; Union St; ⊙breakfast, lunch & dinner) and nearby **Juici Patties** (Map p150; 36 St James St; ⊙breakfast, lunch & dinner) are good for cheap meat and vegetable patties. For bakeries that serve sweeter baked goods like cakes and cookies, try the **Viennese Bakery** (Map p150; 43 St James St) or **Hilton's Bakery** (Map p150; 5 Church St). Ice cream always takes the edge off Montego heat; we like to head to **Devon House I-Scream** (Map p150; Bay West Centre, Howard Cook Dr) or **Calypso Gelato** (Map p156; 75 Gloucester Ave). You're hard pressed to spend more than J$400 at any of these places.

Victorian furnishings are topped by lovely views out to the ocean, themselves topped by a lovely menu of seafood and steaks, all sumptuous, rich and mouth-watering. One of the few places in Jamaica where we blew a lot of money on a meal and didn't feel a little cheated. Lunch is a lighter affair, with sandwiches and fish-and-chips. Worth the trek uphill, even if only for a drink.

Dragon Court   CHINESE **$$**
(Map p146; ☎979-8822; Fairview Shopping Centre, Alice Eldemire Dr; meals US$8-32; ⏱lunch & dinner) This is the best fine-dining Chinese cuisine in MoBay, located in the modern Fairview Shopping Centre. The menu is replete with Chinese standards, with a few standouts including the tempting crispy duckling with plum sauce, and 'reggae fish' with pimentos and other Jamaican spices. Call ahead and make a reservation if you want to sample the sushi.

🍸 Drinking & Entertainment

The nightlife in Montego Bay ranges from the obnoxious to the lethargic, with little bits of 'that was actually pretty fun' sprinkled throughout. The Hip Strip can be surprisingly sedate while upscale hotels mostly have lackluster live bands, so if you're looking for the big party, it may be best to head over to Negril. Local bars outside of the Hip Strip can get lively, but if you plan to venture beyond Fort St after dark, you may want to do so with some Jamaican friends. That said, more locals party on the Hip Strip than you might think – the area is popular with middle-class Jamaicans.

MoBay Proper   BAR
(Map p150; Fort St) Proper is often packed with friendly locals and expats returned to the motherland. It's a friendly, occasionally raucous spot, and probably the easiest bar for tourists to access off the Hip Strip. Beneath a 'chandelier' of Heineken bottles the pool table generates considerable heat, while dominoes are the rage with an older crowd out on the patio.

Reggae Bar   BAR
(Map p156; Gloucester Ave) While it may not win the award for the most imaginatively named bar in Jamaica, this two-story shack, done up in (surprise, surprise) lots of reggae flags and Marley-esque art, does serve some of the cheapest drinks on the Hip Strip. J$80 for some overproof rum? Yes

please. Besides playing pool, listening to reggae and getting drunk, there's not much atmosphere.

Brewery   BAR
(Map p156; Miranda Ridge Plaza) This is a popular sports bar with young and well-to-do Jamaicans, which makes it a good place for getting a bit of local vibe without ever leaving the confines of the Hip Strip. As the night gets later, the crowd gets more local-heavy; by 2am this bar is straight-up Jamaican (which means loud, kind of aggressive and pretty fun if you're into that scene).

Twisted Kilt   PUB
(Map p156; Gloucester Ave; ⏱11am-2am) Every town needs a faux Irish pub, and this is Montego Bay's contribution to the genre. The Kilt is a decent enough place for a beer (although we recommend sitting outside – the interior's kept frigid). The best draw is an extensive martini menu that makes for a nice break from Red Stripe.

Jamaican Bobsled Cafe   BAR
(Map p156; 69 Gloucester Ave; ⏱10am-2am) This watering hole makes a good-natured attempt to capitalize on everybody's favorite fish-out-of-water story – the Jamaican bobsled team immortalized in the film *Cool Runnings*, which is played in a perpetual loop on a corner screen. Honestly, if you can sit through John Candy on repeat through an entire night, you deserve one of the strong rum punches. The actual bobsled is on site, and you can get your picture in it.

Jimmy Buffett's Margaritaville   BAR
(Map p156; Gloucester Ave; after 10pm: US$10) Of all the Margaritavilles in Jamaica (three at last count), this one maybe actually does provide something like a local nightlife experience. Seriously – don't slam the book shut yet! By day, yes, it's a tourist trap. But as night falls a lot of Jamaicans like to come here, and we've seen local couples get on the dance floor and do a Dutty Wine that would make a Kingstonian blush. This hometown crowd sets the Montego Margaritaville a bit apart from its counterparts, although there are still some big ugly tiki heads and a waterslide to carry revelers through the plumbing to flush them ignominiously into the ocean near a floating trampoline.

Blue Beat Jazz & Blues Bar   LOUNGE
(Map p156; Gloucester Ave; ⏱closes 2am) Blue Beat is located next to Marguerite's restau-

rant, and kind of feels like a collection of clichés of what a classy cocktail bar should look like (smooth metal furnishing, dim lighting, dark curtains and a general sense of heavily-cologned polish throughout). It's icy cool inside, and there's a beautiful deck where beautiful people congregate outside. Montego Bay's first jazz and blues martini bar offers live music nightly and Asian-Caribbean fusion cuisine.

Pier One   NIGHTCLUB
(Map p150; Howard Cooke Blvd) If you're into big nightclubs, Pier One is the place to go in Montego Bay. It attracts a largely local crowd, all dressed to impress and dancing as if their lives depended on it. The music is earsplitting, the dance floor is crowded and sweaty (especially on Friday nights) and the light shows will leave you seeing spots for days afterward.

Rum Jungle   LOUNGE
(Map p156; Coral Cliff Casino, Gloucester Ave) There's honestly just about nothing we like about the bar in Coral Cliff Casino. There's cheesy 'African' decor, slot machines jangling away at depressed-looking gamblers... but then, oh, the karaoke. Because this isn't just karaoke – it's like 'Jamaican Idol'. Trust us folks, there are some people in greater Montego Bay who can *sing*. The schedule changes up; when we visited Wednesday night was karaoke night, but we hear this might be shifting to Tuesday or Monday, so ask at your accommodations.

Havana Club   CIGAR BAR
(Map p156; Gloucester Ave) Filled with Jamaican bigwigs, expats and tourists, this spot has good liquor and a genuinely impressive cigar selection.

Groovy Grouper   BAR
(Map p156; Doctor's Cave Beach Club) The beachside location is the main draw here; otherwise the cocktails cost a small fortune.

Montego Bay Yacht Club   PRIVATE CLUB
(Map p146; Montego Bay Freeport) This rum-happy haunt attracts an eclectic crowd that includes crusty old sea-salts and expats eager to talk about their new boats. Nonmembers must be signed in as guests, but this is rarely an issue.

Fairfield Theatre   THEATER
(Map p146; ☎952-0182; Fairfield Rd) The home stage of MoBay's innovative Little Theatre Company; check its Facebook page (just

So you know, some bars on the Hip Strip (Dreamz, Xtatic and probably any other place with misplaced letters from the end of the alphabet) are strip clubs. Oddly enough, they also attract a clientele you might not expect: lots of couples and single women, along with men out for the show. That's just how some roll – drinking, dancing and carrying on while naked women gyrate on stage. Despite the 'normal' crowd at these places, male and female tourists can expect propositions from, hmmm, 'professionals' in these spots, so fair warning.

search for 'Fairfield Theatre') for info on upcoming shows.

Palace Multiplex   CINEMA
(Map p146; ☎979-8359; Fairview Shopping Centre, Alice Eldemire Dr) First-run Hollywood flicks.

🛍 Shopping

Cashing in on the droves of tourists intent on taking home a souvenir, Gloucester Ave is lined with shops containing indistinguishable inventories of rum, cigars, T-shirts and the like.

Craft Markets   CRAFTS
For the largest crafts selection head to the **Harbour Street Craft Market** (Harbour St; ◐7am-7pm), which extends for three blocks between Barnett and Market Sts. **Fantasy Craft Market** (Map p156; ◐8am-7pm), at the southern end of Gloucester Ave, and **Fort Montego Craft Market** (Map p150; ◐8am-7pm), behind the fort, offer less variety and quality. You can expect a hard sell at all of these places, so bring your haggling skills and don't be afraid to walk away from something you don't like.

Gallery of West Indian Art   ART
(Map p146; ☎952-4547; www.galleryofwestindian art.com; 11 Fairfield Rd) In the suburb of Catherine Hall, this is the best quality gallery in town. It sells genuinely original arts and crafts from around the Caribbean including Cuban canvases, hand-painted wooden animals, masks and handmade jewelry. Most of the work here is for sale.

Ambiente Gallery   ART
(Map p150; ☎952-7747; 10 Fort St) Has a fine selection of fine-art prints by regional artists.

Some of the bigger shopping centers around town include **Chatwick Plaza** (Map p146), **Fairview Shopping Centre** (Map p146), **Miranda Ridge Plaza** (Map p156), **MoBay Shopping Centre** (Map p146), **Overton Plaza** (off Map p150), **St James Plaza** (Map p156), **Westgate Shopping Centre** (Map p146) and **West Bay Centre** (Map p146).

ℹ Information

Dangers & Annoyances

The Hip Strip (Gloucester Ave) is safe from criminals, but hustling may be an issue. There are aggressive hucksters in MoBay who will size you up and either try to charm or intimidate you out of a few bucks (or more) if they think you're green. Walk with purpose wherever you go; if you look lost or confused, you'll be an easier mark. That said, don't be afraid to ask for directions (shop-keepers are usually helpful, especially downtown).

Once you get downtown, the main drag (Fort St) is generally fine, but don't wander too far afield from it after dark; east of here, past Orange St, is a squatter neighborhood that's best avoided. Just across from the KFC that sits between the Hip Strip and downtown MoBay is a sparsely-vegetated field fronting a bit of sand known, pretty accurately, as Dump-Up Beach. It is best to avoid this area, especially at night. This is a popular spot for muggings, which are known to occur even in broad daylight. In any case, the water here mixes with untreated runoff that trickles out of downtown drains.

Emergency

Police stations Barnett St (☑952-2333, 952-1557; 14 Barnett St); Catherine Hall (☑952-4997, 953-6309; cnr Southern Cross Rd & Howard Cooke Dr); Church St (☑952-4396, 952-5310; 29 Church St); Union St (☑940-3500; 49 Union St)

Police Tourism Liaison Unit (☑952-1540; Summit Police Station, Sunset Blvd)

Internet Resources

Warning: none of these sites are particularly good at updating.

Official Visitors Guide (www.montego-bay-jamaica.com) The most extensive online resource for MoBay and environs.

Visit Jamaica (www.visitjamaica.com) The official line on the city from the Jamaica Tourism Board.

What's On Jamaica (www.whatsonjamaica.com) Entertainment and culture listings.

Medical Services

You'll find plenty of pharmacies Downtown.

Cornwall Medical Centre (☑979-6107; 19 Orange St) Private clinic.

Cornwall Regional Hospital (☑952-5100; Mt Salem Rd) Has a 24-hour emergency ward.

Doctor's Hospital (☑952-1616; Fairfield Rd) Private hospital southeast of town.

Fontana Pharmacy (☑952-3860; Fairview Shopping Centre) The best-stocked and largest pharmacy in town.

Montego Bay Dental Clinic (☑952-2338; 11 Dome St)

Money

At Donald Sangster International Airport there's a 24-hour money-exchange bureau and a branch of **National Commercial Bank** (☑952-2354) in the arrivals hall, but it doesn't change at good rates. You'll need local currency to take the bus into town, but taxis accept US dollars. The going rate at the time of writing was around US$25.

Better rates can be found on the main strip. Downtown, several bureaus can be found on St James St and Fort St; look for 'cambio' signs. Banks on Sam Sharpe Sq and in the Bay West Centre all have 24-hour ATMs. Flanking the Doctor's Cave Beach Club are ATMs operated by National Commercial Bank and Scotiabank. The cruise-ship terminal is served by a branch of **National Commercial Bank** (☑979-8060) in the Montego Freeport Shopping Centre.

Cambio King (☑971-5260; Gloucester Ave) Currency exchange, northern end of the street.

First Global Bank (☑971-5260; 53 Gloucester Ave)

FX Trader (☑952-3171; 37 Gloucester Ave; ⊙9am-5pm Mon-Sat) Currency exchange.

Western Union (☑926-2454) Branches at the Pelican restaurant on Gloucester Ave, at 19 Church St, and in Shop 9, Overton Plaza, at the top of Dome St.

Post

DHL (☑979-0543; 34 Queens Dr)

FedEx (☑952-0411, 888-991-9081; Chatwick Plaza, 10 Queen's Dr)

Post office Fort St (Map p150; ☑952-7016); White Sands Beach (Map p156; ☑979-5137; Gloucester Ave)

Tourist Information

Jamaica Tourist Board booth (Map p146; ☑952-3009; Donald Sangster International Airport; ⊙for flight arrivals) In the arrivals hall at Donald Sangster International Airport.

Jamaica Tourist Board office (Map p156; ☑952-4425; fax 952-3587; ⊙8:30am-4:30pm Mon-Fri, 9am-1pm Sat) Off Gloucester Ave, opposite the entrance to Cornwall Beach.

TPDCo information booth (Map p150; ☑979-7987; ⊙9am-5pm) At the downtown craft market.

Getting There & Away

Air

Air Jamaica (922-4661, 888-359-2475, in the USA 800-523-5585; www.airjamaica.com; 9 Queen's Dr; 8:30am-4:30pm Mon-Fri) operates jet and prop-plane services between Mo-Bay's Donald Sangster International Airport and Kingston's Norman Manley International Airport and Tinson Pen Aerodrome (US$60 each way, several flights daily). Get tickets at the Montego Bay office or at the airport.

TimAir (952-2516, 979-1114; www.timair.net; domestic terminal, Donald Sangster International Airport), an 'air taxi' service, offers charter flights to Negril (US$179), Ocho Rios (US$362), Port Antonio (US$599) and Kingston (US$483).

Boat

Cruise ships berth at the Montego Freeport, about 3km south of town. Taxis to downtown MoBay cost US$20. See p292 for details on cruise companies serving Montego Bay.

Montego Bay Yacht Club (979-8038; fax 979-8262; Montego Freeport) has hookups, gasoline and diesel, and will handle immigration and customs procedures.

Bus & Minibus

Comfortable **Knutsford Express buses** (Map p146; 971-1822; www.knutsfordexpress.com) run from their own bus terminal near the Courts furniture store in Downtown MoBay to Ocho Rios (J$1200, two hours) and Kingston (J$2000, four hours). Book a Kingston ticket more than 24 hours in advance and get a discount of J$250. Be at the bus station 30 minutes before departure to register your ticket. Departures are at 5am, 9am, 1pm and 5pm Monday to Friday, 6am and 4:30pm Saturday and 8:30am, 1:30pm and 4:30pm Sunday.

Minibuses (ie vans) run directly to Ocho Rios (J$250 to J$300, two hours; onward transfers to Port Antonio and Kingston) and Lucea (J$200, one to 1½ hours; onward transfers to Negril, though some minibuses will continue on to Negril, thus eliminating the need for a transfer).

More land routes can be accessed via share taxis.

Car

Car rental companies with offices at Donald Sangster International Airport:
Bargain (952-0762)
Budget (952-3838)
Hertz (979-0438)
Island Rental Car (952-5771)

Companies with offices in Montego Bay:
Dhana Car Rentals (953-9555; www.mobay.com; 4 Holiday Village Shopping Centre)

Eden (797-9924; www.edancarrental.com; 3 Churchill Ave)

Efay (952-8280; www.efay.com; 3 Churchill Ave)

Ace Rent-a-Car (http://www.acerentacar.com/landing/lp_mbjo01.aspx) books online only.

Public Transportation

Buses, minibuses and route taxis arrive and depart from the **transportation center** off Barnett St at the south end of St James St. There's an **inspector's office** (7am-6pm) inside the gate where you can ask for the departure point of the bus you're seeking.

Montego Bay Metro Line (Map p150; 952-5500; 19A Union St) bus service was introduced in 2001, linking MoBay with the suburbs and outlying towns (a flat fare of US$0.35 applies).

Private Taxi

Jamaica Union of Travelers Association (JUTA; 952-0813) has taxi stands on Gloucester Ave at the Gloucestershire and Coral Cliff hotels and at Doctor's Cave Beach Hotel, downtown at the junction of Market and Strand Sts, and by the bus station. Identify JUTA members by the red plates and JTB decal emblazoned on their vehicles.

A list of official JUTA fares from Montego Bay is posted at the airport. At last visit, certified fares from the airport for up to four passengers: Falmouth (US$75), Kingston (US$200), Negril (US$100), Ocho Rios (US$100) and Port Antonio (US$250).

Shared Taxi

Shared (also known as route or public) taxis are located downtown at the junction of Market and Strand Sts, and by the bus station. Taxis run when full to locations like Falmouth (J$100 to J$150), Lucea (J$200), Anchovy (J$150), Savanna-la-Mar (J$300), Ocho Rios (J$250) and smaller towns in between. You can almost always find a taxi early in the morning or around 4pm to 5pm (ie commuting hours); there will likely be a wait at other times of the day, and long-distance taxi service slacks off after sunset. It's always easier to get a ride to towns on the coast compared to towns in the interior.

Getting Around

You can walk between any place along Gloucester Ave and downtown (it's about 2.5km from Kent Ave to Sam Sharpe Sq). You'll need a vehicle for anywhere further.

To/From the Airport

You'll find taxis waiting outside the arrivals lounge at the airport. There is an official taxi

Route taxis ply set routes and charge set fares for set distances and are the cheapest way to get around Montego Bay. Assuming they have room, route drivers will pick up anyone standing along their route who waves the taxi down.

Route taxis can be recognized by the red license plates and the writing on the side of the driver's door, which indicates the taxi's route (in Montego, the routes are named for neighborhoods: Flankers, Mt Salem etc).

The usual cost for a route is about J$80, perhaps double that if heading to the outer suburbs. There are no official pick-up points, but taxis reliably congregate near Sam Sharpe Sq, the junction of Market and Strand Sts, and by the bus station. Rates go up by as much as 50% after dark, when route taxis become more difficult to find.

Although both route and JUTA drivers use red plates, it's safe to assume cars on the Hip Strip are JUTA vehicles, and those anywhere else are route taxis. Route-taxi drivers will often offer to provide you with private transportation; if you like the driver, we say go for it.

booth immediately outside customs. Your taxi driver will probably call for a porter...who'll expect a tip for taking your luggage the 10m to your car. A tourist taxi to Gloucester Ave costs US$10. Alternatively, you can catch a minibus or route taxi from the gas station at the entrance to the airport (J$80).

Public Transportation

There is no in-town bus service. Montego Bay Metro Line buses (p165) operate to the suburbs, as do minibuses and route taxis. All depart and arrive at the transportation center near the junction of St James and Barnett Sts.

Taxi

Licensed JUTA taxis cruise Gloucester Ave; they charge a steep US$10 minimum. Published fares from Gloucester Ave are US$10 to the airport, US$23 to Greenwood, US$15 to Ironshore, US$15 to Montego Freeport and US$15 to Rose Hall.

EAST COAST TO RIO BUENO

East of Montego Bay the A1 hugs the coast (which here is not particularly scenic) all the way to Falmouth, 37km away.

Ironshore

As you head east of Montego Bay the coast becomes a long stretch of screensaver-worthy beach, speckled with golf courses, all-inclusive resorts, high-end condos and expensive malls, all of which are marketed at wealthy tourists and the Jamaican upper class, many of whom opt to live here

instead of the ritzier suburbs of Kingston. Ironshore, about 8km east of Montego Bay, is the epicenter of this little window of luxury.

🏃 Activities

Most all-inclusive resorts have scuba facilities and snorkeling gear for guests.

Half Moon Equestrian Centre   HORSEBACK RIDING
(☑953-9489; www.horsebackridingjamaica.com) The lovely grounds of this center, just west of Half Moon Village, are a nice slice of the Kentucky bluegrass in paradise; the horses here are well-kept, and many are ex-racehorses. The main draw is the classic bareback **beach ride** (US$80; ☺7am & 4pm) during which you and your horse splash straight into the turquoise sea in a scene worthy of a book cover graced by Fabio, heaving bosoms and tight corsets (almost – you do have to weary distinctly unsexy helmets). For the kiddies there's also a **pony ride** (US$20; ☺9am-noon & 2-5pm). Riding lessons cost US$60 per 45 minutes. Transportation from your hotel can be arranged.

White Witch Golf Course   GOLF
(☑953-2800, 518-0174; www.whitewitchgolf.com; Ritz-Carlton Rose Hall; green fees Ritz-Carlton guests/visitors US$175/185, from 2:30-4:30pm US$109) A par-71 championship course, this is perhaps the most splendid of the three championship-level golf courses around Ironshore. Green fees cover caddy and cart. Rates go down from May through December.

Resort Divers   DIVING

([phone]973-6131; www.resortdivers.com; 2 Gloucester Ave) One of the most well-established outfits on the north coast, located in Montego Bay in the Royal DeCameron Hotel.

Dressel Divers   DIVING

([phone]in Spain +34 963 561 496; www.dresseldivers.com; Rose Hall) Based out of the Iberostar Resort in Rose Hall, which caters to a mainly European (especially Spanish) clientele.

Half Moon Golf Club   GOLF

([phone]953-2560, 953-3105; www.halfmoon.rockresorts.com; Half Moon Resort; green fees US$150) Robert Trent Jones-designed, par-72 course – you pay extra for cart rental (US$45) and caddy (US$20).

SuperClubs Golf Club Montego Bay at Ironshore   GOLF

([phone]953-3681) This is a links-type course known for its blind-shot holes. It was undergoing a change in ownership to the Breezes Resort Group at time of writing.

Dive Seaworld   DIVING

([phone]953-2180; www.diveseaworld.com; Rose Hall) Inexplicably popular, this operation seemed down-at-the-heels when we visited.

🎊 Festivals & Events

Mojo 6 Golf Tournament   GOLF

(www.themojo6.com; ⊙Apr) Major LPGA golfers compete in a short-timeframe 'raceway golf' tournament.

🛏 Sleeping

Coyaba Beach Resort & Club   RESORT $$$

([phone]953-9150, 800-237-3237; www.coyabaresortjamaica.com; r US$300-380; [P][icons]) Coyaba proves high-end resorts in Jamaica don't have to be owned by large chains, gaudy and ostentatious. This classy joint is family run, contemporary and elegant. It has 50 luxurious rooms and junior suites furnished plantation-style with hand-carved beds, floral drapes and rich mahogany reproduction antiques. Water sports are offered, and there's a lovely sundeck, as well as the pretty **Vineyard Restaurant**, which offers splendid nouvelle-Jamaican cuisine. The resort also has an ocean-side bar and grill, and an equestrian-themed polo club that will have you wanting jodhpurs and a lime rickey *now*, dammit. The full-service **SpaSerenity** (⊙9am-6pm Mon-Sat, by appointment Sun) is here.

Half Moon   RESORT $$$

([phone]953-2211, in the USA 877-626-0592; www.halfmoon.rockresorts.com; r from US$400, ste from US$900, villas from US$2000; [P][icons]) One of the great Caribbean resorts, the Half Moon is an exclusive colonial-style affair named for its private, 1.5km-long crescent beach, behind which are 160 hectares of beautifully landscaped gardens containing an 8-hectare nature reserve. With a staff of 750, the place feels more like a utopian village than a resort. The rooms and suites drip with Georgian plantation-era decor, and the villas have hosted the likes of Prince Rainer and the Queen of England. Facilities include gourmet restaurants, squash courts, tennis courts, equestrian center, full-service spa, conference center, championship golf course and the Half Moon Village shopping center.

Sandals Royal Caribbean   RESORT $$$

([phone]953-2231; http://www.sandals.com/main/royal/rj-home.cfm; Mahoe Bay; 3 nights all-incl r from US$1500, ste from US$2200; [P][icons]) This couples-only outpost of the Sandals empire really lays on the nostalgia for the British Empire, albeit in an impressive manner. Reminders about high tea abound, while the entire lobby complex is done up in Georgian accents to the point where it feels like Bath-on-Caribbean. The rest of the hotel does away with overt historicism and opts for a straight up hodgepodge of accents: a Thai restaurant on an Indonesian island reached by an East Asian dragon boat, six more restaurants on shore, rooms executed in plantation chic and suites you can swim to.

Ritz-Carlton Rose Hall   RESORT $$$

([phone]953-2800, in the USA 800-241-3333; www.ritzcarlton.com/resorts/rosehalljamaica; 1 Ritz-Carlton Dr, Rose Hall; r from US$369, ste from US$629; [P][icons]) This Ritz lives up to its namesake both in its luxury branding and the elegance of Rose Hall estate. The front lobby area resembles an imperial mansion; its private beach is studded with lovely white lounging tents plucked from *Lawrence of Arabia*; the rooms mix up-to-the-minute amenities with refined old-world charm. Rich fabrics and mahogany abound, tastefully blended with fresh tropical colors. There are six restaurants and lounges, a tennis center and two courts, a business center, championship golf course, full service spa and fitness center and full convention facilities.

Riu Montego Bay
RESORT $$$

(☎940-8010; www.riu.com; r from US$290, ste US$390, 3-nights all-incl ste per person from $US860; P🅿⊕❄🛜🏊) The Riu is so enormous it's a wonder it doesn't have its own postal code. The list of things to do is as big as the property itself: three restaurants plus multitheme buffets, windsurfing, sailing, snorkeling, diving, catamarans, nightclub, golf course, horseback riding etc. But despite a lot of marble and frilly accents, everything feels a bit midrange; if you're just coming to relax and don't need all those activities, the actual quality of the food and rooms is pretty middling. That said, you can get some incredible deals online (as low as US$110 per person per night in the lowest season), which is certainly value for money.

Atrium
APARTMENTS $$

(☎953-2605; atrium@cwjamaica.com; 1084 Morgan Rd, Rose Hall; apt US$120; ❄🏊) The Atrium bills itself as a collection of villas, but these are more like very modern, comfortable condominium units. Each one is blandly stylish in a freshly-furnished-by-Ikea kinda way, and comes with a kitchen if you want to cook for yourself. Located near the Blue Diamond Shopping Centre.

Cariblue Beach Resort
RESORT $$

(☎953-2022; www.caribluehotel.com; Rose Hall; r US$85-150; ❄🏊) If Pixar made a movie about Ironshore hotels, the Cariblue would be the runty, spunky little hotel that doesn't have the flash of all those big all-inclusives, but plenty of moxie and heart, gosh darn it. We found Cariblue kind of charming after a string of large all-inclusives, but the fact is the simple rooms are a bit underwhelming

and the place feels a little neglected. Very friendly, but neglected. There's a wide range of water sports on hand, including the folk of Dive Seaworld.

🍴 Eating

Scotchies
JERK $

(☎953-8041; Hwy A1; 0.5lb portion US$7; ☺lunch & dinner) Many Jamaicans will tell you that (a) Scotchies serves the best 'sit-down' jerk (ie jerk served in a restaurant as opposed to a street stall) in the northwest, if not all of Jamaica, and (b) the quality has slipped a bit with popularity. We say, in our worst accent, 'Ya mon.' This is very good jerk. Excellent quality. But the locals are right – this is great stuff, but not the best on the island, despite the hype.

Akbar/Thai Garderns
INDIAN, THAI $$

(953-8240; Half Moon Village; mains US$10-24; ☺lunch & dinner; 🍴) Two distinct kitchens serve one big dining room multiple variations of popular Indian or Thai cuisine. We will admit to being snobbishly unprepared for how good the food was here; even discounting the fact there are barely any Indian or Thai restaurants in greater Montego Bay, this is very good stuff. Certainly the best bet for vegetarian food in the area.

Royal Stocks
BRITISH $$

(☎953-9770; Half Moon Village; mains US$12-26; ☺10am-midnight) This pub affects the olde-England vibe, serving pricey (and good) burgers and steaks, Jamaican favorites and an authentic steak-and-kidney pie. With all that said, our favorite reason to come is the ambience; this place seems to attract a lot of hip, cosmopolitan Jamaicans, plus tourists

THE MEANDERING MALLS OF IRONSHORE

Thanks to its position as a major magnet for upper-class Jamaicans and condo-owning/renting expats, Ironshore is filled with high-end shopping centers. That said, land development must be a particularly Darwinian affair here, because these plazas seem to arise with the same frequency that old shopping centers and their shops are abandoned – that is to say, very frequently.

In order from west to east as you proceed along the A1, you'll pass the **Blue Diamond Shopping Centre** before the Riu Montego Bay, then **Golden Triangle**, the largely empty **Holiday Village**, the halfway-empty **Half Moon Shopping Centre**, and the newest additions, **Rose Hall** and **Whittier Village**. And what can you buy at these shopping centers? Well, these places essentially cater to rich locals and expats, as opposed to casual tourists, so pretty much anything you can find at home (clothes, electronics, cosmetics etc) only more expensive, since it's invariably imported. There are a few souvenir shops, and, at some point, some art galleries may open here, but none we've seen yet. If you want handicrafts for tourists, check out the **roadside stalls** that stretch along the A1.

from all of the nearby top resorts craving a more local vibe. TVs broadcast English football if you've got the FA addiction.

☆ Entertainment

169

FREE Bob Marley Experience   CINEMA
(☑953-3449; Half Moon Village) Shows hourly screenings of an engaging documentary on Marley's life in a 68-seat theater. The show may be free, but the accompanying enormous souvenir store proves there's no limits when it comes to commercializing the life of Brother Bob.

Blue Diamond Cinema   CINEMA
(☑953-9020) Screens latest releases in the Blue Diamond Shopping Centre.

❶ Information

Diamond Drugs Pharmacy (☑953-9184; Blue Diamond Shopping Center)

MoBay Hope Medical Center (☑953-3649; www.mobayhope.org; ☺24hr emergency) One of the best hospitals in the area.

National Commercial Bank (ATM; Half Moon Shopping Center)

Scotiabank (☑953-8451; Blue Diamond Shopping Center) Blue Diamond Shopping Center well.

❶ Getting There & Away

A great number of minibuses and route taxis ply the A1 road, traveling to and from Donald Sangster International Airport and Montego Bay's transportation center, Gloucester Ave and downtown. You'll pay about J$120 to travel from MoBay to Ironshore. Private taxis cost US$35. A route taxi can take 45 minutes or more depending on the number of passengers; private taxis make the trip in 20 to 30 minutes.

Rose Hall to Greenwood

East of Ironshore the A1 dips and rises past coastal scrubland, residential estates and several colonial-era great houses. There used to be a nice beach here, but it has been absorbed by the staggeringly enormous Iberostar condo/hotel/shopping complex of which we shall write nothing more, remembering the advice our mothers gave us regarding having something nice to say.

◉ Sights

Greenwood Great House   HISTORICAL SITE
(☑953-1077;   www.greenwoodgreathouse.com; admission US$15; ☺9am-6pm) This marvelous estate sits high on a hill some 11km east

of Ironshore. While the main attraction in these parts is Rose Hall Great House, visiting Greenwood is a far more intimate and, frankly, interesting experience. The furnishings are more authentic, the tour less breakneck than the one in Rose Hall, and there's none of the silly ghost stories – although the exterior edifice is admittedly not as impressive.

Construction of the two-story, stone-and-timber structure was begun in 1780 by the Honorable Richard Barrett, whose family arrived in Jamaica in the 1660s and amassed a fortune from its sugar plantations. (Barrett was a cousin of the famous English poet Elizabeth Barrett Browning.) In an unusual move for his times, Barrett educated his slaves.

Unique among local plantation houses, Greenwood survived unscathed during the slave rebellion of Christmas 1831. The original library is still intact, as are oil paintings, Dresden china, a court-jester's chair and plentiful antiques, including a mantrap used for catching runaway slaves (one of the few direct references we found in any Jamaican historical home to the foundations of the plantation labor market, ie slavery). Among the highlights is the rare collection of musical instruments, containing a barrel organ and two polyphones, which the guide is happy to bring to life. The view from the front balcony down to the sea is stunning.

Rose Hall Great House   HISTORICAL SITE
(☑953-2323; rosehall@cwjamaica.com; adult/child under 12 US$20/10; ☺9am-6pm, last tour 5:15pm) This mansion, with its commanding hilltop position 3km east of Ironshore, is the most famous great house in Jamaica.

Construction was begun by George Ashe in the 1750s and was completed in the 1770s by John Palmer, a wealthy plantation owner. Palmer and his wife Rose (after whom the house was named) hosted some of the most elaborate social gatherings on the island. Slaves destroyed the house in the Christmas Rebellion of 1831 and it was left in ruins for over a century. In 1966 the three-story building was restored to its haughty grandeur.

Beyond the Palladian portico the house is a bastion of historical style, with a magnificent mahogany staircase and doors, and silk wall-fabric that is a reproduction of the original designed for Marie Antoinette during the reign of Louis XVI. Unfortunately, because the house was cleaned out by looters back in the 19th century, almost all of the period furnishings were brought in from

THE WHITE WITCH & RASTA MASSACRES OF ROSE HALL

Here's the skinny on Jamaica's most famous ghost story/murderer: John Rose Palmer, grandnephew of John Palmer, who built Rose Hall, married Anne May Patterson in 1820. Although Annie was half English and half Irish, legend has it that she was raised in Haiti, where she learned vodoo. Legend also says that Anne May was a murderous vixen. The lascivious lady allegedly practiced witchcraft, poisoned John Palmer, stabbed a second husband and strangled her third. Her fourth husband escaped, leaving her to dispose of several slave lovers before she was strangled in her bed by assailants *from the other side*.

Or…not. The famous legend is actually based on a series of distorted half-truths. The inspiration for the story, originally told in writing in 1868 by John Costello, editor of the *Falmouth Post*, was Rose Palmer, the initial lady of Rose Hall. She did have four husbands, the last being John Palmer, to whom she was happily wed for 23 years (she died before her husband, at age 72). Anne Palmer, wife of John Rose Palmer, died peacefully in 1846 after a long, loving marriage. In 1929 novelist HG DeLisser developed the fable into a marvelous suspenseful romance, *The White Witch of Rose Hall*.

With all that said, Rose Hall does occupy a bloody patch of Jamaican history, although you'll see nothing commemorating the following events at the great house. In the early 1960s Rastafarians would walk through the grounds of Rose Hall on the way to their vegetable plots. The Rastas were at odds with property developers who wanted to turn then-defunct Rose Hall into the tourist attraction it is today. Keep in mind, this was pre–Bob Marley days; at the time, Rastas were seen as drug-addled, violent thugs. Police were sent in to arrest some Rastas on Good Friday, 1963, and in the ensuing confrontation eight Rastas were killed in what would be known as the Coral Gardens Massacre. Across the nation, police rounded up anyone with dreadlocks, threw them in jail and sheared their hair. Rastafarians still hold memorial services around the island every Easter to mark the event.

elsewhere, and quite a few are from the wrong century. With that said, the imported furnishings are the genuine article, and many are the work of past leading English master carpenters, so *don't touch*.

Much of the attraction is the legend of Annie Palmer, a multiple murderer said to haunt the house. Her bedroom upstairs has been (re)decorated in crimson silk brocades because, y'know, red is the color of blood. Ooooh! The cellar now houses an English-style pub and has a well-stocked gift shop haunted by the ghosts of tacky souvenirs. There's also a snack bar.

Tours of the house are mandatory and commence every 15 minutes till 5:15pm.

Citizens Beach   BEACH
Just east of the Greenwood Great House is this small patch of public beach, maintained by locals for locals and any tourist who happens to be tripping this way. There's the depressing possibility this land will be bought up by a resort soon, so visit while you can.

🛏 Sleeping & Eating

Dunn's Villa Resort Hotel   HOTEL **$$**
(☎953-7459, in the USA 718-882-3917; www.dunns villaresort.com; Cornwall; r US$115; P ❋ ≋) You'll

find this very friendly, family-run place in the village of Cornwall, in the hills 3km inland of Ironshore (follow the signs from the highway). This well-kept, homey spot has 11 frilly rooms with satellite TV, wide balconies and lots of pink-white color combinations. The spacious public areas are minimally but attractively furnished. There's a Jacuzzi on a raised sundeck. The hosts rent mountain bikes and offer lunch, dinner and weekend brunch poolside.

Royal Reef Hotel & Restaurant   HOTEL **$$**
(☎953-1700; www.royalreefja.com; r US$90-200; P ❋ ≋) On the A1 at Greenwood, this gracious, modern Mediterranean-style hotel has 19 rooms. Its decor includes classical wrought-iron furnishings and exquisite tropical murals. An elevated amoeba-shaped pool is inset in the terra-cotta terrace, which has an outside grill overlooking a tiny beach overgrown by mangroves. The excellent continental cuisine, mostly prepared with Jamaican flavor, is served both alfresco and in an intimate dining room (meals US$20 to US$35).

Hilton Rose Hall   RESORT **$$$**
(☎953-2650, in the USA 866-799-3661; www.rose hallresort.com; r from US$329, ste from US$869;

P♻✳@☂) Huge swathes of land just west of Rose Hall (the great house) are occupied by Rose Hall the resort. Fronted by a beautiful 300m-long beach and dominated by two high-rise buildings, this is a giant property serviced by five restaurants, four bars, an impeccable 18-hole golf course, tennis courts and a water park, **Sugar Mill Falls**, which consists of terraced pools, an 85m waterslide, meandering canals complete with waterfalls, the obligatory swim-up bar and 'dive-in' movie theater.

TOP
CHOICE **Far Out Fish Hut**   SEAFOOD $
(mains $J400-800; ☺lunch & dinner) East of Greenwood Great House, look along the coast for a trailer painted to look like a sea-blue slice of the ocean and you've found the Far Out Fish Hut, one of the finest purveyors of seafood on the north coast. This is a locals' spot where you sit under thatch, with a view of the water, and order very fresh seafood for a very good price. Simple? Yup, and delicious to boot.

❶ Getting There & Away

Minibuses and route taxis ply the A1 road. You'll pay about J$150 to J$200 to travel from MoBay to Rose Hall (35 to 45 minutes).

Falmouth

POP 9500

The capital of Trelawny parish retains the Georgian architecture of old to perhaps a greater degree than any other town in Jamaica. But this is a faded gem, full of faded beauty. It can be difficult to come to Falmouth and appreciate its historical heritage, as said heritage is largely going to rot. At the same time, for anyone with a passing interest in Caribbean and colonial architecture, this place is a bit of a dream.

Located some 37km east of Montego Bay, Falmouth has been the capital of Trelawny parish since 1790, although it underwent a slow economic decline after the abolition of slavery in 1833.

To walk among the cut-stone warehouses at the eastern end of town – places where human beings were inventoried, awaiting sale – is a disquieting experience. Plans for a monument and museum devoted to slavery and its legacy continue to inch forward, but we mean *inch*; in the meantime, the spooky old buildings bear silent witness. There have been several plans to restore the town, but very little effort has been undertaken and many historic buildings are now decrepit. However, several individuals have done fine restoration work, including the **Falmouth Heritage Renewal Society** (☎617-1060; www.falmouthjamaica.org; 9 King St).

Wednesday and Saturday are market days, when everything from bootleg underpants to fresh ginger and homemade root tonics are up for grabs. Much of Trelawny parish shows up for good deals on produce, baby chickens, yam sprouts, coffee beans, bars of soap...you name it. Falmouth is a safe town, but per usual, be careful walking around after dark. FYI, this is the birthplace of speedsters Ben Johnson and Usain Bolt (something in the water?).

History

Falmouth was laid out in 1790 and named for the English birthplace of Sir William Trelawny, then the governor of the island. The streets were planned as a grid and patriotically named after members of the royal family and English heroes. Planters erected their townhouses using Georgian elements adapted to Jamaican conditions.

With its advantageous position, Falmouth became the busiest port on the north coast. Outbound trade consisted mainly of hogsheads (large casks) of wet sugar and puncheons (casks) of rum, while slaves were offloaded for sale in the slave market.

The town's fortunes degenerated when the sugar industry went into decline during the 19th century and it was dealt a further blow with the advent of steamships, which the harbor was incapable of handling. By 1890 the port was essentially dead. The city has struggled along ever since.

Old-timers still wax poetic about the filming of the Steve McQueen movie *Papillon*, which was shot in Falmouth in 1972. Locals were hired en masse for the production. McQueen is remembered by a de facto tour guide named Moses as 'a nice guy who smoked a lot of cigarettes.'

An enormous new cruise-ship dock was being built on the eastern edge of Falmouth at the time of writing. Locals are divided over its impact; some eagerly await the hordes of foreign visitors and their wallets, while others bemoan environmental and cultural jolts to sleepy Falmouth.

◎ Sights & Activities

The best place to orient yourself is **Water Square**, at the east end of Duke St. Named for an old circular stone reservoir dating from 1798, the square (actually a triangle) has a fountain topped by an old waterwheel. Today it forms a traffic roundabout, but back in the day this fountain pumped fresh water before New York City had any such luxury. Many of the wooden shop-fronts in this area are attractively disheveled relics.

The market structure on the east side of Water Sq, which dominates central Falmouth, was once the site of slave auctions. The current structure was built in 1894 and named, in honor of two of Queen Victoria's grandsons, the **Albert George Shopping & Historical Centre**. There is a desultory, dusty **museum** (admission free; ⊙9am-5pm Mon-Sat) with a motley collection of colonial-era artifacts here; but the chances you'll actually find it open are pretty random.

One block east of Water Sq is Seaboard St and the grandiose Georgian **courthouse** in Palladian style, fronted by a double curling staircase and Doric columns, with cannons to the side. The current building, dating from 1926, is a replica of the original 1815 structure that was destroyed by fire. The town council presides here.

Some 50m east along Seaboard St, **Tharp House** sags from age yet is still one of the best examples of an elegant period townhouse. Today housing the tax office, it was formerly the residence of John Tharp, at one time the largest slaveholder in Jamaica.

Continue along Seaboard St to the **Phoenix Foundry**, built in 1810 at the corner of Tharpe and Lower Harbour Sts, with its strange-looking conical roof. Behind the foundry, guarded by locked gates, is the **Central Wharf** where slaves were brought ashore, to be replaced in the holds by sugar, rum and other victuals borne of their back-breaking labor. The crumbling warehouses are on their last legs. The property has been purchased with plans to transform it into a visitors center chronicling the barbarous history of slavery. At the time of writing, there's still no word when the museum might open.

Retrace your steps to Water Sq and cut down Cornwall St. One of the most stately edifices is the restored **Baptist Manse** (cnr Market & Cornwall Sts), formerly the residence of nonconformist Baptist preacher William Knibb, who was instrumental in lobbying for passage of the Abolition Bill that ended slavery. The porticoed **post office** is next door.

At the bottom of colonnaded Market St stands the **Methodist Manse**, a stone-and-wood building with wrought-iron balconies and Adam friezes above the doorways. A diversion along Trelawny St leads one block west to **Barrett House**, which is sadly in a state of advanced disrepair.

On Rodney St, which runs west along the shore, is the historic **police station**, constructed in 1814. The prison here once contained a treadmill: a huge wooden cylinder with steps on the outside. Shackled above the mill, slaves had to keep treading the steps as the cylinder turned. If they faltered, the revolving steps battered their bodies and legs. The ancient lockups are still in use.

On July 31, 1838, slaves gathered outside **William Knibb Memorial Church** (cnr King & George Sts) for an all-night vigil, awaiting midnight and then the dawn of full freedom (to quote Knibbs: 'The monster is dead'), when slave-shackles, a whip and an iron collar were symbolically buried in a coffin. In the grounds of the churchyard you can find Knibb's grave, as well as that of his wife. A plaque inside the church displays the internment of these tools of slavery; to get in, ask for help at the Leaf of Life Hardware store on King St.

The oldest extant building in town is **St Peter's Anglican Church**, built in 1785 and enlarged in 1842. It lies four blocks west along Duke St. The graveyard tombstones are spookily sun-bleached, like bones.

🛏 Sleeping & Eating

Greenside Villa Inn
HOTEL $
(☑954-3127, 865-6894; www.greenside-villa.com; studios US$45-55, additional person US$12) This inn is about 3km west of Falmouth and comes with simple, spacious studio apartments with private bathrooms and kitchenettes with small gas stoves. Meals are cooked on request.

Falmouth Resort
HOTEL $
(☑954-3391; 29 Newton St; r US$40; 🅿❄) This 'resort' offers the only accommodations in the center of Falmouth. If you want to get a feel for bustling Jamaican downtown life, this is a good option. Though it doesn't boast enough polish to qualify as a resort, it's a clean, friendly spot with welcoming, helpful staff. Meals are prepared on request. Take an upstairs room for privacy and a view.

Peter's Highway Bar
JAMAICAN $
(mains J$350-800; ⊙lunch & dinner) On the A1 heading east out of town, this airy roadside

rum dispensary and kitchen doles out good jerk chicken and pork. Welcoming travelers are the flags of many nations hand-painted on the walls, along with a proverb, 'Who God bless no man curse,' above the image of Bob Marley.

Spicy Nice Bakery BAKERY **$**
(Water Sq; ☺breakfast, lunch & dinner) Spice is nice at this bakery, where you can buy freshly baked breads, pastries and spicy meat and vegetable patties.

ℹ Information

Cambio King (☎954-4082; cnr Market & Duke Sts) Currency exchange at good rates. Located upstairs from Marguerite's Supermarket.

Falmouth Hospital (☎954-3250; Rodney St) Emergency services.

National Commercial Bank (☎954-3232; Water Sq)

Police station (☎119, 954-3222; cnr Rodney St & Market St)

Post office (☎954-3050; cnr Cornwall St & Market St)

Scotiabank (☎954-3357; cnr Market St & Lower Harbour St) Scotiabank also operates an ATM in the shopping center near the eastern edge of town.

Trelawny Pharmacy (☎954-3189; 19 Market St)

ℹ Getting There & Away

Buses, minibuses and route taxis arrive and depart on opposite sides of Water Sq for Martha Brae (J$80, 15 to 20 minutes), Montego Bay (J$150, 45 minutes to one hour) and Ocho Rios (J$300, one hour to 80 minutes).

Martha Brae

Situated on a small hill and nearly encircled by the emerald-green waters of the scenic Martha Brae River, this small village 3km due south of Falmouth is justly famous for rafting. The river rises at Windsor Caves in Cockpit Country and spills into the sea at Glistening Waters, east of Falmouth.

A **rafting trip** down a 4.8km stretch of the Martha Brae River is a quiet thrill. The journey takes 90 minutes on 9m-long bamboo rafts, each carrying one or two passengers, poled by a skilled guide. You'll head through a green tunnel of jungle, vines and cold mountain water; the whole experience can be quite romantic, depending on your tolerance of other people (the river gets crowded, as this is the most popular rafting

spot in Jamaica). The upper reaches tumble at a good pace before slowing further downriver, where you stop at 'Tarzan's Corner' for a swing and swim in a calm pool. At the end, after being plied with rum punch, you'll be driven back to your car or tour bus.

Trips begin from Rafters Village, about 1.5km south of Martha Brae. There you'll find an itinerant mento band and picnic area, bar, restaurant, swimming pool, bathrooms, changing rooms and a secure parking lot. Your captain will pause on request if you want to take a dip or climb a tree.

Just about any hotel on the north Jamaican coast, from Negril to Ocho Rios, offers rafting packages on the Martha Brae. Obviously transfer charges will be tacked on, so a smarter method is booking your adventure at the **Rafters Village** (Map p146; ☎952-0889, 940-6398; www.jamaicarafting.com; 66 Claude Clarke Ave, Montego Bay; per raft 1-2 people US$75) office in Montego Bay. Remember to tip your raft guide.

ℹ Getting There & Away

From Martha Brae a well-maintained road winds through the river gorge to Sherwood. A rougher road leads southwest to Good Hope Estate in Cockpit Country and links with another rough road that leads west from Sherwood to the Queen of Spains Valley south of Montego Bay.

Minibuses and route taxis regularly run to Martha Brae from Falmouth (J$100, 15 to 20 minutes).

Glistening Waters

Just a little ways east of Falmouth is one of the most incredible natural wonders of Jamaica, along with a smattering of good-value accommodations, clean beaches and one of the island's more innovative cultural exhibitions. The 25,000-seat Trelawny Greenfield Stadium is located opposite the small village of Rock. In April, the **Jamaica Cricket Festival** (☎992-8423; www.cricketjamaica.com) is held at Greenfield; if you've ever wanted to match jerk chicken with international-level test matches, drop on by.

⊙ Sights & Activities

Glistening Waters (Luminous Lagoon) LAGOON
We tend to roll out eyes whenever a tourism board or travel show describes a place as 'magical,' but Glistening Waters, also known as 'Luminous Lagoon,' actually lives

up to the hype. Located in an estuary near Rock, about 1.6 km east of Falmouth, the water here boasts a singular charm – it glows an eerie green when disturbed. The green glow is due to the presence of microorganisms that produce photochemical reactions when disturbed; the concentrations are so thick that fish swimming by look like green lanterns.

Needless to say, swimming through the luminous lagoon is just awesome, especially on starry nights, when its hard to tell where the water ends and the sky begins. The experience is made all the more surreal thanks to the mixing of salt- and freshwater from the sea and the Martha Brae River; the fresh water 'floats' on the saltwater, so you not only swim through green clouds of phosphorescence, but alternating bands of cold and warm.

Half-hour boat trips are offered from **Glistening Waters Marina** (954-3229; per person US$25; 7-9pm). Again, any hotel from Ocho Rios to Negril should be able to organize a trip out here.

There's a good-value restaurant located at the marina where you can get fresh fish prepared just about any way you like; you're charged based on the size of the fish. The restaurant opens to coincide with the arrival and departure of tour groups.

Outameni　　　　　CULTURAL VILLAGE
(954-4035, 617-0948; www.outameni.com; US$30; shows 3pm) Outameni is an interesting cultural village experience that takes visitors through Jamaican history, from the days of the Taino to colonial settlement, slavery and up to the modern day. The island's different ethnicities, from the Spanish to Indians, Chinese, British and, of course, Africans, are explored via a 90-minute show that incorporates music, dance and film. It's all quite absorbing and seems to be the only experience of its kind on the island; just make sure you book in advance. Located opposite the Breezes resort.

Bear Cay & World Beach　　　　BEACH
A curlicue spit, **Bear Cay**, hooks around the north side of the bay. **World Beach**, the lonesome 3km-long, white-sand beach on the north side, has long been appreciated by savvy travelers for its good snorkeling, sunbathing and solitude. Sea turtles haul themselves up here to lay their eggs at night. This used to be a dangerous beach, but locals banded together into a citizens' watch and quite literally kicked the muggers out; there

were no reported robberies in three years at the time of research. The entire stretch of coast, lined with casuarina pines and a protective coral reef, is a Jamaican treasure that you'd think would qualify for protected-area status. But at the time of writing a portion of the beach was being fenced off, apparently slated for a large resort development.

You can access World Beach from Time 'n Place, or you can rent a boat at Glistening Waters Marina or Fisherman's Inn; picnic meals are available.

Fishing & Boating　　　　FISHING
The river mouth in Glistening Waters is one of the few places in Jamaica that still offers good **fishing** for tarpon, known as the 'silver bullet' for its feisty defense on a line. No license is required. There are at least two dozen captains offering charter services at the **Glistening Waters Marina** (954-3229); call the marina to pre-arrange, or just show up and pick the captain who seems friendliest. Charter prices are notoriously subject to change, but at the time of research a half-day trip ran at least US$400, which can be split between six to eight passengers.

🛏 Sleeping

TOP CHOICE **Time 'n Place**　　　RESORT $
(843-3625; www.mytimenplace.com; cottages US$80; P✳) This delightful spot has four quaint all-hardwood cottages (each housing up to three people) for rent, right on World Beach; a tree-house-like 'Bird's Nest' is also in the works. The cottages, for all their rustic charm, are quite modern and well-presented on the inside. The beach bar and restaurant is a great place to hang out – it was a setting in the movie *How Stella Got Her Groove Back* and has been the backdrop for many a photo shoot. Owner Tony is, to say the least, an eccentric character, and knows about a secret local cavern – he calls it the 'Bottomless Blue Therapeutic Cave' – where you can swim beneath stalagmites by candlelight. Make friends with him and he just might take you there. If you stay for a few days Tony tends to cut you deals, throw in extras – it's a laid-back spot, so just see what's on offer.

Fisherman's Inn　　　HOTEL $$
(954-4078, 954-3427; s/d US$120/125; ✳✳) This well-run, charming hotel at Rock Wharf near Glistening Waters, 2km east of Falmouth, offers 12 spacious and pleasingly furnished rooms with big bathrooms and private patios that look right out on the

Luminous Lagoon. The on-site restaurant does a nice trade in British pub-style fare, and the hotel in general feels like an English country inn, albeit a bit more airy and, well, tropical. Water sports and Glistening Waters tours are offered.

Breezes Trelawny   RESORT $$$
(✆from the USA 877-273-3937; www.breezes.com; all-incl r from US$300; P❄✻@⛱) This gigantic resort tries to set itself apart from Sandals and similar all-inclusive chains by putting an emphasis on marketing to families. Comfortable rooms are arranged ar ound high-rise towers that overlook an enormous pool complex. There's an entire children's center on site, plus four restaurants, six bars, tennis courts, gym, rock-climbing wall, and (this is a bit unique) circus classes that teach you how to juggle, hit the trampoline and do trapeze work for weekly circus shows.

FDR Pebbles   RESORT $$$
(✆617-2500, in the USA 800-337-5437; www.fdrholidays.com; all-incl r from $330; P❄✻@⛱) A good sense of fun pervades this efficiently run, attractive all-inclusive family resort right on the beach. Walkways lined with frangipani, hibiscus and bougainvillea course through the grounds, while the pine and cedar two-story units feature 96 suites. This may be one of the most kid-friendly resorts on the island, employing an entire staff of specially trained nannies.

🍴 Eating

Glistening Waters Marina
Restaurant & Lounge   JAMAICAN $$
(✆954-3229; mains US$11-31; ⊗8am-11pm) A clean, modern place that offers Jamaican and continental fare, from onion rings and steamed fish to lobster and pepper steak. Killer cocktails are served in tall sundae glasses. Diners on a budget should consider the jerk center next door.

❶ Getting There & Away

Minibuses and route taxis frequently travel the A1 road to and from Falmouth, which is about 36km east of Montego Bay and 42km west of Runaway Bay.

Duncans

This small town on a hillside 11km east of Falmouth is a pretty place to base yourself if you want to be removed from resort sprawl, although it appears developers are buying up surrounding real estate at a fast pace so this may not be the case for long. The village is centered on an old stone clock tower in the middle of a three-way junction. The highway diverts ongoing traffic around the town; keep watch for the turnoff from the A1. Minibuses and route taxis pick up and drop off passengers to/from Duncans at the clock tower in the town center.

Kettering Baptist Church, built in 1893, is a creamy-colored building that commemorates William Knibb, a Baptist missionary and a leading abolitionist who founded an emancipation village for freed slaves here in 1840.

During his childhood, singer and activist Harry Belafonte was a frequent visitor to the **Sober Robin**, a cheerfully run-down pub situated on the old road that enters Duncans from the west. The lobby and lounge are atmospheric, with framed photos of classic movie stars, a small bar with table tennis and a pool table, and plenty of books lying about.

The personable Victoria runs the elegant **Victoria's Villa B&B** (✆954-9353; villavictoriaja.com; s incl breakfast & dinner US$60, d incl breakfast & dinner US$80-85; P), a beautiful property overflowing with gardens that resembles a historical home on steroids. Rooms are fluffy and twee; some feel like Jazz Age lounges, others resemble a Victorian grandmother's parlor. Victoria does a great job of making you feel like you've discovered a home away from home, and her cooking, we might add, is phenomenal.

Silver Sands Villa Resort (✆954-7606, 888-745-7245; www.mysilversands.com; 1/2 bedroom cottage from US$160/250, villas per week US$1400-2500; P✻⛱), 1.5km west of Duncans, has more than 100 upscale one- to two-bedroom villas and cottages spread over 90 hectares. The cottages require a minimum three nights booking. The enclosed estate backs a private, 300m-long, white-sand beach which is kept pristine and gorgeous (nonguests can get access for US$25). Each unique villa is privately owned and individually decorated, and has a cook, housekeeper and gardener – this sort of personal service is frankly way above what you get at most all-inclusives. Most of the properties have TVs and their own pools. Weekly rates offer savings and include airport transfers. Facilities include a bar-grill, and there's a grocery store within the 'neighborhood' if you want to self-cater.

Just west of the Silver Sands is the public **Jacob Taylor Beach**, where you'll find a small, mellow craft market and a rum shop.

Rio Bueno

Rio Bueno is a tumbledown fishing village 10km east of Duncans where fishers still tend their nets and lobster pots in front of ramshackle Georgian cut-stone buildings. These are featured in the 1964 movie *A High Wind in Jamaica,* which was filmed here. The town, 52km east of Montego Bay, is set on the west side of a deep, narrow bay that may be the site where Columbus first set foot in Jamaica on May 4, 1494, after anchoring his caravels *Nina, San Juan* and *Cardera.*

You can pick around the 18th-century ruins of **Fort Dundas**, the whitewashed remains of **St Mark's Anglican church** that dates to 1833, and a **Baptist church** erected in 1901 to replace another destroyed in anti-missionary riots of the abolitionist era. All of these sites are currently in states of disrepair. More modern ruins may be found after super-resort Breezes Rio Bueno closes its doors (scheduled to occur as this book heads to print). As of research, it was not clear what would become of the enormous hulk of the 226-room hotel.

Minibuses and route taxis pick up and drop off passengers along the A1 as it passes through town. The stretch of coastal road from here to Discovery Bay is known as the Queen's Hwy.

◉ Sights & Activities

Dornoch Riverhead   RIVER
The source of the Rio Bueno, a cold freshwater pool surrounded by sheer cliffs, lays hidden in a green dream in the interior south of village. This is a lonely landscape, scattered with the crumbling remains and foundations of churches; the ruins certainly far outnumber tourists. There are ruins of an airstrip out this way that locals say used to be a smuggling point for ganja. To get out here you may want to ask for local help – the Hotel Rio Bueno is a good place to start. If you're driving, head for Seaford Town, then ask for directions to the unmarked turn-off to the riverhead. You'll have to walk the last 100m to the pool.

Braco Stables   HORSEBACK RIDING
(✆954-0185; www.bracostables.com; per person with/without transportation US$70/60; ◷rides 10:30am & 2:30pm) If riding a horse bareback into the sea sounds like your cup of tea, Braco Stables offers excellent group rides through sugarcane country that culminate in a bareback ride into the turquoise surf. The ride ends with refreshments at the renovated Braco Great House (clothing required). The stables are well signed from the main road, and also offer combination walking and cycling tours (US$55) of the surrounding countryside.

🛌 Sleeping & Eating

Hotel Rio Bueno   [TOP CHOICE]   HOTEL **$$**
(✆954-0048; Main St; r/ste from US$110/250; P❄) Converted from a Georgian wharfside warehouse, this is the sort of wonderful old place eccentrics dream up for gawking visitors like yourself. In this case, said eccentric is Mr Joe James, a local character who has turned the hotel into a museum/gallery of his paintings, carvings and masks. It has 20 rooms, most with French doors opening onto balconies that overlook the bay. The huge, atmospheric suite has hardwood floors, open-plan layout and lots of light. Rates for larger rooms include breakfast, and much of the artwork is for sale; it makes for a unique Jamaican souvenir.

Lobster Bowl Restaurant   SEAFOOD **$$**
(✆954-0048; Hotel Rio Bueno, Main St; 3-course dinner US$15-38, lunch US$12-20; ◷breakfast, lunch & dinner) This spacious restaurant has an old-time nightclub feel and, again, features the artwork of Joe James. As the name suggests, lobster and seafood figure prominently on the menu, and it's all fresh and prepared with love and attention. An on-site bar becomes a magnet for a motley crew of regular hotel guests and expats in the evening; you're bound to spend a memorable evening here if you've got the stamina for it.

❶ Getting There & Away

Rio Bueno is about 60km east of Montego Bay and 20km west of Runaway Bay. Any taxis plying the A1 between Montego Bay and Runaway Bay will drop you off here; fares vary based on where you're picked up, of course.

WEST COAST TO TRYALL ESTATE

West from Montego Bay the A1 follows the coast, offering little in the way of beaches or attractions. Eight kilometers west of town the road crosses the mouth of the Great

River, then sweeps past Round Hill Hotel & Villa and, further along the A1, Tryall Estate and the world championship Tryall Golf Course. The small wayside village of **Hopewell**, 15km west of Montego Bay, has a bustling daily market; on Saturday the streets are cacophonous with the sounds of higglers from the hills.

TOP CHOICE **Round Hill Hotel & Villas** (956-7050, in the USA 800-972-2159; www.roundhilljamaica.com; d US$660, ste US$800-1200, villa US$1400-4000, daily meal plan per person US$120-140; P[icons]) doesn't need to show off about being luxurious and upmarket, unlike some other Jamaican resorts; it's perfectly secure in its position as one of the most glamorous hotels in the Caribbean. Having celebrated its 50th anniversary in 2003, this hotel still commands a prestige and allure that few others can match (guests have included Queen Elizabeth II, JFK and Clark Gable). The large property is dotted with plantation-chic villas, but the best rooms are the frosty-cool oceanfront accommodations, designed by Ralph Lauren. With access to an infinity pool, each has a kitchen and is exquisitely decorated with antique furniture and stately four-poster bamboo beds. The privately owned villas are furnished to their owners' tastes (Lauren owns one). Many have private pools. Facilities include a gym, tennis courts, water sports (including scuba diving that's open to the public), a beauty salon and a wellness center, which offers all manner of therapies. Nonguests can dine at the wonderful restaurant, which hosts fixed-menu theme nights that run around US$70 a head.

The ruins of the **Tryall Estate** sugar plantation lie 5km west of Hopewell. Much of the estate, including the huge **Tryall Water Wheel** (beside the A1) that drove the cane-crushing mill, was destroyed in the slave rebellion of Christmas 1831. Restored to working condition in the late 1950s, the wheel is still turned by water carried by a 3km-long aqueduct from the Flint River.

Built atop the remains of a small fort that is still guarded by cannons, and magnificently situated amid 890 hectares of lush hillside greenery, the hilltop great house **Tryall Club** (956-5660, in the USA 800-336-4571; www.tryallclub.com; guest house US$550-950, villas from US$1570; P[icons]) is by far one of the most exclusive accommodations on the island. Every conceivable luxury is on hand, and the villa suites, which include magnificent kitchens, living rooms, dining rooms and oversized marble bathrooms, are fully staffed with 24/7 personal service. A newer wing includes over 50 gracious junior suites, which are still miles ahead of most of the competition on the island. More than 55 privately owned, sumptuous estate villas are scattered throughout the estate, each uniquely decorated by individual owners and staffed with a cook, housekeeper and gardener. Other facilities include a gourmet restaurant and bar, tennis, water sports and, of course, golf.

Jamaica's top golf resort, the championship, 6328m par-71 **Tryall Golf Course** (956-5660; www.tryallclub.com) is one of the world's finest courses and reputedly Jamaica's most difficult. Green fees for guests cost US$70 in summer, US$120 in winter. The great house and resort complex are usually closed to nonguests, but you may be able to pre-arrange a go on the links for US$170.

🛈 Getting There & Away

CAR To get to Tryall or Hopewell, simply head west on the coast road/A1/Howard Cooke Hwy from Montego Bay. Hopewell is 15km and Tryall about 20km away from downtown MoBay; with good traffic it shouldn't take more than 20 minutes to get there.

TAXI Any westbound route taxi/van will drop you off at either Tryall or Hopewell (J$150).

INLAND: SOUTH OF MONTEGO BAY

The hill country inland of MoBay is speckled with villages clinging to rocky outcrops, narrow roads and large fields of fruit, vegetables and, deeper in the interior, ganja. This is friendly country, where locals aren't as jaded with tourists as their counterparts on the coast. To really explore this area you need your own wheels; the taxi service between mountain towns is too unreliable unless you have a lot of time on your hands. The hills can be reached either via the B8, which winds south from Reading and crosses a broad upland plateau before dropping onto the plains of Westmoreland, or the B6, which leads southeast from Montpelier (10km south of Reading). Be on the lookout for brightly painted shacks decorated with off-the-wall bric-a-brac (pottery, feathers, whatever); these are often the homes of witchcraft-practicing bush doctors. The southeast quarter of St James parish culminates in the wild Cockpit Country.

Lethe

We love this village for the name alone: the Lethe, in Greek mythology, was one of the rivers surrounding Hades, and to cross it caused you to lose memories of your previous life; it could happen to you in Lethe, Jamaica, if you spend enough time in this hilltop town. The turnoff for Lethe is 3km south of Reading off the B8 (signs show the way). If you pass the sign for Rocklands Bird Feeding Station, you've gone too far. The graceful stone bridge spanning the Great River was built in 1828, and from its pastoral span you can see the overgrown remains of an old sugar mill rotting on the riverbank.

◉ Sights & Activities

Mountain Valley Rafting RAFTING
(☑956-4920) Headquartered at Lethe Estate, this outfit offers tranquil one-hour river trips on the Great River from Lethe. You're piloted 3km downstream aboard long, narrow bamboo rafts poled by an expert rafter, who waxes poetic about the birds, flora and fauna as you glide along. It's a nice way to forget all your worries. Trips cost US$80 for two passengers (children under 12 half price), including lunch and transfers. For an extra US$15 per person you'll get lunch, a plantation tour and a fresh piña colada at the end of the excursion. If you show up under your own steam, you'll pay US$50 for the raft trip alone.

Lethe Estate can arrange special river-raft wedding celebrations in which the bride, groom and guests are carried down the river in specially decorated rafts to the plantation.

Animal Farm FARM
(☑899-0040, 815-4104; www.animalfarmjamaica. com; ☉tours by arrangement Mon-Fri, 10am-5pm Sat & Sun) While disappointingly light on revolutionary pigs corrupted by the acquisition of power (if you haven't read your Orwell, never mind), this Animal Farm does happen to be a great place to take your kids. This pretty little homestead is powered by ecofriendly solar power and pig crap. Skilled guides take guests on bird-watching tours around the grounds (look for the funky-crested 'Rasta fowl'), and on site there's a friendly little petting zoo, donkey stable (rides available), access to swimming in the Great River and lovely views over Cockpit Country.

FREE **Nature Village Farms** PARK
(☑912-9172; naturevillagefarms.com; ☉10am-6pm Mon-Fri, 11am-7pm Sun) It's hard to describe Nature Village Farms. It's certainly not a working farm or a traditional tourist site per se. Let's call it a collection of gardens, landscaped yards, basketball courts, pool halls and tree copses that happens to provide access to the muddy waters of the Great River, which are always nice for a dip. There's an on-site restaurant that serves up excellent, cheap Jamaican fare.

⊨ Sleeping

Lethe Estate HOTEL $
(☑956-4920; letheestate@cwjamaica.com; ste per person US$80; P✳☄) Located on resplendently gardened grounds about 1km from the town center, this is a terrifically relaxing place that feels like a cool hill-country retreat. It offers spacious two- and three-bedroom suites with balconies that overlook the river. The suites are painted in earthy tones, and come nicely decorated with local arts and crafts, fully equipped kitchen and satellite TV. Cooking and nanny services are available.

❶ Getting There & Away

By car or taxi, head west out of Montego Bay on the coast road (A1/Howard Cooke Hwy). In Reading (4km west of downtown MoBay) take the B8 (Long Hill Rd) from Reading toward Anchovy; the signed turnoff for Lethe is about 5km inland. If traffic is light, the trip takes around 30 minutes. Route taxis heading towards Savanna-la-Mar and Black River can drop you off by the turnoff; it's a short, steep hike up to Lethe from there.

Rocklands Bird Feeding Station

Rocklands (☑952-2009; admission US$10; ☉2pm-5pm) is a favorite of birders, who have flocked here since 1958 when it was founded by noted ornithologist Lisa Salmon, who tamed and trained over 20 bird species to come and feed from your hand. Over 140 bird species have been recorded here, but the big draw are those little darting gems: hummingbirds, including the deep purple Jamaican mango hummingbird and ever-popular 'doctorbird,' all best seen around 4pm. You can also spot ground doves, orange- and bananaquits, Jamaican woodpeckers (flickers) and orioles.

The station is run by one Fritz Beckford, a passionate champion of birds who will pour birdseed into your hand or provide you with a sugar-water feeder. Guests sit agog as hummingbirds streak in to hover like tiny helicopters before finally perching on their outstretched fingers. Fritz estimates his feathered friends devour nearly 900kg of seed each year (so much for 'bird-sized' appetites). If you need more avian action, Fritz leads tours from the house into the bush (US$20 per person).

A tremendous way to enjoy the bird feeding station is to spend the night in **Rocklands Bird Sanctuary Cottage** (952-2009; whole house per night US$150; P⁜), a nicely appointed three-bedroom, two-bathroom home that sleeps up to six people and comes with a sweet little Jacuzzi tub.

To get here from Montego Bay take the B8 (Long Hill Rd) from Reading toward Anchovy; turn left about 200m south of the signed turnoff for Lethe on Rock Pleasant Rd. The road leading to Rocklands is agonizingly steep and narrow in places. Alternatively, you can take a bus or route taxi from Montego Bay bound for Savanna-la-Mar or Black River, but be prepared for a tough 30-minute hike to and from your destination. If a taxi sounds better, be prepared to shell out at least US$75 for the round-trip journey.

Montpelier

Passing through Anchovy, you drop south into a broad valley. Citrus fields splotch across the valley, but in the 19th century this was a sugar estate that was at the epicenter of the great slave rebellions that rocked the Western parishes. The great house of the old Montpelier sugar plantation burned down (unrelated to slave rebellion issues) a few years back, but **St Mary's Anglican Church** still stands on a knoll overlooking the remains of the sugar factory. It's a lovely cutstone building, moldering but all the more beautiful for that, with a cornerstone that dates back to 1847.

Want to get out on those roiling waters? **Caliche Rainforest Park & Adventure Tour** (940-1745; http://calicherainforest.shoreadventures.net; rain forest/canyon white-water rafting trip per person US$70/80; ⊙9am & 1pm) sends travelers down some of the Great River's big waters, which start turbulent and grow progressively more tranquil as they approach the sea. Two 2½-hour trips are offered: one over a quiet stretch of river through a tropical rain forest that is appropriate for small children, and a wet-and-wild romp through Class III–IV waters with internationally trained and experienced guides. The experience concludes at a waterfall and swimming hole. **Barrett Adventures** (382-6384; www.barrettadventures.com; Rose Hall; tours incl transfers US$120) offers tours out this way.

The B8 splits at a gas station just south of the church. The main road continues southwest. The road to the southeast (the B6) leads toward Seaford Town.

Catadupa

Twenty years ago the Catadupans had a thriving trade selling crafts and making clothing to order for train passengers headed to the Appleton Rum Estate (you were measured en route to Appleton and clothes were finished and ready to pick up on the way back). Today the village, 3km east of the B6 from the hamlet of Marchmont, is a collection of aging buildings clustered around the disused railroad station where locals eke out a living growing coffee and bananas.

Keep heading along the road here and eventually it plunges into the mountain fastness of Cockpit Country. The last town before the asphalt gives up is one you've heard of...sorta. See, every country has a town or region that is the butt of all the jokes having to do with being remote, a redneck and a rube. In Jamaica, it's the last town before the Cockpits: little **Mocho**. There's not a heck of a lot to see here but stunning scenery, but you'll impress a lot of Jamaicans just by making it this far.

Croydon in the Mountains Plantation   PLANTATION

(979-8267; www.croydonplantation.com) Reached via a side road 1.5km from Catadupa, this 54-hectare working plantation was the birthplace of national hero and icon of the abolitionist movement Sam Sharpe. It can feel more like an Indian or Balinese rural community than Jamaica, with its well-groomed, deep green terraces sprouting fields and orchards of coffee, citrus and pineapples. A 'see, hear, touch and taste' tour is offered from 10:30am to 3pm Tuesday, Thursday and Friday (US$75 including lunch and transfers). Advance reservations are required. It's easy to drive here, and most Montego Bay tour companies can get you out this way.

THE BLUE-EYED, BLOND JAMAICANS OF SEAFORD

Seaford Town is surely one of the great ethno-historical oddities of the Caribbean. Here's the story behind this sprawling hillside burg: between 1834 and 1838 more than 1200 Germans arrived in Jamaica. These settlers were essentially indentured laborers; abolition was coming and plantation owners were looking to swell the white workforce and white population. An initial group of 251 Germans settled on land donated by Lord Seaford of Montpelier, which would become Seaford Town. That land was tangled, harsh wilderness (Lord Seaford may have believed in altering the ethnic makeup of an entire island, but he was also a bit of a cheapskate). Few of the Germans were farmers (another small issue); most were tradespeople or former soldiers. They received free rations for 18 months, but even before those ran out the Germans had settled into a life of poverty. Tropical diseases and social isolation soon reduced their numbers to a fraction of their original. To top all this off, the Germans who *did* stay were promised they would receive the title to the difficult land they had been laboring on after five years, but it took 15 before the land was theirs.

Almost two centuries later there are surprisingly few mulattos in Seaford (although who knows what intermingled genes lay further up the family tree). While fewer than 200 Seaford inhabitants claim German ancestry, these individuals are (more or less) white, working class Jamaicans. That said, don't expect lederhosen and oompah-bands in the jungle. Only a scant few older people speak German. The main evidence of their heritage is their Catholic faith, exemplified by the red, zinc-roofed, old stone **Church of the Sacred Heart**, which sits atop a rise overlooking Seaford. Its precursor was built by Father Tauer in the late 19th century, but was totally demolished in the hurricane of 1912. Take time to browse the graveyard, a stone record of the town's unique population. In front of the church is the **Seaford Town Historical Mini-Museum** (☑640-6486, 333-1507; admission US$2), which tells the tale of Seaford's German origins. There are maps and photographs of the early settlement, plus artifacts spanning 150 years, including curiosities like cricket bats made from the stems of coconut leaves. The building is usually locked; ask around town or at the HEART/NTA (National Training Agency) school for the good Mrs Shakes, who keeps the key to the museum. A pleasant **guest house** (☑995-2607; r J$2000) is located near the same building, and operated by NTA students.

Seaford can be accessed off side roads from the B6; ask for directions at Chesterfield or Marchmont. If you have a GPS, the coordinates are N 18.25°, W -77.9°. It's a gorgeous drive though some of the greenest overgrown jungle mountains in Jamaica, but keep your eyes on the road or you're liable to drive straight off it. Also, note that this is not the only town where German settlers intermixed with locals; in the appropriately named **German Town**, near Albert Town in North Cockpit Country, you'll see a lot of lighter complexions and last names like Stockhausen.

Flagstaff via Maroon Town

Few travelers venture into the hills to the southeast of Montego Bay. The potholed road ascends to the western flanks of Cockpit Country, offering lovely views over the valleys. This is truly wild, isolated Jamaica: a land of big banana groves and small villages utterly isolated by jungle walls and mountains. For all this ruggedness, in many places you're not 30km from the Hip Strip.

This land is steeped in Jamaica's history, particularly its antislavery struggles (although there was also a Taíno settlement at the town of John's Hall, 10km southeast of Montego Bay; now it looks, literally, like a trash dump because it is used as such by

other local municipalities). When you pass through the otherwise nondescript hamlet of **Kensington** 21km southeast of Montego Bay, be on the lookout for a roadside **plaque** that commemorates the site where, in 1831, slaves set fire to the highest ridges of the Kensington plantation, thus initiating the devastating Christmas Rebellion (see boxed text, p153).

At the edge of the rugged Cockpit Country, 5km southeast of Kensington (thanks to the windy roads it's a *long* 5km) you'll find **Maroon Town** (see p255), named for the bands of escaped slaves that once dominated these hills. Despite the name, Maroon Town does not possess many links to modern Maroons, but proceed along the road a little ways and you'll reach **Flagstaff**, which does (all of this land was technically granted to the Trelawny Maroons in 1739).

In Flagstaff you'll want to look up the **Maroon Village Heritage Tour & Trail** (☑326-1868, 421-3473; michael.grizzle@yahoo.com; tours US$20) which sends tourists to visitor centers that focus on Maroon history. You'll also get to head out into Cockpit Country on nature/ history walks past some of the major sites of the Maroon wars, and some lovely flora and fauna as well. The folks who run this outfit can link you up with B&Bs in the area (these are essentially village homestays, so don't expect a lot – except friendliness); rates are variable but shouldn't run over US$40 to US$50. Try to book in advance. After visiting you can drive from here on to the other great Maroon site of Accompong in the southwest. It's a gorgeous trip along the rim of the Cockpits, but fair warning: the road was a bit of a mess at the time of writing.

Locals will likely approach you once you get to Maroon Town offering private tours of the region for around US$20. We prefer the Heritage Tour & Trail, but we did get the sense many of these outfits drew on each others' expertise. If you want to book from Montego Bay, you can try contacting **Michael G** (www.toursbylocals.com/maroontour); otherwise most of the major tour operators we list in Montego Bay can either get you here or link you up with someone who can.

❶ Getting There & Away

By far the easiest way out here is with your own wheels; from Montego Bay take Fairfield Rd, 2.5km south of town, towards Kensington to begin your journey into Maroon country. There will be signs from Kensington to Flagstaff, but take a road map in any case.

NORTH COCKPIT COUNTRY

Look at a road map of Jamaica and you'll notice southwest Trelawny parish, inland of Falmouth is...blank. Just a big green eye of tantalizing mystery peeking at you from the tangle of towns, villages and roads that is the rest of Jamaica's face. So what's that eye? Jamaica's most rugged quarter: a 1295-sq-km limestone plateau known as Cockpit Country, a vast network of eroded limestone studded with thousands of conical hummocks divided by precipitous ravines. From the air, Cockpit Country resembles a bright-green, somewhat ominous egg carton.

Conical hummocks? Precipitous ravines? If it sounds daunting, it is. Overgrown with luxuriant greenery, most of the region remains uninhabited, and much of it remains to be surveyed and otherwise fully explored. No roads penetrate this land (although a rough dirt road cuts across the eastern edge between Clark's Town and Albert Town) and only a few tracks make even halfhearted forays into its interior.

This nearly impenetrable country proved a perfect hideout for the Maroons who, through their ferocity, maintained an uneasy sovereignty from the English colonialists. The southern section is known as 'District of Look Behind,' an allusion to the Maroon practice of ambushing English soldiers, many of whom came to a bloody end in these valleys. It's not hard to see why so many stories of duppies (ghosts) predominate in these misty valleys.

A few valley floors are cultivated by small-holders who grow bananas, yams, corn, manioc and ganja. It's unwise for foreigners to explore here unless accompanied by someone known in the area. You could easily get lost or worse – if you stumble upon a major ganja plot, you're likely to be considered a DEA (Drug Enforcement Agency) agent and the consequences could be serious.

The southern portion of Cockpit Country lies in St Elizabeth parish and is accessed from the south by side roads from the B6. See p225.

Most of the Cockpits are still clad in primary vegetation that, in places, includes rare cacti and other endemic species known only in that specific locale. The northern slopes are typically more lush. The hilltops are relatively sparsely vegetated due to soil erosion. The Cockpits are generally covered in tall scrub, including brambles and scratchbush.

Most of Jamaica's 27 endemic bird species are found in the Cockpits, including black-and yellow-billed parrots, todies and the endangered golden swallow. The Jamaican boa and giant swallowtail butterfly are among other rare species, which include 37 of Jamaica's 62 amphibian and reptile species.

🏃 Activities

Hiking

A few hunters' tracks lead into and even across Cockpit Country. Most are faint paths, often overgrown, and hiking away from these trails can be dangerous going. The rocks are razor sharp and sinkholes are everywhere, often covered by decayed vegetation and ready to crumble underfoot. Never travel alone, as there is no one to hear you call for help should you fall into a sinkhole. Take lots of water: there is none to be had locally.

It is imperative you take a trusted guide, and the best starting point for organizing in advance is the **Southern Trelawny Environmental Agency** (STEA; www.stea.net), based in Albert Town, which has become the main tourism hub in these parts. STEA runs a tourism initiative, **Cockpit Country Adventure Tours** (☑610-0818; www.stea.net), which will set you up with locals who are versed in ecotourism practices and know their way around these hills. You'll still need to bring a machete, stout walking shoes, rain gear and a powerful flashlight in the event of a delay past sunset. Take warm clothing if you plan on overnighting, as nights can get cold. Rates for guides vary based on hikes, but J$2500 for a day trek seems standard.

The easiest – but by no means easy – trail across the Cockpits is an old military trail connecting Windsor (in the north) with Troy (in the south), about 16km as the crow flies. It's an arduous full-day's hike with a guide. It is a more difficult hike southbound, leading gradually uphill; an easier option is to begin in Troy (p229) and take the downhill route.

Spelunking

The Cockpits are laced with mostly uncharted caves that are a tempting draw for spelunkers. This is true adventure travel; guides lead trips into the better-known caverns, but past that, exploring is for experienced and properly outfitted spelunkers only. There is no rescue organization, and you enter caves at your own risk. The most accessible are Windsor Caves at Windsor.

The **Jamaican Caves Organisation** (www.jamaicancaves.org/main.htm) provides resources for the exploration of Jamaican caves, sinkholes and underground rivers. In 2005 the group completed a project to formally classify and evaluate over 70 caves within Cockpit Country.

Jamaica Underground by Alan Fincham is a rare but essential compendium providing the most thorough information available on the island's charted caves; you can check Fincham's website at www.fincham.co.uk.

☞ Tours

Cockpit Country
Adventure Tours   ADVENTURE TOURS
(☑610-0818; www.stea.net/ccat_main.htm; 3 Grants Office Complex, Albert Town; tours US$55-

70) Sponsored by the Southern Trelawny Environmental Agency, local guides are used to lead hikes and cave exploration in the rugged Freeman's Hall district. The most arduous visits the Quashie River and the Quashie Cave, featuring a 'cathedral room' and an underground waterfall.

Sun Venture Tours   HIKING TOURS
(☑in Kingston 960-6685, in Ocho Rios 920-8348; www.sunventuretours.com; 30 Balmoral Ave, Kingston 10) Runs guided hikes and birdwatching trips into the Cockpits for US$85.

❶ Information

Nature Conservancy (☑978-0766; www .nature.org; Unit 5, 32 Lady Musgrave Rd, Kingston 5) Working with Cockpit Country residents to develop stable long-term protection for the region's fragile ecosystem.

Southern Trelawny Environmental Agency (☑610-0818; www.stea.net; 3 Grants Office Complex, Albert Town) Concerns itself with the social aspects of Cockpit Country communities and can arrange private lodging and guides for visitors.

Windsor Research Centre (☑997-3832; www. cockpitcountry.com; Windsor Great House) A science-based operation at Windsor Great House, devoted to monitoring Cockpit Country's fragile environment. The website, replete with up-to-date information about regional ecology, is a joy for nature geeks.

Good Hope Estate

Imagine 'Cotswold-on-Cockpit' and you'll get a sense of what this honey-hued great house and working plantation looks like. The property, 13km south of Falmouth at the western end of Queen of Spains Valley, is set on the northern edge of Cockpit Country, and the views into that checkerboard of deep razor ridges and jungle domes has no rival.

The estate was owned by John Tharp (1744–1804), once the richest man in Jamaica, owner of over 4000 hectares and 3000 slaves in Trelawny and St James parishes. Built around 1755, there is still a collection of 18th-century Jamaican Georgian cut-stone buildings here, including a sugar works and waterwheel.

The great house first became a hotel in the early 1900s when an American banker came to Jamaica looking for antiques and happened upon Good Hope. Today **Good Hope Country House & River Cottage** (☑469-3443; www.goodhopejamaica.com; 10-bedroom house per week US$14,500, 3-bedroom cottage per week US$4400; ⓅⒶ❄❆) is without doubt one of Jamaica's most opulent villa rentals.

After staying here, you'll realize all those other places that pretend to give you the 'lord-of-a-plantation' experience are full of bunk. Here the architecture and mood are fabulous, with high ceilings, gleaming hardwood floors and a two-story cut-stone 'counting house' that is now the honeymoon suite. The house is fully furnished with enough 18th- and 19th-century antiques and fine maps and paintings to open a small museum. Meals, cooked to order, average US$80 per person per day.

The three-bedroom river cottage is a restored 19th-century house set in extensive gardens and perched above an idyllic swimming hole. There are three bedrooms with antique four-poster beds and private bathrooms, a full kitchen, a comfortable living room and an enormous shaded veranda.

David Pinto, an acclaimed ceramist, operates a **pottery studio** (☏954-4635) open to the public on the grounds, and pottery workshops are offered – though you'll need to contact the **Anderson Ranch Arts Center** (☏in the USA 970-923-3181; www.andersonranch.org) in the USA to attend.

If you can't afford to stay at the Good Hope, you can wander the grounds on a **guided horseback ride** (☏469-3443; US$50), which is quite a pleasant way of seeing the edges of, somewhat dualistically, one of the fanciest properties in Jamaica and a slice of its most rugged country. As this ride is often done one-on-one, just you and a guide, you kinda feel like you're in a tropical version of the *Lord of the Rings*.

Windsor

If you want to drive into Cockpit Country...well, you can't really. But you can get a taste of what's on offer by entering the narrow 3km-long valley southeast of Good Hope Estate. This passage, surrounded by towering cliffs, is most easily accessed from Sherwood at the north end. The paved road dead-ends at Windsor near the head of the valley; from here you can hike across the Cockpits to Troy, but this is as far as you can go into this wild country without hiking. And, to be fair, the natural beauty of the wild Cockpit Country interior is on display here in its truest form (minus the machete-and-gun-toting ganja militias – bonus!).

◎ Sights

Usain Bolt was living here at the time of writing but he's supposed to be moving to a home near Bluefields on the south coast; nonetheless, you'll probably see signs touting pride in the fastest man on Earth.

Windsor Caves   CAVES
These caverns may be off-the-beaten-track to most people, but they're a major way point for some 50,000 bats. Their egress and entrance, a massed cloud of skittering airborne mammalian tooth, fur, flap and claw, is a sight to behold (the less said about the smell of their guano, the better). Luckily, the caves were donated to the World Wildlife Fund in 1995 with the proviso that they never be developed, and that's the case today.

The entrance is a 1km hike from the road, ending with a clamber up a narrow rocky path. Beyond the narrow entrance you'll

WORTH A TRIP

WINDSOR GREAT HOUSE

Built in 1705 by John Tharp, Windsor Great House now serves as a hostelry and scientific research center. The home is architecturally impressive, but the main reason to visit is to actually spend the night here. How often do you, budget traveler, get to sleep in a **colonial mansion** (☏997-3832; www.cockpitcountry.com; r incl breakfast US$35-45) that happens to be a biological research station? Decked out with several no-frills cut-stone rooms with shared bathroom (cold water only), the Windsor is a great deal.

It is first and foremost a research center, and resident naturalists Mike Schwartz and Susan Koenig occasionally stage four-course 'Meet the Biologist' dinners (US$40); call for a schedule and reservations. We can't imagine any better way of acquainting yourself with the background story on natural Jamaica – whilst enjoying nice food and wine in, oh yes, a mansion. A bird-banding effort happens the last weekend of each month; to participate you must first become a member (US$20).

It's not marked by a sign; to find it, take a left at the junction at the end of the paved road.

pass into a large gallery full of stalactites and a huge chamber with a dramatically arched ceiling; in rainy season you can hear the roar of the Martha Brae River flowing deep underground.

You'll need a local guide, who can usually be found at **Dango's shop** (www.jamaicancaves.org/dango-jamaica) at the end of the road. It's emblazoned with the epithet 'Jah love is a burning flame'; here you'll likely find cave wardens Martell or Franklyn 'Dango' Taylor. One of them will lead the way with a flashlight or bamboo torch to visit Rat Bat Cave and the Royal Flat Chamber. Depending on how deep into the cave you wish to go and the size of your group, figure on around US$40 per person.

For experienced cavers who arrive with spelunking gear, Martell or Franklyn will lead the way on a remarkable four-hour subterranean excursion through Windsor Cave all the way to its 'back door' at Bamboo Batam. You'll need to bring 30m of rope and basic rappelling equipment, and a desire to wade for an extended period with water up to your waist in total darkness. Eventually, you will emerge and make the return journey in the blessed daylight. For this you'll be charged only US$25 per person, but most people are inclined to tack on a substantial tip.

See p28 for general information about spelunking in Jamaica.

Sleeping & Eating

Last Resort   GUEST HOUSE
(www.jamaicancaves.org/last-resort-jamaica)
An excellent lodge for backpackers and spelunkers run by the Jamaica Caves Organisation, was closed at the time of writing but may be back up and running by the time you read this.

Patrick's Cabin   GUEST HOUSE **$**
(397-6448; r US$225) Very simple, basic accommodations operated by caver and guide Dango Taylor. It's cheap and you get what you pay for, but cheerful and accommodating for all that.

Miss Lilly's   GUEST HOUSE **$**
(788-1022; www.jamaicancaves.org/lillys-jamaica.htm; Coxheath; r with shared bathroom US$40)
In Coxheath at the northern entrance to Windsor Valley, and marked by a sign reading 'Lilly's Bar,' is this useful-things shop, bar, restaurant and guest house all rolled

into one – run by the welcoming and jovial aunt of Usain Bolt, Miss Lilly Bolt. Two simply appointed rooms share a bathroom (cold water only) and have fans, while Miss Lilly cooks some delicious yams in the kitchen, said to be the source of Usain's extreme speed. This is a nice place to chill and meet locals (including a fair few members of the direct and extended Bolt family, and if you're really lucky, the fast man himself), who tend to congregate here for gossip, dominoes and the other social pastimes of Jamaican life.

ⓘ Getting There & Away

Windsor is reached by traveling the road from Falmouth to Martha Brae, then crossing the bridge to the east and turning right to follow the valley south into the hills. Minibuses and route taxis (around J$300) operate between Montego Bay and Brown's Town via Sherwood, from where you can walk or hitchhike the remaining 5km to Windsor.

Albert Town

This small market center lies high in the mountains about 24km inland of Rio Bueno. The B5 climbs through the Cockpits with dramatic views en route. Albert Town is a base for guided hikes into Cockpit Country, set immediately to the west.

The B5 rises southeast from Albert Town to the spine of Jamaica, with vistas of lush, rolling agricultural land interspersed with pine forest. You'll crest the mountains (and the boundary with Manchester parish) just south of Lorrimers, about 14km south of Albert Town.

West of Albert Town, the B10 climbs along the eastern edge of Cockpit Country and beyond Warsop drops dramatically to Troy (p229), a gateway to the Cockpits.

Every year on Easter Monday the wildly entertaining **Trelawny Yam Festival** (www.stea.net) features such highlights as yam-balancing races, best-dressed goat and donkey, and the crowning of the Yam King and Queen. You will learn more about yams than you ever thought possible and (trust us) have a great deal of fun in the process.

The **Southern Trelawny Environmental Agency** (610-0818; www.stea.net; 3 Grants Office Complex) is on the west side of the town square. If you're looking for lodging, its staff can recommend local B&Bs.

Negril & West Coast

Includes »

Best Places to Eat

» Le Vendôme (p201)

» Rockhouse Restaurant & Bar (p202)

» Cosmo's (p201)

» Canoe Bar (p202)

» 3 Dives Jerk Centre (p202)

Best Places to Stay

» Caves (p198)

» Rockhouse (p198)

» Moondance (p193)

» Banana Shout (p198)

» Kuyaba (p194)

Why Go?

Negril is an interesting combination of the best and worst of Jamaica. On one hand there's the 11km Long Beach which, despite being cluttered with hotels, guest houses and resorts, is still perhaps the most beautiful beach in the country, a stretch of snowy powder lapped by a teal bay where the sunsets are simply perfect. On the other hand, the explosion of development has attracted the most obnoxious elements of mass tourism: prostitution (aimed at both genders), extremely persistent hustlers, lots of drugs and a general shattering of innocence.

Many travelers prefer the charms of natural escapes just to the south of Negril, in the sunny reaches of Jamaica's west coast, and the laid-back West End of Negril proper. Here the beach may not be as accessible, but the vibe is more like the Negril that once was. The sunset's just as magnificent from the cliffs, after all...

When to Go
Negril

Apr-Jun It's not wet here as the rest of Jamaica, but small thunderstorms do occur.

Jul-Oct Rooms dip into low-season rates, and short frequent bursts of rain are common.

Nov-Mar It's sunny, clear and dry. Weatherwise, it's the best time to be in town.

Negril & West Coast Highlights

1 Plumbing the grottoes and reefs off **Negril** for some of the island's best scuba diving (p191)

2 Clambering, clawing and occasionally sliding around the slick rocks and white water of **Mayfield Falls** (p209)

3 Gazing into the perfect sunsets that set on fire the sugary sand of **Seven Mile Beach** (Long Beach; p189)

4 Disappearing into the country at one of Jamaica's most scenic and atmospheric caves at **Roaring River Park** (p211)

5 Riding a chestnut horse across the hills east of Negril from **Rhodes Hall Plantation** (p207)

Caribbean Sea

Lance's Bay

Cousins Cove

Davis Cove

Davis Cove

Negril Marine Park

Green Island Harbour

Half Moon Beach

Green Island

Rhodes Hall Plantation **5**

Negril Environmental Protection Area

Orange Bay

Deep Plane

Negril Aerodrome

Bloody Bay

Fish River

March Town

Negril Great Morass Game Sanctuary

Long Bay

Orange Hills

Orange River

Seven Mile Beach (Long Beach)

1 **3**

Sands Club Reef

Great Morass

Shark's Reef

Royal Palm Reserve

The Throne

Delve Bridge

Negril Village

Aweemaway

Negril Environmental Protection Area

South Negril Point

Mt Airy

Retirement

Retreat

Negril Lighthouse

Orange Hill

Negril Hills

Brighton

Negril Marine Park

Homers Cove

Little Bay

Lost Beach

Southwest Point

St John's Point

Caribbean Sea

Pedro Point

Orange Cove

Moskito Cove

Kenilworth

Sandy Bay

A1

Lucea
Lucea Harbour

To Hopewell (2km); Montego Bay (25km)

German Hill (268m) ▲

B9

Flint River

Old Pen (478m) ▲

Blenheim

Dias

Cascade

Pondside

Kingsvale

Dolphin Head (545m) ▲

Dolphin Mountains

Birchs Hill (551m) ▲

Hanover

Westmoreland

❷ Mayfield Falls

Pennycooke

Montego Bay (45km)

Morgans River

Glen Islay

Grange Hill

Frome

Friendship Cross

Blue Hole Gardens

❹ **Roaring River Park**

Cabarita River

B9

Banbury

Whithorn

Petersfield

Little London

Amity Cross

Galloway

B8

Ferris Cross

New Broughton

A2

Robins Point

Hope Wharf

SAVANNA-LA-MAR

Bluff Point

Bluefields Bay

Bluefields

A2

To Black River (32km)

▲
Ⓝ

| 0 | | 4 km |
| 0 | | 2 miles |

History

The Spanish called Negril's bay and adjacent headland 'Punta Negrilla' (Dark Point), referring to the black conger eels that used to proliferate in the local rivers. During the colonial era pirates favored Negril's two bays for safe anchorage during plundering forays. During the War of 1812 between Britain and the US Bloody Bay was the point of assembly and departure for the British naval armada's ill-fated expedition to storm New Orleans. Bloody Bay was also used by 19th-century whalers who butchered their catch here (hence the name). When a road was finally constructed to Negril in 1959, the area slowly began to attract vacationers – as well as a coterie of hippies – but it wasn't until the late 1970s, when the first resorts opened, that Negril began to stake its claim as Jamaica's coolest party destination.

❶ Getting There & Away

Nearly all international air passengers fly into Donald Sangster International Airport in Montego Bay, 81km from Negril. From there you can arrange for a private minivan or taxi, or take public transportation in the form of a minibus or route taxi.

NEGRIL

POP 4200

If you came to Jamaica looking to find a party and lose your inhibitions, look no further than Negril, 81km west of Montego Bay. At night, reggae and dancehall parties thump their tunes across the beach; by day, thousands fall in love with Negril's insouciance and scintillating 11km-long beach sliding gently into calm waters that reflect a palette of light blues and greens. Coral reefs lie just offshore, and you'll want your camera close by to record the consistently peach-colored sunsets that get more applause than live reggae concerts.

Tourism is Negril's only industry, and it shows in the way you're treated here. There's an easygoing rapport between visitors and locals in some places, especially when you start becoming a regular at specific bars and restaurants, but it's hard not to feel like a walking wallet, especially when you first arrive and every hustler and drug dealer can smell your fresh blood.

In spite of Negril's perhaps predictable evolution from a remote, sensual Eden to a big-money resort, the place remains Jamaica's best destination for Dionysian revelry. Let your hair down, sample the local pleasures and let Jamaica happen around you.

History

Only in 1959 was a road cut to Negril, launching the development of what was then a tiny fishing village. Electricity and telephones came later. The sleepy beachfront village soon became a popular holiday spot for Jamaicans. About the same time, hippies and backpackers from abroad began to appear. They roomed with local families or slept on the beach, partook of ganja and magic mushrooms, and generally gave Ne-

Negril – West End

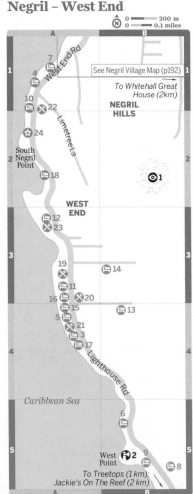

gril its laid-back reputation. In 1977 the first major resort – Negril Beach Village (later renamed Hedonism II) – opened its doors to a relatively affluent crowd seeking an uninhibited Club Med–style vacation. By the mid-1980s Negril was in the throes of a full-scale tourism boom that continues today.

This let-it-all-hang-out tradition still overflows during the March to April Spring Break when US college kids swarm for wet T-shirt contests, drinking competitions and general party time.

Nonetheless, the resort has developed an active and environmentally conscious spirit under the guidance of expat residents, resulting in the creation of the Negril Marine Park within the Negril Environmental Protection Area. The park encompasses the shoreline, mangroves, offshore waters and coral reefs, and is divided into eight recreational zones. Some hotels have taken admirable steps towards implementing green policies, and it is hoped traveler preference for these resorts will lead to a copycatting of environmentally friendly behavior across the beach.

◉ Sights

Seven Mile Beach (Long Beach) BEACH
(Map p202) Also known as Negril Beach or Long Beach, Seven Mile Beach was initially touted on tourism posters as 'seven miles of nothing but you and the sea.' But the once-peaceful place that drew all those blissed-out sensualists in the early 1970s is now only a happy memory. As before, topless sunbathers lie half submerged on lounge chairs in the gentle surf, and the sweet smell of ganja smoke still perfumes the breeze, but otherwise the beach has changed in nearly every way. Today it's cluttered with restaurants, bars and nightspots and every conceivable water sport on offer. The swaying palms, clear waters and nearby coral reefs mean that the beach is still beautiful to behold – some contend it's the most beautiful in the Caribbean – but if you're looking for solitude, look elsewhere.

Bloody Bay Beach BEACH
(Map p195) Another splendid option, with no facilities and few people, save for a few savvy travelers and a smattering of locals enjoying some repose away from the hubbub. There's a jerk shack selling snacks and drinks if you need 'em.

Negril Hills HILLS
This range of low-lying hills rises inland of Negril's West End. The raised limestone upland is wild and smothered in brush. Tiny hamlets sprinkle the single road that provides access from Negril: Whitehall Rd leads

south from Sheffield Rd to the hamlet of Orange Hill, swings east through the hills via the town of Retirement, and eventually links to the A2 for Savanna-la-Mar.

Seemingly a world away from the Negril strip, **Abba Jahnehoy's Garden** (Map p188; ☎371-4050, 578-9578) is a three-story meditation and learning center poised on a hill that offers a splendid panoramic view extending down to the sea. Solar powered and surrounded by a vegetable and root garden, the octagonal building is the work of Janhoi Jaja. He's a gracious Rasta who is more than happy to discuss the ins and outs of Rastafarianism, or reggae or Negril's development or the finer points of numerology (or all of the above) over bowls of his excellent soup, homemade from his garden's produce. Getting there is half the fun, as the garden's located at the end of a series of unmarked dirt roads: either take the Westland Mountain Rd to the top and then ask, or give Janhoi himself a call.

The only other site of note in the hills is **Whitehall Great House** (off Map p188), in ruins following a fire in 1985. Don't be fooled into paying for a tour by the locals who hang out and attempt to attach themselves as self-described 'guides.'

Long Bay Beach Park BEACH
(Map p195) South of Seven Mile Beach, this beach is more peaceful and far less crowded. Here you'll find more sugary sand and picnic tables plus changing rooms, but there's also coarse grass, so it's not quite as picturesque.

Booby Cay ISLAND
This small coral island 1km offshore from Rutland Point was used as a South Seas setting in the Walt Disney movie *20,000 Leagues Under the Sea*. The island is named for the seabirds – 'boobies' in local parlance – that make their nests here. Water-sports concessionaires can arrange boats for about US$35 round trip.

FREE **Negril Lighthouse** LIGHTHOUSE
(Map p188; West End Rd; ☺9am-sunset) The gleaming white, 20m-tall Negril Lighthouse, 5km south of Negril Village, illuminates the westernmost point of Jamaica, at N 18°15', W 78°23'. The lighthouse, erected in 1894 with a prism made in Paris and originally powered by kerosene, is now solar powered and flashes every two seconds. Wilson Johnson, the superintendent, will gladly lead the way up the 103 stairs for a bird's-eye view of the coast.

DON'T MISS

GREAT MORASS

This virtually impenetrable 3km-wide swamp of mangroves stretches 16km from the South Negril River to Orange Bay. The swamp is the island's second-largest freshwater wetland system and forms a refuge for endangered waterfowl. American crocodiles still cling to life here and are occasionally seen at the mouth of the Orange River.

The Great Morass acts like a giant sponge filtering the waters flowing down to the ocean from the hills east of Negril, and is a source of much-needed fresh water. Drainage channels cut into the swamp have lowered the water levels, and sewage and other pollutants have seeped into the region's shallow water table, making their way to sea where they have poisoned the coral reefs and depleted fish stocks.

The easiest way to get a sense of the Great Morass is at the **Royal Palm Reserve** (Map p188; ☎957-3763; www.jpat-jm.net; adult/child US$10/5; ☺9am-6pm). Wooden boardwalks make a 1.5km loop around the reserve. Three distinct swamp forest types are present – royal palm forest, buttonwood forest and bull thatch forest. They're all home to butterflies galore as well as doctorbirds, herons, egrets, endangered black parakeets, Jamaican woodpeckers and countless other birds. Two observation towers provide views over the tangled mangroves.

If driving, take Sheffield Rd east of the roundabout for 10 minutes and turn left after the golf course. Otherwise, local tour operators run trips to the reserve. To explore the Great Morass outside the reserve, negotiate with villagers who have boats moored along the South Negril River (just northeast of Negril Village), or with fishermen at Norman Manley Sea Park, at the north end of Bloody Bay. It costs approximately US$45 for two hours.

(At the time this book went to press, the reserve was closed until further notice, so check the website or call ahead to confirm.)

Kool Runnings Water Park AMUSEMENT PARK
(Map p195; ✆957-5400; www.koolrunnings
.com; Norman Manley Blvd; adult/child US$28/19;
☺11am-7pm Tue-Sun) If you prefer your water fun doled out in a themepark, on this 2
hectares there are 10 different rides, ranging
from the 15m drop of the Jamaica Bobsled
to the tranquil Rio Bueno Lazy River ride.
Food is available at three restaurants, and
children can be easily distracted at Captain
Mikie's Coconut Island.

🏃 Activities

Boat Trips

Several companies offer two- and three-hour
excursions. Tours can be booked at most
hotels. Most trips include snorkeling and
plenty of booze, but try not to mix the two.

Glass-bottom boat rides are a great way to
see the fish life and coral if you don't want
to get wet. There are several to choose from
on Long Beach, and most trips will run you
around US$35.

Wild Thing Watersports CRUISES
(✆957-9930; www.wildthingwatersportsnegril.com)
Day cruises on a 45ft catamaran go to
Rhodes Hall (US$85; Monday, Wednesday
and Friday) and Half Moon Bay (US$65;
Tuesday, Saturday and Sunday). There
are also daily sunset cruises to Rick's Café
(US$55). You'll find the boat at Chances res-
taurant on Negril Beach.

Negril Cruises CRUISES
(✆430-0596) Offers several variations of
long, drunken party cruises; good times.

Stanley's Deep Sea Fishing WILDLIFE CRUISES
(Map p192; ✆957-6341; www.stanleysdeepseafish
ing.com; Negril Yacht Club) Offers whale- and
dolphin-watching cruises.

Cycling

The intense traffic along Norman Manley
Blvd and West End Rd makes cycling a dicey
proposition in town. The best place to ride is
along Ocean Dr or in the Negril Hills, southeast of Negril.

Rusty's X-Cellent Adventures CYCLING
(✆957-0155; http://rusty.nyws.com/bikeshop.
htm; Treetops, Hilton Ave; tours per person without/
with bike rental US$25/35) Offers high-quality
two- to four-hour mountain-bike tours into
the Negril Hills. Exciting single-track routes
follow goat paths to high ridges with awesome views; your guide provides casual instruction and commentary along the way.
All equipment – bikes, helmets, water and
accessories – is included. Tours begin and
end at Treetops (off Map p188), where gnarly
cyclists can also find lodging. Reservations
are required.

Diving & Snorkeling

Negril offers extensive offshore reefs and
cliffs with grottoes, shallow reefs perfect for
novice divers and mid-depth reefs right off
the main beach at Long Beach. Clusters of
dwarf tube sponges are a noteworthy feature. The West End offers caves and tunnels;
its overhangs are popular for night dives.
Hawksbill turtles are still quite common
here.

Visibility often exceeds 30m and seas are
dependably calm. Most dives are in 10m
to 23m of water. (For more general scuba-
diving information, see p26.)

Several sites here will be of interest to
prospective divers. **The Throne** is a 15m-
wide cave with massive sponges, plentiful
soft corals, nurse sharks, octopuses, barracuda and stingrays. **Aweemaway** is a shallow reef area south of the Throne, and has
tame stingrays. **Deep Plane** is the remains
of a Cessna airplane lying at 21m underwater. Corals and sponges have taken up residence in and around the plane, attracting an
abundance of fish, and nurse sharks hang
out at a nearby overhang. **Sands Club Reef**
lies in 10m of water in the middle of Long
Beach. From here, a drift dive to **Shark's
Reef** leads through tunnels and overhangs
with huge sponges and gorgonian corals.

Snorkeling is especially good at the southern end of **Seven Mile Beach (Long Beach)**
and off the **West End**. Expect to pay about
US$5 an hour for masks and fins from conces-
sion stands on the beach. Most of the scuba-
diving providers offer snorkeling tours
(about US$25).

Most all-inclusive resorts have scuba facilities. The following are among the companies offering PADI certification and intro-
ductory 'resort courses'.

Marine Life Divers DIVING
(Map p188; ✆957-3245; www.mldiversnegril.
com; Hotel Samsara, West End Rd; 1-/2-tank dive
US$40/70) English- and German-speaking
instructors.

Negril Scuba Centre DIVING
(www.negrilscubacenter.com; ✆877-7517) Mari-
ner's Negril Beach Club (✆957-4425, 957-9641;
Norman Manley Blvd); West End (Map p188;
✆957-0392; West End Rd); Sunset at the Palms
(Map p195; ✆383-9533; Bloody Bay Beach; 1-/2-
tank dive US$40/70).

Negril Village

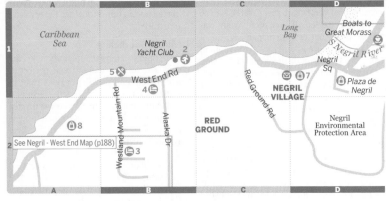

NEGRIL & WEST COAST NEGRIL

Sun Divers DIVING
(Map p195; ☑957-4503; www.sundiversnegril.com; Point Village; 1-/2-tank dive US$45/80) Many trips led by the charismatic Ansel Clarke.

Fishing

The waters off Negril – teeming with tuna, blue marlin, wahoo and sailfish – provide some excellent action for sport-fishing enthusiasts. **Stanley's Deep Sea Fishing** (Map p192; ☑957-0667; www.stanleysdeepseafishing.com; Negril Yacht Club) offers custom fishing-trip charters (US$750/1100/1500 per half/three-quarter/full day for up to four people; for additional passengers add US$50/75/100 per head).

For a more offbeat experience, head out into the briny with a local fisherman; ask around by the bridge over South Negril River, or talk to the fishermen near North Negril River.

Golf

Negril Hills Golf Club GOLF
(☑957-4638; www.negrilhillsgolfclub.com; Sheffield Rd; green fee US$58, club/cart rental US$18/35, caddy US$14; ⊙7:30am-4pm) An 18-hole par-72 course that borders the Great Morass, about 5km east of Negril. If you plop your ball in the water, forget it – the crocodiles will probably get to it first! Facilities here include a clubhouse, pro shop and restaurant.

Horseback Riding

Country Western Horse Rental HORSEBACK RIDING
(Map p192; ☑955-7910; Sheffield Rd; rides US$50; ⊙8am-5pm) Next to the police sta-

tion. The route follows the coast and then continues into the Negril Hills.

Rhodes Hall Plantation HORSEBACK RIDING
(☑957-6422; www.rhodesresort.com; 2hr rides incl hotel transfers from US$70) Based 5km north of Negril at Green Island, offers rides through banana plantations and up into the hills.

Water Sports

The waters off Negril are usually mirror-calm – ideal for all kinds of water sports. Numerous concessions along the beach rent jet skis (about US$40 for 30 minutes), plus sea kayaks, sailboards and Sunfish (about US$20 per hour). They also offer waterskiing (US$25 for 30 minutes), glass-bottom boat rides (US$15) and banana-boat rides (using an inflatable banana-shaped raft towed by a speedboat; US$15).

☞ Tours

Several tour operators offer a standard fare of excursions to the Black River Morass and Appleton Rum Estate (about US$85 to US$95) to the east in St Elizabeth parish, Mayfield Falls (US$65 to US$75) and Roaring River (US$60 to US$70).

Caribic Vacations SIGHTSEEING TOURS
(Map p202; ☑953-9895; www.caribicvacations.com; Norman Manley Blvd) The largest operator. Also has tours to the Royal Palm Reserve.

Clive's Transport Service SIGHTSEEING TOURS
(☑956-2615; www.clivestransportservicejamaica.com) Offers reliable, comfortable tours islandwide and airport transfers (one to

three people US$50) in a nine-passenger minivan.

JUTA Tours   SIGHTSEEING TOURS
(Map p202; ☎957-9197; Negril Crafts Market, Norman Manley Blvd) Run by the Jamaica Union of Travelers Association.

★ Festivals & Events

Jamaica Sprint Triathlon   TRIATHLON
(☎957-4061; ☺Jan) Held at the Couples Swept Away resort's sports complex.

Jamaica Beachfest   SPRING BREAK
(☺Feb-Apr) Starting in late February and now spanning six weeks to early April is Negril's famous Spring Break celebration, featuring live music and plenty of booze.

Unleash the Tiger   MUSIC
(☎957-4005; ☺Feb) A big concert at the Jungle, in observance of Jamaican Carnival.

Negril Music Festival   MUSIC
(☎968-9356; ☺Mar) Three-day reggae and calypso festival.

Negril Ice Cream and Chocolate Festival   FOOD
(☎957-3454) Easter Sunday and Monday.

Epicurean Escape   FOOD
(☎518-5006; Grand Lido Negril; ☺Aug/Sep) Seminars and tastings for foodies, from jerk to champagne.

Reggae Marathon & Half-Marathon
MARATHON
(☎922-8677; www.reggaemarathon.com; ☺Dec) Both a full and a half-marathon with a musical soundtrack staged on Norman Manley Blvd.

🛏 Sleeping

In general, beach properties are more expensive than hotels of equivalent standard in the West End. Unless otherwise noted, all 'Long Beach' beach hotels are on Norman Manley Blvd, and all 'West End' hotels are on the coast road, variously called West End Rd, Lighthouse Rd and Ocean Dr.

LONG BEACH
Moondance   VILLAS $$$
(Map p202; ☎312-981-6344, in the USA 800-621-1120; www.moondanceresorts.com; villas US$600-1900; P❋🗇🞉) The ultimate in Long Beach luxury, the Moondance villas put even the best all-inclusives to shame. You have a choice of gorgeous one- to five-bedroom villas; the one-bedroom honeymoon villa is akin to a lovely tropical home, whereas the three-bedroom 'Dream Walk' home looks like a medieval Chinese palace. For US$125 per adult per night you can get 24-hour all-inclusive service, which covers all food and drink any time of day or night.

Sunset at the Palms   RESORT $$$
(Map p195; ☎957-5350, from the USA 877-734-3486; www.sunsetatthepalms.com; all-incl d US$1500-2100, ste from US$1700; ❋🗇🞉) Sunset at the Palms is proof that an all-inclusive hotel doesn't have to be bland. This ecoconscious resort fairly drips heaps of jungle atmosphere with its all-hardwood, Thai-style cabins raised on stilts amid lush grounds full of croaking tree frogs. The interior decor is several shades of warm earth-tones mixed up with African crafts, crisp white

THE FRAGILE CORAL REEFS

Negril's offshore reefs have been severely damaged by the resort boom and human tinkering with the Great Morass. The percentage of live coral cover is now so low that further coral loss could seriously threaten the functioning of the entire ecosystem.

Reef restoration is an important part of the NEPA project (p208). But nothing can be done to bring back the marine turtles that once favored the beach for nesting.

The **Negril Coral Reef Preservation Society** (NCRPS; Map p202; ☏957-4626; http://negril.com/ncrps), located next to the Negril Crafts Market on Norman Manley Blvd, has established a code of conduct for snorkelers and scuba divers, including the following guidelines:

» Never touch corals; even slight contact can harm them.

» Select points of entry and exit to avoid walking on corals.

» Maintain a comfortable distance from the reef, so as to avoid contact.

» Stay horizontal in the water while you're near or above the reef.

» Move slowly and deliberately in the water – relax as you swim and take your time.

» Take nothing living or dead out of the water, except recent garbage which does not have living organisms on it.

» Never touch, handle or feed marine life except under expert guidance and following locally established guidelines.

sheets, antique-style cabinets and tables, and traces of Asian design sensibility. Facilities include a fitness center and tennis court plus games room, Jacuzzi, swim-up bar and romantic restaurant serving top-notch fusion cuisine.

Kuyaba
HOTEL **$$**

(Map p202; ☏957-4318; www.kuyaba.com; cottage US$77, r US$97, honeymoon ste US$106) With considerable style, this tasteful family-run hotel offers six quaint rustic wooden cabins with filigree trim, done up in bright Caribbean colors. The cottages are nice enough, but the real draws are the deluxe rooms and suite with king-sized bed upstairs in a handsome stone-and-timber house tastefully decorated with terra-cotta floors and modern design touches. The ecoconscious owners are gourmets and run the splendid Kuyaba on the Beach restaurant (p201), attached to the property. There's also a well-stocked gift store and live music 7pm to 9pm nightly.

Negril Yoga Centre
RESORT **$**

(Map p202; ☏957-4397; www.negrilyoga.com; d US$49-84; ❋🛜) A heartening back to hippie days of yore, these rustic yet atmospheric rooms and cottages – most with fridges and fans – surround an open-air, wood-floored, thatched yoga center set in a garden. Options range from a two-story, Thai-style wooden cabin (our favorite) to an adobe farmer's cottage; all are pleasingly if modestly furnished. The staff make their own yogurt, cheese and sprouts, and cook meals on request. Naturally, yoga classes are offered (guests/visitors US$10/15), as are massages (US$60). There's a communal kitchen. This is a good option for women traveling alone and families with children.

Whistling Bird
HOTEL **$$**

(Map p202; ☏957-4403, in the USA 800-276-8054; www.whistlingbird.com; s/d/tr US$140/210/315, all-incl per person from US$125; P❋) A cute family-run place with 24 rooms in bungalows and cottages all decked out with wood-accented decor and wicker furniture. The rooms are all highly individualized, and many have a sort of luxury tree house/chic safari-camp vibe going on. It's low-key and a great place to relax beneath shady bamboo. The all-inclusive add-on gets you two meals, drinks and a massage (that's for two people).

Couples Swept Away
RESORT **$$$**

(Map p195; ☏957-4061; www.couples.com; all-incl per person from US$700; P❋🛜☒) Widely recognized as one of the best all-inclusive resorts in the world, Couples Swept Away is pretty damn magnificent. This adults-only resort boasts the island's best-equipped sports and fitness facility, where you can sweat and look good before cooling off in the waters that lap onto the private beach. Pathways coil through an 8-hectare botanical rush-hour of ferns and heliconias to the suites, which are housed in two-story villas and boast terra-cotta tile floors, deep-red hardwoods and vast louvered windows; the whole energy of the rooms really screams 'billionaire scion of a wealthy Caribbean family,' and there's probably a few of those types lounging around. Maybe they're in the immaculately hip on-site bars and nightclubs, which wouldn't be out of place in London, Berlin and New York. Free golf at Negril Hills Golf Club is included.

Our Past Time
B&B **$$**

(Map p202; ✆957-5422; www.ourpasttimenegril.com; d/studio/2-bedroom apt US$120/130/250; ❄️🐾🛜) A simple B&B for those who don't need the laundry list of amenities at larger resorts, or the nuts party scene at some of the smaller, youth-oriented guest houses. Our Past Time, with its quiet gardens, rooms washed in gentle Caribbean colors and friendly staff (who make some mighty fine meals on demand, we might add) may

be the most genuinely peaceful place to stay on Long Beach.

Firefly Beach Cottages
HOTEL **$$**

(Map p202; ✆957-4358; www.jamaicalink.com; ste & apt US$130-250; cabins from US$50; ❄️🛜) One of the more diverse accommodations in Negril, the Firefly gives you a range of lodgings starting from a crisp, single-occupancy studio apartment to luxurious penthouse suites atop a small apartment complex, to beachside cottages. The on-site 'Secrets Cabins' are a collection of (very) tiny chalets that can sleep two people and are priced for backpackers. Staff are professional and courteous. The nearby beach is *very* nude-friendly.

Merril's Beach Resort
HOTEL **$$**

(Map p202; ✆957-4751; www.merrilsbeach.com; s/d/tr per person gardenside US$90/75/60, beachside US$141/119/108; ❄️) A short distance from Negril Gardens, Merril's (which has multiple incarnations across Negril) is a solid midrange option, with clean white rooms done up in varying themes of nautical and tropical chic. The grounds are lushly landscaped

Negril – Long Bay (North)

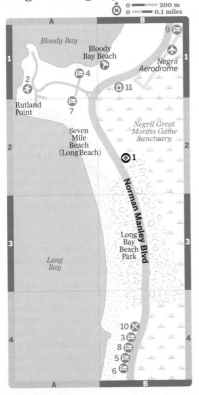

0 ——— 200 m
0 ——— 0.1 miles

Negril – Long Bay (North)

'CALICO' JACK'S LAST STAND

Before you park yourself on the sand, consider the plight of 'Calico Jack' Rackham, a pirate who dallied a little too long on the beach. In 1720 'Calico' Jack (so named for his fondness for calico underwear) and his buccaneers paused in Bloody Bay after a particularly satisfying plundering spree. He and his band of merry men got a little too merry on the local rum, and in the course of their beach party were taken unawares by the British navy, which overwhelmed them after a struggle worthy of the bay's name.

After the battle, the British were shocked to find that two of 'Calico' Jack's cohorts were actually women: Mary Read and Anne Bonney, who had been his mistress. Rackham was executed and his body suspended in an iron suit on what is now called Rackham Cay, at the harbor entrance at Port Royal, as an example to other pirates. The lives of Read and Bonney were spared because they claimed to be pregnant.

and shady. All rooms have verandas. The beach here has been accorded the prestigious Blue Flag award for Merril's attention to the environment. Popular with European tour groups.

Rondel Village RESORT $$
(Map p202; ☎957-4413; www.rondelvillage.com; d US$100-182, 1-/2-bedroom villa US$225-330; ❄❖❂) Rondel's Green Globe Certification attests to its commitment to preserving the environment. This friendly, efficiently run place is graced by walkways lined with an array of indigenous fruit trees. The family-owned Village offers well-appointed studios and beachfront rooms clustered around a small pool and Jacuzzi. You can also choose octagonal one- and two-bedroom villas that sleep up to six and feature marble floors, French doors, satellite TV, DVD and CD players, fully equipped kitchenettes and Jacuzzi. It has a seafront restaurant and popular bar, Irie on the Beach.

White Sands HOTEL $
(Map p202; ☎957-4291, in the USA 305-503-9074; www.whitesandsjamaica.com; r US$69-108, studio/villa US$138/540; ❄❂) This attractive property offers simple yet elegant one-bedroom octagonal units, and an excellent four-bedroom, four-bathroom villa that sleeps eight people and has its own pool: the latter is the real draw, as a group rental is a total steal. There's also a pleasant, well-maintained garden where you can relax while the resident parrot recites dub poetry.

Charela Inn HOTEL $$$
(Map p202; ☎957-4277; www.charela.com; s/d/tr US$163/183/229; ❖❄❂❂) Run by a Jamaican-French couple, Daniel and Sylvie, this engaging spot resembles a Spanish haci-

enda and surrounds a sunny courtyard. The rooms all have contemporary decor with lots of hardwood, plus ceiling fans, hair dryers, telephones and balconies or patios. The on-site Le Vendôme restaurant is one of the finest in Negril.

Mariposa Hideaway HOTEL $$
(Map p202; ☎957-4918; www.mariposahideaway.com; r US$80-140, 2-bedroom apt US$150; ❖❂) A twee Italian-run hotel that feels like a nice marriage between the Mediterranean and the Caribbean. Rooms are all right, but the tiled studios with kitchenettes and family-size apartment, all with cable TV and fridge, are the real standouts. A great bonus here is the Ristorante da Gino, where the grappa starts flowing before noon.

Country Country COTTAGES $$$
(Map p202; ☎957-4273; www.countrynegril.com; cottages US$190-210; ❄) So nice they named it twice, this color-crazy charmer has that mellow Negril vibe down cold. The green-shaded wooden cottages all have gingerbread trim and fretwork; pastels dominate and lend a chic warmth. Some have king-sized beds and separate sitting areas.

Sandals Negril Beach Resort & Spa RESORT $$$
(Map p195; ☎957-5216; www.sandals.com; all-incl r from $US400, ste US$1000-1250; ❖❄❂❂) One of the more tasteful outposts of the Sandals empire, this couples-only resort sprawls over wide lawns trimmed to perfection. At its node is a huge pool with swim-up bar abuzz with happy guests. There are 227 rooms in six categories, including exquisite honeymoon suites in gracious cottages with Edwardian decoration, swim-up suites where your front porch is your pool deck and the impressive two-story sunset lofts, classily

furnished apartments with four-poster beds where the entire wall gives way to grand windows and views of the ocean.

Roots Bamboo
RESORT $

(Map p202; ☑957-4479; www.rootsbamboo.com; camping per person US$15, r US$45, d with porch & shower US$55, with air-con US$70; ❄) First: if you want peace and quiet, look elsewhere. On the other hand, if you need a party – well, stick around, mon. This complex of cottages, campsites and chalets attracts a mixed crowd of the middle-aged and back-packers who share a pretty similar desire to get crazy on the beach; there are regularly scheduled reggae concerts and a perpetual party atmosphere.

Chippewa Village Hotel
HOTEL $

(Map p202; ☑957-4676, from USA 877-670-8426; www.chippewavillageresort.com; cottage d US$60, studio US$80, 1-/2-/3-bedroom apt US$140/180/200; ❄❄@) We love Chippewa for being so endearingly retro; it reminds us of the hotels we associate with family road trips, but plunked into the Caribbean. It's certainly a cheerful choice, with a definite Native Americans Everywhere theme, from the geometric-patterned house decorations to the library filled with black-and-white photos of, it seems, the supporting cast of *Dances With Wolves*. Accommodations are split between rustic octagonal studio units screened in by porches and lofty ceilings and one- to three-bedroom apartments. A small swimming pool under a shade canopy is inset in a wooden sundeck. There's a small restaurant and bar, with American home cooking (for guests only), plus a Jacuzzi, steam room and viewing tower overlooking the Great Morass.

Sunrise Club
HOTEL $

(Map p202; ☑957-4293; www.sunriseclub.com; s/d US$74/98; ⓟ❄@) Easing back onto the Great Morass, this gracious getaway is enhanced by its intimate Southwest style. Older rooms to the rear are simply furnished but have neat bathrooms, while newer rooms have blue mahoe furnishings, and all have screened windows, earth colors, natural hardwoods and rustic architectural touches. The on-site bar gets pretty busy at night and attracts a young clientele. Meal plans available for US$22 to US$38 per person.

Travellers Beach Resort
HOTEL $$

(Map p202; ☑957-9308; www.travellersresorts .com; s/d from US$70/110, ste US$190; ⓟ❄❄❄)

Although overrun during Spring Break, Travellers is a real bargain the rest of the year. The family-owned resort is a lovely little midrange option, professionally run with clean, comfortable rooms that match the amenities of larger top-end resorts.

Idle Awhile
HOTEL $$$

(Map p202; ☑957-9566, in the USA 877-243-5352; www.idleawhile.com; r US$195, ste US$210-335; ⓟ❄❄) This exquisite boutique hotel is highly recommended for airy, delightfully appointed rooms and suites that all drip with contemporary vogue and tropical decor. The interior of the place, from the lobby to the rooms themselves, resembles a fantastically hip loft condo from 1980s Miami, and we mean that as a compliment.

Westport Cottages
GUEST HOUSE $

(Map p202; ☑957-4736, 307-5466; www.westport -cottages.com; s/d US$25/35; ❄) Westport is extremely popular with the backpacking crowd, and owner Joseph Mathews says it's also approved for 'smoke-friendly heartical people,' so you should have an idea of what the vibe here is like. Joseph has 17 very rustic, somewhat stuffy huts with mosquito nets and fans. The well-kept bathrooms and cold showers are outside. A communal kitchen is available, and bicycles (US$5 per day) and snorkeling equipment (free!) are provided.

Beachcomber Club & Spa
HOTEL $$$

(Map p202; ☑957-4170; www.beachcomberclub. com; r US$150-175, 1-bedroom apt US$280, 2-bed-room apt US$405-430; ⓟ❄@) Operating with crisp efficiency, this handsome multi-room hotel has an open-air beachside restaurant, Gambino's, that does great Italian, plus a nightly entertainment schedule, tennis and water sports. Yet for all this, it doesn't feel as corporate as an all-inclusive. All rooms are well furnished in a sort of standard high-midrange-hotel outlay of tans and beiges; suites and apartments have kitchenettes.

Foote Prints on the Sands Hotel
HOTEL $$

(Map p195; ☑957-4300; r US$150-200; ⓟ❄❄❄) If you can get past the bright yellow color scheme on the exterior (seriously, the place looks as if it was crossed with a lemon), you'll find this friendly family-run hotel on the beach to be a good option. The simple rooms and simple grounds are fam-ily-friendly and hearken back to old-school Negril vacations, pre big resorts.

Negril Tree House

RESORT **$$**

(Map p202; ☑957-4287; www.negril-treehouse. com; r US$150-170, ste US$280-350; P✻≋) This unpretentious resort has a very loyal fan base of returning guests who just can't get enough of the professional, friendly service or the 16 octagonal bungalows and ocean-front villas nudging pleasingly up to the beach. More elegant one- and two-bedroom suites have a modernist Mediterranean feel to them, with cushy beds and views, opening onto a wide veranda.

Nirvana on the Beach

RESORT **$$$**

(Map p202; ☑957-4314, in the USA 716-789-5955; www.nirvananegril.com; d cottage US$195-250) The place to stay if you're seeking meditation and the sort of bohemian ambience you get when members of the counterculture decide to open up a tasteful boutique hotel. You can pick from one-, two- and three-bedroom cottages all set in elegantly subdued, yet still vibrantly colorful Zen-like tropical gardens.

Hedonism II

RESORT **$$$**

(Map p195; ☑957-5070; www.hedonismresorts. com; all-incl r per person US$620-925; P✻🤶≋) Famous for its risqué attitude and weekly lingerie parties (and notorious for its sheer tackiness), this adults-only resort has 280 rooms and suites and a *lot* of parties going on, literally a different theme for every night. Sadly, the strange retro decor is somewhat of a turnoff. There are two fine beaches – one for nudes and the other for 'prudes,' a rock-climbing wall, ice-skating rink and, of course, a disco (inset with glass-bottomed Jacuzzi in the roof). Guests include many more single males than females, and thus a third female in a group stays free. What's that? Oh, of course the ceilings are mirrored.

Breezes Grand Negril

RESORT **$$$**

(Map p195; ☑957-5010; www.breezes.com; all-incl d from US$495; P✻🤶≋) We give plenty of points to the full amenities list here, which includes some nine bars, six restaurants (French, Italian, Japanese, Jamaican – take your pick), 9 hectares of gardens, a pillow menu (anti-snoring, 'Swedish foam' etc), diving lessons and several pages worth more of stuff to do. It's the 210 rooms, decked out in a boring Victorian pastiche, that we think need work.

Beaches Negril

RESORT **$$$**

(Map p195; ☑957-9270; www.beaches.com; 3 nights all-incl d US$2000-3200; P✻🤶≋) An-other Sandals all-inclusive resort, this one is primarily aimed at families. It loosely resembles a castle, with thick limestone walls, wrought-iron furniture and lanterns, plus seven restaurants speckled on-site. There are 215 rooms, including 39 junior-suite buildings in quasi-Spanish hacienda style. It has a gigantic pool and lots of facilities for kids. Guests get access to Sandals Negril.

WEST END

TOP CHOICE Caves

HOTEL **$$$**

(Map p188; ☑957-0269, in the USA 800-688-7678, in the UK 0800-688-76781; www.islandoutpost. com/the_caves/; ste incl meals from US$608, all-incl cottage US$920-1865; P✻🤶≋) One of the finest boutique hotels in Jamaica, and one beloved of the Hollywood elite (some of whom are helicoptered in), the Caves offers handcrafted, individually styled one- and two-bedroom wood-and-thatch cottages set in lush gardens above cave-riddled cliffs. Rooms feature exquisite hand-carved furniture, batik fabrics and one-of-a-kind art; many have exquisite alfresco showers. Paths wind down to a free-form Jacuzzi studding the rock face, and then to a cave with molded benches where you can meditate to the reverberations of the waves (or have dinner if you order a day in advance). There's also a sauna, plus an Aveda spa. Rates include all meals and self-service bar.

Rockhouse

HOTEL **$$$**

(Map p188; ☑957-4373; www.rockhousehotel.com; r/studio/villa US$160/185/355; ✻🤶≋) One of the West End's most beautiful and well-run hotels, with luxury thatched rondavels (African huts) built of pine and stone, plus studio apartments that dramatically cling to the cliffside above a small cove. Decor is basic yet romantic, with net-draped poster beds and strong Caribbean colors. Catwalks lead over the rocks to an open-sided, multilevel dining pavilion (with one of the best restaurants in Negril) overhanging the ocean. A dramatically designed pool sits atop the cliffs and looks as if it's about to plunge into the ocean – but you already got that sense the minute you entered this cliffside world. In the lounge is a projection screen where Jamaican films are frequently shown.

Banana Shout

CABINS **$$**

(Map p188; ☑957-0384; www.bananashout.com; 2-/3-/4-person cabins US$200/200/250; P@) Occupying a particularly choice bit of cliff-top turf, these cheerful green and orange cabins – a color combination that works to soothing effect here – are perched over the sea in offbeat and homey seclusion. Tastefully decorated with Jamaican and Haitian art, they're unique and charmingly idiosyncratic, even for the West End. Step outside to a dramatic stairway descending to a sea cave with sundeck and freshwater shower. Two of the cabins include loft bedrooms; one can accommodate up to six people.

Blue Cave Castle — HOTEL $$

(Map p188; ☎957-4845; www.bluecavecastle.com; s/d US$60/125; ✴) Providing perhaps the best view of Long Beach from the West End, this atmospheric, all-stone concoction attracts nudists, travel junkies and freethinkers. The property really does resemble a castle, albeit one built by a mad genius who wanted to create a pastel lighthouse and didn't skimp on the quirkiness while they were at it. Or comfort: bedrooms are equipped with a CD player, ceiling fan and refrigerator and tower rooms open to the stars and the ocean. Stairs from the castle lead down to a blue sea cave.

Villas Sur Mer — COTTAGES $$$

(Map p188; ☎382-3717; www.villassurmer.com; cottages US$260-550; ✴🛜🏊) Sure, there are plenty of hotels in Negril that offer access to the sea – but how many do so via a dramatic cave that looks as if it were carved out by Poseidon himself? Seriously, look at the ocean through that cave and tell us we're wrong. In addition, you've got rooms decorated in a thatched, Greek island–esque style, overlaying everything with a cool blue Hellenic vibe that goes quite well with the Caribbean breezes.

Catcha Falling Star — HOTEL $$$

(Map p188; ☎957-0390; www.catchajamaica.com; 1-/2-bedroom cottage incl breakfast from US$110/320; 🅿@) In inimitable West End style, these pleasant fan-cooled cottages – including several with two bedrooms – sit on the cliffs. Each is named for an astrological sign and the rooms do have the genuine variety of the zodiac; some peek into gardens all afire with tropical flowers while others lip out onto the blue-on-blue vista of ocean and sky. Breakfast (included in rates) is delivered to your veranda, which we just love; other meals by request. A tiered cliff affords easy access to the sea, where clothing-optional bathing can be enjoyed in a private cove.

Tensing Pen — RESORT $$$

(Map p188; ☎957-0387; www.tensingpen.com; r incl breakfast US$140-230, cottages US$330-680, per week US$960-3060) Among the more acclaimed accommodations in Negril is this tranquil, reclusive option with 12 thatched cottages on a hectare of land. Most are 'pillar houses' – an architectural style that has come to be associated with the West End – perched above the coral cliffs and set in natural gardens. All have exquisite bamboo and hardwood details, though otherwise differ markedly in decor. Guests take meals – some of Negril's best cuisine – in an extravagant structure inspired by the architecture of luxury South African hunting lodges. The most expensive cottages are some of the finest rooms in Negril.

Seastar Inn — HOTEL $

(Map p188; ☎957-0553; www.seastarinn.com; s/d incl breakfast US$69/129; 🅿✴🛜) This peaceful modern place is run by a charming Canadian-Jamaican couple. Pretty tiled rooms offset by tastefully frilly interior decor characterize the interior; outside the inn is fuzzed over with fecund trees and lush grounds. Hammocks are strung out over verandas, which is a bit of an issue, as you may never leave them. Cell phones are provided for guests.

Lighthouse Inn 2 — GUEST HOUSE $

(Map p188; ☎957-4052; www.lighthouseinn2.com; cottages s/d/q US$60/80/140) A small, family resort that brings to mind the old-school charms of Negril's heyday, the Lighthouse 2 is the sort of budget place with a gentle, fun vibe that you kind of want to export all over Long Beach, just to bring the madness there down a tick to a manageable level. Deserves special mention for making an effort to accommodate disabled guests. Rooms and apartments are spare but sweet, especially at these prices.

Mi Yard — GUEST HOUSE $

(Map p192; ☎957-4442; www.miyard.com; s/d/tr US$50/60/70; ✴@) With friendly service and yummy meals served till all hours, this agreeable little place offers four simple, clean, albeit somewhat dark, tiled rooms – two have air-con – and two no-frills yet charming wooden Caribbean-style cottages with balconies. Organizes trips across Jamaica.

Judy House — GUEST HOUSE $

(Map p192; ☎957-0671; judyhousenegril.com; s apt US$35, s/d US$50/60; 🛜) The owners describe this place as 'pretty and country,' and we can't really improve on that. Two rough-shod and charming wooden cabins are tucked into clouds of brilliant flowers and yam vines on grounds patrolled by a friendly cat and dog; one of the cabins has air-con, and there's a small apartment for single travelers as well. There's a communal patio for getting to know your neighbor and general consolidation of being Irie. If you just need some tropical seclusion, we highly recommend this spot.

Sundown Cottage
COTTAGE **$**

(Map p188; ☑361-1401, 990-9125; cottage US$80; ❄) This beguiling cottage adjacent to Tensing Pen is an ideal private spot for the couple seeking to, a la Stella, get a groove on. A veritable home away from home, the fan-cooled one-bedroom nest has a kitchenette and sundeck, and a cheerful ambience colored by pastels. Tremendous value.

Moonlight Villa
VILLA **$$**

(Map p188; ☑957-4838; www.moonlightvilla.com; s/d/tr US$80/100/120; Ⓟ) Moonlight has large rooms decked out in a sort of Rasta-university-student-chic design scheme; we're sorry they didn't provide black lights. Each has cable TV, coffeemaker, ceiling fan, and a double and single bed, so mixed groups might find this a very good deal (and to be honest, it's a lovely place no matter how many of you there are). From a wide sunny veranda a stairway descends to the sea.

Xtabi
HOTEL **$**

(Map p188; ☑957-0120; www.xtabi-negril.com; r US$83-90, cottages US$210, extra person US$25; Ⓟ❄🛜) This chic and casual hotel bills itself as 'the meeting place of the gods.' Its clientele is decidedly human, but the setting is truly divine. You can choose from rooms, simple garden cottages or quaint octagonal seafront bungalows perched atop the cliff. They're pleasingly appointed, if nothing fancy. The bar is lively and the restaurant appealing, and the place tends to attract a fun crowd that manages to be livelier than the usual West End folks without becoming too crazy like the folks in Long Beach.

Home Sweet Home
HOTEL **$$**

(Map p188; ☑957-4478, in the USA 800-925-7418; www.homesweethomeresort.com; r US$110, ste US$175-$250, penthouse US$225; ❄🛜) Yet another cliffhanger with a dozen rooms plus two suites, all with private balconies, fans and private showers. The rooms are, natu-

rally, done up in tropical pastels, but for some reason the execution works much better here than it does in other Negril hotels. It features a clifftop bar and restaurant, a Jacuzzi and multi-tiered sundecks overhanging the teal-blue waters. This may be more or less where Stella got her groove back; writer Terry McMillan stayed here while researching the novel of the same name.

Negril Escape Resort & Spa
HOTEL **$$$**

(Map p188; ☑851-6506; www.negrilescape.com; s US$95-240, d US$100-245, tr US$110-340, ste US$490-580; Ⓟ❄@🛜) The 10 spacious cottages here are named and decorated with a different 'ethnic' theme: Romancing the Kasbah, with its Arabian-style pillows and terracotta accents, suggests Morocco; the paper lanterns and bamboo blinds of Oriental Express hint at the Far East; Atlantis features mermaids on its murals (ironically, the most boring cottage is the Negril-themed one). Yoga classes are offered and you're within walking distance of Rick's. There's a huge variety of rooms and seasonal rates.

Jackie's on the Reef
HOTEL **$$**

(off Map p188; ☑957-4997, in the USA 718-469-2785; www.jackiesonthereef.com; r or cottage per person US$175; ❄) This tranquil option is 11km south of the Negril roundabout, just north of the intersection with William Hogg Blvd. It operates as a New Age haven focusing on spiritual renewal. A natural stone 'temple' is divided into four rooms, each with two handmade wooden beds and an outdoor shower and bathroom enclosed within your own private backyard. There's a small cooling pool set in the reef top. The facility is more rustic, and the rooms more austere than rates might suggest, but a lot of guests are really paying for the organic reputation Jackie's has built up with the New Age community.

Summerset Village
COTTAGES **$**

(Map p188; ☑957-4409; www.summersetvillage.net; Summerset Rd; r US$40-50, 1-/2-bedroom cottage US$40/80, Thatch House US$200; ❄🛜) Set about 300m inland on 3 hectares of landscaped grounds, this property defines casual seclusion, as well as odd design choice. In addition to standard rooms, it has octagonal 'towers' (seriously), a vaguely Latin 'hacienda,' a pillared 'chateau' (not as grand as it sounds) and a lovely dark-wood, five-bedroom thatch house, ideal for a group rental. Summerset offers a shuttle to the beach, and has a restaurant and bar on site.

Lighthouse Park
GUEST HOUSE **$**

(Map p188; ☑957-0252, 283-8691; www.lighthouse-park.com; cabins/cottages US$65/120) This old favorite south of the lighthouse consists of wooden cottages and a tasteful apartment suite, perched on a cliff affording excellent sea views. The rooms are fine, but the real draw is the clientele, an eccentric mix of rootsy artist types who tend to be frequent repeat customers.

✖ Eating

Local delicacies (besides hallucinogenic mushroom omelets and ganja muffins) include crab pickled in red peppers. Easier to find is pasta, pizza and plenty of good vegetarian (I-tal) fare. Many places price in US$, so we have followed suit.

LONG BEACH

TOP CHOICE Le Vendôme
FRENCH **$$$**

(Map p202; ☑957-4648; Charela Inn; mains US$30-48; ☺breakfast, lunch & dinner) Trust us: Jamaican-French fusion means more than jerk croissant –although we were surprised such a pairing could end up being so heavenly before we came to the Charela's signature restaurant. Take your table on the terra-cotta terrace with a pleasant garden view and choose from classic French dishes like duck à l'orange and escargots Burgundy-style, or regional creations like curried shrimp or red snapper cooked in coconut milk; what sets everything apart from both traditional French and Jamaican cuisine is the Gallic attention to final execution and the use of locally grown vegetables and spices. There's a daily five-course gourmet dinner (US$45 to US$70) that's a fantastic indulgence.

Cosmo's
SEAFOOD **$**

(Map p195; Norman Manley Blvd; mains J$300-1000; ☺10am-11pm) Our favorite spot for seafood in seaside Negril, Cosmo's eschews fine-dining flash for a few rough-hewn tables, a beachside location and plates of melt-in-your mouth amazing seafood. The curry conch is deliciously spicy – enough kick to wake your mouth up, not so much to be unbearable.

Kuyaba on the Beach
FUSION **$$$**

(Map p202; ☑957-4318; Kuyaba; mains US$18-30; ☺breakfast, lunch & dinner) 'Kuyaba' means 'Celebrate!' in the Arawakan language, which is exactly what happens here each evening at sunset as guests tuck into innovative dishes like crab and pumpkin cakes

with papaya mustard or coconut conch with a mango chutney. The lunch menu is a bit more laid-back: burgers, kebabs and gourmet sandwiches, plus superb pepper shrimp.

Lobster House
ITALIAN **$$**

(Map p202; Sunrise Club; mains US$8-22; ☺breakfast, lunch & dinner) Renowned for its pink gnocchi in a parmesan cream and its signature lobster dishes, this congenial outdoor spot's brick oven has brought it the status of best pizzeria in town – if you need proof, try the Queen Aragosta pizza with lobster tails. Many, however, come for a cup of what is arguably the best espresso on the island, made from the proprietor's vintage 1961 Faema espresso machine.

Ristorante da Gino
ITALIAN **$$**

(Map p202; ☑957-4918; Mariposa Hideaway; mains US$14-18; ☺breakfast, lunch & dinner) Host Gino Travaini proudly serves fresh pasta and homemade bread plus delectable Italian fare in a secluded beachside garden setting with four open pavilions. Specialties include seafood linguine, scaloppini and lobster. Reservations recommended.

Selina's
JAMAICAN **$$**

(Map p202; mains US$5-16; ☺breakfast, lunch & dinner) Negril is in dire need of an all-day breakfast joint, and Selina's provides. This outstanding spot enjoys many repeat customers for the callaloo and cheese omelets, banana pancakes, killer smoothies and hand-roasted Blue Mountain coffee. The lunch menu features salads and burgers, though the pièce de résistance is the cheese-and-vegetable quesadilla. Sundays see a jazz band that draws a mixed crowd of locals and visitors. Make sure you give the Bloody Mary a whirl (and we mean whirl; packs a punch).

Angela's
ITALIAN **$$**

(Map p202; Bar-b-barn Hotel; mains US$6-20; ☺breakfast, lunch & dinner) We don't know why pizza goes so well with the beach, but it does, and the pizza at Angela's is some of the best in Negril. As are the pasta plates and a host of other Italian dishes, all of a quality we frankly weren't expecting on a Jamaican beach.

Norma's on the Beach at Sea Splash
JAMAICAN **$$$**

(Map p202; Sea Splash Resort; mains US$15-32; ☺breakfast, lunch & dinner) This Negril branch of Norma Shirley's celebrated Jamaican culinary empire seems to have escaped the hype surrounding her Kingston flagship, but the 'new world Caribbean' food at this stylish beach restaurant is just as adventurous. Expect to find the likes of lobster, Cornish game hen, jerk chicken and pasta, as well as tricolor 'rasta pasta.'

Bourbon Beach
JERK $

(Map p202; mains J$300-800; ☺lunch & dinner) Though it's best known for its live reggae concerts, those in the know swear by Bourbon's jerk chicken. The sauce is thick and pastelike, and well complemented by a Red Stripe as you wait for a show.

WEST END

On the West End you'll find restaurants that mainly serve cheap Jamaican fare, although some of the nicer resorts have international fusion.

TOP CHOICE Rockhouse
Restaurant & Bar
FUSION $$$

(Map p188; ☎957-4373; Rockhouse Hotel; mains US$15-30; ☺breakfast, lunch & dinner) Lamplit at night, this pricey yet relaxed cliffside spot leads the pack when it comes to nouvelle Jamaican cuisine in the western parishes. Dine and gush over dishes such as vegetable tempura with lime and ginger, specialty pastas and daily specials like watermelon spare ribs and blackened mahimahi with mango chutney. At the very least, stop by for a sinful bananas Foster.

Canoe Bar
FUSION $$

(Map p192; mains J$450-1400; ☺breakfast, lunch & dinner) The Canoe Bar occupies a pretty lovely space within the Jamaican culinary curriculum: a seeming local food shack that happens to be able to pull off excellent fusion techniques, adding a bit of international body to coarse Jamaican flavors (or is that adding Jamaican heat and heft to international fare?). Opt for the pepper-grilled kingfish or rum sautéed shrimp (oh yeah), and make sure to have a side of fluffle (we're not telling).

Sips & Bites
JAMAICAN $$

(Map p188; mains J$350-1500; ☺breakfast, lunch & dinner Sun-Fri) This large, welcoming open-air restaurant serves classic Jamaican fare, and it serves it done right: rich, filling and more compellingly seasoned than in many other Jamaican restaurants. The dishes include oxtail, curried goat, brown stew lobster and conch steaks. Wash it down with the day's special natural juice. Starting bright and

early, hearty Jamaican breakfasts are served, and locals consider them pretty top-quality fare.

3 Dives Jerk Centre
JERK $

(Map p188; West End Rd; quarter-/half-chicken J$350/600; ☺noon-midnight) It's no small tribute to 3 Dives that its jerk overshadows its reputation for lengthy waits (sometimes over an hour). Fortunately, the chefs are more than happy to let you peek into the kitchen, where there's bound to be a pile of super-hot Scotch bonnet peppers threatening to spontaneously combust.

Negril – Long Bay (South)

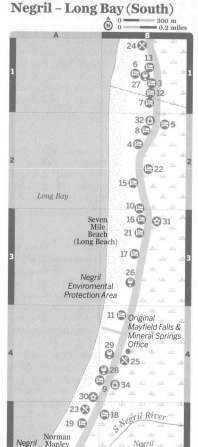

Royal Kitchen Vegetarian Café   I-TAL $
(Map p188; West End Rd; mains J$280-600;
breakfast, lunch & dinner; ✈) The best I-tal
eatery in Negril is popular with legit local
Rastafarians and those who come to collect
their pearls of wisdom. The fare – strictly
vegetarian – is served on simple tables where
you are sure to make friends with inquisitive
passersby. Juices are especially good.

Hungry Lion   JAMAICAN $$
(Map p188; ☎957-4486; mains US$12-32; dinner;
✈) A brightly painted spot that serves intricate fare from a changing menu of mostly
fish and vegetarian dishes, like a vegetarian
shepherd's pie or quesadillas stuffed with
shrimp and cheese. The alfresco rooftop dining room is tastefully decorated with earth
tones and original art, and you'll be eating
in the company of very chill trance music.
Wash everything down by heading to the bar

and ordering off its extensive menu of cocktails and juices.

Sweet Spice Restaurant   JAMAICAN $
(Map p188; Sheffield Rd; J$250-1200; lunch & din-
ner) This unassuming bright-blue clapboard
house is a favorite among several authentic Jamaican restaurants on Sheffield Rd
that are frequented by locals. Portions are
heaped, prices are inexpensive and the food
true blue Jamaican. The menu includes curried goat and fish, conch steak and pepper
steak. No alcohol, but plenty of fruit juices.

Miss Brown's   CAFE $
(off Map p192; Sheffield Rd; mains US$4-28;
6:30am-midnight) Miss Brown's is one of Negril's most famous restaurants, which may
seem a bit odd given the menu. It's all just
mushroom stuff, right? Mushroom omelets
and mushroom tea and mushroom daiqui-
ris...ah. *They're hallucinogenic.* If you come

here (and everyone in Negril seems to do so at least once), make sure you have a trusted driver to get you back to your hotel (or a few hours to kill sitting around).

Rick's Cafe   FUSION **$$$**

(Map p188; ☑957-0380; mains US$20-30; ☺lunch & dinner) You'll be joining the touristy throng at this ever-popular West End institution, but why not? Just for one night. The somewhat pricey menu features steaks, fresh seafood and faux-Cajun fare, and all of it is pretty middling stuff. The loud music precludes having a really intimate meal, but if you're in the mood for a party – or a dip in the pool between courses – this place fits the bill. While you eat, local divers try to outdo each other from the 10m-tall cliffs.

🍷 Drinking & Entertainment

Negril gives Kingston a run for its money when it comes to the after-hours pursuits of cocktails, dancing and live reggae music. There are dozens of bars, one big nightclub and several venues on the beach where live acts keep things throbbing well into the night. Things *really* hop during Spring Break; in point of fact, it never really stops.

Bars & Nightclubs

Nonguests can obtain passes (US$25 to US$50) for entry to the discos in the following upscale all-inclusive resorts: Sandals Negril, Hedonism II, Couples, Beaches Negril and Grand Lido. Once inside the gates you can booze and party to your heart's content without having to shell out another cent, which is actually a pretty decent deal.

The booze starts flowing each evening along Long Beach in time to toast the setting sun, when many bars offer happy-hour incentives to lure you in. In the West End, bars are lively in the early evening before petering out as the beach bars take over.

LONG BEACH

Most bars along the beach are, quite frankly, interchangeable, offering boozers front-row deck chairs for the sunset and barstools for the evening. They all pump reggae music; they all offer cold beer; they're all pretty fun at the end of the day, and the end of the day, ie sunset, is the best time to visit them.

Jimmy Buffett's Margaritaville   BAR

(Map p202) The most ostentatious of the beach bars, Jimmy Buffett's sustains a Spring Break vibe all year long, although it has a bit of a forlorn air on slow nights. There are big-screen TVs, a basketball court, trampolines in the sea, volleyball, swing hammocks and multiple bars waiting to get you trashed. It hosts wet T-shirt contests and the like, and has nightly specials, including karaoke on Sunday.

Jungle   NIGHTCLUB

(Map p202; admission US$5-10; ☺Wed-Sun) If you're looking for a nightclub outside the all-inclusives, head to the Jungle. It's not the most urbane place, with its tacky decor, but the DJs *definitely* know what they're doing; during the high season guest talent from Miami and New York regularly takes command of the turntables. The best nights are Thursday, when women enter free before midnight, and Saturday. There's not much action before midnight.

Alfred's Ocean Palace   BAR

(Map p202) Busiest bar on the beach on some nights. Live music three nights a week.

Legends Beach Resort   BAR

(Map p202) Corny music, cheesy vibes, good times.

Risky Business   BAR

(Map p202; ☺Mon, Thu & Sat) This place goes all out during Spring Break. Occasionally, jazz is featured on Wednesday night. Covers sometimes budge into the expensive US$12 to US$15 range. Sound-system parties rock the beachside.

Sunrise Club   BAR

(Map p202; www.sunriseclub.com) At the hotel of that name, has a cool bar if you want to escape the beach mayhem.

WEST END

All the live-music venues listed below are also terrific bars, even when there are no acts on stage.

Rick's Cafe   BAR

(Map p188) A little pricey and the reggae cover band really lays on the schmaltz, but this two-story restaurant, with sun deck, rope swing and cliff-diving platform still has its kitschy charm. To be sure, it *is* shamelessly touristy (it's been a *long* time since the Rolling Stones have stopped by), but the party-hearty vibe makes Rick's the proper spot from which to launch a big night out.

Sands   BAR

(Map p188) Even if you can't afford to stay at Caves, you can still join sunset cocktails at its classy bar. Sadly, only guests are allowed to stay after 7:30pm.

LTU Pub   BAR
(Map p188) A friendly and comfortable cliff-top haunt centered on a small yet lively tiki bar: the perfect place to strike up a conversation at sunset or enjoy a Bloody Mary before noon.

Mi Yard   BAR
(Map p192; ⊘24hr) Popular with locals, this place draws a late-night crowd into the wee hours, when you can swig shots of white rum and slap down dominoes with locals.

Ivan's Bar   BAR
(Map p188) The bar at Catcha Falling Star serves jerk shrimp that is, we have discovered (after lengthy research), the perfect thing to eat with Red Stripe.

Live Music   ✈
Negril's reggae concerts are legendary, with live performances every night in peak season, when there's sure to be some big talent in town. Several venues offer weekly jams, with a rotation system so they all get a piece of the action. The really big-name acts usually perform at **Hotel Samsara** (Map p188; ☑957-4395).

You will also find sound-system jams where the DJs ('selectors') play shatteringly loud music – usually dancehall with some Euro-disco – on speakers the size of railroad boxcars. The most popular jams are in the Negril Hills, near Little Bay. Most bars start the night playing reggae oldies (ie Bob Marley) early in the evening and bust out the dancehall later.

Information about upcoming events is posted on streetside poles. Covers are usually US$5 to US$10.

The following venues stage free reggae concerts.

Bourbon Beach   LIVE MUSIC
(Map p202; ⊘Tue, Fri & Sun) The best spot for live reggae on Long Beach, Bourbon Beach occasionally hosts big-name acts.

Alfred's Ocean Palace   BAR
(Map p202; ⊘Tue, Fri & Sun) This Negril institution is one of the oldest beach bars. Shows begin around 10pm and continue deep into the night.

Roots Bamboo   LIVE MUSIC
(Map p202; ☑957-4479; ⊘Wed & Sun) With a rotating roster of musicians anchored by a rock-solid 'riddim' section, the house Hurricane Band shows tourists a thing or two about roots music here each Wednesday.

On selected nights big dancehall shows rock the beach.

🛍 Shopping

Locals hawk carvings, woven caps, hammocks, jewelry, macramé bikinis, T-shirts and crafts on the beach and along West End Rd. Competition is fierce. Haggling is part of the fun. Don't be hustled into a purchase you don't want. **Times Square Plaza** (Map p202) has duty-free and jewelry stores, including **Tajmahal's** (Map p202; ☑675-4579), and a **Cigar World** (Map p202; ☑957-3299) selling Cuban cigars, which can also be bought at countless beach shacks on Long Beach. The same shacks (and really, you can't walk without tripping on one) sell beach essentials like towels, lighters, sunscreen and bug spray.

A Fi Wi Plaza   CRAFTS
(Map p192; Negril Village, West End Rd). Probably the best crafts market around.

Ja-Ja Originals   ART
(Map p202; ☑957-4326; Coco La Palm Hotel, Norman Manley Blvd) Original paintings and sculpture by local artists – our preferred place to buy art in Negril.

Kush Art Gallery   CRAFTS
(Map p192; ☑957-0728; West End Rd) Sells Wassi Art pottery and other quality crafts.

Collectibles Art Gallery   ART
(Map p188; ☑957-4486; Hungry Lion, West End Rd) Art gallery showcasing original works.

Kuyaba Arts & Crafts Boutique   CRAFTS
(Map p202; ☑957-4318; Kuyaba, Norman Manley Blvd) At the Kuyaba hotel, with a nice craft selection and Caribbean art and assorted Africana.

Negril Crafts Market   CRAFTS
(Map p202; Norman Manley Blvd) Just north of Plaza de Negril.

Rutland Point Craft Centre   CRAFTS
(Map p195; Norman Manley Blvd) Opposite Couples Negril.

ℹ Information

Dangers & Annoyances
Do not walk between Long Beach and the West End at night. Tourists have been, and continue to be, mugged walking through this area. It's best to avoid dark patches of beach; the locals in Negril, police and civilian, are good about patrolling these areas, but sometimes a mugger slips through. At night you should definitely take taxis.

Hustlers stalk Negril like nowhere else in Jamaica. You can expect to be endlessly offered everything from drugs to the hustlers themselves. Usually – but not always – you can shake them off with a firm 'no,' but Negril hustlers can be pretty in-your-face, and some will try to cop an attitude with you if they think it will intimidate you into giving them some money. Tourist police now patrol the beach but, by law, all Jamaican beaches must permit public access so the hustlers are free to roam, like it or not.

Ganja is smoked in plain view in Negril, but undercover police agents are present and rarely a week goes by without one or more visitors being arrested.

Prostitution is an established part of the local scene and short-term holiday liaisons are a staple. Female visitors should expect to hear a constant litany of well-honed lines enticing you to sample some 'Jamaican steel.'

Emergency
Fire (☑110, 957-4242)
Medical emergency (☑110)
Police emergency (☑119)
Police station (☑957-4268; Sheffield Rd)

Internet Access
There are dozens of internet cafes; many also offer internet-based international calls. It's increasingly the norm for hotels to offer wi-fi or cable connections in their lobbies and front offices, and often, both.

Blue Water Internet (☑884-6030; West End Rd; per 20min J$150; ☺8am-11pm) Very high-tech equipment, this cafe also serves delicious ice cream.

Café Taino (☑957-9813; www.cafetaino.com; Norman Manley Blvd; per 30min J$180) Internet access and international phone calls.

Easy Rock Internet Café (☑957-0816; West End Rd; per hr US$4) Offering an amiable cafe atmosphere; you can plug in your laptop and make international calls.

Sunshine Internet Center (☑957-4236; Sunshine Village, West End Rd; per hr US$4) A businesslike alternative with card readers and disk burning.

Internet Resources
Chamber of Commerce (www.negrilchamberofcommerce.com) Good information about community projects and green initiatives.

Negril (www.negril.com) Commercial site with numerous listings.

Negril Jamaica (www.negriljamaica.com) Operated by the Negril Resort Association.

Negril Jamaica Videos (www.negril-jamaica-videos.com) Another good clearing house of local information.

Negril Message Board (www.negril-message-board.com) A popular online meeting place.

Medical Services
The nearest hospitals are in **Savanna-la-Mar** (☑955-2533) and **Lucea** (☑956-2233), and neither of those is very nice.

Negril Health Centre (☑957-4926; Sheffield Rd; ☺9am-8pm Mon-Fri) Government-operated.

Negril Pharmacy (☑957-4076; Plaza de Negril; ☺9am-7pm Mon-Sat, 10am-2pm Sun)

Money
Banks are open 9am to 2pm Monday to Thursday and 9am to 4pm Friday; 24-hour ATMs are on the north side of Plaza de Negril. While many hotels offer currency exchange, you'll get better rates at banks or a private enterprise. Avoid the black-market currency-exchange touts that hang out around Negril Sq, or go there with a local.

National Commercial Bank (NCB; ☑957-4117; Sunshine Village, West End Rd)

Scotiabank (☑957-4236; West End Rd) Northwest of Plaza de Negril; offers currency exchange and ATMs.

Timetrend (☑995-3242; Norman Manley Blvd) Private currency-exchange business.

Western Union (Hi Lo Supermarket, Sunshine Village, West End Rd)

Post
Airpak Express (☑957-5051; Negril Aerodrome) Handles UPS service.

FedEx (☑957-5533; Negril Aerodrome)

Post office (Map p192; ☑957-9654; West End Rd) Between A Fi Wi Plaza and King's Plaza.

Telephone
There are public phones at the main craft market and at Plaza de Negril. Several internet cafes now offer internet-based international calls. Hotels charge roughly US$4 for three minutes to the USA or Western Europe and US$0.50 per minute locally.

Cable & Wireless office (☑888-957-9700; shop 27, Plaza de Negril; ☺8am-4pm Mon-Fri, 9am-4pm Sat) Public phones and WorldTalk cards.

Tourist Information
Jamaica Tourist Board (☑957-4803/9314; Times Square Plaza, Norman Manley Blvd; ☺9am-5pm Mon-Fri) Dispenses local maps and events information.

Negril Chamber of Commerce (NCC; ☑957-4067; www.negrilchamberofcommerce.com; Sunshine Village, West End Rd; ☺9am-4pm Mon-Fri) Publishes an annual *Negril Guide*. You can pick it up at hotels or at the NCC office west of the post office.

Negril Marine Park office (Map p202; ☑957-3735) Behind the Negril Crafts Market at the south end of Norman Manley Blvd; can provide information on the marine park.

❶ Getting There & Away

Negril Aerodrome (☑957-5016), at Bloody Bay about 11km north of Negril Village, is served by the domestic charter company **TimAir** (☑957-2516; www.timair.net), an 'air taxi' service offering on-demand charter flights for small groups going to Montego Bay, Ocho Rios, Port Antonio and Kingston. See p293 for more details on domestic charter service.

Dozens of minibuses and route taxis run between Negril and Montego Bay. The 1½-hour journey costs about J$350 to J$500 (depending on how honest your minibus driver is) and you will likely need to change vehicles in Lucea. Minibuses and route taxis also leave for Negril from Donald Sangster International Airport in Montego Bay (the price is negotiable, but expect to pay about US$10 to US$15).

In Negril, buses bound for Montego Bay (J$300), Savanna-la-Mar (J$300) and Kingston (J$1000, about five hours with no stops, which is rare) depart from the **transportation center** (Map p192; Sheffield Rd), 1km east of the roundabout. There's an **inspector's office** (☺7am-6pm) inside the gate, where you can ask for the departure point of the bus you're seeking.

A licensed taxi between Montego Bay and Negril will cost about US$80. In MoBay, call the **Jamaica Union of Travelers Association** (JUTA; ☑979-0778).

❶ Getting Around

Negril stretches along more than 16km of shoreline, and it can be a withering walk. At some stage you'll likely need transportation. Upscale resorts at the north end of Long Beach have shuttles to the village, and several hotels on the West End run shuttles to the beach.

Fortunately minibuses and route taxis cruise Norman Manley Blvd and West End Rd all the time. You can flag them down anywhere. The fare between any two points should never be more than J$100 (they'll always take you as far as Negril Sq from either the West End or Long Beach).

Local car-rental companies include **Jus Jeep** (☑957-0094; West End Rd) and **Vernon's Car Rentals** (Plaza de Negril ☑957-4522; Norman Manley Blvd ☑957-4354).

More than a dozen places along Norman Manley Blvd and West End Rd rent motorcycles (US$40 to US$50 per day), scooters (US$25 to US$35) and bicycles (US$10). For bicycle rentals, try **Wright's Bike Rental** (☑957-4908; Norman Manley Blvd) or **Negril Yacht Club** (☑957-9224; West End Rd). The latter also offers scooter rentals, as does **Dependable Bike Rental** (☑957-4354; Vernon's Car Rentals, Norman Manley Blvd).

Tourist taxis display a red license plate. Fares are regulated by the government (about US$4 per 3km) but few drivers use meters. Negotiate your fare before stepping into the cab. Your hotel will call a cab for you, or you can order taxis from **JUTA** (☑957-9197). There are taxi stands at the Negril Crafts Market and in front of Coral Seas Plaza.

NEGRIL TO MAYFIELD FALLS

Northeast from Negril, the new A1 expressway leads to Tryall and on to Montego Bay. The only town of note is Lucea and the main draw in the area is Mayfield Falls.

Green Island Harbour

Immediately north of Negril, the A1 swings around a wide expanse of swampland – the Great Morass. After 16km you pass the shores of a deep cove – Green Island Harbour – where pirogues line the thin, gray-sand shore. Minibuses and route taxis going between Negril and Lucea stop in Green Island Harbour.

Half Moon Beach (☑957-6467; admission free; ☺8am-10pm) is a beautiful, hassle-free stretch of sand beloved by locals and families; hang out here and you get a sense of what originally brought tourists to Negril (speaking of which, there's a disused airstrip near by that was once used for ganja smuggling – another original draw to the area). It's part of the Negril Marine Park; there are healthy reefs just offshore and no motorized watercraft. Nudism is permitted.

Rhodes Hall Plantation (☑957-6883; www.rhodesresort.com), 3km southwest of Green Island Harbour, is a picturesque, 220-hectare fruit-and-coconut plantation with several thatched bars and a restaurant backing a small but attractive beach where hot mineral springs bubble up. Follow the beach west and you'll see a stand of mangroves where Jamaican crocodiles sometimes like to sun themselves. Horseback riding is offered (US$60/70 per one/two hours). This is lovely countryside, flat and crisscrossed with natural water features, and being on horseback is the perfect way to access it.

This protected wilderness zone extends from Green Island on the north coast to St John's Point (south of Negril) and inland to Fish River village and Orange Hill. It also includes a marine park extending out to sea. The intention is to protect the entire Negril watershed (the area drained by the Orange, Fish, Newfound, North Negril and South Negril Rivers), including the Great Morass swampland and all land areas that drain into the Caribbean between Green Island and St John's Point.

The Negril Environmental Protection Area was declared in November 1997, incorporating the Negril Marine Park and embracing uplands, morass, shoreline, offshore lagoon and reefs. It has since been joined by the **Negril Environmental Protection Trust** (NEPT; ☑957-3736; http://nept.wordpress.com), whose remit extends 80 sq miles (more than 207 sq km) from Green Island to Salmon Point, and the **Negril Coral Reef Preservation Society** (http://negril.com/ncrps), which focuses on the ocean side of the protected area (see also p194). In conjunction with the **National Environmental & Planning Agency** (NEPA), the plan establishes guidelines for tourism growth, moratoriums on further cutting or draining of mangrove or wetland areas, the establishment of 'fish management zones,' sewage systems for outlying communities and the reforestation of deforested areas. It also encourages hotels to maintain their beaches through the **Blue Flag Award**, which they can receive if they meet the Blue Flag environmental outfit's strict criteria for water and beach quality as well as environmental management (www.blueflag.org).

In Cousin's Cove, a rustic little village a bit north of Green Island, you'll find **Sweet Breeze** (☑890-6554; www.sweetbreezejamaica. com; camping US$15, cottage US$40), a simple collection of pretty cottages and campsites run by some very friendly locals who can arrange lots of tours in the surrounding region.

Three miles west of Green Island, **Half Moon** (☑957-6467; camping US$10, cabins from US$50) offers camping and five simple but spacious wooden cabins with bare-bones furnishings. The thatched restaurant serves sandwiches, burgers, simple Jamaican snacks (J$250 to J$700) and, if you're very lucky, fresh lobster.

If you've got some cash to blow, there's a beautiful villa to rent near here: the lovely **Cliffhouse** (☑in the USA +1896-956-6076; www .cliffhousejamaica.com; per week US$4000).

Plenty of jerk stalls line the roadside at Green Island Harbour.

Blenheim

This tiny hamlet, 6km inland of Davis Cove, is important as the birthplace of national hero Alexander Bustamante, the island's first prime minister. 'Busta' is honored with a memorial ceremony each August 6. The rustic three-room wooden shack where Bustamante was born has been reconstructed as the **Sir Alexander Bustamante Mu-**seum (☑956-3898; admission J$250; ⊙9am-5pm). It includes memorabilia telling of the hero's life. It has public toilets and a picnic area to the rear.

Lucea

POP 7500

The halfway point between Negril and Mo-Bay, 'Lucy' is a pretty harbor ringed by hills on three sides, small enough for visitors to walk everywhere and charming enough to grab your attention for more than a quick blow-through.

The once-bustling port abounds in old limestone-and-timber structures in 'Caribbean vernacular' style, with gingerbread wood trim, clapboard frontages and wide verandas. The oldest dates to the mid-1700s, but this is a well-preserved town despite all the odds and many buildings look to be on their last legs. That said Lucea is atmospheric enough to have made an appearance in several films, including *Cool Runnings* and *Wide Sargasso Sea*. The **Hanover Historical Society** (☑956-2584; Watson Taylor Dr) is active in the town's preservation.

◉ Sights

Sir Alexander Bustamante Square & Around   NOTABLE BUILDINGS
Bustamante Square is centered on a small fountain fronting the handsome courthouse.

Note the vintage 1932 fire engine beside the courthouse.

The town's restored **courthouse** (✆956-2280; Watson Taylor Dr) has limestone balustrades and a clapboard upper story topped by a clock tower supported by Corinthian columns. The clock was sent to Lucea in 1817 by mistake – it was actually intended for the Caribbean island of St Lucia. It has supposedly worked without a hitch ever since.

On the east side of the square is **Cleveland Stanhope market**, which bustles on Saturdays. A walk north up the main frontage road curls past some of Lucea's finest historical houses, many in a state of near decrepitude, and deposits you atop the headland with a fine view east over Lucea Harbour. At the hillcrest is **Hanover Parish Church**, established in 1725. It's architecturally uninspired but has several interesting monuments; a Jewish section of the walled **cemetery** recalls the days when Lucea had a vibrant Jewish community.

Hanover Museum   MUSEUM
(✆956-2584; admission J$150; ⊙8:30am-5pm Mon-Thu, 8:30am-4pm Fri) A side road that begins 200m west of the church leads to the Hanover Museum, a tiny affair housed in an old police barracks. Exhibits include prisoners' stocks, a wooden bathtub and a miscellany of pots, lead weights and measures, but the poor place is pretty run-down, and thieves have stolen artifacts in the past.

Headland   LANDMARK
On the headland beyond the church is **Rusea High School**, a venerable Georgian-style red-brick building constructed in 1843 as an army barracks. The overgrown remains of **Fort Charlotte** overlook the channel a short distance beyond Rusea High School. It's named after Queen Charlotte, wife of King George III of England. The octagonal fortress still boasts cannons in its embrasures.

🛏 Sleeping & Eating

There are other sleeping options in town, but they were pretty tatty when we visited, so we recommend the following.

Global Villa Guest House   GUEST HOUSE $
(✆956-2916; www.globalvillahotel.com; r US$50-60; ❄) Eight kilometers west of town on the A1, Global Villa is a pretty collection of rooms in a modern house with louvered windows and tiled floors. There's a good res-

taurant serving hearty Jamaican fare on site, and the owners are very gracious.

Tommy's Restaurant   JAMAICAN $
(Main St; mains J$250-800; ⊙breakfast, lunch & dinner; ✔) Between the town square and Hanover Parish Church, this is an ever-popular place that serves healthy natural foods, including tofu dishes, steamed fish and natural juices.

❶ Information

Hanover Parish Library (✆956-2205; internet access per 30min US$1) Internet access, west of downtown.

Lucea Hospital (✆956-2233/3836) On the headland behind Hanover Parish Church, with an emergency department.

National Commercial Bank (✆956-2348; Main St)

Police station (✆956-2222; Sir Alexander Bustamante Sq, Watson Taylor Dr)

Scotiabank (✆956-2553) Faces the roundabout in the center of town.

❶ Getting There & Away

Buses, minibuses and route taxis arrive at and depart Lucea from the open ground opposite the market. Lucea is a midway terminus for public vehicles traveling between Montego Bay and Negril, and you may need to change vehicles here. A bus between Lucea and MoBay or Negril costs about J$250. A minibus or route taxi costs about J$300 to J$350.

Mayfield Falls

The **Dolphin Head Mountains** rise inland of Moskito Cove and are known for their waterfalls. The grandest of these are at Mayfield, near Pennycooke, about 16km south of Moskito Cove (6km east of Lucea). Here, a series of 21 falls and pools beckons you to take a refreshing dip in any of the delightful swimming holes, which are shaded by glades of bamboo and where you can swim through a green underwater tunnel.

Original Mayfield Falls & Mineral Springs (✆792-2074; www.mayfieldfalls.com; adult/child US$15/10; ⊙9am-5pm) is a working tropical farm and tourist attraction, but it was closed for grounds-keeping when we visited and will close if the weather is bad (so call ahead if there have been storms). In the past, to reach the cascades you would cross a bamboo-and-log bridge then follow the sun-dappled river course, clambering over river stones. Water shoes can be rented for US$6.

❶ Getting There & Away

From the A1, take the road inland from Moskito Cove via Cascade. The route is signed but it's quite complex and there are several turnoffs; you should ask your way to be sure. You can also reach Mayfield Falls from Tryall or Hopewell via Pondside, or by turning north at Savanna-la-Mar and taking the Banbury or Amity Cross routes (about 24km) along a road that is deplorably potholed.

Caribic Vacations (☑in Montego Bay 953-9896, in Negril 957-3309) offers excursions out this way (US$65 to US$85).

NEGRIL TO SAVANNA-LA-MAR

Tourism has been slow to develop along the southern shore of Westmoreland, a parish dependent on the sugar industry, with gritty Savanna-la-Mar the only town of any import.

Roads fan out from Savanna-la-Mar through the Westmoreland Plains. This flat, mountain-rimmed area, planted almost entirely in sugarcane, is drained by the Cabarita River, which feeds swamplands at its lower reaches. The fishing is good, and a few crocodiles may still live in more secluded swampy areas, alongside an endemic fish – the 'God-a-me' – that can live out of water in moist, shady spots. The river is navigable by small boat for 19km. In the wetlands you can spot rice paddies, originally planted by Indian workers shipped here to work on the sugar plantations.

Little Bay & Around

Southeast of Retirement, a badly eroded side road loops down to **Homers Cove** (locals call it 'Brighton Beach') and, immediately east, Little Bay, with handsome beaches and peaceful bathing. Little Bay is imbued with the kind of laid-back feel that pervaded Negril before the onset of commercialization. It's a great place to commune with Rastas and other Jamaicans who live by a carefree axiom in ramshackle homes, dependent on fishing and their entrepreneurial wits. The area is popular for reggae and dancehall sound systems that lure the local crowd from miles around.

Between Negril and Little Bay you'll first pass the town of **Orange Hill**, (in)famous around the island as a major marijuana cul-

tivation and distribution center, although you'd never guess it just looking around. Ask around for directions to **Jurassic Park** (admission free; ☉10am-sunset); no, there's not real velociraptors here (damn!), but you will find giant cast-iron sculptures of dinosaurs courtesy of local character Daniel Woolcock. Just look for the giant iron pterodactyl and you've found the entrance.

If you continue on to Little Bay, you may find the seaside **house** (now a private residence) where Bob Marley used to live with one of his girlfriends. The home stands next to imaginatively dubbed **Bob Marley's Spring**, where the legend used to bathe.

A mangrove swamp extends east of Little Bay, beyond which lies the fishing community of **Hope Wharf** and a long sliver of white sand called **Lost Beach**. Crocodiles and marine turtles can be found here. Dolphins and humpback whales frequent the waters offshore year-round.

The annual **Uncle Sam's Donkey Derby** is held on Little Bay beach the first Sunday in February; this donkey race is pretty much the talk of the Western Parishes when it goes down and must not be missed if you're in the area at this time.

Also known as 'Uncle Sam's,' **Garden Park** (☑867-2897; per tent US$10, cabin with shared/private bathroom US$20/30) is a little budget heaven on the cliffs of Little Bay, offering camping amid shady almond trees as well as rustic cabins and communal showers and toilets. Its atmospheric eatery – a gaily decorated bamboo bar festooned with girlie posters, crab shells and other miscellany – serves 'dapper' soup and other simple fisherfolk fare; the conch dishes are lovely. Uncle Sam's also puts on sound-system events. Full-moon parties are held in the Bat Cave, when a cavern is lit up with hundreds of candles, the reggae is cranked up and everyone parties down.

With a wide, sandy beach, **Lost Beach Resort** (☑640-1111, in the USA 800-626-5678; www.lostbeachresort.com; cabin US$79, 1-bedroom apt US$99-129, 2-bedroom apt US$129-149, 3-bedroom apt US$149-179; ⓟ❋@❋⊞❡) is a quiet hotel that's good for families who want a more peaceful environment than Negril. There are exotic hardwood furnishings throughout the spacious one- to three-bedroom suites; we prefer the thatch-and-wood beach cabins, which have loft bedrooms and kitchenettes.

Frome

Frome lies at the heart of Jamaica's foremost sugar estate, in the center of a rich alluvial plain. The area is dominated by the Frome **sugar-processing factory** (☏955-6080), on the B9 north of Savanna-la-Mar and south of the town of Grange Hill. Constructed in 1938, the factory became the setting for a violent nationwide labor dispute. During the Depression of the 1930s many small factories were bought out by the West Indies Sugar Company. Unemployed workers from all over the island converged here seeking work. Although workers were promised a dollar a day, the men who were hired received only 15 cents a day and women only 10 cents. Workers went on strike for higher pay, passions ran high and violence erupted. When the crowds rioted and set fire to the cane fields, the police responded by firing into the crowd, killing four people. The whole island exploded in violent clashes. The situation was defused when labor activist Alexander Bustamante mediated the dispute. His efforts gave rise to the island's first mass labor unions and the first organized political party, under his leadership (see p258).

A **monument** at a crossroads north of the factory gates reads: 'To Labour leader Alexander Bustamante and the Workers for their courageous fight in 1938. On behalf of the Working People of Jamaica.'

Free tours of the factory can be arranged by reservation.

Frome also boasts two attractive churches, including **St Barnabas Anglican Church**, in a vaguely Teutonic style.

Roaring River & Blue Hole

If you're looking for a brief escape from the fun-in-the-sun ethos of Negril, spend an hour or two down the caves at **Roaring River Park** (cave tours adult/child US$15/8; ☺8am-5pm). This natural beauty spot contains mineral waters that gush up from the ground in a meadow full of water hyacinths and water lilies. A stone aqueduct takes off some of the water, which runs turquoise-jade. Steps lead up a cliff face gashed by the mouth of a subterranean passage lit by electric lanterns (you can enter the caves only with guides from the cooperative). Inside, a path with handrails leads down to chambers full of stalagmites and stalactites. Take your swimming gear to sit in the mineral spring

that percolates up inside the cave, or in the 'bottomless' blue hole outside the cave. Harmless fruit bats roost in the recesses.

As you arrive an official guide will meet you to show the way to the ticket office, and then around the gardens and cave; ignore the touts who congregate outside posing as tour guides.

The lane then continues beyond Roaring River for about 1km uphill through the village to **Blue Hole Gardens** (☏955-8823; www.jamaicaescapes.com; admission US$8), a beautiful sinkhole that is surrounded by a landscaped garden full of ginger torch and heliconia on the private property of a Rasta called Esau. Entry is overpriced, but you'll get the chance to take a cool dip with the fish in the turquoise waters. The source of the Roaring River is about 400m further up the road, where the water foams up from beneath a matting of foliage.

This is also a quintessential counterculture lifestyle retreat that offers two very rustic but charming **cottages** (☏401-5312; www.jamaicaescapes.com/villas/bluehole/bluehole. html; cottages US$40-80) set in gardens at the edge of the tumbling brook (the 'waterhouse' cabin sits *over* the stream). Bamboo-enclosed toilets and showers are alfresco. Here you can also rent 'Esau's Mountain Retreat' (US$80), which is a separate cabin in the hills with fully equipped kitchen. Camping is US$10.

If you're hungry, pop into **Lovers Café** (mains US$3-8; ☑), which is known for its veggie feast, I-tal dishes, fruit juices and herbal teas.

🛈 Getting There & Away

Roaring River is at Shrewsbury Estate, about 2km north of the main crossroads in Petersfield (8km northeast of Savanna-la-Mar). You can catch a bus in Savanna-la-Mar as far as Petersfield (J$150, about once every hour). From there it's a hot walk or rough ride down the potholed road through the cane fields. Route taxis and coasters also run to Roaring River from Petersfield (J$100).

Organized tours to Roaring River are offered by companies in Negril (around US$75).

Ferris Cross & Paradise Park

Ferris Cross is a major crossroads hamlet on the A2, 8km east of Savanna-la-Mar. Here the A2 turns southeast and follows the coast to Black River and the south coast. Another road – the B8 – leads northeast to Galloway, where it begins a steep climb to Whithorn and Montego Bay.

A couple of kilometers west of Ferris Cross, **Paradise Park** (☑848-9826; admission US$7; ☺9am-4:30 Mon-Sat) is an 800-hectare farm, where you can ride horses along the inland dunes (US$40 per hour) and swim in a local creek.

Savanna-la-Mar

POP 20,000

Although Savanna-la-Mar is the largest town in western Jamaica and the capital of Westmoreland parish, 'Sav,' as it is locally known, offers few attractions. It has a distressingly high crime rate, and while it's fine to stop here to change minibuses or route taxis, we don't recommend hanging about after dark.

Sav is virtually a one-street town. Its axis is 2km-long Great George St, which runs past several petrol stations; this is where route taxis and minibuses congregate to take passengers on to Negril, Montego Bay, or further east to Black River.

◉ Sights

Savanna-la-Mar Fort   NOTABLE BUILDING
The English colonialists never completed the Savanna-la-Mar Fort at the foot of Great George St. Parts of it collapsed into the swamps within a few years of being built, and these discarded guts now form a small cove where locals swim. A bustling daily market, specializing in vegetables and local fish, has been built into the grounds.

Courthouse   NOTABLE BUILDING
The most interesting building is the Sav courthouse, built in 1925 at the junction of Great George and Rose Sts, where there's a fountain made of cast iron, inscribed with the words, 'Keep the pavements dry.' There doesn't seem to be any deeper meaning to this highly literal commandment.

St George's Parish Church   CHURCH
This church, opposite the courthouse, was built in 1905. It's uninspired, but has a stately **pipe organ** that was dedicated in 1914.

Manning's School   NOTABLE BUILDING
At the north end of town by the roundabout known as Hendon Circle is the very handsome Manning's School, built in 1738 and named after Westmoreland planter Thomas Manning.

🛏 Sleeping & Eating

Lochiel Guest House   GUEST HOUSE $
(☑955-9344; Sheffield Rd; r US$35) On the A2, 2km east of town, is an old stone-and-timber, two-story guest house that looks delightful from the outside. Inside it's a bit run-down, though some of the rooms are appealing. All have utilitarian furniture and hot water in private bathrooms; this place is decent as a last resort, but otherwise move along.

You can buy fresh fish and produce from the market at the base of Great George St, but the sanitary conditions aren't great; otherwise, cheap jerk and food stalls cluster in the center of Sav.

ⓘ Information

National Commercial Bank (☑955-2623; Great George St)

Police station (☑918-1865; Great George St) Near the courthouse.

Post office (☑955-9295; Great George St)

Savanna-la-Mar Hospital (☑955-2133; ☺emergency service 24hr) On the A2 on the northeast side of town.

Scotiabank (☑955-2601; Great George St)

ⓘ Getting There & Away

Buses, minibuses and route taxis operate frequently along the A2/B8 between Montego Bay (US$3, 1½ to two hours) and Negril (US$3, 45 minutes). Public vehicles also depart on a regular basis from the Beckford St transportation center in Kingston (US$10, three hours).

South Coast & Central Highlands

Why Go?

The south of Jamaica is one of the most beautiful, unspoiled areas of the country and yet it remains, compared to Negril and Montego Bay, relatively untouristed. Folks are missing all the boutique hotels, excellent food, dinosaur-esque reptiles and long fields of sun-kissed farmland.

We just don't see how anyone can say they love Jamaica without seeing this, one of her most special sides. The south coast and central highlands contain everything that makes the island lovely – soft beaches, wild mountains, delicious food, kickin' music – with very few megaresorts to speak of and laid-back, low-impact tourism. The locals seem a little friendlier, and crime is certainly less of an issue here than elsewhere on the island. Trust us: you'll come to St Elizabeth parish and see the way the golden light meets the red soil here. It's magic, a uniquely beautiful moment on an already beautiful island.

When to Go

The Accompong Maroon Festival, held January 6, is one of the most compelling celebrations of Afro-Caribbean culture in Jamaica. The summer season (June to August) on the south coast is also not a bad time to visit; rates go down and the region stays relatively dry, especially compared to the rest of the island.

Best Places to Eat

» Little Ochie (p245)

» Strikey's (p242)

» Jack Sprat Café (p242)

Best Places to Stay

» Nuestra Casa Guest House (p240)

» Jake's Place (p240)

» Baboo's Garden (p229)

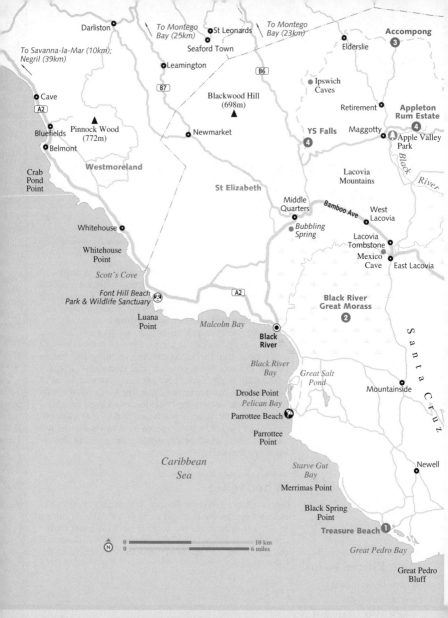

South Coast & Central Highlands Highlights

1 Slowing down the pace at **Treasure Beach** (p238) – a serene, laid-back fishing community known for offbeat hospitality

2 Exploring Jamaica's longest river, the **Black River** (p222), by small watercraft: see crocodiles in their mangrove ecosystem, eat at a riverside shack and discover hidden swimming holes

3 Heeding the call of the ancient *abeng* (goat horn) at the well-preserved Maroon village of **Accompong** (p227), on the cusp of scenic Cockpit Country

4 Soaring over the majestic **YS Falls** (p226) on a zip line, then delving into the island's largest rum distillery **Appleton Rum Estate** (p226) before sampling its wares

5 Watching fishermen pull in with the daily catch, then savoring it on the beach at Jamaica's finest seafood restaurant, **Little Ochie** (p245)

History

People here have always been somewhat different from other Jamaicans. Miskito Indians were brought to Jamaica from Central America to help track Maroons in the 18th century and eventually were given land grants in St Elizabeth. The Miskitos, along with others including 19th-century Scottish castaways and German settlers, are responsible for the high percentage of mixed-race peoples around Treasure Beach.

Jamaica's cool central highlands – rising northeast of St Elizabeth – were popular from the 19th century through the mid-20th century as a vacation retreat, when Christiana and Mandeville became social centers for the wealthy.

ⓘ Getting There & Around

Travel between towns here, especially out in the mountains (with the exception of Mandeville), is not as reliable as on the north coast. Route taxis and minibuses ply the coastal road but run infrequently, and to some areas only a few times per day. The primary transportation centers for the region are Mandeville and Black River, where you can find the most reliable short-hop service and long-distance transportation to Kingston, Negril and Montego Bay. If you book overseas into a place on Treasure Beach, most resorts there will give you a ride from Montego Bay (MoBay) for between US$80 to US$100; it's a four- to five-hour ride.

WHITEHOUSE & AROUND

The green mountains slope steeply down almost directly into cool dollops of sea and sky in southeastern Westmoreland parish, shading the narrow coastal road and the fishing villages that cling to it. This sleepy stretch of hills is known as Surinam Quarters. The main settlements are small towns like Bluefields, Belmont and Whitehouse, which attract visitors who eschew luxury for getting way off the beaten path. Book into a little homestay out here and you may lose yourself in the slow pace of life for a week. Or a month. Or longer, as attested by some truly shaggy long-term expats.

Bluefields & Belmont

Bluefields is appropriately named: look out the door here and it's either big light-blue skies beyond the mountains or sea-blue harbors lapping the rocky beach. In 1519 this was Oristan, one of the first Spanish settlements in Jamaica; Bluefields Bay provided safe anchorage for Spanish explorers, British naval squadrons and pirates. In 1670, long before he became a tacky rum mascot, infamous buccaneer Henry Morgan set out from Bluefields Bay to sack Panama City. Today Bluefields and adjacent Belmont are populated by a quiet collection of fishers, tourists, escape artists, regular artists, expats and returning Jamaicans (the latter two particularly attracted by a small housing construction boom in the hills).

Surinam Quarters is named for the colonists who settled here after the English traded Surinam to the Dutch in exchange for Nieuw Amsterdam (New York) in 1667. Scots also settled in the area after the Battle of Culloden in 1745, and Scottish place names abound.

◉ Sights & Activities

Peter Tosh Monument   MONUMENT
(admission J$700) Many monuments make a political statement, and the memorial to reggae superstar Peter Tosh, plunked a kilometer south of Bluefields in the tiny inlet of Belmont, is no exception. And the cause here is, as Tosh once sang, to 'legalize it.' You can guess what 'it' is, but if not just check all the murals, which depict: a Rasta man with a huge joint; jumbo marijuana leaves; best of all, a red-eyed Lion of Zion on Tosh's actual tomb. In all the world of heraldry, it must be the only symbol you could accurately describe as 'lion; rampant; baked.' Behind the tomb is a garden where they ain't growing oregano. This is a casual place with few visitors, a stark contrast to the tourist maelstrom surrounding fellow Wailer Bob Marley's mausoleum in Nine Miles (p141). It is run by the Tosh family – his nonagenarian mother still lives on the property and will warmly greet you if you ask after her – and your money is taken by a caretaker who will give you a brief tour along with commentary on Tosh's political positions ('I'm like a smoke. Dat why we say legalize it.'). In mid-October the annual **Peter Tosh Birthday Bash**, an informal local affair, features live roots reggae music played deep into the night.

Bluefields Beach Park   BEACH
(☉8am-sunset; admission J$400) Well signed from the Winston Jones Hwy (A2), this

In Bluefields, Belmont, Whitehouse and other fishing villages speckled along the southwest stretch of the A2, the main pedestrian thoroughfare happens to be the highway. While there are back-paths through the villages, these tend to lead directly through residents' yards. This usually isn't a big deal to locals, but at night, when there's no streetlights, you'll get lost pretty quickly.

The alternative – walking along the A2 – can be dangerous at night, given all the blind turns it has and the way folks drive around here. If you can, ask your accommodations about village pathways to get where you want to go; otherwise, always make sure to cross to the opposite side of a blind turn when walking towards traffic.

beach is a swathe of pale sand that frames the dark blue water like a ribbon; a beach as beautiful as it is ignored by foreign tourists (although it's quite popular with locals on weekends). During the early evening and on weekends you'll find a nice collection of food stalls featuring locally caught fresh fish and plenty of Red Stripe.

Belmont Beach BEACH
There are actually two small Belmont Beaches, but one is too rocky to relax on and the other is a major mooring point for fishing boats. That said, if the day is clear the water will be as well, so you can swim out a ways and do some fine snorkeling or spear fishing. All of the accommodations we list in Belmont rent the required equipment.

Bluefields House HISTORICAL SITE
Philip Gosse was one of the great polymaths of his time: the man who both popularised the aquarium and modified its design, and illustrator of gorgeously detailed renditions of Jamaican birdlife. His old home, naught but a ruin located inland from the Bluefields police station, is worth visiting for historical novelty more than anything – to see where the author of *Illustrations of the Birds of Jamaica* and *A Naturalist's Sojourn in Jamaica* once laid his head – although there's a lovely breadfruit tree on site, said to be the first on the island.

☞ Tours

Travelers staying in the area can enjoy day trips and excursions to regional attractions including YS Falls, the Black River Great Morass, Ipswich Caves and Alligator Pond.

Natural Mystic Tours NATURE TOURS
(☏851-3962; www.naturalmystic-jamaica.com) Run by a German expat, leads tours (in English and German) all across the island.

Nature Roots NATURE TOURS
(☏955-8162, 384-6610; www.natureroots.de) Go with Brian the Bush Doctor out on the sea and into the jungle, or stay at his friendly little cottage.

Shafston Tours NATURE TOURS
(☏869-9212; www.shafston.com; Shafston Estate Great House, Bluefields) A good choice for outdoor pursuits such as river kayaking (US$50 per person) and hiking.

🛏 Sleeping & Eating

Multiday villa rentals are a popular lodging option; contact **Sun Villas** (☏in the USA 941-922-9191; www.sunvillas.com/south_coast.htm; per night US$650) or **Bluefields Villas** (☏in the USA 202-232-4010; www.bluefieldsvillas.com; per week US$5250). Both offer fully staffed, exquisitely furnished waterfront properties.

All of the lodging listed here either serves food or can direct you to locals who run their own seasonal restaurants. A favorite is a little roadside shack called the **Belmont Sands Open Edge** (⊙dinner; mains J$400-800) run by Ms Dorrit and famed for its crab backs and curried goat.

TOP CHOICE **Shafston Estate Great House** GUEST HOUSE **$**
(☏869-9212; www.shafston.com; all-incl per person US$50-100; ℗@⊠) Poised on a hilltop with exquisite coastal views stretching as far as Savanna-la-Mar, this wonderfully creaky great house makes you wonder why luxury accommodation costs so much. In the original manor house there are atmospheric, spacious rooms ranging from basic to modest; a few have bathrooms. For even cheaper digs, there are 12 simple yet charming rooms in a newer block with screened windows and clean, tiled communal unisex showers and bathrooms. Relax in a hammock, laze on a sundeck next to the pool and Jacuzzi, chill at the congenial poolside bar or take a ride

ROOTS, ROCK, REAL ART

In many of the shops, restaurants and hotels running from Belmont up to Savanna-la-Mar, you'll see flower-bright bits of wood, canvas and corkboard painted in bright reggae colors displaying Rasta themes: 'Who Jah bless, no man can harm' and similar messages. You'll find the source of this work just off of the A2, near the turnoff for Nature Roots homestay, where a shack is kept by local artist Jah Callo. Callo tends to focus on other Rasta themes, including the beauty of nature and the mystical, redemptive power of Jah's love.

on the zip line – yup, there's one on site. To get here from the A2, take the dirt road opposite Bluefields police station, then it's a precipitous 3km climb over bad roads. Alternatively, owner Frank Lohmann can arrange for airport transfers.

Sunset Cottage HOTEL $
(955-8007; r US$20-50; P) Located on the A2 in Bluefields, this simple, small, immaculately kept hotel overlooks a rocky beach; it's an excellent bargain. The rooms are well kitted out for self-caterers, with pretty kitchenettes and breezy porches. A day spent doing nothing in the on-site gazebo is a day well-spent indeed.

Horizon Cottages HOTEL $$
(955-8823, 942-7633; www.jamaicaescapes.com; cottage US$110; P@) One of the first accommodations in the area, this cozy spot right on the waterfront of Bluefields Bay features two wooden cottages, the Sea Ranch and the Rasta Ranch, each tastefully appointed with local artwork and featuring small kitchenettes and shared hot-water shower in the garden. The beach is private and kayaking is available.

Shades Cottage HOMESTAY $
(955-8102, 441-1830; www.shadescottage.com; r US$25-30;) Run by the hospitable Rasta Bigga (when you meet him, you'll see where the nickname comes from), at Shades Cottage you'll be staying in a 'yard' – a compound of neighborly houses – arranged around a bar where fresh meals and cold beer can be ordered. The rooms are basic and clean, but don't expect the Ritz. This

is a spot that attracts younger travelers and long-term expat types.

Nature Roots HOMESTAY $
(955-8162, 384-6610; www.natureroots.de; r US$25-30) Nature Roots, the home base for the tour outfit of the same name, is located next to Shades Cottage and offers much the same sort of accommodation. A chilled-out spot in a yard with good vibes, easy access to the beach (it's about 50m away) and a lovely, indolent air.

Catch the Vibes Guesthouse GUEST HOUSE $
(851-3962; www.naturalmystic-jamaica.com; cottage s/d US$20/25) Run by the friendly Lydia and perched on a hill in Belmont Village, this pretty cottage is set in a flower garden with a great view over the sea. There's a basic kitchen and a beach only a five-minute walk away. A cooking service and dominoes instruction are provided on request. Natural Mystic Tours is based here. German travelers note: *sie sprechen Deutsch*.

Information

For local information, visit the **Bluefields People's Community Association** (955-8793; www.bluefieldsjamaica.com; Belmont Sq) in Belmont, where internet access is also available.

Getting There & Away

The A2 is the only road that runs through Bluefields and Belmont, and buses will drop you off wherever you ask in either town; otherwise they'll likely leave you in Bluefields' 'square,' a centrally located patch of open land with a small general-purpose shop. Buses and minivans run frequently (every hour during the day) up the coastal road (A2) to Savanna-la-Mar (J$200, one hour), and from there to Montego Bay and Negril, but try to go before late afternoon – you don't want to be stuck in Savanna-la-Mar, especially after dark. In the opposite direction (south) most buses go through Black River (J$350, 1½ to two hours), from where you can get buses or taxis to Treasure Beach or Mandeville, or travel onwards to May Pen, from where you can find reliable transportation to Kingston. Getting stuck in Black River is fine, for the record.

Whitehouse

The small fishing village of Whitehouse is another great place to sample provincial coastal life. It stretches for about 2km along the A2, parallel to a series of beaches where motorized boats and pirogues draw up and unload wahoo, tuna, barracuda, bonito, snapper, kingfish, marlin and lobster taken on the Pedro Banks, about 130km out to sea.

The 2005 opening of the south coast's first large-scale all-inclusive resort was fiercely opposed by local activists striving to preserve the region's unspoilt charm and traditional way of life. At last visit, the Sandals Whitehouse European Village & Spa had not led to an influx of mass developments along the south coast – for now.

◉ Sights & Activities

Make sure to visit the nearby **Font Hill Beach Park** (p220). This pretty sweep of sand isn't terribly big, but it's a good spot where you can venture out in your snorkeling gear. Across the street is the Font Hill Villa and a wildlife sanctuary that serves as a refuge for the vulnerable American crocodiles, many of which have been displaced by large-scale construction projects.

Head down to any of the small beachfronts in Whitehouse and have a chat with the local fishing captains about hiring a boat and going **snorkeling** (around US$40 per hour). Better yet, hop aboard with local fishers for a trip to the fishing banks (typically up to four people for US$80 to US$100). Women should not go unaccompanied.

⌸ Sleeping & Eating

South Sea View Guest House GUEST HOUSE $
(☑963-5172; www.southseaviewjamaica.com; r without/with air-con US$70/90; ✳☀) With a bit of imagination you could call South Sea View Greek Island-ish in its aesthetics, all white-walled and open to the pale-blue sky and winds. Rooms are fresh and modern, with big fluffy king-size beds, tropical murals and cable TV for those days when you need to veg. If the latter is what you're after, a dip in the local cove is worth a try.

Culloden Cove Villa VILLA $$$
(☑472-4608; www.jamaicaholidayvilla.com; Little Culloden; 2-bedroom villa per week US$3720) This excellent rental, 1.5km northwest of Whitehouse, consists of a wonderful three-bedroom house and two-bedroom cottage commanding a pretty position over the pounding blue sea. The atmosphere in both properties is bright and breezy, and you can enjoy excellent meals cooked by your own chef, drink at your own atmospheric bar,

relax under your own shady veranda or on your own beach, and read plenty of books from your own library. The aforementioned cook and 24-hour security personnel are included in the price; stays are one-week minimum.

Sandals Whitehouse
European Village & Spa RESORT $$$
(☑in USA 888-726-3257; www.sandals.com; all-incl r US$490; ℗☀✳☞☀) If, when visiting Jamaica, you want to stay in a European-style village, this all-inclusive resort should hit the spot. It cost over US$100 million to build this place around three villages conceived to look like towns in France, the Netherlands and Italy; the main pool area, for example, is a gigantic Florence-meets-the-tropics-meets-Sandals extravaganza. The well-appointed rooms – all with beachfront views – come in nine categories spread over 20 hectares. The all-inclusive promise is fulfilled by eight restaurants and six bars, as well as a full range of land and water sports, the largest swimming pool in Jamaica at time of writing and a long sandy beach.

Jimmyz Restaurant & Bar SEAFOOD $
(☑390-3477; mains J$200-500; ◉breakfast, lunch & dinner Mon-Sat) On Fisherman's Beach in central Whitehouse, next to a pavilion where local fishers sell their catch to wholesalers, this eatery is popular with old sea salts. The menu has fresh juices, including an exceedingly peppery ginger tonic, and dishes featuring steamed fish, chicken, 'sea puss' (octopus) and a particularly excellent spicy conch stew.

❶ Getting There & Away

To get to or from Whitehouse, follow the same procedure as getting to and away from Bluefields and Belmont (see p216).

Scott's Cove

About 8km southeast of Whitehouse, the A2 sweeps around this deep little inlet marking the border of Westmoreland and St Elizabeth, where dozens of **food and beer stalls** line the shore. Anyone from western Jamaica will tell you this is the best place on the island to buy fried snapper and *bammy* – a pancake of fried cassava – with onions and peppers. It shouldn't cost more than J$500. Most stalls shut after dark.

Font Hill Beach Park & Wildlife Sanctuary

This **sanctuary** (⊙9am-5pm; adult/child J$250/120), situated on almost 1300 hectares southeast of Scott's Cove, is incongruously owned by the Petroleum Corporation of Jamaica, which has not tarnished its natural beauty in the slightest...after it realized that the oil it initially sought offshore didn't exist.

You can only visit the sanctuary if accompanied by a guide, but it's worth it for the good introduction to the odd marsh-and-scrub coastal ecosystem of southwest Jamaica. There's scrubby acacia, logwood thickets and, closer to the shore, a maze of connected lagoons and swamps with a population of a couple of hundred American crocodiles (made all the more vulnerable after being displaced from other parts of the south coast by large-scale construction projects). The bird-watching is fabulous, highlighted by a flock of bald plate pigeons as well as assorted black-billed whistling ducks, jacanas, herons and pelicans.

Two golden-sand beaches (connected by a trail) are fringed by a reef offering great snorkeling and bathing. Dolphins come into the cove, as do turtles for nesting season.

There's a small cafe and bar, changing rooms, picnic booths, volleyball, a boardwalk and a lackluster interpretive center and marina. Horseback rides are also offered.

Font Hill Villas (☑462-9011; www.pcj.com/fonthill/villas.html; r J$3000-8600; ✳@) is a superb option and has a green sensibility about it, maintaining a nice bit of beachfront for guests and locals and working hand in hand with the wildlife reserve. Rooms are sunny, cozy, done up in tropical shades and caressed by cool gusts off the sea thanks to their porches. The owners are very friendly and will help to book tours all across the island. Note that room rates are quoted in J$, a bit of a rarity at this price point.

BLACK RIVER & AROUND

Black River

POP 4230

The capital of St Elizabeth and the parish's largest town occupies an interesting median point in terms of tropical energy. A big city this may be for these parts, but a bustling metropolis it most certainly is not. At the same time it's no sleepy backwater either – Black River may be off the beaten path, but

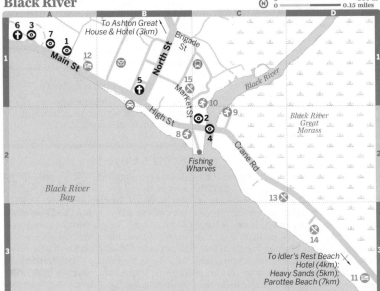

Black River

there's a buzz here, a colorful, open-air chaos offset by Georgian architecture peeling away in a state of elegant rot and buckets of liquid gold sunlight. The namesake river is a slow-moving slick of moldering tannins patrolled by straight-arrow alligators and boats full of curious tourists. Although most visitors understandably opt to stay in nearby Treasure Beach, a few people do use this town as a base for visiting attractions like YS Falls and the Appleton Rum Estate.

The town's Georgian buildings attest to its 19th-century prosperity, when Black River exported local logwood from which Prussian blue dye was extracted for textiles. Locals proudly point out the Waterloo Guest House, which in 1893 became the first house in Jamaica to have electricity installed. The racetrack and spa that attracted the wealthy have sadly not survived the passage of time.

◎ Sights & Activities

Heritage Buildings   HISTORICAL BUILDINGS
Foremost among the historic structures worth checking out is the yellow-brick **Parish Church of St John the Evangelist** (cnr Main & North Sts), built in 1837. From the outside it's a bright, mustard-colored supermarket. The wind-pocked interior is graced by wooden porticoes and a stately balcony,

---

Black River

◎ Sights

---

while the graves around the back cemetery date from the 17th century. Two blocks west are the porticoed **courthouse** and the **town hall**, with lofty pillars, and beyond that a simple **Roman Catholic church**, something of a rare denomination in Jamaica.

Two of the most impressive buildings are both hotels. The 1894 **Invercauld Great House & Hotel** and the **Waterloo Guest House**, both west on Main St, are splendid examples of the Jamaican vernacular style; with their shady wooden verandas and gingerbread trim they look like the sort of place where you should don a safari hat and demand a sherry in an imperious voice.

High Street   STREET
Although it's as frenetic and chaotic as any other High St in Jamaica, Black River's High St (note, High St and Main St are used interchangeably here) is also lined with colonnaded, Georgian timber houses, all musty and fading away in the intense sunshine, which gives it a prettily entropic quality. At the east end is the **Hendricks Building** (2 High St), dating from 1813, a fine example of period British-Caribbean architecture. Immediately east is an old **iron bridge**, a good spot for watching American crocodiles waiting for tidbits thrown by tourists from the riverside berths. Trawlers lie at anchor immediately south of the bridge, from where you can watch fish being hauled ashore onto the wharfs.

Captain Lando   FISHING
(✆387-8008) Give friendly Captain Lando a call; he's happy to arrange charters. Expect to pay around US$60 for a half day trip, although these rates may be higher if he gets a bigger boat.

⛱ Beaches

There are a fair few beaches near Black River. The following spots are public land so visit at your leisure, although you'll need your own wheels to get out here. Both beaches can be accessed from Crane Rd, on the eastern edge of Black River, but make sure to ask for directions.

Heavy Sands   SECLUDED BEACH
Long stretches of dark sand still undiscovered by most international tourists. Just don't swim near the river mouth – crocodiles like to congregate here! You'll be fine in the sea, but beware the tides as there will likely be no one around.

BLACK RIVER GREAT MORASS

An amoeba-ish clump of salt marsh, black waters, leaching tannins, wind-bent reed beds and spider mangroves rise like a mushroom from the mouth of Black River, pushing deep into the Jamaican interior. For its singular scenery and excellent wildlife-viewing opportunities, this 200-sq-km wetland – the Great Morass – is one of Jamaica's most fascinating (yet accessible) natural wonders (see www.jamaicablackriver.com for more information).

The best way to get a feel for the morass is to explore it by small watercraft or tour boat; quick excursions are easily arranged in Black River, but if you are heading on to Treasure Beach, lengthier forays up the river can be arranged there. Along the way, with the right guide, you can eat at delightful riverside shacks, discover hidden swimming holes and, of course, spot some grinning, sunning crocodiles. The morass forms Jamaica's most significant refuge for American crocodiles, and an estimated population of 300 live in the swamps. Several have made a habit of hanging out near the bridge in town, waiting for their next meal of raw chicken parts dispensed from tour operators who have a vested interest in keeping them around.

The crocodiles aren't the only animal to be spotted here, not by a long shot. The interplay of saltwater and freshwater, the generally dry climate of St Elizabeth and the parish's geologic composition all make for a complex ecosystem and a vital preserve for more than 100 bird species, including cinnamon-colored jacanas, egrets, whistling ducks, water hens and seven species of heron.

The culture of this region is unique as well. The impenetrability of the morass has made for an isolation that has preserved folkways lost in other parts of Jamaica. Locals go out in pirogues, tending funnel-shaped bamboo shrimp pots in the traditional manner of their West African forebears.

These interconnecting waterways are navigable for about 30km upriver. Along the way, the mangroves suck water through long tendrils drooping into the water. Beyond the confluence of the YS, Middle Quarters and Black Rivers, the mangroves broaden into marshy meadows of tall sedges and reeds. Feisty game fish are plentiful, including snook and tarpon. On rare occasions, endangered manatees may even be seen near the river estuary.

For an excellent lunch experience, be sure to tell your guide that you want to visit **Sister Lou's River Stop** (⊙lunch), on the Salt Spring tributary, where delicious stuffed crab backs (J$400) and pepper shrimp are served up. It's a great place to have a Red Stripe and watch the river drift by, or look on as local kids jump from a nearby bridge into the river.

Parottee Beach　　SWIMMING BEACH
Is essentially a continuation of Heavy Sands – more dark sand studded with shells and loads of clean ocean. Excellent for swimming, but again, don't swim out too far as you'll likely be on your own out here.

☞ Tours

A trip up the Black River is the main reason many tourists come to, well, Black River. Loads of boats cluster by the old warehouse on the east bank of the river, waiting to chug folks into the vine-laden interior of the Great Morass. You'll be escorted along water that resembles a mossy oil slick, and while nothing can be guaranteed when speaking of spotting wildlife, there's a good chance you'll see white marsh cranes and herons skimming the banks like pterodactyls, sword-beaked, fish-spearing anhinga and, of course, alligators. Thanks to all the visitors these reptiles are tame around people now, and they're pretty small to boot. Many operators let people go swimming in the river with them, which they insist is a safe endeavor. We can't vouch for this, so if you do choose to swim, do so at your own risk.

Black River Safaris (☑965-2513, 965-2086; ⊙tours 9am, 11am, 12:30pm, 2pm & 3:30pm), which offers 60- to 75-minute journeys aboard the *Safari Queen*, is a typical operator. Similar tours and prices are offered by **St Elizabeth River Safari** (☑965-2374, 965-2229; ⊙tours 9am, 11am, 2pm & 3:30pm), behind the Hendricks Building, and **Irie Safaris** (☑965-2211; 12 High St; ⊙tours every 90 min 9am-4.30pm), wharfside from a jetty just southeast of the bus station (Irie can also arrange kayaking trips in the area, which come highly recommended). At the time of writing tours ran around US$20 to US$30; thanks to the price of petrol these rates can swing up and down at short notice.

For a less regimented (and a more authentic) experience, you can easily hire a guide to take you upriver by canoe or boat for about US$50 to US$60 round-trip. Ask near the bridge in town or anywhere in Treasure Beach. If you're continuing on to Treasure Beach, you can hire a boat there for a round-trip tour (US$75) that includes a stop at the Pelican Bar (p243) and a journey up the Black River.

Midday tours are best for spotting crocodiles; early and later tours are better for birding. Take a hat and some mosquito repellent.

🛏 Sleeping

TOP CHOICE **Ashton Great House & Hotel** HOTEL $

(☎965-2036; r from US$60; P❄☲) We just can't figure out how this place is so undervisited. This is a magnificent, large, atmospheric wooden home in a beautiful setting: on 140-hectare grounds on a hill beside the A2. The big rooms are outfitted in tasteful antiquarian style, while Verna, the owner, is a treasure trove of local lore and can expound eloquently on current affairs in Jamaica (she's also a hell of a cook). There's a spacious pool with a children's section. If there are few guests – a condition that seems to be the norm – the house is atmospherically spooky, especially when the bats flit by.

Idlers' Rest Beach Hotel HOTEL $$

(☎965-9000; www.idlersrest.com; r from US$100; P❄🛜) Another fantastic option a little way out of town, Idlers' Rest redefines 'Irie.' Owned by a friendly lawyer, the hotel is a tasteful boutique decorated in a comfy mix of modern chic, Caribbean color and pan-African art. Rooms are cooled by gentle sea breezes and you can wander the local beach while gazing at dolphins frolicking on the waves – sheesh, sometimes Jamaica really *is* paradise. The folks here can arrange tours all around St Elizabeth parish at very reasonable rates.

Waterloo Guest House HOTEL $

(☎965-2278; 44 High St; r US$40-50; P❄@☲) The Waterloo has been in the accommodations business for over 100 years, and has both the style and complacency you'd expect from a centenarian. Facing the shoreline

and the photogenic hulk of a rusting ship, this rickety Georgian edifice is still possessed of offbeat charm and a distinctive claim to fame: it was the first house in Jamaica to be wired for electricity. It doesn't seem to have changed much since. The rooms in the old house are pretty meagerly furnished, while the carpeted, more stylish rooms in the modern annex don't quite have that romantic whiff of yesteryear (that said, they're more comfortable). All have bathrooms with showers. There's a cheerful bar and restaurant on-site serving seafood and (oddly enough) chop suey; the bar gets pretty kickin' on Friday nights.

South Shore Guest House GUEST HOUSE $

(☎965-2172; southshoreg@yahoo.com; 33 Crane Rd; r US$50-80; P❄) This mid-sized hotel has a breezy outdoor bar and restaurant and spacious, basic rooms; the main draw is a pretty veranda fronting a narrow beach. It's a bit utilitarian, but a good option if you need quiet air-conditioning. Meals are prepared to order.

🍴 Eating

Cloggy's on the Beach SEAFOOD $$

(☎634-2424; Crane Rd; mains J$600-2000; ☺lunch & dinner) This beachside joint is your best culinary bet in Black River; it's an all-round pleaser with a relaxed vibe, great bar ambience and excellent chow. It occasionally throws well-attended beach sound-system parties; ask the bartender for the lowdown. Try a cup of conch soup for a revelation, and follow that up with some gorgeous fresh lobster.

Bridgehouse Inn JAMAICAN $$

(14 Crane Rd; mains J$500-1800; ☺breakfast, lunch & dinner) This upscale Jamaican eatery falls a little short in the atmosphere stakes, especially given the prices, but the food – seafood and Jamaican dishes such as curried goat, washed down with health drinks made from beetroot juice and Irish moss – is lovely.

Waterloo Guest House JAMAICAN $

(44 High St; mains J$300-900; ☺breakfast, lunch & dinner) Has a modest restaurant with an inexpensive Jamaican menu, plus an earthy bar serving ice-cream sodas and milk shakes.

There's a supermarket in the Hendricks Building, and another one 100m north. You can buy fruit, vegetables and meats at the open-air **produce market** (Market St; ☺sunrise-sunset).

❶ Information

Black River Hospital (☎965-2212/2224; 45 Main St) A kilometer west of town.

Dr John Brown (☎965-2305; 48 Main St) Medical clinic.

National Commercial Bank (☎965-9027; 9 High St)

Police station (☎965-2232 or 119; North St)

Post office (☎965-2250) Immediately west of the police station.

Scotiabank (☎965-2251; 6 High St)

St Bess Pharmacy (☎634-4526; 1A Brigade St; ◷Mon-Sat)

❶ Getting There & Away

From Black River, public vehicles go to and from Santa Cruz (J$180), Savanna-la-Mar (J$200), Montego Bay (J$250 to J$300) and Treasure Beach (J$200). The transportation center is behind the market, just west of the river. Taxis arrive and depart from a lot at the junction of Main and North Sts.

Middle Quarters

This small village on the A2, 13km north of Black River, is a tiny vortex of good eats. First, it's renowned for women higglers (street vendors) who stand at the roadside selling delicious (spicy) pepper shrimp – pronounced 'swimp' in these parts – cooked at the roadside grills. The shrimp are caught in traps made in centuries-old West African tradition from split bamboo. Around J$300 will buy a spicy bagful. The women come on strong in the sales pitch, but we understand many of these vendors are related, so don't let guilt direct your purchase.

Go jog, jump, or do whatever it takes to get hungry again, because now you have to try a Jamaican trucker favorite: **Howie's Healthy Eating** (☎378-8714; mains J$200-500; ◷24hr), on the A2 at the turnoff for YS Falls. Do you have a great 24-hour diner or greasy spoon in your town? If so, come to Howie's for the same vibe Jamaican-style. The cooking is done in big pots bubbling over wood fires. Choose from a number of soups, stews, fried fish, chicken, of course, and huge helpings of 'swimp'; we opt for the fried chicken.

If you want to shed some of your newly accumulated weight via a quick dip, stop by **Bubbling Spring** (☎850-1606; admission US$15; ◷8am-6pm), 1.5km south of Middle Quarters on the A2. Cool, slightly carbonated spring water is fed into long, shallow pools. If you're driving yourself around this can be a lovely break from the road, but it may be a bit underwhelming if you're coming here by public transportation. Simple Jamaican fare is served at nearby stalls.

Bamboo Avenue

The soothing sound of a million leaves rustling in the wind is one of the quiet pleasures of this photogenic archway of towering bamboo. The 4km-long stretch of the A2 between Middle Quarters and Lacovia is shaded by dense 100-year-old stands of *Bambusa vulgaris*, the largest species of bamboo in Jamaica. Cool and pretty, Bamboo Avenue is the perfect place to stop for a coconut jelly, accompanied by a bag of pepper shrimp brought along from Middle Quarters. In Lacovia ask locals for help finding the **twin tombs** (near the Texaco) where, according to local lore, two young victims of a 1738 duel are buried. One of the dead is identified: Thomas Jordan Spencer, a descendant

❶ YU CYAN WALK DEH

That's patois for 'You can't hike there,' and by 'there' we mean St Elizabeth's many illicit ganja plots. Thanks to the local dry soil, many Jamaicans swear by the potency of St Elizabeth herb. This is all well-and-good news for some folks, but it also means there are a lot of marijuana fields peppered throughout the parish. When hiking here, especially in areas like Bamboo Avenue and the Cockpit Country, stick to main paths (or better yet, hire a guide). For all the 'One Love' language that surrounds marijuana culture, the stuff is not always grown by laid-back hippies and Rastas – there are a lot of bad boys in the industry too. If you're wandering and notice the flora around you is starting to resemble the posters in a university dorm room, backtrack and get out of there. Even the friendliest Rastas who only grow their own are protective of their plots. During our research we met one backpacker who stumbled upon a plot and was robbed at machete-point for his troubles; in retrospect, he believes he got off lucky. Try not to follow in his footsteps.

of the Duke of Marlborough and distant ancestor of Lady Diana Spencer and Winston Churchill. Infrequent minibuses connect Lacovia to Black River and Santa Cruz, but it makes more sense to drive here; it makes for a nice add-on to a trip to Mandeville.

Santa Cruz

POP 7000

Santa Cruz is a bustling market town and the most important commercial center in southwest Jamaica. Black River may be the capital of St Elizabeth parish, but Santa Cruz is arguably the more important settlement thanks to its economic clout. Unfortunately it's less attractive. Back in the day Santa Cruz was a market center for horses and mules bred locally for the British army, and a livestock market is still held on Saturday, but by and large this is a bauxite town that has grown too fast. While there's nothing here to keep the average tourist busy for long, it's a good place to stop for money or a bite to eat, and it's a major transportation hub as well.

Banks include **Scotiabank** (☎966-2230; 77 Main St) and **National Commercial Bank** (☎966-2204; 7 Coke Dr). **Dr Oliver Myers** (☎966-2106; 23 Coke Dr) has a clinic near the **police station** (☎966-2289), 200m south of the town center on the road to Malvern.

Hind's Restaurant & Bakery (☎966-2234; Santa Cruz Plaza, Main St; mains US$1-6; ☺Mon-Sat) sells baked goods and is a clean, simple place to enjoy Jamaican fare such as brown stew and curried goat.

Paradise Patties (Shop 30, Beadles Plaza, Main St) sells veggie and beef patties for cheap (under J$100). **Fruity's** (Shop 27, Philip's Plaza, Main St) serves delicious ice-cream cones.

Santa Cruz is a main stop for buses, minibuses and route taxis going between Kingston, Mandeville and Black River. They arrive and depart from the transportation center on the A2, at the east end of Santa Cruz.

SOUTH COCKPIT COUNTRY

St Elizabeth is the driest parish in Jamaica thanks in part to the rugged Cockpit Country, which joins St Elizabeth to Trelawny parish in a rocky fist-bump and blocks the south coast from the rains whipping off the ocean. South Cockpit Country is as beautiful, rugged and remote as its northern counterpart, and perhaps a better area from which to access the unique, if fading, culture of the Maroons. Few roads penetrate the hills, where the sparse population is mostly involved in subsistence farming and, deeper in the valleys, ganja cultivation. As in North Cockpit Country, we warn you away from trying to discover marijuana plots; if you come upon one uninvited, it could cost you your life. Between the Nassau Mountains and the Cockpit Country is the wide Siloah Valley, carpeted with sugarcane.

The Cockpit Country is easily accessed from the south via the hamlet of Troy. See p229 for more details, including trails and information on hiring guides.

Maggotty

POP 1400

Maggotty is a forgettable town with an unforgettable name, laid out on a bend of the Black River at the western end of the Siloah Valley. It thinks of itself as a sleepy regional center, but it can also be a viable base for exploring YS Falls and the Appleton Rum Estate. Plus, Maggotty is the closest base for trips into the **Black River Gorge**, a rocky rent in the jungle speckled with 28 pretty waterfalls and intermittent natural swimming pools. The name, by the way, can be attributed to the missionary Rev John Hutch, who named Maggotty after his English birthplace.

☉ Sights & Activities

TOP CHOICE **Apple Valley Park**   PARK

(☎487-4521, 894-5947; www.applevalleypark.com; adult/child J$450/350; ☺10am-5pm daily by reservation only) Owned by Patrick Lee and his lovely Chinese-Jamaican family, Apple Valley Park is a little triumph of green sensibility and community tourism. The park grounds consist of an 18th-century home, a manicured lake, an artificial pool and further on, a forest reserve that stretches past the waterfalls and swimming holes of the Black River Gorge. You can kayak and paddleboat in the park itself or hike into the woods or fish or order a meal – it's all relaxing. The prettiness of the place is all the more remarkable when one considers this was once the scarred remains of a bauxite mine; Patrick Lee helped bring the area back to nature after hiring locals and subsequently boosting the surrounding economy, and for this reason we give some of the wear and tear evident on the grounds a pass. The 169-hectare family nature park is only open by appointment, so call ahead. The owners also operate a tractor-pulled jitney from the old train station in Maggotty. Be sure to spend the night at Apple Valley Guesthouse.

☞ Tours

Manfred's Jamaican Mountain Bike Tours — CYCLING TOURS

(✆in Canada 705-745-8210; tours US$900) Based at Apple Valley Park, this operator offers week-long tours of the south coast in January and February, with daily excursions geared to moderate riders (a support vehicle is provided). Over the week, you'll pedal 18km to 42km each day through glorious south-coast scenery to some of the region's most notable attractions, including YS Falls, Treasure Beach, Oxford Cave, Appleton Rum Estate and the Black River mangroves. The cost excludes airfare but includes transfers, gratuity and accommodations. You can rent a bike (US$25 per day or US$100 per week).

🛏 Sleeping & Eating

Apple Valley Guesthouse — GUEST HOUSE $

(per person camping/dm/d US$5/15/20) Patrick and Lucille Lee, the Chinese-Jamaican couple who run Apple Valley Park, keep bunks and private rooms in the 18th-century red-roofed great house south of town. Guests have kitchen privileges, but there is also an open-air restaurant (mains J$200 to J$600) serving traditional Jamaican fare. If you catch carp, silver perch or red snapper yourself, Lucille will cook it for you. Both park and guest house are reached from behind the police station.

Happy Times Restaurant — JAMAICAN $

(✆963-9807; Shakespeare Plaza; mains J$300-500; ◷Mon-Sat) This place serves simple, well-prepared meals, including curried goat, snapper, curried chicken and brown-stew pork.

❶ Getting There & Away

Public vehicles infrequently arrive and depart from opposite Shakespeare Plaza at the north end of Maggotty, connecting to Mandeville and Black River.

Appleton Rum Estate

You can smell the yeasty odor of molasses wafting from the **Appleton Sugar Estate**

and Rum Factory (✆963-9215; www.appletonrumtour.com; factory tour & rum tasting US$18; ◷9am-3:30pm Mon-Sat, closed public holidays) well before you reach it, 1km northeast of Maggotty in the middle of the Siloah Valley. This is the largest distillery in Jamaica and the oldest: the factory has been blending Appleton rums since 1749.

The 45-minute tour of the factory explains how molasses is extracted from sugarcane, then fermented, distilled and aged to produce the Caribbean's own rocket fuel, which you can taste in the John Wray Tavern. Around 17 varieties – including the lethal Overproof – are available for sampling. Unsurprisingly, the well-stocked gift shop does brisk business with visitors whose inhibitions have understandably been lowered over the course of the tour (and by the way, you get a complimentary bottle of the stuff at the end of the tour, so don't get too soused!).

Every tour company in Jamaica can get you onto one of the busloads of tourists that truck to and from (the 'from' part is pretty fun after 17 varieties of rum) the Appleton estate. Otherwise, it's easiest to get here from Maggotty; the factory is 1km east, and taxis will take you there and back for around J$500.

YS Falls

Jamaica prides itself on her waterfalls, but for our J$ the title of most beautiful cascades in the country is a dead heat between Reach Falls (p107) and the south coast stunner. YS, a series of eight **cascades** (✆997-6360; www.ysfalls.com; adult/child US$15/7.50; ◷9:30am-3:30pm Tue-Sun, closed public holidays) hemmed in by limestone cliffs, surrounded by lush jungle and brimming with an energy that is positively Edenic. If you wander around here early in the morning, before the falls are swarmed with tourists, there is, well...a natural mysticism in the air. The waters of YS (*why-ess*; the falls take their name from the original landowners, ranchers John Yates and Richard Scott) look like a whitewater necklace laid over deep green, falling 36m from top to bottom, separated by cool pools just screaming to be swam in.

If you're so inclined, you can **tube** down a bamboo-shaded stretch of river through five mini-rapids for US$6; depending on the flow of the water, this should take about 30 minutes. If you're feeling more daring,

IPSWICH & MEXICO CAVES

If you head about 8km north of YS Falls (you'll probably need a 4WD to do so) you'll find the almost-abandoned hamlet of Ipswich, the equally derelict railway line between Montego Bay and Kingston, and some of the most dramatic caves in Jamaica.

There are two groups of caverns in this area. The first set, known as the **Ipswich Caves** (N 18°11′55.2″, W 77°50′21.6″), also known as Duanwarie Caves, can be accessed from the 'town' of Ipswich; there are three entrances to the cavern system, which are studded with some particularly attractive stalactite, stalagmite and flowstone formations. Be on the lookout for small samples of plant life that have been washed into the cave entrance – the shoots are able to grow right to the point where natural light is snuffed out. Another 10km from here, near the town of Balaclava, you'll find the entrance to **Mexico Cave** (N 18°10′59.2″, W 77°39′21.2″), supposedly the longest in Jamaica (we say 'supposedly' because there is so much karst yet to be explored in the Cockpits), and an equally arresting and more challenging spelunking opportunity.

Getting out here can be a challenge, as public transportation is not a viable option. If you want to DIY, you'll be glad of a 4WD; the turnoff to Ipswich is off the B6, about 3km north of YS Falls. We *strongly* recommend checking with the **Jamaican Caves Organisation** (www.jamaicancaves.org) before coming here; they should be able to hook you up with a guide, which is essential. Natural Mystic Tours and Shafston Tours both lead excursions into the caves from Belmont and Bluefields respectively (see p217).

whiz down a canopy **zip line** (adult/child US$30/20) or just take a dip in the local spring-fed pool.

A tractor-drawn jitney takes visitors to the cascades, where you'll find picnic grounds, a tree house and a rope-swing over the pools. Be careful: the eddies are strong, especially after rains when the falls are torrential. A stone staircase and pathway follow the cascades upriver. There are no lockers, however, so you'll need to keep an eye on your stuff while you bathe. Admission includes a guide. There's a gift store and a cheap restaurant on site.

Almost every tour operator in Jamaica (and the vast majority of the hotels we list in this chapter, plus Montego Bay and Negril) offer trips to YS Falls, but if you want to get here ahead of the crowds, drive yourself (or charter your own taxi) and arrive right when the grounds open.

The YS Falls entrance is just north of the junction of the B6 toward Maggotty. From the A2 (a much smoother road if you're driving) the turnoff is 1.5km east of Middle Quarters; from here you'll head 5.5km north to the falls. On the B6, buses travel via YS Falls from Shakespeare Plaza in Maggotty. On the A2, buses, minibuses and route taxis will drop you at the junction to YS Falls, from where you can walk or catch an Ipswich-bound route taxi and ask to be dropped at the falls (J$80 to J$100).

Accompong

POP 3000

The Maroons and their legacy make up a significant chapter in the Jamaican national narrative, yet the truth of the matter is there are very few actual Maroon communities remaining on the island. Accompong, named for the brother of Maroon hero Cudjoe and embedded in the outer edges of southwestern Cockpit Country, is the sole remaining outpost in western Jamaica. This unique cultural lineage alone makes the town worth a visit, but it is also a good base for exploring the region of Cockpit Country, also known as 'Me No Sen, You No Come,' a landscape that, by dint of its ruggedness, is as responsible for Maroon independence as Maroon battle prowess.

The village still enjoys aspects of quasi-autonomy and is headed by a colonel elected by secret ballot for a period of five years. The colonel appoints and oversees a council, and it is considered proper etiquette to introduce yourself upon visiting (you should be directed to him upon entering the village, but if not, just ask around). For more background on the Maroons, see p255 and http://abengcentral.wordpress.com, a website that serves the Maroon community both within and outside of Jamaica.

⊙ Sights & Activities

If you arrive in Accompong under your own steam you'll be quickly greeted by locals offering to give you a tour of the town; the going rate at time of writing was US$20, which pays for a full tour of everything mentioned here, except the Peace Caves.

Accompong is centered on the tiny Parade Ground, where the Presbyterian church looks over a small **monument** that honors Cudjoe, the Maroon leader (the statue next to it is that of Leonard Parkinson, another Maroon freedom fighter). Opposite the monument, the **Accompong Community Centre & Museum** is a veritable peek into the Afro-Caribbean world's cultural attic: *goombay* drums, a musket, a sword, baskets and other artifacts from the Maroon era stacked alongside Ashanti art and Taíno tools. Other sections of the tour take in a Maroon burial ground, a small herbal garden, **Bickle Village**, studded with traditional thatch-roofed homes, and the **Kindah Tree**, a stately, sacred mango tree where the elders of the community congregate.

There are several tours offered into the beautiful surrounding countryside, including a one-hour trek down to the **Peace Caves** (about US$60), where Cudjoe signed the 1739 peace treaty with the British.

⌖ Tours

There are many hotels in Treasure Beach and Mandeville, and a few in Montego Bay and Negril, that can hook you up with tours into Accompong.

Original Trails of the Maroons   ADVENTURE TOURS
(☑475-3046; http://baboosgarden.wordpress.com, www.jamaicanmaroons.com) Affiliated with Baboo's Garden, this is an excellent ecotourism collaboration between an expat and the local Accompong community. It offers cultural tours of Accompong, and arranges tours with local guides into the rugged interior of the Cockpit Country.

Sun Venture Tours   CULTURAL TOURS
(☑960-6685, 408-6973; www.sunventuretours.com; 30 Balmoral Ave, Kingston 10) An excellent Kingston-based tour operator that specializes in cultural and environmental tours of off-the-beaten-path Jamaica.

Countrystyle Community Tours   CULTURAL TOURS
(☑962-7758; www.countrystylecommunitytourism.com) Based out of Mandeville, Countrystyle puts together individually tailored tours with a focus on community-based tourism.

DON'T MISS

ACCOMPONG MAROON FESTIVAL

In many ways, the best sight in Accompong is...well, Accompong. The village is more than politically autonomous; despite the fact the native Coromantee language has vanished and knowledge of local rituals is fading among the young, Accompong still feels *different* from the rest of Jamaica. Locals will proudly tell you there is no crime, police or taxes in Accompong, and while they may be guilty of some exaggeration, the town certainly feels tranquil compared to settlements of similar size in other parts of Jamaica.

Although it is anything but calm, perhaps the best time to get a sense of Accompong's uniqueness is during the traditional Accompong Maroon Festival, held each January 6. Because the festival is held in early January, a lot of Jamaicans call it 'Maroon New Year,' but it actually marks the signing of the 1739 peace treaty between Cudjoe of the Maroons and the British Empire. The provisions of that agreement guaranteed the Maroons significant personal freedom and 15,000 acres out of which to make their own community; a clerical error reduced said land to 1500 acres, still a source of some tension in these parts. The Maroon Festival celebrates Accompong's nominal independence and is a riot of traditional dancing, drumming, mento bands and local tonics and herbs.

Between the storytellers, chanting, rhythmic drumbeats and appeals to pre-Christian spirits, this is an intense invocation of Afro-Caribbean heritage – perhaps the most raw meshing of Old Africa and the New World many people will see in their lifetime (outside of certain parts of Brazil). The festival culminates in a traditional march to the revered Kindah Tree, where a specially prepared Maroon dish of unsalted and unseasoned pork is consumed with yams; afterwards (because after all, this is still Jamaica) an all-night sound-system party rocks into the wee hours. You'll never see Jamaica so quiet as Accompong sometime around 11am on January 7.

📛 Sleeping & Eating

Most residents of Accompong will offer to put you up for around US$20; meals will be a 'likkle' bit extra.

TOP CHOICE Baboo's Garden   GUEST HOUSE **$**

(☎475-3046; http://baboosgarden.wordpress.com; camping US$15, r US$25; P) Run by American Tony Kuhn, Baboo's Garden is a constantly evolving solar-powered guest house with thatched-roof bungalows and balconies that offer splendid views out over Cockpit Country. There's a very Irie vibe about, and guests will have a good opportunity to interact with local Maroons via an accessible interlocutor in the form of Tony.

Mystic Pass Villas   GUEST HOUSE **$**

(☎770-3680; r US$50-60; P) These simple yet well-kept, thatch-roofed, wooden-floored cottages constitute some surprisingly luxurious digs considering how far off the beaten path Accompong is. There are refreshing outdoor hot showers, worth the price of the stay alone if you've been out hiking. The property is run by the lovely Nervalee; be aware that it can be tough to contact her by phone.

🛍 Shopping

Local artisans still make *goombay* drums here. These – along with an array of medicinal herbs, calabash shells and *abengs* – are for sale in the tiny red-and-green craft shop as you enter town. The hand-carved *goombay* drum is box-shaped and covered with goatskin, and makes a wonderfully deep and resonant racket. A large one will set you back at least US$150.

ℹ Getting There & Away

Route taxis run from Shakespeare Plaza in Maggotty (J$200). If you're driving, the route from Maggotty is well signed, but the winding road is horribly potholed. You can also drive here from Albert Town in North Cockpit Country, although you'll want to get a good road map and some detailed directions.

Quick Step

This remote mountain hamlet 13km north of Siloah offers magnificent views over the portion of the Cockpit Country known as the District of Look Behind (so named for the frequent ambushes endured by British soldiers trying to hunt down Maroons). It's eerie and extremely foreboding, a chaos of honeycombed limestone cliffs hewn into bizarre shapes and cockpits (hillocks separated by canyons), with deep forested bowls up to 150m across.

North of Quick Step the road peters out. Hiking trails lead into the heart of the Cockpits, but you are well advised to hire a guide through the Southern Trelawny Environmental Agency (p182) or the **Jamaican Caves Organisation** (www.jamaicancaves.org). One trail leads to **Windsor Caves**, a full day's hike. It's easy to get lost and this is no place for that. Don't attempt it alone!

Balaclava

Balaclava sits atop a ridge at the east end of the Siloah Valley. If you're climbing uphill from the west, it's worth resting at the ridge crest to take in the view of the valley laid out below: smothered in sugarcane, as flat and green as a billiard table.

An attractive Anglican church and the disused railway station are about the only buildings of interest.

Troy & Around

Three kilometers northeast of Balaclava the B6 turns southeast for Mandeville; another road (the B10) leads north and climbs to Troy on the border with Trelawny parish. The latter is a spectacular drive as you climb through a series of dramatic gorges, with the road clinging to the sheer face of the Cockpits.

Troy, plunked in a valley bottom and surrounded by sugarcane fields, is the southeastern gateway to Cockpit Country. It is also a center for the cultivation of yams, which grow on tall runners spaced throughout the valley. **St Silas Church**, still in use by the locals, is worth a look for its blue-tinted corrugated iron roof.

Auchtembeddie, 5km south of Troy, is a choice spot for cavers, who head to **Coffee River Cave** (N 18°12'43.6", W 77°37'29.2"), known for some magnificent rockfalls and a whole lotta bats. The area is totally undeveloped for tourism, but local guides will escort you for a negotiated fee; again, contact the **Jamaican Caves Organistion** (www.jamaicancaves.org) if you want to attempt cave exploration. This cave is known to flood during the rains, so be especially mindful of the weather if you want to spelunk here.

A dirt road leads 3km north from Troy to Tyre, a hamlet on the edge of the Cockpits. Beyond Tyre the road fades into a bush-enshrouded trail that leads all the way to Windsor (about 24km), see p183. Don't attempt this trek alone, as there are several forks and it is easy to get lost.

To hire a guide, contact the Southern Trelawny Environmental Agency (p182) in Albert Town, 17km northeast of Troy.

Christiana

The harvesting heart of the western highland agricultural yam-basket, Christiana, some 16km north of Mandeville and 900m above sea level, is a pleasant town set in a lovely backdrop of rippling hills and shallow valleys.

The area was settled by German farmers during the 18th and 19th centuries, which is a little bit evident in the complexion of some locals and the local Moravian church, located at the northern end of sinuous Main St. During the 19th century, Christiana became a hill-town resort popular with European dignitaries and Kingstonians escaping the heat of the plains. Today Christiana makes a good base for exploring YS Falls and the Appleton Rum Estate.

This is a fairly sleepy place – farmers go to bed early and get up around 4am or 5am – which you may find refreshing if you're tired of Jamaica's usual cacophony. That said, if you're here on Thursday when the higglers come to sell their produce, the roads are so thick you can hardly drive through town. It's a sight worth seeing.

Around Christiana you'd be forgiven for imagining yourself in the Pyrenees or the Costa Rican highlands. The air is crisp, clouds drift through the vales and pine trees add to the alpine setting. This is an important center for growing Irish potatoes, cacao, yams and coffee, and during picking season you can watch women with baskets moving among the rows, plucking cherry-red coffee berries.

◉ Sights & Activities

Christiana Bottom   VALLEY
The main reason for stopping here is to discover this beautiful riverside valley bottom, located below the town at the base of a shimmering **waterfall**. Two **sinkholes** full of crystal-clear water offer refreshing dips; collectively they're known as the Blue Hole.

You can hike from the center of Christiana, though the going at the lower reaches can be muddy and slippery (but pretty, once you start pressing through a tangle of moss and ferns). Take the road that leads east from the National Commercial Bank; it's 3km from here. Take the first left and then the second left and press on through the green; if you get lost, locals are happy to provide directions.

Gourie Forest Reserve   FOREST
(☉sunrise-sunset) An unexpected bloom of pine trees, plus mahogany and mahoe, grows atop the flinty heads of the Cockpits 3km northwest of Christiana, near Coleyville. This park is laced with **hiking trails** and is most noteworthy for having one of Jamaica's longest cave systems. Two spelunking routes into the **Gourie Caves** have been explored, but this is advanced caving; ask at Hotel Villa Bella for a guide. You'll find magnificent columns, narrow fissures and an icy river with overhead air passages that barely clear 30cm. As such, Gourie should only be attempted in dry weather, as flooding is a distinct possibility. You'll also want to bring warm clothes; the water is seriously cold.

To get to the park from Christiana, turn uphill (southwest) at the radio tower immediately south of the junction that leads west for Coleyville and Troy. Immediately take the left at a Y-fork, then right at the next Y-fork and follow the green wire fence. The road isn't in very good condition, but it's doable in a 2WD if you proceed carefully.

✯✯ Festivals & Events

On Christmas Eve the streets here have traditionally been closed and farming families have poured in for a centuries-old Jonkanoo celebration called **Grand Market Night**, with men on stilts, music in the air and general festivity in the streets. The festivities are sometimes cancelled; call Sherryl McDowell or Audrey Brown at Hotel Villa Bella.

🛏 Sleeping & Eating

TOP CHOICE **Hotel Villa Bella**   HOTEL **$$**
(☎964-2243, from North America 888-790-5264; www.hotelvillabella.com; r US$70-120; 🅿☍) This charming, cozy country inn is one of our favorite midrange rural retreats on the island. Perched on a hill at Sedburgh, at the south end of town, the villa is a former grande dame that retains her original mahogany floors (now somewhat squeaky) and Victorian and deco furniture and trappings.

The polite service matches the old-school elegance of the furnishings, and recalls the days when Christiana was a center for 'old-style tourism.' The rooms don't entirely keep pace with all this grandeur, but they're still lovely, if a little plain. Villa Bella also offers one of the most reasonably priced fine-dining experiences on the island. The superb menu merges Jamaican, Japanese and Chinese cuisines; typical dishes include Chinese-style poached fish in ginger and soy sauce, and sole simmered in coconut milk, spices and lemongrass. Eat on the veranda or the garden terrace, where you can sip homemade ginger beer and admire the flower-filled garden. Afternoon tea is at 4:30pm. And the ackee breakfast: *amazing*.

Main St has numerous undistinguished restaurants and pastry shops. **Akete Vegetarian Restaurant** (Main St; mains J$100-400; ⊙breakfast, lunch & dinner; ✍) is recommended for I-tal food.

❶ Information

Christiana Health Centre (☑964-2749; Main St) Government-run; toward the south end of Main St.

Christiana Pharmacy (☑964-2424; Main St) Well stocked.

Dr Glen Norman Day (☑964-2361; Christiana Plaza) Clinic off Main St.

National Commercial Bank (☑964-2466; Main St)

Police station (☑964-2250; Main St)

Post office (☑964-2279; Main St) Next to the police station.

Scotiabank (☑964-2223; Main St)

❶ Getting There & Away

Christiana is well-served by public transportation from both Kingston and Mandeville; from Mandeville you can access other major towns in the south coast and central highlands. A bus and minibuses also operate from Montego Bay and Ocho Rios via Albert Town.

MANDEVILLE & AROUND

Mandeville

POP 48,000

Mandeville is the official capital and largest town in Manchester parish, and fifth-largest city in the country. But it carries just as many unofficial titles. Sitting at 610m above sea level, it's essentially the capital of the Jamaican hill country, and certainly the largest urban center in the interior. It's also one of the strongest magnets for wealthy, returning-from-overseas Jamaicans, recalling its old role as colonial hill retreat. Stupendously gaudy mansions are studded all around the local Don Figuerero Mountains, cloaked in a year-round early spring/late autumn coolness.

In the topmost hills of Mandeville you'll find neighborhoods laid out in neat grids with spick-and-span cul-de-sacs and consistent street signage – they resemble American suburbs, largely because a lot of the residents used to live in American suburbs before they retired back to Jamaica. Finally, Mandeville is something of a base for volunteer, Peace Corps and NGO types in Jamaica; don't be surprised to see a few young, Western faces (more than you'd normally expect in a non-resort town) wandering the streets.

History

Established only in 1816, Mandeville began life as a haven for colonial planters escaping the heat of the plains. In the 19th century, the city prospered as a holiday retreat for wealthy Kingstonians, and attracted soldiers and British retirees from other colonial quarters. Many early expats established the area as a center for dairy farming and citrus and pimento production. Jamaica's unique seedless citrus fruit, the ortanique, was first produced here in the 1920s and is grown in large quantities.

North American bauxite company Alcan opened operations here in 1940 (in 2000 it sold its operations to a Swiss company, Glencore). Relatively high wage levels lured educated Jamaicans, bringing a middle-class savoir faire to the town.

◉ Sights

Marshall's Pen   HISTORICAL SITE
(☑904-5454; Mike Town Rd; admission US$10; ⊙by appointment) One of the most impressive historical sights in the Central Highlands, Marshall's Pen has a story that manages to encapsulate the sweep of Jamaican history from Taíno times through colonialism to abolition, independence and the modern day. Also: it's a great spot to watch birds.

Taíno people once inhabited this property, and archaeological digs still turn up their artifacts. The stone-and-timber great house itself, built in 1795, dates back to the first British Provost General of Jamaica. Throughout its history the home has been a coffee

Mandeville

◉ Sights
1	Cecil Charlton Park	B4
2	Cenotaph (War Memorial)	B4
3	Mandeville Courthouse	B3
4	Produce Market	B4
	Rectory	(see 3)
5	St Mark's Anglican Church	B4

⬤ Sleeping
6	Golf View Hotel	A2
7	Mandeville Hotel	B4

✖ Eating
8	Devon House I-Scream	B1
9	Flakey Crust	A4
10	Little Ochie	B1
	Manchester Arms Pub & Restaurant	(see 7)
11	New Den	B1

◔ Drinking
12	Club Beavers	A3
13	Link	A2
14	Vineyard	B4

◍ Shopping
15	SWA Craft Centre	A2

plantation and cattle-breeding property (hence Marshall's 'Pen'). Today the 120-hectare grounds are owned by Jamaica's leading ornithologist, Robert Sutton, and Anne Sutton, an environmental scientist. Robert can trace his ancestry to the first child born to English parents in Jamaica in 1655.

The exterior of the building, all cut-stone and Spanish windows surrounded by landscaped gardens, is beautiful. The interior is equally arresting, a honeycomb of wood-paneled rooms brimming with antiques, leather-bound books, Taíno artifacts, historical and original artwork and lots of other museum-quality pieces, many from Japan and China (this may be the best collection of Asian art on the island). You can tour the mini-museum by appointment only.

Marshall's Pen is splendid for bird-watching: more than 100 species have been recorded here, including 25 of the 27 species endemic to Jamaica. It's a treat to don rubber boots and binoculars and set out with the Suttons, their several dogs swarming happily at your heels. Robert is coauthor with Audrey Downer of *Birds of Jamaica: A Photographic Field Guide*. Visiting early morning or late afternoon is best; again, call to make an appointment. You may be able to arrange an overnight stay for around US$40, but this option is essentially only open to dedicated ornithologists.

To get to the property, take Oriole Close off Winston Jones Hwy (A2), about 5km northwest of the town center (there's a sign for 'Somerset Quarries' at the junction). Turn left on Nightingale Dr and then, after about 100m, right on Mike Town Rd; the estate entrance – an unmarked stone gateway – is about 400m further on the right. Take insect repellent.

Countrystyle Community Tours offers tours by appointment.

Cecil Charlton Park   SQUARE
This tiny English-style 'green', also known as Mandeville Sq, lends a slight Cotswoldian village feel to the town center (that's assuming Cotswold greens are dominated by dozens of people hailing taxis, selling produce and

hawking Digicel scratch cards). On the north side is the **Mandeville Courthouse**, the oldest building on the square. Built by slaves in 1817 out of cut limestone, the edifice is fronted by a horseshoe staircase and raised portico supported by Doric columns. The **rectory**, attached to the courthouse, was completed in 1820 and is the oldest home in town.

On the south side is a **produce market** and a **cenotaph** commemorating Jamaican dead from the two world wars.

St Mark's Anglican Church, on the south side of Cecil Charlton Park, was established in 1820. There's a lot of gothic accents, which makes it stand out from other Jamaican churches built around the same period. The building still functions as the parish church for Manchester.

Bloomfield Great House　　GREAT HOUSE
(☎962-7130; bloomfield.g.h@cwjamaica.com; 8 Perth Rd; ⊙noon-10pm Tue-Sat) This immaculate historic home stands atop a hill at the end of a very winding road southwest of the town center. The two-story structure is built in traditional Caribbean vernacular and gleams today thanks to some fine renovations. It is about 170 years old (the exact date is uncertain) and began life as the center of a coffee estate and, later, a citrus plantation, cattle farm and dairy. It's now one of Jamaica's finest art galleries and a premier restaurant.

The **art gallery** features works by many of Jamaica's leading artists and is a popular function space for Mandeville's many well-to-do and the local expat population. Most of the work you see is available for purchase; if you want something cheaper than an original work of art, there's a gift and crafts shop on site that sells woodwork, prints and assorted goodies that are a bit more exciting than the stuff you see in a standard Jamaican souvenir shack.

The entrance is 200m south of Manchester College, on the opposite side of the road at the crossroads.

Mrs Stephenson's Garden　　GARDEN
(☎962-2909; 25 New Green Rd; admission US$5; ⊙by appointment) Carmen Stephenson is testament to the fact that any individual who cares enough to can carve out their own plot of Eden. Her well-manicured garden has been planned and planted, and pruned and mulched, with much loving care and discipline. Keen amateur gardeners descend year-round to admire the layout or gasp at the collection that includes orchids and ortaniques. Casual visitors are welcome during daylight hours.

Huntington Summit　　HISTORICAL SITE
(☎962-2274; George's Valley Rd; admission free, donations accepted; ⊙by appointment) The extravagant Huntington Summit mansion in May Day, about 3km southeast of the town center, forms the yin to Bloomfield Great House's yang. The octagonal home is of palatial proportions, with wraparound plate-glass windows and artificial cascades that tumble into a swimming pool, from where waters feed into a pond in the lounge. The ostentatious furnishings reflect the catholic tastes of its owner, Cecil Charlton, a millionaire farmer, politician and self-promoter who served as the mayor of Mandeville during the 1970s and 1980s.

To get here, take Manchester Rd south to the T-junction; turn right onto Newport Rd then left onto May Day Rd, and left again after 1km onto George's Valley Rd (you can't miss the big green gates on the left). An appointment and a permit are required to visit; call ahead of time to book.

☞ Tours

TOP　Jack Mandora Tours SIGHTSEEING TOURS
CHOICE　(☎530-6902; jackmandoratours@gmail.com) Yup – two excellent destinations in one town. Tours here are actually conducted by the affiliated Real Jamaican Vacations which tailors special packages for small groups (one to four individuals) at good rates (whole day trips are US$150). Affiliated with local **Allison Morris** (☎965-2288, www.real-jamaica-vacations.com), a clever, witty joy who can expound for hours on her beloved home island (and offers steel drumming lessons); her website is a fantastic clearing house of island information.

Countrystyle Community Tours　　CULTURAL TOURS
(☎962-7758, 488-7207; www.countrystylecommunitytourism.com; Astra Country Inn, 62 Ward Ave) Has a 'Marvelous Mandeville' tour (US$60 per person for a full day, including lunch and transfers). It also offers tours further afield and specialist guides.

✯✯ Festivals & Events

Manchester Horticultural Society Show　　OPEN GARDEN
(☎962-2909; ⊙late May) Held at Mrs Stephenson's Garden.

COMMUNITY TOURISM

You won't be long in the Mandeville area before you hear about 'community tourism,' an attempt to create opportunities for locals wishing to participate more fully in Jamaica's tourism industry, while fostering a deeper connection for visitors with the people of communities they might otherwise just pass through.

The dynamo behind the movement is Diana McIntyre-Pike, co-owner and manager of the Astra Country Inn and director of **Countrystyle Community Tours** (☎962-7758, 488-7207; www.countrystylecommunitytourism.com; Astra Country Inn, 62 Ward Ave), a company geared toward providing alternatives to 'sea and sand' vacations. McIntyre-Pike helped to form the Central & South Tourism Committee, which sponsors special-interest tours, community guides, skills training and assistance with tourism development at the local level. She also runs the Countrystyle Institute for Sustainable Tourism, offering courses from community guide training to environmental waste management. 'Whatever development takes place, it must complement our lifestyle, not change our way of life,' she says.

The following tours were conceived to provide experience and insights that capture the 'real Jamaica.' Each day-tour includes lunch and refreshments:

» **Roots Jamaica** (US$50) introduces you to Jamaican hospitality. Spend a day in a country village, receive a community welcome and be entertained in a private home while sampling local food. Visit churches and community centers and listen as elders relate tales of the past.

» **Taste of Jamaica** (US$50) entails a day of village-hopping and learning to cook Jamaican cuisine in a natural setting within the community. Learn the old-time way of making *bammy* (a pancake) from cassava, taste sugarcane and plantain tarts, and sample fruits including naseberry, star apples and ortaniques. There's traditional coffee-making, a visit to Middle Quarters for some pepper shrimp, and the tour concludes with a meal at Little Ochie restaurant (p245) in Alligator Pond.

» **Jamaica Naturally** (US$50) unfurls nature at its best in six villages of the central and south areas of Jamaica. Along the way you'll enjoy the scenic splendor of Resource Village, Gut River, Alligator Pond, Bamboo Avenue, YS Falls, Black River and a dramatic conclusion at Lover's Leap.

In addition, Countrystyle offers 'community experience packages' for lengthier stays. Among them is a three-day all-inclusive package (including choice of one of the above day tours) for US$1000 (US$1200 per couple) and a seven-day B&B package (including all three tours) for US$1050 (US$2000 per couple). If none of these options appeal, Countrystyle does individually tailored tours that can encompass experiences from across the island.

Manchester Golf Week GOLF
(☎925-2325, 962-2403; www.jamaicagolfassociation.com; ⊙late Jul) Contact the Jamaica Golf Association for details.

Sleeping

Kariba Kariba Guest House GUEST HOUSE $
(☎962-8006/3039; 39 New Green Rd; r incl breakfast US$50) North of the town center, Kariba is a beautiful fieldstone home run by a surpassingly friendly English-Jamaican couple. Admittedly, the exterior grounds and lobby are a good deal more attractive than the actual rooms, which are a bit middling, but we're willing to forgive this given the efforts staff make to accommodate guests. The owner can point out nature trails, and also leads customized excursions that give a good sense of rural Jamaican culture.

Mandeview Flats HOTEL $
(☎961-8439; www.mandeview.com; 7 Hillview Dr, Balvenie Heights; s/d from US$60/75; P@≋) With deeply satisfying views over Mandeville's surrounding undulating hillsides, this gleaming small hotel offers 12 clean, fan-cooled rooms (a fan is all you need this high up). Simple, functional and hardly luxury; a quintessential Mandeville hotel.

Golf View Hotel
HOTEL $

(☎962-4477; www.thegolfviewhotel.com; 51/2 Caledonia Rd; s US$70-90, d US$75-95, ste US$110; P※@※) This rambling, conference-oriented property features 60-odd rooms centered on a small pool in a concrete courtyard. We're not bowled over by the grounds, honestly, but once you get to the rooms – the equivalent of a decent midrange hotel anywhere else – this becomes a pretty good option. The interior decor is surprisingly modern; the four-poster beds are pretty comfy and spacious suites have walk-in showers.

Mandeville Hotel
HOTEL $$

(☎962-2460/9764; www.mandevillehoteljamaica .com; Hotel St; r US$80, ste US$110-150, apt US$195-255; P※※) The town's oldest hotel (and one of the oldest in Jamaica, actually) has been operating since 1875, although an unimaginative 1970s renovation has cost it a bit of character. The hotel, and its staff, likes to think of itself as the poshest thing around. but the rooms score a resounding 'just OK'. The spacious suites and self-contained apartments are better quality. An on-site restaurant overlooks a pool and is joined by a pub that gets crowded with Mandeville's moneyed.

✖ Eating

Bloomfield Great House Restaurant & Bar
FUSION $$

(8 Perth Rd; mains J$800-2200; ☉lunch & dinner Mon-Sat) The on-site restaurant at the Bloomfield Great House is one of Jamaica's preeminent eateries and purveyors of Caribbean fusion cuisine. Frankly, we think the setting and the views over Mandeville from the open veranda may be a bit better than the food, which is not quite as grand as the name it's built. But it's still quite good: callaloo fettuccine, jumbo shrimp stuffed with jalapeño pepper, filet mignon and, many say, the best fish-and-chips on the island (no mushy peas though). A Sunday champagne brunch is popular, and the restaurant conveniently offers free pick-up and drop-off from central Mandeville hotels. At the very least, drop by for a drink in the mahogany bar, the only place we found in Jamaica (anywhere, come to think of it) that serves Red Stripe *on tap.*

Little Ochie
SEAFOOD $$

(Leaders Plaza; mains J$500-2000; ☉breakfast, lunch & dinner) The second satellite of what may be Jamaica's most famous restaurant (see p244), this Little Ochie branch is good. Very good. Not as good as its parent, but hey – we can't all approach perfection. The menu is seafood done in all the traditional Jamaican ways (brown stew, escoveitch, jerk etc) so don't expect anything too original, except for the flavors, which are fantastic.

New Den
JAMAICAN $$

(35 Caledonia Rd; mains US$5-25; ☉lunch & dinner Mon-Sat) In the former home of a colonial family with an affinity for wickerwork, this refined Jamaican eatery serves up excellent fish-and-chips, curried or barbecued chicken and plenty of old-school class. If you're especially hungry, try the mixed grill – basically a small farm's worth of meat that ought to satisfy the most carnivorous appetite.

Manchester Arms Pub & Restaurant
JAMAICAN $

(Mandeville Hotel, Hotel St; mains J$500-1500; ☉breakfast, lunch & dinner) The Manchester Arms goes all out to give you that pub-in-the-midst-of-Jamaica feeling, an effort that's vaguely successful. The broad menu encapsulates fairly overpriced Jamaican and continental food, but the setting is pretty lovely, especially for the poolside barbecues held on Wednesday night. Speaking of which, the last Wednesday of every month is Jamaica Night, with Jamaican food and entertainment, including a live mento band.

Flakey Crust
BAKERY

(11A Manchester Rd) Sells fresh-baked breads, pastries and patties.

Devon House I-Scream
ICE CREAM

(Main St) This also has an outlet in Mandeville.

Fresh produce can be found at the **market** on the south side of Cecil Charlton Park, but hygiene is an issue.

♟ Drinking & Entertainment

This town has a reputation for being popular with newlyweds and seniors, which should tell you how exciting the place can get. The Manchester Arms has a quiet English-style pub that's open late, while Bloomfield Great House has live music on Friday night.

Link
BAR

(80 Caledonia Rd) A popular neighborhood bar with a friendly clientele. Manages to be both a locals' haunt and a spot for Jamaican patrons who have lived abroad, plus it's popular with foreign volunteers and expats.

Raging karaoke nights are held on Thursday and Saturday, and on Sunday a DJ spins vintage reggae and American R&B.

Club Beavers BAR
(Ward Ave) A nice open-air bar that doubles as a fun open-air club on weekends and Wednesday nights.

Vineyard WINE BAR
(Manchester Rd; ☺4:30pm-midnight Mon-Thu, 4:30pm until last person leaves Fri-Sun) As chi-chi as Mandeville gets, with flashy small plates and, of course, a good wine menu.

🛍 Shopping

SWA Craft Centre CRAFTS
(☎962-0694; 7 N Racecourse Rd) Behind the Manchester Shopping Plaza, this place trains young women to make a living from crochet, embroidery, weaving and so on. Its most appealing item is the famous 'banana patch' Rastafarian doll.

❶ Information

Fontana Pharmacy (☎962-3129; Manchester Shopping Plaza)

Heart Institute of the Caribbean (☎625-7122/4/6; www.caribbeanheart.com; Unit 7, 1 Brumalia Rd)

Hargreaves Memorial Hospital (☎961-1589; Caledonia Rd) Privately run.

Internet Cafe (☎961-1829; Suite 10, Central Plaza; per 30 min J$200; ☺8:30am-5pm Mon-Fri)

Manchester Parish Library (☎962-2972; 34 Hargreaves Ave; internet per half hr J$100; ☺9:30am-4:30pm Mon-Fri, to 4pm Sat)

Mandeville Hospital (☎962-2067; 32 Hargreaves Ave)

Police station (☎962-2250, 119; Park Cres) On the north side of the green.

Post office (☎962-2339; South Racecourse Rd)

Scotiabank (☎962-1083; cnr Ward Ave & Caledonia Rd)

Western Union (☎962-1037; Brumalia Town Centre, Perth St)

❶ Getting There & Around

Mandeville has direct bus, minibus and route-taxi services from virtually every major town in Jamaica. Most buses, and many minibuses and route taxis, depart and arrive from the transportation center, off Main St. Others depart and arrive near the market on the main square. As usual, there are no set times for departure; vehicles leave when full, which means they do so quickly in the early morning and late afternoon.

You'll probably have to wait a little bit otherwise. Sample fares are J$300 to Kingston, J$400 to Savanna-la-Mar and J$550 to Montego Bay.

Gutters & Spur Tree Hill

Gutters, 16km southeast of Santa Cruz, sits astride the border of Manchester and St Elizabeth parishes at the foot of Spur Tree Hill. From here, the A2 road begins a long, steep switchback climb up the Don Figuerero Mountains to Mandeville.

At the top of the hill you can look out over the Essex Valley and the Santa Cruz Mountains. The valley floor is dominated by the Alpart alumina factory at Nain, 8km to the southwest, and aglitter at night.

You can admire the view midway up the hill at several roadside shacks, some of which serve fine Jamaican food, all for around J$200 to J$500. Try **All Seasons** (☺lunch & dinner) for the jerk (they do a jerk sausage on weekends, so good it should be a controlled substance) and **Neville's Curry Goat** (☺lunch & dinner) for...well, really, do we have to spell it out?

Williamsfield

In the village of Williamsfield, 300m below and northeast of Mandeville, at the base of the Winston Jones Hwy (A2), you can take a free tour of the **High Mountain Coffee Factory** (☎963-4211; Winston Jones Hwy; ☺10am-4pm Mon-Fri, tours by appointment). Both the factory and the tour are pretty small, but the whole affair is fascinating, especially the sections where the tour guides explain how coffee is categorized, tasted, packaged and exported (mainly to Japan). We might add the whole place smells amazing. Obviously, you can purchase fresh bags of coffee (plus Scotch bonnet sauce) after the tour is done.

The **High Mountain 10K Road Race** (www.highmountaincoffe10k.com), Jamaica's largest and longest-running road race, is held here every last Sunday in January.

Shooter's Hill

Shooter's Hill begins 3km northwest of Williamsfield and climbs steadily and steeply (430m in elevation) to Christiana. A lookout point midway offers splendid views. On the west side of the road, atop a hillock, is the Moravian-built **Mizpah Church** topped by a four-faced German clock.

If you've ever eaten at a Jamaican restaurant anywhere in the world, you've undoubtedly seen bottles of spicy Pickapeppa sauce. If you've ever wondered where the stuff is made, ponder no more and come to the **Pickapeppa Factory** (☎603-3439/3441; www.pickapeppa.com; tours J$200; ☻9am-3pm Mon-Thu), on the B6 at the foot of Shooter's Hill. The plant offers 30-minute tours by appointment. There's honestly not much to see but workers stirring giant pots of simmering scallions, mangoes, peppers and some other ingredients – we'd tell you, but then we'd have to kill you. (Joke!)

Mile Gully & Around

The village of Mile Gully sprawls along a valley that runs northwest from Mandeville in the lee of the forested north face of the Don Figuerero Mountains. The B6 leads northwest from Shooter's Hill, winding, dipping and rising past lime-green pastures dotted with guango and silk-cotton trees and criss-crossed with stone walls and hedgerows.

About 1km west of Mile Gully at **Skull Point**, you'll find a venerable blue-and-white 19th-century police station and courthouse at the junction for Bethany, plus the atmospheric remains of a defunct train station. The name has nothing to do with the police station, though; it comes from the local church – or at least the ruins of that church. It's a genuinely creepy place, all rotted and burnt out and infested with bats. The local consensus is the grounds are very much haunted (folks were literally yelling at us from their cars to beware of duppies – ghosts – when we arrived), supposedly by beheaded local slave James Knight.

The Bethany road climbs sharply and delivers you at the **Bethany Moravian Church** – a simple gray stone building dating to 1835, dramatically perched foursquare midway up the hill with fantastic valley views. The church is rather dour close up, but the simple interior boasts a resplendent organ. Another beautiful church – **St Simon's Anglican Church** – sits on a hillside amid meadows at Comfort Hall, 6km west of Mile Gully, with huge spreading trees festooned with old-man's beard.

To the south of the B6, perched atop the Don Figuerero Mountains, at Maidstone, is the humble **Nazareth Moravian Church**, which would look as comfortable on an American prairie as it does in the Jamaican

bush. Founded in 1840, Maidstone is one of Jamaica's post-emancipation pre-planned 'free villages,' an early experiment at the intersection of urban planning and social policy. The annual **Emancipation Day Fair** is celebrated at Maidstone on August 1, with mento bands, Jonkanoo celebrations, and maypole and quadrille dancing.

If you want to spend the night in this quiet, hilltop landscape, pop into **Villa Isabel** (☎322-9281, 469-3476; www.discoverjamaica.com/villa/villaisabel; Mile Gully; r from US$50; ❉☜) in Mile Gully. It's a pretty place with tiled floors, lovely garden and a gazebo. They can arrange tours of the nearby caves, haunted churches and bicycle treks.

Coasters and route taxis operate on the B6 between Mandeville and Maggotty via Mile Gully. If you're driving from Mandeville, the B6 continues west about 8km to Green Hill and a T-junction. About 1.5km north (to the right) of the junction, en route to Balaclava, is a *very dangerous* spot: you'll climb a short hill that tempts you to accelerate. Unfortunately there's an unmarked railway crossing on the crest and a hairpin bend *immediately* after. Drive slowly!

TREASURE BEACH & AROUND

The sun-kissed land southeast of Black River is sheltered from rain for most of the year by the Santa Cruz Mountains, so there is none of the lush greenery of the north coast. Instead, you'll find a thorny, surreally beautiful semidesert, a landscape almost East African in its scorched beauty. Acacia trees and cacti tower over fields of scallions guarded by fencerows of aloe vera. The region remains unsullied by resort-style tourism; here you can slip into a lazy, no-frills tropical lifestyle almost impossible to achieve elsewhere on the island's coast.

Dividing the plains north to south is the aforementioned Santa Cruz range, a steep-faced chain that slopes to the sea and drops 520m at Lover's Leap. The plains are hemmed in to the west by the hills of Surinam Quarters, whose scarp faces fall sharply to the coast; to the north by the Nassau Mountains and Cockpit Country; and to the east by the Don Figuerero Mountains, a wedge-shaped upland plateau dominating Manchester parish. The base of the west-facing escarpment of the Don Figueroos forms the boundary between St Elizabeth and Manchester. Northeast, the Mocho Mountains rise to Christiana and crest at Mt Denham (992m).

Treasure Beach

Treasure Beach puts paid to the misconception that Jamaica is little more than big, expensive resorts and poor ghettos. A smattering of yellow sand, lowland brush, guest houses, private homes, rental villas, fishers, farmers and expats, the area has sufficient tourism infrastructure to be convenient for visitors, yet it's low-key enough so you rarely feel like an interloper. There's hardly any of the hustle you get in Negril, Ocho Rios and Montego Bay, and everyone walks around at night without fear. This is the highlight of Jamaica for many foreign visitors who reject big resort tourism; they return to this spot every year or even settle down, buying

homes and becoming neighbors – much to local pride.

Treasure Beach is the generic name for four coves – Billy's Bay, Frenchman's Bay, Calabash Bay and Great Pedro Bay. It's said Scottish sailors were shipwrecked near Treasure Beach in the 19th century, accounting for the presence of fair skin, green eyes and reddish hair among the local population. The area's residents are known for their strong community spirit. Collectives like the Treasure Beach Women's Group and the Treasure Beach Foundation bring locals and expats together to work on projects relating to housing, education and local culture. There's a burgeoning cultural scene, with artists, poets and other luminaries continuing to put down roots. This creative class, plus events like the Calabash International Literary Festival, continue to shape and guide the national literary dialogue.

With all the buzz that 'quiet' Treasure Beach is generating, it's no surprise develop-

Treasure Beach

ers are hungrily buying up land, and some say it is only a matter of time before the first major resorts appear. A citizens' committee meets each month to regulate impending development. But for the time being, it's just you, the sea and one of the most compelling mixes of expats and Jamaicans on the island.

◉ Sights & Activities

A bicycle is a good means of getting around quiet Treasure Beach; most hotels and guest houses rent them out for a small fee. There is one main road connecting all of the beaches, plus many smaller cow-paths and dirt trails.

Boating & Fishing

With a long history (and a large population) of seafaring fishers, it's no wonder Treasure Beach is a great place from which to take to the sea. The best time to book a trip is during the early morning or late afternoon; the winds tend to pick up during the middle of the day. On bright moonlit evenings it is possible to take to the silvery waters for an enchanting tour of the coast.

Popular boating excursions include the Pelican Bar (p243), Black River Great Morass (p222), and Sunny Island and Little Ochie, both near Alligator Pond (p245).

From Frenchman's Beach, boat captain and fisher **Dennis Abrahams** (☎ 435-3779, 965-3084; dennisabrahams@yahoo.com) offers a sunset cruise by motorboat to Great Pedro Bluff and Billy's Bay, as well as fishing and on-demand trips to the Pelican Bar and Black River Great Morass. Other recommended captains include **Allan Daley** (☎ 423-3673, 366-7394), **Teddy Parchment** (☎ 854-5442) and **Joseph Brown** (☎ 376-9944, 847-1951). Expect to pay around US$35 for a trip out to Pelican Bar and US$70 for a trip to Black River, although bear in mind the shifting cost of petrol makes prices subject to change.

Everyone with a boat in Treasure Beach is involved in some way with the pursuit of fishing, and it's easy to talk someone into taking you to pull a trap or drop a line. Or you can book a fishing trip at **Jake's Place** (☎ 965-3000; per hour up to 6 people US$60), which includes rods and bait. Fish frequently caught include grouper, kingfish and snapper; most restaurants are happy to prepare them for the night's dinner.

☂ Beaches

Several fishing beaches, all sparsely sprinkled with tourists, beckon within easy walking distance of the accommodations we mention in this chapter. Water sports haven't yet caught on, but the waves are good for bodysurfing. Beware, as sometimes a vicious undertow tugs at area beaches.

Great Bay Beach   SECLUDED BEACH

All the way at the eastern 'bottom' of Treasure Beach you'll find Great Bay, a pretty, rural patchwork of fields and beach; this is the least-developed portion of Treasure Beach, where the main business remains a Fishermen's Co-op building.

Jack Spratt Beach   SWIMMING BEACH

At the western edge of Jake's Place brightly painted wooden fishing boats are pulled up on the sand, and there is invariably a fisherman or two on hand tending the nets. This is the safest beach for swimming.

Frenchman's Beach   SWIMMING BEACH

The next beach to the west is Frenchman's Beach, watched over by a landmark buttonwood tree that has long attracted the attention of poets, painters and woodcarvers who ply their wares. Local boat captains congregate here, as does everyone else in the area once the sun starts to set. It's a great place to arrange trips to the Pelican Bar or Black River.

Calabash Bay Beach   SWIMMING BEACH
In the opposite direction from Jake's Place there's Calabash Bay Beach, with a few cook (food shack) and rum shops and a sandy beach.

Old Wharf Beach   SECLUDED BEACH
The most private of the bunch, although still accessible by anyone who makes the effort to totter down to the sand.

If you head east from Great Bay, across Great Pedro Bluff (it's about a 20-minute walk; ask for directions) you'll discover waves of grassy hills studded with tall cacti, seabirds, very few (if any) people and cowpaths. The sunlight seems to melt into this utterly pastoral coastscape, named by locals **Back Seaside**.

Tours

Every hotel in Treasure Beach can hook you up with their own recommended tour guides. If you prefer to look outside of your accommodations, at Jake's Place a man calling himself simply **Andy** (438-1311) rents bicycles (US$25 per day) and kayaks (US$35 per day) and leads tours (from US$50).

Treasure Tours   SIGHTSEEING TOURS
(965-0126; www.treasuretoursjamaica.com) Does tours all around the south coast and across the island.

Festivals & Events

Jake's Off-Road Triathlon   TRIATHLON
(965-0635; www.jakesoffroadtri.com; Apr or May)

Calabash International Literary Festival   LITERARY
(965-3000; www.calabashfestival.org; late May) A daring, acclaimed literary festival at Jake's Place, drawing literary voices both domestically and internationally. (At the time this book went to press, the festival was in hiatus, but was scheduled to resume 2012. Check the website for updates.)

New Year's Eve Bonfire Party   PARTY
At Fisherman's Beach, this boisterous party is an institution in these parts.

Sleeping

New villa rentals open in Treasure Beach all the time. Some provide bona fide luxury and considerable style, while others are more modest and practical, providing good value for groups or families. Details can be found at www.treasurebeach.net, www.jamaicaes

capes.com and www.treasuretoursjamaica.com. Parking is included at all of the accommodations listed here; prices quoted are high-season rates.

TOP CHOICE Nuestra Casa Guest House   GUEST HOUSE $
(965-0152; www.billysbay.com; d US$50;) Nuestra Casa is just gorgeous; it's a pretty house run by the lovely Roger and his mum Lillian, who together with their Jamaican staff are the epitome of hospitality. Their laid-back property consists of a beautiful arid flora garden built into porous rocks, a wide veranda peppered with rockers and highly personalized rooms kitted out in quirky, individual (yet also intellectual; the books on hand are amazing) decor. It's a tremendous deal at these rates, which decrease for longer stays. Meals are prepared by arrangement.

Jake's Place   HOTEL $$
(965-3000, in the USA 800-688-7678, in the UK 020-7440-4360; www.jakeshotel.com; r from US$150, cottages US$225-450;) If there is a quirky, bohemian-chic center to Treasure Beach's laid-back, community-tourism oriented vibe, it's Jake's Place. Jake's was founded by theater-set designer Sally Henzell, which should tell you a bit about the property: a fantastical mix of rooms, suites, cottages and huts decked out like a fairy-tale illustration book with references to Greece and North Africa; mini *ksars* (Moroccan castles), terra-cotta tile floors, tile and glass-brick walk-in showers, exquisite handmade beds, onion-dome curves, blood-red walls and rough-hewn doors inset with colored bottles and glass beads. The place has grown in dribs and drabs, cottage by cottage, and continues to do so. The exquisite pool – lamplit at night – is shaded by a spreading tree and adjoined by two restaurants and a bar. Local bands perform, moonlight poetry readings are hosted and there are nannies on staff if you have kids.

Marblue Villa Suites   BOUTIQUE HOTEL $$
(840-5772, 848-0001; www.marblue.com; junior ste US$134-160, ste US$180-295;) One of Jamaica's most stylish boutique hotels, this well-run, welcoming property pampers its guests with thoughtful service and considerable streamlined luxury. Five one-bedroom villa suites are appointed with furniture designed by the owners, Axel (architect) and Andrea Wichterich. Each veranda suite

features living areas that open to spectacular views of the sea. The Blue Parrot Tiki Lounge, weekly barbecues, two dramatic pools and superb cuisine round out the offerings. Attracts a bohemian crowd, including many of Kingston's best-regarded artists.

Minerva
VILLA **$$$**

(☎965-3374; www.minervahouse.com; per night for 1-8 people US$700; ☎☒) Minerva is one of the more modern properties we've reviewed, not just in Treasure Beach, but in Jamaica. It feels very much like a trendy Manhattan or Melbourne mansion with its cool white walls, polished-stone floors, monochromatic color scheme and furniture plucked from the drawing board of a painfully hip Scandinavian designer. The pool is lovely for lounging, as is the buttery-golden private beach.

Ital Rest
GUEST HOUSE **$**

(☎421-8909, 473-6145; www.italrest.com; r US$50) In the right setting, a lack of electricity rockets a property right into the super-romantic category. Two exquisite all-wood thatched cabins is the sort of setting we're talking about. Hanging here with the Rasta owners as the sun sets, then retiring to a candlelit room with a loved one for a cool-water shower – good times. All rooms have toilets and the upstairs room has a great sundeck. Kitchen facilities are shared, meals are available by request, and there's a small thatched bar and fantastic herbal steam baths.

Kouros Villa
VILLA **$$$**

(☎965-0126; www.treasuretoursjamaica.com; per week for 4 people US$2500, for additional guests US$250; ☒☎) A slice of Santorini on the south coast of Jamaica, Kouros consists of a whitewashed, Greek Island–style great house clustered over a cliff with roof terrace, sundeck, enclosed courtyard and oodles of romance. The interior is as simple and breezy – yet luxurious – as the digs you'd expect in the most romantic Aegean village. Located about halfway between Frenchman's Beach and Billy's Bay.

Waikiki Guest House
GUEST HOUSE **$**

(☎965-3660, 345-9669; s/d US$25/50) Location, location, location: this excellent budget option literally abuts Frenchman's Beach. The rooms are clean and simple; nothing special and nothing to complain about either. The 2nd-floor double in Waikiki's odd concrete tower (prettier than it sounds) is awesome; you can step out onto a little veranda and watch the sun set into the ocean or stumble right onto Eggy's Bar. Waikiki also has a one-bedroom cottage, two two-story cottages and a small house with three bedrooms and kitchen.

Rainbow Point
VILLA **$$$**

(☎965-0126, in the USA 703-948-0651; www.rainbowtreevillas.com; per week for 4 people US$2400; ☒☎☒) This rather appropriately named private property is a veritable riot of colors, with white rooms set off by pastels and cool blues and purples, making for a playful star-of-your-own-'80s-music-video-shot-in-the-Caribbean kind of energy. There's a sundeck pool with a hell of a view and open porches made for chilling out and enjoying the considerable ocean breeze.

Irie Rest Guesthouse
GUEST HOUSE **$**

(☎965-0034, in the USA 954-708-8127; www.irierestguesthouse.com; Billy's Bay Way; d/q/whole house US$40/50/200; ☒☎) Another excellent budget choice, Irie consists of spacious rooms with tile floors outfitted in Rasta chic, arranged around open courtyards and lush gardens. The entire house can be rented for US$200 a night – a great deal if you're in a big group. Did we mention it's a five-minute walk to the beach?

Viking's Rasta Retreat
GUEST HOUSE **$**

(☎292-7268; info@vikingsrastaretreats.com; r US$35-50) Viking's is as rustic as it gets out here, a collection of slightly tatty rooms with kitchenettes and private bathrooms located on a gravel track near Great Bay. The place has a lot of I-tal character; it's run by serious, religiously observant Rastafarians. As such, staying here can be an excellent means of learning about the deeper layers of Rasta belief. Many folks come here because Viking's can also feel like…being on a particularly Jamaican agricultural homestay, where guests chill out in (very) relaxed silence in Treasure Beach's version of the bush.

Shakespeare Cottage
GUEST HOUSE **$**

(☎965-0120; r US$20-30) Two hundred meters east of the Treasure Beach Hotel, this simple budget option has five rooms with fans and bathrooms with cold water only. There's a communal kitchen. The building itself doesn't have much character, but Shakespeare is popular with backpackers so there's a good social vibe going on.

Golden Sands Beach Hotel
HOTEL **$**

(☎965-0167; www.goldensandstreasurebeach.com; r US$40-50, cottages US$60-80; ☒) Golden

TREASURE BEACH FOUNDATION

The **Treasure Beach Foundation** (☑965-0748, 965-3434; www.breds.org; Kingfisher Plaza) – or Breds (short for brethren) – is dedicated to fostering heritage pride, sports, health and education among the community, and represents a partnership between the Treasure Beach community, expats and stakeholders (Jamaican and foreign) in the local tourism industry. Work includes restoring decrepit housing, sponsorship of both a soccer team and a basketball team, the introduction of computer labs at local schools and education for the children of fishers lost at sea.

Sands is one of the few traditional hotels in Treasure Beach, and could be a good choice for those who don't like the intimacy of sharing a guest house, or the length of time needed to book a villa or private house. Rooms vary; some have ceiling fans, others boast sea views, while one- and three-bedroom cottages come with air-con and TV, but they're all clean and quite serviceable.

Bay Villa   VILLA **$**
(☑837-0430; bayvillaja@yahoo.com; d per night US$50, 8 people per week US$1200) This pleasant red-roofed house is in as central a location as you can get in Treasure Beach, across from the Kingfisher Plaza and a quick jaunt to the beach. Rooms are standard Jamaican: tiled floors, clean walls, chintzy furniture and friendly staff if you need someone to help organize more trips in the area.

Treasure Beach Hotel   HOTEL **$**
(☑965-0114; www.jamaicatreasurebeachhotel.com; d US$80-100; ❄️🛏️) This rambling property dotted with palms and nestled on a hillside overlooking the beach has a good variety of midrange-quality rooms, including spacious, deluxe oceanfront suites that have king-size four-poster beds and breezy patios. The Yabba Restaurant is on the premises, and the front desk can hook you up with a good range of tours and activities across the region.

✖️ Eating

TOP CHOICE **Strikey's**   JAMAICAN **$**
(Billy's Bay; mains J$400-800; ⊘dinner, closed summer) The energetic, ever-friendly Chris Strikey has worked as a professional chef in the US and at Jake's Place, but when the tourist season rolls around (roughly December to April), Strikey operates his own food shack, anchored by secret recipes and a hand-built jerk smoker. The man's food is sublime; Jamaican favorites, home-cooked and mouth-watering, especially the jerk. This stuff is elegantly spiced with a fair kick of heat, just enough to create a gorgeous complexity of flavor.

Jack Sprat Café   FUSION **$$**
(mains US$7-20; ⊘10am-11pm) An excellent barefoot beachside eatery affiliated with Jake's Place, this appealing joint features vintage reggae posters, an old jukebox and a lively bar scene that spills onto the tree-shaded patio and Christmas-light-bedecked garden area. There's a diverse menu of Jamaican and Western standards: salads, crab cakes, smoked marlin, conch curry and lobster as well as excellent jerk or garlic shrimp. But for our money it's all about the pizza, quite possibly the best on the island; the jerk sausage topping in particular elicits audible moans of pleasure from satisfied customers. Takes credit cards.

Potsnapper Restaurant   JAMAICAN **$**
(mains J$400-1000; ⊘breakfast, lunch & dinner) Supplied by a steady flow of fresh fish from the morning's catch, this pleasant roadside eatery serves up Jamaican standards – brown stews, goat curry and the like – in a laid-back setting. It's decent, filling Jamaican home cooking.

Jake's Place   FUSION **$$**
(mains US$5-27; ⊘breakfast, lunch & dinner; 🖉) This atmospheric spot serves excellent fare in an open-sided wooden restaurant with low lighting and hip music (you can also dine poolside on the patio out back). The menu shifts daily based on what's growing in the local gardens and what's fresh from the market. Jake's is friendly to vegetarians, although meat eaters will be equally at home; typical dishes include pumpkin soup, baked lamb, stuffed crab and chocolate cake for dessert.

Smurf's Cafe   JAMAICAN **$**
(meals J$300-700; ⊘breakfast, lunch & dinner) Smurf's (look for the namesake blue fairies

on the side of the building, between French-man's and Billy's Bay) is popular with locals and tourists, who pop in for home-cooked Jamaican favorites. Of particular note are the baked goods, pastries and (oh my good-ness) the coffee – fresh roasted and brewed by hand on site, it's the best rocket fuel on Treasure Beach.

Pardy's CAFE $
(mains J$300-500; ✆breakfast & lunch) On the main road across from Waikiki Guest House, Pardy's does some delicious breakfast and lunch-style fare; light sandwiches as the day beats on, and lovely callaloo omelets plus pancakes and French toast served with gen-erous helpings of homemade honey in the morning. The fresh juice goes down a treat too.

🍷 Drinking & Entertainment

At night, Treasure Beach appears like a sleepy place, but local bars party late into the night until the last person leaves. Jake's Place has an infamous poolside cocktail hour, while Jack Sprat Café hosts small con-certs, poetry readings and outdoor movies.

TOP CHOICE **Pelican Bar** BAR
(Caribbean Sea; ✆morning-sunset) The Pelican Bar may be Jamaica's most famous spot for a drink: a thatched hut built on a submerged sandbar 1km out to sea, where you can chill with a Red Stripe while watching dolphins flip in the surf a few meters away. This eat-ery on stilts provides Jamaica's – and per-haps the planet's – most enjoyable spot for a drink. Getting there is half the fun: hire a local boat captain (most charge around US$35), who will call ahead to arrange things if you want to eat. This is essential for those who want to take a meal out here (mains are US$5 to US$15), which is novel but frankly not necessary – you'll get better food on land. We recommend coming here for the beer (or rum, if such is your fancy). The clientele is a mix of enchanted travel-ers and repeat-business fishers who while away the hours playing dominoes, talking on their cell phones, checking the cricket scores or exchanging pleasantries with the self-satisfied owner. In between Red Stripes, or perhaps before your meal of lob-ster, shrimp or fish, feel free to slip into the water for a dip.

Eggy's Bar BAR
Off the main road by Frenchman's Bay, Eggy's is the place to go at sunset; every-one in Treasure Beach, tourists, locals and tourists alike gather here to drink beer, watch the sunset and pass around torpedo-sized spliffs.

Fisherman's Nightclub NIGHTCLUB
Up a dirt road near Jake's Place, with a wooden bar in front where everyone plays dominoes and sips Red Stripe. On some nights sound-system parties go off, attract-ing local youth and selectors (DJs).

Wild Onion NIGHTCLUB
Located in Frenchman's Bay, it attracts a mix of locals and visitors with its spacious dance floor and pool tables.

🛍 Shopping

One of the best craft stores is on the front lawn at Jake's Place, and Kingfisher Plaza is a small shopping center where you can buy essential sundries.

Treasure Beach Women's Group CRAFTS
(☑965-0748; thcs8@yahoo.com; Kingfisher Plaza; ✆9am-3pm Mon-Fri, till 1pm Sat) A wide range of gifts are sold here, including batiks, crafts made from calabash shells and other natural materials, swimwear, sandals and coffee.

ℹ Information

For information online, a good starting point is www.treasurebeach.net. There are no banks serving international travelers here, but there is a 24-hour Scotiabank ATM in Crossroads, 5km north of Treasure Beach.

Breds (☑965-9748;Kingfisher Plaza; per 30min J$200; ✆9am-5pm) Provides internet access.

Dr Valerie M Elliott (☑607-9074; ✆7am-10pm Mon, Tue & Fri) Available on call.

Police station (☑965-0163) Between Cala-bash Bay and Pedro Cross.

ℹ Getting There & Around

There is no direct service to Treasure Beach from Montego Bay, Negril or Kingston. Jake's Place is now served by it's own aerodrome. It's hoped that the building will eventually take public domestic flights, but for now only private charters are landing there – contact Jake's directly for information on fares, and expect them to run for at least a few hundred US dollars.

PUBLIC TRANSPORTATION From Black River you can connect to Treasure Beach via route taxi or minibus (J$200). From Mandeville, you'll need to get a route taxi to Junction or Santa

MALVERN

Straddling the Santa Cruz Mountains at a refreshing 730m, the pretty hamlet of Malvern is located at the end of a dramatic looping 24km drive northeast from Treasure Beach. Years ago Malvern was favored as a summer resort for its temperate climate; today it's an agricultural and educational center.

Much of the appeal of Malvern is its physical beauty, but the town is also notable for historical roots that tend to run under many visitors' radar. In the 18th century these uplands were an important center for coffee cultivation. Sugar estates were absent and the harsh plantation system never took hold. Following emancipation, newly freed slaves settled as independent farmers and continued to grow coffee. In later years citrus farms became important, and cattle now grow fat on the lush pastures. Bauxite mining near Mandeville and Santa Cruz has brought further, much-evident prosperity to the region.

Malvern is dominated by the cream-colored **Hampton College** (a girls' school founded in 1858), about 1km south of Malvern Sq, the village center. **Munro College**, a boys' school founded in 1856, is 6km further south. Each school consists of several buildings, all remarkably well preserved, which lend an elegant, Oxbridge-style accent to these hills.

Cruz (J$150) and another taxi to Treasure Beach (J$200).

PRIVATE TAXI A private taxi will run around US$20 from Black River and US$40 to US$50 from Mandeville. Most hotels and villas arrange transfers from Montego Bay for US$80 to US$100 (up to four people) and can help with car and motorcycle rental, which is quite popular here.

SELF-DRIVE From Black River, take the A2 to Santa Cruz and turn south; follow the many signs to Jack Sprat's.

WALKING It takes about 30 minutes to walk from Jake's Place to Billy's Bay; and 30 minutes to get from Great Bay to Jake's Place.

Lover's Leap

The Santa Cruz Mountains don't tend to slope very gently into the coast even at their most gentle, but at **Lover's Leap** (965-6577; admission US$3; 10am-6pm), 1.5km southeast of Southfield, they positively plunge over 500m into the ocean. This headland provides a very photogenic, end-of-the-world-esque view, and is tipped by a red-and-white-hooped solar-powered **lighthouse**.

Far below, waves crash on jagged rocks and wash onto **Cutlass Beach**. You can hike with a guide (US$20 per group) in these parts: it's a stiff one-hour trek down to the bottom, made more difficult by the mocking stare of herds of smug mountain goats.

Lover's Leap is named for two young slaves who supposedly committed suicide here in 1747. Legend says the woman was lusted after by her owner, who arranged for her lover to be sold to another estate. When the couple heard of the plot, they fled and were eventually cornered at the cliffs, where they chose to plunge to their deaths. The power of this heartbreaking story is not diminished by the children's play area, souvenir shop, small museum and restaurant that have been set up at the spot where they made their sacrifice.

On the road to the site, **Lover's Leap Guesthouse** (965-6004; r US$20-35;) offers well-appointed rooms, some with Jacuzzis, and a small restaurant serving simple meals and snacks.

Alligator Pond

Jamaica is a huge holiday destination for foreigners, but where do Jamaicans go when they want to chill out? Well, if you're from Kingston or the surrounding area, you may very likely drive over to Alligator Pond, hidden at the foot of a valley between two steep spurs of the Santa Cruz and Don Figuerero mountains. This is about as far from packaged-for-foreigners tourism as you can get in Jamaica, but it's got an offbeat Jamaican vacation vibe that's tough not to love.

The hamlet is set behind a deep-blue bay backed by dunes. The main street is smothered in wind-blown sand. Each morning, local women gather on the dark-sand beach to haggle over the catch – delivered by fishers, whose colorful old pirogues line the long shore. Local youths surf wooden planks.

The **Sandy Cays**, about 32km offshore, are lined with white-sand beaches. The snorkeling and scuba diving are good at **Alligator Reef**, about a 20-minute boat ride from shore; you'll need to organize an outing with a local boat captain, who'll likely charge around US$30 to US$40 for the experience. But the main reason to come here is for quite possibly the best dining experience in Jamaica.

TOP CHOICE **Little Ochie** (☑965-4449; www .littleochie.com; mains J$800-2000; ☺8am until last guest leaves) is *the* place to eat in Alligator Pond, if not the island. Since 1989 Evrol 'Blackie' Christian has been running this seafood mecca on the beach with verve, style and an uncompromising commitment to quality, even as his little operation has grown from food shack to veritable culinary beachside extravaganza. Little Ochie, how we love thee; let us count the ways: 1) the setting, wooden tables and chairs shaded by a thatch roof on the beach (not by the beach, mind you; *on* the beach), including some built into thatched-roof old boats raised on stilts. The same boats that pull up on the beach with their catch before you go inside to place your order – name your fish and exactly how you want it cooked. Which brings us to 2) the fish, and any other supporting cast members of *The Little Mermaid*, all chopped, steamed, fried, stewed, and curried into blissfully delicious concoctions. Specialties include fish tea, curried conch, roast fish, lobster prepared seven different ways, and aphrodisiac tonics such as 'Stallion Punch.' You may think you've had escoveitch and jerk fish before you came to Little Ochie, but in reality you've only had pale echoes of this, the 'platonic ideal' of Jamaican seafood.

If you need to stay out here, try the **Sea-Riv Hotel** (☑450-1356, 360-7609; r US$25-40; ☐☒), on the black-sand beach next to a river mouth. There are 18 appealing, fan-cooled rooms, water sports and many in-the-know guides. The other hotel here, **Venus Sunset Lounge & Accommodation** (☑965-4508; r US$25), is nothing to write home about (spartan rooms, cold water), but works in a pinch.

West of Alligator Pond you may see the cranes of **Port Kaiser**, one of the major bauxite shipping ports on the island. Near the port is the **Kaiser Sports Ground**, a cricket pitch where, during the second week of January, the **Rebel Salute** (www.myspace

.com/rebelsalute) goes off. This is one of Jamaica's leading roots reggae festivals; there's (technically) no booze or meat as it is supposed to be strictly I-tal. Expect lots of excellent music, an all-night dance party and the usual aerosol flamethrowers.

Minibuses and route taxis operate between Alligator Pond and the Beckford St transportation center in Kingston (about J$500), and from Mandeville via Gutters (about J$400). Hotels and guest houses in Treasure Beach usually offer 'tours' to Little Ochie for around US$50 round-trip.

Long Bay

Drive east of Alligator Pond and you are entering the polar opposite of the well-developed, hotel-studded north coast. Instead, here you will find 24km of wild coast, undeveloped and unvisited but for a few recreational fishers and hermits. The small ribbons of sand are hemmed in by mountains and mangroves, a nirvana for bird-watchers that remains unexplored by many Jamaicans, let alone tourists. There are crocodiles, too, and endangered manatees gently cruising the swamps. Sadly, some herders graze cattle here, which have invaded the wetlands and introduced exotic species of flora, and locals continue to kill marine turtles that come ashore to lay eggs.

The area is uninhabited, largely because the road that stretches along it is known as a 'lonely road,' broken by rockfalls and potholes and, according to local lore, haunted by duppies and bandits. There used to be a settlement here at **Gut River**, 10km east of Alligator Pond, but the town is now abandoned save for (at time of writing) one lone hermit. Here a mineral spring emerges from a deep cleft and feeds a pond where the occasional flash reveals mullet and big crabs 6m down. The pool grows more shallow toward its mouth, where the water is trapped behind a sandspit that hides a lonely red-sand beach. It's tempting to swim here, but beware strong riptides; no one will be around to save you.

Long Bay extends to Alligator Hole, also known as the Canoe Valley Wetland (see p77), a stupefyingly beautiful spot where you can spy manatees. Past here is a sinkhole known as **God's Well**, which drops to a cave at about 50m. If you thought the lonely road through Long Bay was ghostly, wait till you come to this place, with its palpable air of isolation. You can get here by taking an unmarked inland path about 200m from Milk River. Scuba divers occasionally test the waters, but there are no local dive outfits that provide guides or rent equipment; as such, God's Well is for experienced divers only – the first diver to tackle it died. Bring a buddy, as attempting God's Well solo is folly.

Some divers have been known to do the 'Suicide Run,' a 3km swim to the ocean through the seemingly impenetrable swamps. Yes, the chance of bumping into a crocodile is very real, but locals advise:

'Dem alligators no problem, mon...Dem coward. 'Im see you come close, mon, 'im swim fast, fast can go!'

At the time of writing no public taxis plied this road, which was in awful condition. A 4WD is highly recommended; if you come in a 2WD, go slow. We can't speak to duppies, but we heard enough stories about bandits to suggest that driving this road would be a bad idea at night. In any case the road is so rough that driving in the dark would be a terrifying proposition.

Understand
Jamaica

Jamaica Today

Trouble in Paradise

Jamaicans tend to be passionate people. Their full-bore approach to life is what often attracts and sometimes intimidates visitors to their island. You will see this energy manifest itself in countless ways; in loud laughter, loud music, loud church revivals... What we're saying is 'quiet' is a relative term in Jamaica. And to be fair, it's hard to be subdued when you live on an island so beautiful it's been mistaken by explorers for Eden, where things like music and generosity and smiles that take in the eyes are commonplace.

Yet that same island is a troubled paradise. The easiest way to hear angry patois is to talk politics with a Jamaican; most, including deceptively laid-back Rastas, have well-crafted and informed opinions on current affairs in Jamaica, and even the optimistic ones have their gripes. Jamaica faces many challenges: 20% illiteracy, 35% teen pregnancy, almost half of young women reporting sexual violence or coercion and 1428 reported murders in 2010. Jamaica's citizens are patriotic, but the high hopes and promise they hold for their home are often balanced out by tension, even anxiety, over the future.

Reggae has long been one of the most identifiable elements of the Jamaican brand. Locals and outsiders have understandably tied its rhythms and beats to sun, sand and relaxation. But Bob Marley's timeless message of 'One Love' was topically addressed at factions that were gunning each other down in the streets of Kingston in the 1970s. The powerful message of hope reggae music imparts is rooted in deep national trauma.

Jamaica is a poor but not destitute island (it ranked 80th out of 168 on the 2010 UNDP's Human Development Index), yet at the time of writing, 85% of Jamaicans with a post high-school degree were expected to

» Population:
2.86 million

» GDP:
US$23.93
billion

» GDP per
capita:
US$8400

» Public debt:
123% of GDP

» Inflation rate:
13%

» Unemploy-
ment rate: 13%

Top Films

» **The Harder They Come** (1972) A classic rags-to-rude bwai (rude boy) story of country boy turned Kingston criminal. One of the best soundtracks in film history.

» **Smile Orange** (1976) A hilarious tale of a waiter hustling tourists at Jamaican resorts.

» **Life and Debt** (2001) A powerful documentary on the impact of globalization on the Jamaican economy.

Patois Proverbs

» **Chicken deh merry, hawk deh near** 'Danger stalks those having fun.' Remember when walking home at night!

» **Rockstone a riva bottom cyaan noh sun hot** 'You learn from experience.' Leave the resort!

belief systems
(% of population)

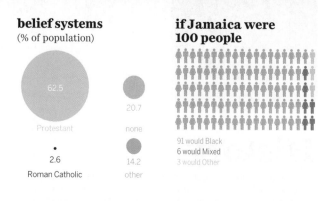

62.5
Protestant

20.7
none

2.6
Roman Catholic

14.2
other

if Jamaica were 100 people

91 would Black
6 would Mixed
3 would Other

emigrate. This is not entirely negative, as remittances now form the largest sector of the economy. But the fact remains: many of Jamaica's most talented citizens are not choosing to stay in Jamaica.

On this island there are as many opinions on how to fix things as there are Jamaicans. Travelers, however, remain well regarded by the average Jamaican. Tourism is the second-largest industry here, testament to the fact that despite the challenges, Jamaicans are determined to share their island with the world.

'Time langa dan rope.'

Huh? Let us translate: time longer than rope (welcome, by the way, to the wonderful world of Jamaican patois). 'Time langa dan rope' is a Jamaican proverb that contains much of the black humor, resilience and resignation that characterizes modern Jamaica. In a sense, Time langa dan rope means things will improve, that perseverance pays off, that there's a light at the end of the tunnel. But the grim imagery of the rope, that visceral symbol of death and/or captivity, comes straight from the island's hard history.

Jamaica doesn't allow for easy answers. On the bright side, the nation has embarked on a debt exchange program that politicians anticipate will spare the economy billions of dollars. Around 84% of school-age children are enrolled in primary school. And the island's beauty and unique cultural position is undeniable; even the most cynical Jamaicans acknowledge their home is worth fighting for. But at the grassroots level are thousands running their small businesses, farming small plots and hawking their CDs to make their lives, and often, the lives of those around them, a little better.

» Guided snorkeling trip US$30 (J$2550)

» Rio Grande raft trip US$65 (J$5525)

» Fresh fish in a touristy restaurant US$15 (J$1275)

» Fresh fish in a local restaurant US$5 (J$425)

» Red Stripe US$4 (J$340)

Best Books

» **Lionheart Gal** (1986) A lively short-story collection that reveals much about patois and the lives of women.

» **White Witch of Rose Hall** (1928) Herbert de Lisser's classic gothic horror, set in colonial Jamaica.

Dos & Don'ts

» Do be formal with strangers. Address people you meet with 'Mr' or 'Miss,' or even 'Sir' or 'Ma'am.'

» Do relax. 'Soon come' is a favorite expression that means 'it'll happen when it happens.'

» Do ask before snapping a photo. Many Jamaicans enjoy being photographed, sometimes for a small fee, but others prefer not to pose for tourists.

» Don't ignore beggars, hustlers or higglers, as it will be taken as an insult. Offer a firm but polite 'sorry' or 'no thank you.'

History

> Out of the past of fire and suffering and neglect, the human spirit
> has survived – patient and strong, quick to anger, quick to forgive,
> lusty and vigorous, but with deep reserves of loyalty and love and
> a deep capacity for steadiness under stress and for joy in all the
> things that make life good and blessed.
> Norman Manley, Jamaica's first prime minister

At first glance, Jamaica's colonial past seems much like that of many
other countries in New World: conquest, settlement, plantocracy. From
the arrival of the Spanish in the 16th century to the present day, the
island's history has been marred with conflict and violence. The enslavement and subsequent demise of Jamaica's original inhabitants, the
peaceful Taínos, led to the establishment of an efficient plantation-based
economic system underpinned by the Atlantic slave trade, with Jamaica
becoming Britain's most prized Crown colony.

The very harshness of slavery become the catalyst for fierce resistance
from slaves, which ranged from disobedience to fight and flight. Again, it
was slavery that paved the way for independence by giving rise to a large
mulatto population, whose clamor for the same rights as their white forebears would not be silenced. Black consciousness and a fierce pride was
born of this pre-independence turbulence, affecting the world over.

It is the legacy of those 300 years that divides the island still, the color
lines still drawn (though less so in the music industry), and with post-independence discontent leading the have-nots to turn upon each other. Yet the
passion and the perseverance of the Jamaican people, which have made
the island and its culture so vital, lead you to imagine a brighter future.

Xaymaca

An Amerindian group, the Arawakan-speaking Taínos, settled the island
around AD 700 to 800. The Taínos are believed to have originated in

*The Story of the
Jamaican People
by Philip Sherlock
and Hazel Ben-
nett offers a new
interpretation of
Jamaica's history
that eschews the
imperial perspec-
tive, instead
looking to Africa
for the keys to
understanding
the island's
complex culture.*

AFRICA

TIMELINE	1494	1503	1511
	Christopher Columbus first lands on Jamaica, which he names Santa Jago; it later becomes his personal property.	Columbus returns to Jamaica for the fourth time, convinced he can forge a passage to Asia. However, his decrepit ships are ruined and he and his party become stranded.	Portuguese settle in Jamaica under the protection of Columbus' descendants.

the Amazon Basin of South America perhaps 2000 years earlier. After developing seafaring skills, they gradually moved north through the Caribbean island chain.

Their communal villages were made up of several family clans, which were headed by a *cacique* (chief). Subsistence farmers to the core, the women gathered food while the men tilled the fields, hunted and fished. Jamaica's fertile soils yielded yams, maize, beans, spices and cassava, which the Taínos leached of poison and baked into cakes and fermented into beer. They called the island 'Xaymaca,' meaning 'land of wood and water.'

Having neither the wheel nor a written language, the Taínos did not use beasts of burden or metals (except for crude gold ornamentation). They honed skills as potters, carvers, weavers and boat builders. (Columbus was impressed with the scale of their massive canoes hewn from silk cotton trees.) They were particularly adept at spinning and weaving cotton into clothing and hammocks – the latter an Amerindian invention.

For recreation, the Taínos got fired up with maize alcohol, smoked dried leaves and snorted a powdered drug through a meter-long tube they called a *tabaco*. They worshipped a variety of gods believed to control rain, sun, wind and hurricanes, and who were represented by *zemes*, idols of humans or animals.

Columbus & Spanish Settlement

Christopher Columbus landed on the island in 1494 on the second of his four voyages to the New World. Anchoring offshore in Bahía Santa Gloria (modern-day St Ann's Bay), he sailed down the coast to a horseshoe-shaped cove (Discovery Bay), where he had his men fire crossbows at a group of Taínos that failed to welcome him. Columbus claimed the island for Spain and christened it Santo Jago. The Taínos soon reappeared with peace offerings and feasted the strange newcomers throughout their brief stay.

In 1503 Columbus returned on his fourth and final voyage, still hell-bent on finding that elusive passage to Asia. Unfortunately, his worm-eaten ships were falling apart and he barely made it to Bahía Santa Gloria. Columbus and his 120 crew were forced to abandon ship and watch both vessels sink.

The hapless explorers spent almost a year marooned (p135) and suffered from disease and malnutrition. Finally, two officers paddled a canoe 240km to Hispaniola, where they chartered a ship to rescue the now broken explorer and his men.

Jamaica became Columbus' personal property and when he died in 1506 it passed to his son Diego, whose direct descendant Don Cristobal Colón de Carvajal y de Gorosabel carries the honorary title of Marquis of

The Killing Time: The Morant Bay Rebellion in Jamaica by Gad Heuman explores the roots and the political aftermath of the rebellion that was brutally suppressed by the British authorities.

Visit the ruins of the first Spanish settlement on the island at the Maima Seville Great House near St Ann's Bay.

1517	1643	1655	1670
The Spanish bring enslaved West Africans to do their bidding on the island in place of the Taínos, whose population has been decimated by European disease and appalling treatment.	Jamaica is sacked by English pirate William Jackson, raising doubt about the security of the Spanish colony.	The English capture Jamaica from the Spanish, who retreat to Cuba.	At the Treaty of Madrid, the Spanish cede Jamaica to the English. Both nations agree to cease trading in each other's territories.

Jamaica to this day. Diego appointed as governor one of his father's lieutenants, Don Juan de Esquivel, who established a capital called Nueva Sevilla (New Seville) near present-day Ocho Rios.

From their arrival the Spaniards had exacted tribute from the Taínos, whom they enslaved and killed off through hard labor and ill-treatment. European diseases decimated the Amerindians too, for they had no resistance to the common cold and influenza. By Esquivel's time, the Taíno population had been virtually wiped out. To replenish the labor pool, in 1517 the Spaniards began importing slaves from West Africa.

In 1534 the Spanish uprooted and created a new settlement on the south coast, Villa de la Vega (Spanish Town). However, the Spaniards never developed the colony and it languished as a post for provisioning ships en route between Spain and Central America.

The English Invasion

On May 10, 1655, an expeditionary force of 38 ships landed 8000 troops on weakly-defended Jamaica as part of Oliver Cromwell's 'Grand Western Design' to destroy the Spanish trade monopoly and amass English holdings in the Caribbean. The Spaniards retreated north over the mountains, from where they set sail to Cuba.

The *cimarrones* (runaways) – freed slaves left in the Spaniards' wake – took to the hills, where they mastered the tactics of guerrilla warfare and fiercely defended their freedom. A small band of Spanish loyalists under General Cristobal Ysassi also fought a guerrilla war against the English with less success. The decisive battle at Rio Bueno (outside Ocho Rios) in 1660 was won by the English under Colonel Edward D'Oyley.

In December 1656 some 1600 English arrived to settle the area around Port Morant near the eastern tip of Jamaica. The region proved too swampy: within a year, three-quarters of the settlers had succumbed to disease. Other settlers fared better, resettling in Port Royal and making it the island's capital, and a viable trading economy began to evolve.

By 1662 there were 4000 colonists on the island, including exiled felons as well as impoverished Scots and Welshmen who arrived as indentured laborers. Settlement hastened as profits began to accrue from cocoa, coffee and sugarcane production.

The Age of the Buccaneers

Throughout the 17th century Britain was constantly at war with France, Spain or Holland. The English sponsored privateers to capture enemy vessels, raid their settlements and contribute their plunder to the Crown's coffers. These 'buccaneers' (from *boucan,* a French word for smoked meat, as they used to hunt wild cattle before turning to the high seas) evolved as a motley band of seafaring miscreants, ex-slaves,

SHARPE

Before his execution on May 23, 1832, Sam Sharpe is quoted as saying 'I would rather die upon yonder gallows than live in slavery.'

1692

Port Royal slides into the harbor after an earthquake. More than 2000 people die.

1693

Kingston is officially founded. It was previously known as Hog Crawle on account of the small pig-raising settlement in the area.

JERRY ALEXANDER/LONELY PLANET IMAGES ©

1700

There are more than five slaves for every English settler on Jamaica. The practice of slavery creates enormous economic bounty for the English, at terrible cost to the enslaved.

» Kingston

heretics, political refugees and escaped criminals. They became the Brethren of the Coast, committed to a life of piracy, and grew into a powerful and ruthless force, feared throughout the Antilles – even by their English sponsors.

Initially, the newly appointed governor of Jamaica, Sir Thomas Modyford, joined with the Spanish in attempts to suppress the buccaneers. But the outbreak of the Second Dutch War against Holland and Spain in March 1664 forced England to rethink its policy. Modyford contrived for the Brethren to defend Jamaica. They left their island of Tortuga, and Port Royal became their base. Their numbers swelled astronomically, and within a decade Port Royal was Jamaica's largest city – a den of iniquity and prosperity.

With England at peace with Spain, buccaneers were now regarded merely as pirates. Mother Nature lent a hand in their suppression when a

Jamaica National Heritage Trust (www.jnht.com) provides a guide to Jamaica's history and heritage, covering all sites of importance on the island.

JAMAICA'S NATIONAL HEROES

Jamaica has its equivalent of George Washington and Joan of Arc – individuals deemed worthy of special status as national heroes, earning the honorific title 'the Right Excellent'. There are seven national heroes:

» Paul Bogle (d 1865) staged a protest in Morant Bay in 1865 that spun out of control and became the Morant Bay Rebellion.

» Alexander Bustamante (1884–1977) was a firebrand trade unionist and founder of the Jamaica Labour Party, who became the independent nation's first prime minister (1962–67).

» Marcus Garvey (1887–1940) is considered the father of 'black power' and was named Jamaica's first national hero in 1980.

» George William Gordon (1820–65), a mixed-race lawyer, assemblyman and post-emancipation nationalist, was a powerful advocate of nationalism and the rights of the poor.

» Norman Manley (1893–1969) founded the People's National Party, fought for political reform and became the self-governing island's first prime minister (1959–62), prior to independence.

» Nanny (dates unknown) was a leader of the Windward Maroons in the 18th century. Folklore attributes her with magical powers.

» Sam 'Daddy' Sharpe (1801–32), a town slave and Baptist deacon, was hanged by British authorities for his role in leading the 1831 slave rebellion that engulfed the western parishes.

» Curiously, the world's most famous Jamaican is not among this venerable pantheon, though a movement is afoot to confer National Hero status on Robert Nesta Marley (1945–1981).

1720	1760	1814	1834
Notorious pirate 'Calico Jack' Rackham is executed in Port Royal, his body hung in a cage above Rackham Cay.	Tacky, a runaway slave, starts an uprising in St Mary that is brutally suppressed with the aid of the local Maroons.	Jamaican sugar production peaks at £34 million. During the latter half of the 18th century and the first half of the 19th, Jamaica is the world's largest producer of sugar.	Slavery is abolished throughout the British Empire, causing economic chaos in Jamaica.

massive earthquake struck Port Royal on June 7, 1692, toppling much of the city into the sea. More than 2000 people – one-third of the Port Royal population – perished and many survivors fled to Kingston, believing the earthquake to be punishment from God.

The Slave Trade

Meanwhile, Jamaica's English planters grew immensely wealthy from sugar, and English merchants from the sordid market in slaves. Wrenched from the Ashanti, Coromantee, Mandingo and Yoruba tribes of West Africa, they were bought from African slave traders and shipped across the Atlantic to Kingston, where they were auctioned off. Of the

THE PIRATE JEWS OF PORT ROYAL

Though the history of the pirate capital gives preference to tales of flamboyant cut-throats such as Blackbeard, who went into battle wearing flaming fuses in his matted beard, and 'Calico Jack' Rackham, with a weakness for calico underwear and carousing, without the likes of Bartholomew the Portuguese and Moses Cohen Henriques, Port Royal would not have even existed.

Since 1511 hidden Jews (see p262) lived in Jamaica as traders under the protection of Columbus' descendants, out of the long reach of the Spanish Inquisition. When wealthy Spanish planters began to clamor for the Spanish Crown's takeover of the island, thus threatening Portuguese lives, the latter, through their contacts in London, promised Oliver Cromwell their support in the English takeover of Jamaica in 1655.

In 1643 Bartholomew the Portuguese assisted the English pirate William Jackson with the sacking of Jamaica. After capturing a Spanish ship off the coast of Cuba he was caught by Spanish men-of-war but escaped overboard, using two empty wine jars as water wings. Having borrowed another ship, he recaptured his original booty – only for the ship to be wrecked in a storm. He returned to Port Royal penniless, in a canoe.

Port Royal grew fabulously wealthy due to the joint efforts of Jewish traders and brigands. The former outfitted the plunderers' ships and used their insider knowledge, gathered from their Jewish merchant contacts in other colonies, to guide the pirates to the most profitable pickings.

A ruthless young Welshman, Henry Morgan pillaged Spanish towns throughout the Americas before sacking Panama City. One of his advisors was Moses Cohen Henriques, a Jewish pirate born in Amsterdam who became a fearless soldier and spy for the Dutch navy, enabling their plunder of the Spanish silver fleet in 1628 and the capture of the Portuguese colony of Recife, Brazil, in 1630. Henriques settled in Port Royal in 1654.

Once Henry Morgan became lieutenant governor of Jamaica and a wealthy land-owner in his own right, he put an end to privateering. Henriques and other buccaneers 'retired', accepting a pardon and a grant of land in exchange for giving up their trade; those who didn't were sent to the gallows.

1845	1865	1872	1891
To fill the labor gap left by the abolition of slavery, 30,000 Indians are brought to Jamaica as indentured laborers.	The Morant Bay Rebellion, led by Paul Bogle, is brutally suppressed by the British authorities.	The administrative capital of Jamaica is moved from Spanish Town to Kingston, the port city outstripping the former in importance.	The Great Exhibition is held in Kingston, drawing over 300,000 visitors – the largest attendance of its time in proportion to the local population.

estimated 11 million slaves who survived the trans-Atlantic crossing, around 1.5 million ended up in Jamaica.

The 'Middle Passage' across the Atlantic lasted anywhere from six to 12 weeks. In cramped and festering holds, many died of disease. Those who survived the voyage were made more presentable and oiled to make them appear healthy before being auctioned. Bidders paid between £25 and £75 for unskilled slaves, perhaps £300 or more for those trained as carpenters or blacksmiths, and no more than a shilling for the most wretched.

From Kingston, slaves were re-exported to other Caribbean islands. The slave ships then returned to England carrying cargoes of sugar, molasses and rum.

Maroon Resistance

By the end of the 17th century Jamaica was also under siege from within. The first major slave rebellion occurred in 1690 in Clarendon parish, where many slaves escaped and joined the descendants of slaves who had been freed by the Spanish in 1655 and had eventually coalesced into two powerful bands (called Maroons, from the Spanish word *cimarrón*): one in the remote Blue Mountains and one in the almost impenetrable Cockpit Country of southern Trelawny, from where they raided plantations and attracted runaway slaves. The eastern community became known as the Windward Maroons; those further west were called Leeward Maroons.

In 1729 the English launched the First Maroon War offensive to eradicate the Maroons. The thickly forested mountains, however, were ill-suited to English-style open warfare and the Maroons had perfected ambush-style guerrilla fighting. Nonetheless, after a decade of costly campaigning, the English gained the upper hand.

The belief that the Maroons fought for the freedom of every black slave is a mistaken one: on March 1, 1739, Colonel Guthrie and Cudjoe, the leader of the Maroons of Cockpit Country, signed a peace treaty granting the Maroons autonomy and 1500 acres of land. In return, the Maroons agreed to chase down runaway slaves and return them to the plantations and to assist the English in quelling rebellions.

The Maroons of the Blue Mountains, under a leader named Quao, signed a similar treaty one year later.

Mavis Campbell's *The Maroons of Jamaica* is a serious study of the origins of the Maroons and their evolution as a culture through to the late-19th century.

A Planters' Plutocracy

During the course of the 18th century Jamaica became the largest sugar producer in the world. The island was jointly ruled by a governor (appointed by the English monarch) and an elected assembly of planters. Jamaica was divided into 13 parishes; today there are 14, including Kingston. The Crown's interests at the parish level were looked after by an appointed custos (the Crown's local representative).

1904	1907	1915	1930
Numerous skilled workers from Jamaica head to Panama to assist with the building of the Panama Canal.	A great earthquake topples much of Kingston on January 14, causing widespread destruction and killing more than 800 people.	Hurricanes devastate the island, and again during 1916 and 1917, natural disasters that compound the hardships being experienced as a result of the demise of trade during WWI.	Haile Selassie is crowned emperor of Ethiopia, encouraging the rise of Rastafarianism in Jamaica.

The planters built sturdy 'great houses' in Georgian fashion high above their cane fields. Many planters were absentee landlords who lived most of the year in England, where they formed a powerful political lobby. In Jamaica the planters lived a life of indolence, with retinues of black servants. Many over-indulged in drink and had sexual relations with slaves – some of the mulatto offspring were freed; known as 'free coloreds,' they were accorded special rights and often sent to study in Europe.

The economic and political life of the times was an exclusively male arena. The planters' wives spent much of their time playing cards, arranging balls and socializing, while the day-to-day care of their children was undertaken by wet nurses, who were often female slaves.

The planter Thomas Thistlewood's diary, *In Miserable Slavery*, paints a graphic picture of Jamaican plantation life.

In Miserable Slavery

By 1700 there were perhaps 7000 English and 40,000 slaves in Jamaica. A century later, the number of whites had tripled and they ruled over 300,000 slaves. Tens of thousands were worked to death, many building factories, houses and roads; most working on plantations; others were domestic servants.

During their few free hours, the slaves cultivated their own tiny plots, allocated by the planters. On Sunday, a rest day, slaves gathered to sell yams and other produce at the bustling markets. In rare instances they might save enough money to buy their freedom, which masters could also grant as they wished.

The planters ran their estates as fiefdoms under the authority of an overseer (the *busha*), who often enjoyed relatively free rein. Some planters showed kindness and nurtured their slaves, but most resorted to violence to terrorize the slave population into obedience. The extreme treatment was eventually regulated, but plantation society remained tied to the rule of the whip.

Port Royal Project (http://nautarch.tamu.edu/portroyal) is a site that offers a fascinating look at the work of maritime archaeologists in the submerged historic neighborhoods of Port Royal, which have lain underwater since the great earthquake of 1692.

Revolt & Reform

Bloody slave insurrections occurred with frightening frequency. The last and largest of the slave revolts in Jamaica was the 1831 Christmas Rebellion, inspired by 'Daddy' Sam Sharpe, an educated slave and lay preacher who incited resistance and pushed for emancipation. The rebellion turned violent – up to 20,000 slaves razed plantations and murdered planters – and was brutally suppressed, with the problem of disenfranchisement left unaddressed. Four hundred slaves were hanged and hundreds more whipped. After much debate, the British Parliament passed antislavery legislation in 1834 and the Jamaican Assembly subsequently agreed to do the same.

1938	1941	1943	1944
Jamaica's first political party, the People's National Party, is formed by Norman Manley, who works with the Bustamante Trade Union to make working-class issues a main focus of Jamaican politics.	Thousands of Jamaican servicemen volunteer to fight for Britain during WWII.	The Jamaica Labour Party (JLP) is formed by Alexander Bustamante.	A new constitution introduces universal suffrage and the first elections are held for a locally based government.

In the 1860s Paul Bogle, a Black Baptist deacon in the hamlet of Stony Gut, preached resistance against the oppression and injustice of the local authorities and planters in St Thomas. He was supported by George William Gordon, a wealthy mulatto planter who had become an assemblyman.

On October 11, 1865, Bogle and 400 supporters marched to the Morant Bay court-house to protest the severe punishment meted out to a vagrant arrested on a petty charge. A riot ensued in which 28 people were killed, and the courthouse and much of the town center were razed. The countryside erupted in riots. Bogle fled with a £2000 bounty on his head, but was soon captured by Maroons and hanged the same day from the center arch of the burned-out courthouse. Gordon was arrested in Kingston, ferried to Morant Bay, condemned by a kangaroo court and also hanged.

Governor Edward Eyre ordered reprisals. The militia swept through St Thomas, razing more than 1000 houses and summarily executing more than 430 people. While some members of the British government believed that Eyre's reaction had been necessary to preserve the Crown colony, others were outraged (a tribunal found that the punishments were 'excessive...reckless...and...positively barbarous'). Eyre was subsequently stripped of his post and the Jamaica House of Assembly was forced to relinquish its power to the British parliament. Thus the island became a Crown colony, leading to reforms of the harsh judicial system.

The resulting transition from a slave economy to one based on paid labor caused economic chaos; most slaves rejected the starvation wages offered on the estates, choosing to fend for themselves. Desperation over conditions and injustice finally boiled over in the 1865 Morant Bay Rebellion, led by a black Baptist deacon named Paul Bogle.

'Come Mr Tallyman, tally me banana...'

In 1866 a Yankee skipper, George Busch, arrived in Jamaica and loaded several hundred stems of bananas, which he transported to Boston and sold at a handsome profit. He quickly returned to Port Antonio, where he encouraged production and soon had himself a thriving export business. Captain Lorenzo Dow Baker followed suit in the west, with his base at Montego Bay. Within a decade the banana trade was booming. Production peaked in 1927, when 21 million stems were exported.

To help pay the passage south to Jamaica, banana traders promoted the island's virtues and took on passengers. Thus, the banana-export trade gave rise to the tourism industry, which continues to grow and flourish.

Pieces of the Past (www.jamaica-gleaner.com/pages/history) is a compendium of thematic essays about Jamaican history.

1945

Reggae superstar Bob Marley is born in Nine Mile, in St Ann's Parish.

1962

Jamaica becomes an independent nation within the British Commonwealth.

1963

At the height of the ska era in Jamaican music, Clement Dodd begins recording Bob Marley and the Wailers.

ANTHONY PIGEON/LONELY PLANET IMAGES © / SCULPTOR: PIERRE ROUZIER

» Statue of Bob Marley

Birth of a Nation

With the Depression of the 1930s, sugar and banana sales plummeted, and the vast majority of Jamaicans were unemployed and destitute. Strikes and riots erupted, spilling over in 1938 when a demonstration at the West Indies Sugar Company factory at Frome, Westmoreland, got out of hand. A battle between police and the unemployed seeking work left several people dead. The situation was defused when a locally born labor leader, Alexander Bustamante, mediated the dispute.

Amid the clamor, the charismatic Bustamante, son of an Irish woman and a mulatto man, formed the Bustamante Industrial Trade Union (BITU) in 1938. That same year, Bustamante's cousin Norman Manley formed the People's National Party (PNP), the first political party in the colony. Separately they campaigned for economic and political reforms. As historians Philip Sherlock and Barbara Preston observed, 'Bustamante swept the Jamaican working class into the mainstream of Jamaican political life and Norman Manley secured the constitutional

Tony Sewall's *Garvey's Children: The Legacy of Marcus Garvey* provides a look at the rise of black nationalism inspired by national hero Marcus Garvey.

UP YOU MIGHTY RACE!

Marcus Garvey was born of working-class parents in St Ann's Bay on August 17, 1887. After traveling to Costa Rica, Panama and England, he returned a firm believer in self-improvement and he founded the Universal Negro Improvement Association (UNIA) in 1914 to unite 'all the Negro peoples of the world to establish a state exclusively their own.' When Jamaica's middle classes proved largely unreceptive to his message, he moved in 1916 to the US, where he received a rapturous welcome and formed a branch of the UNIA in New York. The UNIA is credited for giving birth to the Black Panther movement, which in turn paved the way for the civil rights movement. Garvey, a gifted orator, established a weekly newspaper, the *Negro World*, and built an enormous following under the slogan 'One God! One Aim! One Destiny!'

Garvey set up the Black Star Line, a steamship company, with the aim of eventually repatriating blacks to Africa, though it ultimately failed due to poor management. Garvey's greatest achievement was to instill the post-colonial black community with a sense of self-worth and pride: 'Up you mighty race, you can accomplish what you will.'

Considering Garvey a dangerous agitator, the American and British governments conspired against him, and in 1922 they arrested him on mail-fraud charges. He served two years in Atlanta Federal Prison before being deported to Jamaica, where he founded the reformist People's Political Party. Universal franchise did not then exist in Jamaica, and he failed to gather enough support at the polls. In 1935 he departed for England, where he died in poverty in 1940.

His remains were repatriated to Jamaica in 1964 and interred with state honors in National Heroes Park in Kingston. The advent of reggae music in the 1970s gave rise to a new wave of Garveyism.

1966	1972	1976	1978
On the second stop of his Caribbean trip, HIM Haile Selassie I is greeted by nearly 100,000 chanting Rastafarians at the airport.	Michael Manley launches socialist reforms, and tries to promote Jamaica's self-sufficiency by rejecting close ties with the US and allying Jamaica with Cuba.	In the lead up to the election, tensions between Jamaica's two political parties erupt into open warfare in the street between politically aligned gangs. A state of emergency is declared.	The One Love peace concert is held in Kingston, following Bob Marley's homecoming; 100,000 people attend. The People's National Party and Jamaica Labour Party declare a peacefire in its honor.

changes that put political power in their hands.' Not content with trade union activism, Bustamante formed the Jamaica Labour Party (JLP) in 1943.

Adult suffrage for all Jamaicans and a new constitution that provided for an elected government were introduced in 1944, and Bustamante's JLP won Jamaica's first election. In 1947 virtual autonomy was granted, though Jamaica remained a British colony under the jurisdiction of Parliament and the Crown – a prelude to full independence.

On August 6, 1962, Jamaica finally gained its independence (while remaining part of the British Commonwealth). At midnight the Union Jack came down, replaced by Jamaica's new flag with three new colors: black (for the people), green (for the land) and gold (for the sun).

The Manley-Seaga Era

Post-independence politics have been largely dominated by the legacies of Bustamante and Manley. Manley's son Michael led the PNP toward democratic socialism in the mid-'70s. His policy of taxation to fund social services deterred foreign investment and caused a capital flight at a time when Jamaica could ill afford it. Bitterly opposed factions engaged in open urban warfare before the 1976 election. A controversial state of emergency was declared and the nation seemed poised on the edge of civil war, but the PNP won the election by a wide margin and Manley continued with his socialist agenda.

Unsurprisingly, the US government was hostile to the Jamaica's socialist turn, and when Manley began to develop close ties with Cuba, the CIA purportedly planned to topple the Jamaican government. Businesses pulled out, the economy (tourism in particular) went into sharp decline and the country was under virtual siege. Almost 800 people were killed in the lead-up to the 1980 elections, which were won by the JLP's Edward Seaga. Seaga restored Jamaica's economic fortunes somewhat, severed ties with Cuba and became a staunch ally of the Reagan administration. Relatively peaceful elections in 1989 returned a reinvented 'mainstream realist' Manley to power; he retired in 1992, handing the reins to his deputy, Percival James Patterson – Jamaica's first black prime minister.

David Howard's *Kingston* is an engaging exploration of the capital's history, from Spanish to modern times.

The PNP Years

The Patterson-led PNP triumphed in the 1993 and 1997 elections. In spring 1999 the country erupted in nationwide riots after the government announced a 30% increase in the tax on gasoline. Kingston and Montego Bay, where sugarcane fields were set ablaze, were particularly badly hit. After three days of arson and looting, the government rescinded the tax.

1980	1988	1992	2004
The Jamaica Labour Party's Edward Seaga is elected to power, and begins transforming Jamaica's foreign engagement, cutting ties with Cuba, and positioning himself as a friend of the Reagan administration.	Hurricane Gilbert slams Jamaica, killing 45 people and causing damage estimated at up to US$1 billion.	The Blue Mountains–John Crow National Park is established. Formed during the Cretaceous Period (c 144–65 million years ago), the mountain range itself is the island's oldest geological feature.	At least 15 people are killed by Hurricane Ivan, with Negril being particularly hard-hit. The banana-tree population is ravaged, and the following year banana exports drop by 68%.

In the lead-up to the 2002 elections, violence in West Kingston soared to new heights as criminal posses battled to control electoral turf and profit from the largesse that victory at the polls in Jamaica brings. Rival political gangs turned the area into a war zone, forcing residents to flee, and schools, businesses and even Kingston Public Hospital to close.

In 2004 Hurricane Ivan bounced off Jamaica en route to the Cayman Islands, causing widespread damage, and Edward Seaga – still representing the JLP as opposition leader – retired after over three decades of life in politics. Two years later Prime Minister Patterson resigned, giving way to Portia Simpson-Miller: Jamaica's first female prime minister, and Michael Manley's protégé. 'Mama P' was initially popular with the masses, but 18 years of PNP rule bred voter disillusionment with the party. In the 2007 elections, Bruce Golding of the JLP carried the day, inheriting high rates of crime and illiteracy as well as threats to the environment through deforestation and overdevelopment.

Jamaica carries a debt to foreign banks exceeding US$800 billion. *Life & Debt*, a documentary film by Stephanie Black, takes a provocative look into the island's burden.

The Dudus Affair

In 2009, the US called for the extradition of Christopher 'Dudus' Coke, the don of Tivoli Gardens ghetto and one of the most powerful men in Jamaica, on alleged gun- and drug-running charges. The demand for extradition was originally refused by Prime Minister Bruce Golding, who claimed that the evidence against Dudus was gathered illegally, but after pressure from the US a warrant was issued for Dudus' arrest on 18 May, 2010. Between May 24 and 27 heavy fighting broke out between Dudus' gunmen and the joint police-military force, leaving 67 dead. Dudus himself remained on the run for a month, before being apprehended: disguised as a woman at a road block, enroute to the US embassy to negotiate his surrender, and accompanied by the influential Reverend Al Miller. Dudus demanded that he be extradited immediately. His father, Lester Lloyd Coke, former don of Tivoli Gardens, was burned to death in his Jamaican jail cell (allegedly by accident) while also awaiting extradition to the US, and he wished to avoid a similar fate. His absence left a power vacuum, with new blood fighting over the position of Jamaica's most influential don.

In spite of recent troubles, the Jamaican tourist industry is rapidly recovering (with a greater emphasis on sustainable tourism), Jamaican musicians continue to be major players on the world stage, and Jamaican people's resilience allows them to face the future with resolve and good humor.

2006	2007	2008	2010
Portia Simpson-Miller, of the People's National Party, becomes Jamaica's first female prime minister.	The Cricket World Cup is held in the West Indies. Won by Australia, the tournament was overshadowed by the death of Pakistani coach Bob Woolmer, apparently of heart failure.	At the Beijing Olympic Games, world records are broken by sprinter Usain Bolt in the 100m and 200m and with the Jamaican men's team in the 400m relay.	Christopher 'Dudus' Coke, don of the Tivoli Gardens ghetto, is extradited to the US after an armed standoff between gang members and the Jamaican police and military.

Jamaican Life

Jamaicans are as diverse a people as the island's geography is varied. Far from being confined to the dreadlocked, spliff-puffing Rastafarian vibin' to reggae or the violent 'rude bwai' (rude boy, criminal) of the ghetto, they comprise many social and demographic strata.

Street-level Jamaica can be daunting at first. Poverty blights Jamaica's towns, and tourists mean money. Nevertheless, with reasonable precautions, you'll soon fall under the spell of Jamaica's inimitable charms. Violence rarely impinges on foreigners; it is mostly restricted to drug wars and political gang feuds in the ghettoes of Kingston, Spanish Town and Montego Bay.

What emerges is a panoply of communities: from the sleepy fishing hamlets that line the coasts to the cosmopolitan business sector of the capital, from the bustling market towns to the autonomous Maroon mountain villages. And while you can of course meet Rastas happy to smoke ganja with you, you'll also encounter proud matriarchs presiding over the family-owned rum shop, dancehall enthusiasts delighted to take you to the local sound-system party, bush-medicine doctors who can explain herbal lore, or students who know as much about your own country as you do.

You'll learn to greet strangers with the local salutation 'blessed' – and by the time you leave Jamaica, you'll realize you have been.

The Jamaicans

Many Jamaicans will tell you their island is not part of the Caribbean, but of Africa. And while the vestiges of the slave era unsurprisingly weigh heavily on the national psyche, over the last century the rise of Jamaican nationalism and an explosion in homegrown culture have engendered a proud and vibrant contemporary culture.

Jamaicans are an intriguing contrast. Much of the population comprises the most gracious people you'll ever meet: hardworking, happy-go-lucky, helpful, courteous, genteel and full of humility. However, charged memories of slavery and racism have continued to bring out the spirit of anarchy latent in a former slave society divided into rich and poor. Jamaicans struggling hard against poverty are disdainful of talk about a 'tropical paradise.'

Jamaicans love to debate, or 'reason.' They tend to express themselves forcefully, turning differences of opinion into voluble arguments with some confounding elliptical twists and stream-of-consciousness associations.

Jamaicans' sarcasm and sardonic wit is legendary. The deprecating humor has evolved as an escape valve that hides their true feelings. The saying that 'everyt'ing irie' is black humor, because life is a problem. Often, Jamaican wit is laced with sexual undertones. Jamaicans like to make fun of others, usually, in the subtlest yet no-punches-pulled way, but they accept being the source of similar jokes in good grace.

Understanding Patois

When Jamaicans speak patois, often they drop their 'h's' (thus, *ouse* instead of 'house') and add them in unexpected places (eg, *hemphasize*). Jamaicans usually drop the 'h' from 'th' as well: hence, *t'anks* for 'thanks.' 'The' is usually pronounced as *de* and 'them' as *dem*. They also sometimes drop the 'w,' as in *ooman* (woman).

Cedella Booker's *Bob Marley* is a mother's affectionate portrait of the singer, focusing on the man more than the music.

Living in Jamaica

Many Jamaicans live in the countryside, eking out a marginal existence in ramshackle villages and rural shacks, fishing, working the cane and banana fields and farming – sometimes in pockets of extreme poverty, as in Kingston's ghettoes and shanties. Job opportunities are difficult to come by without a proper education, which doesn't come cheap, so many low-income Jamaicans hustle, waiting for an opportunity to present itself. The average per capita income is only US$4390 (J$371,615) and many Jamaicans are reliant on remittances sent by family members living abroad.

Jamaica has a significant middle class – well educated, entrepreneurial and with a preference for shopping trips to Miami or New York. But many of the middle class live with a surprising lack of contact with the harsh reality in which the majority of Jamaicans live, and they seem to be able to muster little empathy. At the same time, others will employ a part-time gardener or maid not out of necessity, but to share their own good fortune.

> Jamaican proverbs are a proud celebration of heritage and dialect. A sample: 'So cow a grow so him nose hole a open.' This roughly translates to 'Live and learn.'

'Out of Many, One People'

The nation's motto reflects the diverse heritage of Jamaica. Tens of thousands of West Africans, plus large numbers of Irish, Scottish, Germans and Welsh, arrived throughout the colonial period, along with Hispanic and Portuguese Jews and those whom Jamaicans call 'Syrians' (a term for all those of Levantine extraction). In 1838, following emancipation, Chinese and Indian indentured labourers ('coolies') arrived from Hong Kong and India.

Jamaica proclaims itself a melting pot of racial harmony. Still, insecurities of identity have been carried down from the plantation era. As explored in the works of celebrated Jamaican poet and social critic, Louise Bennett (and in *Identity, Race and Protest in Jamaica* by Rex Nettleford), the issue of class lines drawn during the colonial era still exists and is still related to color; lighter-skinned Jamaicans are far more likely to hold better-paid jobs and it is still desirable to 'marry light.' Unlike in the US, solidarity among all people of African descent never existed in Jamaica; the middle classes have always sought to distance themselves from the inhabitants of shanty towns. There is some lingering resentment – as well as prejudice – against whites, particularly among the poorer segment of society, and disillusionment with post-independence Jamaica.

> Traditional folk healing is still very much alive. Healers, called 'balmists,' rely on concoctions of native herbs (bush medicines), the recipes for which span many generations.

Religion & Spirituality

Jamaica professes to have the greatest number of churches per square kilometer in the world. Although most foreigners associate the island with Rastafarianism, more than 80% of Jamaicans identify themselves as Christian.

JEWS IN JAMAICA

Jamaica's Jewish community is the oldest in the New World. The first Jews settled in Jamaica in the early 1500s, following their expulsion from Spain. Though officially forbidden in Spanish colonies, they came as conversos, or 'hidden Jews,' who'd officially converted to Catholicism but continued to practice Judaism in secret. When Spain ceded Jamaica to the British in 1655, the island was settled by Sephardic Jews of Spanish and Portuguese origin, followed by Ashkenazi Jews from Eastern Europe in the 1770s. Allowed to practice their religion freely, the community flourished, its members taking part in commerce, the arts and politics. Though today the island's many synagogues have been reduced to just one (www.ucija.org), the remaining congregation of 100 or so play an active role in the upkeep of their proud heritage.

Based on religious practices derived from West Africa, obeah is similar to Haiti's Vodou or Cuba's Santería, practiced by few but fear-inducing even in those who claim not to believe. Myal is essentially 'white magic' to obeah's 'black magic,' and obeah-men (and women) engage in both. Largely a rural practise, it involves invoking the services of a practitioner who can dispel a curse, bring you good luck, force your partner to be faithful or put a curse on your enemies, using a full arsenal of herbs, powders (including grave dust), specially-shaped candles and power rings to achieve their objective.

The summoning of duppies, or spirits, is central to the practice. Jamaicans believe that your spirit roams the earth for nine days after you die, and in that time it can be summoned to do good or evil. Many Jamaican elders still observe Nine Night, a 'wake' held for nine nights after someone's death to ensure that the spirit of the deceased (duppy) departs to heaven (and doesn't hang around to haunt the living!).

Invoking duppies involves a ritual circle comprised of bottles topped with candles – evil spirits prefer Guinness, whereas good spirits claim Red Stripe; both have a fondness for cream soda. The entrance or 'gateway' to the circle is barred with a cutlass or machete and the circle may contain food offerings to the spirits, as well as chalked symbols.

Non-believers dismiss obeah as superstitious nonsense, and believers keep mum so as not to dilute its power, but everyone knows where the nearest obeah shop is. Judging by the charms you find in many Jamaican homes, it has a powerful grip on the nation's psyche.

Christianity

On weekends, it's common to see adults and children walking along country roads holding Bibles and dressed in their finest outfits. On Sundays in particular, every church in the country seems to overflow with the righteous, and the old fire-and-brimstone school of sermonizing is still the preferred mode. Bible-waving congregations sway to and fro, and wail and shriek 'Hallelujah!' and 'Amen, sweet Jesus!' while guitars, drums and tambourines help work the crowds into a frenzy.

The most popular denomination is the Anglican Church of Jamaica, followed by Seventh-Day Adventists, Pentecostals, Baptists, Methodists and Catholics.

Revivalism

Jamaica has several quasi-Christian, quasi-animist sects that are generically named Revivalist cults after the postemancipation Great Revival, during which many blacks converted to Christianity. The two most important Revivalist branches are Zionism and Pocomania (Pukkumina), the former being more Bible-centered, and the latter involving ancestor worship.

The cults are derived from West African animist beliefs (animism is derived from the Latin word *anima*, or 'soul') based on the tenet that the spiritual and temporal worlds are a unified whole. A core belief is that spirits live independently of the human or animal body and can inhabit inanimate objects and communicate themselves to humans.

Revivalist ceremonies are characterised by the bright, flowing robes of the congregation, chanting, drumming, speaking in tongues and spirit possession. They are held in designated poco yards, led by a 'shepherd' or 'mother,' who interprets the messages of the spirits.

Relatively rare these days, Kumina is the most African of the Revivalist cults, combining evocation of ancestral spirits with call-and-response chanting and intricate drumming rhythms that induce the dancing worshippers to 'catch the spirit.'

Jamaica's most celebrated theatre company is the National Dance Theatre Company, which performs at the Little Theatre in Kingston and incorporates Kumina movements into their routines.

Rastafarianism

Rastafarians, with their uncut, uncombed hair grown into long sun-bleached tangles known as 'dreadlocks' or 'dreads,' are as synonymous with the island as reggae. A faith rather than a church, Rastafarianism has no official doctrine and is composed of a core of social and spiritual tenets. It was developed by charismatic Rastafarian leader Leonard Percival Howell who, in 1940, established the first Rastafarian community, the Pinnacle, at Sligoville northwest of Kingston. His followers adopted the dreadlocked hairstyle of several East African tribes – an allegory of the mane of the Lion of Judah.

Howell's document 'Twenty-One Points' defined the Rastafarian philosophy and creed. One tenet was that the African race was one of God's chosen races, one of the Twelve Tribes of Israel descended from the Hebrews and displaced. Jamaica is Babylon (named after the place where the Israelites were enslaved) and their lot is in exile in a land that cannot be reformed. Another tenet states that God, whom they call Jah, will one day lead them from Babylon – any place that 'downpresses' the masses – to Zion (the 'Promised Land,' or Ethiopia). A third addresses Haile Selassie's status as the Redeemer chosen to lead Africans back to Africa.

Not all Rastafarians wear dreads, and others do not smoke ganja. All adherents, however, accept that Africa is the black race's spiritual home to which they are destined to return.

Rastafarianism evolved as an expression of poor, black Jamaicans seeking fulfilment in the 1930s, a period of growing nationalism and economic and political upheaval. It was boosted by the 'back to Africa' zeal of Marcus Garvey's Universal Negro Improvement Association. He predicted that a black man – a 'Redeemer' – would be crowned king in Africa. Haile Selassie's crowning as emperor of Abyssinia (now Ethiopia) on November 2, 1930, fulfilled Garvey's prophecy and established a fascination with Ethiopia that lies at the core of Rastafarianism.

Many Rastafarians believe that ganja provides a line of communication with God. Through it they claim to gain wisdom and inner divinity through the ability to 'reason' more clearly. The search for truth – 'reasoning' – is integral to the faith and is meant to see through the corrupting influences of 'Babylon.'

Despite its militant consciousness, the religion preaches love and nonviolence, and adherents live by strict biblical codes that advocate a way of life in harmony with Old Testament traditions. Their diet consists of

Reggae Routes by Wayne Chen and Kevin O'Brien Chang is required reading. This lavishly illustrated volume is an insider's guide to reggae and popular Jamaican music in general.

The Sympathetic Dread: The Rastafarians of Jamaica by Joseph Owens and *Rasta Heart: A Journey Into One Love* by Robert Roskind are noteworthy books on Jamaica's most talked-about creed.

A UNIQUE LEXICON

One of the 21 tenets of Rastafarianism is the belief that God exists in each person, and that the two are the same. Thus the creed unifies divinity and individuality through the use of personal pronouns that reflect the 'I and I.' ('One blood. Everybody same, mon!') 'I' becomes the id or true measure of inner divinity, which places everyone on the same plane. Thus 'I and I' can mean 'we,' 'him and her,' 'you and them.' (The personal pronoun 'me' is seen as a sign of subservience, of acceptance of the self as an 'object'.)

Rastafarians have evolved a whole lexicon that has profoundly influenced 'Jamaica talk' and is laced with cryptic intent and meaning. This revisionist 'English' is inspired by Rastafarian reasoning that sees the English language as a tool in the service of Babylon, designed to 'downpress' the black people. In short, they believe the language is biased. Every word is analysed, and in this frame even the most insignificant word can seem tainted. The well-meant greeting 'Hello!' may elicit the response: 'Dis not 'ell and I nuh low!'

vegetarian I-tal food, prepared without salt, and they are teetotalers who shun tobacco and the trappings of Western consumerism.

Jamaica's Sporting Legacy

In 2008 Jamaica's male and female athletes made history at the Beijing Olympics, breaking world records in the 100m sprint, the 200m sprint and the 4 x 100 men's relay. This continued the country's tradition of producing outstanding track-and-field achievements, dating back to sprinter Arthur Wint, Jamaica's first Olympic gold-medal winner (in 1948). At the time of writing, Usain 'Lightning' Bolt is the fastest man on the planet, thanks to his world-record times of 9.58 seconds in the 100m and 19.19 seconds in the 200m sprint, set at the 2009 World Championships.

Jamaica is cricket mad, and you'll come across small fields in even the most remote backwaters, where kids with makeshift balls and bats practice the bowling and swings that may one day bring them fortune and fame. International and regional games are played frequently at **Sabina Park** in Kingston.

Football is Jamaica's second sport. It was given a huge boost by the success of the Reggae Boyz – Jamaica's national soccer team – in qualifying for the 1998 World Cup, though they haven't qualified since. Spirited international matches are played at Kingston's **National Stadium**.

Jamaicans do not lack imagination and you'll find them participating in the most unlikely sports. The Jamaican Bobsleigh Team – inspiring the film *Cool Runnings* – surprised everyone by coming 14th in the 1994 Winter Olympics, beating the likes of France, Russia and the US. In 2010, 27-year-old Newton Marshall became the first black musher to complete Alaska's gruelling 1850km Iditarod Great Sled Race (a dog-sledding event). He finished in 47th place out of 71, and was training for the 2011 Iditarod at the time of research.

The Jamaican Woman: A Celebration by Joanne Simpson provides biographies of 200 women who have made major contributions to Jamaican society.

A Woman's Lot

While Jamaican society can appear oppressively macho to outsiders accustomed to dancehall lyrics, women tend to be strong and independent (in 40% of households, a woman is the sole provider). This spirit often translates into the self-assurance so apparent in Portia Simpson-Miller, former prime minister (2006–07) and current leader of the PNP opposition. Jamaican women attain far higher grades in school and have higher literacy rates than Jamaican men, and middle-class women have attained levels of respect and career performance that are commensurate with their counterparts in North America and Europe. Women also make up about 46% of Jamaica's labor force, although the majority are in extremely low-paying jobs.

The darker side of a Jamaican woman's life is the proliferation of sexual violence. According to statistics, one in four women is subject to a forced sexual encounter during the course of her life.

Jamaican Art

Literature

Through the years Jamaican literature has been haunted by the ghosts of slave history and the ambiguities of Jamaica's relationship to Mother England. Best known, perhaps, is Herbert de Lisser's classic gothic horror, *White Witch of Rose Hall*, which tells of Annie Palmer, the wicked mistress of Rose Hall (see the boxed text, p170) who supposedly murdered three husbands and several slave lovers.

Perry Henzell's *Power Game* is a tale of power politics based on real events in the 1970s, as told by the director of the movie *The Harder They*

One of the most electrifying voices of Jamaican dub poetry is that of Mutabaruka. Learn about his work and read his poems at www .mutabaruka.com.

Come. The poignant novel of that name, written by Michael Thewell, recounts the story of a country boy who comes to Kingston, turns into a 'rude bwai' (armed thug), and becomes fatally enmeshed in the savage drug culture. The mean streets of Kingston are also the setting for the gritty novels of Roger Mais, notably *The Hills Were Joyful Together* and *Brother Man.* Orlando Patterson's *The Children of Sisyphus* mines the same bleak terrain from a Rastafarian perspective.

In recent years, a number of Jamaican female writers have gained notice: they include Christine Craig *(Mint Tea)*, Patricia Powell *(Me Dying Trial)*, Michelle Cliff *(Abeng, Land of Look Behind)* and Vanessa Spence *(Roads Are Down).* *Lionheart Gal*, a lively collection of stories mostly in patois by the Sistren Collective sheds light on the lives of women in Jamaica, while *Anancy and Miss Lou* by Louise Bennett continues the art of classic storytelling in patois.

Jamaica Art by Kim Robinson and Petrine Archer Straw is a well-illustrated treatise on the evolution of the island's art scene.

Film

Jamaica has produced some excellent films, most notably cult classic *The Harder They Come* (1973), starring Jimmy Cliff as a rude bwai in Kingston's ghettoes. *Smile Orange* (1974) tells the story of Ringo, a hustling waiter at a resort – a theme not irrelevant today. *Rockers* (1978), another music-propelled, socially poignant fable is a Jamaican reworking of the *Bicycle Thief* featuring a cast of reggae all-stars.

Jamaica has also had strong links to James Bond movies ever since novelist Ian Fleming concocted the suave macho spy 007 at his home near Oracabessa. The Bond movies *Dr No* and *Live and Let Die* were both shot on location along Jamaica's north coast.

THE BIRTH OF VISUAL NATIONALISM

Until the early 20th century, Jamaica's visual, literary and performing arts largely sought to reflect British trends and colonial tastes. In the 1920s, however, the Jamaican School (a group of local artists) began to develop its own style, shaped by realities of Jamaican life and divided into two main groups: the painters who were schooled abroad, and island-themed 'intuitives.'

Jamaican Independence leader Norman Manley's wife, Edna, an inspired sculptor and advocate for indigenous Jamaican art, became a leading catalyst for change. Edna Manley's bitter opposition to the 'anaemic imitators of European traditions' pushed her to aspire to an 'expression of the deep-rooted, hidden pulse of the Country – that thing which gives it its unique life.' Through the example of seminal works like *Negro Aroused* (1935), which can be seen in the National Gallery in Kingston, and *Pocomania* (1936), which synthesized African and Jamaican archetypes within a deeply personal vision of the national psyche, Manley provided an electrifying example of the potential of Jamaican art. On a grassroots level, Manley organized free art classes and volunteer-run training courses to energize and organize rising talent.

Out of this fertile ground emerged – almost simultaneously – three of Jamaica's great painters. Self-taught artist John Dunkley was 'discovered' by Manley in his brilliantly decorated Kingston barber shop. His inimitable style, articulated through brooding landscapes of sinister tropical foliage, never-ending roads and furtive reptiles and rodents, brought form to an apocalyptic vision that resonated with the historical traumas of the Jamaican people. In contrast, Albert Huie produced intricately detailed and beautifully composed works like *Crop Time* (1955) and *Coconut Piece* (1966), depicting an idyllic dreamscape of rural scenes far removed from the urban strife of Kingston, where he lived and worked. More rooted in his immediate surroundings, David Pottinger's primary interest is in the urban landscape. His portrayals of downtown life, such as *Trench Town* (1959), reveal the desolate melancholy of poverty while also suggesting the indomitable spirit of life.

The Lunatic (1991), based on the Anthony Winkler novel, is a humorous exploration of the island's sexual taboos.

Rick Elgood's emotionally engaging 1997 film *Dancehall Queen* found an international audience for its tale of redemption for a struggling, middle-aged street vendor, who escapes the mean streets of Kingston through the erotic intoxication of dancehall music. Jamaica's highest-grossing film of all time is Chris Browne's 2000 crime drama *Third World Cop*, in which old friends straddling both sides of the law must come to terms with each other. The gangster film *Shottas* (2002) follows in its footsteps, featuring two criminals from Kingston who decide to try their luck in the US. *One Love* (2003) explores Jamaica's social divides against the backdrop of a controversial romance between a Rasta musician and a pastor's daughter.

The Afflicted Yard (http://afflict edyard.com) is an edgy website out of Kingston featuring commentary and photography.

>

Music

Most travelers experience, on some level, a destination before they get there. That history strongly informs how you eventually experience a place. You've probably had sushi before you got to Japan; drank Guinness before you arrived in Ireland; watched Hollywood films before you came to the USA. And – excuse our presumption – we assume you've been listening to Jamaican music long before you reached the island.

There are few places as defined by their music as Jamaica. The island's most iconic image is of Bob Marley, and for many it is impossible to hear the word 'Jamaica' and not have the beginnings of some tune filter into our minds. Of course, there is more to Jamaican music than 'Brother Bob,' although it was the reggae revolution of the late 1960s to the early 1980s that put Jamaican music on the map and made it inexorably distinct from other Caribbean hot spots.

The sound of Jamaica comes from many places, although it lacks much of the Spanish influence that is so prominent in other Caribbean nations: African folk rhythms, gospel harmonies, 20th-century brass, all brought together through the application and exploitation of limited production means and a hell of a lot of hard work and guts. It's the unstoppable urge to *create* that gives Jamaican music such incredible vitality.

Remember the first time you heard reggae and figured that sound must be what Jamaica is all about? You weren't totally off. Over the past 50 years Jamaican music has had a massive effect on global culture disproportionate to the country's size and population. Somehow the poorest and most disenfranchised citizens of one small nation have developed institutions and art forms that have influenced the music of countries around the world. Perhaps this Jamaican proverb gives the best answer: 'Mi likkle but mi talawah,' or I may be little, but I am powerful.

Rethinking the National Motto

Most historical overviews of Jamaican music present a neat linear chronology from mento (indigenous Jamaican folk music; 1930s and '40s) to

Jahworks (www.jahworks.org) is an online zine dedicated to Caribbean (mostly Jamaican) music and culture. The writing is intelligent, informed and entertaining.

For an outstanding biography of Bob Marley that captures the Jamaica of his times, check out Timothy White's *Catch a Fire*.

OUR TOP REGGAE PLAYLIST

007 (Shanty Town) Desmond Decker & the Aces
Picture of Selassie I Khari Kill
Legalize It Peter Tosh
One Love Bob Marley & the Wailers
Cool Rasta The Heptones
The Harder They Come Jimmy Cliff
Rivers of Babylon The Melodians
Pass the Koutchie The Mighty Diamonds
Funky Kingston Toots & the Maytals
Is This Love Bob Marley

Even if you're not a prude, you might find some Jamaican dancing to be, hmmmm, 'explicit.' Don't get us wrong, there's lots of sweet, embraceable slow-dancing during oldies parties, but head to a modern nightclub or sound-system party and you'd be forgiven for raising an eyebrow. If you want to attempt some of Jamaica's more risqué dance moves, here's our guide:

» **Dutty Wine** For females only. Bend over. Raise posterior in air. Proceed to whip head around in rapid circles while rotating butt – extra points if you can go clockwise in one direction, counterclockwise in the other. (Note: you don't really win anything, except increased attention.) If especially talented, follow with the splits; just never, ever stop rotating head and butt. Serious warning: doctors say the Dutty Wine can cause ligament injury, and urban legends persist about women *dying* from too much Dutty Wine.

» **Daggering** We'll leave it to you to figure out the word etymology of the raunchiest type of Jamaican dancing (at the time of writing). To 'dagger,' – have rough drysex on dance floor. Start vertical, get horizontal. Rinse, repeat.

Jamaican R&B ('50s), to ska (its first popular music; early '60s), to rocksteady (a short intermediate step; mid-'60s), to reggae (the apex of its achievements; late '60s to late '70s) and finally dancehall (more club and sound-system oriented than its predecessors; post-1981). But this view of Jamaican music is oversimplified, and obscures much more than it illuminates. The Jamaican national motto is 'Out of Many, One People.' We could be clever and change 'people' to 'music' and pretend that is the true meaning of Jamaican music, but we'd be lying. Jamaican music styles are distinct, yet they constantly blend. This syncretism is the magic of Jamaican music.

The Stone that the Builder Refused

In the song 'Trench Town,' Bob Marley asked if anything good could ever come out of Trench Town. Posing a rhetorical question he must have heard a thousand times from the Jamaican upper classes, Marley challenged the very ideological foundation Jamaican society was built on – the notion that one set of people (the poor masses of African descent) would be denied their freedom and sense of human worth by the minority that was Jamaica's ruling elite. In one of the song's next verses, Marley exhorts us to 'pay tribute to Trench Town,' defiantly demanding respect for his hometown, spitting the old paternalism back in the face of his oppressors while at the same time encouraging the ghetto to escape the shackles of 'mental slavery.'

'The stone that the builder refused shall become the head corner stone' (Psalm 118:22) is a line Marley employed in more than one song. The moral, as in so much of the sweep of Jamaican history and art, is that of redemption: the rejected coming back to be the exalted one; the last shall be first. It is this basic message to the masses – to take pride in who you are, to recognize that divinity is kin to your soul, that change can happen – that is the source of Marley's impact in the developing world. Of course his music has rocked the developed world as well, and while much of that impact is simple aesthetic appreciation, his message of hope and the powerful simplicity of its delivery is pretty universal. Who else's music is played with such frequency in both Western university dorm rooms and the back alleys of Dakar? Acknowledging his singular place in the history of the last century, in 1999 *Time Magazine* named *Exodus* 'album of the century,' while the BBC rated 'One Love' the song of the millennium.

SCENE

Whaddat (www
.whaddat.com)
covers the
Jamaican
entertainment
scene from a
local perspective.
Check out the
latest dancehall
happenings,
interviews with
current stars,
fashions and
photographs.

Dancehall Culture

The modern sound of Jamaica is definitely dancehall: rapid-fire chanting over bass-heavy beats. It's simplistic to just call dancehall Jamaican rap, because the formation of the beats, their structure and the nuances of the lyrics all have deep roots in Jamaica's musical past.

Whether dancehall started in the late 1970s (with the rise of DJs such as The Lone Ranger, Yellowman and Josey Wales) or the mid-1980s (with the advent of digital production techniques and the famous Sleng Teng rhythm) is a matter of some debate. However, as a cultural space where social dances were held, dancehall's roots go back to the slavery era. Jamaicans have always utilized public spaces as places to listen to music; dancehall as a genre has (literally) amplified the listening experience with sound systems and speakers.

www.dancehall reggae.com has the latest word on the scene and is a great source of information on the next sound-system party.

Dancehall is visible and audible in every aspect of daily life in Jamaica: from roadside cassette vendors and bars and taverns blasting IRIE FM, to the nightly news and political rallies. Jamaicans come from miles away to makeshift dancehalls to hear 'champion' sound systems. Outside the dancehall, people linger in the shadows of kerosene lanterns. Vendors and card sharks hustle and groove while the DJs tempt youths to buy a ticket and join the show, while in the heat of the dance, the sound systems engage in a 'sound clash,' dueling with custom records to win the crowd's favor and boost their reputation.

To find a sound-system show, listen to the radio to figure out what's going on – IRIE FM (105.1, 107.7) is a good place to start. Ask locals, especially those working in your hotel or guest house, where you can find a dancehall session or stage show. Once you've found a show, head out late as lots of Jamaicans don't start the party until 3am.

An alternative to dancehall sessions is nightclub events, which are usually sort of a hybrid between a dancehall session and a typical North

---

DANCEHALL & ANTI-GAY LYRICS

Some of the most popular lyrics in dancehall and reggae are full of murderous sentiment aimed at homosexuals (commonly referred to as 'Batty Boys' and 'chi-chi men'). Lyrics encourage listeners to hang, burn, shoot and beat gays and lesbians, and anger and boycotts in the West have been met with outright recalcitrance from some dancehall artists; Sizzla's 'Nah Apologize' is a specific refusal to apologize for homophobic lyrics.

Some dancehall artists have expressed contrition for these lyrics, but often there seems to be a retraction from said artists, or tabloids in Jamaica that accuse performers of 'bowing to gays' (a pun – to 'bow' in patois is to perform oral sex). In 2007, the Stop Murder Music campaign, organized by J-Flag (Jamaica Forum for Lesbians, All-Sexuals and Gays), and the UK-based OutRage! and Black Gay Men's Advisory Group, succeeded in convincing some dancehall artists, including Sizzla, Beenie Man and Capleton, to sign the Reggae Compassionate Act. The contract called for an end to hate lyrics in dancehall music, but soon after it was publicized the signatory artists either denied they had signed the document, claimed it was homosexual propaganda or appeared to walk back on their commitment.

There are many equivocations and excuses for homophobic dancehall lyrics, with some artists saying 'fire' is a metaphor for spiritual cleansing, while producers argue, perhaps more convincingly, that the nature of head-to-head sound-system parties forces performers to come up with increasingly outlandish lyrics (at sound-system shows emcees shout across the crowd, trying to win listeners to their camp; doing so requires flair, a brash attitude and clever or outrageous lyrics, sometimes both). Whatever the case may be, homophobic lyrics are common in dancehall, and music is omnipresent in Jamaica; sadly, you may well hear some of this hate speech while traveling on the island.

American or European club event. Hot nightclubs include the Building (formerly known as Asylum) and the Quad in Kingston, or Pier One in Montego Bay. Spend some time in Negril: the hotels that dot Seven Mile Beach frequently have live reggae shows or sound-system events.

Experiencing Jamaican Music

Outside of oldies bands playing watered-down reggae and mento in resort hotels, it may be easier for you to experience live Jamaican music in your hometown than while on vacation in Jamaica. Why? For one, the heart of Jamaica's music scene is in Kingston, which all but the most adventurous tourists avoid. The city lacks the visitor-friendly infrastructure (like good public transportation and pedestrian-friendly streets) that would encourage the traveler wanting to get a taste of the music culture. Aside from the Bob Marley Museum (which rarely offers live music), Kingston has no equivalent of Beale Street in Memphis or Frenchmen Street in New Orleans – and neither does Montego Bay or Negril.

If you're hell-bent on seeing a dancehall, it's recommended you go in a group with a 'guide,' a local you can trust. Street dances in Kingston are the most vibrant, but visitors are rare and, while on the whole peaceful, sound-system parties are not policed events. Check out our Kingston Weekly Party Planner p60.

Jamaican Music Glossary

bashment	a party where *dancehall* music is played
dancehall	music genre wherein selectors (DJs) toast (chant) over *riddims* (beats)
dub	a subgenre of reggae with more emphasis on electronic mixing of beats, adding reverb, echo, drum-and-bass and other production techniques, plus remastering and 'dubbing' instrumental and vocal sections
jonkanoo	a carnival parade with West African and Bahamian origins; also a name for the kind of dancing that accompanies the party
mento	indigenous folk music that predates modern Jamaican genres. The sound is acoustic: guitar, fiddle, banjo, drums and a large *mbira*, a wooden box with metal keys, also known as a rhumba box that lays down the bassline.
ragga	a popular modern form of *reggae* with an emphasis on digital sounds
reggae	Jamaica's most famous native music. Generally played in 4/4 time with one or two chords, a highly-tuned drum, and a strong, dominant bass. The guitar is (usually) played on the second and fourth beat; this 'plink...plink' sound is known as a 'skank.' This is the most basic structure; there are countless variations and syncopations on the above.
rhythm track	you'll notice many beats in Jamaican music sound like clones; that's because many producers replicate popular chord sequences and bass lines, otherwise known as rhythm tracks
riddim	can just mean 'rhythm', but also refers to instrumental versions of songs, the beat that a *selector* toasts over
rockas	slang for both music and enjoying music
rocksteady	the genre bridge between *ska* and *reggae*, rocksteady is characterized by strong bass lines and a mellow sound
roots reggae	sub-genre of *reggae* that focuses on Rastafarian spirituality and social change

Reggae Explosion: The Story of Jamaican Music, by Chris Salewcz and Adrian Boot, traces the evolution of Jamaican music in words and (amazing) photographs.

Solid Foundation: An Oral History of Reggae is an intensely readable study of Jamaican music in the words of the people who created it.

REGGAE

The Maytals' 1968 song 'Do the Reggay' was one of the first records to use the term 'reggae'. Prior to this the music was known as rocksteady.

Seven-inch 45 rpm records (the ones with the big hole) are the primary product of Jamaica's record plants and the mainstay of the sound-system dances.

selector	basically, a DJ (in the sense that he or she 'selects' the *riddims* at the *bashment*)
ska	in the late 1950s Jamaican musicians took mento, mixed it with calypso from Trinidad, married the result to American R&B, had jazz over for a ménage à trois and bam: ska was born
slackness	while 'slack' can refer to any kind of vulgarity (particularly sexual), it is often used as an adjective to describe *dancehall* lyrics; many older musicians see this as a degradation of the old-school subtle lyrical suggestions of sensuality
soca	combination of soul and calypso music
sound system	mobile disco/party using giant speakers, such as a *dancehall*
toasting	When a selector/DJ (ie the toaster) starts a rhythmic chant over a pre-laid beat (ie a *riddim*). There's a convincing case to be made that this is the origin of modern rap and hip-hop. Has strongly discernible African roots; listen to any West African chanting circle and you'll hear the connection.

Natural Jamaica

The Archipelago

At 11,425 sq km (about equal to the US state of Connecticut, or one-twentieth the size of Great Britain) Jamaica is the third-largest island in the Caribbean and the largest of the English-speaking islands. It is one of the Greater Antilles, which make up the westernmost Caribbean islands.

It's important to note there is a distinction between Jamaica the island and Jamaica the country. The nation is actually an archipelago, with the main island of Jamaica overwhelmingly the dominant land mass. Other small islands in the chain, called cays, are all uninhabited except for some temporary stints by local fishers, include the Port Royal Cays south of Port Royal (such as Lime Cay), the Pedro Banks, an important fishing area 160km to the southwest, and the Morant Cays, which lay off the east coast.

'Mainland' Jamaica is rimmed by a narrow coastal plain, except for the southern broad flatlands. Mountains form the island's spine, rising gradually from the west and culminating in the Blue Mountains in the east, which are capped by Blue Mountain Peak at 2256m. The island is cut by about 120 rivers, many of which are bone dry for much of the year but spring to life after heavy rains, causing great flooding and damage to roads. Coastal mangroves, wetland preserves and montane cloud forests form small specialized ecosystems that contain a wide variety of the island's wildlife.

Caves

Two-thirds of the island's surface is composed of soft, porous limestone (the compressed skeletons of coral, clams and other sea life), in places several miles thick and covered by red-clay soils rich in bauxite (the principal source of aluminum). The constant interplay of water and soft rock makes Jamaica an especially good destination for spelunkers.

Animals

Mammals

Jamaica has few mammal species. Small numbers of wild hogs and feral goats still roam isolated wilderness areas, but the only native land mammal is the endangered Jamaican coney (or hutia), a large brown rodent akin to a guinea pig. Habitat loss now restricts the highly social, nocturnal animal to remote areas of eastern Jamaica.

The mongoose is the one you're most likely to see, usually scurrying across the road. This weasel-like mammal was imported from India in 1872 to rid sugarcane fields of rats. Unfortunately, they proved more interested in feeding on snakes, a natural predator of the rat. It is now considered a destructive pest.

CAVING

If you're into caving, refer to Alan Fincham's *Jamaica Underground*, which plumbs the depths of Cockpit Country.

BIRDS

Amphibians & Reptiles

Jamaica harbors plenty of both. The largest are American crocodiles (called 'alligators' in Jamaica), found along the south coast, but also in and around Negril's Great Morass and adjacent rivers. Abundant until big-game hunters appeared around the turn of the century, crocs are now protected. Crocodile river-safaris are big business in Black River.

Jamaica has 24 species of lizard, including the Jamaican iguana, which hangs on to survival in the remote backwaters of the Hellshire Hills. Geckos can often be seen hanging on ceilings by their suction-cup feet. Local superstition shuns geckos, but their presence in your hotel room means less bugs.

Jamaica has five snake species, none poisonous and all endangered thanks mostly to the ravages of the mongoose, which has entirely disposed of a sixth species – the black snake. The largest is the Jamaican boa, or yellow snake – a boa constrictor (called *nanka* locally) that can grow 2.5m in length.

There are 17 frog and one toad species. Uniquely, none of Jamaica's 14 endemic frog species undergoes a tadpole stage; instead, tiny frogs emerge in adult form directly from eggs. All over Jamaica you'll hear the whistle frog living up to its name. While it makes a big racket, the frog itself is smaller than a grape.

Insects

Jamaica has mosquitoes, bees and wasps, but most bugs are harmless. A brown scarab beetle called the 'newsbug' flies seemingly without control and, when it flies into people, locals consider it a sign of important news to come. Diamond-shaped 'stinky bugs' are exactly that, advertising themselves with an offensive smell.

Jamaica has 120 butterfly species and countless moth species, of which 21 are endemic. The most spectacular butterfly is the giant swallowtail, *Papilio homerus*, with a 15cm wingspan. It lives only at higher altitudes in the John Crow Mountains and the eastern extent of the Blue Mountains (and in Cockpit Country in smaller numbers). Fireflies (called 'blinkies' and 'peeny-wallies') are also common.

Bird-watchers should turn to *Birds of Jamaica: A Photographic Field Guide* by Audrey Downer and Robert Sutton. James Bond's classic *Birds of the West Indies*, another reference for serious bird-watchers, was republished as *Peterson Field Guide to Birds of the West Indies*.

TIPS FOR TRAVELERS

» Never take 'souvenirs' such as shells, plants or artifacts from historical sites or natural areas.

» Keep to the footpaths. When hiking, always follow designated trails. Natural habitats are often quickly eroded, and animals and plants are disturbed by walkers who stray from the beaten path.

» Don't touch or stand on coral. Coral is extremely sensitive and is easily killed by snorkelers and divers who make contact. Likewise, boaters should never anchor on coral – use mooring buoys (see p194).

» Try to patronize hotels, tour companies and merchants that act in an environmentally sound manner, based on their waste generation, noise levels, energy consumption and the local culture.

» Many local communities derive little benefit from Jamaica's huge tourism revenues. Educate yourself on community tourism and ways you can participate. Use local tour guides wherever possible.

» Respect the community. Learn about the customs of the region and support local efforts to preserve the environment and traditional culture.

When it comes to sheer variety of color and song, birds are Jamaica's main animal attraction. Over 255 bird species call Jamaica home, 26 of which are endemic to the archipelago. Many, such as the Jamaican blackbird and ring-tailed pigeon, are endangered.

Stilt-legged, snowy-white cattle egrets are ubiquitous, as are 'John crows,' or turkey vultures, feared by some as signs of ill fortune in Jamaica and the subject of folk songs and proverbs. The patoo (a West African word) is the Jamaican name for the owl, which many islanders regard as a harbinger of death. Jamaica has two species: the screech owl and the endemic brown owl. There are also four endemic species of flycatcher, a woodpecker and many rare species of dove.

In the extensive swamps, bird-watchers can spot herons, gallinules and countless other waterfowl. Pelicans can be seen diving for fish, while magnificent frigate birds soar high above like juvenile pterodactyls.

Jamaica has four of the 16 Caribbean species of hummingbird. The crown jewel of West Indian hummingbirds is the streamertail, the national bird, which is indigenous to Jamaica. This beauty boasts shimmering emerald feathers, a velvety black crown with purple crest and long, slender, curved tail-feathers. It is known locally as the 'doctorbird,' apparently for its long bill, which resembles a 19th-century surgical lancet. The red-billed streamertail inhabits the west, while the black-billed lives in the east. Its image adorns the Jamaican two-dollar bill and is the logo of Air Jamaica.

Jamaica is a great island for bird-watching; a good place to begin research on the subject is **Windsor Great House** (☎997-3832; www.cockpitcountry.com; Windsor) in the Cockpit Country, run by professional ornithologists, and in the east the bird-oriented **Hotel Mocking Bird Hill** (☎993-7134, 993-7267; www.hotelmockingbirdhill.com/gvt.html; Port Antonio), which offers customized bird-watching tours.

Marine Life

Coral reefs lie along the north shore, where the reef is almost continuous and much of it is within a few hundred meters of shore.

Over 700 species of fish zip in and out of the reefs: wrasses, parrotfish, snappers, bonito, kingfish, jewelfish and scores of others. Smaller fry are preyed upon by barracuda, giant groupers and tarpon. Sharks are frequently seen, though most of these are harmless nurse sharks. Further out, the deep water is run by sailfish, marlin and manta rays.

Three species of endangered marine turtle – the green, hawksbill and loggerhead – lay eggs at the few remaining undeveloped sandy beaches.

About 100 endangered West Indian manatee – a shy, gentle creature once common around the island – survive in Jamaican waters, most numerously in the swamps of Long Bay on the south coast.

Lepidopterists should refer to *An Annotated List of Butterflies of Jamaica* by A Avinoff and N Shoumatoff.

Plants

Jamaica is a veritable garden, with some 3582 plant species (including 237 orchids and 550 species of fern), of which at least 912 are endemic. Although much of the island has been cultivated for agriculture, there are large stretches, especially in the interior, where the flora has largely been undisturbed since human settlement. Probably the most famous indigenous plant species is pimento (allspice), the base of many Jamaican seasonings.

Introduced exotics include bougainvillea, brought from London's Kew Gardens in 1858; ackee, the staple of Jamaican breakfasts, brought from West Africa in 1778; mangos, which arrived in 1782 from Mauritius; and breadfruit, introduced in 1779. Closer cousins to local plants are cocoa, cashew and cassava, native to Central America and the West Indies. A native pineapple from Jamaica was the progenitor of Hawaii's pineapples (the fruit even appears on the Jamaican coat of arms).

NATURAL JAMAICA

Needless to say, ganja (marijuana) is grown beneath tall plants in remote areas to evade the helicopters of the Jamaica Defense Force. The harvest season runs from late August through October. Rastafarians will tell you the plant was first cultivated off the grave of King Solomon in Ethiopia, while historians say it was likely imported by laborers from India.

Tree Species

The national flower is the dark-blue bloom of the lignum vitae tree, whose timber is much in demand by carvers. The national tree is blue mahoe, which derives its name from the blue-green streaks in its beautiful wood. You'll also want to keep your eyes peeled for the dramatic flowering of the vermilion 'flame of the forest' (also called the 'African tulip tree').

Logwood, introduced to the island in 1715, grows wild in dry areas and produces a dark blue dye. Native species include rosewood, palmetto, mahogany, silk cotton (said to be a habitat for duppies, or ghosts), cedar and ebony; the latter two have been logged to decimation during the past two centuries. Over the last decade, deforestation has also led to the deterioration of more than a third of Jamaica's watersheds.

The Nature Conservancy (www.nature.org/wherewework/caribbean/jamaica) has been instrumental in protecting the Blue Mountains-John Crow National Park.

National Parks

Jamaica's embryonic park system comprises four national parks: Blue Mountains-John Crow National Park, Montego Bay Marine Park, Port Antonio Marine Park and Negril Marine Park.

The 780-sq-km Blue Mountains-John Crow National Park (Jamaica's largest) includes the forest reserves of the Blue and John Crow mountain ranges. Both marine parks are situated around resort areas and were developed to preserve and manage coral reefs, mangroves and offshore marine resources.

There is also a fistful of other wilderness areas with varying degrees of protection, such as the Portland Bight Protected Area.

Proposals to turn Cockpit Country into a national park have been met with stiff resistance from the Maroons who live there and fear increased governmental authority will infringe on their hard-won autonomy.

THE MARVELLOUS MANGROVES

The spidery mangrove, which grows along the Jamaican coast, is crucially important to coastal preservation, besides functioning as a nursery for countless marine and amphibian species. There are four species of mangrove in Jamaica: the red, black, white and button. If you're in a coastal area, look for the trees' pneumataphores, which look like rounded branches sticking out of the mud in which the mangroves grow. These are actually, in effect, snorkels; when the tides rise the pneumataphores stay above the water, breathing in oxygen for the trees.

By acting as a shield between the ocean and the mainland, mangroves maintain the integrity of the Jamaican coast; it is estimated their destruction, due to agriculture, resort development, timber cutting, human settlement and pollution has resulted in the erosion of up to 80 million tons of topsoil per year. This habitat destruction obviously sets off an ecological chain reaction/disaster; as mangroves die, so too do the nurseries of important fisheries like the snook, jack and tarpon. As a result, the **National Environment & Planning Agency** (NEPA; www.nepa.gov.jm), in concert with local community organizations, has identified over a dozen areas for mangrove rehabilitation across the country; check the agency's website for more information.

Environmental Issues

Today, the island the Taínos called Xaymaca (or 'Land of Wood and Water') faces significant environmental issues. The aggregation of government agencies into the **National Environmental & Planning Agency** (NEPA; ☑754-7540; www.nepa.gov.jm; 10 Caledonia Ave, Kingston 5), and its partnering with the University of the West Indies at Mona on research issues, has been a positive step. But in Jamaica, the fact remains that top-down policy enactment can occur very slowly, and the nation's environment is on a tight schedule.

In the mid-1990s, Jamaica had the highest rate of deforestation (5% per year) of any country in the world and, although there is now greater awareness of the problem, it is still a threat. Many of Jamaica's endemic wildlife species are endangered, largely due to habitat loss, including the American crocodile, Jamaican boa, Jamaican iguana, coney, green parrot and giant swallowtail butterfly.

Bauxite mining – the island's second-most lucrative industry after tourism – is considered to be the single largest cause of deforestation in Jamaica. Bauxite can only be extracted by opencast mining, which requires the wholesale destruction of forests and topsoil. The access roads cut by mining concerns are then used by loggers, coal burners and yam-stick traders to get to trees in and around designated mining areas, extending the deforestation. Deforestation has also ravaged the Blue Mountains, where farmers felled trees to clear land to grow lucrative coffee plants.

To visit Cockpit Country in an ecologically responsible manner, check out the Southern Trelawny Environmental Agency's website www.stea.net.

NEPA is entrusted with responsibility for promoting ecological consciousness among Jamaicans and management of the national parks and protected areas under the Protected Areas Resource Conservation Project (PARC).

The following organizations are also taking the lead in bringing attention to ecological issues:

Cockpit Country (www.cockpitcountry.com)

Environmental Foundation of Jamaica (☑960-6744; 1B Norwood Ave, Kingston 5)

Institute of Jamaica (JCDT; ☑922-0620; www.instituteofjamaica.org.jm; 10-16 East St, Kingston)

Jamaican Caves Organisation (www.jamaicancaves.org)

Jamaica Conservation & Development Trust (JCDT; ☑960-2848; jcdt .org.jm; 29 Dumbarton Ave, Kingston 10)

Jamaica Environment Trust (☑960-3693; www.jamentrust.org; 58 Half Way Tree Rd, Kingston 10)

Jamaica Institute of Environmnetal Professionals (☑898-1693; http://jiep.org/drupal; 173 Constant Spring Rd, Kingston 8)

Jamaica Sustainable Development Networking Programme (☑968-0323; 115 Hope Rd, Kingston 6)

North Jamaica Conservation Association (☑973-4305; http://sites .google.com/site/njcajamaica; Runaway Bay)

>

Food & Drink

Jamaican cuisine manages to have the weight and heft of a peasant's diet with its heavy starches, and the colorful flavor you associate with a floating garden and cultural entrepôt in the midst of the Caribbean. The Taínos started the show with callaloo, cassava, corn, sweet potatoes and tropical fruits; the Spanish tossed in escoveitch; Africans added their oils, stews, smoked meat and rubs; Indians brought curries and rotis; the Chinese added a dash of heat and the English wrapped it all up in a meat pie.

A top Jamaican food website is www.jamaicans .com/cooking which serves up a wide selection of dishes, kept fresh by a recipe of the month.

But what really makes Jamaican cuisine special, to borrow a phrase from furious dancehall remixes, is that all these distinct foods got the Jamaican 'one-drop.' They were radically reinvented with homegrown spark and funk. Jamaicans love to give playful one-drop names for unique food creations, such as 'Solomon gundy' for pickled herring, 'blue drawers' for duckunoo pudding, 'mannish water' for goat soup and 'fevergrass' for a type of herbal tea.

Put it this way: ackee and saltfish for breakfast, curried goat for lunch and a light I-tal vegetarian dinner will teach you more about Jamaica than a month at an all-inclusive resort.

Eating in Jamaica

Jamaican Favorites

Jerk: Barbecue from Jamaica by Helen Willinsky brings to life the visceral joy of preparing a toothsome jerk marinade. You can almost smell the wood smoke and pimento (allspice).

Ackee & Saltfish

The Jamaican breakfast of champions. Ackee fruit bears an uncanny resemblance to scrambled eggs when cooked, while the saltfish is just that: salty, flaky fish that adds a savory depth to the pleasing blandness of the ackee. Can be oily, but in a good way (like the way a nice plate of scrambled eggs is a little oily). Usually served with johnny cakes and callaloo; the cakes add too much starch for our taste.

Breadkind

A sort of catch-all term for starch accompaniments, which can include yams, breadfruit, *bammy* (cassava flatbread), *festival* (sweet fried cornbread), johnny cakes (dumplings) and steamed bananas, among

---

PRICE RANGES

The following price structure is based on the cost of an average meal at a Jamaican restaurant.

» **Budget $**   <US15 (J$1275)
» **Midrange $$**   US$15-25 (J$1275-2125)
» **Top end $$$**   >US$25 (J$2125)

> » **Rundown chicken** Cooked in spicy coconut milk, and is usually enjoyed for breakfast with johnny cakes. Some say the dish is named for the method by which the chicken is caught.
>
> » **Fish tea** 'Warm up yuh belly' with this favorite local cure-all. Essentially, fish broth.
>
> » **Matrimony** A Christmas dessert made from purple star apples, which ripen in the winter.

others. While not technically breadkinds, rice and peas (rice and beans) is also a major addition.

Brown Stew

Often more of a sauce than a stew, brown stew dishes are a nice combination of savory and sweet (and slightly tangy); it's a good choice for those who don't like hot food.

Curry

All kinds of curry are popular in Jamaica, but goat curry is king, chopped into small bits with meat on the bone. While the curry has Indian roots, it's not as hot as its motherland cuisine.

Escoveitch

Imported from Spain by Spanish Jews, escoveitch is a marinade, most commonly used on fish, made of vinegar, onions, carrots and Scotch bonnet peppers. Delicious.

Jerk

The island's signature dish, jerk is both a tongue-searing marinade and spice rub for meats and fish, and the method of smoking them slowly in an outdoor pit. The classic jerk pit is an oil drum cut in half, and the meat is best cooked over a fire of pimento wood for its unique flavor. Every chef has a secret ingredient, but allspice, a dark berry which tastes like a mixture of cinnamon, clove and nutmeg, is essential.

Oxtail

Simmered with butter beans and served with rice, stewed oxtail is a national obsession.

Patties

Delicious meat pies; fillings can include spicy beef, vegetables, fish and shrimp. A Jamaican favorite is a patty sandwich – a patty squeezed between two thick slices of coco bread (a sweet bread baked with coconut milk).

Fruits & Vegetables

'All fruits ripe' is a Jamaican expression meaning 'all is well,' which is also the state of Jamaican fruit. This island is a tropical-fruit heaven. Sampling them all and finding your favorites is a noble, healthy and rewarding task. Don't just taste the obvious, like coconut, banana, papaya and mango. Savor your first star apple, soursop, ortanique, naseberry, ugli or tinkin' toe. For more information, see p280.

Norma Benghiat and John Demers's *Food of Jamaica: Authentic Recipes from the Jewel of the Caribbean* is a comprehensive exploration of the island's cuisine.

Be warned! The ubiquitous ackee fruit is poisonous if eaten before it's fully mature. Never open an ackee pod; when the fruit is no longer deadly, the pod will open itself and ask to be eaten.

JAMAICAN FRUIT PRIMER

ackee	Its yellow flesh is a tasty and popular breakfast food, invariably served with saltfish.
callaloo	A spinachlike vegetable, usually served shredded and steamed or lightly boiled. It also finds its way into spicy pepperpot stew. Excellent in omelets.
cho cho	Also known as christophine or chayote; a pulpy squashlike gourd served in soups and as an accompaniment to meats. Also used for making hot pickles.
guava	A small ovoid or rounded fruit with an intense, musky sweet aroma. It has a pinkish granular flesh studded with regular rows of tiny seeds. It is most commonly used in nectars and punches, syrups, jams, chutney and even ice cream.
guinep	A small green fruit (pronounced gi-nep) that grows in clusters, like grapes, and can be bought from July through November. Each 'grape' bears pink flesh that you plop into your mouth whole. It's kind of rubbery and juicy, and tastes like a cross between a fig and a strawberry. Watch for the big pip in the middle.
jackfruit	A yellow fruit from the large pods of the jackfruit tree. Jackfruit seeds can be roasted or boiled.
mango	A lush fruit that comes in an assortment of sizes and colors, from yellow to black. Massage the glove-leather skin to soften the pulp, which can be sucked or spooned like custard. Select your mango by its perfume.
naseberry	A sweet, yellow and brown fruit that tastes a bit like peach and comes from an evergreen tree. Also known as sapodilla.
ortanique	An unusual citrus discovered in the Christiana market, believed to be a cross between a sweet orange and a tangerine.
papaya	Cloaks of many colors (from yellow to rose) hide a melon-smooth flesh that likewise runs from citron to vermilion. The central cavity is a trove of edible black seeds. Tenderness and sweet scent are key to buying papayas.
Scotch bonnet pepper	Celebrated for its delicious citrus sparkle just before your entire mouth and head go up in flames, Scotch bonnets are small hot peppers that come in yellow, orange and red.
soursop	An ungainly, irregularly shaped fruit with cottony pulp that is invitingly fragrant yet acidic. Its taste hints at guava and pineapple.
star apple	A leathery, dark-purple, tennis-ball-sized gelatinous fruit of banded colors (white, pink, lavender, purple). Its glistening seeds form a star in the center. The fruit is mildly sweet and understated.
sweetsop	A heart-shaped, lumpy fruit packed with pits and a sweet, custardlike flesh.
tinkin' toe	The Jamaican name for a popular brown fruit that smells like stinky feet. Its scientific name is *Hymenaea courbaril*. Consider it the durian of Jamaica!
ugli	A fruit that is well named. It is ugly on the vine – like a deformed grapefruit with warty, mottled green or orange skin. But the golden pulp is delicious: acid-sweet and gushingly juicy.

I-tal

Thanks to the Rastafarians, Jamaica is veggie-friendly. The Rastafarian diet is called I-tal (for 'vI-tal') cooking, and in its evolved form has an endless index of no-nos. For instance: no salt, no chemicals, no meat or dairy (the latter is 'white blood'), no alcohol, cigarettes or drugs (ganja doesn't count). Fruits, vegetables, soy, wheat gluten and herbs prevail. Because of the popularity of the I-tal diet many restaurants offer I-tal options on their menus. Popular dishes include eggplant curry, whipped sweet potatoes and steamed vegetables.

Drinks

Nonalcoholic Drinks

Coffee

Jamaican Blue Mountain coffee is considered one of the most exotic and expensive coffees in the world. It's relatively mild and light-bodied with a musty, almost woody flavor and its own unmistakable aroma. Most upscale hotels and restaurants serve it as a matter of course. The majority of lesser hotels serve lesser coffees from other parts of the country or – sacrilege! – powdered instant coffee. Be careful if you ask for white coffee (with milk), which Jamaicans interpret to mean 50% hot milk and 50% coffee.

Tea

'Tea' is a generic Jamaican term for any (usually) hot, nonalcoholic drink, and Jamaicans will make teas of anything. Irish moss is often mixed with rum, milk and spices. Ginger, mint, ganja and even fish are brewed into teas. Be careful if tempted by 'mushroom tea': the fungus in question is hallucinogenic, so unless you're in search of an LSD-like buzz, steer clear.

Cold Drinks

A Jamaican favorite for cooling off is 'skyjuice': a shaved-ice cone, flavored with sugary fruit syrup and lime juice, that is sold at streetside stalls, usually in a small plastic bag with a straw. You may also notice 'bellywash,' the local name for limeade.

Ting, a bottled grapefruit soda, is Jamaica's own soft drink, although Pepsi is pretty popular too (Pepsi decidedly won the cola wars in Jamaica; Coke is surprisingly difficult to find).

Coconut water straight from the nut is sold for about US$1 from streetside vendors.

Roots tonics, made from the roots of plants such as raw moon bush, cola bark, sarsaparilla and dandelion, are widely available in small shops, or sold roadside in handmade batches. They taste like dirt...but in a good way.

For the finer points of I-tal cuisine, see Laura Osbourne's *The Rasta Cookbook: Vegetarian Cuisine Eaten with the Salt of the Earth.*

It's only natural that food itself gets celebrated, with events such as the Portland Jerk Festival, the Jamaica Coffee Festival and the Trelawny Yam Festival.

FOOD & DRINK DRINKS

MANNISH UP

If you've been partying all night and need to get home – and if you're a guy – Jamaicans may serve you 'mannish water,' which serves two purposes, to wit: a) it's alleged to make you a cogent-enough drunk to drive home (though this is unproven and unwise), and b) it makes you, well, 'mannish,' assuming you've got someone to get mannish with. It's basically made from goat parts, brain included, plus lots of starches. But for our dollars, if you really want to man up, find some cow cod soup. It's tough to find on any restaurant menu, which is perhaps unsurprising given the ingredients: bull penis, Scotch bonnet peppers and bananas (because the bull penis wasn't phallic enough, we guess). *Cooked in white rum!* If that doesn't make you mannish, see a doctor.

Alcoholic Drinks

Rum

Jamaica's rums range from mellow bottles seasoned with coconut and peppermint, to the knockout blow of overproof (151 proof) white rum. Overproof may come in a shot glass, but if you down it in one go you're heading home early. It's best enjoyed mixed with Ting or ginger beer and sipped.

For the latest word on rum, check out the Ministry of Rum (www.ministryof rum.com).

Beer

Red Stripe is Jamaica's famous beer, the one crisp and sweet antidote to spicy jerk creations. If you hear locals calling for 'policemen,' don't panic: the beer is named for the 'natty trim' – a conspicuous red seam – on the trouser legs of the uniform of the Jamaican police force. Should you tire of Red Stripe, Real Rock is a slightly heavier, tastier local lager, while the malty Dragon Stout is also popular. Heineken and Guinness are both brewed under license locally.

Self-Catering

Food at grocery stores is usually expensive, as many canned and packaged goods are imported. Dirt-cheap fresh fruits, vegetables and spices sell at markets and roadside stalls islandwide. Wash all produce thoroughly! You can always buy fish (and lobster, in season) from local fishermen.

Cooking Courses

Culinary courses are sometimes offered in all-inclusive resorts. Outside, consider contacting the **Hotel Mocking Bird** (☏993-7134, 993-7267; www .hotelmockingbirdhill.com/gvt.html; Port Antonio) in Port Antonio or **Countrystyle Community Tours** (☏962-7758; www.countrystyletourism .com) in Mandeville.

Survival Guide

>

Directory A-Z

Accommodations

If you're traveling on a shoestring, head to a simple guest house, where rooms can be had for up to US$90 (J$7650). Midrange hotels are priced between US$90 (J$7650) and US$200 (J$17,000): if this is your budget, you'll enjoy a wide range of choice in appealing small hotels, many with splendid gardens, sea views or both. If traveling with your family or a group, consider one of the hundreds of villas available to rent across the island. And if you've decided to splurge on something sumptuous, Jamaica's luxury hotels rank among the finest in the world; top-end rates start from US$200 (J$17,000).

Throughout this book and unless otherwise stated, prices are for double rooms

in high season and refer to European Plan, or room only with bathroom. US dollars are the preferred currency for accommodations, but guest houses that charge around US$70 or less for a night are usually happy to convert your bill to Jamaican dollars if you prefer to pay that way. Don't forget to check if the quoted rate includes tax and service charge; if not, the compulsory 6.25% to 15% GCT (General Consumption Tax; and possibly a 10% to 15% service charge) may be added to your bill.

Low season (summer) is usually mid-April to early-December; the high season (winter) is the remainder of the year, when hotel prices increase by 40% or more and popular hotels are often booked solid. All-inclusive packages are usually based on three-day minimum stays.

All-Inclusive Resorts

Rates for all-inclusive resorts presented in this book are guidelines based on unpublicized 'rack' or 'standard' rates. (Note: in this book, reviews for all-inclusive options will include a mention of 'all-incl' in the practicalities details where costs are shown.) You will likely spend considerably less depending on the source of booking, season and current specials, which are perpetually publicized.

Major all-inclusive resort chains include the following:

Breezes (☑877-273-3937; www.breezes.com) Also operates Starfish, Grand Lido and Hedonism resorts.

Couples (☑in the USA 800-268-7537 or 954-416-1280, in the UK 1582-794-420; www.couples.com)

Franklyn D Resorts (☑in the USA 800-654-1337, 973-4124; www.fdrholidays.com) Family-oriented.

Riu (☑in the USA 888-666-8816, in Canada 866-845-3765, in Spain 34-971-269-460; www.riu.com)

Sandals (☑in the USA 888-726-3257, in Europe 44-207-581-9895, in the UK 08000-22-30-30; www.sandals.com)

B&Bs

A B&B (bed and breakfast) is usually a lodging where the owner plays live-in host and provides breakfast in the quoted room rate. In Jamaica, some establishments purporting to be B&Bs actually charge for breakfast, and true B&Bs are few and far between.

Camping

Jamaica is not developed for campers, and it's unsafe to camp in much of the wild. Many budget properties will let you pitch a tent on their lawns for a small fee. Some even rent tents and have shower, toilet and laundry facilities.

BOOK YOUR STAY ONLINE

For more accommodations reviews by Lonely Planet authors, check out hotels.lonelyplanet.com/Jamaica. You'll find independent reviews, as well as recommendations on the best places to stay. Best of all, you can book online.

Guest Houses

Most guest houses are inexpensive and good places to mix with the locals. Some are indistinguishable from hotels.

Homestays

You can make your own arrangements to stay with individuals or families who do not rent rooms as a normal practice. The following agencies coordinate homestays:

Countrystyle Community Tours (⚑962-7758; www .countrystyletourism.com) Can arrange homestays in central Jamaica as part of community tours.

Southern Trelawny Environmental Agency (⚑610-0818; www.stea.net; 3 Grants Office Complex, Albert Town) Coordinates homestays in Cockpit Country.

Hotels

Hotels in Jamaica run the range from for-locals business style places with little atmosphere, to boutique properties run by generations of the same Jamaican family.

Island Outpost properties (⚑in the USA 800-688-7678, in the UK 800-6887 6781; www .islandoutpost.com, twitter .com/iohotels) offers travelers some quintessentially Caribbean boutique hotels that are unpretentious and gracious.

Villa Rentals

Jamaica boasts hundreds of private villas for rent. Rates start as low as US$100 per week for budget units with minimal facilities. More upscale villas begin at about US$750 weekly and can run to US$10,000. Rates fall as much as 30% in summer. A large deposit (usually 25% or more) is required. Try the following:

Caribbean Way (⚑877-953-7400, in North America 514-393-3003; www.caribbean way.com; 5530 St Patrick St, Suite 2210, Montreal, Quebec, Canada H4E 1A8).

PRACTICALITIES

» The *Jamaica Gleaner* is the high-standard newspaper; its rival is the *Jamaica Observer*. The best domestic magazine is Air Jamaica's *Sky Writings*.

» There are 30 radio stations and seven TV channels; most hotels have satellite TV.

» Metric and imperial measurements are both used. Distances are measured in meters and kilometers, and gas in liters, but coffee (and ganja) is most often sold by the pound.

Jamaican Association of Villas & Apartments (JAVA; ⚑800-845-5276, in North America 773-463-6688; www .villasinjamaica.com; 2706 W Agatite #2, Chicago, IL)

Jamaican Treasures (⚑877-446-7188, in North America 305-767-2596; www .jamaicantreasures.com; 14629 SW 5th St, Pembroke Pines, FL).

Sun Villas (⚑888-625-6007, 544-9497, in the USA 941-922-9191; www.sunvillas.com; 1410 South Lake Shore Dr, Sarasota, FL)

Villascaribe (⚑800-645-7498, in North America 404-815-9855; www.villascaribe .com; 730 Peachtree St NE, Suite 580, Atlanta, GA)

Business Hours

The following are standard hours for Jamaica; exceptions are noted in reviews.

Banks 9:30am to 4pm Monday to Friday.

Bars From around 6pm until the last guest leaves. Jamaicans tend to go out late. Although some clubs and drinking establishments claim to have set opening hours, you'll often find that they stay open until the last customer stumbles out, or the owner decides it's time to call it a night.

Businesses 8:30am to 4:30pm Monday to Friday.

Restaurants Breakfast dawn to 11am, lunch noon to 2pm, dinner 5:30pm to 11pm.

Shops 8am or 9am to 5pm Monday to Friday, to noon or 5pm Saturday, late-night shopping to 9pm Thursday and Friday.

Children

All-inclusive resorts cater to families and have an impressive range of amenities for children. Many hotels offer free accommodations or reduced rates for young children in their parents' room; many provide a babysitter/nanny by advance request. Increasingly, resorts and upscale hotels offer free childcare centers.

It's a good idea to pre-arrange necessities such as cribs, babysitters, cots and baby food at hotels other than family resorts. Many car-rental agencies in Jamaica do not offer safety seats. One agency that does is Island Car Rentals (p295). Negril, Ocho Rios and Montego Bay are perhaps the best towns for children. Each is replete with kid-friendly attractions and activities, most notably Dunn's River Falls (outside Ocho Rios), Kool Runnings Water Park (Negril), Aquasol Theme Park (Montego Bay) and horseback riding (all three).

In general, it's safe for children and pregnant women to go to Jamaica. However, because some vaccines are not approved for use in children and pregnant women, these travelers should be particularly careful not to drink tap water or consume any questionable food or beverage. Breastfeeding in public is somewhat taboo but not illegal.

Lonely Planet's *Travel with Children* gives you the low-down on preparing for family travel.

Climate

Coastal temperatures are consistently warm, and while temperatures fall steadily with increasing altitude, even in the Blue Mountains the thermometer averages 18°C or more. The annual rainfall averages 1980mm, but nationwide there are considerable variations, with the east coast receiving considerably more rain than elsewhere. Despite wet and dry seasons, rain can fall any time of year and normally comes in short, heavy showers, often followed by sun. Jamaica lies in the Caribbean 'hurricane belt.' Officially the hurricane season lasts from June 1 to November 30; August and September are peak months.

See also p19.

Customs Regulations

Entering Jamaica

You are allowed to import: 25 cigars, 200 cigarettes and two liters of alcohol duty-free. You may bring a 'reasonable' amount of duty-free goods for personal use; anything deemed in excess of 'reasonable' may incur an import tax.

You may need to show proof that laptop computers and other expensive items (especially electronics) are for personal use; otherwise you may be charged import duty.

For more information, see **Jamaica Customs** (www .jacustoms.gov.jm).

Electricity

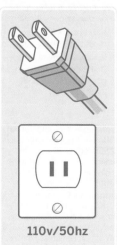

110v/50hz

110v/50hz

Embassies & Consulates

If your country isn't represented in this list, check 'Embassies & High Commissions' in the yellow pages of the Greater Kingston telephone directory.

Australia ((☑868-628-069518; Herbert Street, St Clair, Port of Spain, Trinidad and Tobago)

Canada High Commission (☑926-1500; www.canada international.gc.ca/jamaica -jamaique; 3 West Kings House Rd, Kingston); Consulate (☑952-6198; 29 Gloucester Ave, Montego Bay)

France (☑946-4000; 13 Hillcrest Ave, Kingston 6)

Germany (☑631-7935, emergency 819-4351; www .kingston.diplo.de; 10 Waterloo Rd, Kingston 10)

Italy (☑968-8464; 10 Surbiton Rd, Kingston 10)

Japan (☑929-7534; www .jamaica.eab-japan.go.jp; NCB Tower, Nth Tower, 6th floor, 2 Oxford Rd, Kingston 5)

Netherlands (☑926-2026; Victoria Mutual Bldg, 53 Knutsford Blvd, Kingston 5)

UK High Commission (☑936-0700; www.ukinja maica.fco.gov.uk/en/; 28 Trafalgar Rd, Kingston)

US Embassy (☑702-6000, after hr 702-6055; http://king ston.usembassy.gov; 142 Old Hope Rd, Kingston); Consulate ☑953-0602, 952-5050; Unit EU-1, Whitter Village, Ironshore)

Gay & Lesbian Travelers

There is a gay scene in Kingston, but it is an underground affair. Jamaica, overwhelmingly, is adamantly homophobic. Sexual acts between men are prohibited by law and punishable by up to 10 years in prison and hard labor. Many reggae dancehall lyrics by big-name stars seem intent on instigating violence against gays. Law enforcement in most cases looks the other way, and gay-bashing incidents are almost never prosecuted.

Nonetheless, many hoteliers are tolerant of gay visitors, and you should not

BAD TRIP

If you want to smoke (marijuana), we recommend doing so at your hotel or at least in a trusted bar or restaurant. Tourists have been reported as suffering harmful side effects from ganja, especially from ganja cakes. This is also true of hallucinogenic wild mushrooms. Apparently drinking alcohol while on mushrooms can induce a 'bad trip' – and the same term may end up describing your vacation.

be put off from visiting the island. Just realize that displaying your sexuality openly could have life-threatening consequences. Check these websites for gay-friendly businesses and general information on the Jamaican LGBT scene.

Gay Journey (http://gayjourney.com/hotels/jamaica.htm)

Gay Jamaica Watch (http://gayjamaicawatch.blogspot.com)

J-FLAG (www.jflag.org)

Purple Roofs (www.purpleroofs.com/caribbean/jamaica.html)

Health

Availability & Cost of Health Care

Acceptable health care is available in most major cities and larger towns throughout Jamaica, but may be hard to locate in rural areas. Most travelers will find the quality of health care will not be comparable to that in their home country. To find a good local doctor, your best bet is to ask the management of the hotel where you are staying or contact your embassy in Kingston or Montego Bay.

Many doctors and hospitals expect payment in cash, regardless of whether you have travel health insurance. If you develop a life-threatening medical problem, you'll probably want to be evacuated to a country with state-of-the-art medical care. Since this may cost tens of thousands of dollars, be sure you have insurance to cover this before you depart.

Many pharmacies are well supplied, but important medications may not be consistently available. Be sure to bring along adequate supplies of all prescription drugs.

No See Ums

No see ums, also known as midges (or *Ceratopogonidae* if you're an entymologyst) are tiny (hence the name) biting flies that live near water. Females are blood suckers, and while their bites are not painful, they are awfully itchy. No see ums congregate in large swarms near bodies of water, puddles etc; to avoid them, wear insect repellent and skirt their swarm areas, as the bugs won't fly too far from their 'home' body of water.

Traveler's Diarrhea

Throughout most of Jamaica tap water has been treated and is safe to drink, but in some far-flung rural areas it is safest to avoid it unless it has been boiled, filtered or chemically disinfected (with iodine tablets). Eat fresh fruits or vegetables only if cooked or peeled; be wary of dairy products that might contain unpasteurized milk; and be highly selective when eating food from street vendors. If you develop diarrhea, be sure to drink plenty of fluid, preferably an oral rehydration solution containing lots of salt and sugar.

ABC of Healthy Travel by E Walker et al, and *Medicine for the Outdoors* by Paul S Auerbach, are other valuable resources.

Internet Resources

Lonely Planet (www.lonelyplanet.com) A good place to start.

MD Travel Health (www.mdtravelhealth.com) Provides complete travel health recommendations for every country, updated daily, at no cost.

World Health Organization (www.who.int/ith/) Publishes a superb book called *International Travel and Health*, which is revised annually and is available online on its website at no cost.

Internet Access

Wi-fi is appearing in more and more Jamaican hotels, but internet access is still almost nonexistent in rural areas. Most town libraries now offer internet access (US$1 for

WATER

Water is generally safe to drink from faucets throughout the island except in the most far-flung rural regions. It is safest, however, to stick with bottled water. It's a good idea to avoid ice, particularly ice sold at street stands as 'bellywash,' 'snocones' or 'skyjuice,' shaved-ice cones sweetened with fruit juice. Unless you're certain that the local water is not contaminated, you shouldn't drink it. Vigorous boiling for one minute is the most effective means of water purification. At altitudes greater than 2000m, boil for three minutes. In Jamaica's backwaters, clean your teeth with purified water rather than tap water.

30 minutes), though you may find there's only one or two terminals and waits can be long. Most towns have at least one commercial entity where you can get online. Jamaican businesses aren't very good at maintaining (or even creating) their web presence, so don't rely too heavily on online research before your trip.

Internet Resources

Dancehall Reggae (www.dancehallreggae.com) The place to go for the latest on the island's music scene.

Jamaica Gleaner (www.jamaica-gleaner.com) Best news source from the island's most reliable newspaper.

Jamaica National Heritage Trust (www.jnht.com) Excellent guide to Jamaica's history and heritage.

Jamaica Yellow Pages (www.jamaicayp.com) Handy online version of the Jamaican phone directory.

Lonely Planet (www.lonelyplanet.com) Succinct summaries on travel in Jamaica, plus the popular Thorn Tree bulletin board, travel news and a complete online store.

Visit Jamaica (www.visitjamaica.com) The tourist board's presentation of Jamaica to travelers, with plenty of destination, attractions and lodging information.

Legal Matters

Jamaica's drug and drink-driving laws are strictly enforced. Don't expect leniency because you're a foreigner. Jamaican jails are Dickensian hellholes! If you are arrested, insist on your right to call your embassy in Kingston to request its assistance.

Maps

The Jamaican Tourist Board (JTB) publishes a *Discover Jamaica* road map (1:350,000). No topographical details are shown.

The best maps are Hildebrandt's Jamaica map (1:300,000) and ITMB Publishing's maps (1:250,000), available online or at travel bookstores.

The most accurate maps are the Jamaica Ordnance Survey maps published by the **Survey Department** (☏922-6630; 231-1/2 Charles St, PO Box 493, Kingston 10).

Money

The unit of currency is the Jamaican dollar, the 'jay,' which uses the same symbol as the US dollar ($). Jamaican currency is issued in bank notes of J$50, J$100, J$500, J$1000 and (rarely) J$5000. Prices for hotels and valuable items are usually quoted in US dollars, which are widely accepted.

Commercial banks have branches throughout the island. Those in major towns maintain a foreign-exchange booth. Most city bank branches throughout Jamaica have 24-hour ATMs linked to international networks such as Cirrus or Plus. In more remote areas, look for ATMs at gas stations. Traveler's checks are widely accepted in Jamaica, although some hotels, restaurants and exchange bureaus charge a hefty fee for cashing them. Major credit cards are accepted in larger towns and businesses throughout the island, although local groceries and the like will not be able to process them even in Kingston.

Tipping

A 10% tip is normal in hotels and restaurants. Some restaurants automatically add a 10% to 15% service charge to your bill. Check your bill carefully, as the charge is often hidden. Some all-inclusive resorts have a strictly enforced no-tipping policy. Outside Kingston, tourist taxi drivers often ask for tips but it is not necessary; JUTA (Jamaica Union of Travelers Association) route taxis do not expect tips.

Safe Travel

The Jamaica Tourist Board publishes a pocket-size pamphlet, *Helpful Hints for Your Vacation*, containing concise tips for safer travel.

JTB hotline (☏929-9200) Use for emergency assistance.

US State Department (☏202-663-1225; www.travel.state.gov) publishes travel advisories that advise US citizens of trouble spots.

British Foreign & Commonwealth Office (☏0845-850-2829; www.fco.gov.uk; Travel Advice Unit, Consular Division, Foreign & Commonwealth Office, 1 Palace St, London SW1E 5HE).

Crime

Jamaica has one of the highest murder rates for any country not in the throes of war, and Kingston and Spanish Town have the worst reputations in the Caribbean for violent crime. Although the vast majority of violent crimes occur in ghettoes far

---

SMART TO LEAVE YOUR SMARTPHONE AT HOME

If you have a smartphone (eg iPhone or Android) or Blackberry, leave it at home or at least in your hotel room (or preferably, hotel safe). They're all the rage among Jamaican thieves, who seem disconcertingly willing to shoot someone over the gadgets.

from tourist centers, visitors are sometimes the victims of robberies and scams. Crime against tourists has dropped in recent years, however, and the overwhelming majority of visitors enjoy their vacations without incident.

Keep hotel doors and windows securely locked at night, and lock car doors from the inside while driving. Don't open your hotel door to anyone who can't prove their identity. If you're renting an out-of-the-way private villa or cottage, check in advance with the rental agency to establish whether security is provided. And don't assume you're entirely safe at all-inclusive resorts: readers have reported security issues even there.

Carry as little cash as you need when away from your hotel. Keep the rest in a hotel safe. You can rely on credit cards and traveler's checks for most purchases, but you'll need cash for most transactions in rural areas and at gas stations.

Many local police are members of the communities they serve. Reports suggest there are times when they can't be trusted to act with impartiality.

Drugs
Ganja (marijuana) is everywhere in Jamaica and you're almost certain to be approached by hustlers selling drugs. Cocaine is also widely available (Jamaica is the major stop on the Colombia–US drug route). The street sale of drugs is a sad pandemic that has corroded society and led to frightening levels of violence.

Despite their ubiquity and cultural eminence, drugs are strictly illegal and penalties are severe. Roadblocks and random searches of cars are common, undertaken by well-armed police in combat gear. Professionalism is never guaranteed, and 'dash' – extortion – is often extracted to boost wages.

Harassment
Usually the traveler's biggest problem is the vast army of hustlers (mostly male) who harass visitors, notably in and around major tourist centers. A hustler is someone who makes a living by seizing opportunities, and the biggest opportunity in Jamaica is you.

It's important to be polite but firm in repressing unwanted advances; never ignore them, which is taken as an insult. Aggressive persistence is the key to their success and trying to shake them off can be a wearying process. Hustlers often persist in the hope that you'll pay just to be rid of them. Try pretending to be a tourist from a non-English-speaking country (few Jamaicans speak Croatian). If harassment continues, seek the assistance of a tourist police officer or the local constabulary.

Telephone
Jamaica's country code is ☑876. To call Jamaica from the US, dial ☑1-876 + the seven-digit local number. From elsewhere, dial your country's international dialing code, then ☑876 and the local number.

For calls within the same parish in Jamaica, just dial the local number. Between parishes, dial ☑1 + the local number. We have included only the seven-digit local number in Jamaica listings in this book.

Cell Phones
You can bring your own cellular phone into Jamaica (GSM or CDMA), but if your phone is locked by a specific carrier, don't bother. Another option is to purchase an inexpensive cellular phone (from US$35) at a **Digicel** (☑888-344-4235; www.digiceljamaica.com), **Claro** (☑621-1000; www.claro.com.jm) or **Lime** (☑888-225-5295; www.timeforlime.com.jm) outlet and purchase a prepaid phone card. These are sold in denominations of up to J$1000, and you'll find them at many gas stations and stationery shops.

Time
In fall (autumn) and winter, Jamaican time is five hours behind Greenwich Mean Time, and the same as in New York (Eastern Standard Time). Jamaica does not adjust for daylight saving time. Hence, from April to October, it is six hours behind London and one hour behind New York.

Toilets
There are few public toilets, and those that do exist are best avoided. Most restaurants have restrooms, but many require you make a purchase before you can use them.

Tourist Information

The **Jamaica Tourist Board** (JTB; www.visitjamaica .com) has offices in key cities around the world. You can request maps and literature, including hotel brochures, but they do not serve as reservation agencies.

Travelers with Disabilities

Very few allowances have been made in Jamaica for travelers with disabilities. Some useful resources:

Council for Persons with Disabilities (☏922-0585; www.mlss.gov.jm; 4 Ellesmere Rd, Kingston 5)

Disabled Peoples' International (☏268-461-1273; www.dpinorthamericacarib bean.org; PO Box W1529, Potters Main Rd, St John's, Antigua)

Visas

For stays of six months or less, no visas are required for citizens of the EU, the US, Commonwealth countries, Mexico, Japan and Israel. Nationals of Argentina, Brazil, Chile, Costa Rica, Ecuador, Greece and Japan don't need a visa for stays of up to 30 days.

All other nationals require visas (nationals of most countries can obtain a visa on arrival, provided they are holding valid onward or return tickets and evidence of sufficient funds).

Women Travelers

Many Jamaican men display behavior and attitudes that might shock visiting women, often expressing disdain for the notion of female equality or women's rights. Despite this, women play pivotal roles in Jamaican society (see p265).

If you're single, it may be assumed you're on the island seeking a 'likkle love beneat' de palms.' Protests to the contrary will likely be met with wearying attempts to get you to change your mind. If you go along with the flirting, your innocent acceptance will be taken as a sign of acquiescence. Never beat about the bush out of fear of hurting the man's feelings.

Rape is not uncommon in Jamaica and occasionally involves female tourists. Women traveling alone can reduce unwanted attention by dressing modestly when away from the beach. Women should avoid walking alone at night and otherwise traveling alone in remote areas.

Work

Visitors are admitted to Jamaica on the condition that they 'not engage in any form of employment on the island.' Professionals can obtain work permits if sponsored by a Jamaican company, but casual work is very difficult to obtain.

The adjacent terminal serves domestic flights. The terminals aren't linked by walkways and are a three-minute walk apart. Charter airlines, including Air Jamaica Express, provide connecting shuttles.

Norman Manley International Airport (KIN; ☑924-8452; www.nmia .aero) Around 11km southeast of downtown Kingston, Manley also handles international flights. There's a JTB desk in the arrivals hall, a money-exchange bureau before customs, and a taxi-information booth as you exit customs. Beyond customs there's a bank and Island Car Rentals. Ahead is the JUTA (Jamaica Union of Travelers Association) taxi office, a **police station** (☑924-8002), an ATM, a telephone office and the Otahetis Café.

The following major airlines have offices in Jamaica:
Air Canada (www.aircanada .com) Kingston (☑800-677-2485); Montego Bay (☑952-5160)
Air Jamaica (www.airja maica.com) Kingston (☑888-359-2475); Montego Bay (☑940-9411)
American Airlines (www .aa.com) Kingston (☑800-744-0006; 26 Trafalgar Rd); Montego Bay (☑971-7379)
British Airways (www .britishairways.com) Kingston (☑800-247-9297)
Caribbean Airlines (www .caribbean-airlines.com) Kingston (☑800-744-2225)
Cayman Airways (www .caymanairways.com) Kingston (☑800-422-9626); Montego Bay (☑924-8809)
COPA Airlines (www.copaair .com) Kingston (☑800-234-2672)
Delta Airlines (www.delta .com) Kingston (☑800-221-1212); Montego Bay (☑971-1284)
International AirLink Montego Bay (☑888-247-5465)
Northwest Airlines (www .nwa.com) Montego Bay (☑952-4033)

Transportation

GETTING THERE & AWAY

Entering the Country

Expect a wait in the immigration halls at the airports in Kingston and Montego Bay. There are often only two or three immigration officers on hand to process the planeloads of passengers and often multiple flights land within minutes of each other, increasing the burden on officials. See p290 for information about visa requirements.

Passport

Canadian citizens do not technically need passports for visits to Jamaica of up to six months, but most airlines will refuse boarding if you do not bring your passport. In any case, you *do* need two pieces of identification, including proof of citizenship or permanent residency, such as a passport, birth certificate or driver's license with photo ID. All other nationalities must bring a passport.

Air

In North America and Europe (and to a lesser extent, Australia and the Asia Pacific) there are a plethora of travel agencies that specialize in organizing vacations to Jamaica and the Caribbean.

Airports & Airlines

Jamaica's international airports are in Montego Bay and Kingston. For flight arrival and departure information, call the airports, visit their websites or call the airline directly.

Donald Sangster International Airport (MBJ; ☑952-3124; www.mb jairport.com) The majority of international visitors arrive here, 3km north of Montego Bay. There's a Jamaica Tourist Board (JTB) information booth in the arrivals hall and a 24-hour money-exchange bureau immediately beyond immigration. There is also a transportation information counter plus desks representing tour companies, hotels and rental cars immediately as you exit customs. A **police station** (☑952-2241) is outside.

US Airways (www.usairway
.com) Montego Bay (☎940-
0171)

Virgin Atlantic (www.virgin
-atlantic.com) Montego Bay
(☎974-2323)

Tickets

The cost of plane tickets
to Jamaica varies widely,
depending on such variables
as time of year, weather and
traffic in the region. Higher
fares normally apply in 'high
season,' from mid-December
through mid-April, with even
higher fares for peak times
such as Christmas and
around the New Year. You can
save 20% or more by traveling in low season; weekday
flights offer savings, too.

Charter Flights

Charter flights from the US,
Canada, UK and Europe offer
another option for getting
to Jamaica. Fares are often
cheaper than on regularly
scheduled commercial air-
lines, but you usually have
to go and come back on a
specific flight, and you'll
probably have no flexibility to
extend your stay.

Although charter compa-
nies do most of their business booking package tours
that include both accommodations and airfare, they will
often find themselves with a
few empty seats on planes
they've chartered. The seats
will sometimes be sold for
bargain prices a week or two
prior to departure.

In the US you can some-
times find these seats adver-
tised in the travel pages of
larger Sunday newspapers,
such as the *New York Times*
and the *Boston Globe*.

Sea

Jamaica is a popular destination on the cruise roster,
mainly for passenger liners
but also for private yachters.
Arrival by freighter is even an
option.

For maps and charts of the
Caribbean, contact **Bluewa-**

ter Books & Charts (☎800-
942-2583; www.bluewaterweb
.com). The **National Ocean-
ic & Atmospheric Admin-
istration** (☎888-990-6622;
www.nauticalcharts.noaa.gov)
sells US government charts.

Cruise Ship

More than 800,000 cruise-
ship passengers sail to
Jamaica annually, making
it one of the world's largest
cruise-ship destinations.
Most ships hit four or five
ports of call, sometimes
spending a night, other
times only a few hours. The
typical cruise-ship holiday is
the ultimate package tour.
While the majority of mainstream cruises take in fine
scenery along the way, the
time spent on the islands is
generally limited and the opportunities to experience a
sense of island life are more
restricted. Port visits are
usually one-day stopovers at
either Ocho Rios or Montego
Bay, with Falmouth expected
to become a port of call by
the time you read this. Some
travel agencies that specialize in cruise booking include:
Cruise411 (☎800-553-7090;
www.cruise411.com)
Cruises at Cost (☎800-
274-3866; cruisesatcost.biz)

Cruise Outlet (☎800-775-
1884; www.thecruiseoutlet.com)

Flying Wheels Travel (☎507-
451-5005; www.flyingwheels
travel.com) Specializes in
booking disabled-accessible
Caribbean cruises.

Freighter

Several freighters that ply
between North America and
Europe call in Jamaica,
and some take paying pas-
sengers. Most have plush
cabins and passengers are
well looked after by stewards.
Book early:

Freighter World Cruises
(☎626-449-3106, 800-531-
7774; www.freighterworld.com;
Suite 335, 180 South Lake Ave,
Pasadena CA 91101)

**Hamburg-Sud Reiseagen-
tur** (☎040-370 5155; www
.hamburgsued-reiseagentur.de;
Ost-West Strasse 59-61, 20457
Hamburg, Germany)

Maris USA (☎203-222-1500,
800-996-2747; www.freighter
cruises.com; 84-1320 State Rt
9, Champlain, NY, USA)

**NSB Frachtschiff-Touris-
tik** (☎0421-338-8020; www
.reederei-nsb.de; Cioenstrasse
22, D-28195 Bremen, Germany)

Private Yacht

Many yachters make the
trip to Jamaica from North

OFF THE BOAT

While the cruise-lines' optional land tours are conve-
niently packaged to take in many of the island's sightseeing highlights, they also move quickly and tend to
shield visitors from interaction with the local people. In
addition, a fair percentage of the money paid for these
tours stays with the organizers rather than going into
the local economy. If you venture out on your own,
you're likely to enjoy a richer cultural experience. If
you want to tour the island, consider hiring a local taxi
driver, who will likely shed light on local issues and give
you a more colorful tour. Wander the streets of the main
town, poke into little shops, eat at local restaurants
and buy mementos from street vendors, or veer off the
beaten track. Visit small businesses and chat with the
owners, buy local rums and other souvenirs in small
shops instead of on board – you'll help fuel the local
economy (and save money in the process).

America. Upon arrival in Jamaica, you *must* clear customs and immigration at Montego Bay, Kingston, Ocho Rios or Port Antonio. In addition, you'll need to clear customs at *each* port of call. Yachts frequently call at the following places:

Errol Flynn Marina (☑715-6044; www.errolflynnmarina .com; Port Antonio) GPS N 18.168889°, W -76.450556°

Montego Bay Yacht Club (☑979-8038; www.mobay yachtclub.com; Sunset Dr, Montego Bay) GPS N 18.462452°, W -77.943267°

Royal Jamaican Yacht Club (☑924-8685; www.rjyc .org.jm; Norman Manley Dr, Kingston) GPS N 17.940939°, W -76.764939°

GETTING AROUND

Air

There are four domestic airports: **Tinson Pen Aerodrome** in Kingston, **Ian Fleming International Airport**, formerly Boscobel Aerodrome, near Ocho Rios, **Negril Aerodrome** and **Ken Jones Aerodrome** at Port Antonio (though Ken Jones Aerodrome wasn't receiving flights at time of writing). Montego Bay's **Donald Sangster International Airport** (MBJ; ☑952-3124; www.mbjairport.com) has a domestic terminal adjacent to the international terminal. It's a bit of a walk – Air Jamaica Express provides a shuttle.

In Kingston, most domestic flights use Tinson Pen, 3km west of downtown, but it's a 40-minute ride to the domestic airstrip from Norman Manley International Airport.

Airlines in Jamaica

Air Jamaica (Jamaica ☑922-3460; North America ☑800-523-5585; www.airja maica.com) offers a daily ser-

vice between Kingston and Montego Bay, and between Montego Bay and Ocho Rios through its domestic air service, Air Jamaica Express.

Typical one-way fares (for purchase outside Jamaica) are US$165 for Kingston to Montego Bay (five daily).

TimAir (☑952-2516; www .timair.net; domestic terminal, Donald Sangster International Airport) has (ridiculously expensive) charter flights between its hub in Montego Bay and Kingston (US$638/ J$54,000), Mandeville (US$435/J$38,820), Negril (US$324/J$27,426), Ocho Rios (US$355/J$30,050) and Port Antonio (US$754/ J$63,826). Rates are for two passengers; fares go up or down for fewer or more passengers.

Helicopter

You can charter your own helicopter for transportation or for personalized tours from **Jamaica Customised Vacations & Tours** (☑616-272-8257; www.jcvtt.com; 19 Austin Ave, Mt Salem, Montego Bay; tours per person from US$460). Tours depart from Montego Bay, Negril and Ocho Rios.

Bicycle

Mountain bikes and 'beach cruisers' (bikes with fat tires, suitable for riding on sand) can be rented at most major resorts (US$10 to US$30 per day). Road conditions are hazardous and Jamaican drivers are not considerate to bicyclists. For serious touring, bring your own mountain or multipurpose bike. You'll need sturdy wheels to handle the potholed roads.

Bus & Public Transportation

Traveling by public transportation could be the best – or worst – adventure of your trip to Jamaica. An extensive transportation network links virtually every village and comprises several options that range from standard public buses to private taxis, with minibuses and route taxis in between.

For the adventurous traveler who doesn't mind getting up close and personal with fellow passengers without the comfort of air-conditioning, and is unfazed by the wild and often dangerous manoeuvres of the drivers, this is the cheapest way to get around Jamaica. There is usually no set timetable – buses leave when the driver considers them full – and passengers are crammed in with little regard for comfort. Taxis and buses tend to fill quickly early in the morning (before 8am) and around 5pm as people depart for work and home.

Public buses, minibuses and route taxis depart from and arrive at each town's transportation station, which is usually near the main market. Locals can direct you to the appropriate bus or vehicle, which should have its destination marked above the front window (for buses) or on its side.

Public buses and minibuses are regulated by the **Ministry of Transport & Works** (☑754-2584; www .mtw.gov.jm; 138 Maxfield Ave, Kingston 10).

CLIMATE CHANGE & TRAVEL

Every form of transport that relies on carbon-based fuel generates CO_2, the main cause of human-induced climate change. Modern travel is dependent on aeroplanes, which might use less fuel per kilometer per person than most cars but travel much greater distances. The altitude at which aircraft emit gases (including CO_2) and particles also contributes to their climate change impact. Many websites offer 'carbon calculators' that allow people to estimate the carbon emissions generated by their journey and, for those who wish to do so, to offset the impact of the greenhouse gases emitted with contributions to portfolios of climate-friendly initiatives throughout the world. Lonely Planet offsets the carbon footprint of all staff and author travel.

Buses

Large buses are few and far between in Jamaica due to the narrow twisting roads, but the big, comfortable, air-conditioned **Knutsford Express**, which runs between Montego Bay, Ocho Rios and Kingston (see the Getting There & Away sections for those respective cities) is a notable exception. Throughout the island there are bus stops at most road intersections along routes, but you can usually flag down a bus anywhere except in major cities. When you want to get off, shout 'One stop!' The conductor will usually echo your request with, 'Let off!'

Minibuses

Private minibuses, also known as 'coasters,' have traditionally been the workhorses of Jamaica's regional public transportation system. All major towns and virtually every village in the country are served.

Licensed minibuses display red license plates with the initials PPV (public passenger vehicle) or have a JUTA (Jamaica Union of Travelers Association) insignia. JUTA buses are exclusively for tourists. They usually depart their point of origin when they're full. They're often overflowing, with people hanging from open doors, and the drivers seem to have death wishes.

Route Taxis

These communal taxis are the most universal mode of public transportation, reaching every part of the country. They operate like minibuses, picking up as many people as they can squeeze in along their specified routes.

Most route taxis are white Toyota Corolla station wagons marked by their red license plates. They should have 'Route Taxi' marked on the front door, and they are not to be confused with similar licensed taxis, which charge more. Avoid any taxi that lacks the red license plate.

Costs

Taking public transportation is terrifically inexpensive. Buses and minibuses charge in the neighborhood of J$100 per 50km, and route taxis charge about J$150 to J$250 per 50km. A minibus from Kingston to Negril at the time of writing (basically crossing the country) was around J$900 – a little over US$10.

Car & Motorcycle

Automobile Associations

There is no national roadside organization to phone when you have car trouble. Most car-rental agencies have a 24-hour service number in case of breakdowns and other emergencies. If you do break down, use a local mechanic only for minor work; otherwise the car-rental company may balk at reimbursing you for work it hasn't authorized. If you can't find a phone or repair service, seek police assistance. *Never* give your keys to strangers.

Driver's License

To drive in Jamaica, you must have a valid International Driver's License (IDL) or a current license for your home country or state, valid for up to six months. In the US you can obtain an IDL by applying with your current license to any Automobile Association office.

Fuel & Spare Parts

Many gas stations close at 7pm or so. In rural areas, stations are usually closed on Sunday. At time of writing, gasoline cost about US$1.85/ J$157 per liter. Most gas stations only accept cash for payment, although a growing number of modern gas stations in larger towns accept credit cards.

Rental

Several major international car-rental companies operate in Jamaica, along with dozens of local firms. Car-rental agencies are listed in the local yellow pages.

INTERNATIONAL RENTAL COMPANIES

Avis (www.avis.com.jm); Donald Sangster International Airport (☎952-0762); Norman Manley International Airport (☎924-8542)

Budget (www.budgetjamaica .com); Donald Sangster International Airport (☎952-3838); Norman Manley International Airport

(☎924-8762); Ocho Rios (☎974-1288)

Hertz (www.hertz.com); Donald Sangster International Airport (☎979-0438); Norman Manley International Airport (☎924-8028)

Jamaica Airport Car Rental (www.jamaicaairport carrental.com) Clearing house on local car rentals.

Thrifty (☎952-1126; www .thrifty.com; Donald Sangster International Airport)

DOMESTIC RENTAL COMPANIES

Local rental agencies often provide better daily rates than the international chains, but cars are sometimes road-worn.

Reputable agencies include the following:

Beaumont Car Rentals Kingston (☎926-0311; 56C Brentford Rd); Montego Bay (☎971-8476; www.beaumont -car-rental.com; 34 Queens Dr)

Caribbean Car Rentals (☎974-2513, in North America ☎877-801-6797, in UK ☎0800- 917-9904; www.caribbean carrentals.net; 31 Hope Rd, Kingston)

Island Car Rentals (www .islandcarrentals.com); Donald Sangster International Airport (☎952-7225); Kingston (☎926-8012; 17 Antigua Ave); Norman Manley International Airport (☎924-8075); North America (☎866-978- 5335).

COSTS

High-season rates begin at about US$45 (J$4000) per day and can run as high as US$150 (J$12,700) or more, depending on the vehicle. Cheaper rates apply in the low season. Some companies include unlimited distance, while some set a limit and charge a fee for excess kilometers driven. Most firms require a deposit of at least US$500 (J$40,000), but accept a credit-card imprint. Keep copies of all your paperwork. Renters must be 21 years old (some companies

will rent only to people aged 25 or older).

RESERVING
You can reserve a car upon arrival, but in the high season be sure to make your reservation in advance. Reconfirm before your arrival.

Before signing, go over the vehicle with a fine-tooth comb to identify any dents and scratches. Make a note of each one before you drive away. You're likely to be charged for the slightest mark that wasn't noted before. Don't forget to check the cigarette lighter and interior switches, which are often missing.

WHAT KIND OF CAR
Most of the companies rent out modern Japanese sedans. A big car can be a liability on Jamaica's narrow, winding roads. Some companies also rent 4WD vehicles, which are highly recommended if you intend to do any driving away from main roads.

Stick shift is preferable because frequent and sudden gear changes are required when potholes and kamikaze chickens appear out of nowhere. Remember that you'll be changing gears with your *left* hand. If this is new to you, you'll soon get the hang of it.

INSURANCE
Check in advance whether your current insurance or credit card covers you for driving while abroad. All rental companies will recommend damage-waiver insurance, which limits your liability in the event of an accident or damage. This costs about US$12 to US$40 (J$1000 to J$3500) per day and is a valuable investment.

Road Conditions
Jamaica's roads run the gamut from modern multilane highways to barely passable tracks. You can expect

any road with the designation 'A' to be in fairly good condition. 'B' roads are generally much more narrow and often badly potholed, but still passable in the average rental car. Minor roads, particularly those in the Blue Mountains and Cockpit Country, can be hellish. If you plan to drive off the major routes, it's essential to have a stalwart 4WD vehicle.

Signage on main roads is good, but directional signs are few and far between as soon as you leave them. Many B roads are not shown on maps. And what may appear on a map to be a 30-minute journey may take several hours. More often than not there are no signs to indicate sharp curves, steep ascents or work in progress. In addition roads are often poorly lit, if at all.

Road Hazards
Jamaicans undergo a psychological mind flip when they get behind the wheel, shifting from laid-back folks who rarely rush anything to some of the world's rudest and most dangerously aggressive drivers. Cars race through towns and play chicken with one another with daredevil folly. Use extreme caution and drive defensively, especially at night when you should be prepared to meet oncoming cars that are either without lights or blinding you with high-beams (there's never a middle ground for some reason). Use your horn liberally, especially when approaching blind corners.

Road Rules
» Always drive on the left. Remember: 'Keep left, and you'll always be right.'

» Jamaica has a compulsory seatbelt law.

» Speed limits range from 50km to 80km and vary from place to place across the island.

Hitchhiking

Hitchhiking is common enough among Jamaicans but, because public transportation is absurdly cheap, few tourists stick out their thumbs.

Hitchhiking is never entirely safe in any country in the world and we don't recommend it, especially in Jamaica where there are a lot of bad men looking to take advantage of naive tourists. Travelers who decide to hitchhike should understand that they are taking a small but potentially serious risk. If you choose to take that risk, you will be safer if you travel in pairs and let someone know where you are planning to go.

Local Transportation

Bicycle

Bicycle rentals are commonly available in resort towns for US$15 to US$30 (J$1000 to J$2500) per day but the frenetic nature of Jamaican traffic may preclude you from having the pleasant experience that you had in mind.

If you want to do any serious riding, consider bringing your own bike. However, you need to be prepared to fix your own flats and broken chains. Bike shops are virtually nonexistent.

Buses

Kingston's **municipal bus system** (Jamaica Urban Transport Co Ltd; ☏749-3196; fares US$0.30-0.50; ⏱5am-10pm) operates a fleet of Mercedes-Benz and Volvo buses, including some for disabled travelers. Buses stop only at official stops. Students, children, disabled passengers and pensioners pay half fare.

Motor Scooter & Motorcycle

Dozens of companies hire motorcycles and scooters; they're available at any resort town. These companies are far more lax than the car-rental companies; you may not even have to show your driver's license. If you are not an experienced motorcycle driver, it might be better to rent a scooter, which is far easier to handle. Scooters cost about US$35 to US$50 (J$3000 to J$4000) per day and motorcycles cost about US$45 to US$60 (J$4000 to J$5000) per day; note that deposits can be high.

Road conditions in Jamaica are hazardous. If the rental agency has helmets available, *wear one!*

Route Taxi

Route taxis, which are generally white Toyota Corolla station wagons with red PPV license plates, provide vital transportation on both the local and national level. You can generally flag them down anywhere.

Taxi

Licensed taxis – called 'contract carriages' – have red PPV license plates (those without such plates are unlicensed). They're expensive, but affordable if you share the cost with other passengers.

Jamaica Union of Travelers Association (JUTA; www.jutatoursjamaica.com; ☏957-4620) operates island-wide and is geared almost exclusively to the tourist business. Other taxicab companies are listed in the yellow pages and in regional chapters of this book.

The Transport Authority has established fixed rates according to distance (different rates apply for locals and tourists, who pay more). Licensed cabs should have these posted inside. Taxis are also supposed to have meters, but many don't use them.

TAXI FARES

The following were typical fares in 2010, based on up to four people per taxi:

ROUTE	FARE
Around Montego Bay	US$35 flat fare
Kingston-Ocho Rios	US$120-150
Kingston-Port Antonio	US$100-120
Montego Bay-Ocho Rios or Negril	US$80
Norman Manley International Airport-Kingston (Uptown)	US$35
Donald Sangster International Airport-Montego Bay	US$25

Glossary

For culinary terms, see p278.
For music terms, see p271.

all-inclusive resort – resort hotel where all activities, meals, beverages, entertainment etc are included in the room rate

Antilles – the Caribbean islands

Arawak people – see *Taíno people*

Babylon – term used by *Rastafarian* people for oppression or corruption; sometimes used to denote the police; named after the place where the Israelites were enslaved

cay – coral isle

dreadlocks – uncut, uncombed hair, as worn by *Rastafarian* people

higgler – street vendor

I-tal – a form of vegetarian cuisine that excludes salt, chemicals, meat or dairy

jerk shack – a shack where meat or fish is served or prepared using the method of smoking meat with the jerk marinade and spice rub

jitney – a small bus that carries passengers over a regular route on a flexible schedule

JLP – Jamaica Labour Party

JTB – Jamaica Tourist Board

JUTA – Jamaica Union of Travelers Association

Maroons – community of escaped slaves who resisted the British during the colonial period; also their contemporary descendants

MoBay – slang for Montego Bay

NEPA – National Environment & Planning Agency

Ochi – slang for Ocho Rios

PADI – Professional Association of Dive Instructors

parish – one of 14 political districts

pirogue – canoe hollowed out of a large tree trunk; long wooden fishing boat

PNP – People's National Party

Rastafarian – adherent of the religious philosophy Rastafarianism, whose main tenets hold that those of African descent are one of the 12 lost tribes of Israel, that Emperor Haile Selassie is divine, and that he will lead Rastafarians to *Zion*; also called a Rasta

rum shop – local bar, usually utilized by the working class

spliff – joint; marijuana rolled in paper

Taíno people – Arawakan-speaking people; indigenous pre-Columbian inhabitants of Jamaica

Xaymaca – term used to describe Jamaica by *Taíno people*

Zion – the Promised Land (Ethiopia) in the Rastafarian religion

behind the scenes

SEND US YOUR FEEDBACK

We love to hear from travelers – your comments keep us on our toes and help make our books better. Our well-traveled team reads every word on what you loved or loathed about this book. Although we cannot reply individually to postal submissions, we always guarantee that your feedback goes straight to the appropriate authors, in time for the next edition. Each person who sends us information is thanked in the next edition – and the most useful submissions are rewarded with a free book.

Visit **lonelyplanet.com/contact** to submit your updates and suggestions or to ask for help. Our award-winning website also features inspirational travel stories, news and discussions.

Note: We may edit, reproduce and incorporate your comments in Lonely Planet products such as guidebooks, websites and digital products, so let us know if you don't want your comments reproduced or your name acknowledged. For a copy of our privacy policy visit lonelyplanet.com/privacy.

OUR READERS

Many thanks to the travelers who used the last edition and wrote to us with helpful hints, useful advice and interesting anecdotes:

B Antonello Balacco, Marianne Barstein, Jaka Bobnar, Leon Boerboom, Steve Brookwell, Jay Brown, Jill Browning **C** Kimberley Carannante, Roz Cunningham, Asa Cusack **D** Anna Du Vent **E** Emile Erens **G** Tanya Gerri **H** Astrid Haldorsen, Katy Hinton, Lukas Horn **J** Anne Jaumees **K** Andrey Knyazev, Ewelina Kopiczko **L** Beth Lawrence, Robert Lockett **M** Noriko Manabe, Chantal Mantha, Pauline Messing, John Miatech, Pascale Mulet, Dennis Mullings **O** Elena Obukhova **R** Raphael Richards, Anna Rohleder **S** Andreea Sleahtenea, Matthew Sussman **W** Margaret & Anton Walker **V** Jeremy Verity **Z** Janne Zwat

AUTHOR THANKS

Adam Karlin

Thanks: Julian and Alex for friendship, laughs and perspective; Steve and Roger for tons of valuable advice; Rachel for her companionship and constant support; every Jamaican who passed along a genuine smile and warmth; Jennye and Bruce, my awesome editors; mom and dad for the usual. And big ups to Anna Kaminski for helping make this Jamaica book what it is.

Anna Kaminski

Many thanks to Lindsey and her faithful 4WD; Steve, Newton, Paul, Paddy and Sarah – my partners in crime; Lois, Kala, Troy and Copper – big up yuhself!; Mrs Ritgard, Miss Rose and Miss Joy – my home away from home, yet again; Gad Heuman; Nancy; assorted prison staff, the Jamaica National Heritage Trust staff; Helen, Andy and Emily – one love!; Mr Ainsley Cohen Henriques; Mrs Twyman; Juggler and Rocky; Roger and Lillian; and my fellow author Adam – for the memorable trip!

ACKNOWLEDGMENTS

Climate map data adapted from Peel MC, Finlayson BL & McMahon TA (2007) 'Updated World Map of the Köppen-Geiger Climate Classification', *Hydrology and Earth System Sciences*, 11, 163344.

Cover photograph: View of sea from boat, Negril, Westmoreland, Jamaica, Michael Lawrence/Lonely Planet Images

Many of the images in this guide are available for licensing from Lonely Planet Images: www.lonelyplanetimages.com.

This Book

The 6th edition of *Jamaica* was researched and written by Adam Karlin (coordinating author) and Anna Kaminski. This guidebook was commissioned in Lonely Planet's Oakland office and was produced by the following:
Commissioning Editor Jennye Garibaldi
Coordinating Editor Gina Tsarouhas
Coordinating Cartographers Valeska Canas, Mark Griffiths

Coordinating Layout Designer Carlos Solarte
Managing Editors Bruce Evans, Annelies Mertens
Managing Cartographer Alison Lyall
Managing Layout Designer Chris Girdler
Assisting Editors Andrew Bain, Janice Bird, Andrea Dobbin, Asha Ioculari, Craig Kilburn, Bella Li, Matty Soccio
Assisting Cartographers Ildiko Bogdanovits, Joelene Kowalski

Cover Research Aude Vauconsant
Internal Image Research Sabrina Dalbesio

Thanks to Helen Christinis, Laura Crawford, Ryan Evans, Lisa Knights, Anna Metcalfe, Kathleen Munnelly, Susan Paterson, Martine Power, Averil Robertson, Gerard Walker, Juan Winata

index

how to use this book

These symbols will help you find the listings you want:

- ◉ Sights
- 🏖 Beaches
- 🏃 Activities
- 🥾 Courses
- ☞ Tours
- 🎊 Festivals & Events
- 🛏 Sleeping
- 🍴 Eating
- 🍷 Drinking
- ☆ Entertainment
- 🛍 Shopping
- ⓘ Information/ Transport

These symbols give you the vital information for each listing:

- ☏ Telephone Numbers
- ⊙ Opening Hours
- Ⓟ Parking
- ⊖ Nonsmoking
- ❄ Air-Conditioning
- @ Internet Access
- ☎ Wi-Fi Access
- ⚊ Swimming Pool
- ✔ Vegetarian Selection
- 📄 English-Language Menu
- 👪 Family-Friendly
- 🐾 Pet-Friendly
- ⊟ Bus
- ⚓ Ferry
- Ⓜ Metro
- Ⓢ Subway
- ⊖ London Tube
- 🚃 Tram
- ⊞ Train

Reviews are organised by author preference.

Look out for these icons:

- TOP CHOICE — Our author's recommendation
- FREE — No payment required
- 🌱 — A green or sustainable option

Our authors have nominated these places as demonstrating a strong commitment to sustainability – for example by supporting local communities and producers, operating in an environmentally friendly way, or supporting conservation projects.

Map Legend

Sights
- Beach
- Buddhist
- Castle
- Christian
- Hindu
- Islamic
- Jewish
- Monument
- Museum/Gallery
- Ruin
- Winery/Vineyard
- Zoo
- Other Sight

Activities, Courses & Tours
- Diving/Snorkelling
- Canoeing/Kayaking
- Skiing
- Surfing
- Swimming/Pool
- Walking
- Windsurfing
- Other Activity/ Course/Tour

Sleeping
- Sleeping
- Camping

Eating
- Eating

Drinking
- Drinking
- Cafe

Entertainment
- Entertainment

Shopping
- Shopping

Information
- Post Office
- Tourist Information

Transport
- Airport
- Border Crossing
- Bus
- Cable Car/ Funicular
- Cycling
- Ferry
- Metro
- Monorail
- Parking
- S-Bahn
- Taxi
- Train/Railway
- Tram
- Tube Station
- U-Bahn
- Other Transport

Routes
- Tollway
- Freeway
- Primary
- Secondary
- Tertiary
- Lane
- Unsealed Road
- Plaza/Mall
- Steps
- Tunnel
- Pedestrian Overpass
- Walking Tour
- Walking Tour Detour
- Path

Boundaries
- International
- State/Province
- Disputed
- Regional/Suburb
- Marine Park
- Cliff
- Wall

Population
- Capital (National)
- Capital (State/Province)
- City/Large Town
- Town/Village

Geographic
- Hut/Shelter
- Lighthouse
- Lookout
- Mountain/Volcano
- Oasis
- Park
- Pass
- Picnic Area
- Waterfall

Hydrography
- River/Creek
- Intermittent River
- Swamp/Mangrove
- Reef
- Canal
- Water
- Dry/Salt/ Intermittent Lake
- Glacier

Areas
- Beach/Desert
- Cemetery (Christian)
- Cemetery (Other)
- Park/Forest
- Sportsground
- Sight (Building)
- Top Sight (Building)

OUR STORY

A beat-up old car, a few dollars in the pocket and a sense of adventure. In 1972 that's all Tony and Maureen Wheeler needed for the trip of a lifetime – across Europe and Asia overland to Australia. It took several months, and at the end – broke but inspired – they sat at their kitchen table writing and stapling together their first travel guide, *Across Asia on the Cheap*. Within a week they'd sold 1500 copies. Lonely Planet was born.

Today, Lonely Planet has offices in Melbourne, London and Oakland, with more than 600 staff and writers. We share Tony's belief that 'a great guidebook should do three things: inform, educate and amuse'.

OUR WRITERS

Adam Karlin

Coordinating Author, Plan Your Trip, Port Antonio & Northeast Coast, Montego Bay & Northwest Coast, Negril & West Coast, Jamaica Today, Music, Natural Jamaica, Food & Drink, Survival Guide Adam Karlin has always covered the edges of the Caribbean for Lonely Planet – Miami, New Orleans, the Florida Keys – and he jumped at the chance to travel deep into the heart of the region. In Jamaica he barreled down mountain roads on crazy taxis, watched a silly amount of beautiful sunsets, traded many stories for more shots of overproof rum, tasted some truly sublime jerk and turned 30. Adam has worked on over two dozen guidebooks for Lonely Planet.

Read more about Adam at:
lonelyplanet.com/members/adamkarlin

Anna Kaminski

Kingston & Around, Blue Mountains & Southeast Coast, Ocho Rios & North Coast, History, Jamaican Life The Caribbean first captured Anna's imagination when she studied the history and literature of the region at the University of Warwick and joined the Caribbean Riddims Society for the raucous parties and the great food. She'd spent a year studying in Puerto Rico and island-hopping in the Leeward Islands before finally coming to Jamaica in 2006, where she was thrown in the deep end by an NGO in Downtown Kingston. She spent five months becoming intimately acquainted with the city's ghettos and prisons while penning articles for the *Caribbean Times* on the shortcomings of the Jamaican justice system. Anna often finds herself hurtling along Jamaica's potholed roads in search of food; a connoisseur of Jamaican cuisine, she is prepared to travel great distances for that perfect piece of jerk pork.

Published by Lonely Planet Publications Pty Ltd
ABN 36 005 607 983
6th edition – October 2011
ISBN 978 1 74179 462 5
© Lonely Planet 2011   Photographs © as indicated 2011
10 9 8 7 6 5 4 3 2
Printed in China